Third Grade Math
with Confidence

Instructor Guide

Third Grade Math with Confidence

Instructor Guide

KATE SNOW

WELL-TRAINED MIND PRESS

Names: Snow, Kate (Teacher), author.

Title: Third grade math with confidence. Instructor guide / Kate Snow.

Other titles: Instructor guide

Description: [Charles City, Virginia] : Well-Trained Mind Press, [2023] | Series: Math with confidence | For instructors of third grade math students.

Identifiers: ISBN: 978-1-944481-28-5 (paperback)

Subjects: LCSH: Mathematics--Study and teaching (Elementary) | LCGFT: Teachers' guides. | BISAC: JUVENILE NONFICTION / MATHEMATICS / Arithmetic.

Classification: LCC: QA107.2 .S663 2023 | DDC: 372.7--dc23

Reprinted September 2024 by Bradford & Bigelow.

3 4 5 6 7 8 9 10 B&B 30 29 28 27 26 25 24

Table of Contents

Welcome to Third Grade Math with Confidence!

Third Grade Math with Confidence is a complete math curriculum that will give your child a solid foundation in math. It's **playful, hands-on, and fun** with thorough coverage of third-grade math skills:

- multiplication and division facts to 100
- adding and subtracting four-digit numbers
- multi-step word problems
- perimeter and area of rectangles
- adding and subtracting fractions
- geometry, money, elapsed time, and measurement

The incremental, confidence-building lessons will help your child develop a strong understanding of math, step by step. Daily review ensures she will fully master what she has learned in previous lessons. With this blend of **deep conceptual understanding and traditional skill practice,** you'll give your child a thorough third-grade math education.

Fun activities like Fraction Diner, the Chocolate Shop, Escape the Maze, and Division Crash will help your child develop a **positive attitude** toward math. You'll also find optional enrichment lessons at the end of each unit, with suggestions for delightful math picture books and real-world math activities that help your child appreciate the importance of math in real life.

Besides this Instructor Guide, *Third Grade Math with Confidence* also includes **two colorful, engaging Student Workbooks.** You'll find three workbook pages for each lesson. First, you'll use the Lesson Activities page to teach your child a new topic. Then, your child will complete the Practice and Review pages to practice the new concept and review previously-learned skills. Workbook Part A covers Units 1-8, and Workbook Part B covers Units 9-16.

Many parents worry about their ability to teach math as their children move beyond the primary years. If that's the case for you, don't worry: I promise to guide you every step of the way! *Third Grade Math with Confidence* is full of features that will help you teach math with confidence all year long:

- **Scripted, open-and-go lessons** help you clearly explain and teach new math concepts
- **Explanatory notes** help you understand more deeply how children learn math so you feel well-equipped to teach your child
- **Unit Wrap-ups and Checkpoints** at the end of each unit provide assessment and give you guidance on whether your child is ready to move on to the next unit

In the next section, you'll learn how the curriculum is organized and how to get your materials ready. Invest a little time reading this section now (and getting your Math Kit ready), and you'll be ready to teach math like a pro all year long.

Wishing you a joyful year of third grade math!
Kate Snow

Introduction

The Goals of *Third Grade Math with Confidence*

Third Grade Math with Confidence aims to help children become confident and capable math students, with a deep understanding of math concepts, proficiency and fluency with fundamental skills, and a positive attitude toward math.

Deep conceptual understanding

You'll focus on one main topic per unit so your child can build deep conceptual knowledge of the new material. (Educators call this a *mastery approach* to new content.) Each new lesson builds on the previous one so your child gradually develops thorough understanding.

Proficiency with fundamental skills

Children need lots of practice to master the basic skills necessary for proficiency in math. *Third Grade Math with Confidence* provides continual, ongoing review of these core skills so your child fully grasps them by the end of the year. (Educators call this a *spiral approach* to review, because children periodically revisit topics, just as the curve of a spiral returns to the same point on a circle.)

Positive attitude

The lessons in *Third Grade Math with Confidence* include games, pretend activities, and lots of hands-on learning so your child enjoys and even looks forward to math time. Optional enrichment lessons at the end of each unit (with a picture book suggestion and math extension activity) provide a break from the usual routine and help your child appreciate how math is used in real life.

What's New in Third Grade

If you used earlier levels of *Math with Confidence*, you'll find two major changes in *Third Grade Math with Confidence*. First, the lessons are still grouped into units, but they are no longer grouped into weeks. This change gives you more flexibility with your schedule and allows the number of lessons in each unit to vary depending on what skills need to be covered. You'll now find an enrichment lesson (with math application activities and a picture book suggestion) at the end of each unit rather than each week. As in earlier levels, these lessons are optional.

Second, every regular lesson now includes a **Lesson Activities page in the workbook** (in addition to Practice and Review). These pages provide visual aids, practice exercises, and game boards all in one place to streamline your teaching. The Lesson Activities pages are designed for you to complete with your child during your hands-on teaching time. They are **not** meant for your child to complete independently.

Overview

You'll need three books to teach *Third Grade Math with Confidence*. All three books are essential for the program.

- This Instructor Guide contains the scripted lesson plans for the entire year (Units 1-16).
- Workbook Part A contains the workbook pages for the first half of the year (Units 1-8).
- Workbook Part B contains the workbook pages for the second half of the year (Units 9-16).

Units

Third Grade Math with Confidence is organized into 16 units. Each unit focuses on developing thorough understanding of one main concept, such as multiplication, area and perimeter, or fractions. Units vary in length from 6 to 12 lessons, and there are a total of 144 lessons. The final lesson in each unit is an optional enrichment lesson.

The preview for each unit includes the following:

- **Overview.** A brief summary of what you'll teach your child.
- **What Your Child Will Learn.** A detailed list of objectives for the unit.
- **Lesson List.** The full list of lessons included in the unit.
- **Extra Materials.** This section gives you a heads-up if you need any extra materials for the unit. You'll sometimes need to supplement your regular math materials with a few everyday household items, such as markers, tape, or scissors. The optional enrichment lessons also usually require some extra materials.
- **Teaching Math with Confidence.** These notes help you understand more deeply how children learn math so that you're well-prepared to teach the new concepts.

Lessons

Each lesson includes several short and varied activities to keep your child engaged and attentive. You'll need both the Instructor Guide and Student Workbook for every lesson. Most pilot families spent an average of 25-35 minutes on each lesson, with 10-15 minutes of parent-led instruction and 15-20 minutes of independent work. However, this will vary depending on your teaching style and your child's learning style—and whether you have any toddlers interrupting you!

The Instructor Guide contains the scripted, open-and-go lesson plans. Within the Instructor Guide:

- **Bold text** indicates what you are to say.
- *Italic text* provides sample answers.
- Gray-highlighted text indicates explanatory notes.

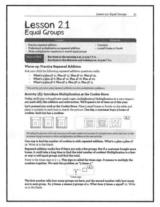

The Student Workbook includes three workbook pages for each lesson. First, you'll use the Lesson Activities page to teach your child the new concept or skill. Then, your child will complete the Practice and Review pages to reinforce what he learned in the lesson and review previously-learned skills. (Some Review pages will have the Lesson Activity page for the next Lesson on their reverse side. Hold on to those pages for use in the next lesson.)

 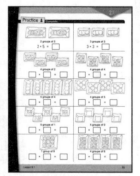 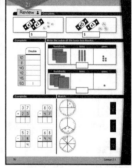

Memory work and warm-up activity with parent

Each lesson begins with a few memory work review questions and a quick warm-up activity. The memory work questions are listed at the top of each lesson. Reviewing a few questions daily helps your child master these important facts and vocabulary words. The warm-up activity eases your child into math time and helps start the lesson on a confident and positive note.

Memory Work

Warm-up Activity

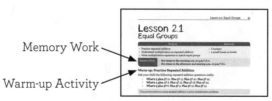

Lesson activities with parent

Next, you'll use the scripted lesson plan and Lesson Activities page to teach your child new concepts and skills. The Instructor Guide and Lesson Activities workbook pages are lettered so that it's easy to see how they align. Some activities are only in the Instructor Guide, without a matching section on the Lesson Activities page.

Instructor Guide

Student Workbook

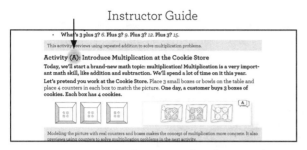
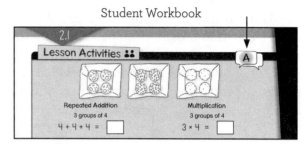

The activity headings and images in the Instructor Guide are lettered to help you find the matching activity in the Student Workbook.

Instructor Guide

Some activities in the Instructor Guide do not have a letter. These activities do not have a matching section in the Student Workbook, and they are completed either orally or with hands-on materials instead.

Independent practice

Last, your child will complete the Practice and Review workbook pages. Most third-graders will be able to complete these workbook pages independently, but some may need help reading and interpreting the directions.

Try to check the workbook pages as soon as your child finishes them. This immediate feedback shows your child that you value his work, and it helps prevent mistakes from becoming ingrained habits. You'll find answer keys for the Practice and Review pages at the end of each unit.

Enrichment Lessons (Optional)

Optional enrichment lessons are scheduled at the end of each unit. The Instructor Guide provides suggestions for a related picture book and enrichment activity, while the Student Workbook includes a two-page Unit Wrap-up for your child to complete.

Many parents and children find that the enrichment lessons are their favorite part of the program. (Siblings often enjoy participating in them, too!) However, these lessons are completely optional. You are free to choose the ones that sound the most fun for your family, or skip them entirely if your schedule is too full.

Picture book

Most of the suggested books relate to the math studied in the unit, but some expose your child to other interesting math topics. **The picture books are not required.** You do not need to buy every book or track down every book in your library system. You can also use a book on a similar topic as a substitute.

Enrichment activity

The enrichment activities help your child understand and appreciate how math is used in everyday life. You'll find suggestions for art projects, real-life applications, and more to make math come alive for your child.

Unit Wrap-up (review and assessment)

The Unit Wrap-ups provide two pages of additional exercises for the concepts and skills your child learned in the unit. You can use them to casually review the unit, or you can use them as tests to assess your child's progress more formally. Either way, children and parents often find it very satisfying to see this concrete evidence of growth. If you live in a state where you're required to provide evidence of learning, you may want to save them for your child's portfolio.

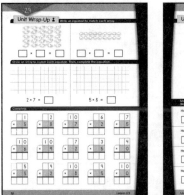 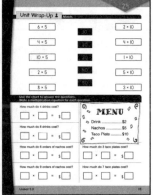

Your child is not expected to fully master every skill from every unit before moving on to the next unit. See below for more on pacing and assessing your child's progress.

Pacing and Checkpoints

Just as children learn to crawl, walk, and talk at different times, they are developmentally ready to learn math at different times, too. *Third Grade Math with Confidence* provides lots of flexibility so your child can learn at her own pace. You know your child best, and you are always welcome to slow down or speed up the pace of the lessons based on your child's needs.

Is My Child Ready to Start *Third Grade Math with Confidence*?

Your child is ready to begin this program if he can:

- Count by 1s, 2s, 5s, and 10s to 1,000.
- Read, write, and compare 3-digit numbers.
- Understand place-value in 3-digit numbers.
- Know the addition and subtraction facts mostly by heart. (He should be able to recall the answers to most within 3 seconds or so.)
- Know how to use place-value strategies to solve mental math problems like 55 + 37, 36 + 8, 90 – 42, or 74 – 6.
- Know how to add and subtract two- and three-digit numbers with the standard written process. (You might know this method as "stack math" or "borrowing and carrying.")

All of these skills are reviewed in the first few units, so don't worry if your child needs a refresher on a few of them. However, if your child is shaky on many of these skills, *Second Grade Math with Confidence* may be a better fit for her. Math skills build incrementally, and it will be difficult for your child to develop proficiency and confidence with the new third-grade skills if she has a weak foundation.

If your child is not fluent with the addition and subtraction facts but knows the rest of the skills listed above, she is probably ready to begin *Third Grade Math with Confidence*. Make sure to add 5 minutes of daily addition and subtraction facts practice to each lesson until your child becomes more fluent with the facts. *Addition Facts that Stick* and *Subtraction Facts That Stick* (also available from Well-Trained Mind Press) provide quick games to help your child master these essential skills.

How Do I Know Whether to Stick with a Lesson (or Unit) or Move On?

Most children need lots of exposure to a new concept or skill before they fully grasp it. Each lesson in *Third Grade Math with Confidence* gently builds on the previous one, but your child doesn't need to completely master every lesson before moving on to the next. The program includes many opportunities for practice and review before your child is expected to achieve full proficiency with a topic.

In general, continue teaching new lessons until you reach the end of a unit. At the end of each unit, you'll find a Checkpoint that provides guidance on whether your child is ready to move on to the next unit.

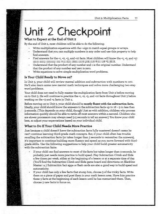

Each Checkpoint is divided into three parts:

- **What to Expect at the End of the Unit** This list of skills tells you what third graders typically are able to do at the end of each unit.
- **Is Your Child Ready to Move On?** This section tells you what your child needs to have mastered before moving on to the next unit.
- **What to Do if Your Child Needs More Practice** If your child isn't quite ready to move on, this section gives you options for reviewing and practicing the skills your child needs to master before the next unit. (This section is omitted if no specific skills are necessary for the next unit.)

For most units, your child is not expected to fully master all of the material from the current unit before moving on. For example, in Unit 2, your child will learn the ×2, ×5, and ×10 multiplication facts. He'll continue to practice multiplication as he studies mental addition and subtraction in Unit 3, but he does not need to be completely fluent with these multiplication facts before starting the new unit.

Scheduling

Third Grade Math with Confidence includes 144 lessons. 128 are regular lessons, and 16 are optional enrichment lessons. You're welcome to adjust the number of lessons you teach per week to best fit your family's schedule. Some families prefer to teach math 5 days per week, while others prefer to teach math 4 days per week and leave one day open for co-ops, errands, or field trips.

Use the following guidelines to plan your year:

- If you teach 4 lessons per week and teach all the enrichment lessons, *Third Grade Math with Confidence* will take you 36 weeks.
- If you teach 4 lessons per week and skip the enrichment lessons, *Third Grade Math with Confidence* will take you 32 weeks.
- If you teach 5 lessons per week and teach all the enrichment lessons, *Third Grade Math with Confidence* will take you 29 weeks.
- If you teach 5 lessons per week and skip the enrichment lessons, *Third Grade Math with Confidence* will take you 26 weeks.

Use this list as a rough guide to planning your year, but don't set it in stone. You'll generally be able to cover one lesson per day, but you may occasionally find that you want to split a lesson over two days.

How Can I Adjust the Lessons to Best Fit My Child and My Schedule?

Children vary tremendously in how quickly they learn new math concepts and skills. Use these suggestions to adjust the lessons to best fit your child's needs and your family's schedule.

- If your student is a fast processor or picks up math skills quickly, you may be able to **condense lessons** and teach more than one lesson in one day. If so, teach the concepts that are new to your child. Then, have your child complete a selection of exercises on the corresponding Practice and Review pages.
- If your child has a slower processing speed or takes a while to grasp math concepts and skills, some lessons may take longer than you would like (or longer than your child is able to stay engaged and attentive). If that's the case, **set a timer** for your desired lesson length, stop when the timer goes off, and continue the next day where you left off. In the elementary years, you are setting a foundation for a lifetime of proficiency and confidence in math. It's okay not to rush through these essential skills.
- If your child doesn't have the stamina to complete the Practice and Review pages at the same time, **split the lesson into two parts.** Do the Lesson Activities page and Practice page during one part of the day, and then have your child complete the Review page at a different time of the day.
- **Adjust your use of manipulatives** (like base-ten blocks, play money, or fraction circles) to fit your child's learning style. If your child readily understands a skill and doesn't enjoy using manipulatives, allow her to solve the problems without them. If your child learns best with a lot of visual and hands-on reinforcement, allow her to use manipulatives to model problems as much as she needs. Cut out some of the practice problems if the extra manipulative work makes the exercises take too long.
- Games provide a fun way to practice math skills, and they can be a great way to bond with your child. However, if your child doesn't enjoy games, or you don't have time for a game on a particular day, **choose a few problems from the game** for your child to solve instead. That way, he'll still get the extra practice that the game was meant to provide.
- Don't worry if you have a bad day every once in a while. Extra tiredness, oncoming illness, or just plain grumpiness can make for a less-than-cheerful math lesson. It's perfectly normal for children to occasionally get frustrated, and it doesn't mean that you're a bad math teacher or need to change the way you teach. If emotions rise during math, just **cut the lesson short and resume later** in the day or the next day. Most of the time, you'll find that the next day goes much better.

What You'll Need

You'll use simple household items to make math hands-on, concrete, and fun in *Third Grade Math with Confidence*. Most lessons only require materials from your Math Kit, but you'll also sometimes use everyday objects to enhance the lessons.

How to Create Your Math Kit

You'll use materials from your Math Kit in most lessons. Stick the following materials in a box or basket so they're always ready to go, and keep them handy when you're teaching.

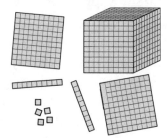

Base-ten blocks

- **Base-ten blocks.** Base-ten blocks provide a concrete way for children to understand place value. Each block represents a different value in our number system (ones, tens, hundreds, or thousands). Look for a set with at least 50 units, 20 rods, 10 flats, and 1 large cube, either online or at school supply stores. You can also photocopy and color Blackline Master 12 (page 571) instead, but children usually find real blocks easier to maneuver.
- **50 small counters.** Any type of small object (such as plastic tiles, Legos, blocks, plastic bears, coins, or dried beans) is fine. You can also use the units from your set of base-ten blocks. You'll occasionally need 2 colors, so make sure at least 10 of the counters are a different color than the rest.
- **Coins (20 pennies, 20 nickels, 20 dimes, 10 quarters).** You can use toy coins, but children often enjoy using real coins more. (If you live outside the U.S., you can use your local currency's coins instead. See the materials note on page 10 for more details.)
- **Play money (20 each of one-dollar bills, ten-dollar bills, and hundred-dollar bills; 10 each of five-dollar bills, twenty-dollar bills, and thousand-dollar bills).** Play money from a toy cash register or board game works well, or you can copy and cut out the play money on Blackline Master 13.
- **Clock with hands.** Your clock should have clear, easy-to-read numbers, tick marks along the edge for each minute, and hands your child can easily move. If your family's clocks don't meet these criteria, you may want to buy an inexpensive plastic geared teaching clock.
- **Fraction circles.** Either plastic or wood is fine, and you can find them online or at school supply stores. If you don't have access to fraction circles, photocopy and color Blackline Master 7 (page 551) instead.
- **1-foot (or 30-centimeter) ruler.** You will teach your child to measure with both inches and centimeters this year, so make sure your ruler is labeled with both units.
- **2 packs of playing cards and 2 dice.** You'll use playing cards or dice for many of the games. Any standard 52-card decks and regular, six-sided dice will work fine.
- **Blank paper.** Any kind of paper is fine, including plain copy paper.
- **Pencils.** Keep sharp pencils on hand for lessons and workbook pages.
- **1 page protector and 1 dry erase marker.** Place the dot array (Blackline Master 5) in a plastic page protector so you can write on it with a dry-erase marker.
- **Binder with about 10 plastic page protectors.** (Recommended, but not required.) You'll use Blackline Masters often throughout the book. Some are for modeling important concepts, while others provide helpful reference information. Many pilot-test families found it easiest to keep track of these pages in plastic page protectors in a binder. Storing the pages in a binder also makes it easy for your child to refer to them as he completes the Practice and Review pages.

See page 531 for the full guide to the Blackline Masters. You may want to copy or print the Blackline Masters now so that you don't have to worry about it when you reach the corresponding lessons. **If you prefer to print the Blackline Masters rather than copy them from the book, you can download digital copies at welltrainedmind.com/mwc.**

 You will occasionally need to save items for future lessons. This symbol will alert you if you need to save anything.

Other Supplies Needed

You'll only need your Math Kit for most lessons, but occasionally you'll need a few other common household items. You'll find these items listed in three different places in the curriculum to make sure you always know what you need:

- The preview for each unit lists all extra household items needed.
- The top of each lesson lists all supplies you'll need to teach that lesson. These lists include items from your Math Kit as well as extra household items. (Note that many lessons require paper, slips of paper, pencils, or a dry-erase marker. To save space, they are not listed unless you need more than 3 slips of paper or pieces of paper.)
- You'll find the complete list of household items needed throughout the year on pages 529-530.

Don't feel you have to gather every extra household item now. Most are common things like markers, tape, or scissors, so you can grab them right before you begin the lesson.

Note for Families Living Outside the U.S.

Math with Confidence uses American money and the U.S. customary measurement system, but it's designed to be easy to adapt to use anywhere in the world. Here are some tips for adapting the program to wherever your family lives.

- When you teach lessons with money, change the language in the lessons to match whatever currency you use. Use your country's coins in place of the American coins. For paper bills, use money from your country's currency, play money from a board game or a toy cash register, or the generic bills on Blackline Master 13. Write your country's currency symbol in place of the dollar sign.
- The measurement lessons cover both metric units (such as meters, grams, liters) and U.S. customary units (such as feet, pounds, cups). Even if you use the metric system, do teach these lessons. They often include important foundational measurement skills, and they'll help your child understand measurement concepts more deeply.

Helpful Resources

You'll find an appendix of helpful resources at the back of this book:

- Complete Picture Book List
- Scope and Sequence
- Complete Memory Work List
- Materials List
- Blackline Masters

Unit 1
Review Addition and Subtraction

Overview

Your child will review several essential skills she learned in second grade:

- comparing numbers
- understanding the relationship between addition and subtraction
- addition and subtraction word problems
- adding and subtracting numbers to 100 with the written algorithms.

These gentle introductory lessons help your child start the year on a positive, confident note. They also refresh your child's memory if you took a break from math for the summer.

Your child will also deepen her understanding of the numbers to 100 as she learns to approximate numbers' positions on the number line and round two-digit numbers to the nearest ten. She'll also think more abstractly about addition and subtraction as she finds missing numbers in equations, and she'll learn to solve multi-step word problems.

What Your Child Will Learn

In this unit, your child will learn to:

- Round two-digit numbers to the nearest ten
- Compare numbers and addition and subtraction expressions with the <, >, and = signs
- Find missing numbers in addition and subtraction equations
- Solve one- and two-step addition and subtraction word problems
- Review adding and subtracting two-digit numbers with the addition and subtraction algorithms
- Review bar graphs

Lesson List

Lesson 1.1	Round to the Nearest Ten	Lesson 1.5	Review Word Problems
Lesson 1.2	Review Comparing	Lesson 1.6	Two-Step Word Problems
Lesson 1.3	Find Missing Numbers in Equations, Part 1	Lesson 1.7	Review Written Addition
		Lesson 1.8	Review Written Subtraction
Lesson 1.4	Find Missing Numbers in Equations, Part 2	Lesson 1.9	Review Bar Graphs
		Lesson 1.10	Enrichment (Optional)

Extra Materials Needed for Unit 1

- 6 toothpicks
- White crayon
- Marker or highlighter
- Markers or colored pencils
- 10 slips of paper
- For optional Enrichment Lesson:
    - × *Fun with Roman Numerals*, written by David A. Adler and illustrated by Edward Miller III. Holiday House, 2009.

You will also need items from your Math Kit in this unit (and every unit!). If you haven't yet made your Math Kit, see page 9 for instructions on how to assemble it.

The suggested picture books are listed at the beginning of each unit so you have time to buy them or request them from the library. They are a delightful way to enjoy math, but they are not required. You may also be able to find some of the books available online as video read-alouds.

Teaching Math with Confidence:
How to Teach Your Child to Understand and Solve Word Problems

When children read stories, they often read for the main idea, without worrying about every detail. This approach doesn't work when reading math! In this unit, you'll teach your child how to read word problems slowly and carefully so that she fully comprehends them. You'll also prompt her to identify the goal in word problems and read them twice before solving.

How to Read Word Problems

1. Read the problem.
2. Identify the goal.
3. Read the problem again.
   - Read slowly and carefully.
   - Imagine what's happening.
   - Stop after each sentence to make sure you understand it.
4. Solve.

Third-graders vary widely in both their reading comprehension skills and their enthusiasm for word problems. Some children love solving problems about real-life situations, but others find them challenging. If your child struggles with word problems, adjust your word problem instruction to best fit her needs:

- If your child is still working on becoming a proficient reader, **read the word problems aloud to her.** Keep reading instruction separate from math lessons so that your child can focus on math rather than decoding the words.
- Some third-graders may have already developed the habit of looking for keywords, like "more" or "in all." Looking for keywords short-circuits the process of deeply understanding the structure of these problems. It also doesn't always work, both in real life and on standardized tests! **Discourage your child from looking for keywords** and reassure her that the steps for reading word problems will help her understand and solve the problems.
- If your child has trouble understanding a word problem, act out or **pantomime the sequence of events** to make the problem more concrete.
- If your child feels overwhelmed by the number of words in a problem, encourage her to **underline the important information and the goal of the problem.** Underlining helps to visually simplify the problem.

You'll teach your child to solve a variety of one- and two-step word problems this year, including problems with multiplication and division. By learning how to methodically read word problems now, she'll be better-prepared to tackle these new types of problems with confidence. There's no magic formula for solving word problems, but learning to read them slowly and carefully makes a huge difference!

Lesson 1.1
Round to the Nearest Ten

Purpose	Materials
• Set a positive tone for the year and preview what your child will learn • Introduce the concept of rounding • Learn to round two-digit numbers to the nearest ten	• Playing cards • Counters

Warm-up: Introduce the Workbooks

Today, you'll begin your new math book. Let's take a look at your workbooks and see what you'll learn this year. Briefly page through both workbooks with your child. **What are you most excited to learn about in math this year?** *Answers will vary.*

Show your child the Lesson 1.1 workbook pages. **This year, your lessons will have three pages. The first page is the Lesson Activities page. This page has sample problems, fun hands-on activities, and games.** Point out the icon with two heads at the top of the page. **We'll complete the Lesson Activities pages together.**

Point out the icon with one head at the top of the Practice and Review pages. **You'll complete the Practice and Review pages on your own. The Practice page gives you independent practice with the new skills from the lesson. The Review page reviews topics that you've already learned.**

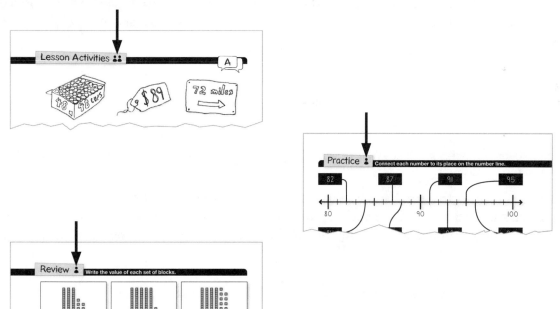

You will complete the Lesson Activities page with your child.
Your child will complete the Practice and Review pages independently.

The lesson plans recommend that you write the answers on the Lesson Activities page, and your child write the answers on the Practice and Review workbook pages. Feel free to adjust this based on your child. It's fine for your child to write the answers on the Lesson Activities pages or for you to scribe some or all of your child's answers on the Practice and Review pages.

Activity (A): Introduce Rounding

Today, you'll learn how to round numbers to the nearest ten. When we say the "nearest ten," we mean the numbers that we say when we count by 10s. In everyday conversation, we often round numbers instead of telling exact amounts. Show your child the pictures in part A. Discuss each picture with your child and tell how you might round the number in each picture:

- **If I buy a pack of 48 cups for a party, I might say that I bought about 50 cups.**
- **If something costs $89, I might say that it cost about $90.**
- **If it's 72 miles to the aquarium, I might say that the aquarium is about 70 miles away.**

Activity (B): Use the Number Line to Round to the Nearest Ten

Show your child the printed number line in part B. **Let's pretend there are 62 children in a hockey league. About where would 62 go on this number line?** *Child points between 60 and 70.* **62 is between 60 and 70. Is 62 closer to 60 or 70?** *60.* **How do you know?** *Answers will vary.*

Here's one way to tell. 65 is halfway between 60 and 70. Draw a light tick mark halfway between 60 and 70 on the number line and label it 65. **62 is less than 65, so it is closer to 60 than 70. That means 62 rounded to the nearest ten is 60. There are about 60 children in the league.** Have your child write 60 in the chart.

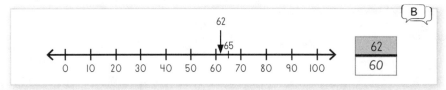

> Framing rounding in this way helps your child develop deeper number sense and begin to think about distances on the number line.

Have your child use the same approach to complete the chart. For 45, say: **45 is 5 more than 40, and it's 5 less than 50. It's exactly in between! Mathematicians have agreed that we round in-between numbers to the higher number. So, 45 rounded to the nearest ten is 50.**

62	69	87	23	18	51	45	96
60	70	90	20	20	50	50	100

Activity (C): Play Round to the Nearest Ten Crash

Play Round to the Nearest Ten Crash.

Round to the Nearest Ten Crash

Materials: Deck of playing cards with 10s, jacks, queens, and kings removed (36 cards total); 10 counters of two different colors each

Object of the Game: Have the most counters on the game board at the end of the game.

Shuffle the cards and place the stack face down on the table. Give 10 counters of one color to one player and 10 counters of a different color to the other player.

On your turn, flip over the top two cards. Use the cards to make a two-digit number. Round the number to the nearest ten, and place a counter on the square that matches the rounded number. For example, if you flip over a 7 and 9, you can make 97 or 79. If you make 97, place a counter on 100, since 97 rounds to 100. If you make 79, place a counter on 80, since 79 rounds to 80.

If the other player already has a counter on the square, you may "crash" into their counter, remove it, and place your own counter on the square. Continue until you have used all the cards in the deck. Whoever has more counters on the board wins the game.

Independent Practice and Review

Have your child complete the Lesson 1.1 Practice and Review pages.

Many third-graders will need some time to build up the stamina necessary to complete the Practice and Review pages on their own. If needed, break up the work and have your child complete the Review page at a different time of day than the Practice page.

Lesson 1.2
Review Comparing

Purpose	Materials
• Practice addition facts • Review the <, >, and = signs • Complete numbers and addition and subtraction expressions	• 2 decks of playing cards • 6 toothpicks • Counters

Warm-up: Addition Least to Greatest

Play one round of Addition Least to Greatest.

Addition Least to Greatest

Materials: 2 decks of cards, with jacks, queens, and kings removed (80 cards total)

Object of the Game: Win the most cards.

Shuffle the cards and deal 5 cards to both players. Place the rest of the deck in a face-down pile.

Choose who will go first. Player 1 chooses two cards from his hand, places them face-up on the table, and names their sum. For example, if you play a 4 and a 3, the sum is 7. Then, Player 1 picks up two new cards to replenish his hand.

Player 2 then chooses any two cards from her hand whose sum is greater than Player 1's sum. She places them on top of Player 1's cards, names their sum, and takes 2 new cards to replenish her hand. For example, if Player 1 played a 4 and a 3, Player 2 can play any two cards with a sum greater than 7.

Sample first turn for Player 1.   Sample first turn for Player 2.
Player 2 places her cards directly on top of
Player 1's cards. She may play any pair of numbers
with a greater sum than the previous pair of cards.

Continue alternating turns until one player can no longer play a greater sum. The player who played last takes all of the face-up cards. The player who was unable to play new cards chooses two cards from their hand and starts a new round.

Play until you have used all the cards. Whoever has won the most cards wins the game.

Activity (A): Review the <, >, and = Signs

Today, we'll review comparing. Show your child the first inequality in part A. **This sign is called the greater-than sign. We read this mathematical statement as** *87 is greater than 42.* Have your child create the greater-than sign from toothpicks. Write 87 and 42 on slips of paper and place them next to the toothpick sign.

The next sign is called the less-than sign. We read this mathematical statement as *42 is less than 87.* Have your child create the less-than sign from toothpicks. Reverse the position for the slips of paper.

People often get confused by the greater-than and less-than signs, since they look so much alike! Remember, the small, pointy part of the sign always points to the lesser number, and the big, wide part of the sign always opens toward the greater number. You can pretend that the sign is an alligator's mouth that wants to chomp the bigger number!

The last sign is the equals sign. We read this equation as *42 equals 42.* Have your child create the equals sign from toothpicks. Write 42 on another slip of paper and arrange the slips as shown.

The equals sign has 2 lines like the greater-than and less-than signs. But the two lines open equally wide on both sides, just like the amounts on either side are equal to each other.

Have your child write the correct sign between the number pairs at the bottom of part A. If he has trouble writing the signs, have him first construct each sign with toothpicks before writing it.

Mathematical statements with an equals sign are called *equations*. They tell that two amounts are equal to each other. Listen to how the word equation starts like the word equal. That can help you remember that equations tell that two amounts are equal.

Mathematical statements that use the greater-than or less-than sign are called *inequalities*. Inequalities tell that one amount is greater than or less than another amount. The prefix in- means "not." So, the word inequality means "not an equality."

Which of the mathematical statements in part A are equations? *42 equals 42 and 38 equals 38.*

Which of the mathematical statements in part A are inequalities? *87 is greater than 42, 42 is less than 87, 60 is less than 100, and 49 is greater than 47.*

Activity (B): Complete Equations and Inequalities with <, >, or =

Show your child part B. **We can think of the two sides of equations and inequalities like two sides of a scale. Let's pretend the counters are weights, and that the printed scale is a real scale!**

Put 5 counters on the left side of the printed scale, and 4 counters on the right side. **Which side would be heavier, the side with 5 counters or the side with 4 counters?** *The side with 5 counters.* Break a toothpick in half and use the two halves to construct a greater-than sign between the two sides of the scale. 5 is greater than 4. Write ">" in the blank.

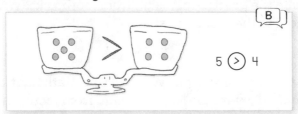

To make this activity more kinesthetic, have your child hold out his hands and pretend to be a scale. Place 5 counters in his left hand and 4 counters in his right hand. **Which side weighs more?** *The side with 5 counters.* Have him tip his hands like a scale to show that 5 counters weigh more than 4 counters.

The next problem tells us to put 3 plus 3 counters on the left side. What's 3 plus 3? *6.* Write 6 below 3 + 3 and have your child put 6 counters on the left side of the scale. (He may need to overlap them or stack them.)

It tells us to put 7 counters on the right side. Have your child put 7 counters on the right side. **Which side has more counters?** *The side with 7 counters.* Use the toothpick halves to construct a less-than sign between the two sides of the scale. **3 plus 3 is less than 7.** Write "<" in the blank.

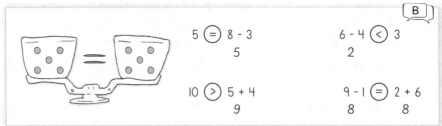

Writing the sum keeps your child from having to remember it while he compares the numbers. It also builds good habits for solving algebraic equations when he's older.

The next problem tells us to put 5 counters on the left side. Have your child put 5 counters on the left side. **It tells us to put 8 minus 3 counters on the right side. What's 8 minus 3?** *5.* Put 5 counters on the right side of the scale and write 5 below 8 – 3.

Which side has more counters? *They're equal!* Use the toothpick halves to construct an equals sign between the two sides of the scale. **5 equals 8 minus 3.** Write "=" in the blank. Have your child complete part B.

Independent Practice and Review

Have your child complete the Lesson 1.2 Practice and Review pages.

Many answers are possible for the problems at the bottom of the Practice page. For example, for the first problem (7 + 6 < ___), your child can write any number greater than 13 to make the statement true.

The optional starred problems provide extra challenge and give your child the chance to stretch his skills. If your child struggles with the challenge problems or feels frustrated by them, feel free to skip them.

Lesson 1.3
Find Missing Numbers in Equations, Part 1

Purpose	Materials
• Review addition facts • Review fact families and Part-Total Diagrams • Use the Part-Total Diagrams and the relationship between addition and subtraction to find missing numbers in equations	• 2 decks of playing cards • White crayon • Marker or highlighter

Warm-up: Addition Least to Greatest

Play one round of Addition Least to Greatest. See Lesson 1.2 (page 16) for full directions.

Activity (A): Review Fact Families and Part-Total Diagrams

Today, we'll review how addition and subtraction are related. Then, you'll use that relationship to find secret numbers in equations.

This Part-Total Diagram shows that we can join 8 and 4 to make 12. What two addition equations match the Part-Total Diagram? *8 plus 4 equals 12. 4 plus 8 equals 12.* Write "8 + 4 = 12" and "4 + 8 = 12" in the blanks.

The diagram also shows we can split 12 into a group of 8 and a group of 4. What two subtraction equations match the Part-Total Diagram? *12 minus 4 equals 8. 12 minus 8 equals 4.* Write "12 − 4 = 8" and "12 − 8 = 4" in the blanks.

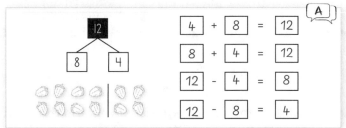

This group of addition and subtraction equations is a *fact family*. The fact family tells the addition and subtraction relationships between 8, 4, and 12. Briefly review addition and subtraction vocabulary:

- **What do we call the result when we add numbers together?** *The sum.*
- **What do we call the numbers that we add together?** *The addends.*
- **What do we call the result when we subtract a number from another number?** *The difference.*

Have your child complete the Part-Total Diagrams.

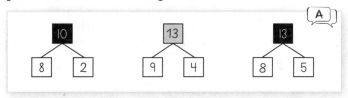

Activity (B): Find the Secret Number in Addition and Subtraction Equations

I'm going to write a secret number in each equation in white crayon. Your job is to use the Part-Total Diagrams to find the secret numbers. Once you find the secret number, you can color over it with a marker to reveal it! Use a white crayon to secretly complete the highlighted blanks:

$$\boxed{7} + 6 = 13 \qquad 12 - \boxed{3} = 9 \qquad \boxed{15} - 8 = 7 \;\; \text{B}$$

> If you don't have a white crayon, write the numbers in pencil and cover each with a counter or small slip of paper. Have your child remove the counter or slip of paper after she figures out the secret number.

Read the first equation aloud: ***What plus 6 equals 13?* You know one part and the total, and you want to find the other part. What is the total?** *13.* **What is one of the parts?** *6.* Write 13 and 6 in the Part-Total Diagram.

> If your child "just knows" the answer and doesn't want to use the Part-Total Diagram to help solve the problem, ask her to pretend to be the teacher and teach you how to use the Part-Total Diagram to find the answer.

You know the total and one part, so, you can subtract 13 minus 6 to find the missing part. What's 13 minus 6? *7.* Write 7 in the Part-Total Diagram. Have your child use a marker to color over the blank in the equation and reveal the 7.

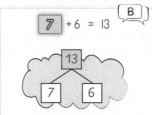

> If your child has trouble understanding how the Part-Total diagram matches the equation, model the problem with counters. Place 7 counters under a piece of paper and place 6 counters next to the piece of paper. **The counters under the paper plus the 6 counters next to the paper equal 13 counters. How many counters must be under the paper?** *7.*

Read the next equation aloud: ***12 minus what equals 9?* What is the total?** *12.* **What is one of the parts?** *9.* Write 12 and 9 in the Part-Total Diagram. **How can you find the missing part?** *Subtract 12 minus 9.* **So, what's the missing number?** *3.* Write 3 in the Part-Total Diagram. Have your child use a marker to reveal the 3.

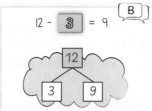

> If your child has trouble, model the problem with counters. Place 12 counters on the table. Secretly take 3 and place them under a piece of paper. **I had 12 counters and took some away. Now, there are 9 left. How many did I take away?** *3.*

Read the final equation aloud: *What minus 8 equals 7?* **In this problem, we know both of the parts. We want to find the total. What are the parts?** *8 and 7.* Write 8 and 7 in the Part-Total Diagram as shown. **How can we find the missing number?** *Add 8 plus 7.* **So, what's the missing number?** *15.* Write 15 in the Part-Total Diagram. Have your child use a marker to reveal the 15.

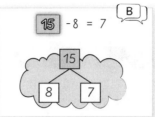

If your child has trouble, model the problem with counters. Place 15 counters under a piece of paper. Slide 8 out from under the paper, and show your child that 7 are left. **I had some counters and took 8 away. Now, there are 7 left under the paper. How many did I start with?** *15.*

For the final three equations, have your child make up her own equations with missing numbers for you to find. Have her first write each complete equation on scrap paper. Then, have her transfer the equation to the Lesson Activities page. She should write the secret number (in the highlighted box) in white crayon and the other numbers in pencil. After you figure out the secret number, use a marker to reveal it.

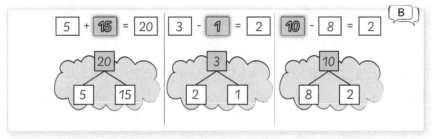

Sample equations and Part-Total Diagrams. Your child may choose different equations.

Independent Practice and Review

Have your child complete the Lesson 1.3 Practice and Review workbook pages. If she has trouble finding any of the missing numbers in the equations, suggest she draw Part-Total diagrams to help.

If possible, check your child's work as soon as she finishes, and have her correct any mistakes. Children benefit from immediate accountability, and your prompt attention shows that you value your child's work and effort.

Lesson 1.4
Find Missing Numbers in Equations, Part 2

Purpose	Materials
• Introduce and practice memory work • Find missing numbers in addition or subtraction equations	• Memory Work (Blackline Master 1) • White crayon • Marker or highlighter

In this lesson, you'll introduce your child to the Memory Work list. Store this list (and other Blackline Masters) in a binder so that you always have them available for easy reference. You'll add more helpful resources to the math binder throughout the year. See the Introduction (pages 9-10) for more on organizing Blackline Masters.

All Blackline Masters are available at the back of the book. **You can also find all Blackline Masters at well-trainedmind.com/mwc for easy printing.**

Warm-up: Introduce and Practice Memory Work

Show your child the list of memory work on Blackline Master 1. **You'll memorize these important vocabulary words and facts this year. You already know some of them, and some of them are new. We'll practice them throughout the year so that you memorize all of them.**

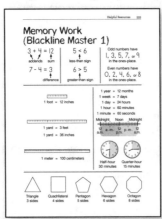
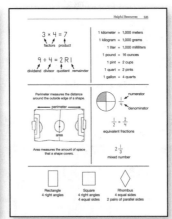

The first page of Blackline Master 1 reviews the memory work children learned in *Second Grade Math with Confidence.* If you didn't use *Second Grade Math with Confidence,* you do not need to stop and help your child memorize all these items now. He'll have plenty of opportunities to learn these memory work items over the course of the year. The second page of Blackline Master 1 has new memory work items that will be introduced over the course of this year.

Today, we'll review just a few memory work questions. Ask your child the following questions. If he has trouble with any of the questions, allow him to peek at the Memory Work list to find the correct answer.

- **What do we call the result when we add numbers together?** *The sum.*
- **What do we call the numbers that we add together?** *The addends.*
- **What do we call the result when we subtract a number from another number?** *The difference.*
- Write the < sign. **What does this sign mean?** *Less than.*
- Write the > sign. **What does this sign mean?** *Greater than.*
- **If a number has 1, 3, 5, 7, or 9 in the ones-place, is the number even or odd?** *Odd.*
- **If a number has 0, 2, 4, 6, or 8 in the ones-place, is the number even or odd?** *Even.*

If your child is not familiar with even and odd numbers, explain that even numbers of objects can be evenly divided into two groups, but odd numbers of objects can't. Also name some two- or three-digit numbers and have him tell whether the numbers are even or odd.

Activity (A): Understand Two Ways to Write Addition and Subtraction Equations

In the last lesson, you found secret numbers in equations. Today, you'll use the idea of a scale to find more secret numbers in equations.

Read the first equation aloud: *3 plus 4 equals what?* **There are 3 blue marbles and 4 green marbles on the left side of the scale. How many would you have to put on the right side to make the scale balance?** *7.* Write 7 in the blank. Have your child draw 7 marbles on the right side.

$$3 + 4 = \boxed{7}$$

Read the second equation aloud: *What equals 3 plus 4?* **This time, there are 3 blue marbles and 4 green marbles on the right side of the scale. How many would you have to put on the left side to make the scale balance?** *7.* Write 7 in the blank. Have your child draw 7 marbles on the left side.

$$\boxed{7} = 3 + 4$$

Both equations mean the same thing. The numbers are just written in a different order. Does this second equation look funny to you? *Answers will vary.* It can take a little time to get used to seeing equations written this way!

We can write the numbers in subtraction problems on both sides of the equals sign, too. Repeat with the subtraction equations in part A.

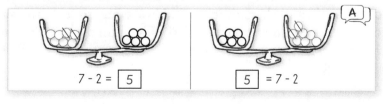

$$7 - 2 = \boxed{5} \qquad \boxed{5} = 7 - 2$$

Activity (B): Find the Secret Number in Addition and Subtraction Equations

I'm going to write a secret number in each equation in white crayon again. This time, we'll use the scale to find the secret numbers. Use a white crayon to secretly complete the blank in each equation:

Read aloud the first equation: *What equals 4 plus 4?* How many marbles would you have to put on the left side to make the scale balance? *8.* Have him draw 8 marbles on the left side of the scale. Then, have him use a marker to reveal the secret number in the equation.

Have your child solve the next equation in the same way.

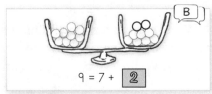

Read aloud the next equation: *9 equals 7 plus what?* There are 9 marbles on the left side of the scale, and 7 marbles on the right side. **How many marbles would you have to add to the right side to make the scale balance?** *2.* Have him draw 2 more marbles on the right side of the scale. Then, have your child use a marker to reveal the secret number.

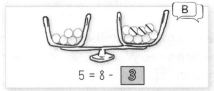

Read aloud the next equation: *5 equals 8 minus what?* There are 5 marbles on the left side of the scale, and 8 marbles on the right side. **How many marbles would you have to subtract from the right side to make the scale balance?** *3.* Have him cross out 3 of the marbles on the right side of the scale and reveal the secret number.

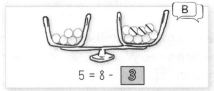

Watch out, these last two equations are tricky! Read aloud the next equation: ***4 equals what minus 2?*** There are 4 marbles on the left side of the scale. Imagine we put some marbles on the right side of the scale and then subtract 2. **How many marbles should we put on the right side to make the scale balance in the end?** *6.* Have him draw 6 marbles on the right side of the scale and then cross out 2 of the marbles. Then, have your child use a marker to reveal the secret number.

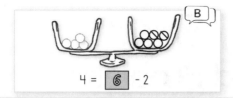

$$4 = \boxed{6} - 2$$

If your child struggles with this problem, suggest he try a few possibilities for the missing number. For ex-ample: **If you put 10 marbles on the right side and subtract 2, how many marbles would be left?** *8.* **Would the scale be balanced?** *No, the right side would be too heavy.* **Let's try a smaller number.**

Have your child solve the final problem in the same way.

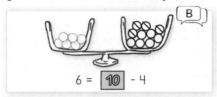

$$6 = \boxed{10} - 4$$

Independent Practice and Review

Have your child complete the Lesson 1.4 Practice and Review workbook pages.

The Review pages review many of the skills covered in *Second Grade Math with Confidence* so that your child is ready to extend these skills later in the year. For example, in the Lesson 1.4 Review page, he'll prac-tice identifying fractional parts. He'll continue to practice writing simple fractions on the Review pages in Units 1-5, and then he'll study fractions in depth in Unit 6. If you find that your child has forgotten one of the skills included on the Review pages, briefly explain it to him.

Lesson 1.5
Review Word Problems

Purpose	Materials
• Practice memory work • Learn strategies for reading word problems • Review addition and subtraction word problems	• Memory Work (Blackline Master 1) • Markers or colored pencils

All of the word problems in this lesson involve simple numbers so that your child can focus on understanding the structure of the problems. If she would like more challenge, cross out the numbers in the problems and replace them with harder numbers.

Warm-up: Practice Memory Work

Ask your child the following questions. If she has trouble with any of the questions, allow her to peek at the Memory Work list to find the correct answer.

- **How many months are in a year?** *12.*
- **How many days are in a week?** *7.*
- **How many hours are in a day?** *24.*
- **How many minutes are in an hour?** *60.*
- **How many seconds are in a minute?** *60.*
- **Are times in the morning a.m. or p.m.?** *A.m.*
- **Are times in the afternoon and evening a.m. or p.m.?** *P.m.*
- **What is another name for 12 a.m.?** *Midnight.*
- **What is another name for 12 p.m.?** *Noon.*
- **How many minutes equal a half-hour?** *30.*
- **How many minutes equal a quarter-hour?** *15.*

Discuss any items that are unfamiliar to your child.

Activity (A): Learn Reading Strategies for Word Problems

Today, we'll review how to solve addition and subtraction word problems. Reading math is very different than reading a story. When you read a story, you can enjoy the story even if you don't fully understand every word or detail. But in word problems, every detail matters. You need to fully understand every sentence before you try to solve the problem.

Following these steps will help you understand and solve word problems. Read aloud the steps in the box.

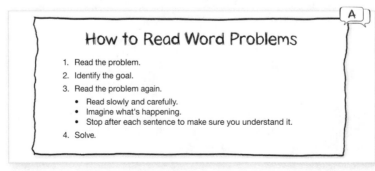

How to Read Word Problems

1. Read the problem.
2. Identify the goal.
3. Read the problem again.
   - Read slowly and carefully.
   - Imagine what's happening.
   - Stop after each sentence to make sure you understand it.
4. Solve.

Activity (B): Use Part-Total Diagrams to Solve Word Problems

Have your child read aloud the first word problem in part B. **What's the goal?** *Find how much money I have at the end.* Then, have her read the problem again slowly and describe what she imagines. For example: *I imagine I have some money, and then I get some more!*

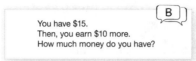

> If your child is not a proficient reader, read the problem aloud to her instead. See the Unit 1 **Teaching Math with Confidence** for more on how to support your child as she solves word problems.

> If your child immediately knows the answers to the word problems in this lesson, don't require her to follow every step for reading word problems. Instead, simply introduce the steps in this lesson and revisit them when she solves two-step word problems in Lesson 1.6.

We'll use the Part-Total Diagram to solve the problem.

- **You start with $15. That's one part.** Write 15 in the Part-Total Diagram.
- **Then, you earn $10 more. That's the other part.** Write 10 in the Part-Total Diagram.
- **We know two parts. How do we find the total?** *Add 15 and 10.* Have your child write an equation to match: 15 + 10 = 25. Write 25 in the Part-Total Diagram.
- **Last, label and draw a box around your answer.** Have your child write a dollar sign before the 25 and draw a box around the complete answer.

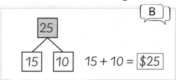

> Labeling the answers reminds your child to think about whether her answers are reasonable. Drawing a box around the answers makes it easier for you to check her work.

Have your child read aloud the next word problem. **What's the goal?** *Find how much the markers cost.* Then, have her read the problem again slowly and describe what she imagines.

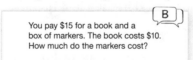

We'll use a Part-Total Diagram again to solve this problem.

- **The book and markers together cost $15. That's the total that gets split into parts.** Write 15 in the top of the Part-Total Diagram.
- **The book costs $10. That's one part.** Write 10 in the diagram.
- **We know the total and one part. How do we find the other part?** *Subtract 15 minus 10.* Have your child write an equation to match: 15 – 10 = 5. Write 5 in the Part-Total Diagram.
- Have your child write a dollar sign before the 5 and draw a box around the complete answer.

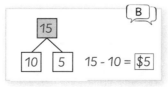

Activity (C): Review Comparison Word Problems

Have your child read aloud the word problem. **What's the goal?** *Find how many more inches you have of red ribbon than blue.* Then, have her read the problem again slowly. **Instead of imagining this problem, let's draw a sketch to visualize it.** Use a red marker or colored pencil to draw a line. Label it as shown. **This is just a sketch, so it's okay that the line isn't actually 10 inches.**

Now, I'll draw the blue line. Should it be longer or shorter than the red line? *Shorter.* Use a blue crayon or colored pencil to draw a line that is shorter than the red line. Label it as shown.

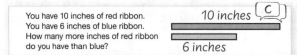

Give your child a moment to look at the picture and try to solve the problem. **How many more inches of red ribbon are there?** *4 inches.* **How do you know?** *Sample answer: I subtracted 10 minus 6.*

This is a comparison word problem. You knew both lengths, and you found the difference between them. To compare two numbers, we start with the greater number and then subtract the lesser number.

> If your child is confused by the terms "greater" and "lesser," you may use "bigger" and "smaller" instead. "Bigger number" and "smaller number" are not precise mathematical terms, but they're more familiar to children.

What's the greater number in this problem? *10.* **What's the lesser number?** *6.* Write the numbers in the blanks and have your child complete the equation. Have her label her answer with "inches" and draw a box around the complete answer.

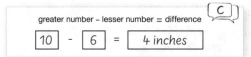

What do we call an answer to a subtraction problem? *The difference.* **That's because the answer to a subtraction problem tells how "different" the numbers are from each other! The difference between 10 inches and 6 inches is 4 inches.**

Independent Practice and Review

Have your child complete the Lesson 1.5 Practice and Review workbook pages. Have your child draw Part-Total Diagrams as needed to solve the word problems.

Lesson 1.6
Two-Step Word Problems

Purpose	Materials
• Practice memory work • Solve two-step word problems • Find a missing part out of three parts	• Memory Work (Blackline Master 1) • How to Read Word Problems (Blackline Master 2)

Warm-up: Practice Memory Work

Ask your child the following questions. If he has trouble with any of the questions, allow him to peek at the Memory Work list to find the correct answer.

- **How many sides does a triangle have?** *3.*
- **How many sides does a quadrilateral have?** *4.*
- **How many sides does a pentagon have?** *5.*
- **How many sides does a hexagon have?** *6.*
- **How many sides does an octagon have?** *8.*

If your child is not familiar with these shapes, you may want to have him briefly construct each type of polygon with popsicle sticks or toothpicks to give him hands-on practice with these definitions.

Activity (A): Use Reading Strategies to Solve Two-Step Word Problems

In the last lesson, we reviewed word problems. What do you remember about the steps for reading word problems? *Sample answer: You read them twice and imagine what's happening.* Show your child the steps for reading word problems on Blackline Master 2 and briefly review them.

Add Blackline Master 2 to your Math Binder. Keep the binder open to this page as you complete the rest of the lesson. Encourage your child to refer to this page any time he has trouble with a word problem.

It only took one step to solve the word problems in the last lesson. Today, you'll solve problems with two or three steps. These problems are more complicated, so it's even more important that you read them slowly and carefully before solving.

Have your child read aloud the first word problem, identify the goal, and then read the problem again slowly. Stop him after each sentence and ask him to describe what he imagines. For example: *"Oscar has $11 to spend at the carnival."* *I imagine a boy with some money in his hand.*

Now, let's solve the problem. Use the following dialogue to help your child solve the problem.

- **Oscar starts with $11 and spends $4. What equation matches that part of the problem?** *11 minus 4 equals 7.* Write "11 − 4 = 7."
- **Now, Oscar has $7. He spends $3. What equation matches that part of the problem?** *7 minus 3 equals 4.* Write "7 − 3 = 4."
- **So, how much money does Oscar have left?** *$4.* Write a dollar sign next to the 4 and draw a box around the answer.

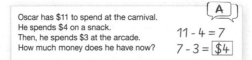

You could also write "11 − 4 − 3 = 4" to solve this word problem. This is a valid equation, since the quantities on either side of the equals sign are the same. However, writing each step as a separate equation reinforces the idea that your child should think through each step of the problem. Write two equations for this sample problem, but allow your child to write his equations either way.

Do not allow your child to write all the steps in one long, horizontal equation like "11 − 4 = 7 − 3 = 4." This is not a valid equation, since the quantities on each side of the equals signs do not actually equal each other.

Repeat with the other word problem.

Activity (B): Draw Part-Total Diagrams to Solve Two-Step Word Problems

Have your child read aloud the ice cream word problem. Have him identify the goal and then read the problem again slowly. Stop him after each sentence and ask him to describe what he imagines. For example: *"4 cones were chocolate. 5 were vanilla. The rest were strawberry."* *I imagine 3 groups of ice cream cones. Each group has a different flavor.*

This problem is about parts of a total, so we can use a Part-Total Diagram to solve it. 3 different parts make up the total: chocolate, vanilla, and strawberry. So, the Part-Total Diagram has boxes for all 3 parts.

What's the total number of ice cream cones the shop sold? *12.* Write 12 as the total. **4 of the cones were chocolate.** Write 4 as one part. **5 of the cones were vanilla.** Write 5 as another part.

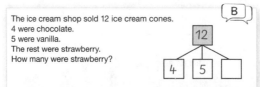

We want to find how many cones were strawberry. That's the missing part. First, let's add 4 plus 5 to find out how many ice cream cones are not strawberry. Write "4 + 5 = " and have your child complete the equation: 4 + 5 = 9.

Now, let's subtract 12 minus 9 to find out how many ice cream cones are strawberry. Write "12 – 9 = " and have your child complete the equation: 12 – 9 = 3. **So, 3 cones are strawberry.** Write 3 in the Part-Total Diagram. Have your child label and box the answer.

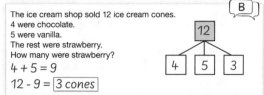

If your child is confused, use counters to model the problem. Place 12 counters on the table. Have your child separate the counters into groups to match the problem.

Have your child solve the other word problem in part B in the same way.

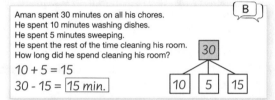

If your child immediately knows the answer, ask him to complete the Part-Total Diagram and write the matching equations anyway. Explain that practicing with easier numbers will help him solve more challenging problems in the future.

Independent Practice and Review

Have your child complete the Lesson 1.6 Practice and Review workbook pages.

Lesson 1.7
Review Written Addition

Purpose	Materials
• Practice memory work • Learn strategies for reading word problems • Review addition and subtraction word problems	• Memory Work (Blackline Master 1) • Markers or colored pencils • 10 slips of paper

You will need 10 slips of paper to play Leaf Fight. Use brown paper (or orange, red, and yellow) if you'd like the slips to look more like leaves.

This lesson provides a quick review of the written process for adding two-digit numbers, which was covered in depth in *Second Grade Math with Confidence.* If your child struggles with this process and needs practice to become more fluent with it, break the lesson into two days:

- Day 1: Complete the problems in part A of the Lesson Activities. Use base-ten blocks to concretely model each step, and encourage your child to refer to the Addition Algorithm diagram. Have your child solve half of the Practice problems and half of the Review exercises.

- Day 2: Review the process with base-ten blocks and play Leaf Fight (in part B of the Lesson Activities). Have your child complete the remaining exercises on the Practice and Review pages.

Warm-up: Practice Memory Work

Ask your child the following questions. If she has trouble with any of the questions, allow her to peek at the Memory Work list to find the correct answer.

- **How many inches equal 1 foot?** *12.*
- **How many feet equal 1 yard?** *3.*
- **How many inches equal 1 yard?** *36.*
- **How many centimeters equal 1 meter?** *100.*

If your child is not familiar with any of these units, show her a ruler so that she can concretely see their lengths. If your family does not use inches, feet, and yards, see the note in the Introduction (page 10) for how to handle U.S. customary units like these.

Activity (A): Review Written Addition

Algorithms are step-by-step methods for solving problems. They're like recipes for math. Today, we'll review how to use the addition algorithm to add two-digit numbers.

The *addition algorithm* is another name for the traditional process for adding numbers vertically on paper. (You may also know it as "carrying the 1" or "stack math.")

Computer programmers write algorithms to tell computers and robots how to work. They make diagrams like this to show the steps in their algorithms. Let's pretend that you're a robot programmed to follow this program.

Use the following dialogue to review how to add two-digit numbers.

- Model 39 and 57 with base-ten blocks on the Place-Value Chart.

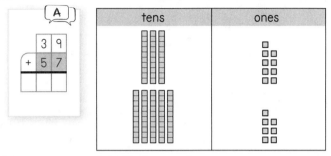

- **Which place do we start with?** *The ones-place.*
- **What's the first step?** *Add the digits.* **9 plus 7 is 16. The sum is greater than 9, so I need to trade.** Trade 10 unit blocks for 1 rod and place the rod horizontally in the tens-column.

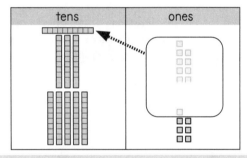

Placing the new rod horizontally makes it visually distinct from the other rods.

- **What's the final step for the ones-place?** *Record your work.* **We added 1 more rod to the tens-place, so I write a 1 above the tens-place.** Write 1 above the tens-place. **There are 6 units left in the ones-place, so I write a 6 in the ones-place.** Write 6 in the answer's ones-place.

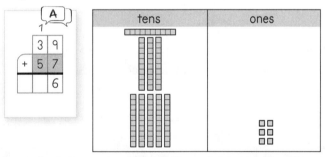

- **Now, we go back to the beginning and follow the steps for the tens-place. I have to make sure to add together all 3 of the digits in the tens-place. 1 plus 3 plus 5 equals 9, so I write 9 in the tens-place.** Write 9 in the answer's tens-place.

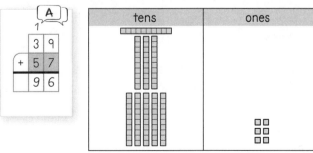

Have your child use the algorithm to complete the addition problems. For 57 + 52 and 76 + 84, help her trade 10 rods for 1 flat and record her work as shown.

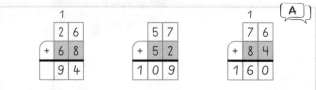

Use the Addition Algorithm diagram and base-ten blocks to support your child as she completes the problems. If she has trouble, model every step with base-ten blocks and discuss how the blocks match the written numbers. If she readily remembers the process, cover the Addition Algorithm diagram and challenge her to complete the problems without looking at it.

Activity (B): Play Leaf Fight

Play Leaf Fight. Model the problems with base-ten blocks as needed.

The silliness of this activity makes solving these problems feel more relaxed and fun. But, if you'd rather not encourage throwing (or if you're teaching this lesson in a place where it's not practical), put the paper wads in a bowl and draw 2 wads each turn instead. Replace the wads in the bowl after each turn.

Leaf Fight

Materials: 10 slips of paper

Object of the Game: Win the most points.

Write the numbers on the leaves in part B on separate slips of paper:

Crumple the slips of paper and place them on the table. Both players count down in unison from 10 while throwing the crumpled wads of paper at each other. When you reach 1, both players stop and pick up the 2 closest wads of paper.

Both players unfold their paper wads and write their numbers in neighboring blank grids on the scorecard. Then, they find the sum. Whoever has the greater sum wins a point.

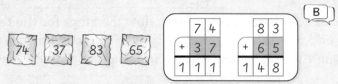

Sample play. The player whose sum is 148 wins the point.

Crumple up your numbers and add them back to the pile of "leaves." Repeat until you have filled in all of the blank grids. Whoever wins more points wins the game.

 Save these paper slips for Lesson 1.8.

Independent Practice and Review

Have your child complete the Lesson 1.7 Practice and Review page. If needed, allow your child to use the Addition Algorithm diagram as she completes the addition problems.

The Practice section is short, since your child practiced lots of two-digit addition in the Lesson Activities. As a result, there is only 1 page of Practice and Review in this lesson.

You'll find a reference copy of the Addition Algorithm on Blackline Master 4. Place this page inside your math binder so your child can refer to it as needed.

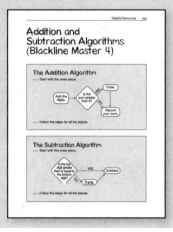

Lesson 1.8
Review Written Subtraction

Purpose	Materials
• Review telling time to the hour, half-hour, or quarter-hour • Review using the subtraction algorithm to subtract two-digit numbers	• Clock • Base-ten blocks • Place-Value Chart (Blackline Master 3) • 10 slips of paper with numbers for Leaf Fight (from Lesson 1.7)

Memory Work
- **What do we call the result when we add numbers together?** *The sum.*
- **What do we call the numbers that we add together?** *The addends.*

Memory Work Note

You'll find suggested memory work review questions at the beginning of each lesson from this point forward. You'll review memory work daily, and you'll add new topics to the rotation as your child studies them. If you know your child already has a memory work item fully memorized, feel free to replace the suggested question with an item that he doesn't know as well. Or, if you know your child needs more practice with a particular fact, review it every day until he knows it more thoroughly.

This lesson provides a quick review of the written process for subtracting two-digit numbers, which was covered in depth in *Second Grade Math with Confidence*. If your child struggles with this process and needs practice to become more fluent with it, break the lesson into two days:

- Day 1: Complete the problems in part A of the Lesson Activities. Use base-ten blocks to concretely model each step, and encourage your child to refer to the Subtraction Algorithm diagram. Have your child solve half of the Practice problems and half of the Review exercises.

- Day 2: Review the process with base-ten blocks and play Leaf Fight (in part B of the Lesson Activities). Have your child complete the remaining exercises on the Practice and Review pages.

Warm-up: Review Telling Time to the Hour, Half-Hour, or Quarter-Hour

Don't worry if your child forgot how to tell time over the summer. This tricky skill requires lots of practice. In this warm-up, you'll briefly review telling time to the hour, half-hour, or quarter-hour. You'll review telling time to 5 minutes and to the minute later in the year.

Show your child a clock and have him identify the hour hand and minute hand. Set the clock to the following times and have him tell each time: 2:00, 2:30, 3:00, 3:15, 4:00, 4:45.

If your child has trouble identifying the hour, encourage him to think of each hour as "owning" part of the clock. For example, for 2:30, use your finger to trace lines on the clock as shown. **The 2 o'clock hour owns this part of the clock. If the hour hand is in this area, the hour is 2.**

Activity (A): Review Written Subtraction

In the last lesson, we reviewed how to use the addition algorithm to add two-digit numbers. Today, we'll review how to use the subtraction algorithm to subtract two-digit numbers.

Let's pretend again that you're a robot. You're programmed to follow this Subtraction Algorithm program.

As with addition, use the Subtraction Algorithm diagram and base-ten blocks to support your child as needed. If he has trouble, model and discuss every step. If he can easily perform written subtraction, you do not need to use the base-ten blocks.

Use the following dialogue to review how to subtract two-digit numbers.

- Model 72 with base-ten blocks on the Place-Value Chart.

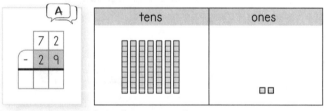

- **Which place do we start with?** *The ones-place.*
- **The first step says: Is the top digit greater than or equal to the bottom digit? Is 2 greater than or equal to 9?** *No.*

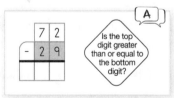

- **So, we need to trade.** Trade 1 rod for 10 unit blocks and place the 10 unit blocks in the ones-column. **Now, we have 6 tens.** Cross out the 7 and write 6 above it. **We have 12 ones.** Cross out the 2 and write 12 above it.

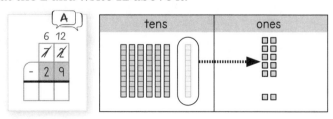

- **The final step for the ones-place is to subtract. 12 minus 9 is 3.** Remove 9 unit blocks and write 3 in the answer's ones-place.

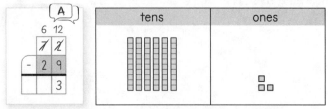

- **Now, we go back to the beginning and follow the steps for the tens-place. 6 is greater than 2, so now I subtract 2 tens.** Remove 2 rods and write 4 in the answer's tens-place.

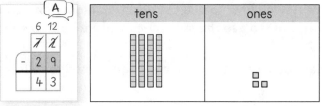

Have your child use the subtraction algorithm to complete the problems.

Activity (B): Play Leaf Fight

Use the slips of paper from Lesson 1.7 to play Leaf Fight. Game play is the same as in Lesson 1.7, except that both players find the difference (rather than the sum) between their numbers. Whoever has the greater answer wins the point. See Lesson 1.7 (page 34) for full directions. Model the problems with base-ten blocks as needed.

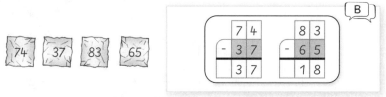

Sample play. The player whose answer is 37 wins the point.

Independent Practice and Review

Have your child complete the Lesson 1.8 Practice and Review page. If needed, allow your child to use the Subtraction Algorithm diagram as he completes the subtraction problems.

The Practice section is short, since your child practiced lots of two-digit subtraction in the Lesson Activities.

You'll find a reference copy of the Subtraction Algorithm on Blackline Master 4. Allow your child to refer to it as needed.

Lesson 1.9
Review Bar Graphs

Purpose	Materials
• Review writing money amounts • Review bar graphs • Approximate amounts on bar graphs • Use addition and subtraction to solve word problems about a bar graph	• Play money • 6 slips of paper • Markers or colored pencils

Memory Work • **What do we call the result when we subtract a number from another number?** *The difference.*

Warm-up: Review Writing Money Amounts

You'll review the rules for writing money amounts in this warm-up. Your child will learn more about money in Unit 7. If your family lives outside the U.S., see the note in the Introduction (page 10) for how to adapt money lessons to your currency.

Show your child the following amounts of money. Have her tell you the value of the money and then write its value on a slip of paper. Remind your child about the rules for writing money amounts as needed.

- 1 ten-dollar bill, 1 five-dollar bill, and 2 one-dollar bills. *17 dollars. $17.* **The dollar sign always comes before the number.** Also have your child write this amount with a decimal point: *$17.00.* **The little dot is called a decimal point. It separates the dollars from the cents. The zeros show that there aren't any extra cents.**
- 1 five-dollar bill, 2 dimes, and 3 pennies. *5 dollars and 23 cents. $5.23.*
- 1 five-dollar bill and 3 pennies. *5 dollars and 3 cents. $5.03.* **The number of cents can be any number from 0 to 99. Putting a place-holder zero before the 3 makes the number of cents easier to read. Make sure you always include a place-holder zero if there are fewer than 10 cents.**
- 2 quarters and 4 pennies. *54 cents. $0.54.* Also have your child write this amount with a cents sign: *54¢.*

$17	$5.23	$5.03	$0.54
$17.00			54¢

Activity (A): Review Bar Graphs

Today, we'll make bar graphs. Arjun made a chart that shows how many points each person on his basketball team scored in one game. Use the following questions to review graph vocabulary:

- **What's the title of the graph?** *Points Scored in Last Night's Game.*
- Run your finger along the graph's horizontal axis. **This line is the horizontal axis. What's this axis labeled?** *Name.*
- Run your finger along the graph's vertical axis. **This line is the vertical axis. What's this axis labeled?** *Points.*

Have your child use the numbers in the chart to draw bars on the bar graph. If she's not sure how to draw bars for the odd numbers, explain that she should draw the top of the bar half-way between the lines. For example: **7 is halfway between 6 and 8, so draw the top of the bar halfway between the lines for 6 and 8.**

Encourage your child to mark the line for the top of the bar first, draw the sides of the bar second, and shade the bar last. This method helps children draw the bars evenly.

Use the following questions to discuss the bar graph:

- **Who scored the most points?** *Brynn.*
- **Who scored the fewest points?** *Claire.*
- **How many more points did Dan score than Eve?** *3.* **How do you know?** *Sample answer: 7 minus 4 equals 3.*
- **How many fewer points did Arjun score than Brynn?** *4.* **How do you know?** *Sample answer: 10 minus 6 equals 4.*
- **How many points did the players score in all?** *30.* **How do you know?** *Sample answer: I added up all the points.*

Activity (B): Draw a Bar Graph with Approximate Amounts

Arjun also made a chart of how many points each player has scored so far this season. The vertical axis is marked in multiples of 10, but not all of the numbers in the chart are multiples of 10. So, you'll need to approximate where the tops of some of the bars go.

Have your child use the chart to complete the bar graph. Encourage her to use logical reasoning to approximate the height of each bar. For example: **35 is halfway between 30 and 40, so draw the top of the bar halfway between the lines for 30 and 40. Or, 19 is just a little less than 20, so draw the top of the bar a little below 20.**

Accept any reasonable height for the bars in the graph. For example, for 6, any bar that is below the line for 10 and higher than the halfway point between 0 and 10 is acceptable.

Activity (C): Use a Bar Graph to Solve Word Problems

Have your child read the first word problem, identify the goal, and then read the problem again slowly. When she's ready to solve the problem, ask: **How will you solve the problem?** *Sample answer: Subtract 35 minus 19.*

If she's not sure, point out that this problem asks her to compare Brynn's points with Dan's points. So, she should subtract the lesser amount from the greater amount.

Do you want to solve the problem with the subtraction algorithm or mental math? *Answers will vary.* **Either way is fine. If you want to solve the problem with the subtraction algorithm, write the problem vertically. If you want to solve the problem with mental math, write the problem horizontally.** Have your child write and solve the equation, either vertically with the subtraction algorithm or horizontally with mental math. Make sure she labels and boxes her complete answer.

Your child may also write the equation horizontally.

Encourage your child to write one digit per box in the printed grid. This will help her line up the digits correctly if she's using the subtraction algorithm.

Have your child complete the other word problem.

Your child may also write the equation horizontally.

Independent Practice and Review

Have your child complete the Lesson 1.9 Practice and Review workbook pages.

Lesson 1.10
Enrichment (Optional)

Purpose	Materials
• Practice memory work • Introduce Roman numerals • Write Roman numerals • Summarize what your child has learned and assess your child's progress	• *Fun with Roman Numerals,* written by David A. Adler and illustrated by Edward Miller III

The final lesson in each unit is an optional enrichment lesson. The purpose of these enrichment lessons is to help your child enjoy math, develop a positive attitude toward math, and appreciate how math is used in everyday life. Feel free to adapt the enrichment activity directions to fit your family. Simplify them if you're short on time, or use different materials if you don't have the exact items listed. Or, if your child is particularly excited about a project, make the project more elaborate and spend more time on it.

Warm-up: Review Memory Work

Quiz your child on any of the memory work items that he struggled with during this unit.

Math Picture Book: *Fun with Roman Numerals*

Read *Fun with Roman Numerals,* written by David A. Adler and illustrated by Edward Miller III. As you read, discuss the examples of Roman numerals and help your child understand this different number system.

Enrichment Activity: Write Numbers in Roman Numerals

If you didn't read *Fun with Roman Numerals,* use this dialogue to introduce Roman numerals. If you read the book, skip straight to making a chart of Roman numerals to 20 and writing your child's birth year with Roman numerals.

In ancient Rome, people didn't write numbers the same way that we do. Instead, they used letters to represent numbers. Show your child the following chart.

Roman Numeral	Value
I	1
V	5
X	10
L	50
C	100
D	500
M	1,000

The Romans added and subtracted to combine the letters and show other numbers. Here are the main rules they used for combining the letters.

Rule 1: When letters are repeated, add the values. The Romans never repeated V, L, or D, and they never repeated a letter more than 3 times. Show your child the following examples.

III = 3   XX = 20   CCC = 300

Rule 2: When a letter with a smaller value comes after a letter with a larger value, add the values.

VI = 6	VII = 7	XV = 15
5 + 1 = 6.	5 + 2 = 7.	10 + 5 = 15.

Rule 3: When a letter with a larger value comes after a letter with a smaller value, subtract the values.

IV = 4	IX = 9	XL = 40
5 - 1 = 4.	10 - 1 = 9.	50 - 10 = 40.

Roman numerals have several other subtleties, but these are the main rules for finding their values.

Help your child use these rules and examples to create a chart showing the Roman numerals for 1-20.

1	2	3	4	5	6	7	8	9	10
I	II	III	IV	V	VI	VII	VIII	IX	X

11	12	13	14	15	16	17	18	19	20
XI	XII	XIII	XIV	XV	XVI	XVII	XVIII	XIX	XX

Also help your child write his birth year using Roman numerals. For example, if your child was born in 2017: **We use 2 M's to show the 2 thousands. Then, we write XVII for the 17.**

2017 = MMXVII

Unit Wrap-up

Have your child complete the Unit 1 Wrap-up.

The Enrichment lessons have a two-page Unit Wrap-up rather than the usual Lesson Activities, Practice, and Review pages. The Unit Wrap-ups are completely optional, but children (and parents!) often find it very satisfying to see this concrete evidence of growth. You can use the Unit Wrap-ups to casually review the material from the unit, or you can use them as tests to assess progress more formally. If you live in a state where you're required to provide evidence of learning, you may want to save them for your child's portfolio.

Unit 1 Answer Key

1.1 Practice

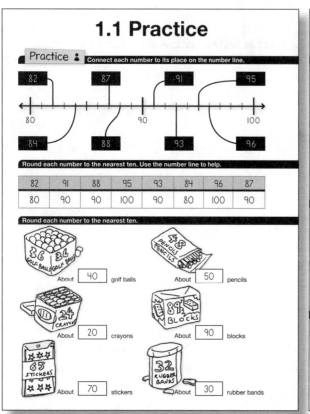

1.1 Review

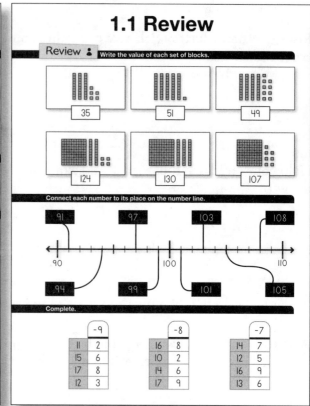

1.2 Practice

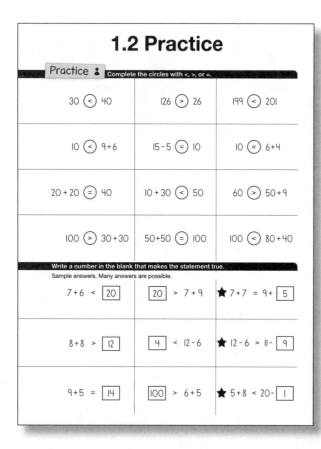

1.2 Review

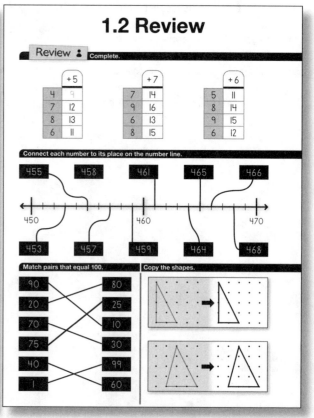

Unit 1 Answer Key

1.3 Practice

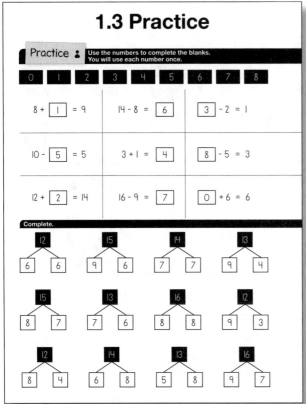

Practice ⦿ Use the numbers to complete the blanks.
You will use each number once.

| 0 | 1 | 2 | 3 | 4 | 5 | 6 | 7 | 8 |

8 + $\boxed{1}$ = 9   14 - 8 = $\boxed{6}$ $\boxed{3}$ - 2 = 1

10 - $\boxed{5}$ = 5   3 + 1 = $\boxed{4}$ $\boxed{8}$ - 5 = 3

12 + $\boxed{2}$ = 14   16 - 9 = $\boxed{7}$ $\boxed{0}$ + 6 = 6

Complete.

12 → 6, 6
15 → 9, 6
14 → 7, 7
13 → 9, 4

15 → 8, 7
13 → 7, 6
16 → 8, 8
12 → 9, 3

12 → 8, 4
14 → 6, 8
13 → 5, 8
16 → 9, 7

1.3 Review

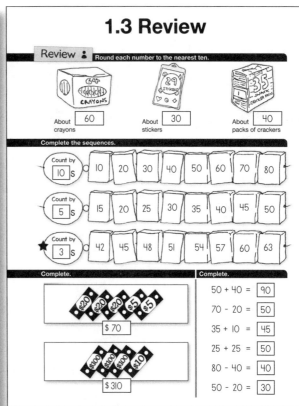

Review ⦿ Round each number to the nearest ten.

About 60 crayons   About 30 stickers   About 40 packs of crackers

Complete the sequences.

Count by 10 s: 10 20 30 40 50 60 70 80

Count by 5 s: 15 20 25 30 35 40 45 50

★ Count by 3 s: 42 45 48 51 54 57 60 63

Complete.

$ 70

$ 310

Complete.

50 + 40 = $\boxed{90}$
70 - 20 = $\boxed{50}$
35 + 10 = $\boxed{45}$
25 + 25 = $\boxed{50}$
80 - 40 = $\boxed{40}$
50 - 20 = $\boxed{30}$

1.4 Practice

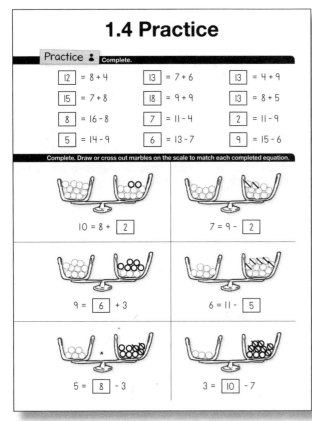

Practice ⦿ Complete.

$\boxed{12}$ = 8 + 4 $\boxed{13}$ = 7 + 6 $\boxed{13}$ = 4 + 9

$\boxed{15}$ = 7 + 8 $\boxed{18}$ = 9 + 9 $\boxed{13}$ = 8 + 5

$\boxed{8}$ = 16 - 8 $\boxed{7}$ = 11 - 4 $\boxed{2}$ = 11 - 9

$\boxed{5}$ = 14 - 9 $\boxed{6}$ = 13 - 7 $\boxed{9}$ = 15 - 6

Complete. Draw or cross out marbles on the scale to match each completed equation.

10 = 8 + $\boxed{2}$ 7 = 9 - $\boxed{2}$

9 = $\boxed{6}$ + 3   6 = 11 - $\boxed{5}$

5 = $\boxed{8}$ - 3   3 = $\boxed{10}$ - 7

1.4 Review

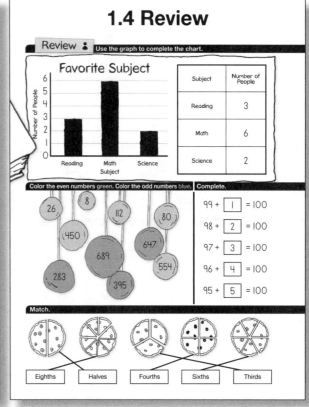

Review ⦿ Use the graph to complete the chart.

Favorite Subject

Subject	Number of People
Reading	3
Math	6
Science	2

Color the even numbers green. Color the odd numbers blue. | Complete.

26   8   112   80
450   647
689
283   554
395

99 + $\boxed{1}$ = 100
98 + $\boxed{2}$ = 100
97 + $\boxed{3}$ = 100
96 + $\boxed{4}$ = 100
95 + $\boxed{5}$ = 100

Match.

Eighths   Halves   Fourths   Sixths   Thirds

Unit 1 Answer Key

1.5 Practice

Practice 👤 Solve. Write the equations you use.

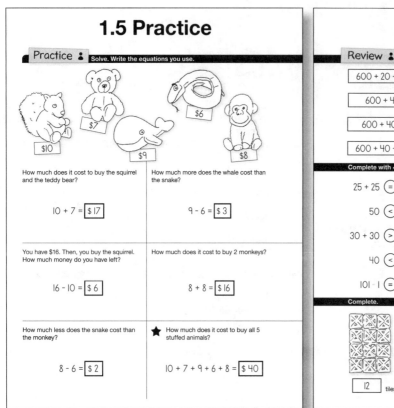

$10 $7 $9 $6 $8

How much does it cost to buy the squirrel and the teddy bear?

10 + 7 = $17

How much more does the whale cost than the snake?

9 - 6 = $3

You have $16. Then, you buy the squirrel. How much money do you have left?

16 - 10 = $6

How much does it cost to buy 2 monkeys?

8 + 8 = $16

How much less does the snake cost than the monkey?

8 - 6 = $2

★ How much does it cost to buy all 5 stuffed animals?

10 + 7 + 9 + 6 + 8 = $40

1.5 Review

Review 👤 Match.

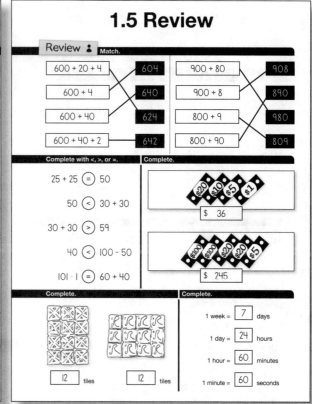

600 + 20 + 4 — 604
600 + 4 — 640
600 + 40 — 624
600 + 40 + 2 — 642

900 + 80 — 908
900 + 8 — 890
800 + 9 — 980
800 + 90 — 809

Complete with <, >, or =.   Complete.

25 + 25 ⊜ 50

50 ⊘ 30 + 30

30 + 30 ⊗ 59

40 ⊘ 100 - 50

101 - 1 ⊜ 60 + 40

$ 36

$ 245

Complete.   Complete.

12 tiles   12 tiles

1 week = 7 days

1 day = 24 hours

1 hour = 60 minutes

1 minute = 60 seconds

1.6 Practice

Practice 👤 Solve. Complete the Part-Total diagram to match.

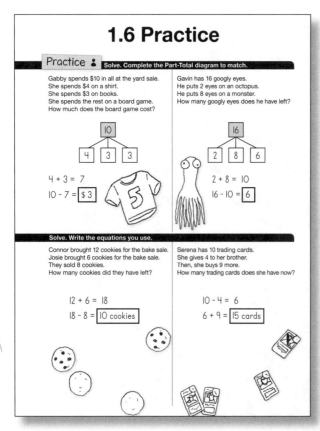

Gabby spends $10 in all at the yard sale. She spends $4 on a shirt. She spends $3 on books. She spends the rest on a board game. How much does the board game cost?

10 | 4 3 3

4 + 3 = 7
10 - 7 = $3

Gavin has 16 googly eyes. He puts 2 eyes on an octopus. He puts 8 eyes on a monster. How many googly eyes does he have left?

16 | 2 8 6

2 + 8 = 10
16 - 10 = 6

Solve. Write the equations you use.

Connor brought 12 cookies for the bake sale. Josie brought 6 cookies for the bake sale. They sold 8 cookies. How many cookies did they have left?

12 + 6 = 18
18 - 8 = 10 cookies

Serena has 10 trading cards. She gives 4 to her brother. Then, she buys 9 more. How many trading cards does she have now?

10 - 4 = 6
6 + 9 = 15 cards

1.6 Review

Review 👤 Draw a shape to match each description.

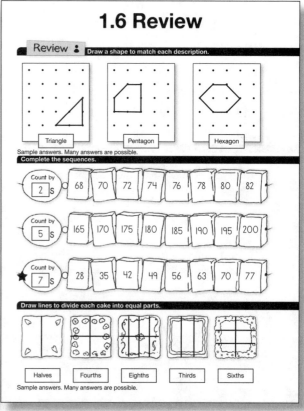

Triangle   Pentagon   Hexagon

Sample answers. Many answers are possible.

Complete the sequences.

Count by 2s | 68 | 70 | 72 | 74 | 76 | 78 | 80 | 82

Count by 5s | 165 | 170 | 175 | 180 | 185 | 190 | 195 | 200

★ Count by 7s | 28 | 35 | 42 | 49 | 56 | 63 | 70 | 77

Draw lines to divide each cake into equal parts.

Halves   Fourths   Eighths   Thirds   Sixths

Sample answers. Many answers are possible.

Unit 1 Answer Key

1.7 Practice/Review

Practice Complete.

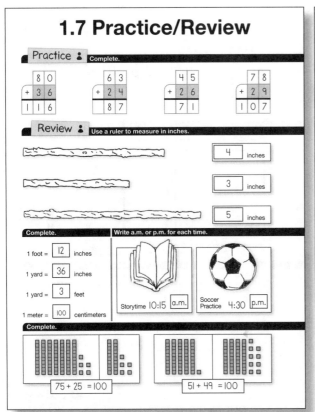

	8	0
+	3	6
1	1	6

	6	3
+	2	4
	8	7

	4	5
+	2	6
	7	1

	7	8
+	2	9
1	0	7

Review Use a ruler to measure in inches.

4 inches

3 inches

5 inches

Complete.

1 foot = 12 inches

1 yard = 36 inches

1 yard = 3 feet

1 meter = 100 centimeters

Write a.m. or p.m. for each time.

Storytime 10:15 a.m.

Soccer Practice 4:30 p.m.

Complete.

75 + 25 = 100

51 + 49 = 100

1.8 Practice/Review

Practice Complete.

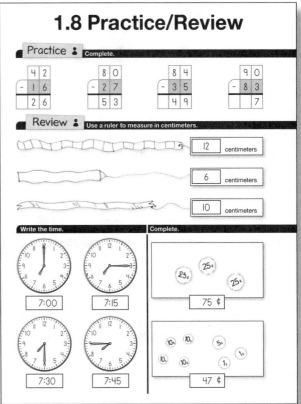

	4	2
−	1	6
	2	6

	8	0
−	2	7
	5	3

	8	4
−	3	5
	4	9

	9	0
−	8	3
		7

Review Use a ruler to measure in centimeters.

12 centimeters

6 centimeters

10 centimeters

Write the time.

7:00

7:15

7:30

7:45

Complete.

75 ¢

47 ¢

1.9 Practice

Practice Use the chart to make a bar graph.

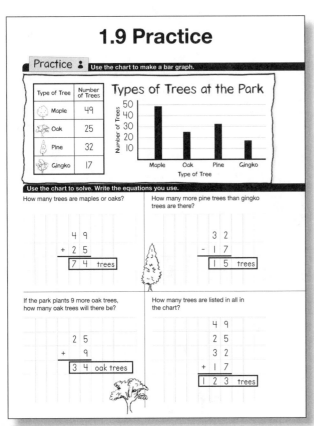

Type of Tree	Number of Trees
Maple	49
Oak	25
Pine	32
Gingko	17

Types of Trees at the Park

Use the chart to solve. Write the equations you use.

How many trees are maples or oaks?

	4	9
+	2	5
	7	4	trees

How many more pine trees than gingko trees are there?

	3	2
−	1	7
	1	5	trees

If the park plants 9 more oak trees, how many oak trees will there be?

	2	5
+		9
	3	4	oak trees

How many trees are listed in all in the chart?

	4	9
	2	5
	3	2
+	1	7
1	2	3	trees

1.9 Review

Review Use a ruler to draw a line that matches each length.

5 inches

9 centimeters

Complete.

	3	7
+	5	6
	9	3

	8	4
+	1	7
1	0	1

	9	2
−	3	5
	5	7

	8	0
−	4	7
	3	3

Round to the nearest ten.

16	20
27	30
43	40
85	90
96	100

Write each amount of money two ways.

$ 0.75   75 ¢

$ 0.45   45 ¢

Write the time.

3:15

10:30

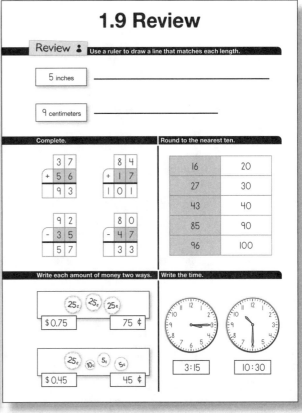

Unit 1 Answer Key

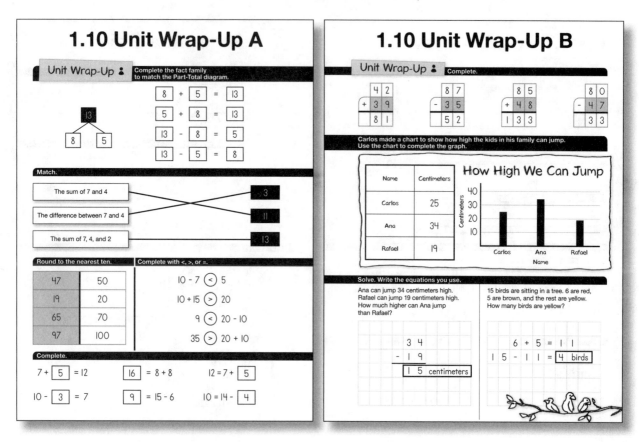

1.10 Unit Wrap-Up A

Unit Wrap-Up 👤 Complete the fact family to match the Part-Total diagram.

13
8   5

8 + 5 = 13
5 + 8 = 13
13 - 8 = 5
13 - 5 = 8

Match.

The sum of 7 and 4 ⟶ 11
The difference between 7 and 4 ⟶ 3
The sum of 7, 4, and 2 ⟶ 13

Round to the nearest ten.

47	50
19	20
65	70
97	100

Complete with <, >, or =.

10 - 7 (<) 5
10 + 15 (>) 20
9 (<) 20 - 10
35 (>) 20 + 10

Complete.

7 + [5] = 12   [16] = 8 + 8   12 = 7 + [5]
10 - [3] = 7   [9] = 15 - 6   10 = 14 - [4]

1.10 Unit Wrap-Up B

Unit Wrap-Up 👤 Complete.

```
  4 2        8 7        8 5        8 0
+ 3 9      - 3 5      + 4 8      - 4 7
  8 1        5 2      1 3 3        3 3
```

Carlos made a chart to show how high the kids in his family can jump. Use the chart to complete the graph.

Name	Centimeters
Carlos	25
Ana	34
Rafael	19

How High We Can Jump

Solve. Write the equations you use.

Ana can jump 34 centimeters high. Rafael can jump 19 centimeters high. How much higher can Ana jump than Rafael?

```
  3 4
- 1 9
[1 5] centimeters
```

15 birds are sitting in a tree. 6 are red, 5 are brown, and the rest are yellow. How many birds are yellow?

6 + 5 = 1 1
1 5 - 1 1 = [4] birds

Unit 1 Checkpoint

What to Expect at the End of Unit 1

By the end of Unit 1, most children will be able to do the following:

- Round two-digit numbers to the nearest ten, either mentally or with a number line.
- Complete equations and inequalities with the <, >, or = sign.
- Find missing numbers in addition or subtraction equations. Some children will still feel confused by these equations, especially equations where the "problem" is on the right side of the equals sign.
- Solve one- and two-step addition and subtraction word problems. Most children will feel confident with one-step problems, but some will still feel intimidated by and need help with multi-step problems.
- Add and subtract two-digit numbers with the algorithms. Many children will make occasional mistakes with the math facts or forget a step as they solve the problems.
- Interpret and draw bar graphs.

Is Your Child Ready to Move on?

In Unit 2, you will introduce your child to multiplication. She will learn to use repeated addition to find answers to multiplication problems, and she'll begin to master the ×2, ×5, and ×10 facts.

Before moving on to Unit 2, your child should be **mostly fluent with the addition facts.** Ideally, your child should know the answers to the addition facts up to 9 + 9 in less than 3 seconds. (This depends on your child, though! Children who process information quickly should be able to rattle off most answers within a second, but children who are slower processors may always need 3-5 seconds to tell an answer.) You know your child best, so adjust your expectations based on your individual child.

What to Do If Your Child Needs More Practice

Just because a child doesn't have the addition facts fully mastered doesn't mean she can't continue learning third-grade math concepts. But, if your child often has trouble recalling the addition facts (or takes longer than 3 seconds to remember the answers), it's important to continue building more fluency and speed as you move forward with third-grade skills. Use the following suggestions to help your child build automatic recall with the addition facts:

- If your child can find answers to most of the facts but takes longer than 3 seconds, she probably just needs more practice to build speed. Play Addition Least to Greatest (either at the beginning of a lesson or at a separate time of day) a few times per week. Addition War also provides lots of quick practice. (To play Addition War, see the directions for Multiplication War in Lesson 7.4 (page 224). Game play is the same, except that whoever has the greater sum wins all the cards.) Addition fact apps or flash cards are also a good way to build speed and automatic recall.
- If your child has only a few facts that stump her, choose 3 of the tricky facts. Write them on a piece of paper and post them in your math lesson area. Have her practice these 3 facts at the beginning of each lesson until she has memorized them. Then, choose 3 new facts to focus on.

- If your child has trouble finding answers to many of the addition facts or often counts on her fingers to find the answers, she may not be ready to tackle *Third Grade Math with Confidence. Addition Facts That Stick* provides a systematic approach to mastering the facts. You can use *Addition Facts That Stick* on its own for a few weeks to reinforce the specific facts that your child needs to practice. Or, if you want to continue to move forward with *Third Grade Math with Confidence,* use the activities from *Addition Facts that Stick* for 5-10 minutes per day outside of your regular math time.

Unit 2
Multiplication, Part 1

Overview

In Unit 2, your child will learn to write multiplication equations to match equal groups and arrays. He'll learn several important multiplication properties and vocabulary words, and he'll begin to master the ×1, ×2, ×5, and ×10 facts. He'll also begin solving simple multiplication word problems.

This unit is the first of three multiplication units in *Third Grade Math with Confidence*. Your child will learn the ×3 and ×4 facts in Unit 4, and then he'll tackle the rest of the multiplication facts in Unit 8. He'll also learn several mental multiplication techniques along the way. By the end of the year, he'll have a solid foundation in multiplication and be ready to learn the written process for multi-digit multiplication in fourth grade.

What Your Child Will Learn

In this unit, your child will learn to:

- Write multiplication equations with the × sign for equal groups and arrays
- Understand that you can multiply numbers in any order
- Find answers for the ×1, ×2, ×5, and ×10 facts
- Understand that any number times zero equals zero
- Solve simple multiplication word problems

Lesson List

Lesson 2.1	Equal Groups	Lesson 2.6	Multiplication Word Problems
Lesson 2.2	Arrays	Lesson 2.7	×5 Facts
Lesson 2.3	×2 Facts	Lesson 2.8	×5 Facts on the Clock
Lesson 2.4	Multiply by 1 or Zero	Lesson 2.9	Enrichment (Optional)
Lesson 2.5	×10 Facts		

Extra Materials Needed for Unit 2

- 5 small boxes or bowls
- For optional Enrichment Lesson:
  - × *2 × 2 = Boo!: A Set of Spooky Multiplication Stories*, by Loreen Leedy. Holiday House, 1995.
  - × 24 small snack items, such as raisins, pieces of cereal, or small candies.

The suggested picture book is about Halloween. If your family does not observe Halloween, a good substitute is *Too Many Kangaroo Things to Do*, written by Stuart J. Murphy and illustrated by Kevin O'Malley. HarperCollins, 1996.

Teaching Math with Confidence:
Using Strategies (Not Skip-Counting) to Master the Multiplication Facts

In Unit 2, you'll begin teaching your child the multiplication facts. But that doesn't mean you have to break out the flash cards and timed tests! Instead, you'll teach your child simple strategies for finding the answers, just as you did for the addition and subtraction facts in *First Grade Math with Confidence* and *Second Grade Math with Confidence*.

In this unit, you'll focus on the ×1, ×2, ×5, and ×10 facts. Children usually find these facts easiest to learn, so beginning with them helps build your child's confidence with multiplication. These facts are also helpful stepping stones for mastering the more difficult multiplication facts.

Your child already knows the skip-counting sequences for 2, 5, and 10, so he may be inclined to simply skip-count to find the answers. For example, to find 7 × 5: *5, 10, 15, 20, 25, 30, 35. I counted by 5 seven times, so 7 times 5 is 35.*

It's fine if your child sometimes uses a skip-counting approach when he's first making sense of multiplication. But in the long run, skip-counting is slow, inefficient, and error-prone, just like counting one by one to solve addition or subtraction problems. That's why you'll teach your child to use strategies to find the answers instead. In this unit, you'll introduce the following multiplication strategies:

- **×2 facts:** Multiplying a number times 2 is the same as doubling it. So, you can double the number to find the answer. For example, to find 2 × 6, you can double 6 to find that the product is 12.
- **×10 facts:** You'll teach your child to use place-value thinking to find these facts. For example, 8 × 10 means "8 groups of 10." 8 tens equal 80, so 8 × 10 = 80.
- **×5 facts:** You'll show your child how to combine 5s into groups of 10 to find answers to these facts. For example, 4 × 5 means 4 groups of 5. Every 2 groups of 5 equal 10, so 4 fives equal 2 tens, or 20.

At first, your child will probably need to think through these strategies slowly and deliberately. Then, with practice, he'll become more automatic at finding their answers. A few children will know all these multiplication facts by heart by the end of the unit, but most will need more practice (and many reminders to "use your strategies") before mastering them. Your child will continue to practice the ×2, ×5, and ×10 in warm-up games and review workbook pages throughout the year until he has them fully mastered.

Lesson 2.1
Equal Groups

Purpose	Materials
• Practice repeated addition • Understand multiplication as repeated addition • Write multiplication equations to match equal groups	• Counters • 5 small boxes or bowls

Memory Work	• **Are times in the morning a.m. or p.m.?** *A.m.* • **Are times in the afternoon and evening a.m. or p.m.?** *P.m.*

Warm-up: Practice Repeated Addition

Ask your child the following repeated addition questions orally:

- **What's 5 plus 5?** *10.* **Plus 5?** *15.* **Plus 5?** *20.* **Plus 5?** *25.*
- **What's 4 plus 4?** *8.* **Plus 4?** *12.* **Plus 4?** *16.* **Plus 4?** *20.*
- **What's 3 plus 3?** *6.* **Plus 3?** *9.* **Plus 3?** *12.* **Plus 3?** *15.*

This activity previews using repeated addition to solve multiplication problems.

Activity (A): Introduce Multiplication at the Cookie Store

Today, we'll start a brand-new math topic: multiplication! Multiplication is a very important math skill, like addition and subtraction. We'll spend a lot of time on it this year.

Let's pretend you work at the Cookie Store. Place 3 small boxes or bowls on the table and place 4 counters in each box to match the picture. **One day, a customer buys 3 boxes of cookies. Each box has 4 cookies.**

Modeling the picture with real counters and boxes makes the concept of multiplication more concrete. It also previews using counters to solve multiplication problems in the next activity.

One way to find the number of cookies is with repeated addition. What's 4 plus 4 plus 4? *12.* Write 12 in the blank.

Repeated addition works fine if there are only a few groups. But if a customer bought more boxes, it could take a long time to find the total number of cookies! Multiplication is a faster way to add equal groups and find the total.

Point to the times sign in 3 × 4. **This sign is called the times sign. It means to multiply the numbers together. We read this problem as "3 times 4."**

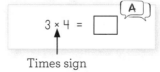

Times sign

The first number tells how many groups we have, and the second number tells how many are in each group. So, 3 times 4 means 3 groups of 4. What does 3 times 4 equal? *12.* Write 12 in the blank.

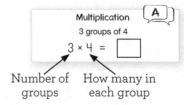

Have your child help you write a repeated addition equation and multiplication equation for the other cookie pictures.

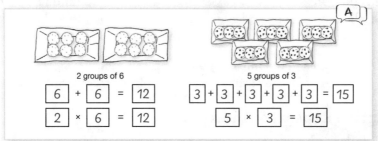

This definition of the first and second numbers is only a convention, and not a hard-and-fast mathematical definition. (In fact, some math programs describe 3 × 4 in the opposite way, with 3 as the size of the groups and 4 as the number of groups.) As your child will learn in Lesson 2.2, we can multiply in any order, and so the final answer does not depend on the order of the factors. It's fine if your child writes multiplication equations in either order, as long as she understands the underlying concept of equal groups.

Activity (B): Multiply at the Cookie Store

Let's pretend that you work at the Cookie Store, and I'm the customer buying cookies. I'd like 3 boxes of 6, please. Have your child fill 3 boxes or bowls with 6 counters each.

What multiplication problem matches my order? *3 times 6.* **How many cookies are in my order?** *18.* If your child isn't sure, prompt her to add 6 + 6 + 6. Write the matching multiplication equation in the chart.

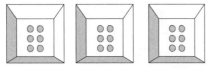

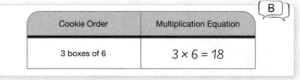

Cookie Order	Multiplication Equation
3 boxes of 6	3 × 6 = 18

Repeat with the other cookie orders in part B. Have your child create each order with counters. Then, write the matching equation in the chart.

Cookie Order	Multiplication Equation
3 boxes of 6	3 × 6 = 18
4 boxes of 4	4 × 4 = 16
1 box of 8	1 × 8 = 8
2 boxes of 7	2 × 7 = 14
5 boxes of 2	5 × 2 = 10

Independent Practice and Review

Have your child complete the Lesson 2.1 Practice and Review pages.

Lesson 2.2
Arrays

Purpose	Materials
• Review rows and columns • Write multiplication equations to match arrays • Draw arrays	• Dot array and L-cover (Blackline Master 5)

Memory Work	• **What is another name for 12 a.m.?** *Midnight.* • **What is another name for 12 p.m.?** *Noon.*

You will need the dot array and L-cover (Blackline Master 5) for the first time in this lesson. Before the lesson, cut out the L-cover along the dotted lines and place the dot array in a plastic page protector. Keep the dot array and L-cover in your math binder.

Warm-up: Review Rows and Columns on the Dot Array

In the last lesson, you learned how to write multiplication equations for equal groups. Today, you'll learn how to write multiplication equations for arrays.

Show your child the dot array and L-cover (Blackline Master 5). **This is called the dot array. An array is a group of objects arranged in rows and columns.**

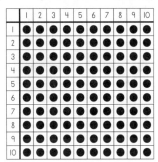

Slide the L-cover over the dot array so that 4 rows of 3 are showing. **The numbers on the top and side tell the number of rows and columns so you don't have to count. How many rows are in this array?** *4.* **How many columns are in this array?** *3.*

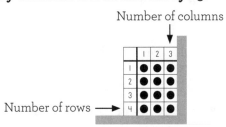

Use the L-cover to show your child the following arrays. Have your child tell how many rows and columns are in each array.

         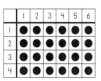

2 rows and 5 columns.   3 rows and 3 columns.   4 rows and 6 columns.

Activity (A): Write Multiplication Equations for Arrays

Bakers often arrange cupcakes and muffins in arrays. We can think of each row of muffins as a group. How many rows of muffins are there? *3.* **How many muffins are in each row?** *5.* **So, we have 3 groups of 5. What multiplication problem means 3 groups of 5?** *3 times 5.* **How many muffins are there in all?** *15.* Write the matching multiplication equation in the blanks.

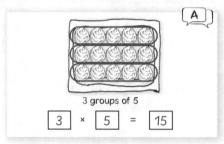

Or, we can think of each column as a group of muffins. **How many columns of muffins are there?** *5.* **How many muffins are in each column?** *3.* **So, we have 5 groups of 3. What multiplication problem means 5 groups of 3?** *5 times 3.* **How many muffins are there in all?** *15.* Write the matching multiplication equation in the blanks.

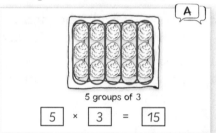

The answer to a multiplication problem is called the *product.* **What do you notice about the products in these two problems?** *They're equal!* **We can multiply numbers in any order, just like we can add numbers in any order.** Complete the other equations to match the arrays.

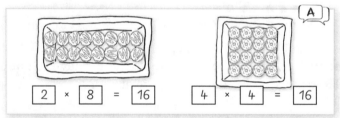

Your child may write the factors in multiplication equations in either order.

Activity (B): Draw Arrays at the Window Factory

Builders often create arrays when they lay bricks, lay tiles, or install windows. Briefly look around your home for bricks, tiles, or panes of glass arranged in arrays.

Let's pretend you design windows at a window factory. Each window is made from an array of glass squares. Your job is to draw the plan for each window before it's made and find how many glass squares are needed.

The first order is for a window with 3 rows and 3 columns. Demonstrate how to draw a box around 3 rows and 3 columns of squares, as shown. **How many squares of glass are in this window?** 9. Write 9 in the chart.

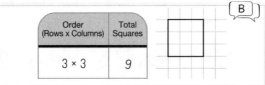

Repeat with the other window orders.

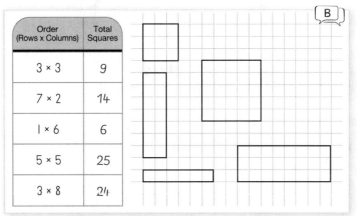

Order (Rows x Columns)	Total Squares
3 × 3	9
7 × 2	14
1 × 6	6
5 × 5	25
3 × 8	24

This activity previews finding area. Your child will study area in Unit 9.

Independent Practice and Review

Have your child complete the Lesson 2.2 Practice and Review pages.

Lesson 2.3
×2 Facts

Purpose	Materials
• Review doubling numbers • Introduce ×2 facts • Multiply in any order to find ×2 facts	• Dot array and L-cover (Blackline Master 5) • Paper • Playing cards • Counters

Memory Work
- **How many minutes equal a half-hour?** *30.*
- **How many minutes equal a quarter-hour?** *15.*

Warm-up: Review Doubling Numbers

What does it mean to double something? *Sample answer: Make it twice as much.* Have your child double the following numbers:

- **Double 3.** *6.*
- **Double 6.** *12.*
- **Double 5.** *10.*
- **Double 8.** *16.*
- **Double 9.** *18.*

- **Double 7.** *14.*
- **Double 10.** *20.*
- **Double 20.** *40.*
- **Double 40.** *80.*
- **Double 50.** *100.*

If your child has trouble, model the questions with counters or base-ten blocks.

Double 3 is 6.   Double 20 is 40.

Activity (A): Introduce the ×2 Multiplication Facts

The multiplication facts are the multiplication problems from 1 × 1 up to 10 × 10. This year, you'll learn the multiplication facts so that you know them by heart, just like you know the addition and subtraction facts. Today, you'll start learning the ×2 facts.

See the Unit 2 **Teaching Math with Confidence** for more on how *Math with Confidence* approaches mastering the multiplication facts.

Show your child the list of ×2 facts in part A. **This list of multiplication facts is called the "times 2 table."** Show 1 × 2 on the dot array. **What's 1 times 2?** *2.* Write 2 in the blank.

Show 2 × 2 on the dot array. **What's 2 times 2?** *4.* Write 4 in the blank.

Repeat with the rest of the ×2 facts. Encourage your child to add 2 to each previous answer to find the next answer.

1 × 2 = 2	6 × 2 = 12
2 × 2 = 4	7 × 2 = 14
3 × 2 = 6	8 × 2 = 16
4 × 2 = 8	9 × 2 = 18
5 × 2 = 10	10 × 2 = 20

What patterns do you notice? *Sample answers: The answers are the even numbers in order. The answers are the numbers we say when we count by 2s. The answers are doubles.*

Noticing and discussing patterns in multiplication tables helps children memorize them more easily and quickly. You'll discuss each multiplication table in this way.

Activity (B): Multiply in Any Order to Find ×2 Facts

Use a piece of paper to cover the completed ×2 table.

Covering the completed table prevents your child from referring to it during the next activity.

If we think of each row as a group, we have 2 groups of 6. What's 6 plus 6? *12.* Point to each group of 2 as you ask: **So, what's 2 times 6?** *12.* Write 12 in the blank. **You can also think of 2 times 6 as double 6. Double 6 is 12, so 2 times 6 is 12.**

2 groups of 6
2 × 6 = 12

If we think of each column as a group, we have 6 groups of 2. Point to each group of 2 as you ask: **What's 2 plus 2?** *4.* **Plus 2?** *6.* **Plus 2?** *8.* **Plus 2?** *10.* **Plus 2?** *12.* **So, what's 6 times 2?** *12.* Write 12 in the blank.

6 groups of 2
6 × 2 = 12

Did the total number of goldfish change when we switched the order of the numbers? *No.* **6 times 2 and 2 times 6 both have the same total number of goldfish. The two equations just describe the array in two different ways.**

We can multiply numbers in any order, just like we can add numbers in any order. This helps find answers to the ×2 facts.

10 times 2 means 10 groups of 2. Adding up 10 groups of 2 would take a while! Instead, let's think of this as 2 groups of 10 and double 10 to find the answer. What's double 10? *20.* **So, what's 10 times 2?** *20.* Write 20 in both blanks. Repeat with the other multiplication problems.

10 × 2 = 20	8 × 2 = 16	9 × 2 = 18
2 × 10 = 20	2 × 8 = 16	2 × 9 = 18

Activity (C): Play Multiplication Crash (×2)

Play Multiplication Crash.

Multiplication Crash (×2)

Materials: Deck of playing cards with jacks, queens, and kings removed (40 cards total); 10 counters of two different colors each

Object of the Game: Have the most counters on the game board at the end of the game.

Shuffle the cards and place the stack face down on the table. Give 10 counters of one color to one player and 10 counters of a different color to the other player.

On your turn, flip over the top card. Multiply the card by 2, say the matching multiplication fact, and place a counter on the matching square. For example, if you flip over a 7, say "2 times 7 equals 14" and place a counter on 14.

If the other player already has a counter on the square, you may "crash" into their counter, remove it, and place your own counter on the square. Continue until all the squares are filled. Whoever has more counters on the board at the end wins the game.

Learning the multiplication facts by heart requires lots of practice! You'll find many quick games like this throughout the program to provide short, fun, and targeted multiplication practice sessions.

Independent Practice and Review

Have your child complete the Lesson 2.3 Practice and Review pages.

Lesson 2.4
Multiply by 1 or Zero

Purpose	Materials
• Practice ×2 facts • Understand that any number multiplied by 1 equals the original number • Understand that any number multiplied by zero equals zero	• Playing cards • Counters

Memory Work	
	• Write the < sign. **What does this sign mean?** *Less than.* • Write the > sign. **What does this sign mean?** *Greater than.*

The Student Workbook usually includes a new game board every time the Instructor Guide calls for you to play a game. You do not need to save the game boards unless otherwise noted. Due to space constraints, some of the game boards have fairly small boxes. If your usual counters are too big for the boxes, choose one of these options:

1. Use unit blocks (from your set of base-ten blocks).
2. X out each box on the game board with a pencil rather than placing a counter.
3. Place the game board in a plastic page protector and mark turns with a dry erase marker.

Warm-up (A): Play Multiplication Bingo (×2)

In the last lesson, you learned the ×2 facts. Today, you'll practice the ×2 facts and learn about multiplying by 1 or zero. Play Multiplication Bingo.

Multiplication Bingo (×2)

Materials: Deck of playing cards with jacks, queens, and kings removed (40 cards total); counters

Object of the Game: Be the first player to fill an entire column, row, or diagonal.

Shuffle the cards and place the stack face down on the table. Have each player choose which game board to use.

Have your child turn over the top card and multiply the number on the card times 2. For example, if the card is a 5, your child says, "5 times 2 equals 10." Then, each of you uses a counter to cover a square containing that product on your game board.

Continue until one of you wins by filling an entire column, row, or diagonal.

Activity (B): Multiply by 1

Point to 3 × 1. **What does 3 times 1 mean?** *3 groups of 1.* **What do 3 groups of 1 equal?** *3.* Write 3 in the blank.

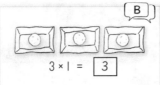

Point to 1 × 3. **What does 1 times 3 mean?** *1 group of 3.* **What does 1 group of 3 equal?** *3.* Write 3 in the blank.

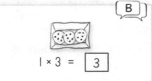

What do you notice about the answers? *They're the same.* **Any number times 1 just equals the number.** Have your child use similar reasoning to complete part B.

$$6 \times 1 = \boxed{6} \qquad 1 \times 7 = \boxed{7} \qquad 250 \times 1 = \boxed{250}$$

> If your child has trouble with any of the problems, encourage him to think about the definition of multiplication. For example: **What does 1 times 7 mean?** *1 group of 7.* **If I have 1 group of 7 apples, I just have 7 apples. So, 1 times 7 equals 7.**

Activity (C): Multiply by Zero

Point to 3 × 0. **What does 3 times 0 mean?** *3 groups of 0.* **What do 3 groups of 0 equal?** *0!* Write 0 in the blank.

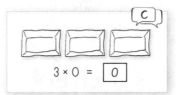

What does 0 times 3 mean? *0 groups of 3.* **If I have 0 groups, that means I don't have anything! So, what does 0 times 3 equal?** *0.* Write 0 in the blank.

$$0 \times 3 = \boxed{0}$$

What do you notice about the answers? *They're both zero.* **Any number times 0 equals 0.** Have your child complete the remaining problems.

$$6 \times 0 = \boxed{0} \qquad 0 \times 7 = \boxed{0} \qquad 250 \times 0 = \boxed{0}$$

Independent Practice and Review

Have your child complete the Lesson 2.4 Practice and Review pages.

Lesson 2.5
×10 Facts

Purpose	Materials
• Practice ×2 facts • Use place-value thinking to find answers to ×10 facts • Practice ×10 facts • Introduce vertical multiplication problems	• Base-ten blocks • Cards • Counters

Memory Work	• If a number has 1, 3, 5, 7, or 9 in the ones-place, is the number even or odd? *Odd.* • If a number has 0, 2, 4, 6, or 8 in the ones-place, is the number even or odd? *Even.*

Warm-up: Practice ×2 Facts

Do a brief oral review of the ×2 facts.

- 2 × 2 = *4*
- 5 × 2 = *10*
- 8 × 2 = *16*
- 10 × 2 = *20*
- 1 × 2 = *2*

- 9 × 2 = *18*
- 4 × 2 = *8*
- 3 × 2 = *6*
- 7 × 2 = *14*
- 6 × 2 = *12*

Activity (A): Use Place-Value Thinking to Find ×10 Facts

Today, you'll use what you know about place value to find answers to the ×10 facts.

Put 4 rods on the table to match the diagram. **4 times 10 means 4 groups of 10. What do 4 tens equal?** *40.* **So, what's 4 times 10?** *40.* Write 40 in both blanks.

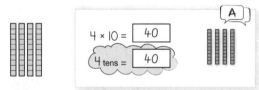

Have your child use place-value thinking to complete part A. Model the problems with base-ten blocks as needed.

6 × 10 = 60	9 × 10 = 90	8 × 10 = 80
3 × 10 = 30	7 × 10 = 70	10 × 10 = 100

What patterns do you notice? *Sample answers: All the numbers have a 0 in the ones-place. The digit in the answer's tens-place is the same as the number you multiply by 10.*

Activity (B): Play Tic-Tac-Toe Crash (×10)

Play Tic-Tac-Toe Crash (×10).

Tic-Tac-Toe Crash (×10)

Materials: Deck of playing cards with 10s, jacks, queens, and kings removed (36 cards total); 10 counters of two different colors each

Object of the Game: Be the first player to fill three boxes in a row, either horizontally, vertically, or diagonally.

Shuffle the cards and place the stack face down on the table. On your turn, flip over the top card. Multiply the number on the card by 10, say the matching multiplication fact, and place one of your counters on the box that matches the product. For example, if you draw a 9, say "9 times 10 equals 90" and place a counter on the box with 90.

If the other player already has a counter on the square, you may "crash" into their counter, remove it, and place your own counter on the square. Play then passes to the other player. Continue until one player has completed an entire row, column, or diagonal.

Activity (C): Introduce Vertical Multiplication

In second grade, you learned to write addition and subtraction problems horizontally or vertically. We can write multiplication equations horizontally or vertically, too.

Show your child the vertical multiplication problems in part C. **When you write an answer for a vertical multiplication problem, write the tens-place for the product directly below the tens-place for the factors. Write the ones-place for the product directly below the ones-place for the factors.**

What's 10 times 2? *20.* Write 20 as shown, from left to right. **We read vertical multiplication problems from top to bottom. We say equals when we get to the line that separates the problem from the answer. This problem says 10 times 2 equals 20.**

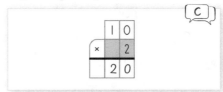

Have your child complete part C. Watch to make sure that she writes each digit in the correct place, and help as needed.

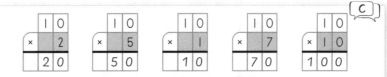

Independent Practice and Review

Have your child complete the Lesson 2.5 Practice and Review pages.

Lesson 2.6
Multiplication Word Problems

Purpose	Materials
• Review ×10 facts • Introduce the terms *factor* and *product* • Solve multiplication word problems	• None

Memory Work	• **What do we call the result when we add numbers together?** *The sum.* • **What do we call the numbers that we add together?** *The addends.* • **What do we call the result when we subtract a number from another number?** *The difference.*

Warm-up: Practice ×10 Facts

Do a brief oral review of the ×10 facts.

- 3 × 10 = *30*
- 7 × 10 = *70*
- 6 × 10 = *60*
- 2 × 10 = *20*
- 5 × 10 = *50*

- 8 × 10 = *80*
- 10 × 10 = *100*
- 1 × 10 = *10*
- 9 × 10 = *90*
- 4 × 10 = *40*

Activity (A): Introduce Multiplication Vocabulary

Today, you'll learn important multiplication vocabulary words and solve multiplication word problems. The numbers that we multiply are called *factors*. We call the result of multiplication the *product*.

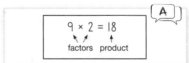

One way to remember this is to imagine putting the numbers into a multiplication factory. The factors are the numbers that we put into the factory. The product is the answer that we get out of the factory.

Activity (B): Solve Multiplication Problems at the Store

Let's pretend we're shopping for school supplies. You get to choose how many we buy of each item. You can choose any number from 1 to 10.

How many packs of scissors should we buy? *Sample answer: 4.* Write your child's response in the blank. **How many scissors are in each pack?** *2.* **So, what multiplication problem tells how many scissors we will get?** *Sample answer: 4 × 2.* **How many scissors is that in all?** *Sample answer: 8.* Write the matching multiplication equation in the blanks.

Sample multiplication equation for the total number of scissors in 4 packs.
Your child may choose a different number of packs of scissors.

If your child has trouble naming the matching multiplication equation, use counters to model the problem. For example, if your child chooses 4 packs of scissors, place 4 groups of 2 on the table. **There are 4 groups of 2, so the matching multiplication problem is 4 times 2.**

Have your child choose quantities for the other items on the list. Then, have him write a matching multiplication equation.

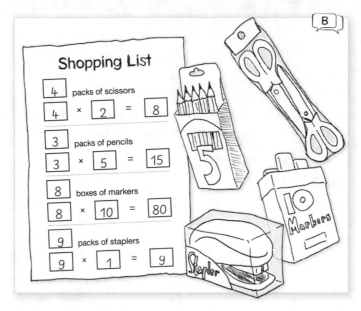

Sample answers. Your child may choose different quantities for each item.

Activity (C): Solve Multiplication Word Problems

What do you remember about the steps for reading word problems? *Sample answer: You read them twice and imagine what's happening.*

Have your child read the first word problem, identify the goal, and then read the problem again slowly.

How many bags of erasers does Julius have? *2.* **How many erasers are in each bag?** *8.* **So, what multiplication problem tells how many erasers he has?** *Sample answer: 2 times 8.* **How many erasers is that in all?** *16.* Have your child write and solve the matching multiplication equation.

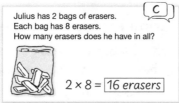

Have your child solve the second word problem in the same way.

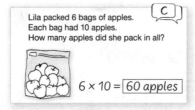

Independent Practice and Review

Have your child complete the Lesson 2.6 Practice and Review pages.

Lesson 2.7
×5 Facts

Purpose	Materials
• Preview the ×5 facts by counting nickels and five-dollar bills • Create groups of 10 to find answers to the ×5 facts • Practice ×5 facts	• Play money • Dot array and L-cover (Blackline Master 5) • Playing cards • Counters

Memory Work
- **What do we call the numbers in a multiplication equation that we multiply together?** *Factors.*
- **What do we call the result when we multiply two numbers?** *The product.*

Warm-up: Count Coins and Paper Bills by 5s

Place nickels and five-dollar bills on the table. Have your child count out the following amounts of play money.

- **May I have 30¢, please?** *Child gives you 6 nickels.*
- **May I have 40¢, please?** *Child gives you 8 nickels.*
- **May I have 45¢, please?** *Child gives you 9 nickels.*
- **May I have $25, please?** *Child gives you 5 five-dollar bills.*
- **May I have $50, please?** *Child gives you 10 five-dollar bills.*
- **May I have $35, please?** *Child gives you 7 five-dollar bills.*

Activity (A): Introduce ×5 Facts

In the last lesson, you practiced the ×10 facts. Today, you'll learn the ×5 facts.

Show 1 × 5 on the dot array. **What's 1 times 5?** *5.* Write 5 in the blank.

$1 × 5 = \boxed{5}$

Show 2 × 5 on the dot array. **What's 2 times 5?** *10.* Write 10 in the blank.

$2 × 5 = \boxed{10}$

Continue with the rest of the ×5 facts. Encourage your child to add 5 to each previous answer to find the next answer.

$1 × 5 =$ $\boxed{5}$		$6 × 5 =$ $\boxed{30}$
$2 × 5 =$ $\boxed{10}$		$7 × 5 =$ $\boxed{35}$
$3 × 5 =$ $\boxed{15}$		$8 × 5 =$ $\boxed{40}$
$4 × 5 =$ $\boxed{20}$		$9 × 5 =$ $\boxed{45}$
$5 × 5 =$ $\boxed{25}$		$10 × 5 =$ $\boxed{50}$

What patterns do you notice? *Sample answers: The answers are the numbers we say when we count by 5. All the numbers have a 0 or 5 in the ones-place.*

Activity (B): Create Groups of 10 to Find ×5 Facts

Use a piece of paper to cover part A.

This array has 4 rows of 5. Combining 5s into groups of 10 makes it easier to find the total number of marbles. Draw rings around groups of 10. **What's 4 times 5?** *20.* If your child's not sure, point out that there are 2 groups of 10. Write 20 in the blank.

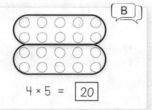

Draw rings around groups of 10 in the second array. **4 groups of 5 equal 20. 5 groups of 5 is just 1 more group of 5. What's 20 plus 5?** *25.* Write 25 in the blank.

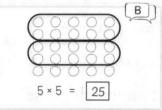

Using 4×5 as a stepping stone to figure out 5×5 helps your child avoid relying on skip-counting to find answers for the ×5 facts. See the Unit 2 **Teaching Math with Confidence** for more on why it's important to avoid skip-counting.

The next problems are arranged like stairsteps. The answers to the problems on the lower steps can help you solve the problems on the higher steps. Always solve these problems from the bottom to the top.

Show 8 × 5 on the dot array. Have your child draw rings around groups of 10. **What's 8 times 5?** *40.* If she's not sure, point out that she created 4 groups of 10. Write 40 in the blank.

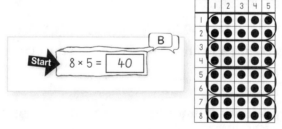

Show 9 × 5 on the dot array. **You just found that 8 groups of 5 equal 40. 9 groups of 5 is just 1 more group of 5. So, what's 9 times 5?** *45.* Write 45 in the blank.

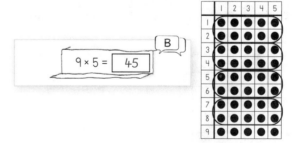

Repeat with 6 × 5 and 7 ×5.

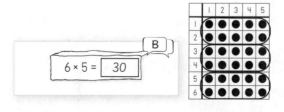

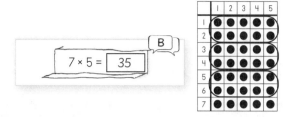

Activity (C): Play Multiplication Cover Up (×5)

The dark line on the game board separates the answers to the first 5 facts from the next 5 facts. You can use the dark line to help find the answers to the ×5 facts. For example, let's say I wanted to find the answer to 6 times 5. Which box is sixth? *Child points to box with 30.* **The box with 30 is sixth, so it has the answer to 6 times 5.**

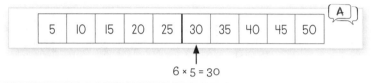

> If you used earlier levels of *Math with Confidence*, point out that the dark line is like the dark line in the middle of the ten-frame.

Play Multiplication Cover Up. Encourage your child to use the position of the boxes on the game board to help find the answers.

Multiplication Cover Up (×5)

Materials: Deck of playing cards with jacks, queens, and kings removed (40 cards total); counters

Object of the Game: Cover all the spaces on your game board first.

Shuffle the cards and place the stack face down on the table.

On your turn, flip over the top card. Multiply the number on the card by 5, say the matching multiplication fact, and place a counter on the matching square on your game board. For example, if you flip over a 7, say "7 times 5 equals 35," and place a counter on 35.

If you already have a counter on the square, say the matching multiplication fact but do not place a new counter. Whoever fills all the squares on their game board first wins the game.

> Games with the answers in order (like Multiplication Cover Up in this lesson or Multiplication Crash in Lesson 2.3) make your child more familiar with the possible answers for a set of facts. Games with the answers mixed up (like Multiplication Bingo in Lesson 2.4) encourage your child to use strategies to find answers. Both types of games are helpful for developing fluency with the multiplication facts, and you'll find both types throughout the program.

Independent Practice and Review

Have your child complete the Lesson 2.7 Practice and Review pages.

Lesson 2.8
×5 Facts on the Clock

Purpose	Materials
• Practice telling time to the quarter hour • Multiply by 5 to identify minutes on the clock • Review telling time to 5 minutes • Understand patterns in the ×5 facts • Practice ×2, ×5, and ×10 facts in the context of a pretend restaurant	• Clock • Counters • Play money

Memory Work	• **What do we call the result when we multiply two numbers?** *The product.* • **What do we call the numbers in a multiplication equation that we multiply together?** *Factors.*

In this lesson, you'll teach your child the connection between the printed numbers on the clock and the ×5 facts. Telling time is an important application of the ×5 facts, and the clock can also be a helpful memory aid for learning the ×5 facts by heart.

Warm-up: Practice Telling Time to the Quarter Hour

Set a clock to the following times and have your child tell each time: 11:00, 11:30, 12:00, 12:45, 1:00, 1:15.

Activity (A): Multiply by 5 to Identify Minutes on the Clock

Today, you'll learn how you can use the ×5 facts to tell the time. When the minute hand points to the 12, it is 0 minutes past the hour. Write :00 in the blank above the 12.

When the minute hand points to the 1, how many minutes have passed since the start of the hour? *5 minutes.* Write :05 in the blank next to the 1. Repeat with the rest of the blanks in order.

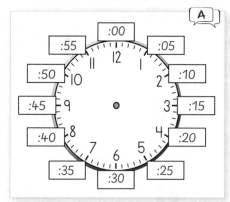

What do you notice about the minute numbers? *Sample answers: They're the numbers we say when we count by 5s. They're the answers to the ×5 facts.*

The printed numbers tell how many groups of 5 minutes have passed since the start of the hour. You can multiply the printed number by 5 to tell how many minutes have passed since the start of the hour!

Cover the minute numbers with counters. Point to a printed number and have your child tell the matching ×5 fact. Then, have him remove the counter to check his answer. For example, if you point to the 7: *7 times 5 equals 35.*

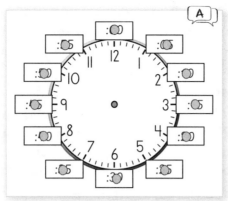

Repeat in random order until your child has removed all the counters. For 11 × 5, challenge your child to use what he knows about counting by 5s to find the answer. For the 12, say: **5 times 12 is 60. 60 minutes equal 1 hour. Once 60 minutes have passed, the new hour begins.**

Activity (B): Understand Patterns in the ×5 Facts

Which of the printed numbers on the clock are even? *2, 4, 6, 8, 10, 12.* Have your child name the matching ×5 multiplication fact for each even number: *2 times 5 equals 10, 4 times 5 equals 20, etc.*

What do these products have in common? *Sample answers: They all have a zero in the ones-place. They're all the numbers you say when you count by 10.* **When you multiply 5 by an even number, the product always has a 0 in the ones-place. That's because every 2 groups of 5 can be put together to make a 10.**

Which of the printed numbers on the clock are odd? *1, 3, 5, 7, 9, 11.* Have your child name the matching ×5 multiplication fact for each odd number: *1 times 5 equals 5, 3 times 5 equals 15, etc.*

What do these products have in common? *Sample answers: They all have a 5 in the ones-place.* **When you multiply 5 by an odd number, the product always has a 5 in the ones-place. After you put groups of 5 together to make as many 10s as possible, you always have one group of 5 left over.**

Activity (B): Play Pretend Restaurant

Let's play Pretend Restaurant! The prices are already printed on the menu, but you get to choose what food the restaurant sells. Have your child tell you what food he would like the restaurant to serve. Write the dishes next to each price. Place play money on the table.

Sample menu.

Let's pretend you're the waiter, and I'm the customer. Pretend to order 6 of the five-dollar item and have your child find the total cost. For example: **I'd like to buy 6 sandwiches, please. How much do I owe you?** *$30.* Use play money to pay for your order and have your child pretend to serve you the food.

Repeat with the following orders:

- **I'd like 7 of the two-dollar items. How much do I owe you?** *$14.*
- **I'd like 3 of the ten-dollar items. How much do I owe you?** *$30.*
- **I'd like 8 of the five-dollar items. How much do I owe you?** *$40.*
- **I'd like 9 of the five-dollar items. How much do I owe you?** *$45.*

If you have time, reverse roles and have your child place some orders at the Pretend Restaurant, too.

If your child is ready for more challenge, try some combination orders. For example: **I'd like 3 orders of sushi and 4 ice cream cones, please. How much do I owe you?** *$38.*

Independent Practice and Review

Have your child complete the Lesson 2.8 Practice and Review pages.

Lesson 2.9
Enrichment (Optional)

Purpose	Materials
• Practice memory work • Discuss multiplication strategies in the context of Halloween • Discover that there can be multiple ways to create arrays with a given number of items • Summarize what your child has learned and assess your child's progress	• *2 × 2 = Boo!: A Set of Spooky Multiplication Stories,* by Loreen Leedy • 24 small snack items, such as raisins, pieces of cereal, or small candies

If you're completing this activity in the fall, candy corn is a fun snack option.

Warm-up: Review Memory Work

Quiz your child on all memory work introduced through Unit 2. See pages 527-528 for the full list.

Math Picture Book: *2 × 2 = Boo!: A Set of Spooky Multiplication Stories*

Read *2 × 2 = Boo!: A Set of Spooky Multiplication Stories,* by Loreen Leedy. As you read, discuss the multiplication strategies that the characters use.

If your family does not observe Halloween, a good substitute is *Too Many Kangaroo Things to Do*, written by Stuart J. Murphy and illustrated by Kevin O'Malley.

Enrichment Activity: Make Arrays of Snacks

Give your child 24 small snack items (such as raisins, pieces of cereal, or small candies). Challenge her to arrange the 24 items in as many different arrays as she can find. Also have her write a multiplication equation to match each array.

1 × 24 = 24 or 24 × 1 = 24.

2 × 12 = 24 or 12 × 2 = 24.   3 × 8 = 24 or 8 × 3 = 24.   4 × 6 = 24 or 6 × 4 = 24.

Your child does not need to arrange each array "both ways." For example, if she creates an array with 4 rows and 6 columns, she does not need to create an array with 6 columns and 4 rows as well.

Unit Wrap-up

Have your child complete the Unit 2 Wrap-up.

Unit 2 Answer Key

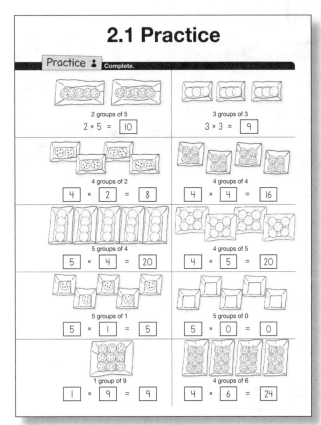

2.1 Practice

Practice 👤 Complete.

2 groups of 5
$2 \times 5 = \boxed{10}$

3 groups of 3
$3 \times 3 = \boxed{9}$

4 groups of 2
$\boxed{4} \times \boxed{2} = \boxed{8}$

4 groups of 4
$\boxed{4} \times \boxed{4} = \boxed{16}$

5 groups of 4
$\boxed{5} \times \boxed{4} = \boxed{20}$

4 groups of 5
$\boxed{4} \times \boxed{5} = \boxed{20}$

5 groups of 1
$\boxed{5} \times \boxed{1} = \boxed{5}$

5 groups of 0
$\boxed{5} \times \boxed{0} = \boxed{0}$

1 group of 9
$\boxed{1} \times \boxed{9} = \boxed{9}$

4 groups of 6
$\boxed{4} \times \boxed{6} = \boxed{24}$

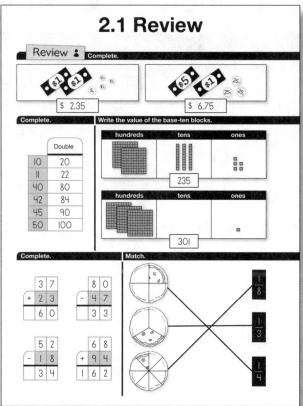

2.1 Review

Review 👤 Complete.

$ 2.35

$ 6.75

Complete.

	Double
10	20
11	22
40	80
42	84
45	90
50	100

Write the value of the base-ten blocks.

hundreds	tens	ones

235

hundreds	tens	ones

301

Complete.

$\begin{array}{c} 3\ 7 \\ +\ 2\ 3 \\ \hline 6\ 0 \end{array}$

$\begin{array}{c} 8\ 0 \\ -\ 4\ 7 \\ \hline 3\ 3 \end{array}$

$\begin{array}{c} 5\ 2 \\ -\ 1\ 8 \\ \hline 3\ 4 \end{array}$

$\begin{array}{c} 6\ 8 \\ +\ 9\ 4 \\ \hline 1\ 6\ 2 \end{array}$

Match.

$\frac{1}{8}$

$\frac{1}{3}$

$\frac{1}{4}$

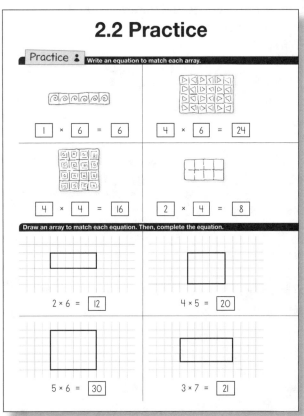

2.2 Practice

Practice 👤 Write an equation to match each array.

$\boxed{1} \times \boxed{6} = \boxed{6}$

$\boxed{4} \times \boxed{6} = \boxed{24}$

$\boxed{4} \times \boxed{4} = \boxed{16}$

$\boxed{2} \times \boxed{4} = \boxed{8}$

Draw an array to match each equation. Then, complete the equation.

$2 \times 6 = \boxed{12}$

$4 \times 5 = \boxed{20}$

$5 \times 6 = \boxed{30}$

$3 \times 7 = \boxed{21}$

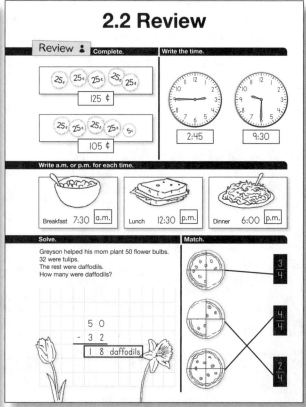

2.2 Review

Review 👤 Complete.

125 ¢

105 ¢

Write the time.

2:45

9:30

Write a.m. or p.m. for each time.

Breakfast 7:30 a.m.

Lunch 12:30 p.m.

Dinner 6:00 p.m.

Solve.

Greyson helped his mom plant 50 flower bulbs.
32 were tulips.
The rest were daffodils.
How many were daffodils?

$\begin{array}{c} 5\ 0 \\ -\ 3\ 2 \\ \hline 1\ 8 \end{array}$ daffodils

Match.

$\frac{3}{4}$

$\frac{4}{4}$

$\frac{2}{4}$

Unit 2 Answer Key

2.3 Practice

Practice 👤 Complete.

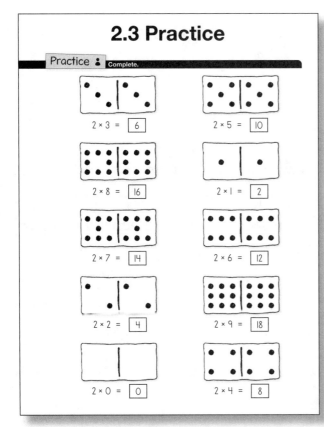

2 × 3 = 6   2 × 5 = 10

2 × 8 = 16   2 × 1 = 2

2 × 7 = 14   2 × 6 = 12

2 × 2 = 4   2 × 9 = 18

2 × 0 = 0   2 × 4 = 8

2.3 Review

Review 👤 Complete the sequences.

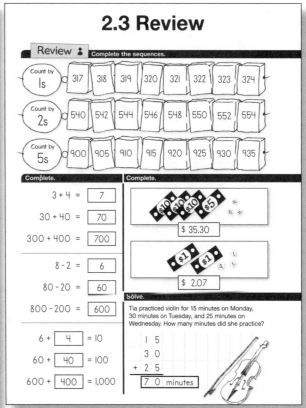

Count by 1s: 317 318 319 320 321 322 323 324

Count by 2s: 540 542 544 546 548 550 552 554

Count by 5s: 900 905 910 915 920 925 930 935

Complete.

3 + 4 = 7

30 + 40 = 70

300 + 400 = 700

8 - 2 = 6

80 - 20 = 60

800 - 200 = 600

6 + 4 = 10

60 + 40 = 100

600 + 400 = 1,000

Complete.

$ 35.30

$ 2.07

Solve.

Tia practiced violin for 15 minutes on Monday, 30 minutes on Tuesday, and 25 minutes on Wednesday. How many minutes did she practice?

```
   1 5
   3 0
 + 2 5
   7 0  minutes
```

2.4 Practice

Practice 👤 Match.

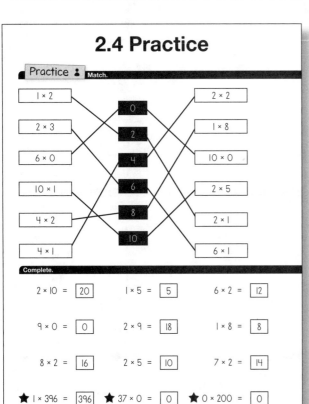

1 × 2   2 × 2
2 × 3   1 × 8
6 × 0   10 × 0
10 × 1   2 × 5
4 × 2   2 × 1
4 × 1   6 × 1

0 2 4 6 8 10

Complete.

2 × 10 = 20   1 × 5 = 5   6 × 2 = 12

9 × 0 = 0   2 × 9 = 18   1 × 8 = 8

8 × 2 = 16   2 × 5 = 10   7 × 2 = 14

★ 1 × 396 = 396   ★ 37 × 0 = 0   ★ 0 × 200 = 0

2.4 Review

Review 👤 Complete the sequences.

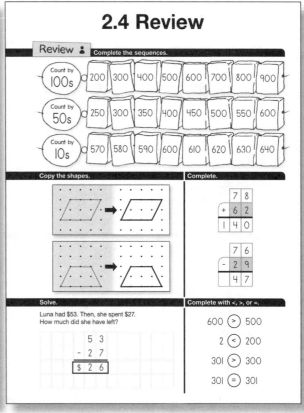

Count by 100s: 200 300 400 500 600 700 800 900

Count by 50s: 250 300 350 400 450 500 550 600

Count by 10s: 570 580 590 600 610 620 630 640

Copy the shapes.

Complete.

```
   7 8
 + 6 2
 1 4 0
```

```
   7 6
 - 2 9
   4 7
```

Solve.

Luna had $53. Then, she spent $27. How much did she have left?

```
   5 3
 - 2 7
 $ 2 6
```

Complete with <, >, or =.

600 > 500

2 < 200

301 > 300

301 = 301

Unit 2 Answer Key

2.5 Practice

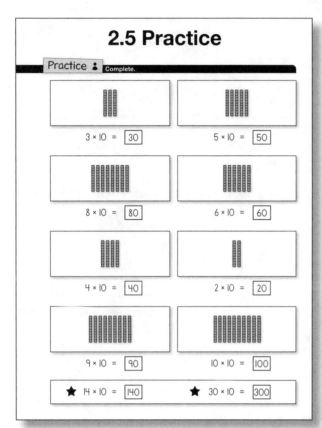

Practice Complete.

3 × 10 = 30

5 × 10 = 50

8 × 10 = 80

6 × 10 = 60

4 × 10 = 40

2 × 10 = 20

9 × 10 = 90

10 × 10 = 100

★ 14 × 10 = 140   ★ 30 × 10 = 300

2.5 Review

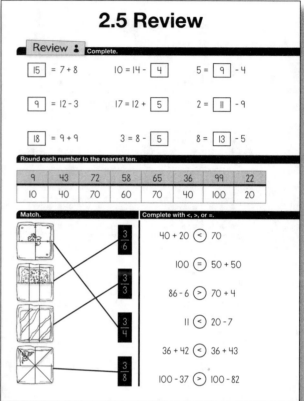

Review Complete.

15 = 7 + 8   10 = 14 - 4   5 = 9 - 4

9 = 12 - 3   17 = 12 + 5   2 = 11 - 9

18 = 9 + 9   3 = 8 - 5   8 = 13 - 5

Round each number to the nearest ten.

9	43	72	58	65	36	99	22
10	40	70	60	70	40	100	20

Match.   Complete with <, >, or =.

$\frac{3}{6}$ 40 + 20 $<$ 70

$\frac{3}{3}$ 100 $=$ 50 + 50

                                86 - 6 $>$ 70 + 4

$\frac{3}{4}$ 11 $<$ 20 - 7

                                36 + 42 $<$ 36 + 43

$\frac{3}{8}$ 100 - 37 $>$ 100 - 82

2.6 Practice

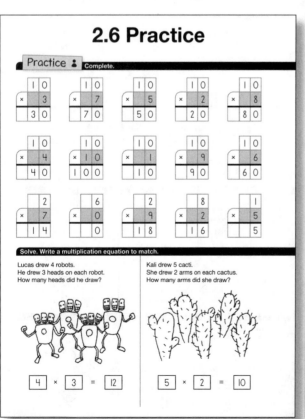

Practice Complete.

1 0		1 0		1 0		1 0		1 0
× 3		× 7		× 5		× 2		× 8
3 0		7 0		5 0		2 0		8 0

1 0		1 0		1 0		1 0		1 0
× 4		× 10		× 1		× 9		× 6
4 0		1 0 0		1 0		9 0		6 0

2		6		2		8		1
× 7		× 0		× 9		× 2		× 5
1 4		0		1 8		1 6		5

Solve. Write a multiplication equation to match.

Lucas drew 4 robots.
He drew 3 heads on each robot.
How many heads did he draw?

Kali drew 5 cacti.
She drew 2 arms on each cactus.
How many arms did she draw?

4 × 3 = 12   5 × 2 = 10

2.6 Review

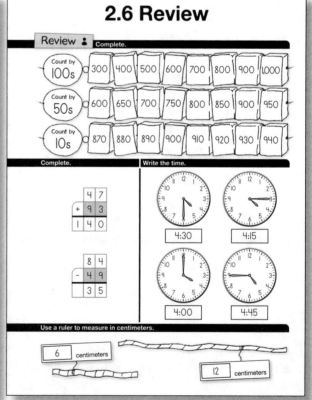

Review Complete.

Count by 100s: 300 400 500 600 700 800 900 1,000

Count by 50s: 600 650 700 750 800 850 900 950

Count by 10s: 870 880 890 900 910 920 930 940

Complete.   Write the time.

| 4 7 |
| + 9 3 |
| 1 4 0 |

| 8 4 |
| - 4 9 |
| 3 5 |

4:30   4:15

4:00   4:45

Use a ruler to measure in centimeters.

6 centimeters

12 centimeters

Unit 2 Answer Key

2.7 Practice

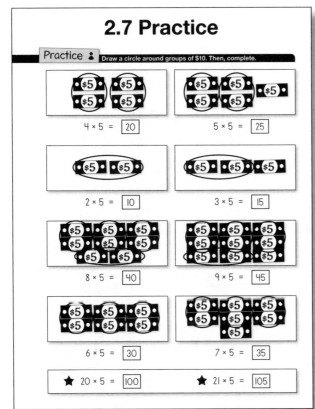

Practice 👤 Draw a circle around groups of $10. Then, complete.

4 × 5 = 20

5 × 5 = 25

2 × 5 = 10

3 × 5 = 15

8 × 5 = 40

9 × 5 = 45

6 × 5 = 30

7 × 5 = 35

★ 20 × 5 = 100   ★ 21 × 5 = 105

2.7 Review

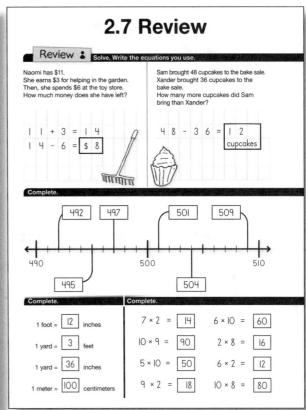

Review 👤 Solve. Write the equations you use.

Naomi has $11.
She earns $3 for helping in the garden.
Then, she spends $6 at the toy store.
How much money does she have left?

1 1 + 3 = 1 4
1 4 - 6 = $ 8

Sam brought 48 cupcakes to the bake sale.
Xander brought 36 cupcakes to the bake sale.
How many more cupcakes did Sam bring than Xander?

4 8 - 3 6 = 1 2 cupcakes

Complete.

492   497   501   509

490   495   500   504   510

Complete.

1 foot = 12 inches

1 yard = 3 feet

1 yard = 36 inches

1 meter = 100 centimeters

Complete.

7 × 2 = 14   6 × 10 = 60

10 × 9 = 90   2 × 8 = 16

5 × 10 = 50   6 × 2 = 12

9 × 2 = 18   10 × 8 = 80

2.8 Practice

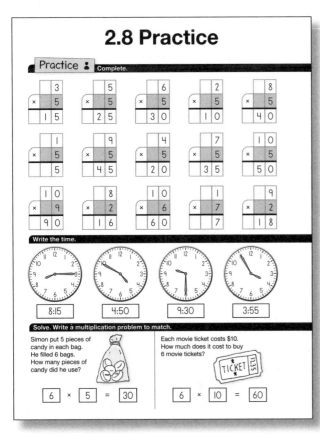

Practice 👤 Complete.

3 × 5 = 15

5 × 5 = 25

6 × 5 = 30

2 × 5 = 10

8 × 5 = 40

1 × 5 = 5

9 × 5 = 45

4 × 5 = 20

7 × 5 = 35

10 × 5 = 50

10 × 9 = 90

8 × 2 = 16

10 × 6 = 60

1 × 7 = 7

9 × 2 = 18

Write the time.

8:15   4:50   9:30   3:55

Solve. Write a multiplication problem to match.

Simon put 5 pieces of candy in each bag.
He filled 6 bags.
How many pieces of candy did he use?

6 × 5 = 30

Each movie ticket costs $10.
How much does it cost to buy 6 movie tickets?

6 × 10 = 60

2.8 Review

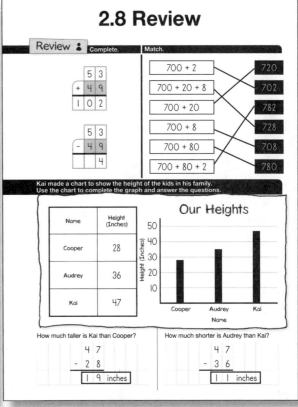

Review 👤 Complete.   Match.

5 3
+ 4 9
1 0 2

5 3
- 4 9
    4

700 + 2
700 + 20 + 8
700 + 20
700 + 8
700 + 80
700 + 80 + 2

720
702
782
728
708
780

Kai made a chart to show the height of the kids in his family.
Use the chart to complete the graph and answer the questions.

Name	Height (Inches)
Cooper	28
Audrey	36
Kai	47

Our Heights

How much taller is Kai than Cooper?

4 7
- 2 8
1 9 inches

How much shorter is Audrey than Kai?

4 7
- 3 6
1 1 inches

Unit 2 Answer Key

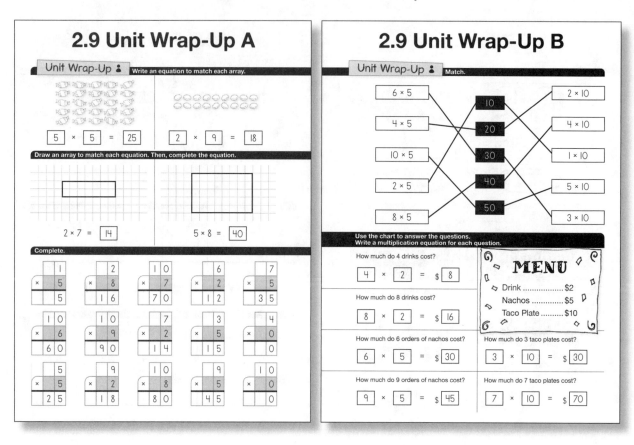

2.9 Unit Wrap-Up A

Unit Wrap-Up 👤 Write an equation to match each array.

$5 \times 5 = 25$ $2 \times 9 = 18$

Draw an array to match each equation. Then, complete the equation.

$2 \times 7 = 14$ $5 \times 8 = 40$

Complete.

1	
× 5	
5	

	2
× 8	
1 6	

1	0
×	7
7	0

	6
×	2
1	2

	7
×	5
3	5

1	0
×	6
6	0

1	0
×	9
9	0

	7
×	2
1	4

	3
×	5
1	5

	4
×	0
	0

	5
×	5
2	5

	9
×	2
1	8

1	0
×	8
8	0

	9
×	5
4	5

1	0
×	0
	0

2.9 Unit Wrap-Up B

Unit Wrap-Up 👤 Match.

6 × 5	10	2 × 10
4 × 5	20	4 × 10
10 × 5	30	1 × 10
2 × 5	40	5 × 10
8 × 5	50	3 × 10

Use the chart to answer the questions.
Write a multiplication equation for each question.

How much do 4 drinks cost?

$4 \times 2 = \$ 8$

How much do 8 drinks cost?

$8 \times 2 = \$ 16$

How much do 6 orders of nachos cost?

$6 \times 5 = \$ 30$

How much do 9 orders of nachos cost?

$9 \times 5 = \$ 45$

MENU

Drink $2
Nachos $5
Taco Plate $10

How much do 3 taco plates cost?

$3 \times 10 = \$ 30$

How much do 7 taco plates cost?

$7 \times 10 = \$ 70$

Unit 2 Checkpoint

What to Expect at the End of Unit 2

By the end of Unit 2, most children will be able to do the following:

- Write multiplication equations with the × sign to match equal groups or arrays.
- Understand that you can multiply numbers in any order and use this property to help find answers.
- Find answers for the ×1, ×2, ×5, and ×10 facts. Most children will know the ×1, ×2, and ×10 facts fairly fluently but will still need more practice with the ×5 facts.
- Understand that the product of any number and 1 is the original number. Understand that the product of any number and zero is zero.
- Write equations to solve simple multiplication word problems.

Is Your Child Ready to Move on?

In Unit 3, your child will review mental addition and subtraction with numbers to 100. He'll also learn some new mental math techniques and solve more challenging two-step word problems.

Your child does not need to fully master the multiplication facts from Unit 2 before moving on to Unit 3. He will continue to practice the ×1, ×2, ×5, and ×10 facts throughout Unit 3 before working on the ×3 and ×4 facts in Unit 4.

Before moving on to Unit 3, your child should be **mostly fluent with the subtraction facts.** Ideally, your child should know the answers to the subtraction facts up to 18 – 9 in less than 3 seconds. (This depends on your child, though! Just as with addition, children who process information quickly should be able to rattle off most answers within a second. Children who are slower processors may always need 3-5 seconds to tell an answer.) You know your child best, so adjust your expectations based on your individual child.

What to Do If Your Child Needs More Practice

Just because a child doesn't have the subtraction facts fully mastered doesn't mean he can't continue learning third-grade math concepts. But, if your child often has trouble recalling the subtraction facts (or takes longer than 3 seconds to remember the answers), it's important to continue building more fluency and speed as you move forward with third-grade skills. Use the following suggestions to help your child build greater automaticity with the subtraction facts:

- If your child can find answers to most of the facts but takes longer than 3 seconds, he probably just needs more practice to build speed. Play Subtraction Climb and Slide a few times per week, either at the beginning of a lesson or at a separate time of day. (You'll find the Subtraction Climb and Slide game board and directions on Blackline Master 14.) Subtraction fact apps or flash cards are also a good way to build speed and automaticity.
- If your child has only a few facts that stump him, choose 3 of the tricky facts. Write them on a piece of paper and post them in your math lesson area. Have him practice these 3 facts at the beginning of each lesson until he has memorized them. Then, choose 3 new facts to focus on.

- If your child has trouble finding answers to many of the subtraction facts or often counts on his fingers to find the answers, he may not be ready to tackle *Third Grade Math with Confidence. Subtraction Facts That Stick* provides a systematic approach to mastering the facts. You can use *Subtraction Facts That Stick* on its own for a few weeks to reinforce the specific facts that your child needs to practice. Or, if you want to continue to move forward with *Third Grade Math with Confidence,* use the activities from *Subtraction Facts that Stick* for 5-10 minutes per day outside of your regular math time.

Unit 3
Mental Math and Word Problems

Overview

Your child will review and practice mental addition and subtraction with numbers to 100. She'll also learn how to make change, add up to find differences, and solve more-challenging two-step word problems.

This unit provides a quick review of the mental addition and subtraction skills covered in *Second Grade Math with Confidence*. If your child used *Second Grade Math with Confidence*, she'll likely find this unit a pleasant review. If your child did not use *Second Grade Math with Confidence* (or struggles with mental math), she may need more than one lesson to practice each new mental math skill before moving on to the next one. If you find your child needs a slower pace, you'll find suggestions for splitting the mental math lessons over two days.

What Your Child Will Learn

In this unit, your child will learn to:

- Find the value of groups of tens and mentally add tens
- Add up to identify missing addends and make change
- Review strategies for mentally adding and subtracting one- and two-digit numbers
- Mentally find differences between close numbers by adding up
- Solve two-step word problems

Lesson List

Lesson 3.1	Review Mental Addition with Tens	Lesson 3.5	More/Less Word Problems
Lesson 3.2	Add Up to Find Missing Addends and Make Change	Lesson 3.6	Review Two-Digit Mental Addition
Lesson 3.3	Review One-Digit Mental Addition	Lesson 3.7	Review Two-Digit Mental Subtraction
Lesson 3.4	Review One-Digit Mental Subtraction	Lesson 3.8	Add Up to Find Differences
		Lesson 3.9	More Two-Step Word Problems
		Lesson 3.10	Enrichment (Optional)

Extra Materials Needed for Unit 3

- For optional Enrichment Lesson:
    - *Counting on Katherine: How Katherine Johnson Saved Apollo 13*, written by Helaine Becker and illustrated by Dow Phumiruk. Henry Holt and Co., 2018.

Teaching Math with Confidence:
Using Strategies (Not Skip-Counting) to Master the Multiplication Facts

In this unit, your child will review how to mentally add and subtract numbers to 100. Besides the real-life usefulness of these skills, mental math also serves another purpose in *Math with Confidence:* helping your child develop deeper number sense. As she breaks numbers apart and puts them together again, she will develop a stronger understanding of place value and the relationships between numbers.

Use the following suggestions to adjust mental math lessons to your child's needs so she can reap the full benefits of these skills:

- Model the strategies presented in the lesson, but **allow your child to use any efficient and accurate strategy** that makes sense to her. Children often make up their own strategies for solving mental math problems, and that's perfectly fine.
- Mental math is meant to help your child develop her number sense, not make her a memory champion. If your child finds it hard to keep the numbers in her head, **allow her to write down any in-between steps** in her solving process.
- Some children won't need base-ten blocks to model these problems. Many will need them only at first, and others will need them for most problems. **Allow your child to use base-ten blocks to model the problems as much as she needs.** If you suspect she's ready to solve the problems without blocks, challenge her to try imagining the blocks instead.
- In this program, problems written horizontally are meant to be solved mentally, and problems written vertically are meant to be solved with the algorithms. **Don't allow your child to rewrite mental math problems vertically** and solve them with the addition or subtraction algorithm. Skipping mental math and going straight to the algorithm short-circuits all the number sense growth that mental math provides.

Lesson 3.1
Review Mental Addition with Tens

Purpose	Materials
• Practice ×10 facts • Identify the value of groups of tens • Use place-value thinking to mentally add tens	• Play money • Counters

Memory Work
- **How many months are in a year?** *12.*
- **How many days are in a week?** *7.*

Warm-up: Practice ×10 Facts

Do a brief oral review of the ×10 facts.

- 3 × 10 = *30*
- 7 × 10 = *70*
- 6 × 10 = *60*
- 2 × 10 = *20*
- 5 × 10 = *50*

- 8 × 10 = *80*
- 10 × 10 = *100*
- 1 × 10 = *10*
- 9 × 10 = *90*
- 4 × 10 = *40*

Activity (A): Identify the Value of Groups of Tens

In previous grades, you learned many ways to add and subtract numbers in your head. This is called mental math. Mental math is important because it helps you understand numbers more deeply. It's helpful in real life, too. In this unit, you'll review mental math strategies for addition and subtraction and learn some new strategies, too.

Today, we'll review mental math with tens. **Let's pretend you have 13 ten-dollar bills, and you want to know how much they're worth.** Place 13 ten-dollar bills on the table to match the picture. **How much do 10 tens equal?** *100.* **How much do 3 tens equal?** *30.* Write 100 and 30 in the blanks.

So, how much do 13 tens equal? *130.* If your child's not sure, suggest she add 100 plus 30. Write 130 in the blank.

Make sure to model the problem with play money as directed, even if your child understands the picture in the workbook. The play money makes the problem more concrete and prepares her to use money to solve the other problems in the lesson if needed.

Have her use the same approach to complete part A. Model the exercises with play money as needed.

One way to solve these problems is to simply tack on a zero to the number of tens. At this point, teaching this "trick" (rather than focusing on the underlying place-value concepts) short-circuits the learning process and reduces these problems to a rule to memorize. If your child discovers this pattern on her own and understands why it occurs, it's fine for her to use it.

Activity (B): Mentally Add Tens

Let's pretend you have $70. Then, you earn $50 more. Place a group of 7 ten-dollar bills and a group of 5 ten-dollar bills on the table to match the picture. **What's 7 tens plus 5 tens?** *12 tens.* If your child's not sure, rephrase the question: **We have 7 ten-dollar bills and 5 ten-dollar bills. How many ten-dollar bills is that?** *12.* Write 12 in the blank.

So, what does 70 plus 50 equal? *120.* Write 120 in the blank.

Some children may prefer to "complete a 100" to solve this problem. For example, to solve 70 plus 50: *70 plus 30 is 100. 100 plus 20 more is 120.* It's fine for your child to use either strategy, as long as she understands why it works and can apply it confidently. See the Unit 3 **Teaching Math with Confidence** (page 82) for more about modifying mental math lessons to best fit your child's needs.

We can use this problem to help solve a harder problem. Write 120 on the bottom step of the first stairstep problem. Add 3 one-dollar bills to the play money on the table. **If 70 plus 50 equals 120, what does 70 plus 53 equal?** *123.* Write 123 in the blank. Add 1 ten-dollar bill to the table. **If 70 plus 53 equals 123, what does 70 plus 63 equal?** *133.* Write 133 in the blank.

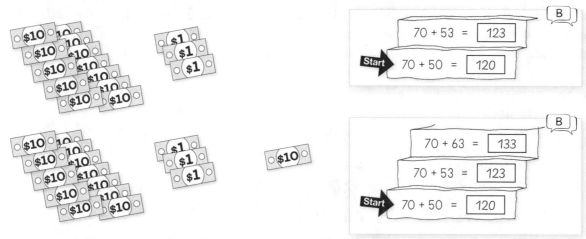

Have your child complete the other stairstep problem. Model the problems with play money as needed.

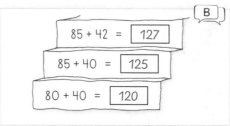

Activity (C): Play Four in a Row

Play Four in a Row. Model the problems in the game with play money as needed.

Four in a Row

Materials: 20 counters per player, with a different color for each player

Object of the Game: Be the first player to place counters in 4 squares in a row, either horizontally, vertically, or diagonally.

On your turn, choose one addition problem on the board and say its answer. Use 2 counters to cover the box with the problem as well as the box with the problem's answer. For example, if you choose the box with 90 + 30, cover the box with 90 + 30 and one of the boxes with 120.

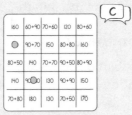

Sample first play

Play then passes to the other player. Continue until one player covers 4 boxes in a row, either horizontally, vertically, or diagonally.

One square in the game does not have a match (since the game board has an odd number of squares). If your child discovers this square, tell her it is a "stopper" and that neither player may play a counter on this square.

Note that you only need to place 4 counters in a row to win, even though there are 5 rows and columns on the game board. The extra row and column provide more opportunities to win.

Independent Practice and Review

Have your child complete the Lesson 3.1 Practice and Review pages.

Lesson 3.2
Add Up to Find Missing Addends and Make Change

Purpose	Materials
• Practice ×5 facts • Add up to find missing addends • Add up to make change	• Clock • Base-ten blocks • Play money

Memory Work	• **How many hours are in a day?** *24.* • **How many minutes are in an hour?** *60.* • **How many seconds are in a minute?** *60.*

Warm-up: Review ×5 Facts on the Clock

Show your child a clock. (The clock can be set to any time.) Point to the printed 4 on the clock and say the matching ×5 multiplication fact: **4 times 5 equals what?** *20.*

Repeat with the rest of the numbers from 1-10, in random order. Point to one at a time, say the matching ×5 fact, and have your child tell the answer to the fact.

Activity (A): Add Up to Find Missing Addends

In the last lesson, you used mental math to add tens. Today, you'll use mental math to find missing addends and make change at the Pretend Store.

Read aloud the first equation: *38 plus what equals 40?* Model 38 with base-ten blocks to match the picture. **How many more ones do I need to complete the group of 10?** *2.* Add 2 unit blocks. **So, 38 plus 2 equals 40.** Write 2 in the blank.

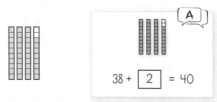

Make sure to model the problem with base-ten blocks as directed, even if your child understands the picture in the workbook. The base-ten blocks make the problems more concrete and prepare him to use base-ten blocks if needed to help solve the other problems in the lesson.

Read aloud the second equation: ***38 plus what equals 70?*** Again, model 38 with base-ten blocks. **To solve this problem, we'll add up in 2 steps. How many more ones do I need to complete the group of 10?** *2.* Add 2 unit blocks. **How many more tens do I need to reach 70?** *3 tens.* Add 3 rods. **We added 32 in all. So, 38 plus 32 equals 70.** Write 32 in the blank.

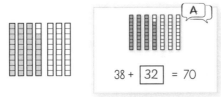

$$38 + \boxed{32} = 70$$

Repeat with the third equation. Help your child add 2 units and 6 rods to reach 100.

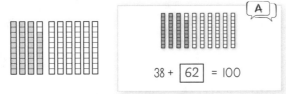

$$38 + \boxed{62} = 100$$

Have your child complete part A. Use base-ten blocks to model the problems as needed.

$$49 + \boxed{1} = 50 \qquad 67 + \boxed{3} = 70 \qquad 52 + \boxed{28} = 80$$

$$76 + \boxed{14} = 90 \qquad 85 + \boxed{15} = 100 \qquad 27 + \boxed{73} = 100$$

Activity (B): Add up to Make Change at the Pretend Store

The prices and items for the Pretend Store are printed in part B. If you'd like to make the activity more hands-on, choose 5 items from around your house and label them with the prices listed.

You can add up to make change, too. Let's pretend that I'm a customer at the Pretend Store, and you're the clerk. I'd like to buy the roller skates, but I don't have the right bills. Here's $80. Give your child 4 twenty-dollar bills.

The roller skates cost $76, but I gave you $80. I gave you too much money, so you need to give me back the extra. 76 plus what equals 80? *4.* **I gave you $4 extra. May I have $4 change, please?** Have your child give you 4 one-dollar bills as change.

Repeat with the other items. Use twenty-dollar bills to pay for each item, and have your child add up to figure out how much change to give you.

Give your child $60. He should give you $5 in change.

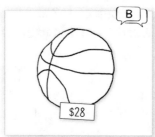

Give your child $40. He should give you $12 in change.

Give your child $100. He should give you $6 in change.

Give your child $80. He should give you $19 in change.

This activity is meant as an introduction to making change. Don't worry if he doesn't fully grasp the concept yet. He'll practice more (and learn to make change with both dollars and cents) in Unit 7.

Independent Practice and Review

Have your child complete the Lesson 3.2 Practice and Review pages.

Lesson 3.3
Review One-Digit Mental Addition

Purpose	Materials
• Practice telling time to 5 minutes • Review strategies for mentally adding one-digit numbers to two-digit numbers	• Clock • Base-ten blocks • Counters • Die

Memory Work	• **How many inches equal 1 foot?** *12.* • **How many feet equal 1 yard?** *3.* • **How many inches equal 1 yard?** *36.*

If your child did not use *Second Grade Math with Confidence* or struggled with mental math last year, she may need two days to practice the skills in this lesson. Here's a suggested plan:

- Day 1: Do the Warm-up and Activity A. Have your child solve half of the problems on the Practice and Review pages. Help her model the problems with base-ten blocks as needed.
- Day 2: Review the strategies in Activity A and play Climb and Slide. Have your child solve the remaining problems on the Practice and Review pages.

Warm-up: Practice Telling Time to 5 Minutes

Set a clock to the following times and have your child tell each time: 1:30, 1:40, 1:55, 2:00, 2:05, 2:15, 2:25, 3:50, 5:10.

Activity (A): Review Two Strategies for Adding One-Digit Numbers

Today, we'll review how to mentally add one-digit numbers to two-digit numbers. I'll show you two strategies. Then, you can use whichever strategy you prefer.

Have your child model 49 plus 3 with base-ten blocks. **One way to find 49 plus 3 is to use related addition facts. 49 has 4 tens and 9 ones, so we can split it into 40 and 9.** Write 40 in the box below the 4 rods.

What's 9 plus 3? *12.* Write 12 in the box below the unit blocks.

What's 40 plus 12? *52.* **So, 49 plus 3 equals 52.** Write 52 in the blank.

 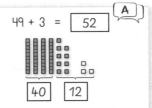

Another way to solve the problem is to complete a 10. First, I add 1 unit to complete the group of 10. Move 1 unit block as shown. **49 plus 1 equals 50.** Write 50 in the blank. **Then, I add on the other 2 units.** Write 2 in the blank. **What's 50 plus 2?** *52.* Write 52 in the blank.

 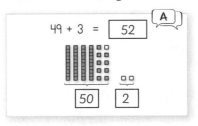

Which strategy do you like better: using related addition facts or completing a 10? *Answers will vary.* **Either way is fine!** Have your child use whatever strategy she prefers to complete part A.

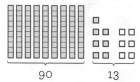

If your child has trouble with 97 + 6, model the problem with base-ten blocks and discuss how she can apply her preferred strategy to solve it.

- If your child prefers using related addition facts: **What's 7 plus 6?** *13.* **What's 90 plus 13?** *103.*

- If your child prefers **completing a 10: In this problem, you don't just complete a 10. You also complete a 100! First, I add 3 to complete the 100.** Move 3 unit blocks as shown. **97 plus 3 equals 100. Then, I add on the other 3 units. 100 plus 3 equals 103.**

You will teach your child many specific mental math strategies in this program, but different strategies "click" better for different children. Your child can use any strategy to solve mental math problems, as long as her strategy is efficient, accurate, and reliable.

Activity (B): Play Climb and Slide

Play Climb and Slide. Use base-ten blocks to model the problems as needed.

Climb and Slide

Materials: 2 different-colored counters to use as game tokens; die

Object of the Game: Be the first player to reach the Finish square.

Each player chooses a counter to use as a game token and places it on the Start square.

On your turn, roll the die and advance your token the corresponding number of squares. Say the answer to the problem on your landing square.

If you land on a square at the bottom of a ladder, "climb" the ladder and place your game token on the square at the top of the ladder. If you land on a square at the top of a slide, slide down the slide and place your game token on the square at the bottom of the slide.

The first player to reach Finish wins the game.

Independent Practice and Review

Have your child complete the Lesson 3.3 Practice and Review pages.

Lesson 3.4
Review One-Digit Mental Subtraction

Purpose	Materials
• Practice ×2 facts • Review how to mentally subtract a one-digit number from a multiple of 10 • Review how to mentally subtract a one-digit number from any two-digit number	• Base-ten blocks • Die

Memory Work · **How many centimeters equal 1 meter?** *100.*

Here's a suggested plan if your child needs two days to learn the skills in this lesson:

- Day 1: Do the Warm-up and Activities A and B. Have your child solve half of the problems on the Practice and Review pages. Help him model the problems with base-ten blocks as needed.
- Day 2: Review the strategies in Activities A and B and play Roll and Subtract. Have your child solve the remaining problems on the Practice and Review pages.

Warm-up: Practice ×2 Facts

Do a brief oral review of the ×2 facts.

- 10 × 2 = *20*
- 1 × 2 = *2*
- 9 × 2 = *18*
- 4 × 2 = *8*
- 3 × 2 = *6*

- 7 × 2 = *14*
- 6 × 2 = *12*
- 2 × 2 = *4*
- 5 × 2 = *10*
- 8 × 2 = *16*

Activity (A): Review Subtracting a One-Digit Number from a Multiple of 10

Today, we'll review how to subtract one-digit numbers from two-digit numbers. First, we'll review how to subtract one-digit numbers from a multiple of 10.

Let's subtract 6 from 70. Model 70 with base-ten blocks. Cover 6 of the units on one rod with a slip of paper. **What's 70 minus 6?** *64.* Write 64 in the blank.

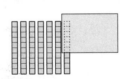

70 - 6 = [64]

If your child starts to count the visible units one-by-one, prompt him to think of the pairs that make 10: **6 and what make 10?** *4.* **I covered 6 units, so there must be 4 showing.**

Have your child complete part A in the same way. Use base-ten blocks as needed.

80 - 5 = [75]   30 - 2 = [28]   100 - 7 = [93]

Activity (B): Review Subtracting a One-Digit Number from any Two-Digit Number

Let's subtract 6 from 72. Model 72 with base-ten blocks. **We'll subtract in 2 steps. First, we subtract the loose ones.** Cover 2 of the units with a slip of paper. **72 minus 2 equals 70.**

We want to subtract 6 ones, and we have already subtracted 2. How many more do we need to subtract? *4*. Use another slip of paper to cover 4 units on 1 of the rods. **What's 70 minus 4?** *66*. Write 66 in the blank.

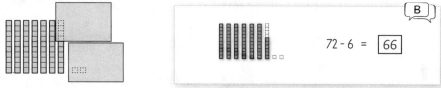

Have your child complete part B in the same way. Model the problems with base-ten blocks as needed.

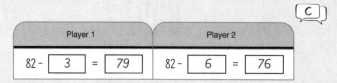

Activity (C): Play Roll and Subtract

Play Roll and Subtract.

Roll and Subtract

Materials: Die

Object of the Game: Win the most points.

Roll and Subtract has 5 rounds. On your turn, roll the die and write your roll in the blank in the first equation on your scorecard. Then, complete the subtraction problem. Whoever has the greater difference wins a point. If the differences are equal, both players win a point.

For example, if Player 1 rolls a 3 in the first round and Player 2 rolls a 6, Player 1 wins the point.

Player 1	Player 2
82 - 3 = 79	82 - 6 = 76

Player 1 wins the point, since 79 is greater than 76.

Play until you have completed the entire scorecard. Whoever has won more points wins the game.

Independent Practice and Review

Have your child complete the Lesson 3.4 Practice and Review pages.

Lesson 3.5
More/Less Word Problems

Purpose	Materials
• Practice completing a chart to solve more/less word problems • Make charts to solve one-step and two-step more/less word problems	• None

Memory Work	
	• **Are times in the morning a.m. or p.m.?** *A.m.* • **Are times in the afternoon and evening a.m. or p.m.?** *P.m.*

In the word problems in this lesson, you know the difference between two quantities, as well as one of the quantities. Your goal is to find the other quantity. These problems are usually called "more/less problems," even though they may use words like *longer, shorter, older, younger,* or *fewer* to describe the relationships between the quantities.

Warm-up (A): Complete a Chart to Solve More/Less Word Problems

Have your child read each clue one at a time and use the clue to complete a line from the chart.

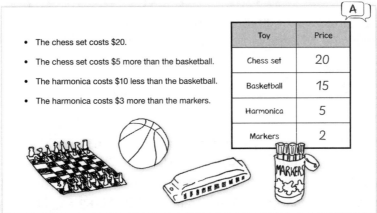

If your child isn't sure whether to add or subtract, have her first decide which item is more expensive. For example: **The chess set costs $5 more than the basketball. Which costs more, the chess set or the basketball?** *The chess set.* **How much more?** *$5.* **So, subtract $5 from the price of the chess set to find how much the basketball costs.**

Activity (B): Make Charts to Solve More/Less Word Problems

In the warm-up activity, you completed a chart about how much more or how much less things cost than each other. Today, you'll learn how to make your own charts to solve more/less word problems.

Have your child read aloud the first word problem. **What's the goal?** *Find how many points her sister scored.* Then, have your child read the problem again slowly. **Making a chart helps organize the information in more/less word problems.** Start a simple chart as shown.

Brielle scored 10 points in a game.
She scored 5 fewer points than her sister.
How many points did her sister score?

Person	Points
Brielle	10
Sister	

The problem says that Brielle scored 5 fewer points than her sister. Who scored more points? *The sister.* **How many more points?** *5.* **So, how can you find Brielle's sister's score?** *Sample answer: Add 5 to Brielle's score.* Write 10 + 5 = below the problem. Have your child complete the equation, write "points" after the sum, and draw a box around the complete answer. **How many points did her sister score?** *15.* Write 15 in the chart.

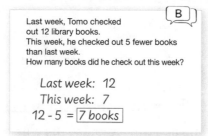

Person	Points
Brielle	10
Sister	15

10 + 5 = $\boxed{15 \text{ points}}$

> Identifying which quantity is greater helps children know whether to add or subtract the difference between the two quantities. If you know the greater number, you subtract to find the lesser number. If you know the lesser number, you add to find the greater number.

Have your child make a simple list to solve the other word problem in part B.

Last week, Tomo checked out 12 library books.
This week, he checked out 5 fewer books than last week.
How many books did he check out this week? **B**

Last week: 12
This week: 7
12 - 5 = $\boxed{7 \text{ books}}$

Activity (C): Make Charts to Solve Two-Step More/Less Word Problems

Have your child read aloud the first word problem in part C. Remind her to follow the steps for reading word problems. **What's our goal in this problem?** *Find how old Grace is.* Begin a simple chart as shown.

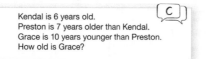

Kendal is 6 years old.
Preston is 7 years older than Kendal.
Grace is 10 years younger than Preston.
How old is Grace? **C**

Name	Age

Let's read one sentence at a time. After we read each sentence, we'll add the information in the sentence to the chart. *Kendal is 6 years old.* Write "Kendal" and "6" in the chart.

Preston is 7 years older than Kendal. Write "Preston" in the chart. **How old is Preston?** *13.* **How do you know?** *Sample answer: I added 6 plus 7.* Write "6 + 7 = 13" and write 13 in the chart.

Grace is 10 years younger than Preston. Write "Grace" in the chart. **How old is Grace?** *3.* **How do you know?** *Sample answer: I subtracted 13 minus 10.* Write "13 − 10 = 3" and write 3 in the chart.

Remind me, what's our goal in this problem? *Find how old Grace is.* **So, what's the answer to the problem?** *3 years old.* Write "3 years old" and draw a box around the complete answer.

Name	Age
Kendal	6
Preston	13
Grace	3

6 + 7 = 13
13 - 10 = $\boxed{3 \text{ years old}}$

Have your child make a chart to organize the information in the other word problem in part C. After she makes the chart ask: **What's the goal in this problem?** *Find how many points Jake scored in both games.* **How can you use the information in the chart to answer the question?** *Sample answer: Add 9 plus 5.* Have your child write a matching equation and complete the problem.

C

On Monday, Jake scored 9 points at his basketball game.
On Tuesday, he scored 4 fewer points than Monday.
How many points did he score in both games?

Day	Points
Monday	9
Tuesday	5

$9 - 4 = 5$ points
$9 + 5 = \boxed{14 \text{ points}}$

Independent Practice and Review

Have your child complete the Lesson 3.5 Practice and Review workbook pages.

Lesson 3.6
Review Two-Digit Mental Addition

Purpose	Materials
• Answer questions that involve *sum*, *difference*, or *product* • Review using place-value thinking to mentally add two-digit numbers	• Base-ten blocks • Playing cards

Memory Work	• **What do we call the result when we multiply two numbers?** *The product.* • **What do we call the result when we subtract a number from another number?** *The difference.* • **What do we call the result when we add numbers together?** *The sum.*

Here's a suggested plan if your child needs two days to learn the skills in this lesson:

- Day 1: Do the Warm-up and Activity A. Have your child solve half of the problems on the Practice and Review pages. Help him model the problems with base-ten blocks as needed.
- Day 2: Review the strategies in Activity A, and then complete Activities B and C. Have your child solve the remaining problems on the Practice and Review pages.

Warm-up: Review Math Vocabulary

Ask your child the following questions to review and apply math vocabulary:

- **What's the sum of 8 and 5?** *13.*
- **What's the difference between 8 and 5?** *3.*
- **What's the product of 8 and 5?** *40.*
- **What are two numbers with a sum of 10?** *Sample answer: 7 and 3.*
- **What are two numbers with a difference of 10?** *Sample answer: 70 and 80.*
- **What are two numbers with a product of 10?** *Sample answer: 2 and 5.*
- **What are three numbers with a sum of 10?** *Sample answer: 1, 4, and 5.*

Activity (A): Review Two-Digit Mental Addition

Today, we'll review how to mentally add two-digit numbers. I'll show you two strategies. Then, you can use whichever strategy you prefer.

Model 48 + 23 with base-ten blocks. **One way to add 48 plus 23 is to split both addends. 48 has 4 tens and 8 ones, so we can split it into 40 and 8. 23 has 2 tens and 3 ones, so we can split it into 20 and 3.**

We can add numbers in any order and still get the same sum. Let's add the tens and ones separately. Then, we'll combine them to find the answer.

- Point to the rods. **What's 40 plus 20?** *60.* Write 60 in the blank.
- Point to the unit blocks. **What's 8 plus 3?** *11.* Write 11 in the blank.
- Point to the all the blocks. **What's 60 plus 11?** *71.* Write 71 in the blank.

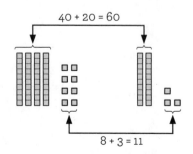

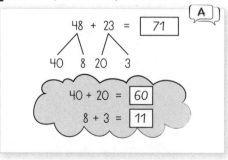

When we split both addends, we have to remember four different numbers as we add! Many people find adding in their heads easier if they only split the second addend. Let's try that strategy for this problem, too.

Point to the 4 rods and 8 units, and the 2 rods. **What's 48 plus 20?** *68.* Write 68 in the blank.

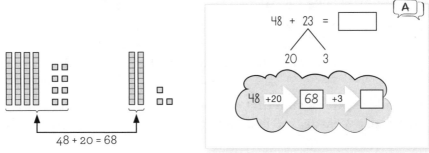

Point to the 3 unit blocks. **What's 68 plus 3?** *71.* Write 71 in both blanks.

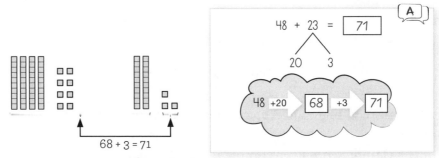

You get the same answer no matter which strategy you use. Have your child use either method to complete the last two questions in part A. He may draw part-total lines below the addends as needed.

35 + 57 = 92   89 + 15 = 104

Activity (B): Prepare to Play Close to 100

We're going to play a game called Close to 100. In this game, you get 4 cards. You use the cards to make 2 two-digit numbers. Your goal is to make a sum as close to 100 as possible.

Before we play, let's investigate how to arrange the cards so that your sum is as close to 100 as possible. Place a 7, 4, ace, and 6 from a deck of playing cards on the table. (Any suit is fine.) **Aces count as 1s.**

Using real cards (rather than just looking at the cards printed in the workbook) allows your child to physically manipulate the digits.

Here's one way to arrange the cards. Make the numbers 47 and 61 from the cards. **What's the sum of 47 and 61?** *108.* Write 108 in the blank. **How close is 108 to 100?** *8.* Write 8 in the blank.

4 7 + 6 1 = 108

How close to 100?   8

If your child isn't sure how close 108 is to 100, say: **To find the difference, subtract the lesser number from the greater number. What's 108 minus 100?** *8.*

Here's another way to arrange the cards. Make the numbers 14 and 76 from the cards. **What's the sum of 14 and 76?** *90.* Write 90 in the blank. **How close is 90 to 100?** *10.* Write 10 in the blank.

     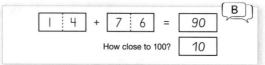

If your child isn't sure, say: **You can add up to find the difference, just like you did when you made change from $100. 90 plus what equals 100?** *10.*

Which pair of addends creates a sum that's closer to 100? *47 and 61.* **That's as close as we can get to 100 with these 4 cards. 108 is 8 away from 100, so your score for this play would be 8 points.**

Activity (C): Play Close to 100

Play Close to 100.

Close to 100

Materials: 2 decks of playing cards, with 10s, jacks, queens, and kings removed (72 cards total)

Object of the Game: Score fewer points than the other player.

Shuffle the cards and place the stack face down on the table. On your turn, take 4 cards off the top of the deck and use them to make 2 two-digit numbers. (Aces count as 1s.) Write your sum on the scorecard and figure out how close to 100 the number is. This difference is your score.

For example, if you have an 8, ace, 4, and 4, your best play is to create 14 and 84. Their sum is 98. The difference between 100 and 98 is 2, so you score 2 points.

Sum	Score (How close to 100?)
14 + 84 = 98	2

Your sum may be greater than, less than, or equal to 100. Aim to create numbers whose sum is as close to 100 as possible so that you score as few points as possible.

Play then passes to the other player. Continue until both players have completed all 3 rounds. Add up each player's total points. The player with fewer points wins.

Advanced Variation: To make this game more challenging, give each player 6 cards instead of 4. Have each player choose 4 of the 6 cards to use to make the numbers.

Independent Practice and Review

Have your child complete the Lesson 3.6 Practice and Review pages.

Lesson 3.7
Review Two-Digit Mental Subtraction

Purpose	Materials
• Practice ×5 facts • Review how to mentally subtract a two-digit number from a two-digit number	• Base-ten blocks • Die • Counters

Memory Work
- **How many sides does a triangle have?** *3.*
- **How many sides does a quadrilateral have?** *4.*

Here's a suggested plan if your child needs two days to learn the skills in this lesson:

- Day 1: Do the Warm-up and Activity A. Have your child solve half of the problems on the Practice and Review pages. Help her model the problems with base-ten blocks as needed.
- Day 2: Review the strategies in Activity A and play Climb and Slide. Have your child solve the remaining problems on the Practice and Review pages.

Warm-up: Practice ×5 Facts

Do a brief review of the following ×5 facts.

- 6 × 5 = *30*
- 10 × 5 = *50*
- 8 × 5 = *40*
- 7 × 5 = *35*
- 9 × 5 = *45*

If your child has trouble with any of the facts, model them on the dot array and have her use a dry erase marker to draw circles around groups of 10.

Activity (A): Review Two-Digit Mental Subtraction

A few lessons ago, we reviewed how to subtract a one-digit number from a two-digit number. Today, we'll review how to subtract a two-digit number from a two-digit number.

Model 64 with base-ten blocks. **Let's subtract 25 from 64 in two steps. First, we subtract the tens. What's 64 minus 20?** *44.* Use a slip of paper to cover 2 rods. Write 44 in the blank.

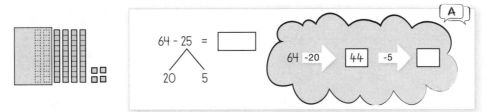

Then, we subtract the ones. What's 44 minus 5? *39.* Use 2 slips of paper to cover the 4 loose units and 1 unit on a rod. **So, what's 64 − 25?** *39.* Write 39 in both blanks.

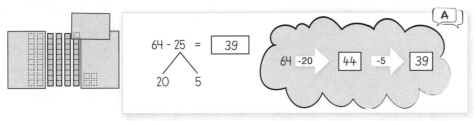

Have your child complete part A. Have her split the second number in each equation into tens and ones, and remind her to subtract in 2 steps. Model the problems with base-ten blocks as needed.

$$90 - 17 = \boxed{73}$$

$$10 \quad 7$$

$$73 - 45 = \boxed{28}$$

$$40 \quad 5$$

A

Activity (B): Play Climb and Slide

Play Climb and Slide. See Lesson 3.3 (page 90) for full directions. Use base-ten blocks to model the problems as needed.

Independent Practice and Review

Have your child complete the Lesson 3.7 Practice and Review pages.

Lesson 3.8
Add Up to Find Differences

Purpose	Materials
• Practice finding missing addends to the next decade • Add up to mentally find differences between two-digit numbers • Subtract two-digit numbers mentally	• Base-ten blocks • Playing cards

Memory Work
- **How many sides does a hexagon have?** *6.*
- **How many sides does an octagon have?** *8.*
- **How many sides does a pentagon have?** *5.*

Warm-up: Review Finding Missing Addends to the Next Decade

Ask your child the following questions:

- **37 plus what equals 40?** *3.*
- **48 plus what equals 50?** *2.*
- **96 plus what equals 100?** *4.*

- **55 plus what equals 60?** *5.*
- **83 plus what equals 90?** *7.*

Activity (A): Add Up to Find Differences

You have already learned how to mentally subtract two-digit numbers. You've also learned how to add up to find missing addends. Today, you'll combine the two skills and learn how to add up to solve subtraction problems.

Read aloud the first equation in part A: *52 minus 49 equals what?* I could subtract in two steps to find the answer. But, when the two numbers in a subtraction problem are close together, it's usually easier to add up to find the missing part. To solve this problem, I think **"49 plus what equals 52?"**

$$52 - 49 = \boxed{} \quad \text{[A]}$$

Model 49 with base-ten blocks. **I'll add up in two steps. How many more ones do I need to complete the group of 10?** *1.* Add 1 unit block. **How many more ones do I need to reach 52?** *2.* Add 2 more unit blocks. **49 plus 3 equals 52. So, 52 minus 49 equals 3.** Write 3 in both blanks.

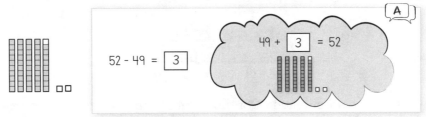

Have your child complete part A. Use base-ten blocks as needed.

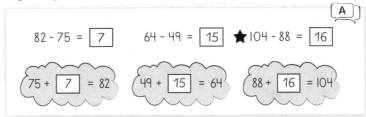

Activity (B): Prepare to Play Close to Zero

We're going to play a game called Close to Zero. It's like Close to 100, but your goal is to make the difference between the two numbers as close to zero as possible.

Before we play, let's investigate how to arrange your cards so that the difference is as close to zero as possible. Place a 6, 3, 8, and 9 from a deck of playing cards on the table. (Any suit is fine.)

Here's one way to arrange the cards. Make the numbers 89 and 63 from the cards. **What's the difference between 89 and 63?** *26.* Write 26 in the blank.

  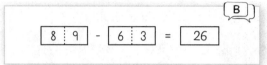

Can you find a way to arrange the cards so that the difference is closer to 0? Give your child some time to experiment with the cards and look for a pair of numbers whose difference is closer to zero. There are several different possible ways.

Activity (C): Play Close to Zero

Play Close to Zero. Model the problems with base-ten blocks as needed.

Close to Zero

Materials: 2 decks of playing cards, with 10s, jacks, queens, and kings removed (72 cards total)

Object of the Game: Score fewer points than the other player.

Shuffle the cards and place the stack face down on the table. On your turn, take 4 cards off the top of the deck. Use them to make 2 two-digit numbers. Write the difference between the two numbers on the scorecard. This difference is your score.

For example, if you have an 8, ace, 4, and 3, your best play is to create 38 and 41. The difference between 38 and 41 is 3, so you score 3 points.

Difference	Score (How close to zero?)
41 - 38	3

Play then passes to the other player. Continue until both players have completed all 3 rounds. Add up each player's total points. The player with fewer points wins.

Advanced Variation: To make this game more challenging, give each player 6 cards instead of 4. Have each player choose 4 of the 6 cards to use.

Independent Practice and Review

Have your child complete the Lesson 3.8 Practice and Review workbook pages.

Lesson 3.9
More Two-Step Word Problems

Purpose	Materials
• Practice mental math • Solve two-step comparison and more/less word problems	• None

Memory Work	• **What is another name for 12 a.m.?** *Midnight.* • **What is another name for 12 p.m.?** *Noon.*

Warm-up (A): Practice Mental Math

Ask your child the following mental math questions:

- 36 + 8 = *44*
- 49 + 31 = *80*
- 53 − 8 = *45*
- 64 − 38 = *26*
- 82 − 77 = *5*

> If your child has trouble keeping the numbers in her head, write each problem horizontally on paper. Don't write the problems vertically or allow your child to use the addition or subtraction algorithms to solve them. See the Unit 3 **Teaching Math with Confidence** (page 82) for more explanation.

Activity (A): Solve Two-Step Comparison Word Problems

Today, we'll solve more word problems. Have your child read aloud the first word problem. **What's our goal in this problem?** *Find how many more pages Taylor read on Tuesday than on Wednesday.* **To find how many more pages Taylor read on Tuesday than on Wednesday, we first need to know how many pages she read each day. It can be hard to remember all the numbers, so let's make a list of how many pages she read each day.**

How many pages did she read on Tuesday? *15.* **How do you know?** *Sample answer: I added 9 and 6.* Write "Tuesday" and "9 + 6 = 15" as shown.

How many pages did she read on Wednesday? *12.* Write "Wednesday" and "12" as shown.

Taylor read 9 pages on Tuesday morning and 6 pages on Tuesday afternoon.
She read 12 pages on Wednesday.
How many more pages did she read on Tuesday than Wednesday?   A

Tuesday: 9 + 6 = 15
Wednesday: 12

How can we find out how many more pages she read on Tuesday than Wednesday? *Subtract 15 minus 12.* If your child's not sure, remind her that she can subtract the lesser number from the greater number to find the difference.

Write "15 − 12 =" and have your child complete the equation. Remind her to write "pages" after the 3 and draw a box around the complete answer.

15 - 12 = 3 pages

Have your child complete the other word problem. If she's not sure how to begin, suggest she write down much money Jonah has and the amount that he needs.

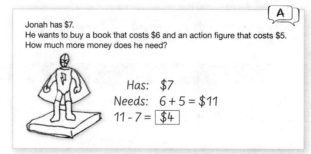

Jonah has $7.
He wants to buy a book that costs $6 and an action figure that costs $5.
How much more money does he need?

A

Has: $7
Needs: 6 + 5 = $11
11 - 7 = $4

Activity (B): Solve Two-Step Part-Total Word Problems

Have your child read aloud the next word problem. **What's our goal in this problem?** *Find how many cupcakes with chocolate sprinkles were left.* **To find how many cupcakes with chocolate sprinkles were left, we first have to know how many there were at the start.**

The events in this problem happen in two steps. First, she makes cupcakes. Then, she eats some cupcakes. So, let's think through each step. How many rainbow sprinkle cupcakes were there at the start? *8.* **Write "Rainbow sprinkle cupcakes: 8." How many chocolate cupcakes were there at the start?** *7.* **How do you know?** *Sample answer: I subtracted 15 minus 8.* Write "Chocolate sprinkle cupcakes: 15 – 8 = 7."

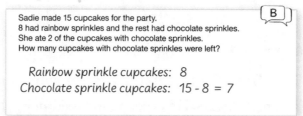

Sadie made 15 cupcakes for the party.
8 had rainbow sprinkles and the rest had chocolate sprinkles.
She ate 2 of the cupcakes with chocolate sprinkles.
How many cupcakes with chocolate sprinkles were left?

B

Rainbow sprinkle cupcakes: 8
Chocolate sprinkle cupcakes: 15 - 8 = 7

If your child isn't sure, draw a Part-Total Diagram as shown. **At the start, there were a total of 15 cupcakes. 8 had rainbow sprinkles and the rest had chocolate sprinkles. So, we can subtract 15 minus 8 to find how many had chocolate sprinkles.**

15

8

Then, Sadie ate 2 of the cupcakes with chocolate sprinkles. How can we find out how many cupcakes were left at the end? *Subtract 7 minus 2.* Write "7 – 2 =" and have your child complete the equation. Remind her to write "cupcakes" after the 5 and draw a box around the complete answer.

7 - 2 = 5 cupcakes

Have your child solve the final word problem in the same way.

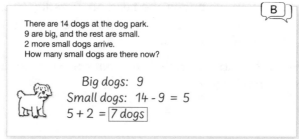

There are 14 dogs at the dog park.
9 are big, and the rest are small.
2 more small dogs arrive.
How many small dogs are there now?

B

Big dogs: 9
Small dogs: 14 - 9 = 5
5 + 2 = 7 dogs

When you solve a word problem on the Practice and Review pages, you may sometimes see right away how to solve the problem. If that's the case, you don't have to write out all this information. But if the problem is complicated or you feel confused, listing the important information can be a big help.

If your child needs extra support with word problems but doesn't want to write anything extra, encourage her to underline the important information in each problem instead. See the Unit 1 **Teaching Math with Confidence** (page 12) for more tips on teaching word problems.

Independent Practice and Review

Have your child complete the Lesson 3.9 Practice and Review workbook pages. Your child does not have to list the information for each problem, but encourage her to do so if needed.

Lesson 3.10
Enrichment (Optional)

Purpose	Materials
• Practice memory work • Learn about the life of a famous mathematician and appreciate perseverance in problem-solving • Create multi-step addition and subtraction word problems • Summarize what your child has learned and assess your child's progress	• *Counting on Katherine: How Katherine Johnson Saved Apollo 13*, written by Helaine Becker and illustrated by Dow Phumiruks.

Warm-up: Review Memory Work

Quiz your child on all memory work introduced through Unit 3. See pages 527-528 for the full list.

Math Picture Book: *Counting on Katherine: How Katherine Johnson Saved Apollo 13*

Read *Counting on Katherine: How Katherine Johnson Saved Apollo 13*, written by Helaine Becker and illustrated by Dow Phumiruk. As you read, discuss the perseverance Katherine Johnson showed in solving difficult problems.

Enrichment Activity: Create Your Own Multi-Step Word Problems

You've solved a lot of word problems in this unit! Today, you get to make up your own addition and subtraction word problems.

Tell your child the following word problem answers, and challenge him to create an addition or subtraction word problem to match each answer. Encourage him to create a variety of word problem types, including problems with multiple steps.

- 9 hamsters. *Sample answer: I have 4 brown hamsters and 5 spotted hamsters. How many hamsters do I have?*
- 10 miles. *Sample answer: I walked 5 miles. Then, I walked another 2 miles. Then, I walked 3 miles more. How far did I walk?*
- 30 watermelons. *Sample answer: I had 40 watermelons. Then, I ate 10 watermelons. How many did I have left?*
- 12 green balloons. *Sample answer: I had 20 balloons. 6 were red, and the rest were green. Then, 2 of the green balloons popped. How many green balloons were left?*
- 15 years old. *Sample answer: I'm 12. I'm 3 years younger than my brother. How old is my brother?*
- $6. *Sample answer: I bought a hamburger for $8, a drink for $5, and an ice cream sundae. I paid $19. How much did the ice cream sundae cost?*

This enrichment activity is meant to encourage your child's silliness and creativity, and to show him that math doesn't always have to be serious! If your child struggles to come up with word problems that match the given answers, it's fine for him to simply make up 5-8 word problems with his own answers instead.

Unit Wrap-up

Have your child complete the Unit 3 Wrap-up.

Unit 3 Answer Key

3.1 Practice

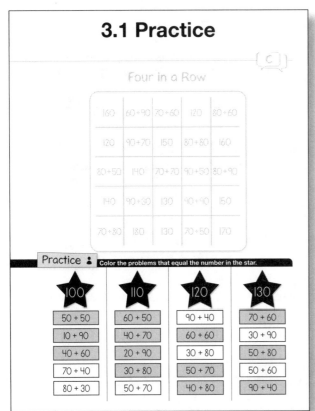

Four in a Row

160	60+90	70+60	120	80+60
120	90+70	150	80+80	160
80+50	140	70+70	90+50	80+90
140	90+30	130	90+90	150
70+80	180	130	70+50	170

Practice 🖉 Color the problems that equal the number in the star.

⭐ 100

| 50 + 50 |
| 10 + 90 |
| 40 + 60 |
| 70 + 40 |
| 80 + 30 |

⭐ 110

| 60 + 50 |
| 40 + 70 |
| 20 + 90 |
| 30 + 80 |
| 50 + 70 |

⭐ 120

| 90 + 40 |
| 60 + 60 |
| 30 + 80 |
| 50 + 70 |
| 40 + 80 |

⭐ 130

| 70 + 60 |
| 30 + 90 |
| 50 + 80 |
| 50 + 60 |
| 90 + 40 |

3.1 Review

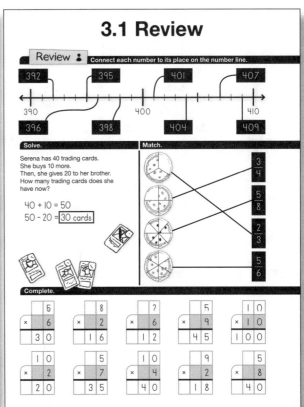

Review 👤 Connect each number to its place on the number line.

392   395   401   407
396   398   404   409

Solve.

Serena has 40 trading cards.
She buys 10 more.
Then, she gives 20 to her brother.
How many trading cards does she have now?

40 + 10 = 50
50 - 20 = 30 cards

Match.

3/4
5/8
2/3
5/6

Complete.

×	5
	6
	30

×	8
	2
	16

×	?
	6
	12

×	5
	9
	45

×	10
	10
	100

×	10
	2
	20

×	5
	7
	35

×	10
	4
	40

×	9
	2
	18

×	5
	8
	40

3.2 Practice

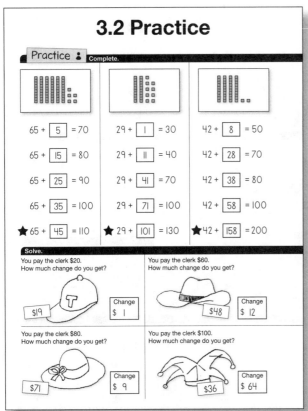

Practice 🖉 Complete.

65 + 5 = 70   29 + 1 = 30   42 + 8 = 50
65 + 15 = 80   29 + 11 = 40   42 + 28 = 70
65 + 25 = 90   29 + 41 = 70   42 + 38 = 80
65 + 35 = 100   29 + 71 = 100   42 + 58 = 100
⭐ 65 + 45 = 110   ⭐ 29 + 101 = 130   ⭐ 42 + 158 = 200

Solve.

You pay the clerk $20.
How much change do you get?
$19   Change $ 1

You pay the clerk $60.
How much change do you get?
$48   Change $ 12

You pay the clerk $80.
How much change do you get?
$71   Change $ 9

You pay the clerk $100.
How much change do you get?
$36   Change $ 64

3.2 Review

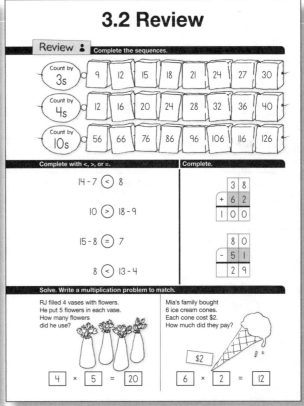

Review 👤 Complete the sequences.

Count by 3s: 9 | 12 | 15 | 18 | 21 | 24 | 27 | 30

Count by 4s: 12 | 16 | 20 | 24 | 28 | 32 | 36 | 40

Count by 10s: 56 | 66 | 76 | 86 | 96 | 106 | 116 | 126

Complete with <, >, or =.

14 - 7 < 8
10 > 18 - 9
15 - 8 = 7
8 < 13 - 4

Complete.

	3	8
+	6	2
1	0	0

	8	0
-	5	1
	2	9

Solve. Write a multiplication problem to match.

RJ filled 4 vases with flowers.
He put 5 flowers in each vase.
How many flowers did he use?

4 × 5 = 20

Mia's family bought 6 ice cream cones.
Each cone cost $2.
How much did they pay?

6 × 2 = 12

Unit 3 Answer Key

3.3 Practice

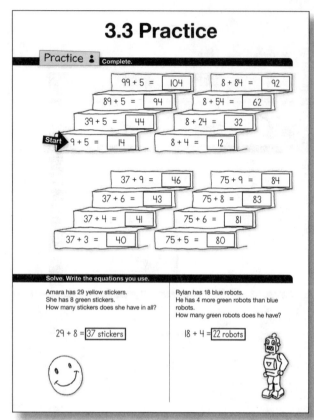

Practice 👤 Complete.

99 + 5 =	104	8 + 84 =	92
89 + 5 =	94	8 + 54 =	62
39 + 5 =	44	8 + 24 =	32
Start 9 + 5 =	14	8 + 4 =	12

37 + 9 =	46	75 + 9 =	84
37 + 6 =	43	75 + 8 =	83
37 + 4 =	41	75 + 6 =	81
37 + 3 =	40	75 + 5 =	80

Solve. Write the equations you use.

Amara has 29 yellow stickers.
She has 8 green stickers.
How many stickers does she have in all?

29 + 8 = 37 stickers

Rylan has 18 blue robots.
He has 4 more green robots than blue robots.
How many green robots does he have?

18 + 4 = 22 robots

3.3 Review

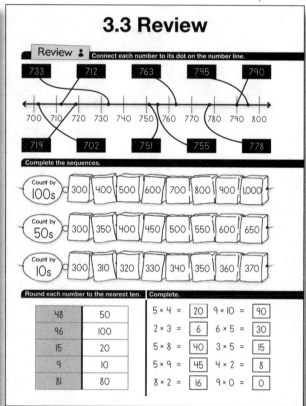

Review 👤 Connect each number to its dot on the number line.

733   712   763   795   790

700 710 720 730 740 750 760 770 780 790 800

719   702   751   755   778

Complete the sequences.

Count by 100s: 300 400 500 600 700 800 900 1,000

Count by 50s: 300 350 400 450 500 550 600 650

Count by 10s: 300 310 320 330 340 350 360 370

Round each number to the nearest ten.

48	50
96	100
15	20
9	10
81	80

Complete.

5 × 4 =	20	9 × 10 =	90
2 × 3 =	6	6 × 5 =	30
5 × 8 =	40	3 × 5 =	15
5 × 9 =	45	4 × 2 =	8
8 × 2 =	16	9 × 0 =	0

3.4 Practice

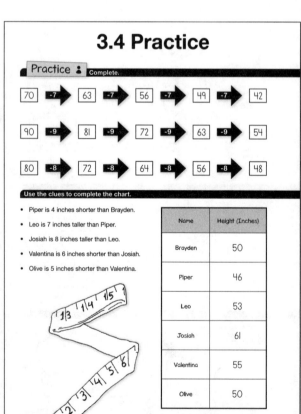

Practice 👤 Complete.

70 -7→ 63 -7→ 56 -7→ 49 -7→ 42

90 -9→ 81 -9→ 72 -9→ 63 -9→ 54

80 -8→ 72 -8→ 64 -8→ 56 -8→ 48

Use the clues to complete the chart.

- Piper is 4 inches shorter than Brayden.
- Leo is 7 inches taller than Piper.
- Josiah is 8 inches taller than Leo.
- Valentina is 6 inches shorter than Josiah.
- Olive is 5 inches shorter than Valentina.

Name	Height (Inches)
Brayden	50
Piper	46
Leo	53
Josiah	61
Valentina	55
Olive	50

3.4 Review

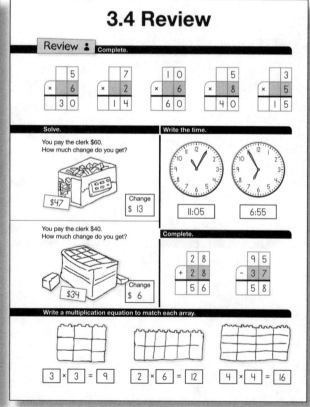

Review 👤 Complete.

×	5		×	7			1 0		×	5		×	3
	6			2		×	6			8			5
3 0			1 4			6 0			4 0			1 5

Solve.

You pay the clerk $60.
How much change do you get?

$47   Change $ 13

You pay the clerk $40.
How much change do you get?

$34   Change $ 6

Write the time.

11:05   6:55

Complete.

```
  2 8
+ 2 8
  5 6
```

```
  9 5
- 3 7
  5 8
```

Write a multiplication equation to match each array.

3 × 3 = 9   2 × 6 = 12   4 × 4 = 16

Unit 3 Answer Key

3.5 Practice

Practice 👤 Use the clues to complete the chart.

- Ben is 3 years older than Leena.
- Leena is 5 years younger than Seth.
- Seth is 8 years younger than Mira.

Name	Age
Ben	8
Leena	5
Seth	10
Mira	18

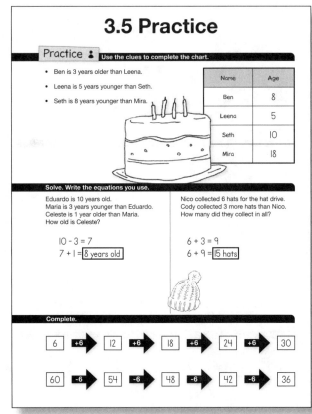

Solve. Write the equations you use.

Eduardo is 10 years old. Maria is 3 years younger than Eduardo. Celeste is 1 year older than Maria. How old is Celeste?

$10 - 3 = 7$
$7 + 1 = \boxed{8 \text{ years old}}$

Nico collected 6 hats for the hat drive. Cody collected 3 more hats than Nico. How many did they collect in all?

$6 + 3 = 9$
$6 + 9 = \boxed{15 \text{ hats}}$

Complete.

$6 \xrightarrow{+6} 12 \xrightarrow{+6} 18 \xrightarrow{+6} 24 \xrightarrow{+6} 30$

$60 \xrightarrow{-6} 54 \xrightarrow{-6} 48 \xrightarrow{-6} 42 \xrightarrow{-6} 36$

3.5 Review

Review 👤 Complete the sequences.

Count by 1s: 593 594 595 596 597 598 599 600

Count by 2s: 586 588 590 592 594 596 598 600

Count by 10s: 530 540 550 560 570 580 590 600

Color the problems that match the number in the star.

★20	★30	★40	★50
5 × 4	10 × 3	8 × 5	10 × 5
10 × 2	2 × 8	1 × 40	9 × 5
7 × 2	6 × 5	4 × 10	50 × 1

Solve.

Ramona bought 5 books. Each book cost $5. How much did she pay?

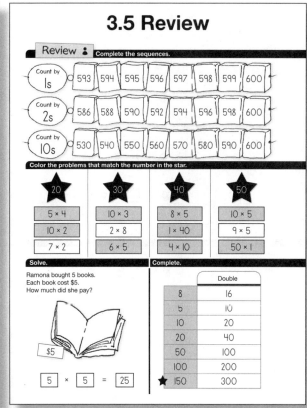

$\boxed{5} \times \boxed{5} = \boxed{25}$

Complete.

	Double
8	16
5	10
10	20
20	40
50	100
100	200
★150	300

3.6 Practice

Close to 100

Sum	Score (How close to 100?)	Sum	Score (How close to 100?)
Player 1 Total		Player 2 Total	

Practice 👤 Match.

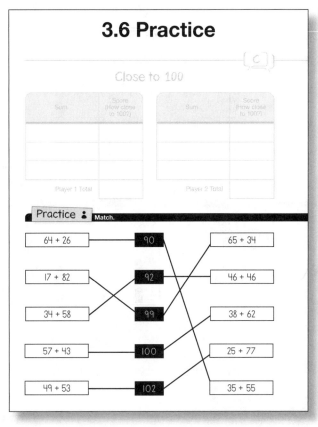

64 + 26	90	65 + 34
17 + 82	92	46 + 46
34 + 58	99	38 + 62
57 + 43	100	25 + 77
49 + 53	102	35 + 55

3.6 Review

Review 👤 Complete.

| 2 × 8 = 16 | 4 × 5 = 20 | 10 × 9 = 90 | 7 × 5 = 35 | 2 × 6 = 12 |
| 10 × 4 = 40 | 9 × 5 = 45 | 5 × 5 = 25 | 3 × 1 = 3 | 9 × 2 = 18 |

Use the pictograph to complete the chart.

Favorite Color of Apple

Red	🍎🍎🍎
Yellow	🍎🍎🍎🍎
Green	🍎🍎

🍎 = 2 people

Color	Number of People
Red	6
Yellow	8
Green	4

Use the key to color the shapes.

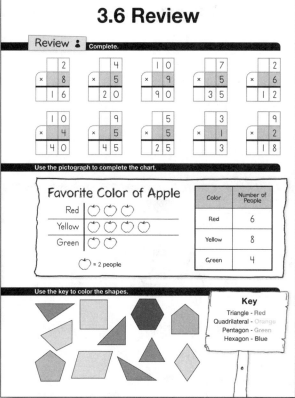

Key

Triangle - Red
Quadrilateral - Orange
Pentagon - Green
Hexagon - Blue

Unit 3 Answer Key

3.7 Practice

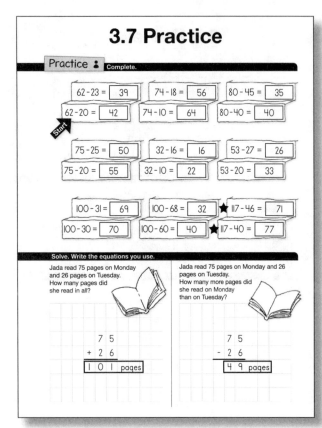

Practice 👤 Complete.

Start →

62 - 23 = 39	74 - 18 = 56	80 - 45 = 35
62 - 20 = 42	74 - 10 = 64	80 - 40 = 40

75 - 25 = 50	32 - 16 = 16	53 - 27 = 26
75 - 20 = 55	32 - 10 = 22	53 - 20 = 33

100 - 31 = 69	100 - 68 = 32	★ 117 - 46 = 71
100 - 30 = 70	100 - 60 = 40	★ 117 - 40 = 77

Solve. Write the equations you use.

Jada read 75 pages on Monday and 26 pages on Tuesday. How many pages did she read in all?

```
  7 5
+ 2 6
-----
1 0 1   pages
```

Jada read 75 pages on Monday and 26 pages on Tuesday. How many more pages did she read on Monday than on Tuesday?

```
  7 5
- 2 6
-----
  4 9   pages
```

3.7 Review

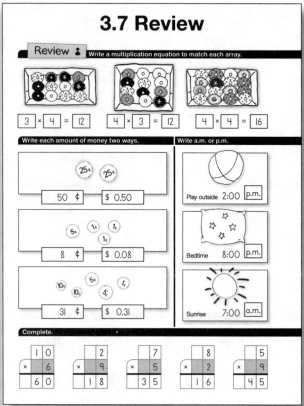

Review 👤 Write a multiplication equation to match each array.

3 × 4 = 12   4 × 3 = 12   4 × 4 = 16

Write each amount of money two ways.

25¢ 25¢
50 ¢ $ 0.50

5¢ 1¢ 1¢ 1¢
8 ¢ $ 0.08

10¢ 5¢ 1¢ 10¢ 5¢
31 ¢ $ 0.31

Write a.m. or p.m.

Play outside 2:00 p.m.

Bedtime 8:00 p.m.

Sunrise 7:00 a.m.

Complete.

×	1 0		2		7		8		5
	6		9		5		2		9
	6 0		1 8		3 5		1 6		4 5

3.8 Practice

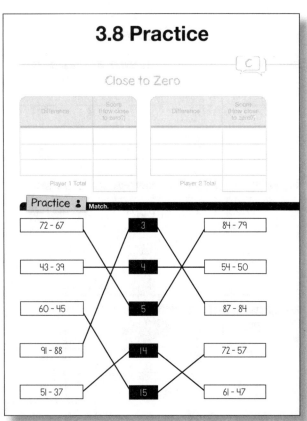

Close to Zero

Difference	Score (How close to zero)		Difference	Score (How close to zero)
Player 1 Total			Player 2 Total	

Practice 👤 Match.

72 - 67			84 - 79
43 - 39	**3**		54 - 50
60 - 45	**4**		87 - 84
91 - 88	**5**		72 - 57
51 - 37	**14**		61 - 47
	15		

3.8 Review

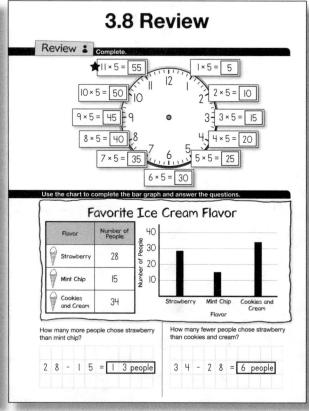

Review 👤 Complete.

★ 11 × 5 = 55   1 × 5 = 5
10 × 5 = 50   2 × 5 = 10
9 × 5 = 45   3 × 5 = 15
8 × 5 = 40   4 × 5 = 20
7 × 5 = 35   5 × 5 = 25
6 × 5 = 30

Use the chart to complete the bar graph and answer the questions.

Favorite Ice Cream Flavor

Flavor	Number of People
🍦 Strawberry	28
🍦 Mint Chip	15
🍦 Cookies and Cream	34

How many more people chose strawberry than mint chip?

2 8 - 1 5 = 1 3 people

How many fewer people chose strawberry than cookies and cream?

3 4 - 2 8 = 6 people

Unit 3 Answer Key

3.9 Practice

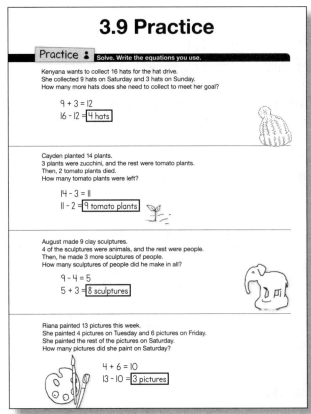

Practice 👤 Solve. Write the equations you use.

Kenyana wants to collect 16 hats for the hat drive.
She collected 9 hats on Saturday and 3 hats on Sunday.
How many more hats does she need to collect to meet her goal?

$9 + 3 = 12$
$16 - 12 = \boxed{4 \text{ hats}}$

Cayden planted 14 plants.
3 plants were zucchini, and the rest were tomato plants.
Then, 2 tomato plants died.
How many tomato plants were left?

$14 - 3 = 11$
$11 - 2 = \boxed{9 \text{ tomato plants}}$

August made 9 clay sculptures.
4 of the sculptures were animals, and the rest were people.
Then, he made 3 more sculptures of people.
How many sculptures of people did he make in all?

$9 - 4 = 5$
$5 + 3 = \boxed{8 \text{ sculptures}}$

Riana painted 13 pictures this week.
She painted 4 pictures on Tuesday and 6 pictures on Friday.
She painted the rest of the pictures on Saturday.
How many pictures did she paint on Saturday?

$4 + 6 = 10$
$13 - 10 = \boxed{3 \text{ pictures}}$

3.9 Review

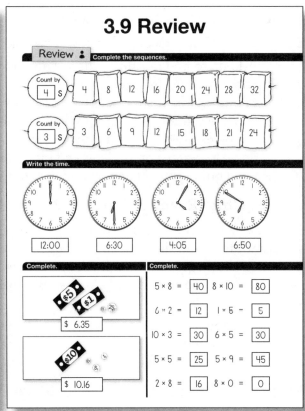

Review 👤 Complete the sequences.

Count by 4 s: 4, 8, 12, 16, 20, 24, 28, 32

Count by 3 s: 3, 6, 9, 12, 15, 18, 21, 24

Write the time.

12:00   6:30   4:05   6:50

Complete.

$ 6.35

$ 10.16

Complete.

$5 \times 8 = \boxed{40}$ $8 \times 10 = \boxed{80}$

$6 \times 2 = \boxed{12}$ $1 \times 5 = \boxed{5}$

$10 \times 3 = \boxed{30}$ $6 \times 5 = \boxed{30}$

$5 \times 5 = \boxed{25}$ $5 \times 9 = \boxed{45}$

$2 \times 8 = \boxed{16}$ $8 \times 0 = \boxed{0}$

3.10 Unit Wrap-Up A

Unit Wrap-Up 👤 Complete. Then, color each answer in black on the 100 Chart to make a picture.

$52 + 25 = \boxed{77}$ $65 - 6 = \boxed{59}$

$6 + 57 = \boxed{63}$ $50 - 16 = \boxed{34}$

$48 + 26 = \boxed{74}$ $62 - 25 = \boxed{37}$

$59 + 9 = \boxed{68}$ $93 - 17 = \boxed{76}$

$28 + 47 = \boxed{75}$ $61 - 9 = \boxed{52}$

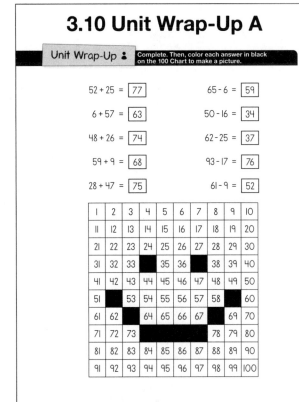

1	2	3	4	5	6	7	8	9	10
11	12	13	14	15	16	17	18	19	20
21	22	23	24	25	26	27	28	29	30
31	32	33	■	35	36	■	38	39	40
41	42	43	44	45	46	47	48	49	50
51	■	53	54	55	56	57	58	■	60
61	62	■	64	65	66	67	■	69	70
71	72	73	■				78	79	80
81	82	83	84	85	86	87	88	89	90
91	92	93	94	95	96	97	98	99	100

3.10 Unit Wrap-Up B

Unit Wrap-Up 👤 Complete.   Solve.

10 tens = $\boxed{100}$

15 tens = $\boxed{150}$

11 tens = $\boxed{110}$

18 tens = $\boxed{180}$

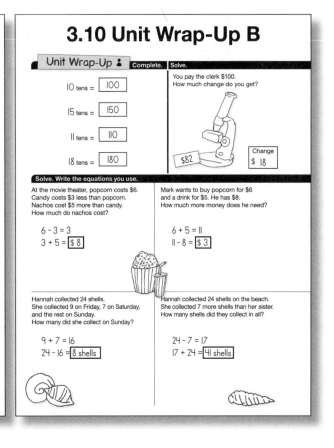

You pay the clerk $100.
How much change do you get?

$82   Change $ 18

Solve. Write the equations you use.

At the movie theater, popcorn costs $6.
Candy costs $3 less than popcorn.
Nachos cost $5 more than candy.
How much do nachos cost?

$6 - 3 = 3$
$3 + 5 = \boxed{\$ 8}$

Mark wants to buy popcorn for $6
and a drink for $5. He has $8.
How much more money does he need?

$6 + 5 = 11$
$11 - 8 = \boxed{\$ 3}$

Hannah collected 24 shells.
She collected 9 on Friday, 7 on Saturday,
and the rest on Sunday.
How many did she collect on Sunday?

$9 + 7 = 16$
$24 - 16 = \boxed{8 \text{ shells}}$

Hannah collected 24 shells on the beach.
She collected 7 more shells than her sister.
How many shells did they collect in all?

$24 - 7 = 17$
$17 + 24 = \boxed{41 \text{ shells}}$

Unit 3 Checkpoint

What to Expect at the End of Unit 3

By the end of Unit 3, most children will be able to do the following:

- Add up to find missing addends and make change. Some children will feel uncertain about making change.
- Mentally add or subtract one- or two-digit numbers to 100. Many children will be able to solve these problems completely in their heads, but some will still need to use base-ten blocks in order to find the answers, especially for subtraction.
- Solve two-step comparison and more/less word problems. Many children will still need quite a bit of support and coaching to solve these problems.

Is Your Child Ready to Move on?

In Unit 4, your child will learn the ×3 and ×4 facts. Before moving on to Unit 4, your child should understand the concept of multiplication and be able to write multiplication equations to match equal groups or arrays. She will use the ×2 facts as stepping stones to the ×3 and ×4 facts, so she should also be able to find answers to the ×2 facts within several seconds.

Your child does not need to have the ×2 facts completely mastered, and she does not need to have full fluency with the ×5 or ×10 facts before starting Unit 4. She'll continue to practice them throughout the unit.

What to Do If Your Child Needs More Practice

If your child can't find the answers to the ×2 facts within several seconds, spend a day or two practicing the ×2 facts before moving on to Unit 4.

Activities for Practicing the ×2 Facts

- Multiplication Crash (×2) (Lesson 2.3)
- Multiplication Bingo (×2) (Lesson 2.4)

Unit 4
Multiplication, Part 2

Overview

In Unit 2, your child learned about the concept of multiplication and began to master the ×2, ×5, and ×10 facts. In this unit, your child will learn the ×3 and ×4 facts. He'll also use multiplication to interpret pictographs, and he'll learn how to mentally multiply two-digit numbers by 2.

This unit is the second of three multiplication units in *Third Grade Math with Confidence*. Your child will tackle the rest of the multiplication facts in Unit 8.

What Your Child Will Learn

In this unit, your child will learn to:

- Find answers for the ×3 and ×4 facts
- Mentally multiply two-digit numbers by 2 (for example, 2 × 36)
- Use multiplication to interpret pictographs

Lesson List

Lesson 4.1	×3 Facts	Lesson 4.5	Pictographs
Lesson 4.2	Multiples	Lesson 4.6	Introduce the Multiplication Table
Lesson 4.3	Multiply Two-Digit Numbers by 2	Lesson 4.7	Enrichment (Optional)
Lesson 4.4	×4 Facts		

Extra Materials Needed for Unit 4

- Crayons or colored pencils
- For optional Enrichment Lesson:
    - *Minnie's Diner*, written by Dayle Ann Dodds and illustrated by John Manders. Candlewick, 2007.

Teaching Math with Confidence:
Using Related Facts as Stepping Stones for the ×3 and ×4 Facts

Trying to learn all of the multiplication facts by rote memorization is very difficult and tedious. It's usually much faster and easier for children to use the facts they've already learned as stepping stones for mastering the harder facts. It's a bit like crossing a river: it's much less work to make short hops between stepping stones than to try to leap across the entire stream!

In this unit, your child will learn the ×3 and ×4 facts. You'll teach him two different ways to find answers for these facts.

One way is to use the facts within the same table as stepping stones. For example, say you want to find 6 × 3. If you know 5 × 3 = 15, you can simply add 15 + 3 to find that 6 × 3 = 18.

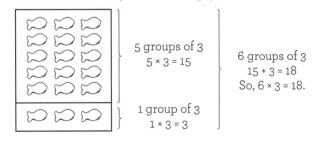

5 groups of 3
5 × 3 = 15

1 group of 3
1 × 3 = 3

6 groups of 3
15 + 3 = 18
So, 6 × 3 = 18.

Another way to find answers to multiplication facts is to use a related fact from a *different* multiplication table. In this unit, your child will learn to use the ×2 facts to help find answers for the ×3 and the ×4 facts.

- **×3 facts:** Your child will multiply numbers by 3 by adding another group to the corresponding ×2 facts. For example, he'll use 2 × 8 to find 3 × 8. Since 2 × 8 is 2 groups of 8, he can add another group of 8 to find that 3 groups of 8 equals 24.

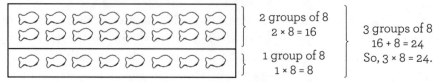

2 groups of 8
2 × 8 = 16

1 group of 8
1 × 8 = 8

3 groups of 8
16 + 8 = 24
So, 3 × 8 = 24.

- **×4 facts:** Your child will double the ×2 facts to find answers to the related ×4 facts. For example, he'll use 2 × 8 to find 4 × 8. Since 2 × 8 is 2 groups of 8, he can double 16 to find that 4 groups of 8 equals 32.

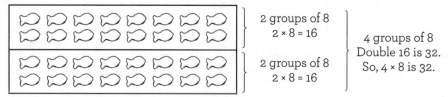

2 groups of 8
2 × 8 = 16

2 groups of 8
2 × 8 = 16

4 groups of 8
Double 16 is 32.
So, 4 × 8 is 32.

You will teach your child many specific multiplication fact strategies in this program, but different strategies "click" better for different children. He may use any approach he wants to find answers to the multiplication facts, as long as his strategy is efficient, accurate, and reliable. As your child practices the ×3 and ×4 facts, always encourage him to use efficient strategies like these rather than skip-counting from zero to find every answer. See the Unit 2 Teaching Math with Confidence (page 52) for more on why it's important to avoid skip-counting.

Lesson 4.1
×3 Facts

Purpose	Materials
• Practice ×2 facts • Introduce ×3 facts • Use ×2 facts to find answers to ×3 facts	• Multiplication Strategies chart (Blackline Master 6) • Dot array and L-cover (Blackline Master 5) • Playing cards • Counters

Memory Work
- **What do we call the result when we multiply two numbers?** *The product.*
- **What do we call the numbers in a multiplication equation that we multiply together?** *Factors.*

Warm-up: Practice ×2 Facts

In Unit 2, you learned the ×1, ×2, ×5 and ×10 facts. Show your child the Multiplication Strategies chart (Blackline Master 6). Read aloud the strategies for the ×1, ×2, ×5, and ×10 facts and briefly discuss the examples. **In this unit, you'll learn the ×3 and ×4 facts. You'll learn the rest of the multiplication facts in Unit 8.**

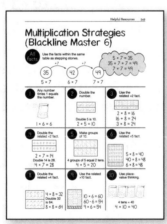

Add the Multiplication Strategies chart to your child's math binder. Encourage her to refer to it any time she has trouble remembering a multiplication fact strategy.

Today, you'll use the ×2 facts to help find the answers to the ×3 facts. We'll warm up by practicing the ×2 facts. Do a brief oral review of the ×2 facts. Encourage your child to respond as quickly as possible for each fact.

- 2 × 5 = *10*
- 2 × 3 = *6*
- 2 × 1 = *2*
- 2 × 6 = *12*
- 2 × 4 = *8*
- 2 × 9 = *18*

- 2 × 2 = *4*
- 2 × 7 = *14*
- 2 × 10 = *20*
- 2 × 8 = *16*

Activity (A): Introduce ×3 Facts

This list of multiplication facts is called the "times 3 table." Use the dot array to model 3 × 1. **What's 3 times 1?** *3.* Write 3 in the blank.

$3 \times 1 =$ 3

Continue in the same way with the rest of the ×3 facts. Use the dot array to model each problem.

$3 \times 1 =$ 3	$3 \times 6 =$ 18
$3 \times 2 =$ 6	$3 \times 7 =$ 21
$3 \times 3 =$ 9	$3 \times 8 =$ 24
$3 \times 4 =$ 12	$3 \times 9 =$ 27
$3 \times 5 =$ 15	$3 \times 10 =$ 30

Encourage your child to add 3 to the previous product to find the next product. For example, to find 3 × 7, she can add 3 to 18 to find that 3 × 7 = 21.

What patterns do you notice? *Sample answers: The answers are the numbers we say when we count by 3s. The products alternate between even and odd.*

Activity (B): Use ×2 Facts to Find Answers to ×3 Facts

Use a piece of paper to cover the completed ×3 table.

Have you ever used stepping stones to get across a stream? Discuss your child's experiences with stepping stones. **When you cross a river, it's much easier to make short hops between stepping stones than to try to leap across the entire stream. Multiplication facts are the same way. It's easier to use facts you've already learned as stepping stones than it is to memorize every fact on its own.**

One way to find the answers to the ×3 facts is to use the ×2 facts as stepping stones. Let's use 2 times 8 to figure out 3 times 8. What does 2 times 8 equal? *16.* Write 16 in the blank.

3 times 8 is just 1 more group of 8. So, we can add 16 plus 8 to find 3 times 8. What's 16 plus 8? *24.* Write 24 in the blank.

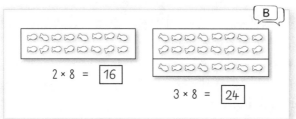

$2 \times 8 =$ 16

$3 \times 8 =$ 24

See the Unit 4 **Teaching Math with Confidence** (pages 113-114) for more on the benefits of using stepping stones to learn the multiplication facts.

Let's use 2 times 7 to figure out 3 times 7. Use the dot array to model 3 × 7. Draw a ring around 2 rows of 7. **What's 2 times 7?** *14*. Write 14 in the blank. **So, what's 3 times 7?** *21*. If your child's not sure, suggest she add 14 plus 7. Write 21 in the blank.

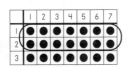
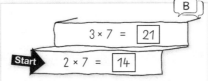

Let's use 2 times 9 to figure out 3 times 9. Use the dot array to show 3 × 9. Draw a ring around 2 groups of 9. **What's 2 times 9?** *18*. Write 18 in the blank. **So, what's 3 times 9?** *27*. If your child's not sure, suggest she add 18 plus 9. Write 27 in the blank.

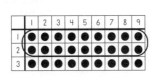
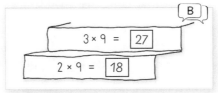

Activity (C): Play Multiplication Cover Up (×3)

Play Multiplication Cover Up (×3). See Lesson 2.7 (page 69) for general directions. Multiply the number on your card by 3, say the matching multiplication fact, and place a counter on the matching square on your game board. For example, if you flip over a 7, say "3 times 7 equals 21" and place a counter on 21.

Model the problems with the dot array as needed. Encourage your child to use the positions of the boxes on the game board to help find the answers.

Independent Practice and Review

Have your child complete the Lesson 4.1 Practice and Review workbook pages.

Lesson 4.2
Multiples

Purpose	Materials
• Review multiplication vocabulary • Introduce the term *multiple* • Identify multiples of 2, 3, 4, and 5 • Practice ×3 facts	• Playing cards • Counters • Multiplication Strategies chart (Blackline Master 6) • Dot array and L-cover (Blackline Master 5), optional

Memory Work
- **How many minutes equal a half-hour?** *30.*
- **How many minutes equal a quarter-hour?** *15.*

Warm-up (A): Review Factor and Product

What do we call the numbers that we multiply together? *Factors.* Write "factors" in the first blank. **What do we call the result of a multiplication problem?** *Product.* Write "product" in the other blank.

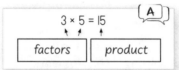

If your child has trouble remembering these vocabulary words, say: **Imagine putting the numbers into a multiplication factory. The factors are the numbers that we put into the factory. The product is the answer that we get out of the factory.**

Activity (B): Introduce Multiples

In the last lesson, you learned the ×3 facts. Today, you'll practice the ×3 facts more and learn a new multiplication vocabulary word: *multiple.*

In everyday conversation, *multiple* just means more than one. I might say that I have *multiple* copies of a book or that we have *multiple* bowls in the cabinet.

These numbers are some of the multiples of 5. Have your child read aloud the list of numbers: *5, 10, 15, …*

What do you notice about the multiples of 5? *Sample answers: They're the answers to the ×5 facts. They're the numbers we say when we count by 5s.*

All of these numbers are multiples of 5. There are several different ways to think about the multiples of 5.

- **You can think of them as the numbers you say when you count by 5s.**
- **You can think of them as the numbers you get if you start at 0 and add 5 over and over.**

- **You can think of them as the products you can get when you multiply a number by 5.** Point to the first few numbers in the list and have your child say the corresponding multiplication fact.

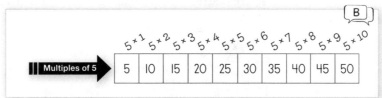

> The mathematical definition of multiples involves division and divisibility, which your child hasn't studied yet. In third grade, your child will name examples of multiples rather than memorizing a definition. He'll learn more about the connection between multiples and divisibility in fourth grade.

These are only some of the multiples of 5. I could keep counting by 5s and continue this list forever!

Point to the multiples of 2. **These numbers are the multiples of 2.** Read the first few multiples aloud. Have your child help you complete the missing multiples. He may count by 2s or add 2 to the previous number to find the multiples.

Point to the next list and have your child read the first few numbers aloud: *3, 6, 9, …*

These numbers are the multiples of what number? *3.* If your child's not sure, ask: **What number are we counting by in this sequence?** *3.* Write 3 in the blank. Have your child complete the missing multiples. If he's not sure what to do, suggest he count by 3s or add 3 to the previous number. Then, repeat with the final list of multiples.

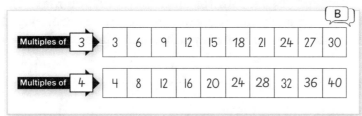

> Your child will learn the ×4 facts in Lesson 4.4.

Did you notice that some numbers appear in more than one list? *Answers will vary.* Have your child circle 12 each time it appears in the lists. **12 is a multiple of 2, a multiple of 3, and a multiple of 4!**

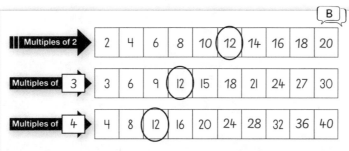

> It's fine if your child doesn't fully understand why 12 is a multiple of all 3 numbers. He will explore factors and multiples in greater depth in fourth grade.

Activity (C): Play Tic-Tac-Toe Crash (×3)

In the last lesson, you learned how to use the ×2 facts to find answers to the ×3 facts.
Read aloud the ×3 strategy on the Multiplication Strategies chart (Blackline Master 6).
Briefly discuss the example.

Play Tic-Tac-Toe Crash (×3). Use the dot array as needed to model the problems. Encourage your child to use the related ×2 facts to find the answers.

Tic-Tac-Toe Crash (×3)

Materials: Deck of playing cards with 10s, jacks, queens, and kings removed (36 cards total); 10 counters of two different colors each

Object of the Game: Be the first player to fill three boxes in a row, either horizontally, vertically, or diagonally.

Shuffle the cards and place the stack face down on the table. On your turn, flip over the top card. Multiply the number on the card by 3, say the matching multiplication fact, and place one of your counters on the box that matches the product. For example, if you draw a 9, say "9 times 3 equals 27" and place a counter on the box with 27.

If the other player already has a counter on the square, you may "crash" into their counter, remove it, and place your own counter on the square. Play then passes to the other player. Continue until one player has completed an entire row, column, or diagonal.

Independent Practice and Review

Have your child complete the Lesson 4.2 Practice and Review workbook pages.

Lesson 4.3
Multiply Two-Digit Numbers by 2

Purpose	Materials
• Review telling time to the minute • Introduce multiplying two-digit numbers by 2 • Mentally multiply two-digit numbers by 2	• Clock • Play money

Memory Work   • **Name the multiples of 3 in order.** *3, 6, 9...* Stop your child when she reaches 30.

In this lesson, you'll teach your child how to multiply two-digit numbers by 2. These mental multiplication problems help your child understand the properties of multiplication more deeply and also build your child's confidence with multiplication. If your child feels intimidated by the larger numbers, reassure her that she already knows all the skills needed to solve these problems.

Warm-up: Review Telling Time to the Minute

Set a clock to the following times and have your child tell each time: 1:30, 1:31, 1:34, 1:39, 1:40, 1:43, 1:46, 1:52.

If your child has trouble, encourage her to use the nearby 5-minute marks to help tell time to the minute. For example, for 1:31: **The minute hand is 1 tick mark past 1:30. Each tick mark represents 1 minute, so the clock now shows 1:31.**

Activity (A): Multiply Tens by 2 at the Pretend Store

You have learned a lot about multiplication already this year! Today, you'll learn to multiply two-digit numbers by 2 in your head.

Let's pretend you work at the Pretend Store, and that I'm buying things for my house. I want 2 of everything!

Each throw pillow costs $20. Place 2 ten-dollar bills on the table. **I'd like 2 pillows, please. How much do I owe you?** *$40.* If your child's not sure, suggest she add 20 plus 20. **2 times 20 equals 40.** Add 2 more ten-dollar bills to the table, and pretend to pay for the pillows with the 4 ten-dollar bills. Write 40 in the blank.

Repeat with the lamp and picture. Model each price with ten-dollar bills. Then, double the number of ten-dollar bills and use the bills to pretend to pay for each item.

Activity (B): Multiply Two-Digit Numbers by 2

Multiplying a number by 2 is the same as doubling the number. Each vase costs \$26, and I'd like to buy 2 vases. So, we can double 26 to find how much I owe you.

Place 2 ten-dollar bills and 6 one-dollar bills on the table. **Let's double the tens and ones separately. Then, we'll combine them to find the answer.**

- Add 2 more ten-dollar bills to the table. **What's 2 times 20?** *40.* Write 40 in the blank.
- Add 6 more one-dollar bills to the table. **What's 2 times 6?** *12.* Write 12 in the blank.
- Point to the all the bills. **What's 40 plus 12?** *52.* **So, 2 vases cost \$52.** Write 52 in the blank and pretend to pay your child the \$52.

Have your child use the same reasoning to complete part B. Draw part-total lines to split each two-digit number into tens and ones before your child multiplies the number by 2. Model the exercises with play money as needed.

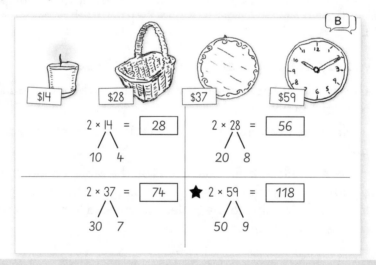

It's fine if your child prefers to use addition to find the answers rather than doubling the tens and ones separately.

Independent Practice and Review

Have your child complete the Lesson 4.3 Practice and Review workbook pages.

Lesson 4.4
×4 Facts

Purpose	Materials
• Practice multiplying two-digit numbers by 2 • Introduce ×4 facts • Double ×2 facts to help find answers to ×4 facts	• Play money, optional • Dot array and L-cover (Blackline Master 5) • Playing cards • Counters

Memory Work	• **What do we call the result when we subtract a number from another number?** *The difference.* • **What do we call the result when we multiply two numbers?** *The product.* • **What do we call the numbers that we add together?** *The addends.*

Warm-up: Practice Multiplying Two-Digit Numbers by 2

Have your child solve the following mental multiplication problems. Model the exercises with play money as needed.

- **2 times 12?** *24.*
- **2 times 14?** *28.*
- **2 times 15?** *30.*

- **2 times 16?** *32.*
- **2 times 18?** *36.*
- **2 times 25?** *50.*

This warm-up prepares your child to double the ×2 facts to find answers to the ×4 facts.

Activity (A): Introduce ×4 Facts

This list of multiplication facts is called the "times 4 table." Use the dot array to model 4 × 1. **What's 4 times 1?** *4.* Write 4 in the blank.

$$4 \times 1 = \boxed{4}$$

Continue in the same way with the rest of the ×4 facts. Use the dot array to model each problem.

$$4 \times 1 = \boxed{4} \qquad 4 \times 6 = \boxed{24}$$
$$4 \times 2 = \boxed{8} \qquad 4 \times 7 = \boxed{28}$$
$$4 \times 3 = \boxed{12} \qquad 4 \times 8 = \boxed{32}$$
$$4 \times 4 = \boxed{16} \qquad 4 \times 9 = \boxed{36}$$
$$4 \times 5 = \boxed{20} \qquad 4 \times 10 = \boxed{40}$$

Encourage your child to add 4 to the previous product to find the next product. For example, to find 4 × 7, he can add 4 to 24 to find that 4 × 7 = 28.

What patterns do you notice? *Sample answers: The answers are all even. The answers go up by 4 each time.*

Activity (B): Double ×2 Facts to Find Answers to ×4 Facts

Use a piece of paper to cover the completed ×4 table in part A.

One way to find answers to the ×4 facts is to use the ×2 facts as stepping stones. Let's use 2 times 7 to figure out 4 times 7. What's 2 times 7? *14.* **Write 14 in the blank.**

2 times 7 means 2 groups of 7. 4 times 7 means 4 groups of 7. So, you can double 14 to find 4 times 7. What's double 14? *28.* **4 times 7 is 28. Write 28 in the blank.**

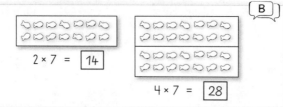

Let's use 2 times 6 to find 4 times 6. Use the dot array to model 4 × 6. Draw rings around the dots as shown. **What's 2 times 6?** *12.* **Write 12 in the blank. So, what's 4 times 6?** *24.* If your child's not sure, suggest he double 12. Write 24 in the blank.

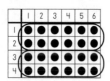 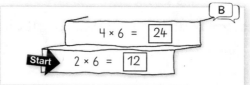

Let's use 2 times 9 to find 4 times 9. Use the dot array to model 4 × 9. Draw rings around the dots as shown. **What's 2 times 9?** *18.* **Write 18 in the blank. So, what's 4 times 9?** *36.* If your child's not sure, suggest he double 18. Write 36 in the blank.

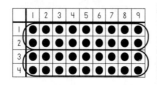 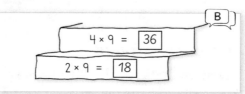

Activity (C): Play Multiplication Crash (×4)

Play Multiplication Crash. See Lesson 2.3 (page 60) for the general directions. On your turn, flip over the top card. Multiply the card by 4, say the matching multiplication fact, and place a counter on the matching square. For example, if you flip over a 7, say "7 times 4 equals 28" and place a counter on 28.

Independent Practice and Review

Have your child complete the Lesson 4.4 Practice and Review workbook pages.

If your child starts to count the tiles in the arrays one by one, encourage him to use the matching ×2 fact to help find the answers more efficiently. For example, for 4 × 8, draw a line to split the array in half as shown. Then ask: **What's 2 times 8?** *16.* **What's double 16?** *32.* **So, 4 times 8 is 32.**

$4 \times 8 =$ [32]

Lesson 4.5
Pictographs

Purpose	Materials
• Practice ×4 facts • Review pictographs	• Multiplication Strategies chart (Blackline Master 6) • Playing cards • Counters

Memory Work • **Name the multiples of 4 in order.** *4, 8, 12...* Stop your child when she reaches 40.

Warm-up (A): Play Multiplication Undercover (×4)

In the last lesson, you learned how to use the ×2 facts to find answers to the ×4 facts. Read aloud the ×4 strategy on the Multiplication Strategies chart (Blackline Master 6). Briefly discuss the example.

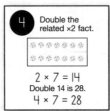

Today, you'll practice the ×4 facts more and use multiplication to interpret pictographs. Play Multiplication Undercover.

Multiplication Undercover (×4)

Materials: Deck of playing cards with jacks, queens, and kings removed (40 cards total); counters

Object of the Game: Uncover all the spaces on your game board first.

Shuffle the cards and place the stack face down on the table. Each player takes 10 counters and covers every number on her game board.

On your turn, flip over the top card. Multiply the card by 4, say the matching multiplication fact, and remove a counter from the matching square on your game board. For example, if you flip over a 7, say "7 times 4 is 28" and remove the counter on the 7th spot on the game board. After you remove the counter, check that you said the correct product.

If you have already removed the counter on that square, say the matching multiplication fact but do not remove any counters. Whoever removes all their counters first wins the game.

As you play, encourage your child to use the uncovered squares to help figure out the answers on the covered squares.

Activity (B):
Use Multiplication to Interpret a Pictograph with an Increment of 10

Luke helped sell donuts and pony ride tickets at the Harvest Festival. Briefly discuss any experiences your child has with festivals or carnivals. **He made a pictograph to show how many donuts were sold. The word "pictograph" is a combination of "picture" and "graph." A pictograph is like a bar graph, but it uses pictures or symbols instead of bars.**

Use the following questions to discuss the pictograph:

- **What's the title of the graph?** *Donut Sales.*
- **What days did they sell donuts?** *Friday, Saturday, and Sunday.*
- Point to the key at the bottom of the pictograph. **This part is called the key, because it's the key to understanding the pictograph. In this pictograph, each picture equals 10 donuts.**

Key

Since each picture stands for 10 donuts, we multiply the number of pictures by 10 to find how many donuts were sold. The Friday row has 3 pictures, so we multiply 3 times 10 to find out how many donuts were sold. Write "3 × 10" in the chart. **What's 3 times 10?** *30.* Write 30 in the chart.

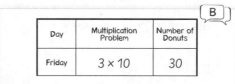

If your child doesn't understand why you multiplied by 10, place 3 groups of 10 counters on the table. **Each picture stands for 10 donuts. So, since we have 3 groups of 10, we can multiply 3 times 10 to find the total number of donuts.**

Have your child use the same reasoning to complete the chart for Saturday and Sunday. Then, use the following questions to discuss the pictograph:

- **Which day did they sell the most donuts?** *Saturday.*
- **Which day did they sell the fewest donuts?** *Friday.*
- **How many more donuts did they sell on Saturday than Sunday?** *10 donuts.*
- **How many fewer donuts did they sell on Friday than Saturday?** *30 donuts.*
- **How many donuts did they sell in all?** *140 donuts.*

Day	Multiplication Problem	Number of Donuts
Friday	3 × 10	30
Saturday	6 × 10	60
Sunday	5 × 10	50

Activity (C):
Use Multiplication to Interpret a Pictograph with an Increment of 5

Luke also made a graph about how many pony ride tickets were sold. Each pony ride at the festival costs 1 ticket. **What does each picture stand for in this pictograph?** *5 tickets.* Have your child use multiplication to complete the chart.

Pony Rides

Day	Multiplication Problem	Number of Tickets
Friday	5 × 5	25
Saturday	4 × 5	20
Sunday	2 × 5	10

Friday (pictures), Saturday (pictures), Sunday (pictures)

= 5 tickets

Then, use the following questions to discuss the pictograph:

- **Which day did they sell the most pony ride tickets?** *Friday.*
- **Which day did they sell the fewest pony ride tickets?** *Sunday.*
- **How many more pony ride tickets did they sell on Saturday than Sunday?** *10 tickets.*
- **How many fewer pony ride tickets did they sell on Saturday than Friday?** *5 tickets.*
- **How many pony ride tickets did they sell in all?** *55 tickets.*

Independent Practice and Review

Have your child complete the Lesson 4.5 Practice and Review workbook pages.

Lesson 4.6
Introduce the Multiplication Table

Purpose	Materials
• Practice multiplication facts • Introduce the multiplication table • Use patterns to find missing numbers in the multiplication table	• Die • Counters • Crayons or colored pencils

Memory Work
- **What do we call the numbers in a multiplication equation that we multiply together?** *Factors.*
- **What do we call the result when we multiply two numbers?** *The product.*

Children often feel overwhelmed by the number of multiplication facts they need to learn. In this lesson, you'll use the multiplication table to show your child that he's already familiar with 84 out of the 100 multiplication facts!

Warm-up (A): Play Dice Tic-Tac-Toe

Play Dice Tic-Tac-Toe.

Dice Tic-Tac-Toe

Materials: Die; counters of two different colors each

Object of the Game: Be the first player to fill three boxes in a row, either horizontally, vertically, or diagonally.

On your turn, roll the die. Find the column in the game board that matches your roll, and choose a multiplication problem in that column. Say the answer to the problem and cover the problem with one of your counters. If you roll a 6, you may choose a problem in any column.

Sample play. You may choose any problem in the column that matches your roll.

Play then passes to the other player. Continue until one player covers 3 boxes in a row, either horizontally, vertically, or diagonally.

If you'd like to make the game longer, play until one player has 4 or 5 in a row.

Activity (B): Introduce the Multiplication Table

This chart is called the multiplication table. After we complete the missing numbers, it will show all the multiplication facts from 1 × 1 up to 10 × 10. The numbers along the top and left edges are the factors. The numbers inside the chart are the products.

Point to the box for 3 × 2. **To figure out what product goes in this box, you multiply the factor at the beginning of the row times the factor at the top of the column.**

What factor is at the beginning of the row? *3.* **What factor is at the top of the column?** *2.* **What's 3 times 2?** *6.* Write 6 in the box.

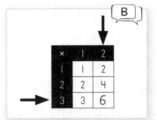

In this book, the first factor tells the row, and the second factor tells the column. So, the product of 3 × 2 is in the box in the third row and second column of the table.

You can also use patterns to help complete the empty boxes. Point to the ×4 row. **The numbers in this row are the multiples of 4. Each number is 4 more than the previous number.** Point to the box for 4 × 5. **So, you can add 4 to 16 to find what number belongs in this box. What's 16 plus 4?** *20.* Write 20 in the box.

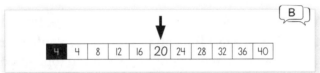

If your child is visually overwhelmed by the chart, cover the rows below the ×4 row with a piece of paper.

Point to the ×5 column. **The numbers in this column are the multiples of 5. Each number is 5 more than the previous number.** Point to the box for 7 × 5. **So, you can add 5 to 30 to find what number belongs in this box. What's 30 plus 5?** *35.* Write 35 in the box.

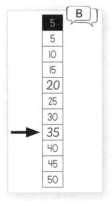

Have your child complete the other empty boxes. He may multiply the factors or use patterns to find the answers.

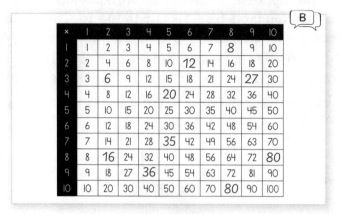

Activity (B): Color the Facts Already Studied in the Multiplication Table

The multiplication table has 10 rows and 10 columns, so there are 100 multiplication facts to learn. You've already learned a lot of them! Let's color the facts you have already studied. Have your child use this key to color the table. Some colors will overlap.

- ×1 row and ×1 column: Red
- ×2 row and ×2 column: Orange
- ×3 row and ×3 column: Yellow
- ×4 row and ×4 column: Green
- ×5 row and ×5 column: Blue
- ×10 row and ×10 column: Purple

How many multiplication facts are left for you to study? *16.* **You've already studied 84 of the 100 multiplication facts!** Draw a line diagonally from the top left corner of the multiplication table to the bottom right corner.

The products are arranged in the same way on either side of this line. Point to the box for 7 × 6. **Can you find the box with the same product?** *Child points to box for 6 × 7.*

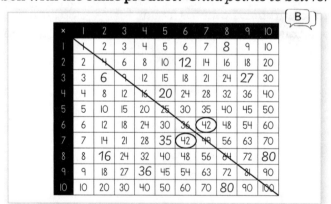

Why do those two boxes have the same product? *Sample answer: We can multiply numbers in any order, so they both have the same answer.* Have your child identify a few more pairs of matching products.

There are 16 multiplication facts left to study, but some of them are matching pairs, like 7 × 6 and 6 ×7. You don't have many left to learn!

Your child will tackle these last few multiplication facts in Unit 8.

Independent Practice and Review

Have your child complete the Lesson 4.6 Practice and Review workbook pages.

Lesson 4.7
Enrichment (Optional)

Purpose	Materials
• Practice memory work • Understand multiplying by 2 in a real-life context • Continue a doubling pattern • Summarize what your child has learned and assess your child's progress	• *Minnie's Diner,* written by Dayle Ann Dodds and illustrated by John Manders • Play money

Warm-up: Review Memory Work

Quiz your child on all memory work introduced through Unit 3. See pages 527-528 for the full list.

Math Picture Book: *Minnie's Diner*

Read *Minnie's Diner,* written by Dayle Ann Dodds and illustrated by John Manders. Each time Minnie doubles the order, have your child name the matching multiplication problem. For example, when she doubles the order of 4 specials: *2 times 4 equals 8.*

One Grain of Rice (the suggested picture book in Week 6 of *Second Grade Math with Confidence*) is also about doubling. If you already own *One Grain of Rice,* you can read it again instead of reading *Minnie's Diner.*

Enrichment Activity: Double Your Money

Let's pretend that you get an allowance that doubles every week. The first week you get $1. Place 1 one-dollar bill on the table.

How much money will you get the second week? *$2.* Add another one-dollar bill to the table.

How much money will you get the third week? *$4.* Add 2 one-dollar bills to the pile.

Week 1.

Week 2.

Week 3.

With your child, begin a simple chart to show how much money she receives each week.

Week	1	2	3
Allowance	$1	$2	$4

How many weeks do you think it will take until you get over $1000 per week? *Answers will vary.* Continue doubling the play money and recording the new amount until you reach $1,024.

Week	1	2	3	4	5	6	7	8	9	10	11
Allowance	$1	$2	$4	$8	$16	$32	$64	$128	$256	$512	$1,024

Use play money to model doubling these quantities and help your child as needed. Your child is not expected to know how to mentally double three-digit numbers.

Unit Wrap-up

Have your child complete the Unit 4 Wrap-up.

Unit 4 Answer Key

4.1 Practice

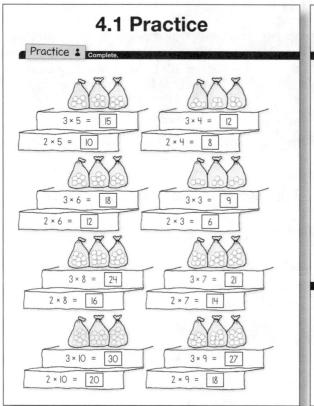

4.1 Review

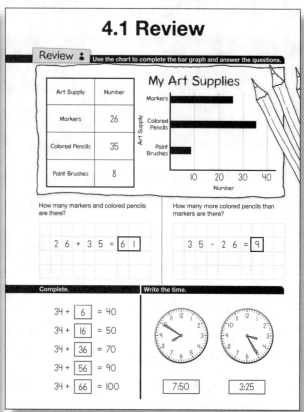

4.2 Practice

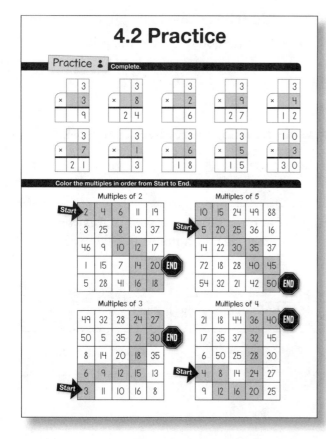

4.2 Review

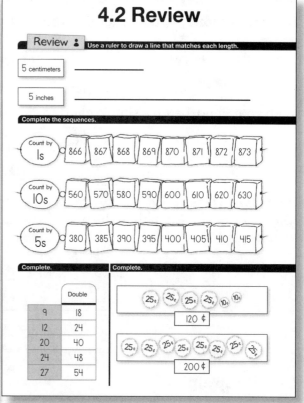

Unit 4 Answer Key

4.3 Practice

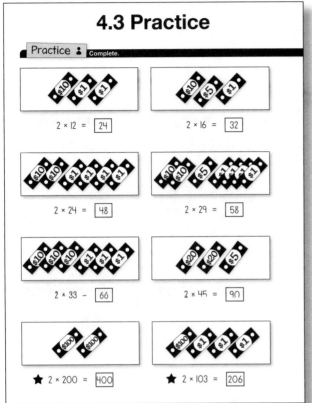

Practice — Complete.

$2 \times 12 = \boxed{24}$

$2 \times 16 = \boxed{32}$

$2 \times 24 = \boxed{48}$

$2 \times 29 = \boxed{58}$

$2 \times 33 = \boxed{66}$

$2 \times 45 = \boxed{90}$

★ $2 \times 200 = \boxed{400}$

★ $2 \times 103 = \boxed{206}$

4.3 Review

Review — Use the pictograph to complete the chart.

Books I've Read

Mystery
Fantasy
Science

= 2 books

Type of Book	Number
Mystery	6
Fantasy	4
Science	8

Write the time.

8:10   8:12

8:19   8:23

Solve.

You pay the clerk $60.
How much change do you get?

$45

Change
$ 15

Complete the sequences.

Count by 4s | 4 | 8 | 12 | 16 | 20 | 24 | 28 | 32

Count by 6s | 6 | 12 | 18 | 24 | 30 | 36 | 42 | 48

4.4 Practice

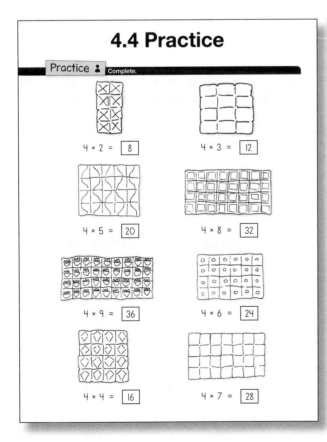

Practice — Complete.

$4 \times 2 = \boxed{8}$

$4 \times 3 = \boxed{12}$

$4 \times 5 = \boxed{20}$

$4 \times 8 = \boxed{32}$

$4 \times 9 = \boxed{36}$

$4 \times 6 = \boxed{24}$

$4 \times 4 = \boxed{16}$

$4 \times 7 = \boxed{28}$

4.4 Review

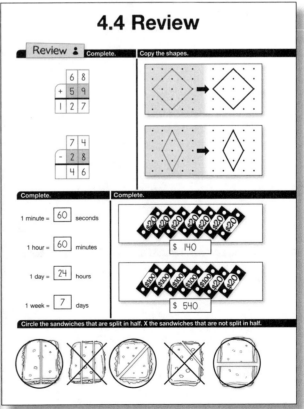

Review — Complete.

Copy the shapes.

$$\begin{array}{r} 6\ 8 \\ +\ 5\ 9 \\ \hline 1\ 2\ 7 \end{array}$$

$$\begin{array}{r} 7\ 4 \\ -\ 2\ 8 \\ \hline 4\ 6 \end{array}$$

Complete.

1 minute = $\boxed{60}$ seconds

1 hour = $\boxed{60}$ minutes

1 day = $\boxed{24}$ hours

1 week = $\boxed{7}$ days

Complete.

$ 140

$ 540

Circle the sandwiches that are split in half. X the sandwiches that are not split in half.

Unit 4 Answer Key

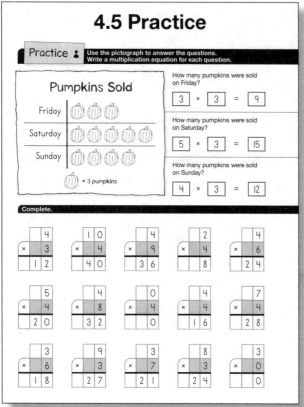

4.5 Practice

Practice Use the pictograph to answer the questions. Write a multiplication equation for each question.

Pumpkins Sold

Friday	🎃 🎃 🎃
Saturday	🎃 🎃 🎃 🎃 🎃
Sunday	🎃 🎃 🎃 🎃

🎃 = 3 pumpkins

How many pumpkins were sold on Friday?
$3 \times 3 = 9$

How many pumpkins were sold on Saturday?
$5 \times 3 = 15$

How many pumpkins were sold on Sunday?
$4 \times 3 = 12$

Complete.

	4		1 0		4		2		4
×	3	×	4	×	9	×	4	×	6
1 2		4 0		3 6		8		2 4

	5		4		0		4		7
×	4	×	8	×	4	×	4	×	4
2 0		3 2		0		1 6		2 8

	3		9		3		8		3
×	6	×	3	×	7	×	3	×	0
1 8		2 7		2 1		2 4		0

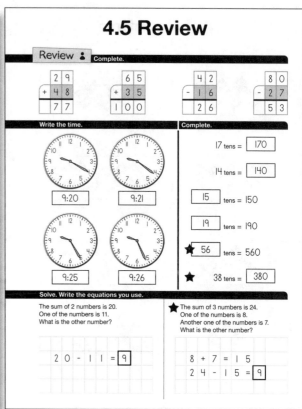

4.5 Review

Review Complete.

	2	9			6	5			4	2			8	0
+	4	8		+	3	5		-	1	6		-	2	7
	7	7			1 0 0				2	6			5	3

Write the time.

9:20   9:21

9:25   9:26

Complete.

17 tens = 170

14 tens = 140

15 tens = 150

19 tens = 190

⭐ 56 tens = 560

⭐ 38 tens = 380

Solve. Write the equations you use.

The sum of 2 numbers is 20. One of the numbers is 11. What is the other number?

$2 0 - 1 1 = 9$

⭐ The sum of 3 numbers is 24. One of the numbers is 8. Another one of the numbers is 7. What is the other number?

$8 + 7 = 1 5$
$2 4 - 1 5 = 9$

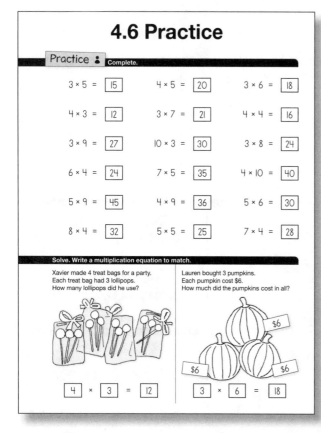

4.6 Practice

Practice Complete.

$3 \times 5 = 15$ $4 \times 5 = 20$ $3 \times 6 = 18$

$4 \times 3 = 12$ $3 \times 7 = 21$ $4 \times 4 = 16$

$3 \times 9 = 27$ $10 \times 3 = 30$ $3 \times 8 = 24$

$6 \times 4 = 24$ $7 \times 5 = 35$ $4 \times 10 = 40$

$5 \times 9 = 45$ $4 \times 9 = 36$ $5 \times 6 = 30$

$8 \times 4 = 32$ $5 \times 5 = 25$ $7 \times 4 = 28$

Solve. Write a multiplication equation to match.

Xavier made 4 treat bags for a party. Each treat bag had 3 lollipops. How many lollipops did he use?

$4 \times 3 = 12$

Lauren bought 3 pumpkins. Each pumpkin cost $6. How much did the pumpkins cost in all?

$3 \times 6 = 18$

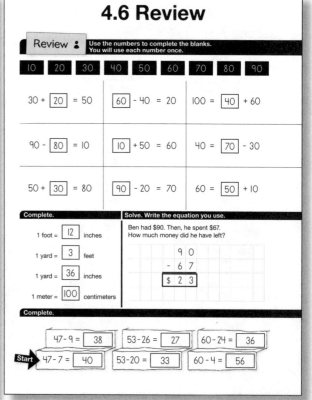

4.6 Review

Review Use the numbers to complete the blanks. You will use each number once.

| 10 | 20 | 30 | 40 | 50 | 60 | 70 | 80 | 90 |

$30 + 20 = 50$ $60 - 40 = 20$ $100 = 40 + 60$

$90 - 80 = 10$ $10 + 50 = 60$ $40 = 70 - 30$

$50 + 30 = 80$ $90 - 20 = 70$ $60 = 50 + 10$

Complete.

1 foot = 12 inches

1 yard = 3 feet

1 yard = 36 inches

1 meter = 100 centimeters

Solve. Write the equation you use.

Ben had $90. Then, he spent $67. How much money did he have left?

	9	0
-	6	7
$	2	3

Complete.

$47 - 9 = 38$ $53 - 26 = 27$ $60 - 24 = 36$

Start $47 - 7 = 40$ $53 - 20 = 33$ $60 - 4 = 56$

Unit 3 Answer Key

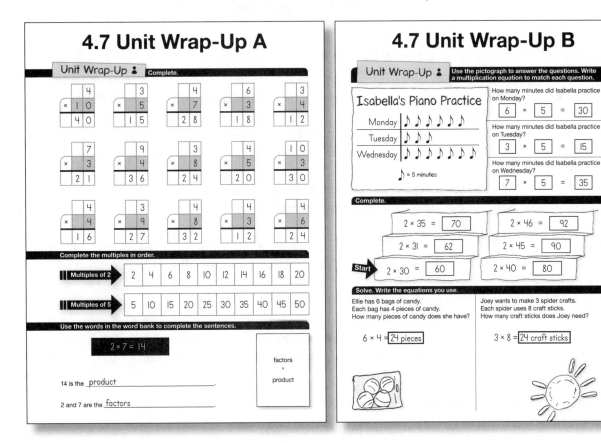

4.7 Unit Wrap-Up A

Unit Wrap-Up 👤 **Complete.**

	4
×	1 0
	4 0

	3
×	5
	1 5

	4
×	7
	2 8

	6
×	3
	1 8

	3
×	4
	1 2

	7
×	3
	2 1

	9
×	4
	3 6

	3
×	8
	2 4

	4
×	5
	2 0

	1 0
×	3
	3 0

	4
×	4
	1 6

	3
×	9
	2 7

	4
×	8
	3 2

	4
×	3
	1 2

	4
×	6
	2 4

Complete the multiples in order.

Multiples of 2 | 2 | 4 | 6 | 8 | 10 | 12 | 14 | 16 | 18 | 20 |

Multiples of 5 | 5 | 10 | 15 | 20 | 25 | 30 | 35 | 40 | 45 | 50 |

Use the words in the word bank to complete the sentences.

2 × 7 = 14

14 is the _product_ .

2 and 7 are the _factors_

factors
∘
product

4.7 Unit Wrap-Up B

Unit Wrap-Up 👤 **Use the pictograph to answer the questions. Write a multiplication equation to match each question.**

Isabella's Piano Practice

Monday ♪ ♪ ♪ ♪ ♪ ♪
Tuesday ♪ ♪ ♪
Wednesday ♪ ♪ ♪ ♪ ♪ ♪ ♪

♪ = 5 minutes

How many minutes did Isabella practice on Monday?
| 6 | × | 5 | = | 30 |

How many minutes did Isabella practice on Tuesday?
| 3 | × | 5 | = | 15 |

How many minutes did Isabella practice on Wednesday?
| 7 | × | 5 | = | 35 |

Complete.

2 × 35 = 70

2 × 46 = 92

2 × 31 = 62

2 × 45 = 90

Start → 2 × 30 = 60

2 × 40 = 80

Solve. Write the equations you use.

Ellie has 6 bags of candy.
Each bag has 4 pieces of candy.
How many pieces of candy does she have?

6 × 4 = 24 pieces

Joey wants to make 3 spider crafts.
Each spider uses 8 craft sticks.
How many craft sticks does Joey need?

3 × 8 = 24 craft sticks

Unit 4 Checkpoint

What to Expect at the End of Unit 4

By the end of Unit 4, most children will be able to do the following:

- Find answers for the ×3 and ×4 facts. Most children will know the facts with smaller factors (like 3 × 3 or 4 × 5) quite well, but they will need more practice with the facts with larger factors (like 3 × 8 or 4 × 7).
- Mentally multiply two-digit numbers by 2. Many children will still need to model these problems with play money or base-ten blocks and carefully think through each problem.
- Use multiplication to interpret pictographs. Some children will still need to be reminded to look at the key before drawing conclusions.

Is Your Child Ready to Move on?

In Unit 5, your child will review reading, writing, comparing, adding, and subtracting three-digit numbers. He'll also learn some new mental math techniques for three-digit numbers and learn to round numbers to the nearest hundred.

Before moving on to Unit 5, your child should be **mostly fluent at adding and subtracting two-digit numbers with the addition and subtraction algorithms.** It's fine if he sometimes has trouble remembering a few of the addition or subtraction facts or forgets one of the steps.

What to Do If Your Child Needs More Practice

If your child needs more practice adding and subtracting two-digit numbers, make up a two-digit addition problem and a two-digit subtraction problem for him to solve at the beginning of every lesson in Unit 5. Make sure to include problems that require trading. If needed, model the problems with base-ten blocks and use the Addition and Subtraction Algorithm diagrams (from Blackline Master 4) to remind him of the steps.

Unit 5
Numbers to 1,000

Overview

In Unit 5, your child will review the numbers to 1,000. She'll develop deeper number sense with three-digit numbers as she rounds numbers to the nearest hundred and learns new mental addition, subtraction, and multiplication techniques.

Your child will also review how to add and subtract three-digit numbers, and she'll learn how to estimate to check whether her answers are reasonable. In Unit 11, your child will extend these skills to four-digit numbers.

What Your Child Will Learn

In this unit, your child will learn to:

- Round three-digit numbers to the nearest hundred
- Mentally add up to find missing addends to 1,000 or the next hundred
- Use place-value thinking to add and subtract groups of tens (for example, 670 + 40 or 510 − 30)
- Use the addition and subtraction algorithms to add and subtract three-digit numbers
- Use estimation to check whether answers are reasonable
- Solve mental multiplication problems that involve groups of 10 (for example, 4 × 30 or 17 × 10)

Lesson List

Lesson 5.1	Round to the Nearest Hundred	Lesson 5.6	Subtract Three-Digit Numbers
Lesson 5.2	Add Up to Find Missing Addends	Lesson 5.7	Subtract Across Zero and Estimate Differences
Lesson 5.3	Add and Subtract Groups of Ten	Lesson 5.8	Multiply Tens, Part 1
		Lesson 5.9	Multiply Tens, Part 2
Lesson 5.4	Add Three-Digit Numbers	Lesson 5.10	Enrichment (Optional)
Lesson 5.5	Estimate Sums		

Extra Materials Needed for Unit 5

- 12 slips of paper
- Paper clip
- For optional Enrichment Lesson:
  - × *Betcha! Estimating,* written by Stuart J. Murphy and illustrated by S. D. Schindler. HarperCollins, 1997.
  - × 3 clear jars or bowls
  - × 3 sets of small objects (such as crackers, blocks, or cotton balls) with 50-150 objects in each set

Teaching Math with Confidence: Place Value and Mental Multiplication

Up until this point, your child's study of place value has mostly focused on trading (for example, trading 10 ones for 1 ten or 1 hundred for 10 tens). In this unit, your child will develop a deeper understanding of the place value system as she learns to mentally multiply tens. For example, to find 23 × 10: 20 tens equal 200, and 3 tens equal 30. So, 23 times 10 equals 230.

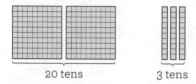

23 tens equal 230, so 23 × 10 = 230.

Multiplying by tens gently introduces your child to a new way to think about place value. Since the value of each place is 10 times the value of the next-smaller place, "sliding" a number to the left by one place is the same as multiplying the number by 10. In the same way, "sliding" a number to the right by one place is the same as dividing the number by 10.

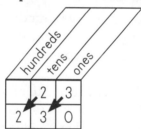

23 × 10 = 230. Multiplying a number by 10 slides each digit one place to the left.

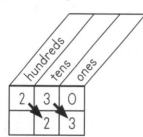

230 ÷ 10 = 23. Dividing a number by 10 slides each digit one place to the right.

This principle underlies many of the multiplication and division skills your child will learn in future grades. (It's especially important when your child tackles decimals!) The multiplication lessons in this unit are meant to simply introduce your child to this new way to look at the place value system. Don't worry if your child doesn't grasp the idea immediately. With repeated exposure and practice, she'll develop a deeper understanding of place value and be ready to apply place-value concepts to multi-digit multiplication and division.

Lesson 5.1
Round to the Nearest Hundred

Purpose	Materials
• Review three-digit numbers • Review writing three-digit numbers in expanded form • Learn to round three-digit numbers to the nearest hundred	• Base-ten blocks • Play money

Memory Work · **How many centimeters equal 1 meter?** *100.*

Warm-up (A): Review Place Value in Three-Digit Numbers

We're beginning a unit on the numbers to 1,000 today. Let's warm up with some place value riddles. I'll only use each number once, so cross off each number after you use it.

- **This number has 1 digit.** *8.*
- **This number has 2 digits.** *99.*
- **This number has 4 digits.** *1,000.*
- **This number equals 200 plus 10 plus 7.** *217.*
- **This number equals 200 plus 70 plus 1.** *271.*
- Put 6 flats and 3 rods on the table. **This number matches these base-ten blocks.** *630.*
- Put 6 flats and 3 unit blocks on the table. **This number matches these base-ten blocks.** *603.*
- Put 4 hundred-dollar bills and 5 ten-dollar bills on the table. **This number matches these bills.** *450.*
- **This number is between 860 and 870.** *864.*
- **This number is between 300 and 400.** *375.*
- **This number is 1 more than 700.** *701.*
- **This number is 1 less than 700.** *699.*

Activity (B): Review Expanded Form

Today, we'll review how to write three-digit numbers in expanded form. You'll also learn how to round numbers to the nearest hundred.

If your child can confidently write three-digit numbers in expanded form, have her write 324 and 506 in expanded form and move on to part C.

Point to the 3 in 324 and the printed base-ten blocks. **Which base-ten blocks match the 3?** *The 3 flats.* **The 3 is in the hundreds-place, so it has a value of 300.**

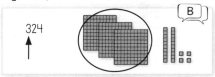

Point to the 2 in 324. **Which base-ten blocks match the 2?** *The 2 rods.* **The 2 is in the tens-place, so it has a value of 20.**

Point to the 4 in 324. **Which base-ten blocks match the 4?** *The 4 unit blocks.* **The 4 is in the ones-place, so it has a value of 4.**

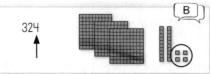

When you write a number in expanded form, you s-t-r-e-t-c-h the number to show the value of each of its digits. So, the expanded form of 324 is 300 plus 20 plus 4. Write "300 + 20 + 4" in the blank. Repeat with 506.

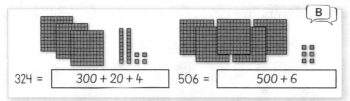

324 = [300 + 20 + 4]   506 = [500 + 6]

Make sure your child writes the addends in expanded form in the same order as the digits. She does not need to write the value of any placeholder zeros. For example, for 506, she should write 500 + 6, not 500 + 0 + 6.

Activity (C): Introduce Rounding to the Nearest Hundred

In Unit 1, you learned how to round numbers to the nearest ten. Today, you'll learn how to round numbers to the nearest hundred. When we say the "nearest hundred," we mean the numbers that we say when we count by 100s. Have your child count from 100 to 1,000 by hundreds: *100, 200...*

There are 628 cotton balls in the carton. 628 is between 600 and 700. Draw a tick mark halfway between 600 and 700 on the number line and label it 650. **650 is halfway between 600 and 700. It's 50 more than 600, and 50 less than 700. Is 628 greater than or less than 650?** *Less than.* **So, is 628 closer to 600 or 700?** *600.*

628 is less than 650, so it is closer to 600 than 700. 628 rounded to the nearest hundred is 600. We can say that there are about 600 cotton balls in the carton. Write 600 in the blank.

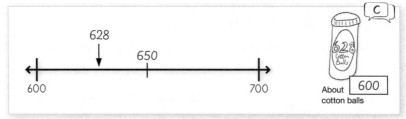

Have your child use the same approach to round 693 and 655 to the nearest hundred.

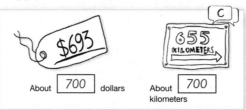

Activity (D): Use the Number Line to Round to the Nearest Hundred

Let's pretend 482 people bought tickets to a concert. About where would 482 go on this number line? *Child points between 400 and 500.* Draw a tick mark halfway between 400 and 500 on the number line and label it 450. **Is 482 greater than or less than 450?** *Greater than 450.* **So, 482 rounded to the nearest hundred is 500. About 500 people went to the concert. Write 500 in the chart.**

482 is closer to 500 than 400, so 482 rounded to the nearest hundred is 500.

Have your child use the same approach to round the rest of the numbers in the chart to the nearest ten. For 850, say: **850 is exactly between 800 and 900! Remember, mathematicians have agreed that we round in-between numbers to the higher number. So, 850 rounded to the nearest hundred is 900.**

482	249	301	532	299	850	940	984
500	200	300	500	300	900	900	1,000

Independent Practice and Review

Have your child complete the Lesson 5.1 Practice and Review pages.

Lesson 5.2
Add Up to Find Missing Addends

Purpose	Materials
• Practice finding pairs that make 1,000 • Add up to find missing addends to the next hundred • Add up to find missing addends to 1,000	• Play money

Memory Work · **Name the multiples of 3 in order.** *3, 6, 9...* Stop your child when he reaches 30.

In Lesson 3.2, your child added up to find missing addends to 100 or the next multiple of 10. In this lesson, he'll use the same reasoning to find missing addends with larger sums.

Warm-up: Find Pairs That Make 1,000

Let's pretend that we have $1,000 to share. How many hundred-dollar bills equal $1,000? *10.* Place 10 hundred-dollar bills on the table. **If we share the money equally, how much money do we each get?** *$500.* Have your child split the money between the two of you.

What's another way we could split the money? Have your child find several other ways to split the 10 hundred-dollar bills. Encourage him to use the pairs that make 10 to reason about the hundred-dollar bills. For example: **3 and 7 make 10. So, if I get $300, how much money do you get?** *$700.*

Sample answer. If one person gets $300, the other gets $700.

We could also trade 1 hundred-dollar bill for 10 ten-dollar bills. Trade 1 hundred-dollar bill for 10 ten-dollar bills. **Now we have many more ways to share the money! Here's one way.** Give your child 1 ten-dollar bill and keep the rest for yourself. **How much money do each of us get?** *I get $10, but you get $990!* Have your child find several other ways to split the money.

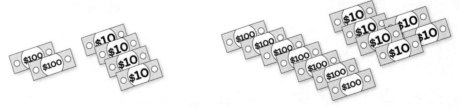

Sample answer. If one person gets $240, the other person gets $760.

Activity (A): Add Up to Find Missing Addends to the Next Hundred

In Unit 3, you learned how to add up to find missing addends and make change. Today, you'll add up to find missing addends with larger sums.

Let's pretend you want to buy something that costs $300. Briefly discuss what your child might buy for $300. **You have saved $280. We want to find how much more money you need.** Give him 2 hundred-dollar bills and 8 ten-dollar bills.

Use ten-dollar bills (rather than twenty-dollar bills) to reinforce place value.

80 plus what equals 100? *20.* Write 20 in the blank. **300 is the next hundred after 280. So, 280 plus what equals 300?** *20.* Write 20 in the blank. Give your child 2 ten-dollar bills. **Now you have enough to pay $300!**

Have your child complete part A. Model each problem with play money and frame it in the same way as above. For example: **You want to buy something that costs $700. You already have $650. How much more money do you need?**

Do not require your child to use money to find the answers if he can solve the problems mentally.

Activity (B): Add Up to Find Missing Addends to 1,000

This time, you want to buy something that costs $1,000. Briefly discuss what your child might buy that costs $1,000. **You have saved $680. We want to find how much more money you need.** Give him 6 hundred-dollar bills and 8 ten-dollar bills.

To solve this problem, we'll add up in 2 steps. First, let's find how many more tens you need to reach the next hundred. 680 plus what equals 700? *20.* Write 20 in the blank, and give your child 2 ten-dollar bills.

Now, you have $700. Let's find how many more hundreds you need to reach 1,000. 700 plus what equals 1,000? *300.* Write 300 in the blank, and give your child 3 hundred-dollar bills. **We added 2 tens and 3 hundreds to reach 1,000. 20 plus 300 is 320, so you needed $320 to reach $1,000.** Write 320 in the blank.

Have your child complete part B. Model each problem with play money and frame it in the same way as above.

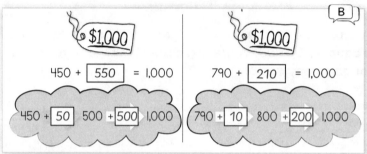

Independent Practice and Review

Have your child complete the Lesson 5.2 Practice and Review pages. Allow him to model the problems with play money if needed.

Lesson 5.3
Add and Subtract Groups of Ten

Purpose	Materials
• Practice ×4 facts • Mentally add groups of ten to three-digit numbers • Mentally subtract groups of ten from three-digit numbers	• Playing cards • Counters • Base-ten blocks • Slips of paper

Memory Work
- **Are times in the morning a.m. or p.m.?** *A.m.*
- **Are times in the afternoon and evening a.m. or p.m.?** *P.m.*

In Unit 3, your child mentally added and subtracted in two steps. In this lesson, she'll use similar reasoning to mentally add and subtract larger numbers.

Warm-up (A): Play Multiplication Crash (×4)

Play Multiplication Crash. See Lesson 4.4 (page 124) for directions.

Activity (B): Add Tens in 2 Steps

Today, you'll learn how to mentally add and subtract multiples of 10, like 40, 70, or 90.

Model 480 + 50 with base-ten blocks to match the picture. **Here's how I add 480 plus 50 in two steps. First, I add 2 tens to complete the hundred.** Move two rods to make a group of 100. **What's 480 plus 20?** *500.* Write 500 in the blank.

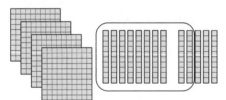
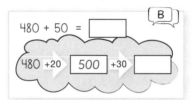

Then, I add the other 3 tens. What's 500 plus 30? *530.* Write 530 in both blanks.

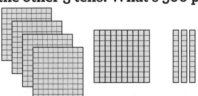
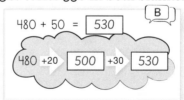

Make sure to model the problem with real base-ten blocks so that you can concretely demonstrate the steps.

Have your child complete part B. Model the problems with base-ten blocks as needed.

290 + 30 = 320		760 + 70 = 830	
180 + 80 = 260		370 + 40 = 410	

Activity (C): Subtract Tens in 2 Steps

We can subtract tens in two steps, too. Point to 330 – 50 and have your child model 330 with base-ten blocks. **First, I subtract the rods.** Cover the 3 rods with a slip of paper. **What's 330 minus 30?** *300.* Write 300 in the blank.

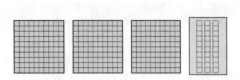
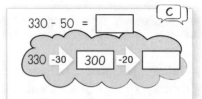

We want to subtract 5 tens, and we have already subtracted 3 tens. So, we need to subtract 2 more tens. Use another slip of paper to cover 2 rods on 1 of the flats. **What's 300 minus 20?** *280.* Write 280 in both blanks.

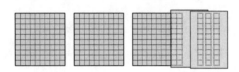
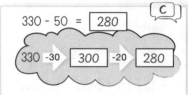

Have your child complete part C. Model the problems with base-ten blocks and encourage her to subtract in two steps.

210 - 40 = 170	550 - 60 = 490	
430 - 50 = 380	820 - 90 = 730	

Independent Practice and Review

Have your child complete the Lesson 5.3 Practice and Review pages.

Lesson 5.4
Add Three-Digit Numbers

Purpose	Materials
• Practice ×5 facts • Use the addition algorithm to add three-digit numbers	• Clock • Base-ten blocks • Place-Value Chart (Blackline Master 3) • 12 slips of paper

Memory Work	
	• **How many inches equal 1 foot?** *12.* • **How many feet equal 1 yard?** *3.* • **How many inches equal 1 yard?** *36.*

In Lesson 1.7, your child reviewed the addition algorithm for two-digit numbers. In this lesson, he'll review how to use this step-by-step procedure to add three-digit numbers.

If your child can confidently and accurately add three-digit numbers with the addition algorithm, you may skip this lesson. Or, make it a quick review: Skip part A and move directly to playing Leaf Fight in part B.

Warm-up: Review ×5 Facts on the Clock

Show your child a clock. (The clock can be set to any time.) Point to the printed 7 on the clock and say the matching ×5 multiplication fact: **7 times 5 equals what?** *35.*

Repeat with the rest of the numbers from 1-10, in random order. Point to one number at a time, say the matching ×5 fact, and have your child tell the answer to the fact.

Activity (A): Add Three-Digit Numbers

In Unit 1, you reviewed how to use the addition algorithm to add two-digit numbers. Today, you'll use the addition algorithm to add three-digit numbers.

To add three-digit numbers, we use the same steps that we use for two-digit numbers.

Model 287 and 436 with base-ten blocks on the Place-Value Chart.

- **Which place do we start with?** *The ones-place.*
- **What's the first step?** *Add the digits.* **What's 7 plus 6?** *13.* **The sum is greater than 9, so we need to trade.** Trade 10 unit blocks for 1 rod and place the rod horizontally in the tens-column. Have your child write a 1 above the tens-place and a 3 in the answer's ones-place.

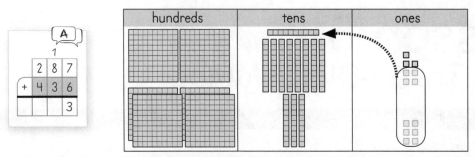

- **Now, we go back to the beginning and follow the steps for the tens-place. What's 1 plus 8 plus 3?** *12.* Trade 10 rods for 1 flat and place the flat in the hundreds-column. Have your child write 1 above the hundreds-place and a 2 in the answer's tens-place.

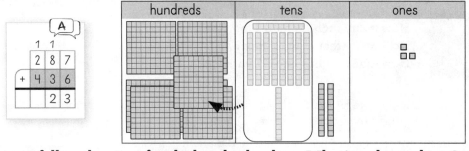

- **Last, we follow the steps for the hundreds-place. What's 1 plus 2 plus 4?** *7.* Have your child write 7 in the answer's hundreds-place.

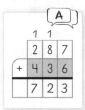

Have your child complete the other problem in part A in the same way.

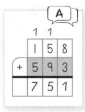

Activity (B): Play Leaf Fight

Play Leaf Fight. See Lesson 1.7 (page 34) for general directions. Use the numbers listed in part B as the numbers for your slips of paper: 153, 237, 309, 195, 288, 342, 424, 571, 90, 466, 510, 87.

Independent Practice and Review

Have your child complete the Lesson 5.4 Practice and Review workbook pages.

The Practice section is short, since your child practiced lots of three-digit addition in the Lesson Activities. As a result, there is only one page of Practice and Review in this lesson.

Lesson 5.5
Estimate Sums

Purpose	Materials
• Practice rounding to the nearest hundred • Estimate answers to three-digit addition problems • Practice adding three-digit numbers • Compare estimates with exact answers	• None

Memory Work
- **What is another name for 12 a.m?** *Midnight.*
- **What is another name for 12 p.m.?** *Noon.*

Warm-up (A): Practice Rounding to the Nearest Hundred

In the last lesson, you used the addition algorithm to add three-digit numbers. Today, you'll learn how to use rounding to estimate sums.

Have your child orally round the playground items' prices to the nearest hundred.

- Tire swing: *$200*
- Swing: *$100*
- Slide: *$400*
- Climbing net: *$200*
- Spiral slide: *$500*

Activity (A): Estimate Sums and Add Three-Digit Numbers

Read aloud the first word problem: ***How much does it cost to buy a tire swing and spiral slide?*** Have your child identify the price of each item. Write the prices in the blank grid below the problem. (Do not have her solve the problem yet.)

When I buy expensive things like these, I estimate the total cost before I go to pay. I don't want to be surprised at the check-out! When I estimate, I'm not trying to find the exact answer. I'm just trying to get a rough idea of the total so I know whether I can afford it.

Let's estimate the total cost of the tire swing and spiral slide. What's 235 rounded to the nearest hundred? *200.* Write 200 as shown. **What's 467 rounded to the nearest hundred?** *500.* Write 500 as shown. **What's 200 plus 500?** *700.* Write 700 as shown.

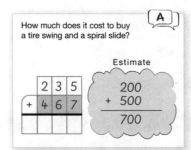

We estimate that the tire swing and spiral slide will cost about $700. Now, add their prices to find the exact cost. Have your child use the addition algorithm to add the prices.

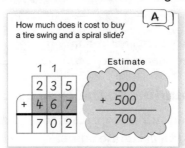

> If your child has trouble, use base-ten blocks to model the problem and talk through each step with the Addition Algorithm diagram (as in Lesson 5.4).

After your child finds the sum, say: **We estimated they would cost $700, and they actually cost $702. Our estimate was very close to the exact answer! Not all estimates are that close!**

> If your child is interested, discuss why the estimate is so close to the actual total: **We rounded 235 down 35 to 200, and we rounded 467 up 33 to 500. The 35 and 33 nearly cancel each other out!** Your child does not need to fully understand the relationship between the estimate and exact sum.

Repeat with the next problem. Have your child estimate the total cost of the climbing net and tire swing. Then, have her add to find the exact cost. After your child finds the sum, say: **We estimated the climbing net and tire swing would cost $400, and they actually cost $461.**

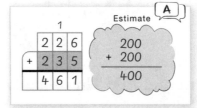

Our estimate wasn't quite as close this time, but it still gave a rough idea of the total cost. If the clerk told me that they cost $600, I would know that he had made a mistake and needed to check his math!

> If your child is interested, discuss why the estimate is so much less than the actual total: **We rounded both numbers down, so our estimate was less than the actual total.**

Repeat with the next problem. Have your child estimate the total cost of the regular slide and spiral slide. Then, have her add to find the exact cost. After your child finds the sum, say: **We estimated the regular slide and spiral slide would cost $900, and they actually cost $825. This estimate isn't exact, but it gives me an idea of the total cost. If I only wanted to spend**

$500 on playground equipment, I would know that buying the two slides would be out of my budget.

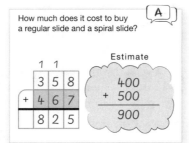

If your child is interested, discuss why the estimate is so much more than the actual total: **We rounded both numbers up, so our estimate was more than the actual total.**

Have your child solve the final problem in the same way. If needed, remind her that she can follow the usual steps in the addition algorithm to find the sum of three addends. After she finds the sum, discuss how close her sum is to her estimate.

Independent Practice and Review

Have your child complete the Lesson 5.5 Practice and Review workbook pages.

On the Practice page, your child will use estimation to check whether answers are reasonable. Encourage your child to look more closely at the incorrect problems and see if she can find the mistake. Also point out that it's possible to make mistakes and still have an answer that looks reasonable. For example, if you add the digits in the ones-place incorrectly, your answer may be reasonable, but still wrong!

Lesson 5.6
Subtract Three-Digit Numbers

Purpose	Materials
• Review even and odd numbers • Use the subtraction algorithm to subtract three-digit numbers	• Base-ten blocks • Place-Value Chart (Blackline Master 3) • Paper clip

Memory Work	• **If a number has 1, 3, 5, 7, or 9 in the ones-place, is the number even or odd?** *Odd.* • **If a number has 0, 2, 4, 6, or 8 in the ones-place, is the number even or odd?** *Even.*

Children often find multi-digit subtraction more difficult than multi-digit addition, so most children will need a refresher on the subtraction algorithm. If your child can confidently and accurately subtract three-digit numbers with the subtraction algorithm, skip part A and move directly to playing Spin to Win in part B.

Warm-up: Review Even and Odd

Have your child tell whether the following numbers are even or odd.

- **10.** *Even.*
- **11.** *Odd.*
- **56.** *Even.*
- **98.** *Even.*
- **215.** *Odd.*
- **417.** *Odd.*

- **254.** *Even.*
- **683.** *Odd.*
- **702.** *Even.*
- **999.** *Odd.*
- **1,000.** *Even.*

Activity (A): Subtract Three-Digit Numbers

In Unit 1, you used the subtraction algorithm to subtract two-digit numbers. Today, you'll use the algorithm to subtract three-digit numbers.

To subtract three-digit numbers, we use the same steps as for two-digit numbers. Point to 432 – 287. Model 432 with base-ten blocks on the Place-Value Chart. Use the following dialogue to demonstrate how to find the difference.

- **Which place do we start with?** *The ones-place.*
- **Is the top digit greater than or equal to the bottom digit?** *No.* **2 is less than 7, so we need to trade.** Trade 1 rod for 10 unit blocks and place the 10 unit blocks in the ones-column. **Now, we have 2 tens.** Cross out the 3 and write 2 above it. **We have 12 ones.** Cross out the 2 and write 12 above it.

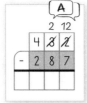

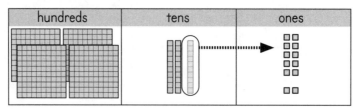

- **The final step for the ones-place is to subtract. 12 minus 7 is 5.** Remove 7 unit blocks and write 5 in the answer's ones-place.

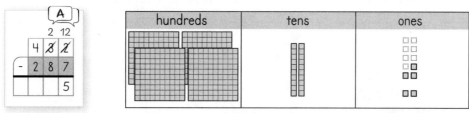

- **Now, we follow the steps for the tens-place. 2 is less than 8, so we need to trade.** Trade 1 flat for 10 rods and place the 10 rods in the tens-column. **Now, we have 3 hundreds.** Cross out the 4 and write 3 above it. **We have 12 tens.** Write a 1 next to the 2 above the tens-place.

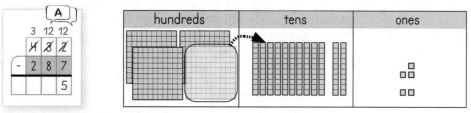

- **The final step for the tens-place is to subtract. 12 minus 8 is 4.** Remove 8 rods and write 4 in the answer's tens-place.

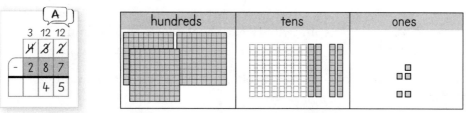

- **Last, we follow the steps for the hundreds-place. 3 minus 2 is 1.** Remove 2 flats and write 1 in the answer's hundreds-place.

Have your child complete the other problem in part A in the same way. Model each step with base-ten blocks and help your child carefully record the trades.

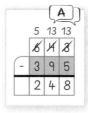

Activity (B): Play Spin to Win

Play Spin to Win. Model the problems with base-ten blocks as needed.

Spin to Win

Materials: Paper clip

Object of the Game: Win the most points.

On your turn, place one end of the paper clip in the center of the top spinner. Place the point of a pencil through the paper clip so that it touches the center of the circle. Spin the paper clip and write this number on the top line of your first blank grid. Then, move the paper clip and pencil to the bottom spinner. Spin again, and write this number on the next line. Subtract the lesser number from the greater number.

For example, if you spin 943 and 281:

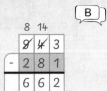

Then, have the other player spin twice, write the value of each spin in the next blank grid, and find the difference. Whoever has the greater difference wins a point.

Continue until you have filled in all the blank grids. Whoever has won more points wins the game.

Independent Practice and Review

Have your child complete the Lesson 5.6 Practice and Review workbook pages.

The Practice section is short, since your child practiced lots of three-digit subtraction in the Lesson Activities. As a result, there is only one page of Practice and Review in this lesson.

Lesson 5.7
Subtract Across Zero and Estimate Differences

Purpose	Materials
• Practice identifying the value of groups of tens • Use the subtraction algorithm to subtract three-digit numbers across zero • Estimate answers to three-digit subtraction problems • Compare estimates with exact answers	• Base-ten blocks • Place-Value Chart (Blackline Master 3)

Memory Work
- **How many sides does a triangle have?** *3.*
- **How many sides does a quadrilateral have?** *4.*

Warm-up: Practice Identifying the Value of Groups of Ten

Have your child tell you the value of the following groups of ten.

- **8 tens.** *80.*
- **10 tens.** *100.*
- **11 tens.** *110.*
- **16 tens.** *160.*
- **20 tens.** *200.*

If your child has trouble, model the questions with base-ten blocks. For example, for 11 tens, place 11 rods on the table and separate them into a group with 10 rods and a group with 1 rod. **How much do 10 tens equal?** *100.* **How much does 1 ten equal?** *10.* **So, you can add 100 plus 10 to find the value of 11 tens.**

Activity (A): Subtract Across Zero

In the last lesson, you used the subtraction algorithm to subtract three-digit numbers. Today, you'll practice subtracting across zero in three-digit subtraction problems.

Children sometimes find these problems confusing. But if you follow the usual steps in the subtraction algorithm, they're not so hard!

Model 704 with base-ten blocks on the Place-Value Chart. Use the following dialogue to demonstrate how to subtract 326 from 704.

- **We start with the ones-place. Is the top digit greater than or equal to the bottom digit?** *No.*
  4 is less than 6, so we need to trade. But, there aren't any tens in the tens-place! We need to trade 1 hundred for 10 tens first.

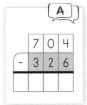

hundreds	tens	ones

- **We'll trade in two steps. First, we trade 1 hundred for 10 tens.** Have your child trade 1 flat for 10 rods and place the rods in the tens-column. Also have her record the trade as shown.

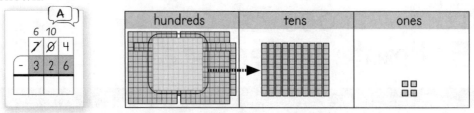

- **Next, we trade 1 ten for 10 ones.** Have your child trade 1 rod for 10 units and place the units in the ones-column. Also have her record the trade.

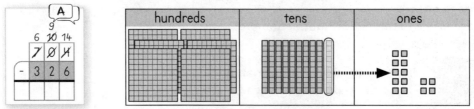

- **Now that you've traded, you're ready to subtract.** Help your child follow the steps in the subtraction algorithm to complete the problem.

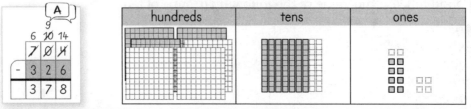

Trading in two steps (and recording each trade separately) helps your child understand what she's doing and helps prevent mistakes.

In the next problem, the greater number has zeros in both the tens-place and the ones-place. You'll need to trade twice again so that you have some tens in the tens-place and some ones in the ones-place.

Model 500 with base-ten blocks on the Place-Value Chart. Have your child trade 1 flat for 10 rods, place the rods in the tens-column, and record the trade.

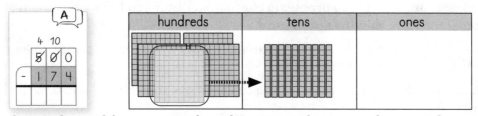

Then, have her trade 1 rod for 10 units, place the units in the ones-column, and record the trade.

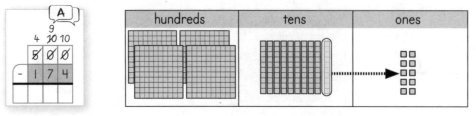

Now, you're ready to subtract! Have your child follow the steps in the subtraction algorithm to complete the problem.

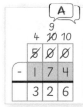

hundreds	tens	ones

Activity (B): Estimate Sums and Add Three-Digit Numbers

Read aloud the first word problem in part B: *How much more does a spiral slide cost than a climbing net?* Have your child find the price of each item. Write the prices in the blank grid below the problem. (Do not have her solve the problem yet.)

Before you solve the problem, let's estimate the answer. Estimating the answer before you solve helps you know whether your answer is reasonable. If your answer is very far off from your estimate, then you know that you need to check your work.

What's 467 rounded to the nearest hundred? *500.* Write 500 as shown. **What's 226 round-ed to the nearest hundred?** *200.* Write 200 as shown. **What's 500 minus 200?** *300.* Write 300 as shown.

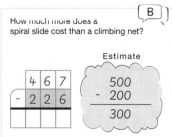

We estimate the spiral slide costs about $300 more than the climbing net. Now, subtract to find the exact answer. Have your child use the subtraction algorithm to find the difference.

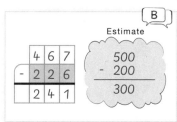

If your child has trouble, use base-ten blocks to model the problem and talk through each step.

After your child finds the difference, say: **We estimated the spiral slide costs about $300 more than the climbing net. It actually costs $241 more. $241 is within a hundred dollars of $300, so that seems like a reasonable answer.**

Whether or not an answer is "reasonable" depends on the numbers involved. When you find the difference between two-digit numbers, your answer should generally be within 10-20 of your estimate. But when you find the difference between numbers in the millions, it's fine if your answer is a few million off from your estimate! For three-digit numbers, most answers should be within about 100 of the estimate.

If your child is interested, discuss the reason why the estimate is $59 off from the answer. **We rounded 467 up 33 to 400, and we rounded 226 down 26 to 200. 33 plus 26 is 59, so that's why our estimate is 59 away from the actual answer.** Your child does not need to fully grasp the relationship between the estimate and exact sum.

Repeat with the next problem. **Before you buy something, it's good to have an idea about how much money you'll have left after you buy it!** Have your child round each number to the nearest hundred and subtract to estimate how much money will be left. Then, have her subtract to find the exact amount. After your child finds the difference, say: **We estimated you'd have about $400 left, and you'd actually have $374 left. That's pretty close!**

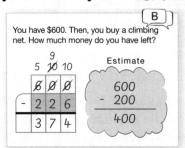

If your child is interested, discuss why the estimate is $26 off from the answer. **We rounded 226 down 26 to 200, so our estimate is 26 away from the actual answer.**

Have your child solve the final problem in the same way.

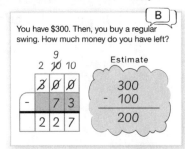

If your child is interested, discuss why the estimate is $27 off from the answer. **We rounded 73 up 27 to 100, so our estimate is 27 away from the actual answer.**

Independent Practice and Review

Have your child complete the Lesson 5.7 Practice and Review workbook pages.

Lesson 5.8
Multiply Tens, Part 1

Purpose	Materials
• Practice multiplication facts • Mentally multiply two-digit numbers by 10	• Die

Memory Work	• **How many sides does a hexagon have?** *6.* • **How many sides does an octagon have?** *8.* • **How many sides does a pentagon have?** *5.*

This lesson provides a gentle introduction to multiplying two-digit numbers by 10. If your child finds the concept easy and the lesson goes very quickly, you may want to combine it with Lesson 5.9 and teach both lessons in one day. If so, have your child skip the Lesson 5.8 Practice page, and choose a selection of problems from Review pages 5.8 and 5.9 for your child to complete.

Warm-up (A): Play Roll and Multiply

Play Roll and Multiply.

Roll and Multiply

Materials: Die

Object of the Game: Have the greater total score.

On your turn, roll the die. Write your roll in the blank in one of the blanks on your scorecard. (You may choose any blank.) Then, find the product of the two numbers. This product is your score.

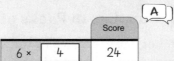

If you roll a 6, roll again (since your child hasn't yet learned how to multiply these numbers by 6.)

Take turns until both players have completed all of the equations. Then, each player finds the sum of all their products. Whoever has the greater total score wins.

Activity (B): Multiply Numbers by 10

In this unit, you've practiced mental addition and subtraction with numbers in the hundreds. In this lesson and the next lesson, you'll learn mental multiplication with numbers in the hundreds. Today, you'll learn how to multiply numbers times 10.

14 times 10 means "14 groups of 10." How much do 14 tens equal? *140.* **So, 14 times 10 equals 140.** Write 140 in both blanks.

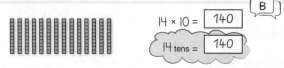

If your child's not sure, ask: **How much do 10 tens equal?** *100.* **How much do 4 tens equal?** *40.* **So, you can add 100 plus 40 to find the value of 14 tens.**

23 times 10 means "23 groups of 10." Instead of counting out 23 rods, let's use flats and rods. Place 2 flats and 3 rods on the table. **10 tens equal 1 hundred, so 20 tens equal 200. How much do 23 tens equal?** *230.* Write 230 in both blanks.

20 tens   3 tens

$23 \times 10 =$ [230]

Have your child complete the other problems in part B. Model the problems with base-ten blocks as needed.

Your child may discover he can solve these problems by simply tacking a zero on to the number of tens. If he discovers this pattern on his own and understands why it occurs, it's fine for him to use it. Otherwise, simply encourage him to use place-value thinking and reason through the problems, since this mental effort will help him understand the place-value system more deeply. See the Unit 5 **Teaching Math with Confidence** for more on the connection between multiplying by tens and place value.

Activity (C): Pretend to Buy Supplies in Packs of 10

Show your child the shopping list. **Let's pretend we're buying snacks for a sports league. There are lots of kids in the league, so we'll need a lot of snacks! Each snack comes in a pack of 10.** Have your child write and complete a multiplication equation to match each quantity on the shopping list.

Independent Practice and Review

Have your child complete the Lesson 5.8 Practice and Review workbook pages.

Lesson 5.9
Multiply Tens, Part 2

Purpose	Materials
• Practice mentally multiplying numbers by 10 • Use place-value thinking to mentally multiply groups of tens	• Base-ten blocks • Counters

Memory Work	• **What do we call the result when we multiply two numbers?** *The product.* • **What do we call the result when we subtract a number from another number?** *The difference.* • **What do we call the result when we add two numbers?** *The sum.*

Warm-up: Practice Multiplying Numbers by 10

Have your child solve the following multiplication problems. Model them with base-ten blocks as needed.

- **8 times 10.** *80.*
- **10 times 10.** *100.*
- **18 times 10.** *180.*
- **20 times 10.** *200.*

- **25 times 10.** *250.*
- **28 times 10.** *280.*
- **30 times 10.** *300.*
- **32 times 10.** *320.*

Activity (A): Multiply Tens

In the last lesson, you learned how to multiply numbers times 10. Today, you'll learn how to mentally multiply numbers times groups of 10.

3 times 40 means "3 groups of 40." Place 3 groups of 4 rods on the table to match the diagram. **One way to find the answer is use repeated addition. What's 40 plus 40 plus 40?** *120.*

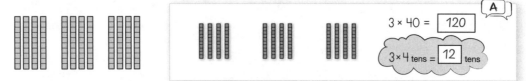

When you have a lot of groups, repeated addition takes a long time! Multiplication is faster. First, we multiply to find the number of tens. We have 3 groups. Each group has 4 tens. What's 3 times 4? *12.* **So, we have 12 tens.** Write 12 in the blank. **How much do 12 tens equal?** *120.* **So, 3 times 40 equals 120.**

> If your child finds the idea of finding the "number of tens" confusing, make the idea more concrete and ask her to find the "number of rods" instead.

Have your child complete part A. Encourage her to multiply to find the number of tens rather than using repeated addition. Model the exercises with base-ten blocks as needed.

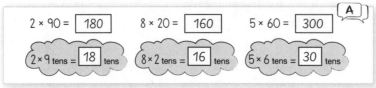

You may have learned to solve these problems with a procedural rule, such as, "Multiply the non-zero digits and then tack on the zero." If your child discovers this pattern on her own and understands why it occurs, it's fine for her to use it. Otherwise, simply encourage her to use place-value thinking to reason through the problems. See the Unit 5 **Teaching Math with Confidence** for more on how reasoning about multiplication and place value helps your child develop a deeper understanding of the place value system.

Activity (B): Play Four in a Row

Play Four in a Row. See Lesson 3.1 (page 85) for directions. Model the problems with base-ten blocks as needed.

One square in the game will not have a match (since the game board has an odd number of squares). When you discover this square, tell your child that it is a "stopper" and that neither player may play a counter on this square.

Independent Practice and Review

Have your child complete the Lesson 5.9 Practice and Review workbook pages.

Lesson 5.10
Enrichment (Optional)

Purpose	Materials
• Practice memory work • Introduce real-life estimation strategies • Estimate quantities • Summarize what your child has learned and assess your child's progress	• *Betcha! Estimating*, written by Stuart J. Murphy and illustrated by S. D. Schindler • 3 clear jars or bowls • 3 sets of small objects (such as crackers, blocks, or cotton balls) with 50-150 objects in each set

Warm-up: Review Memory Work

Quiz your child on all memory work introduced through Unit 5. See pages 527-528 for the full list.

Math Picture Book: *Betcha! Estimating*

Read *Betcha! Estimating*, written by Stuart J. Murphy and illustrated by S. D. Schindler. As you read, discuss the estimation strategies that the characters use and talk about how the estimates compare to the actual quantities.

> This book uses double-digit multiplication for one of the estimation situations. Your child is not expected to understand how to multiply double-digit numbers at this point.

Enrichment Activity: Estimation Jars

Put approximately 50-150 small objects in 3 clear jars or bowls.

Give every member of your family a chance to estimate how many objects are in each jar. Then, have your child count how many objects are in each jar and compare the estimates to the actual quantities.

Unit Wrap-up

Have your child complete the Unit 5 Wrap-up.

Unit 5 Answer Key

5.1 Practice

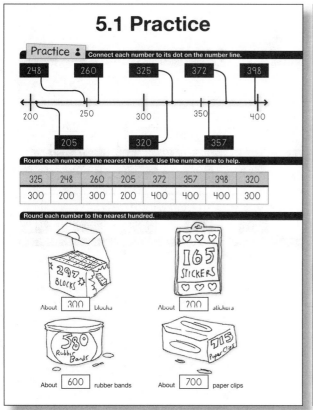

5.1 Review

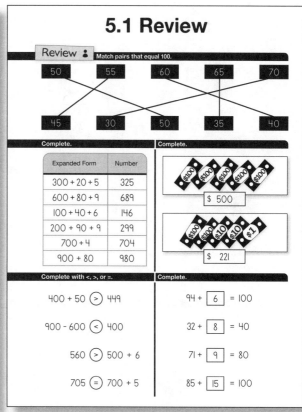

5.2 Practice

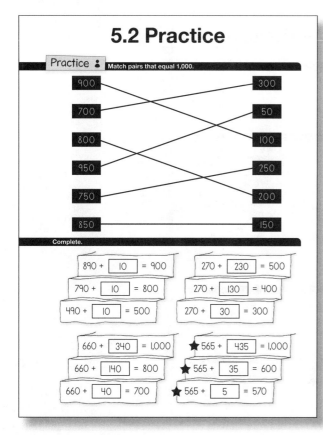

5.2 Review

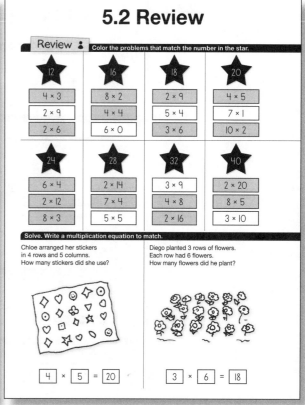

Unit 5 Answer Key

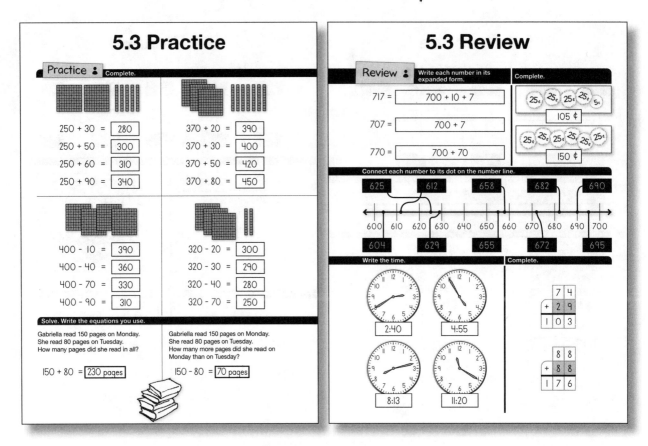

5.3 Practice

Practice · Complete.

250 + 30 = 280
250 + 50 = 300
250 + 60 = 310
250 + 90 = 340

370 + 20 = 390
370 + 30 = 400
370 + 50 = 420
370 + 80 = 450

400 - 10 = 390
400 - 40 = 360
400 - 70 = 330
400 - 90 = 310

320 - 20 = 300
320 - 30 = 290
320 - 40 = 280
320 - 70 = 250

Solve. Write the equations you use.

Gabriella read 150 pages on Monday. She read 80 pages on Tuesday. How many pages did she read in all?

150 + 80 = 230 pages

Gabriella read 150 pages on Monday. She read 80 pages on Tuesday. How many more pages did she read on Monday than on Tuesday?

150 - 80 = 70 pages

5.3 Review

Review · Write each number in its expanded form.

717 = 700 + 10 + 7
707 = 700 + 7
770 = 700 + 70

Complete.

105 ¢

150 ¢

Connect each number to its dot on the number line.

625   612   658   682   690

600 610 620 630 640 650 660 670 680 690 700

604   629   655   672   695

Write the time.

2:40   4:55

8:13   11:20

Complete.

```
  7 4
+ 2 9
1 0 3
```

```
  8 8
+ 8 8
1 7 6
```

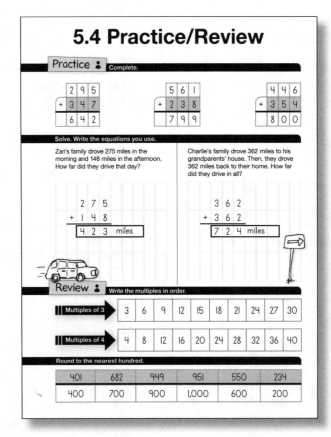

5.4 Practice/Review

Practice · Complete.

```
  2 9 5
+ 3 4 7
  6 4 2
```

```
  5 6 1
+ 2 3 8
  7 9 9
```

```
  4 4 6
+ 3 5 4
  8 0 0
```

Solve. Write the equations you use.

Zari's family drove 275 miles in the morning and 148 miles in the afternoon. How far did they drive that day?

```
  2 7 5
+ 1 4 8
  4 2 3  miles
```

Charlie's family drove 362 miles to his grandparents' house. Then, they drove 362 miles back to their home. How far did they drive in all?

```
  3 6 2
+ 3 6 2
  7 2 4  miles
```

Review · Write the multiples in order.

| Multiples of 3 | 3 | 6 | 9 | 12 | 15 | 18 | 21 | 24 | 27 | 30 |
| Multiples of 4 | 4 | 8 | 12 | 16 | 20 | 24 | 28 | 32 | 36 | 40 |

Round to the nearest hundred.

401	682	949	951	550	234
400	700	900	1,000	600	200

Unit 5 Answer Key

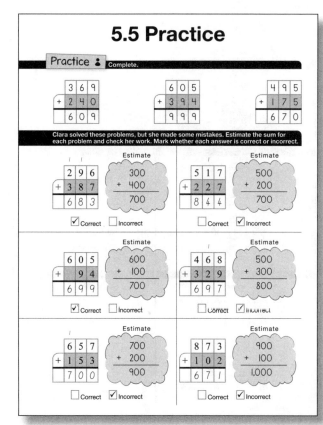

5.5 Practice

Practice Complete.

	3	6	9
+	2	4	0
	6	0	9

	6	0	5
+	3	9	4
	9	9	9

	4	9	5
+	1	7	5
	6	7	0

Clara solved these problems, but she made some mistakes. Estimate the sum for each problem and check her work. Mark whether each answer is correct or incorrect.

Estimate

	2	9	6
+	3	8	7
	6	8	3

300
+ 400
700

☑ Correct ☐ Incorrect

Estimate

	5	1	7
+	2	2	7
	8	4	4

500
+ 200
700

☐ Correct ☑ Incorrect

Estimate

	6	0	5
+		9	4
	6	9	9

600
+ 100
700

☑ Correct ☐ Incorrect

Estimate

	4	6	8
+	3	2	9
	6	9	7

500
+ 300
800

☐ Correct ☑ Incorrect

Estimate

	6	5	7
+	1	5	3
	7	0	0

700
+ 200
900

☐ Correct ☑ Incorrect

Estimate

	8	7	3
+	1	0	2
	6	7	1

900
+ 100
1,000

☐ Correct ☑ Incorrect

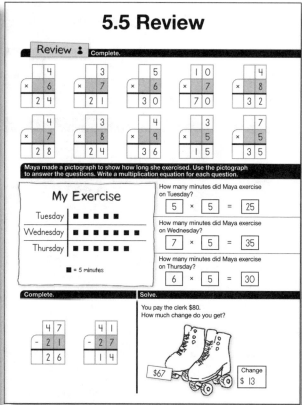

5.5 Review

Review Complete.

×		4	
		6	
	2	4	

×		3	
		7	
	2	1	

×		5	
		6	
	3	0	

×	1	0	
		7	
	7	0	

×		4	
		8	
	3	2	

×		4	
		7	
	2	8	

×		3	
		8	
	2	4	

×		4	
		9	
	3	6	

×		3	
		5	
	1	5	

×		7	
		5	
	3	5	

Maya made a pictograph to show how long she exercised. Use the pictograph to answer the questions. Write a multiplication equation for each question.

My Exercise

Tuesday	■ ■ ■ ■ ■
Wednesday	■ ■ ■ ■ ■ ■ ■
Thursday	■ ■ ■ ■ ■ ■

■ = 5 minutes

How many minutes did Maya exercise on Tuesday?

$5 \times 5 = 25$

How many minutes did Maya exercise on Wednesday?

$7 \times 5 = 35$

How many minutes did Maya exercise on Thursday?

$6 \times 5 = 30$

Complete.

	4	7
-	2	1
	2	6

	4	1
-	2	7
	1	4

Solve.

You pay the clerk $80.
How much change do you get?

$67

Change
$ 13

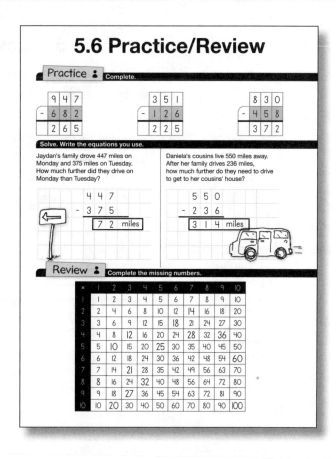

5.6 Practice/Review

Practice Complete.

	9	4	7
-	6	8	2
	2	6	5

	3	5	1
-	1	2	6
	2	2	5

	8	3	0
-	4	5	8
	3	7	2

Solve. Write the equations you use.

Jaydan's family drove 447 miles on Monday and 375 miles on Tuesday. How much further did they drive on Monday than Tuesday?

	4	4	7
-	3	7	5
		7	2	miles

Daniela's cousins live 550 miles away. After her family drives 236 miles, how much further do they need to drive to get to her cousins' house?

	5	5	0
-	2	3	6
	3	1	4	miles

Review Complete the missing numbers.

×	1	2	3	4	5	6	7	8	9	10
1	1	2	3	4	5	6	7	8	9	10
2	2	4	6	8	10	12	14	16	18	20
3	3	6	9	12	15	18	21	24	27	30
4	4	8	12	16	20	24	28	32	36	40
5	5	10	15	20	25	30	35	40	45	50
6	6	12	18	24	30	36	42	48	54	60
7	7	14	21	28	35	42	49	56	63	70
8	8	16	24	32	40	48	56	64	72	80
9	9	18	27	36	45	54	63	72	81	90
10	10	20	30	40	50	60	70	80	90	100

Unit 5 Answer Key

5.7 Practice

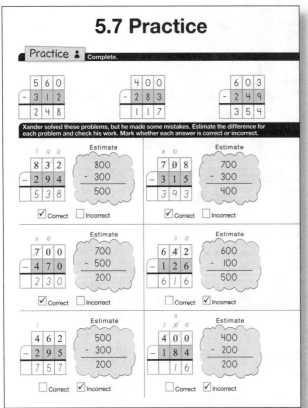

Practice 👤 Complete.

5 6 0 − 3 1 2 **2 4 8**	4 0 0 − 2 8 3 **1 1 7**	6 0 3 − 2 4 9 **3 5 4**

Xander solved these problems, but he made some mistakes. Estimate the difference for each problem and check his work. Mark whether each answer is correct or incorrect.

⁷ ¹² ¹²
8 3 2
− 2 9 4
5 3 8

Estimate
800
− 300
500

☑ Correct ☐ Incorrect

⁶ ¹⁰
7 0 8
− 3 1 5
3 9 3

Estimate
700
− 300
400

☑ Correct ☐ Incorrect

⁶ ¹⁰
7 0 0
− 4 7 0
2 3 0

Estimate
700
− 500
200

☑ Correct ☐ Incorrect

³ ¹²
6 4 2
− 1 2 6
6 1 6

Estimate
600
− 100
500

☐ Correct ☑ Incorrect

¹
4 6 2
− 2 9 5
7 5 7

Estimate
500
− 300
200

☐ Correct ☑ Incorrect

³ ⁹ ¹⁰
4 0 0
− 1 8 4
1 6

Estimate
400
− 200
200

☐ Correct ☑ Incorrect

5.7 Review

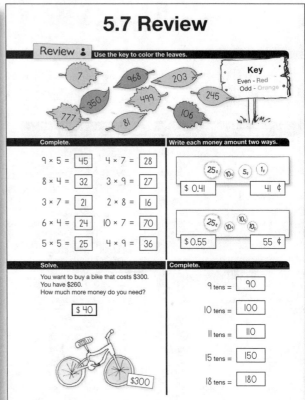

Review 👤 Use the key to color the leaves.

7   968   203   350   499   245   777   81   106

Key
Even - Red
Odd - Orange

Complete.

$9 \times 5 = 45$ $4 \times 7 = 28$
$8 \times 4 = 32$ $3 \times 9 = 27$
$3 \times 7 = 21$ $2 \times 8 = 16$
$6 \times 4 = 24$ $10 \times 7 = 70$
$5 \times 5 = 25$ $4 \times 9 = 36$

Write each money amount two ways.

25¢ 10¢ 5¢ 1¢
$ 0.41   41 ¢

25¢ 10¢ 10¢ 10¢
$ 0.55   55 ¢

Solve.
You want to buy a bike that costs $300.
You have $260.
How much more money do you need?

$ 40

Complete.
9 tens = 90
10 tens = 100
11 tens = 110
15 tens = 150
18 tens = 180

5.8 Practice

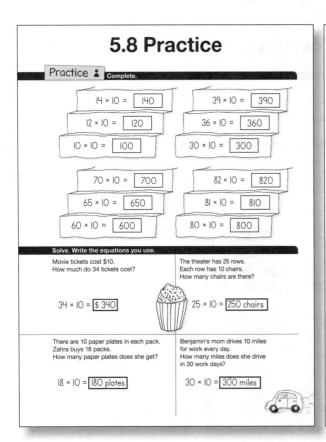

Practice 👤 Complete.

$14 \times 10 = 140$ $39 \times 10 = 390$
$12 \times 10 = 120$ $36 \times 10 = 360$
$10 \times 10 = 100$ $30 \times 10 = 300$

$70 \times 10 = 700$ $82 \times 10 = 820$
$65 \times 10 = 650$ $81 \times 10 = 810$
$60 \times 10 = 600$ $80 \times 10 = 800$

Solve. Write the equations you use.

Movie tickets cost $10.
How much do 34 tickets cost?

$34 \times 10 = $ $ 340$

The theater has 25 rows.
Each row has 10 chairs.
How many chairs are there?

$25 \times 10 = 250$ chairs

There are 10 paper plates in each pack.
Zahra buys 18 packs.
How many paper plates does she get?

$18 \times 10 = 180$ plates

Benjamin's mom drives 10 miles
for work every day.
How many miles does she drive
in 30 work days?

$30 \times 10 = 300$ miles

5.8 Review

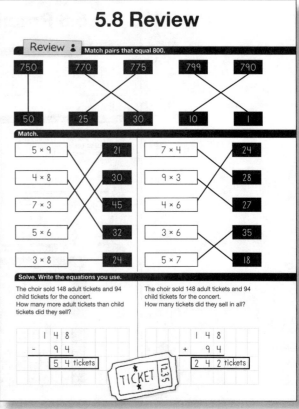

Review 👤 Match pairs that equal 800.

750   770   775   799   790

50   25   30   10   1

Match.

5×9 21
4×8 30
7×3 45
5×6 32
3×8 24

7×4 24
9×3 28
4×6 27
3×6 35
5×7 18

Solve. Write the equations you use.

The choir sold 148 adult tickets and 94
child tickets for the concert.
How many more adult tickets than child
tickets did they sell?

1 4 8
− 9 4
5 4 tickets

The choir sold 148 adult tickets and 94
child tickets for the concert.
How many tickets did they sell in all?

1 4 8
+ 9 4
2 4 2 tickets

TICKET
12.35

Unit 5 Answer Key

5.9 Practice

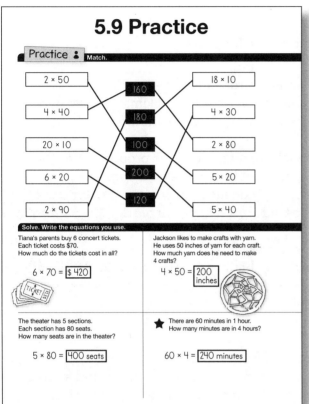

5.9 Review

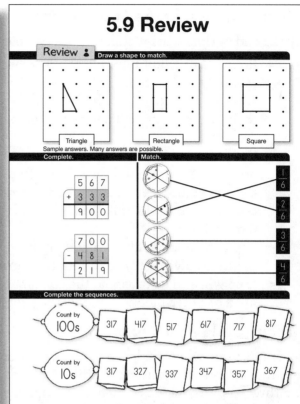

5.10 Unit Wrap-Up A

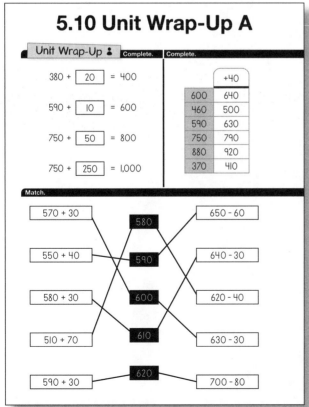

5.10 Unit Wrap-Up B

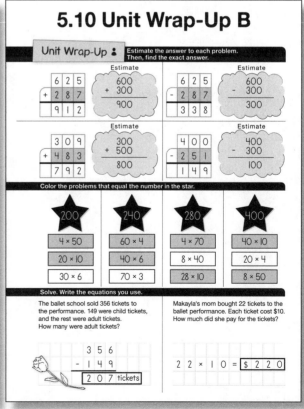

Unit 5 Checkpoint

What to Expect at the End of Unit 5

By the end of Unit 5, most children will be able to do the following:

- Round three-digit numbers to the nearest hundred.
- Mentally add up to identify missing addends in problems like 560 + ___ = 600 or 780 + ___ = 1,000. Many children will be able to solve these problems completely in their heads. Some will need base-ten blocks, especially when finding a missing addend to 1,000.
- Use place-value thinking and base-ten blocks to mentally solve problems like 380 + 50 or 410 – 30. Most children will still find these problems quite challenging.
- Use the addition and subtraction algorithms to add and subtract three-digit numbers. Some children will still need to model the trades with base-ten blocks when subtracting across zero.
- Use estimation to check whether answers are reasonable.
- Begin to solve mental multiplication problems that involve groups of 10. Some children will still be grasping the concept of multiplying groups of tens, and they may need base-ten blocks to model the problems.

Is Your Child Ready to Move on?

In Unit 6, your child will learn to compare fractions, find equivalent fractions, and add and subtract simple fractions. Your child does not need to have mastered adding and subtracting three-digit numbers or mental multiplication with tens before moving on to Unit 6.

Unit 6
Fractions

Overview

In Unit 6, your child will study fractions. First, he'll review how to read and write fractions. Then, he'll learn how to add and subtract fractions with the same denominator, find simple equivalent fractions, and compare fractions. You'll also introduce him to mixed numbers.

The activities in this unit are very concrete, and your child will use hands-on materials and pictures throughout the unit to make sense of fractions. In fourth grade, he'll reason about fractions more abstractly and learn step-by-step fraction arithmetic techniques.

What Your Child Will Learn

In this unit, your child will learn to:

- Read and write fractions to match pictures and hands-on materials
- Identify the numerator and denominator in fractions and understand what each number means
- Add and subtract fractions with the same denominator
- Use pictures and hands-on materials to find equivalent fractions, including fractions equal to 1/2 or 1 whole
- Compare fractions by reasoning about the numerator and denominator or by comparing the fractions to 1/2
- Write mixed numbers to match pictures or hands-on materials

Lesson List

Lesson 6.1   Understand Fractional Parts   Lesson 6.6   Equivalent Fractions, Part 1
Lesson 6.2   Read and Write Fractions   Lesson 6.7   Equivalent Fractions, Part 2
Lesson 6.3   Fractions Equal to One Whole   Lesson 6.8   Compare Fractions, Part 1
Lesson 6.4   Add Fractions   Lesson 6.9   Compare Fractions, Part 2
Lesson 6.5   Subtract Fractions   Lesson 6.10   Mixed Numbers
                                               Lesson 6.11   Enrichment (Optional)

Extra Materials Needed for Unit 6

- Markers or colored pencils
- Paper clip
- 4 sheets of paper
- Measuring cups (1/4-cup, 1/3-cup, 1/2-cup, and 1-cup)
- Water
- For optional Enrichment Lesson:
    × *Fraction Action*, written and illustrated by Loreen Leedy. Holiday House, 1994.
    × Ingredients for pumpkin bread or another recipe. See the recipe in Lesson 6.11 (page 204) for suggested ingredients.

Teaching Math with Confidence:
How to Help Your Child Confidently Understand Fractions

Many children and adults have much more trouble understanding fractions than whole numbers. That's because fractions pose a more demanding cognitive challenge than whole numbers. When you read a whole number, you only have to process one number. The one number conveys the overall value of the quantity.

3 apples

The number 3 tells you the quantity of apples all on its own.

When you read a fraction, you have to process two numbers: the numerator and the denominator. Neither number on its own tells you the value of the fraction. It's the relationship between the two numbers that determines the fraction's value.

$\dfrac{3}{8}$

You need to take both the 3 and the 8 into account to understand how much pizza there is.
On their own, neither the 3 nor the 8 tell the amount of pizza.

You may have learned an "x out of y parts" definition for fractions (for example, that 3/8 means "3 out of 8 parts"). This definition makes fractions even more difficult for children to understand, because they cannot see all the "parts" in many real-life fraction situations. For example, in the above picture, all you see is 3 pieces of pizza. There's no visual reference for the 8.

Math with Confidence uses a different fraction definition to make fractions easier for children to process and understand. You'll teach your child that the numerator (top number) tells how many fractional parts there are. The denominator (bottom number) tells how many equal parts the whole was split into, so it tells the kind of fractional parts in question.

For example, say you have 3/8 of a pizza. The "3" tells that there are 3 fractional parts of the pizza. The "8" tells that the pizza was split into 8 equal parts, so each equal part is an eighth.

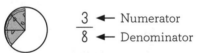

$\dfrac{3}{8}$ ← Numerator
    ← Denominator

This definition helps your child interpret fractions the same way he interprets whole numbers. With this definition, the numerator tells the quantity of parts. The denominator simply tells the kind of parts, or the unit. Just as 3 apples means "3 of the units called apples," 3/8 means "3 of the units called eighths."

3 apples

quantity unit

$\dfrac{3}{8}$ ← quantity
    ← unit

This definition also proves especially helpful as children learn to add and subtract fractions. Your child will learn in Lessons 6.4 and 6.5 that he can simply add and subtract the fractional parts just like whole numbers.

As your child gets older, he'll learn there are other ways to interpret fractions as well. (For example, you can think of a fraction as a number on the number line, or as the numerator divided by the denominator.) For now, focus on helping him understand this concrete definition of the numerator and denominator.

Since this definition is rooted in counting fractional pieces, it will help him use what he knows about whole numbers to make sense of fractions. It will also help reduce the cognitive load required to understand fractions. Once he has this solid, real-world understanding of the numerator and denominator, he'll be ready to reason about fractions more abstractly and learn the algorithms for fraction arithmetic in future grades.

Lesson 6.1
Understand Fractional Parts

Purpose	Materials
• Practice ×3 facts • Review the names of fractional parts and divide shapes into these parts • Understand that fractional parts don't have to look identical	• 2 decks of playing cards • Counters

Memory Work
- **How many minutes equal a half-hour?** *30.*
- **How many minutes equal a quarter-hour?** *15.*

Warm-up (A): Escape the Maze (×3)

Play Escape the Maze.

Escape the Maze (×3)

Materials: 5s, 6s, 7s, 8s, and 9s from 2 decks of playing cards (40 cards total); counters

Object of the Game: Reach your End square before the other player reaches theirs.

Shuffle the cards and place the stack face down on the table. Decide which player will go first. Each player chooses a counter to use as a game token and places it on their Start square.

On your turn, flip over the top card. Multiply the number by 3 and say the product. For example, if you draw a 7: "3 times 7 equals 21." If your counter is connected to a square with 21, you may move your counter to that square.

For example, if Player 1 draws a 7 on her first turn, she may move her counter to the 21. If she draws a 9 for her first turn, she may move to the 27. Or, if she draws a 6, she may move to the 18. But, if she draws a 5 or 8, she may not move and skips her turn (since 15 and 24 are not adjacent to her current position).

You may only move to squares that are adjacent to your current position. You may also choose not to move. (This is a good strategy if moving would take you farther from your end square.) Take turns drawing cards and moving the counters until one player lands on their End square.

Cooperative Variation: Play together with just one counter. Place the counter on the Player 1 starting square. Choose one of the following challenge levels and see if you can escape the maze in the corresponding number of turns.

- Math Master: 12 turns
- Math Whiz: 10 turns
- Math Superstar: 8 turns

Activity (B): Discuss Real-Life Examples of Fractions

We're starting a new unit on fractions today! What do you remember about fractions from last year? *Answers will vary.*

Here are some ways we use fractions in real life. Discuss each picture with your child.

- **We use fractions to measure ingredients for recipes. This recipe says to use one and one-half cups of flour and three-fourths of a cup of sugar.**
- **Composers use fractions to tell musicians how long to hold their notes. The note with an empty middle is called a half note, and the note with a colored middle and flag at the top is called an eighth note.**
- **When the minute hand goes halfway around the clock, 30 minutes has passed. We call 30 minutes a half-hour.**
- **We often use fractions to describe lengths. This sign says that the nature trail is two and a half miles long.**

Your child will learn how to read and write fractions in Lesson 6.2, so you do not need to explain how to read and understand the sample fractions.

Activity (C): Divide Rectangles into Fractional Parts

Today, we'll review how to split shapes into fractional parts. Let's pretend that you and I want to share the first chocolate bar equally. When we split the whole bar into 2 equal parts, we call the parts halves. Have your child draw a line to split the chocolate bar into 2 equal pieces.

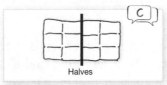

There are many ways to split the chocolate bar into 2 equal parts. Accept any answer as long as each part contains an equal number of smaller squares.

Have your child draw lines to split the rest of the chocolate bars into the fractional parts listed.

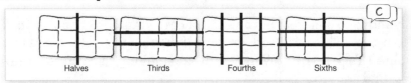

Sample answers. There are many different ways to divide the fractions into the fractional parts.

Activity (D): Identify Fourths

Fractional parts don't have to all look the same, but they must be equal to each other. Let's see which of these chocolate bars are divided into fourths.

Is the first bar divided into four parts? *Yes.* **Are all the parts equal to each other?** *Yes.* **How do you know?** *Sample answer: Each part has 3 small squares.* **So, this chocolate bar is divided into fourths.** Circle the chocolate bar.

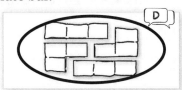

Is the next bar divided into four parts? *Yes.* **Are all the parts equal to each other?** *No.* **How do you know?** *Sample answer: One part has 4 small squares, one part has 2 squares, and the other parts have 3 squares.* **So, this chocolate bar is not divided into fourths.** X the chocolate bar.

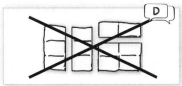

Discuss the rest of the chocolate bars in the same way with your child. Circle the bars that are cut into fourths, and X the bars that are not cut into fourths.

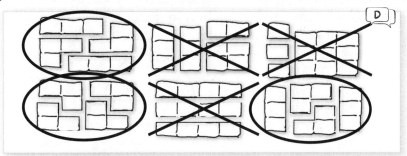

X the bar that is cut into 3 equal pieces, since it is cut into thirds instead of fourths.

Independent Practice and Review

Have your child complete the Lesson 6.1 Practice and Review workbook pages.

Lesson 6.2
Read and Write Fractions

Purpose	Materials
• Practice identifying fractional parts of circles • Draw lines to split circles into fractional parts • Identify the numerator and denominator in a fraction and understand what each number means • Read and write fractions	• Fraction circles • Markers or colored pencils

Memory Work · **Name the multiples of 4 in order.** *4, 8, 12...* Stop your child when he reaches 40.

You will need fraction circles for the first time in this lesson. If you do not have plastic or wooden fraction circles, use the paper fraction circles on Blackline Master 7 instead.

If your fraction circles have fractions printed on one side, flip the circles over so that only the blank side shows. If they have fractions printed on both sides, cover the fractions with a small piece of masking tape.

Warm-up: Introduce Fraction Circles

In the last lesson, we split rectangles into fractional parts. We can also split other shapes into fractional parts. Show your child the following fraction circles and organize them as shown. Have your child tell what fractional parts each circle is split into.

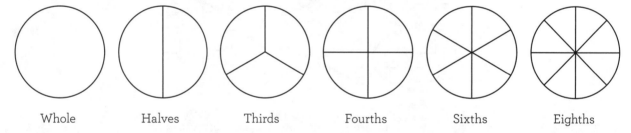

Whole   Halves   Thirds   Fourths   Sixths   Eighths

You will only need halves, thirds, fourths, sixths, eighths, and one whole circle for this unit.

With your child, spend a few minutes comparing the sizes of the pieces and finding combinations of pieces that equal other pieces. For example: **Which piece is biggest? Which piece is smallest? How many fourths does it take to make a half?**

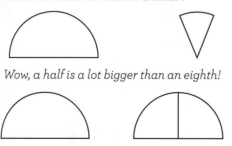

Wow, a half is a lot bigger than an eighth!

If I put 2 fourths together, they make a half.

Activity (A): Draw Lines to Split Circles into Fractional Parts

Today, we'll pretend we work at the Fraction Diner. At the Fraction Diner, customers can order their pancakes cut into fractional parts. They can also ask for different toppings on each part!

We'll need to draw fractional parts on some of the pancakes. Drawing fractional parts for circles can be tricky, so let's practice first. Have your child trace the lines on the circles in part A and split each circle into fractional parts.

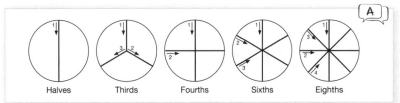

Without guidance, children often draw haphazard lines that come from the center of the circle like spokes in a wheel. Always encourage your child to use this sequence of strokes so that the parts turn out roughly equal to each other.

Activity (B): Introduce Numerator and Denominator

The first customer asked to have his pancake cut into fourths. He asked for chocolate chips on one-fourth of the pancake and blueberries on three-fourths of the pancake.

Point to the 1 in 1/4. **The top number tells the number of parts. It's called the** *numerator.* **Do you hear how numerator starts like the word number? That's because it tells the number of parts.**

Point to the 4 in 1/4. **The bottom number tells how many equal parts the whole was split into. It's called the** *denominator.* **It comes from a Latin word that means to name something. That's because it names what kind of parts the whole was split into, like fourths, halves, or sixths.**

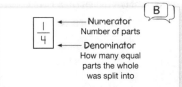

See the Unit 6 **Teaching Math with Confidence** to learn how this definition of fractions helps reduce the cognitive load required to understand fractions.

When you read fractions, always point to the corresponding numbers as you name them. For example, when you say "one-fourth," point to the 1 as you say "one" and the 4 as you say "fourth." This reinforces the idea that the top number in a fraction tells the quantity of parts, while the bottom number tells the kind of parts.

Point to 3/4 on the guest check. **We read this fraction as three-fourths. The customer wants 3 parts to have blueberries, so the numerator is 3. The pancake was split into 4 equal parts, so the denominator is 4.**

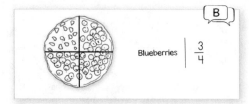

Activity (C): Read Fractions at the Fraction Diner

Time to put toppings on some pancakes! This customer wants strawberries on one-eighth of her pancake. She wants chocolate chips on seven-eighths of her pancake. Have your child find the fraction circle divided into eighths. Have him pretend to put strawberries on one-eighth and chocolate chips on the other seven-eighths.

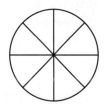
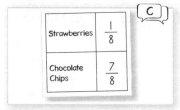

Now, let's color the pancake on the workbook page to match.

- **First, draw lines to split the pancake into eighths.** Have your child draw lines that split the pancake into eighths.
- **Next, draw red dots on one-eighth of the pancake to stand for the strawberries.** Have your child use a red crayon or colored pencil to draw dots on one-eighth of the circle.
- **Last, draw brown dots on seven-eighths of the pancake to stand for the chocolate chips.** Have your child use a brown crayon or colored pencil to draw brown dots on seven-eighths of the circle.

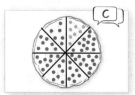

Looks delicious! Repeat this process with the other pancake orders. Have your child draw yellow circles to represent bananas and blue dots to represent blueberries.

Activity (D): Write Fractions for Pancake Toppings

Now, you get to be the server and write down the orders! Point to the first pancake in part D. **How many parts of the pancake have blueberries?** *5.* **How many parts was the whole pancake split into?** *6.* **So, each part of the pancake is a sixth. Five-sixths of the pancake has blueberries.** Have your child write 5/6 in the blank.

How many parts of the pancake have strawberries? *1.* **How many parts was the whole pancake split into?** *6.* **One-sixth of the pancake has strawberries.** Have your child write 1/6 in the blank.

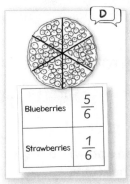

The fraction blanks in this book always have a horizontal line (and not a diagonal one) so your child can easily see which number is on top and which number is on the bottom.

Have your child complete the other guest checks in the same way.

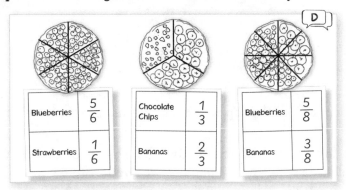

Independent Practice and Review

Have your child complete the Lesson 6.2 Practice and Review workbook pages.

Your child may notice some equivalent fractions as he completes the Practice workbook page. (For example, he may notice 3/6 is the same as 1/2 of a waffle.) Have him write the fraction that best matches the parts shown on the page. He'll learn about equivalent fractions in Lesson 6.6.

Lesson 6.3
Fractions Equal to One Whole

Purpose	Materials
• Practice writing fractions • Understand that fractions equal to one whole have a numerator that is the same as the denominator • Find pairs of fractions equal to one whole	• Fraction circles

Memory Work
- **What do we call the numbers in a multiplication equation that we multiply together?** *Factors.*
- **What do we call the result when we multiply two numbers?** *The product.*

Warm-up (A): Practice Writing Fractions

In the last lesson, you learned to read and write fractions. You also learned special names for the top and bottom numbers in fractions.

How many pieces of the first pizza are left? *5.* **How many pieces was the whole pizza cut into?** *6.* **So, each piece is one-sixth of the pizza. What fraction of the pizza is left?** *Five-sixths.* **Write 5/6 in the blank.**

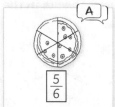

Point to the 5. What do we call the top number? *The numerator.* **It tells the number of parts. There are 5 parts.**

Point to the 6. What do we call the bottom number? *The denominator.* **It tells how many equal parts the whole was split into. This pizza was split into 6 equal parts.**

If your child has trouble pronouncing these long words, clap out the syllables for each word: **Nu-mer-a-tor. De-nom-i-na-tor.** Being able to pronounce math vocabulary helps builds children's confidence that they can understand and apply the concepts that these intimidating words represent.

Have your child write fractions to match the other pizzas.

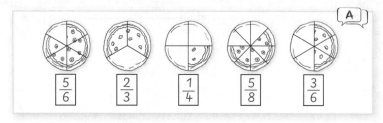

Activity (B): Write Fractions for One Whole

Today, you'll learn about fractions equal to one whole. Have your child model the first pizza in part B with fraction circles. **How many pieces of pizza are there?** *4.* **How many pieces was the whole pizza cut into?** *4.* **So, what fraction of the pizza is shown?** *Four-fourths.* Write 4/4 in the blank. Repeat with the rest of the pizzas. Have your child model each pizza with fraction circles as well.

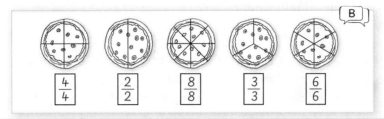

Representing the fractions with fraction circles allows your child to kinesthetically feel how the pieces come together to form one whole.

Use the following questions to discuss the pizzas:

- **What do all these pizzas have in common?** *Sample answers: They're all the same size and shape.*
- **How are these pizzas different from each other?** *They're cut into different fractional parts.*
- **If you were going to choose one of these pizzas to buy, which one would you choose?** *Sample answers: I'd choose the one cut into halves, so I could have really big pieces! I'd choose the one cut into eighths, so I could share the pizza with a lot of people. I'd choose the one cut into sixths, so each person in our family could have 1 piece.*

The purpose of this question is to nudge your child to think about the real-life implications of different fractional parts. Accept any reasonable answer.

What do you notice about the numerator and denominator in these fractions? *In each fraction, the numerator and denominator are the same.*

When the numerator and denominator are equal, it means that you split the pizza into a certain number of fractional parts and still have all of them. If the numerator and denominator are the same, the fraction is equal to one whole.

Activity (C): Play Fraction Four in a Row

We're going to play Fraction Four in a Row today. We'll match pairs of fractions that equal one whole.

Let's pretend I chose 5/6 as my first fraction. Place the fraction circle split into sixths on the table. Separate the circle into 5/6 and 1/6 as shown. **Five-sixths and one-sixth equal six-sixths, so the matching fraction is one-sixth.**

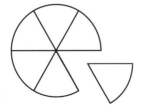

Play Four in a Row. Keep the fraction circles available for your child to use to find the pairs.

Fraction Four in a Row

Materials: 20 counters per player, with a different color for each player

Object of the Game: Be the first player to place counters in 4 squares in a row, either horizontally, vertically, or diagonally.

On your turn, choose a pair of fractions that equal one whole. Your fractions must have the same denominator. Cover both fractions with a counter. For example, you could choose 3/4 and 1/4, since 3/4 and 1/4 equal one whole.

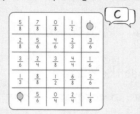

Play then passes to the other player. Continue until one player covers 4 boxes in a row, either horizontally, vertically, or diagonally.

One square in the game does not have a match (since the game board has an odd number of squares). When you discover this fraction, tell your child that it is a "stopper" and that neither player may play a counter on this square.

This activity previews adding fractions. Your child will learn to add fractions with the same denominator in Lesson 6.4.

Independent Practice and Review

Have your child complete the Lesson 6.3 Practice and Review workbook pages.

Lesson 6.4
Add Fractions

Purpose	Materials
• Use hands-on materials to add fractions with the same denominator • Add fractions with the same denominator	• Fraction circles • Paper • Paper clip

Memory Work	
	• **What do we call the top number in a fraction?** *The numerator.* • **What does the numerator tell?** *The number of parts.* • **What do we call the bottom number in a fraction?** *The denominator.* • **What does the denominator tell?** *How many equal parts the whole was split into.*

You may have learned how to add fractions with a rule such as "Add the top numbers and keep the bottom number the same." Teaching this rule without focusing on the underlying fraction concepts prevents your child from developing deeper number sense with fractions. So, give your child time to logically think through the problems in this lesson, and don't tell him a rule for adding fractions with the same denominator. If he discovers this pattern on his own and understands why it occurs, it's fine for him to use it.

Warm-up: Add Fractions with Fraction Circles

Several of the lessons in this unit begin with informal fraction circle activities that preview the concept covered in the lesson. This gives your child concrete, hands-on experience with the new concept before he applies it to written fractions.

Organize the fraction circles as shown.

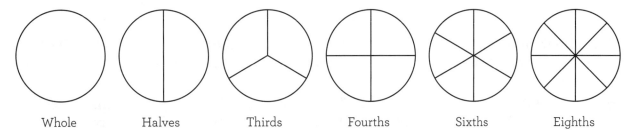

| Whole | Halves | Thirds | Fourths | Sixths | Eighths |

I have two-eighths of a cake. Slide 2 eighths under a piece of paper.

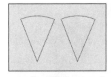

Then, I get three-eighths more. How much of the cake do I have now? *Five-eighths.* If your child is not sure, encourage him to visualize the pieces under the paper to find the answer. After your child tells you the answer, remove the paper so he can check his answer.

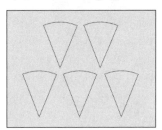

Repeat with the following amounts. Model each problem with fraction circles. Hide the fraction circles under the paper and reveal them after your child tells the sum.

- **I have one-sixth of a cake. Then, I get one-sixth more. How much of the cake do I have now?** *Two-sixths.*
- **I have one-third of a cake. Then, I get two-thirds more. How much of the cake do I have now?** *Three-thirds, or one whole cake.*
- **I have one-fourth of a cake. Then, I get one-fourth more. How much of the cake do I have now?** *Two-fourths.*
- **I have three-eighths of a cake. Then, I get four-eighths more. How much of the cake do I have now?** *Seven-eighths.*

Activity (A): Add Fractions with the Same Denominator

Numbers like 1, 2, and 3 are called whole numbers, because they stand for whole things. You can use what you know about adding whole numbers to add fractions, too.

What does 1 apple plus 2 apples equal? *3 apples.* **Write 3 in the blank.**

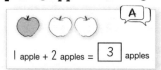

Point to the fraction addition problem and read it aloud: ***One-fourth plus two-fourths.*** **What does one-fourth plus two-fourths equal?** *Three-fourths.* **Write 3 in the blank. Just like 1 apple plus 2 apples equal 3 apples, 1 fourth plus 2 fourths equal 3 fourths.** Have your child write 3/4 in the blank.

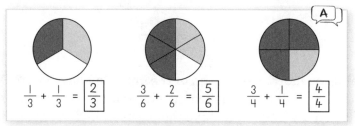

When fractions have the same denominator, you can add the fractional parts just like whole numbers. When you're older, you'll learn how to add fractions with different denominators.

Have your child complete part A. Read each equation aloud. Encourage your child to use what he knows about whole-number addition to help find the answers. For example, for 3/6 + 2/6: **You know 3 pencils plus 2 pencils equal 5 pencils. So, what does 3 sixths plus 2 sixths equal?** *5 sixths.*

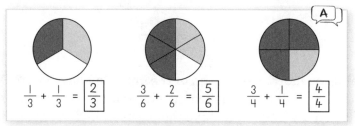

Activity (B): Play Spin a Pizza

Play Spin a Pizza. If needed, model the addition problems with fraction circles to help your child find the sums.

Spin a Pizza

Materials: Paper clip

Object of the Game: Win the most points.

Place one end of the paper clip in the center of the spinner on the game board. Place the point of a pencil through the paper clip so that it touches the very center of the circle.

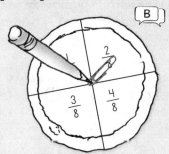

On your turn, hold the pencil upright and spin the paper clip so that it spins freely around the circle. Write the fraction it lands on in the first box on your scorecard. Spin again and write this fraction in the next box. Add to find the sum of the two fractions. For example, if you spin 1/8 and 4/8:

Then, the other player spins twice, writes the two fractions on his scorecard, and finds their sum. Whoever has the greater sum wins a point.

Continue until you complete the score cards. Whoever wins more points wins the game.

This game requires simple fraction comparisons with eighths. If your child has trouble with any of the comparisons, model them with fraction circles. He will learn more about comparing fractions in Lessons 6.8 and 6.9.

Independent Practice and Review

Have your child complete the Lesson 6.4 Practice and Review workbook pages.

Lesson 6.5
Subtract Fractions

Purpose	Materials
• Use hands-on materials to subtract fractions from one whole • Subtract fractions with the same denominator	• Fraction circles • Counters • Die

Memory Work
- **What do we call the top number in a fraction?** *The numerator.*
- **What does the numerator tell?** *The number of parts.*
- **What do we call the bottom number in a fraction?** *The denominator.*
- **What does the denominator tell?** *How many equal parts the whole was split into.*

In the last lesson, your child used fraction circles to add fractions with the same denominator. In this lesson, she'll use the same approach to subtract fractions with the same denominator. As in Lesson 6.4, give your child plenty of time to logically think through the problems, and don't tell her a rule for completing the problems.

Warm-up: Subtract from One Whole with Fraction Circles

Let's pretend the fraction circles are pizzas. Ask your child the following questions. Use the fraction circles to model the questions.

- Arrange 2 halves in a circle. **If I eat one-half of a pizza, how much is left?** *One-half.* Remove 1 half.

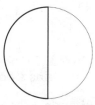

- Arrange 8 eighths in a circle. **If I eat three-eighths of a pizza, how much is left?** *Five-eighths.* Remove 3 eighths.
- Arrange 4 fourths in a circle. **If I eat three-fourths of the pizza, how much is left?** *One-fourth.* Remove 3 fourths.
- Arrange 3 thirds in a circle. **If I eat two-thirds of a pizza, how much is left?** *One-third.* Remove 1 third.
- Arrange 6 sixths in a circle. **If I eat five-sixths of a pizza, how much is left?** *One-sixth.* Remove 5 sixths.
- Arrange 6 sixths in a circle. **If I eat zero-sixths of a pizza, how much is left?** *Possible answers: All of it! Six-sixths. One whole.*
- Arrange 6 sixths in a circle. **If I eat six-sixths of a pizza, how much is left?** *Possible answers: None! Zero-sixths.* Remove 6 sixths.

Activity (A): Subtract Fractions with the Same Denominator

In the last lesson, you learned to add fractions with the same denominator. Today, you'll learn to subtract fractions with the same denominator.

You can use what you know about subtracting whole numbers to subtract fractions. What does 3 apples minus 1 apple equal? *2 apples.* Write 2 in the blank.

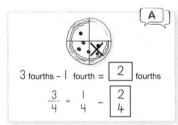

Point to the fraction subtraction problem and read it aloud: ***Three-fourths minus one-fourth. What does three-fourths minus one-fourth equal?*** *Two-fourths.* Write 2 in the blank. **Just like 3 apples minus 1 apple equals 2 apples, 3 fourths minus 1 fourth equals 2 fourths.** Have your child write 2/4 in the blank.

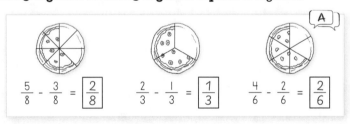

When fractions have the same denominator, you can subtract the fractional parts just like whole numbers. When you're older, you'll learn how to subtract fractions with different denominators.

Have your child solve the rest of the problems in part A in the same way. Read each equation aloud. Encourage your child to use what she knows about whole-number subtraction to help find the answers. For example, for 5/8 – 3/8: **You know 5 pencils minus 3 pencils equals 2 pencils. So, what does 5 eighths minus 3 eighths equal?** *2 eighths.*

$$\frac{5}{8} - \frac{3}{8} = \boxed{\frac{2}{8}} \qquad \frac{2}{3} - \frac{1}{3} = \boxed{\frac{1}{3}} \qquad \frac{4}{6} - \frac{2}{6} = \boxed{\frac{2}{6}}$$

Activity (B): Play Treasure Hunt

Play Treasure Hunt. Model the problems with fraction circles as needed.

Treasure Hunt

Materials: Counters; die

Object of the Game: Win the most counters.

Have each player choose a different-colored counter to use as a game token and place it on one of the Start circles. Place 12 counters in a pile next to the game board. These counters are the treasure chest.

On your turn, roll the die and advance your token the corresponding number of circles clockwise around the path.

- If you land on a circle with a math problem, say the answer to the problem and take 1 counter from the treasure chest.
- If you land on a circle with directions, follow the directions. If you gain treasure, take it from the treasure chest. If you lose treasure, put it back in the treasure chest.
- If you land on a Start circle, roll again.

Play until all of the counters are gone from the treasure chest. The player who has more counters from the treasure chest wins the game.

Independent Practice and Review

Have your child complete the Lesson 6.5 Practice and Review workbook pages.

Lesson 6.6
Equivalent Fractions, Part 1

Purpose	Materials
• Practice ×4 facts • Understand that fractions with different numerators and different denominators can have the same value • Identify pairs of equivalent fractions	• Playing cards • Counters • Fraction circles

Memory Work	
	• **What do we call the top number in a fraction?** *The numerator.* • **What does the numerator tell?** *The number of parts.* • **What do we call the bottom number in a fraction?** *The denominator.* • **What does the denominator tell?** *How many equal parts the whole was split into.*

Warm-up (A): Play Multiplication Crash (×4)

Play Multiplication Crash. See Lesson 4.4 (page 124) for full directions.

Activity (B): Identify Equivalent Fractions at the Fraction Diner

In the last two lessons, you learned how to add and subtract fractions. Today, we're going back to the Fraction Diner to learn about fractions that are equal to each other.

One day, the chef was preparing two pancake orders when he noticed something interesting. The pancakes were cut in different ways, but both pancakes had the same amount covered with bananas! Have your child write a fraction to match each pancake.

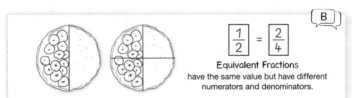

$$\frac{1}{2} = \frac{2}{4}$$

Equivalent Fractions have the same value but have different numerators and denominators.

What do both the pancakes have in common? *They both have bananas on the same amount of the pancake.* **How are these pancakes different from each other?** *They're cut into different fractional parts.*

We say that one-half and two-fourths are *equivalent* to each other, because they equal the same amount. Fractions that equal the same amount are called *equivalent fractions*. They have different numerators and different denominators, but the same value. You can order bananas on one-half or two-fourths of your pancake, but you'll still get the same amount of your pancake covered with bananas.

Have your child model 1/2 and 2/4 with fraction circles. Stack the fourths on top of the half to demonstrate that the two fractions are equal.

Listen to how *equal* and *equivalent* start the same way. Have your child say both words. **That can help you remember that fractions that are equal to each other are equivalent fractions.**

The chef started looking for more orders like this. Show your child the next group of pancakes in part B. **Which two pancakes in this group have the same amount covered with chocolate chips?** *Child points to pancakes with chocolate chips on 3/4 and 6/8.* Circle these pancakes and X the other pancake. Have your child write a fraction to match each of the circled pancakes.

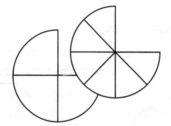

> Identifying pairs of equivalent fractions visually helps children understand the essential idea that equivalent fractions represent the same amount of an object.

Have your child model 3/4 and 6/8 with fraction circles. Then, stack the two models on top of each other to confirm that they are equal.

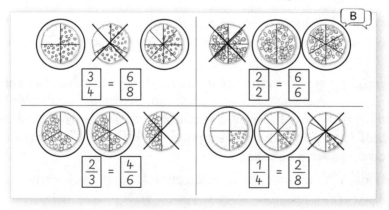

> Stacking the fractions on top of each other allows your child to kinesthetically feel how the fractions are the same part of the whole circle.

Have your child complete the other exercises in part B in the same way. Once your child identifies the pair of equivalent fractions, have him model each with fraction circles and stack the pieces on top of each other to confirm that the fractions are equal.

Independent Practice and Review

Have your child complete the Lesson 6.6 Practice and Review workbook pages.

Lesson 6.7
Equivalent Fractions, Part 2

Purpose	Materials
• Practice identifying whether pairs of fractions are equivalent • Fold paper and draw lines to create equivalent fractions • Match equivalent fractions visually	• 4 sheets of paper • Markers or colored pencils • Die • Counters

Memory Work	
	• **What do we call the top number in a fraction?** *The numerator.* • **What does the numerator tell?** *The number of parts.* • **What do we call the bottom number in a fraction?** *The denominator.* • **What does the denominator tell?** *How many equal parts the whole was split into.*

Warm-up: Identify Pairs of Equivalent Fractions with Fraction Circles

In the last lesson, you learned about equivalent fractions. If two fractions are equivalent to each other, what does that mean? *Sample answers: They look different but have the same value. They're equal to each other.*

Use fraction circles to model the following pairs of fractions. Have your child tell whether the fractions in each pair are equivalent to each other or not.

- 1/2 and 4/8. *Equivalent.*

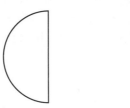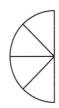

1/2 and 4/8 equal the same portion of the circle, so they are equivalent.

- 1/2 and 2/3. *Not equivalent.*

1/2 and 2/3 do not equal the same portion of the circle, so they are not equivalent.

- 1/2 and 2/4. *Equivalent.*
- 6/6 and 8/8. *Equivalent.*
- 1/3 and 1/4. *Not equivalent.*
- 1/3 and 2/6. *Equivalent.*

Activity (A): Fold Paper to Create Equivalent Fractions

In the last lesson, you told whether or not fractions were equivalent to each other. Today, we'll fold paper to create equivalent fractions.

Let's make a paper version of the first waffle! Have your child fold a piece of paper in half, draw a line along the fold line, and draw red circles on half of the paper.

You and your child will make 4 waffles like this, so encourage your child to draw the strawberries quickly. She can also simply draw a red squiggle to stand for the strawberries.

One-half of the waffle has strawberries. But, the chef could also cut the waffle a different way! Have your child fold the piece of paper in half in the other direction and draw a line along the fold line. **What fraction matches the strawberries now?** *Two-fourths.* Have your child draw a matching line on the printed waffle and complete the equivalent fraction.

Folding paper gives your child concrete experience with creating equivalent fractions and helps her understand how the fractional parts relate to each other (for example, that each half is split into 2 fourths).

The next waffle has blueberries on two-thirds. Help your child fold a piece of paper into thirds and draw blue dots on two of the thirds. Then, have your child fold the piece of paper in half in the other direction and draw a line along the fold line. **What fraction matches the blueberries now?** *Four-sixths.* Have your child draw a line to match on the printed waffle and complete the equivalent fraction.

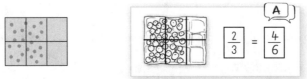

To fold the paper into thirds, roll it into a loose cylinder. Align the edges, and then press down in the middle of the cylinder. It's okay if your thirds aren't perfectly equal.

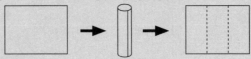

The next waffle has chocolate chips on three-fourths. Help your child fold a piece of paper into fourths and draw brown dots on three of the fourths. Then, have your child fold the piece of paper in half in the other direction and draw a line along the fold line. **What fraction matches the chocolate chips now?** *Six-eighths.* Have your child draw a line to match and complete the equivalent fraction.

To fold the paper into fourths, fold it in half twice in the same direction.

The last waffle has bananas on one-half. Help your child fold a piece of paper in half and draw yellow circles on one of the halves. Then, have your child fold the piece of paper in thirds in the other direction and draw a line along the fold lines. **What fraction matches the bananas now?** *Three-sixths.* Have your child draw a line to match and complete the equivalent fraction.

Activity (B): Play Roll and Cover

Play Roll and Cover. As your child rolls and covers the shapes, make sure she names the equivalent fractions aloud. For example, if she rolls a 2: *One-third equals two-sixths.*

Roll and Cover

Materials: Die; counters

Object of the Game: Be the first player to cover all the shapes on your side of the game board.

On your turn, roll the die. Find the fraction that matches your roll in the key. Then, find a box on your game board that shows a fraction equivalent to the fraction you rolled. Use a counter to cover the box. For example, if you roll a 2, the matching fraction in the key is 1/3. So, cover a box with 2/6.

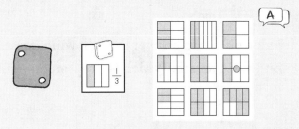

Sample play.

If you roll a 6, you may cover any box. If you roll a fraction and there is no matching uncovered box, play passes to the other player.

Play until one person has covered every box on their side of the game board.

Independent Practice and Review

Have your child complete the Lesson 6.7 Practice and Review workbook pages.

Lesson 6.8
Compare Fractions, Part 1

Purpose	Materials
• Use hands-on materials to compare fractions • Compare fractions with the same denominator or the same numerator	• Fraction circles

Memory Work	• **What do we call the top number in a fraction?** *The numerator.* • **What does the numerator tell?** *The number of parts.* • **What do we call the bottom number in a fraction?** *The denominator.* • **What does the denominator tell?** *How many equal parts the whole was split into.*

Your child will learn how to compare fractions with the same denominator or same numerator in this lesson. He'll learn another strategy for comparing fractions in Lesson 6.9.

Warm-up: Explore Comparing Fractions with Fraction Circles

Organize the fraction circles as shown.

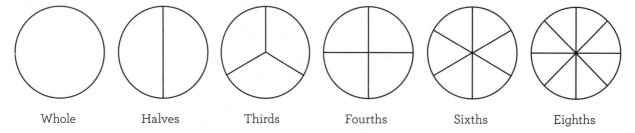

| Whole | Halves | Thirds | Fourths | Sixths | Eighths |

Have your child use the fraction circles to answer the following questions.

- Show your child 1 sixth and 1 fourth. **Which is greater, one-sixth or one-fourth?** *One-fourth.*

- **Which is greater, two-sixths or two-fourths?** *Two-fourths.*

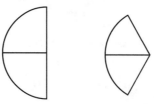

- **Which is greater, two-sixths or one-third?** *They're equal.*

- **Which is greater, three-eighths or one-half?** *One-half.*

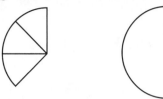

- **Which is greater, four-eighths or one-half?** *They're equal.*

Activity (A): Compare Fractions with the Same Denominator

You already know how to tell whether whole numbers are greater than, less than, or equal to each other. Today, you'll learn to tell whether fractions are greater than, less than, or equal to each other.

One-third of the cherry pie is left, and two-thirds of the pumpkin pie is left. Which pie has more left? *The pumpkin pie.* **How do you know?** *Sample answers: I can see that there's more. There are 2 pieces of pumpkin pie and just 1 piece of cherry pie.* Write < between the fractions. **Both pies are cut into thirds. 1 is less than 2, so one-third is less than two-thirds.**

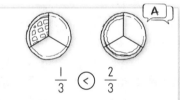

These fractions have the same denominator. When two fractions have the same denominator, we know that they're cut into the same kind of fractional parts. To compare them, we can just think about how many we have of each part.

Repeat with the next pair of pies. **Both pies are cut into fourths. 3 is greater than 1, so three-fourths is greater than one-fourth.** Write > between the fractions.

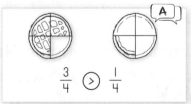

The rest of the pairs of fractions in part A don't have pictures. First, you'll predict which fraction is greater. Then, we'll use the fraction circles to check your prediction.

Point to 1/8 and 5/8 and have your child read each fraction aloud. **Which fraction do you think is greater?** *5/8.* **How do you know?** *Sample answer: 5 is greater than 1.* Have your child model both fractions with fraction circles and check his prediction. Write < in the blank.

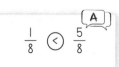

Predicting the answer before modeling the fractions with fraction circles helps your child begin to visualize fractions and understand them more abstractly.

Have him compare the other pairs of fractions in the same way.

$$\frac{3}{6} \, \boxed{>} \, \frac{2}{6} \qquad\qquad \frac{3}{6} \, \boxed{>} \, \frac{1}{6}$$

Activity (B): Compare Fractions with 1 as the Numerator

Only one piece is left in each of these pies! Have your child write the matching fraction below each pie.

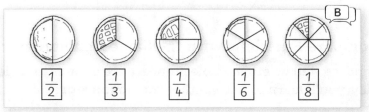

Point to 1/2 and 1/8. **Which fraction is greater, one-half or one-eighth?** *One-half.* If your child's not sure, have him look at the matching pie pictures. Write > in the blank.

$$\frac{1}{2} \, \boxed{>} \, \frac{1}{8}$$

Both fractions have the same numerator. When you compare fractions with different denominators, make sure you think about how big each fractional part is.

Sometimes, kids look at fractions like 1/2 and 1/8 and think that 1/8 must be greater, since 8 is greater than 2. Why isn't that true? *Sample answer: An eighth is a lot smaller than a half.*

One way to think about it is to imagine taking a pie and splitting it between 2 people. Now, imagine taking the same pie and splitting it between 8 people! You get much bigger slices of pie when the pie is split between 2 people.

Have your child complete the other exercises in the same way.

$$\frac{1}{2} \, \boxed{>} \, \frac{1}{8} \qquad\qquad \frac{1}{4} \, \boxed{<} \, \frac{1}{3} \qquad\qquad \frac{1}{6} \, \boxed{>} \, \frac{1}{8}$$

Activity (C): Compare Fractions with the Same Numerator

Model 1/8 and 1/3 with fraction circles. **Which is greater, one-eighth of a pie or one-third of a pie?** *One-third.* Write < in the blank.

$$\frac{1}{8} \, \boxed{<} \, \frac{1}{3}$$

Model 2/8 and 2/3 with fraction circles. **You already know out that one-third is greater than one-eighth. So, which is greater: two-thirds or two-eighths?** *Two-thirds.* Write < in the blank. Have your child use similar reasoning to compare the final pair of fractions in the column.

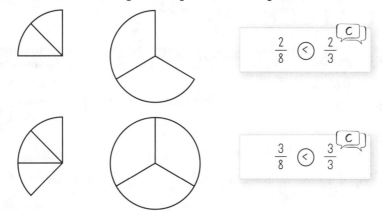

$$\frac{2}{8} \; \textless \; \frac{2}{3}$$

$$\frac{3}{8} \; \textless \; \frac{3}{3}$$

Repeat with the other columns. Model the fractions with fraction circles, and encourage your child to use the first pair of fractions in each column to help compare the other pairs. For example: **One-fourth is greater than one-sixth. So, two-fourths must be greater than two-sixths.**

$\frac{1}{4} \; \textgreater \; \frac{1}{6}$		$\frac{1}{6} \; \textgreater \; \frac{1}{8}$
$\frac{2}{4} \; \textgreater \; \frac{2}{6}$		$\frac{3}{6} \; \textgreater \; \frac{3}{8}$
$\frac{3}{4} \; \textgreater \; \frac{3}{6}$		$\frac{5}{6} \; \textgreater \; \frac{5}{8}$

Independent Practice and Review

Have your child complete the Lesson 6.8 Practice and Review workbook pages. Encourage him to use the pictures to help find the answers. Or, he may model the fractions with fraction circles to make the comparisons more concrete.

Your child may use fraction circles as needed to solve the fraction addition and subtraction problems on the Review page.

Lesson 6.9
Compare Fractions, Part 2

Purpose	Materials
• Find fractions equivalent to 1/2 • Identify whether fractions are greater than, less than, or equal to 1/2 • Use 1/2 as a benchmark for comparing fractions • Compare fractions with a variety of strategies	• Fraction circles • Playing cards

Memory Work • **What do we call fractions that look different but have the same value?** *Equivalent fractions.*

Warm-up: Find Fractions Equivalent to 1/2

Organize the fraction circles as shown.

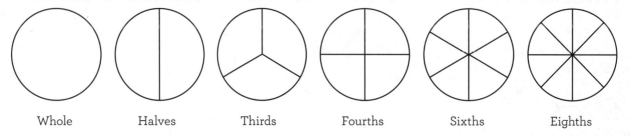

| Whole | Halves | Thirds | Fourths | Sixths | Eighths |

Show your child 1 half. **How many fourths are equivalent to one-half?** *2.* If your child's not sure, split the fourths into two equal groups. Then, place 1 half on top of 2 of the fourths to demonstrate that they are equal. **Two-fourths equal one-half.**

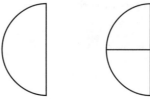

How many sixths are equivalent to one-half? *3.* **Three-sixths equal one-half.**

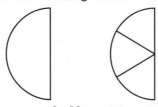

How many eighths are equivalent to one-half? *4.* **Four-eighths equal one-half.**

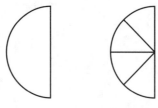

Activity (A): Greater Than, Less Than, or Equal to 1/2?

In the last lesson, you learned to compare fractions with the same denominator or the same numerator. Today, you'll learn how to compare fractions that don't have the same denominator or numerator.

Show your child part A. **First, let's complete the chart to show whether each of these fractions is less than, greater than, or equal to one-half. You'll predict whether each fraction is less than, greater than, or equal to one-half. Then, we'll use the fraction circles to check your prediction.**

Point to 2/6. **Do you predict two-sixths is less than, greater than, or equal to one-half?** *Less than one-half.* **How do you know?** *Sample answer: Three-sixths is equal to one-half, so two-sixths must be less than one-half.* Have your child model 1/2 and 2/6 with fraction circles to check her prediction. Write 2/6 in the column labeled "Less than 1/2".

Predicting the answer before modeling the fractions with fraction circles helps your child begin to visualize fractions and understand them more abstractly. Don't worry if she sometimes makes incorrect predictions, or if she has trouble articulating her reasoning. Many third-graders will still need to rely on fraction circles for comparing fractions at this point.

Continue in the same way with the rest of the fractions. For each fraction, have your child predict whether it is less than, greater than, or equal to 1/2. Then, have her model the fraction with fraction circles and check her prediction.

Less than $\frac{1}{2}$			Equal to $\frac{1}{2}$			Greater than $\frac{1}{2}$		
$\frac{2}{6}$	$\frac{1}{4}$	$\frac{1}{8}$	$\frac{3}{6}$	$\frac{4}{8}$	$\frac{2}{4}$	$\frac{7}{8}$	$\frac{2}{3}$	$\frac{3}{4}$
$\frac{1}{3}$	$\frac{3}{8}$	$\frac{1}{6}$				$\frac{5}{6}$	$\frac{4}{6}$	$\frac{6}{8}$
							$\frac{5}{8}$	

Activity (B): Use 1/2 as a Benchmark for Comparing Fractions

We want to figure out which is greater, five-eighths or one-third. This is a tricky one! It helps if you think about whether each fraction is greater than, less than, or equal to one-half.

$$\frac{5}{8} \bigcirc \frac{1}{3}$$

Is one-third greater than, less than, or equal to one-half? *Less than one-half.* **Is five-eighths greater than, less than, or equal to one-half?** *Greater than one-half.* If your child isn't sure about either question, have her look at the chart in part A.

Five-eighths is greater than one-half, and one-third is less than one-half. So, which fraction must be greater? *Five-eighths.* Write > in the blank. Have your child model 5/8 and 1/3 with fraction circles to check.

> If your child finds this logic confusing, use whole numbers to explain the reasoning: **It's as if you were comparing 2 and 7 by comparing them to 5. 2 is less than 5, and 7 is greater than 5, so 7 must be greater than 2.**

Next, we'll compare three-sixths and four-eighths. Is three-sixths greater than, less than, or equal to one-half? *Equal to one-half.* **Is four-eighths greater than, less than, or equal to one-half?** *Equal to one-half.* If your child isn't sure, have her look at the chart in part A.

So, since both fractions are equal to one-half, they must be equal to each other, too! Write = in the blank. Have your child model 3/6 and 4/8 with fraction circles to check.

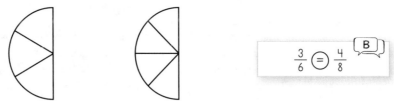

Have your child use similar reasoning to complete part B. For each problem, encourage her to first think about whether the fractions are greater than, less than, or equal to one-half.

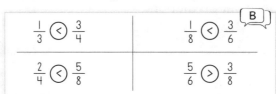

Activity: Play Fraction War

> If the lesson is running long, skip playing Fraction War. You will have the opportunity to play the game again at the beginning of Lesson 6.10.

Play Fraction War. Encourage your child to use logical reasoning and explain her thinking as she compares the fractions. If she's not sure about which fraction is greater, model both fractions with fraction circles to check.

> Most of these fractions can be compared using the strategies your child has already learned, but there are a few pairs (for example, 2/3 and 6/8) that your child may need to model with fraction circles in order to confidently compare them. She will learn how to use common denominators to compare any pair of fractions in fourth grade.

Fraction War

Materials: Aces, 2s, 3s, 4s, 6s, and 8s from a deck of cards

Object of the Game: Win the most cards.

Shuffle the cards and deal them face down in two piles.

Both players flip over their top two cards and use the cards to create a fraction. (The numerator must be less than or equal to the denominator. For example, if you flip over a 4 and 6, make 4/6, not 6/4.)

Whoever has the greater fraction wins all 4 cards.

Sample play. The player with 4/6 wins, since 4/6 is greater than 1/8.

If the fractions are equal, leave the cards face-up on the table and have both players flip over their next two cards. Whoever has the greater fraction wins all the face-up cards.

Play until the piles run out. Whoever has won more cards wins the game.

Independent Practice and Review

Have your child complete the Lesson 6.9 Practice and Review workbook pages.

Lesson 6.10
Mixed Numbers

Purpose	Materials
• Practice comparing fractions • Read and write mixed numbers • Understand fractions and mixed numbers in the context of measuring cups	• Playing cards (24 cards total) • Fraction circles • Measuring cups (1/4-cup, 1/3-cup, 1/2-cup, and 1-cup) • Water

Memory Work	• **What do we call fractions that look different but have the same value?** *Equivalent fractions.*

The final activity in this lesson involves measuring water with measuring cups, so you may want to do it in the kitchen or near a sink. If you use the metric system and do not use cups as a unit of measure, skip this activity. You'll teach your child about liters in Unit 16.

Warm-up: Play Fraction War

Play Fraction War. See Lesson 6.9 (page 201) for directions. Encourage your child to use logical reasoning and explain his thinking as he compares the fractions. If he's not sure about which fraction is greater, model both fractions with fraction circles to check.

Activity (A): Write Mixed Numbers

In real life, we often have a mix of whole objects and parts of an object. Let's pretend we had a pizza party and we have some leftover pizzas. How many whole pizzas do we have left? *2.* **What part of a pizza do we have left?** *One-fourth.* Write 2 and 1/4 in the blanks below the pizzas.

So, we have 2 and one-fourth of a pizza left. Here's how I write 2 and one-fourth. Write 2 1/4 in the blank as shown.

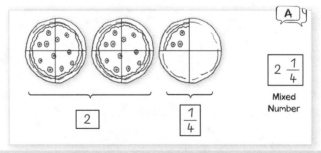

Make sure to say "and" between the whole number and fraction in mixed numbers.

Numbers that show a whole number and a fraction are called *mixed numbers*. That's because they're a mix of a whole number and a fraction.

Have your child write mixed numbers to match the rest of the pizzas in part A.

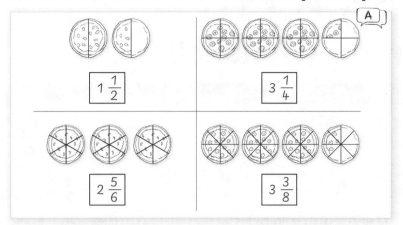

Activity (B): Pretend to Measure with Measuring Cups

We often use fractions and mixed numbers in recipes. Show your child a set of measuring cups. Have him read the fraction printed on each cup.

How many halves make one whole? *2.* **So, 2 half-cups equal 1 whole cup.** Have your child pour 2 half-cups of water into the 1-cup measure to check that this is true. Repeat with 3 third-cups and 4 fourth-cups.

Let's pretend we're measuring out the ingredients for this recipe. Have your child pantomime measuring each ingredient in the list. For example, for 1 1/3 cups sugar, have him pretend to scoop and pour 1 cup and 1/3 of a cup of sugar. For 3/4 cup of vegetable oil, have him pretend to pour oil into the 1/4 cup 3 times.

Lesson 6.11 includes the full pumpkin bread recipe for you and your child to bake together as an enrichment activity.

Independent Practice and Review

Have your child complete the Lesson 6.10 Practice and Review workbook pages.

Lesson 6.11
Enrichment (Optional)

Purpose	Materials
• Review memory work • Read and understand fractions in many real-life contexts • Read fractions and mixed numbers in a recipe • Summarize what your child has learned and assess your child's progress	• *Fraction Action,* written and illustrated by Loreen Leedy • Ingredients for pumpkin bread or another recipe

Warm-up: Review Memory Work

Quiz your child on all memory work introduced through Unit 6. See pages 527-528 for the full list.

Math Picture Book: *Fraction Action*

Read *Fraction Action,* written and illustrated by Loreen Leedy. As you read, discuss the many ways fractions are represented in the book. Also look for the questions written on the blackboard throughout the book and encourage your child to answer them.

Fraction Action introduces finding fractions of a set. Your child is not expected to know this skill yet.

Enrichment Activity: Use Measuring Cups and Spoons to Follow a Recipe

Bake the following recipe for pumpkin bread with your child. Have your child read the fractions in the recipe and find the matching measuring cups and spoons.

If you do not have these ingredients on hand, feel free to use a different recipe instead. Try to choose a recipe with a variety of different fractions.

Pumpkin Bread

Mix together in a large bowl:

- 1 1/3 cups sugar
- 1 1/4 cups canned pumpkin puree
- 3/4 cup vegetable oil
- 2 eggs
- 1/2 teaspoon vanilla

Mix together in a separate medium bowl:

- 1 1/2 cups flour
- 1 1/2 teaspoons cinnamon
- 1 teaspoon baking soda
- 1 teaspoon salt
- 1 teaspoon ginger
- 1/4 teaspoon baking powder

Dump the flour mixture into the pumpkin mixture and stir until combined. If you like, mix in:

- 1/2 cup chocolate chips
- 2/3 cup chopped walnuts

Grease a 9-inch by 5-inch loaf pan. Pour the batter into the pan and bake for 1 hour at 350° F. Let cool before eating.

Recipe adapted from *Joy of Cooking,* by Irma S. Rombauer, Marion Rombauer Becker, Ethan Becker, John Becker, and Megan Scott. Scribner, 2019.

Unit Wrap-up

Have your child complete the Unit 6 Wrap-up.

Unit 6 Answer Key

6.1 Practice

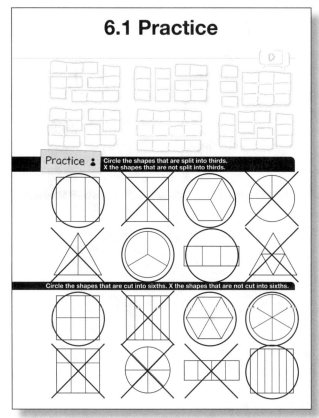

6.1 Review

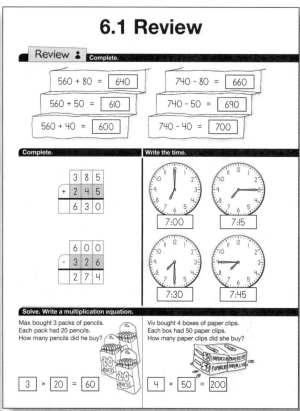

6.2 Practice

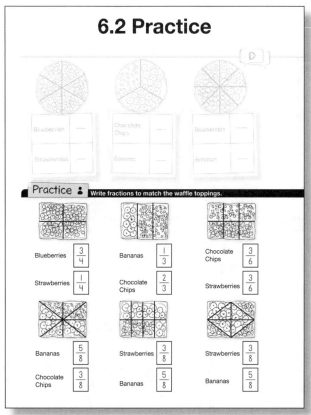

6.2 Review

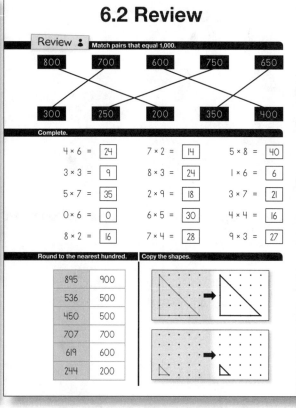

Unit 6 Answer Key

6.3 Practice

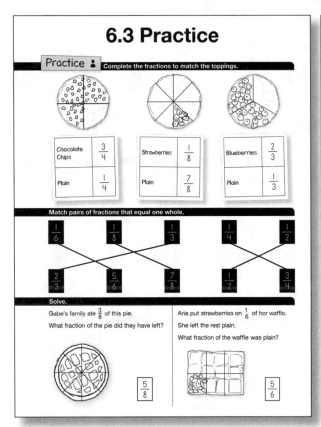

6.3 Review

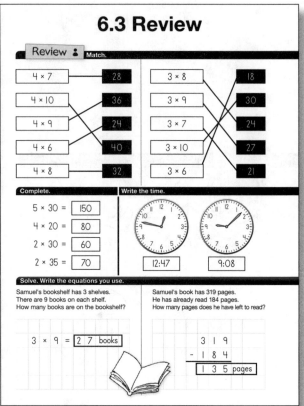

6.4 Practice

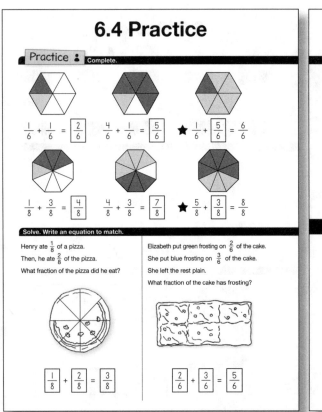

6.4 Review

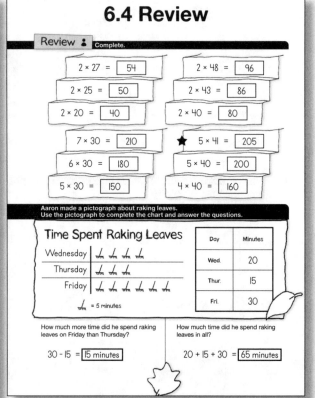

Unit 6 Answer Key

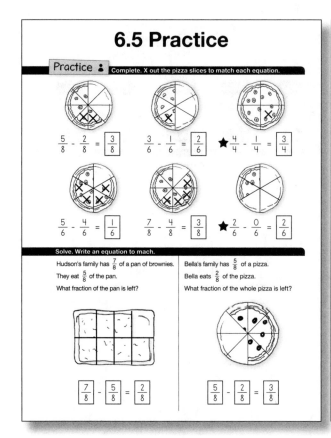

6.5 Practice

Practice 👤 Complete. X out the pizza slices to match each equation.

$\frac{5}{8} - \frac{2}{8} = \boxed{\frac{3}{8}}$ $\frac{3}{6} - \frac{1}{6} = \boxed{\frac{2}{6}}$ ★ $\frac{4}{4} - \frac{1}{4} = \boxed{\frac{3}{4}}$

$\frac{5}{6} - \frac{4}{6} = \boxed{\frac{1}{6}}$ $\frac{7}{8} - \frac{4}{8} = \boxed{\frac{3}{8}}$ ★ $\frac{2}{6} - \frac{0}{6} = \boxed{\frac{2}{6}}$

Solve. Write an equation to mach.

Hudson's family has $\frac{7}{8}$ of a pan of brownies.
They eat $\frac{5}{8}$ of the pan.
What fraction of the pan is left?

$\frac{7}{8} - \frac{5}{8} = \boxed{\frac{2}{8}}$

Bella's family has $\frac{5}{8}$ of a pizza.
Bella eats $\frac{2}{8}$ of the pizza.
What fraction of the whole pizza is left?

$\frac{5}{8} - \frac{2}{8} = \boxed{\frac{3}{8}}$

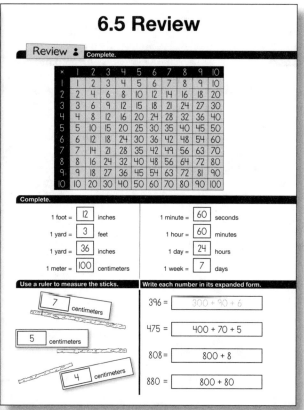

6.5 Review

Review 👤 Complete.

Complete.

1 foot = $\boxed{12}$ inches   1 minute = $\boxed{60}$ seconds

1 yard = $\boxed{3}$ feet   1 hour = $\boxed{60}$ minutes

1 yard = $\boxed{36}$ inches   1 day = $\boxed{24}$ hours

1 meter = $\boxed{100}$ centimeters   1 week = $\boxed{7}$ days

Use a ruler to measure the sticks.

$\boxed{7}$ centimeters

$\boxed{5}$ centimeters

$\boxed{4}$ centimeters

Write each number in its expanded form.

396 = 300 + 90 + 6

475 = 400 + 70 + 5

808 = 800 + 8

880 = 800 + 80

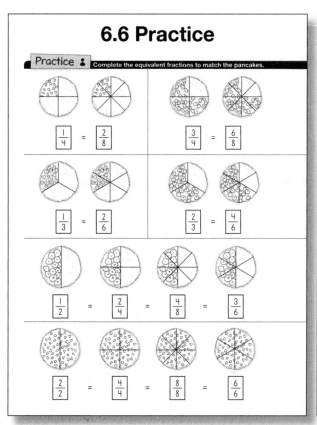

6.6 Practice

Practice 👤 Complete the equivalent fractions to match the pancakes.

$\frac{1}{4} = \frac{2}{8}$ $\frac{3}{4} = \frac{6}{8}$

$\frac{1}{3} = \frac{2}{6}$ $\frac{2}{3} = \frac{4}{6}$

$\frac{1}{2} = \frac{2}{4} = \frac{4}{8} = \frac{3}{6}$

$\frac{2}{2} = \frac{4}{4} = \frac{8}{8} = \frac{6}{6}$

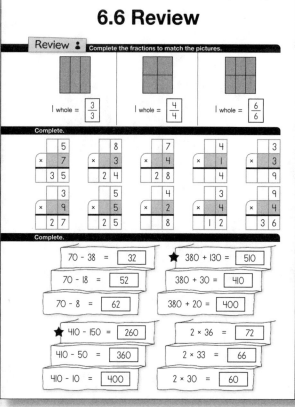

6.6 Review

Review 👤 Complete the fractions to match the pictures.

1 whole = $\frac{3}{3}$ 1 whole = $\frac{4}{4}$ 1 whole = $\frac{6}{6}$

Complete.

5 × 7 = 35	8 × 3 = 24	7 × 4 = 28	4 × 1 = 4	3 × 3 = 9

| 3 × 9 = 27 | 5 × 5 = 25 | 4 × 2 = 8 | 3 × 4 = 12 | 9 × 4 = 36 |

Complete.

70 − 38 = $\boxed{32}$ ★ 380 + 130 = $\boxed{510}$

70 − 18 = $\boxed{52}$ 380 + 30 = $\boxed{410}$

70 − 8 = $\boxed{62}$ 380 + 20 = $\boxed{400}$

★ 410 − 150 = $\boxed{260}$ 2 × 36 = $\boxed{72}$

410 − 50 = $\boxed{360}$ 2 × 33 = $\boxed{66}$

410 − 10 = $\boxed{400}$ 2 × 30 = $\boxed{60}$

Unit 6 Answer Key

6.7 Practice

Practice : Color the second shape in each pair to match the first shape. Then, complete the fraction.

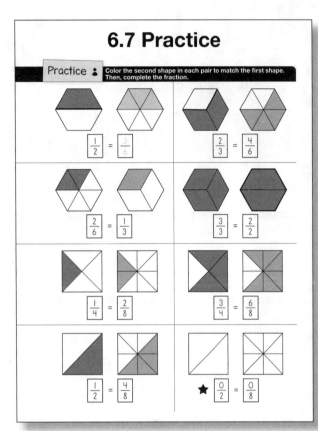

$\frac{1}{2} = \frac{3}{6}$ $\frac{2}{3} = \frac{4}{6}$

$\frac{2}{6} = \frac{1}{3}$ $\frac{3}{3} = \frac{2}{2}$

$\frac{1}{4} = \frac{2}{8}$ $\frac{3}{4} = \frac{6}{8}$

$\frac{1}{2} = \frac{4}{8}$ ★ $\frac{0}{2} = \frac{0}{8}$

6.7 Review

Review : Match pairs that equal 1,000.

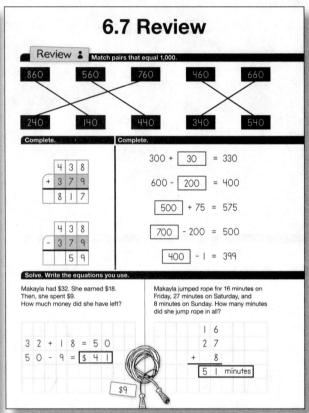

| 860 | 560 | 760 | 460 | 660 |

| 240 | 140 | 440 | 340 | 540 |

Complete.

$$\begin{array}{r} 4\ 3\ 8 \\ +\ 3\ 7\ 9 \\ \hline 8\ 1\ 7 \end{array}$$

$$\begin{array}{r} 4\ 3\ 8 \\ -\ 3\ 7\ 9 \\ \hline 5\ 9 \end{array}$$

Complete.

$300 + \boxed{30} = 330$

$600 - \boxed{200} = 400$

$\boxed{500} + 75 = 575$

$\boxed{700} - 200 = 500$

$\boxed{400} - 1 = 399$

Solve. Write the equations you use.

Makayla had $32. She earned $18. Then, she spent $9. How much money did she have left?

$32 + 18 = 50$
$50 - 9 = \boxed{\$\ 41}$

$9

Makayla jumped rope for 16 minutes on Friday, 27 minutes on Saturday, and 8 minutes on Sunday. How many minutes did she jump rope in all?

$$\begin{array}{r} 1\ 6 \\ 2\ 7 \\ +\quad\ 8 \\ \hline 5\ 1 \text{ minutes} \end{array}$$

6.8 Practice

Practice : Write <, >, or =. Use the pictures to help.

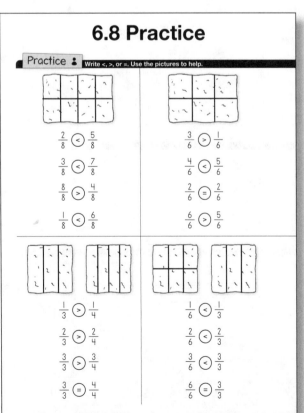

$\frac{2}{8} < \frac{5}{8}$ $\frac{3}{6} > \frac{1}{6}$

$\frac{3}{8} < \frac{7}{8}$ $\frac{4}{6} < \frac{5}{6}$

$\frac{8}{8} > \frac{4}{8}$ $\frac{2}{6} = \frac{2}{6}$

$\frac{1}{8} < \frac{6}{8}$ $\frac{6}{6} > \frac{5}{6}$

$\frac{1}{3} > \frac{1}{4}$ $\frac{1}{6} < \frac{1}{3}$

$\frac{2}{3} > \frac{2}{4}$ $\frac{2}{6} < \frac{2}{3}$

$\frac{3}{3} > \frac{3}{4}$ $\frac{3}{6} < \frac{3}{3}$

$\frac{3}{3} = \frac{4}{4}$ $\frac{6}{6} = \frac{3}{3}$

6.8 Review

Review : Complete.

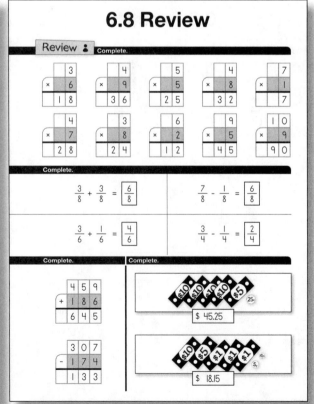

Complete.

$\frac{3}{8} + \frac{3}{8} = \frac{6}{8}$ $\frac{7}{8} - \frac{1}{8} = \frac{6}{8}$

$\frac{3}{6} + \frac{1}{6} = \frac{4}{6}$ $\frac{3}{4} - \frac{1}{4} = \frac{2}{4}$

Complete.

$$\begin{array}{r} 4\ 5\ 9 \\ +\ 1\ 8\ 6 \\ \hline 6\ 4\ 5 \end{array}$$

$$\begin{array}{r} 3\ 0\ 7 \\ -\ 1\ 7\ 4 \\ \hline 1\ 3\ 3 \end{array}$$

$ 45.25

$ 18.15

Unit 6 Answer Key

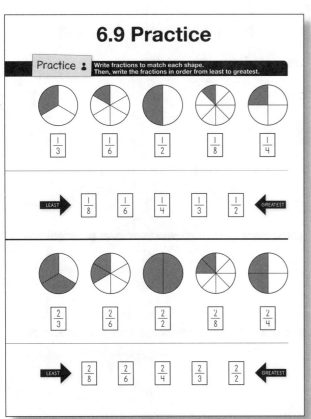

6.9 Practice

Practice 🖉 Write fractions to match each shape.
Then, write the fractions in order from least to greatest.

$\frac{1}{3}$ $\frac{1}{6}$ $\frac{1}{2}$ $\frac{1}{8}$ $\frac{1}{4}$

LEAST ➡ $\frac{1}{8}$ $\frac{1}{6}$ $\frac{1}{4}$ $\frac{1}{3}$ $\frac{1}{2}$ ⬅ GREATEST

$\frac{2}{3}$ $\frac{2}{6}$ $\frac{2}{2}$ $\frac{2}{8}$ $\frac{2}{4}$

LEAST ➡ $\frac{2}{8}$ $\frac{2}{6}$ $\frac{2}{4}$ $\frac{2}{3}$ $\frac{2}{2}$ ⬅ GREATEST

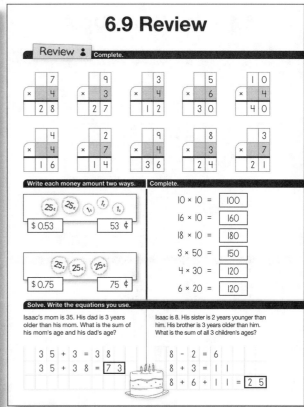

6.9 Review

Review 🖉 Complete.

×	7
4	
2	8

×	9
3	
2	7

×	3
4	
1	2

×	5
6	
3	0

×	1 0
4	
4	0

×	4
4	
1	6

×	2
7	
1	4

×	9
4	
3	6

×	8
3	
2	4

×	3
7	
2	1

Write each money amount two ways.

$ 0.53   53 ¢

$ 0.75   75 ¢

Complete.

$10 × 10 = \boxed{100}$

$16 × 10 = \boxed{160}$

$18 × 10 = \boxed{180}$

$3 × 50 = \boxed{150}$

$4 × 30 = \boxed{120}$

$6 × 20 = \boxed{120}$

Solve. Write the equations you use.

Isaac's mom is 35. His dad is 3 years older than his mom. What is the sum of his mom's age and his dad's age?

3 5 + 3 = 3 8
3 5 + 3 8 = $\boxed{7\ 3}$

Isaac is 8. His sister is 2 years younger than him. His brother is 3 years older than him. What is the sum of all 3 children's ages?

8 - 2 = 6
8 + 3 = 1 1
8 + 6 + 1 1 = $\boxed{2\ 5}$

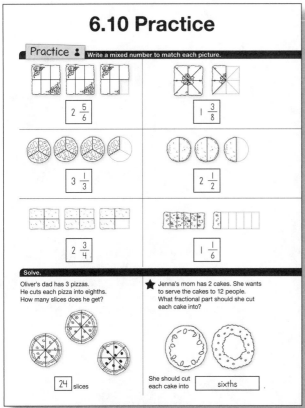

6.10 Practice

Practice 🖉 Write a mixed number to match each picture.

$2\frac{5}{6}$

$1\frac{3}{8}$

$3\frac{1}{3}$

$2\frac{1}{2}$

$2\frac{3}{4}$

$1\frac{1}{6}$

Solve.

Oliver's dad has 3 pizzas. He cuts each pizza into eighths. How many slices does he get?

$\boxed{24}$ slices

⭐ Jenna's mom has 2 cakes. She wants to serve the cakes to 12 people. What fractional part should she cut each cake into?

She should cut each cake into $\boxed{\text{sixths}}$.

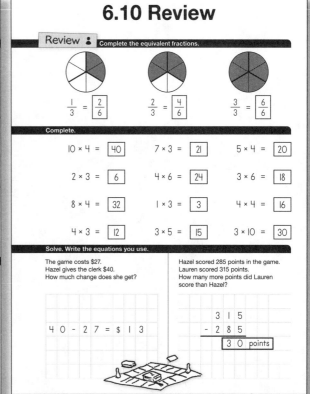

6.10 Review

Review 🖉 Complete the equivalent fractions.

$\frac{1}{3} = \frac{2}{6}$

$\frac{2}{3} = \frac{4}{6}$

$\frac{3}{3} = \frac{6}{6}$

Complete.

$10 × 4 = \boxed{40}$

$7 × 3 = \boxed{21}$

$5 × 4 = \boxed{20}$

$2 × 3 = \boxed{6}$

$4 × 6 = \boxed{24}$

$3 × 6 = \boxed{18}$

$8 × 4 = \boxed{32}$

$1 × 3 = \boxed{3}$

$4 × 4 = \boxed{16}$

$4 × 3 = \boxed{12}$

$3 × 5 = \boxed{15}$

$3 × 10 = \boxed{30}$

Solve. Write the equations you use.

The game costs $27. Hazel gives the clerk $40. How much change does she get?

4 0 - 2 7 = $ 1 3

Hazel scored 285 points in the game. Lauren scored 315 points. How many more points did Lauren score than Hazel?

```
  3 1 5
- 2 8 5
  ___
  3 0  points
```

Unit 6 Answer Key

6.11 Unit Wrap-Up A

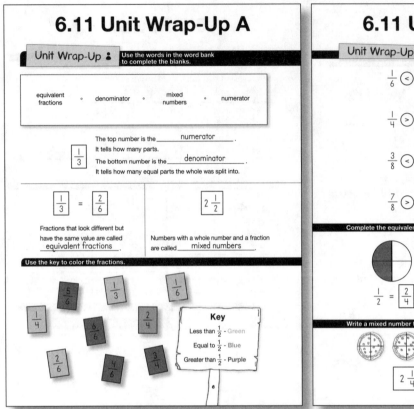

Unit Wrap-Up 👤   Use the words in the word bank to complete the blanks.

| equivalent fractions | ○ | denominator | ○ | mixed numbers | ○ | numerator |

The top number is the __numerator__.
It tells how many parts.

$\frac{1}{3}$

The bottom number is the __denominator__.
It tells how many equal parts the whole was split into.

$\frac{1}{3} = \frac{2}{6}$

$2\frac{1}{2}$

Fractions that look different but have the same value are called __equivalent fractions__

Numbers with a whole number and a fraction are called __mixed numbers__

Use the key to color the fractions.

$\frac{5}{6}$ $\frac{1}{3}$ $\frac{1}{6}$
$\frac{1}{4}$ $\frac{6}{6}$ $\frac{2}{4}$
$\frac{2}{6}$ $\frac{4}{6}$ $\frac{3}{4}$

Key
Less than $\frac{1}{2}$ - Green
Equal to $\frac{1}{2}$ - Blue
Greater than $\frac{1}{2}$ - Purple

6.11 Unit Wrap-Up B

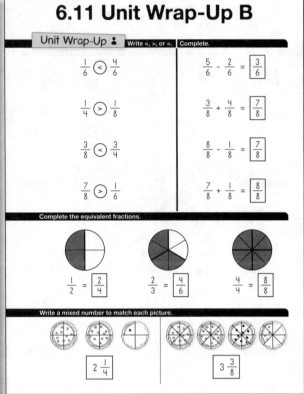

Unit Wrap-Up 👤   Write <, >, or =.   Complete.

$\frac{1}{6}$ < $\frac{4}{6}$ $\frac{5}{6} - \frac{2}{6} = \frac{3}{6}$

$\frac{1}{4}$ > $\frac{1}{8}$ $\frac{3}{8} + \frac{4}{8} = \frac{7}{8}$

$\frac{3}{8}$ < $\frac{3}{4}$ $\frac{8}{8} - \frac{1}{8} = \frac{7}{8}$

$\frac{7}{8}$ > $\frac{1}{6}$ $\frac{7}{8} + \frac{1}{8} = \frac{8}{8}$

Complete the equivalent fractions.

$\frac{1}{2} = \frac{2}{4}$ $\frac{2}{3} = \frac{4}{6}$ $\frac{4}{4} = \frac{8}{8}$

Write a mixed number to match each picture.

$2\frac{1}{4}$ $3\frac{3}{8}$

Unit 6 Checkpoint

What to Expect at the End of Unit 6

By the end of Unit 6, most children will be able to do the following:

- Read and write fractions to match pictures or hands-on materials.
- Identify the numerator and denominator in fractions and understand what each number means. Some children will still have trouble remembering the terms, but most will understand that the top number tells the number of parts, and the bottom number tells how many equal parts the whole was split into.
- Add and subtract fractions with the same denominator. Most children will be able to solve these problems without pictures or fraction circles, but it's fine if your child still needs the extra support.
- Understand the concept of equivalent fractions and use hands-on materials or pictures to find equivalent fractions. Know that fractions with the same numerator and denominator are equivalent to one whole.
- Compare fractions by reasoning about the numerator and denominator, or by comparing the fractions to 1/2. Most children will be able to easily compare fractions with the same denominator, but many will need fraction circles to accurately compare other pairs of fractions.
- Understand how to write mixed numbers to match real-life situations.

Is Your Child Ready to Move on?

In Unit 7, your child will learn how to add and subtract money amounts. Before moving on to Unit 7, your child should have already mastered the following skills:

- Add up to make change with dollars.
- Know the steps in the addition and subtraction algorithm, and use the algorithms to add and subtract three-digit numbers. It's okay if your child sometimes makes mistakes or forgets a step.

What to Do If Your Child Needs More Practice

If your child is having trouble with any of the above skills, spend a few days practicing the corresponding review activities below before moving on to Unit 7.

Activities for Making Change

- Make Change at the Pretend Store (Lesson 3.2)

Activities for Adding and Subtracting Three-Digit Numbers

- Leaf Fight (Lesson 5.4)
- Spin to Win (Lesson 5.6)

This page is intentionally left blank.

Unit 7
Money

Overview

In Unit 7, your child will apply her addition and subtraction skills to money. She'll practice her mental math skills as she makes change with dollars and cents and mentally adds and subtracts money amounts. She'll also reinforce her understanding of the addition and subtraction algorithms as she uses them to add and subtract dollars and cents.

What Your Child Will Learn

In this unit, your child will learn to:

- Round prices to the nearest dollar
- Convert dollars to cents, and convert cents to dollars
- Add up to make change with dollars and cents
- Solve mental addition and subtraction problems with money
- Use the addition and subtraction algorithms to add and subtract dollars and cents

Lesson List

Lesson 7.1	Understand Place Value in Money Amounts	Lesson 7.4	Mental Addition with Money
Lesson 7.2	Convert Dollars and Cents	Lesson 7.5	Mental Subtraction with Money
Lesson 7.3	Make Change with Dollars and Cents	Lesson 7.6	Add Money
		Lesson 7.7	Subtract Money
		Lesson 7.8	Enrichment (Optional)

Extra Materials Needed for Unit 7

- 5 small sticky notes or slips of paper
- 3 small office items (such as a pencil, eraser, and ruler)
- 3 slips of paper
- Paper clip
- For optional Enrichment Lesson:
    - × *Follow the Money!*, written and illustrated by Loreen Leedy. Holiday House, 2002.
    - × Toy catalog or access to a website with items your child would like to buy.

Teaching Math with Confidence: Extending Place Value to Money

Before beginning this unit, most children will think of money amounts as having two chunks: the dollars and the cents, separated by a decimal point. During this unit, your child will refine this understanding and learn that each digit in a money amount has a value based on its place. For example, at the beginning of the unit, most children will understand the printed amount $2.38 to have two chunks: 2 dollars and 38 cents. By the end of the unit, she'll also recognize the value of each digit: the 2 has a value of 2 dollars, the 3 has a value of 30 cents, and the 8 has a value of 8 cents.

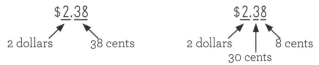

Two different ways to understand money amounts.
Your child will develop a place-value understanding of money in this unit.

Some children will immediately see how to extend place-value concepts to money, but many will need hands-on, explicit teaching to make the connection. To help your child grasp the concept, you'll use sticky notes to relabel the Place-Value Chart to show the value of each place in money amounts. You'll use bills and coins that match the labels so that each digit in the written money amount matches the number of bills or coins in the corresponding column. For example, to represent $2.38, you'll use 2 one-dollar bills, 3 dimes, and 8 pennies (and not any quarters or nickels!)

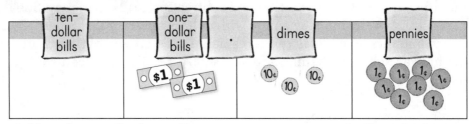

Once your child understands place value in money amounts, she'll apply the concept to add and subtract money. Since each place has 10 times the value of the next-smaller place, she'll find that she can use the familiar algorithms to add and subtract money amounts just like whole numbers.

$$
\begin{array}{r}
\overset{1\ \ 1}{1.89} \\
+4.37 \\
\hline
\$6.26
\end{array}
\qquad
\begin{array}{r}
\overset{6\ 11}{7\cancel{1}9} \\
-3.45 \\
\hline
\$3.74
\end{array}
$$

In fourth grade, your child will learn about decimal place value. She'll learn that the "dimes-place" and "pennies-place" in money amounts are called the tenths-place and hundredths-place in decimal numbers. By first exploring this idea with the familiar context of money, your child will be well-prepared to tackle the more abstract concept of decimal place value next year.

Lesson 7.1
Understand Place Value in Money Amounts

Purpose	Materials
• Review counting out a given amount of money • Understand place value in written money amounts • Round prices to the nearest dollar	• Play money • Place-Value Chart (Blackline Master 3) • 5 small sticky notes or slips of paper • Die • Counters

Memory Work	• **What do we call the result when we multiply two numbers?** *The product.* • **What do we call the numbers in a multiplication equation that we multiply together?** *Factors.*

Warm-up (A): Review Counting Out Money

We're starting a new unit on money. Today, you'll review reading and writing money amounts and learn how to round to the nearest dollar.

The box of cereal costs 2 dollars and 38 cents. The little dot is called a decimal point. It separates the dollars from the cents.

There are lots of different ways you can make $2.38 with paper bills and coins. Place play money on the table and have your child find several different combinations of bills and coins that equal $2.38.

Some possible ways to make $2.38.

Activity (A): Understand Place Value in Money Amounts

In money amounts, the value of each digit depends on its place, just like in whole numbers. Let's put new labels on the columns in the Place-Value Chart to show money place value. Label 5 small sticky notes or slips of paper as shown.

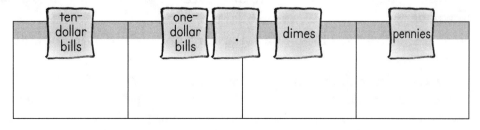

Relabeling the familiar Place-Value Chart helps your child connect place value in whole numbers with place value in money amounts. See the Unit 7 **Teaching Math with Confidence** for more details.

Place the labels on the Place-Value Chart as shown. Then, arrange 2 one-dollar bills, 3 dimes, and 8 pennies on the chart. **In $2.38, the 2 stands for 2 one-dollar bills. The 3 stands for 3 dimes, and the 8 stands for 8 pennies.**

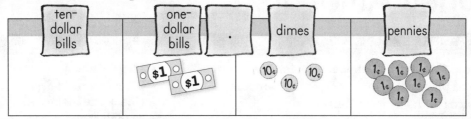

This is a simplified explanation of decimal place-value. In fourth grade, your child will learn that these decimal places are called the tenths-place and hundredths-place.

In the warm-up, you found that you could pay $2.38 with many different combinations of paper bills and coins. Every combination had the same value as 2 one-dollar bills, 3 dimes, and 8 pennies.

Have your child read the prices of the other items and pretend to pay for them with one-dollar bills, dimes, and pennies. For example, she should give you 9 one-dollar bills, 1 dime, and 2 pennies for the almonds.

Using only one-dollar bills, dimes, and pennies prepares your child to use place-value thinking to add and subtract money amounts later in the unit.

Children are often confused by zeros in money amounts. These prices include many zeros so that your child becomes confident at interpreting them. If needed, explain that the zeros are place-holder zeros, just like in whole numbers.

 Save these Place-Value Chart labels for future lessons.

Activity (B): Round Prices to the Nearest Dollar

You have already learned how to round numbers to the nearest ten or hundred. At the store, people often round money amounts to the nearest dollar so they can estimate how much the bill will be.

The cereal costs $2.38. Is $2.38 closer to 2 dollars or 3 dollars? *2 dollars.* **How do you know?** *Answers will vary.*

Here's one way to tell. One dollar equals 100 cents. 50 cents is half of a dollar, so $2.50 is halfway between $2 and $3. $2.38 is less than $2.50, so it is closer to $2 than $3. Write $2 in the blank. Have your child use the same approach to round the rest of the prices to the nearest dollar.

Cereal	Almonds	Broccoli	Grapes	Cucumber	Apple
$2	$9	$4	$6	$1	$1

If your child is not sure about the broccoli, say: **$3.50 is exactly halfway between $3 and $4. Remember, mathematicians have agreed that we round in-between numbers to the higher number.**

Activity (C): Play Race to $10.00

Play Race to $10.00.

Race to $10.00

Materials: One-dollar bills, dimes, and pennies; die; counters

Object of the Game: Be the first person to have $10.00.

Place one-dollar bills, dimes, and pennies on the table. Have each player choose a different-colored counter to use as a game token and place it on one of the Start squares. Start a simple scorecard on a separate sheet of paper.

On your turn, roll the die and advance your token the corresponding number of squares along the path. You may move in either direction. The best strategy is to move to the square with the greater value.

Take the money amount listed on the square. If you have more than 10 pennies, trade them for 1 dime. If you have more than 10 dimes, trade them for 1 one-dollar bill. Count how much money you have and write your new total on the scorecard. Play then passes to the other player.

Elena	Mom
$ 2.00	$ 0.50
$ 2.05	$ 1.50
$ 2.45	$ 3.50

Sample scorecard after first few rolls.

If you land on one of the start squares, roll again. The first player to have $10.00 wins the game.

Have your child place her money on the Place-Value Chart so that she can easily find how much money she has after each turn. Have her record her own score so that she practices writing money amounts.

Independent Practice and Review

Have your child complete the Lesson 7.1 Practice and Review workbook pages.

Lesson 7.2
Convert Dollars and Cents

Purpose	Materials
• Review counting coins • Convert cents to dollars • Convert dollars to cents • Add and subtract cents	• Play money • 2 dice

Memory Work	• **What do we call fractions that look different but have the same value?** *Equivalent fractions.*

Warm-up: Count Coins in Cents

Mix up 7 quarters, 2 dimes, 3 nickels, and 4 pennies on the table. **It's usually easiest to count a pile of coins if you follow three steps: sort, order, and count.** Help your child sort the coins by type, put the piles in order from greatest value to least value, and then count them. **How many cents are the coins worth?** *214¢.*

Leave the coins out for the next activity.

Activity (A): Convert Cents to Dollars

Today, you'll learn how to convert cents to dollars and dollars to cents.

In the warm-up, you found that the coins were worth 214¢. 100 cents equal 1 dollar. So, we can split the coins into groups of 100 cents to find how many dollars the coins are worth. Help your child group the coins into piles with a value of 100¢. **How many dollars and cents are the coins worth?** *$2.14.* Write $2.14 in the blank.

214 ¢ = $ 2.14

Let's figure out how many dollars and cents 139¢ is worth. How many hundreds are in 139? *1.* If your child's not sure, point out that there is a 1 in the hundreds-place. **Each group of 100 cents equals 1 dollar. 139 is 39 cents more than 1 dollar, so 139 cents equals $1.39.** Write $1.39 in the blank.

139 ¢ = $ 1.39

139¢ and $1.39 are equivalent to each other, just like one-half is equivalent to two-fourths. They have the same value, but they express that value with different numbers and units. We converted the money amount from cents to dollars. We changed the units, but we didn't change the value. Have your child use similar reasoning to complete part A.

139 ¢ = $ 1.39   201 ¢ = $ 2.01
400 ¢ = $ 4.00   445 ¢ = $ 4.45

If your child has trouble with these problems, model them with coins and group the coins into piles with a value of $1.00.

Do you notice a pattern for converting cents to dollars and cents? *Sample answer: You put the decimal point between the hundreds-place and tens-place.* **When you convert cents to dollars, each group of 100 cents equals 1 dollar. So, the number of hundreds of cents equals the number of dollars. The leftover tens and ones equal the remaining cents. To convert cents to dollars, put a decimal point between the hundreds-place and tens-place.**

Activity (B): Convert Dollars to Cents

We can also convert dollars and cents to cents. Let's say I have $2.25 and want to know how many cents my money is worth. Discuss why you might need coins rather than paper bills, like for a vending machine, laundromat, or arcade.

Each dollar equals 100 cents. How many cents do 2 dollars equal? *200.* **So, how many cents do 2 dollars and 25 cents equal?** *225.* If your child isn't sure, suggest he add 200 and 25. Write 225¢ in the blank.

$ 2.25 = | 225 ¢ | B

Have your child complete part B. Model the problems with play money as needed.

$3.50 =	350 ¢		$3.79 =	379 ¢	B
$5.00 =	500 ¢		$5.07 =	507 ¢	

Do you notice a pattern for converting dollars and cents to cents? *Sample answer: You take out the decimal point.* **Each dollar equals 100 cents. So, the number of dollars becomes the hundreds-place in the number of cents. The cents become the tens and ones in the number of cents. To convert dollars and cents to cents, remove the decimal point.**

Activity (C): Add and Subtract Cents

Converting between cents and dollars makes it easier to mentally add and subtract money. Show your child the equations with dollar signs in part C. **All those dollar signs, zeros, and decimal points can look confusing! But if you think about these problems in cents, they're much simpler.**

$0.80 + $0.40 = | $ | $1.30 - $0.60 = | $ | C

Have your child read the addition equation aloud: *80 cents plus 40 cents.* **What's 80 cents plus 40 cents?** *120 cents.* Write 120¢ in the blank at the bottom. **Now, let's convert 120 cents to dollars. 120 cents equals how many dollars and cents?** *1 dollar and 20 cents.* Write $1.20 in the blank at the top.

$0.80 + $0.40 = | $ 1.20 | C

80¢ + 40¢ = | 120 ¢ |

Have your child read the subtraction equation aloud: *1 dollar and 30 cents minus 60 cents.* **1 dollar and 30 cents equals how many cents?** *130 cents.* **What's 130 minus 60?** *70 cents.* Write 70¢ in the blank. **Now, we can just write 70 cents with a decimal point and dollar sign.** Write $0.70 in the blank.

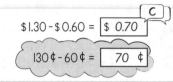

Activity (D): Play Roll and Add

Play Roll and Add.

Roll and Add

Materials: 2 dice

Object of the Game: Win the greater number of points.

Start a simple scorecard on a separate piece of paper.

On your turn, roll 2 dice. Find the matching money amounts on the game board and mentally add them. Write their sum on your scorecard. For example, if you roll a 1 and a 4, the matching amounts are $0.40 and $0.70. Their sum is $1.10, so write $1.10 on the scorecard.

James	Dad
$ 1.10	

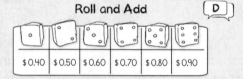

Sample play.

Then, the other player rolls both dice, finds the matching money amounts, and records their sum. Whoever has the greater sum wins a point. If the sums are equal, both players win a point.

Play 5 rounds. Whoever wins more points wins the game.

Independent Practice and Review

Have your child complete the Lesson 7.2 Practice and Review workbook pages.

Your child may use mental math to complete the word problems at the bottom of the Practice page. He does not need to write the equations he uses.

Lesson 7.3
Make Change with Dollars and Cents

Purpose	Materials
• Practice making change from $1 • Add up to make change with dollars and cents	• 3 small office items (such as a pencil, eraser, and ruler) • 3 slips of paper • Play money

Memory Work · **Name the multiples of 3 in order.** *3, 6, 9...* Stop your child when she reaches 30.

Warm-up: Make Change from $1

Write the following prices on a slip of paper and place each on a small office item.

I'd like to buy the item that costs 95¢, please. Give your child 1 one-dollar bill. **How much change do I get?** *5¢.* If she's not sure, say: **One dollar equals 100 cents. So, you can use the pairs that make 100 to help find the change. 95 plus what equals 100?** *5.* **So, my change is 5¢.** Have your child give you 5¢ in change.

Repeat with the other items. For the 75¢ item, your child should give you 25¢ in change. For the 40¢ item, your child should give you 60¢ in change.

Activity (A): Add Up to Make Change with Dollars and Cents

Today, you'll learn how to make change with both dollars and cents. Let's pretend that I'm a customer, and you're the clerk. I'd like to buy the Rubik's cube, but I don't have exact change. Here's $9. Give your child 1 five-dollar bill and 4 one-dollar bills.

You can add up to the next dollar to find how much change to give me. 8 dollars and 90 cents plus what equals 9 dollars? *10 cents.* Write $0.10 in the blank.

So, you need to give me 10¢ in change. Write $0.10 in the blank. Have your child give you 10¢ as change.

If your child seems confused, place 8 one-dollar bills and 9 dimes on the table. **100 cents equal 1 dollar. 90 plus what equals 100?** *10.* **If you had ten cents more, you could trade the coins for 1 dollar, and you'd have 9 dollars.**

Now, I'd like to buy the deck of cards. The cards cost \$3.50, but I only have a five-dollar bill. Give your child 1 five-dollar bill.

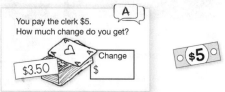

You can add up in two steps to find how much change to give me. First, think about how many cents it takes to reach the next dollar. 3 dollars and 50 cents plus what equals 4 dollars? *50 cents.* Write \$0.50 in the blank, and have your child give you 50¢. **\$4 plus what equals \$5?** *\$1.* Write \$1.00 in the blank, and have your child give you \$1.00. **So, my change is \$1.50.** Write \$1.50 in the blank.

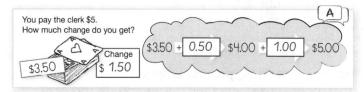

Activity (B): Make Change at the Pretend Store

The prices and items for the Pretend Store are printed in part B. If you'd like to make the activity more hands-on, choose 6 items from around your house and label them with the prices instead.

Show your child the items and prices in Part B. Pretend to buy the items at the store with the money amounts listed below. Have your child add up to figure out how much change to give you for each item.

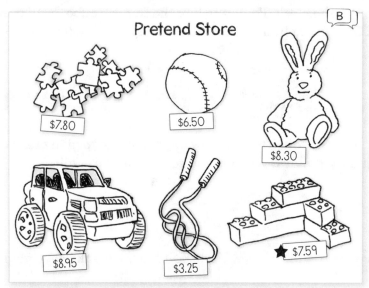

- For the jigsaw puzzle, give your child 1 five-dollar bill and 3 one-dollar bills. She should give you \$0.20 in change.
- For the baseball, give your child 1 five-dollar bill and 2 one-dollar bills. She should give you \$0.50 in change.
- For the stuffed rabbit, give your child 1 ten-dollar bill. She should give you \$1.70 in change.

- For the toy car, give your child 1 ten-dollar bill. She should give you $1.05 in change.
- For the jump rope, give your child 1 five-dollar bill. She should give you $1.75 in change.
- For the blocks, give your child 1 ten-dollar bill. She should give you $2.41 in change.

Independent Practice and Review

Have your child complete the Lesson 7.3 Practice and Review workbook pages.

Lesson 7.4
Mental Addition with Money

Purpose	Materials
• Practice multiplication facts • Mentally add dollars and cents	• 2 decks of playing cards • Play money

Memory Work	• **What do we call the top number in a fraction?** *The numerator.* • **What do we call the bottom number in a fraction?** *The denominator.* • **What does the numerator tell?** *The number of parts.* • **What does the denominator tell?** *How many equal parts the whole was split into.*

In Lessons 7.4 and 7.5, your child will learn to mentally add and subtract money amounts. This skill is useful for real life problem-solving, and it also prepares your child to add and subtract written money amounts in Lessons 7.6 and 7.7.

Warm-up: Play Multiplication War

Play Multiplication War.

The cards in this War game are separated into two decks so that your child gets practice with the more challenging ×2, ×3, ×4, and ×5 facts.

Multiplication War

Materials: 2s, 3s, 4s, 5s, 6s, 7s, 8s, and 9s from 2 decks of cards (64 cards total)

Object of the Game: Win the most cards.

Shuffle together the 2s, 3s, 4s, and 5s, and place them face down in a pile. Shuffle together the 6s, 7s, 8s, and 9s, and place them face down in a separate pile.

2s, 3s, 4s, and 5s   6s, 7s, 8s, and 9s

On your turn, flip over the top card in each pile. Find the product of the numbers. Then, the other player flips over the new top card in each pile and finds the product of those numbers. Whoever has the greater product wins all 4 cards. For example, if Player 1 flips over a 3 and a 7 and Player 2 flips over a 4 and 6, Player 2 wins all 4 cards (since 24 is greater than 21).

The player who flipped over 4 and 6 wins, since the product of 4 and 6 is greater than the product of 3 and 7.

If the products are equal, leave the cards face-up on the table and have both players flip over another card from each pile. Whoever has the greater product wins all eight face-up cards.

Play until the piles run out. Whoever has won more cards wins the game.

Activity (A): Mentally Add Prices at the Yard Sale

In Unit 3, you learned how to add whole numbers with mental math. Today, you'll learn how to mentally add dollars and cents.

We're going to pretend you're having a yard sale today. I'll be the customer. At a yard sale, people sell things they no longer need. Briefly discuss your child's experiences with yard sales. **Which item at the yard sale is the most expensive?** *The tricycle.* **Which item is the least expensive?** *The teapot.*

I'd like to buy the tennis racket and the vase. The tennis racket costs $7.00 and the vase costs $1.40. Model both prices with play money. Point to the matching printed equation.

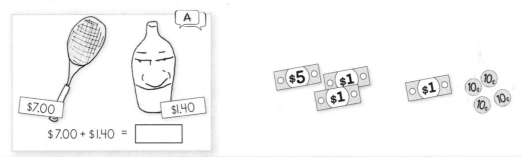

Use dimes (rather than other coins) so that your child can use his whole-number place-value skills to help solve the problems.

I'll add the dollars and cents in two steps, just like we added tens and ones in two steps when we added two-digit numbers. Point to the paper bills. **What's $7.00 plus $1.00?** *$8.00.* Write $8.00 in the blank.

Point to all the paper bills and coins. **What's $8.00 plus $0.40?** *$8.40.* Write $8.40 in both blanks. **I owe you $8.40 for the tennis racket and vase.** Use the play money to pretend to buy the tennis racket and vase.

Allow your child to use any efficient and accurate strategy to mentally add the money amounts. It's fine if he prefers to add the cents before the dollars. See the Unit 3 **Teaching Math with Confidence** (page 82) for more tips on teaching mental math.

Next, I'd like to buy the vacuum cleaner and picture, please. The vacuum cleaner costs $3.90 and the picture costs $4.30. Model both prices with play money as shown. Point to the matching printed equation.

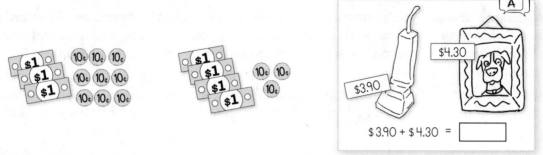

I'll add the dollars and cents in two steps, again. What's $3.90 plus $4.00? *$7.90.* Write $7.90 in the blank.

What's $7.90 plus $0.30? *$8.20.* Write $8.20 in both blanks. **I owe you $8.20 for the vacuum cleaner and picture.** Use the play money to pretend to buy both items.

If your child has trouble adding $7.90 and $0.30, say: **Let's add the dimes in two steps. What's $7.90 plus $0.10?** *$8.00.* **What's $8.00 plus $0.20?** *$8.20.*

Now it's your turn to be the customer! Have your child choose a pair of items to buy and mentally add their prices to find the total cost. Then, have him pretend to pay for the items. Repeat several times.

If your child has trouble keeping the numbers in his head, write the matching equations horizontally on scrap paper.

Independent Practice and Review

Have your child complete the Lesson 7.4 Practice and Review workbook pages.

Your child may use mental math to complete the word problems at the bottom of the Practice page. He does not need to write the equations he uses.

Lesson 7.5
Mental Subtraction with Money

Purpose	Materials
• Practice subtracting tens • Mentally subtract dollars and cents	• Play money • Die • Counters

Memory Work
- **Are times in the morning a.m. or p.m.?** *A.m.*
- **Are times in the afternoon and evening a.m. or p.m.?** *P.m.*

Warm-up (A): Practice Subtracting Tens

Have your child solve these problems mentally:

- 100 − 40 = 60
- 200 − 30 = 170
- 310 − 30 = 280
- 450 − 60 = 390

Activity (A): Mentally Subtract Money

In the last lesson, you learned to mentally add money in two steps. First, you added the dollars. Then, you added the cents. Today, you'll learn to mentally subtract money in two steps.

Have your child read aloud the first problem: *6 dollars minus 2 dollars.* **Let's pretend you have $6.00. Then, you spend $2.00.** Give your child 6 one-dollar bills. Then, have your child pretend to pay you 2 one-dollar bills. **If you have $6.00 and spend $2.00, how much money do you have left?** *$4.00.* Write $4.00 in the blank.

Children sometimes struggle with money problems simply because they feel visually overwhelmed by the dollar sign, decimal point, and placeholder zeros. Reading the problems aloud helps your child understand the meaning of each problem.

Have your child read aloud the next problem: *7 dollars and 50 cents minus 4 dollars.* Give your child 7 one-dollar bills and 5 dimes. Have your child pretend to pay you 4 one-dollar bills. **How much do you have left?** *$3.50.* Write $3.50 in the blank.

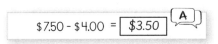 

Have your child read aloud the next problem: *5 dollars and 50 cents minus 2 dollars and 20 cents.* Give your child 5 one-dollar bills and 5 dimes. **Let's subtract the dollars first, and then the cents.** Have your child give you 2 one-dollar bills. **What's $5.50 minus $2.00?** *$3.50.* Write $3.50 in the blank.

Now, we need to subtract the cents. What's $3.50 minus $0.20? *$3.30.* **So, you have $3.30 left.** Write $3.30 in both blanks.

Have your child read aloud the next problem: *3 dollars minus 1 dollar and 20 cents.* **This time, let's try subtracting mentally before we act out the problem with money.**

What's $3.00 minus $1.00? *$2.00.* Write $2.00 in the blank. **Now, we need to subtract the cents. What's $2.00 minus $0.20?** *$1.80.* If she's not sure, suggest she first convert both amounts to cents: **What's 200¢ minus 20¢?** *180¢.* **How many dollars and cents does 180¢ equal?** *$1.80.*

$3.00 - $1.20 = $1.80 $3.00 −$1.00 $2.00 −$0.20 $1.80

Then, give your child 3 one-dollar bills, and have your child pretend to pay you $1.20. Have her give you 2 one-dollar bills, and give her $0.80 in change.

Use the same approach to solve $4.10 − $2.70: **What's $4.10 minus $2.00?** *$2.10.* Write $2.10 in the blank. **What's $2.10 minus $0.70?** *$1.40.* If she's not sure, suggest she first convert both amounts to cents: **What's 210¢ minus 70¢?** *140¢.* **How many dollars and cents does 140¢ equal?** *$1.40.*

Then, give your child 4 one-dollar bills and 1 dime. Have your child pretend to pay you $2.70. Have her give you 3 one-dollar bills, and give her $0.30 in change.

★ $4.10 - $2.70 = $1.40 $4.10 −$2.00 $2.10 −$0.70 $1.40

Activity (B): Play Shopping Spree

We're going to play Shopping Spree to practice subtracting money. This game is the opposite of Race to $10.00. Instead of trying to earn $10.00, the goal is to spend $10.00. Play Shopping Spree.

> To add more fun to the game, have your child pretend to buy something on each turn. For example, if she lands on $0.70: *I'll buy a candy bar!*

Shopping Spree

Materials: One-dollar bills and dimes; die; counters

Object of the Game: Be the first person to spend $10.00.

Give each player 10 one-dollar bills in "spending money." Place a small pile of dimes on the table to serve as the change in the "cash register."

Have each player choose a different-colored counter to use as a game token and place it on one of the Start squares. Start a simple scorecard on a separate sheet of paper. Write $10.00 as the starting score for each player.

Jaden	Mom
$ 10.00	$ 10.00

On your turn, roll the die and advance your token the corresponding number of squares along the path. You may move in either direction. The best strategy is to move to the square with the greater value.

Take the amount listed from your spending money. Pretend to spend the amount of money listed on the square and place it in the cash register. Figure out how much money you now have and write this new amount on the scorecard.

If you do not have the correct change, trade 1 one-dollar bill for 10 dimes from the cash register before paying. If you land on one of the start squares, roll again.

Play then passes to the other player. The first player to reach $0.00 (or land on a spot that is worth more than the player has) wins the game.

Jaden	Mom
$ 10.00	$ 10.00
$ 8.00	$ 7.80
$ 6.60	$ 5.30

Sample first few plays.

Have your child record her own score so that she practices writing money amounts. Encourage her to use mental subtraction (rather than counting the remaining bills and coins) to find how much money she has after each turn.

Independent Practice and Review

Have your child complete the Lesson 7.5 Practice and Review workbook pages.

Your child may use mental math to complete the word problems at the bottom of the Practice page. She does not need to write the equations she uses.

Lesson 7.6
Add Money

Purpose	Materials
• Practice trading pennies for dimes, and dimes for dollars • Model the addition algorithm with money • Use the addition algorithm to add dollars and cents	• Play money • Place-Value Chart (Blackline Master 3), with money labels from Lesson 7.1 • Paper clip

Memory Work	• **What do we call numbers that have a whole number and a fraction?** *Mixed numbers.*

Warm-up: Practice Trading Money Amounts

Place 2 one-dollar bills, 9 dimes, and 15 pennies on the table. **Let's organize this money to make it easier to count. First, let's trade 10 pennies for a dime.** Help your child trade 10 of the pennies on the table for 1 dime from your supply.

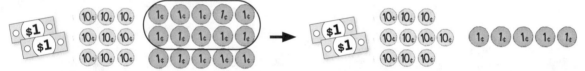

Now, let's trade 10 dimes for a one-dollar bill. Help your child trade 10 dimes on the table for 1 one-dollar bill from your supply. **Now, it's easier to count the money. What's the value of this money?** *$3.05.*

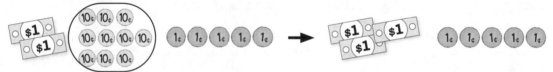

Today, you'll learn how to use the Addition Algorithm to add money amounts. You'll need to trade 10 pennies for 1 dime or 10 dimes for 1 one-dollar bill in some of the problems.

Activity (A): Use the Addition Algorithm to Add Money Amounts

Let's pretend you want to buy the crayons and coloring book. Let's estimate the total cost before we find the exact total. Have your child round each price to the nearest dollar and estimate the sum.

Now, let's find the exact cost. **We'll follow the usual steps in the addition algorithm, and we'll use play money to show the steps.** Model $1.89 and $4.37 with one-dollar bills, dimes, and pennies. Arrange them on the Place-Value Chart as shown.

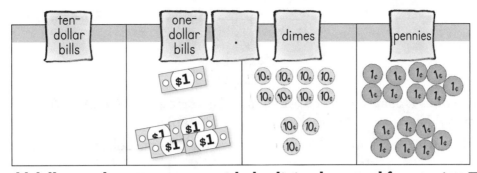

When we add dollars and cents, we start with the digits that stand for pennies. The first step is to add the digits. What's 9 plus 7? *16.* The sum is greater than 9, so I need to trade 10 pennies for 1 dime. Trade 10 pennies for 1 dime and place the dime in the Dimes column.

I added a dime, so I write a 1 above the digits that stand for dimes. Write 1 as shown. There are 6 pennies left, so I write a 6 below the digits that stand for pennies. Write 6 as shown.

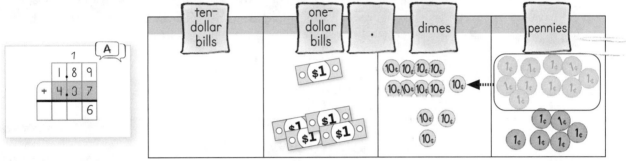

Now, we add the digits that stand for dimes. What's 1 plus 8 plus 3? *12.* The sum is greater than 9, so I need to trade 10 dimes for 1 dollar. Trade 10 dimes for 1 one-dollar bill.

I added a one-dollar bill, so I write a 1 above the digits that stand for one-dollar bills. Write 1 as shown. There are 2 dimes left, so I write a 2 below the digits that stand for dimes. Write 2 as shown.

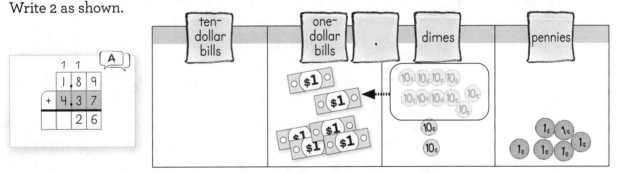

Now, I add the digits that stand for one-dollar bills. What's 1 plus 1 plus 4? *6.* Write 6 as shown.

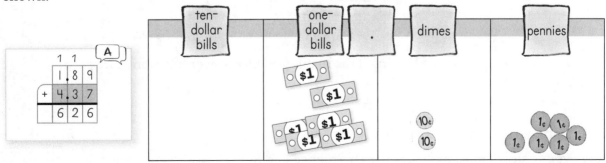

The last step is to write the dollar sign and decimal point. Write a dollar sign in front of the number. The decimal point separates the dollars and the cents, so I write it directly below the other decimal points. Write a decimal point as shown.

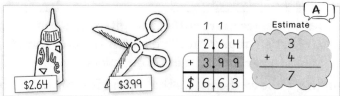

So, how much does it cost to buy the crayons and coloring book? *$6.26.* **We estimated that the answer would be around $6, so that seems reasonable.**

Have your child use the addition algorithm to solve the other problem in part A.

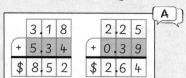

Use play money to support your child as needed as he completes the problem. If he has trouble, model every step with one-dollar bills, dimes, and pennies, and discuss how the money matches the written numbers. If he fully understands the process, allow him to solve the problem without modeling it.

Activity (B): Play Spin to Win

Play Spin to Win. Model the problems with play money as needed.

Spin to Win

Materials: Paper clip
Object of the Game: Win the most points.

Place one end of the paper clip in the center of the spinner. Place the point of a pencil through the paper clip so that it touches the very center of the circle.

There are 5 rounds in the game. For each round, hold the pencil upright and spin the paper clip so that it spins freely around the circle. Write the amount it lands on in the top line of the first blank grid. Then, spin again, and write this amount in the second line of the grid. Add to find the sum of the two spins.

Then, have the other player spin twice, write the value of each spin in the neighboring blank grid, and find the sum. Whoever has the greater sum wins a point.

	3 .	1	8			2 .	2	5
+	5 .	3	4		+	0 .	3	9
$	8 .	5	2		$	2 .	6	4

Sample first round. The player whose sum is $8.52 wins the point.

Continue until you have filled in all the blank grids. Whoever has won more points wins the game.

Independent Practice and Review

Have your child complete the Lesson 7.6 Practice and Review workbook page.

The Practice section is short, since your child practiced lots of addition with money in the Lesson Activities. As a result, there is only one page of Practice and Review in this lesson.

Lesson 7.7
Subtract Money

Purpose	Materials
• Review sum, difference, and product • Model the subtraction algorithm with money • Use the subtraction algorithm to subtract dollars and cents	• Play money • Place-Value Chart (Blackline Master 3), with money labels from Lesson 7.1

Memory Work	• **What do we call the result when we multiply two numbers together?** *The product.* • **What do we call the result when we add numbers together?** *The sum.* • **What do we call the result when we subtract a number from another number?** *The difference.*

Warm-up: Review Sum, Difference, and Product

Ask your child the following questions:

- **What's the sum of 5 and 7?** *12.*
- **What's the product of 5 and 7?** *35.*
- **What's the difference between 5 and 7?** *2.*

Activity (A): Use the Subtraction Algorithm to Subtract Money Amounts

In the last lesson, you learned how to use the addition algorithm to add dollars and cents. Today, you'll learn how to use the subtraction algorithm to subtract dollars and cents.

Let's pretend you have $7.19. Give your child 7 one-dollar bills, 1 dime, and 9 pennies. **You want to buy the markers. Let's estimate how much money you will have left before we find the exact amount.** Have your child round each money amount to the nearest dollar and estimate their difference.

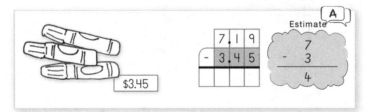

Now, let's find the exact amount you'll have left. We'll follow the usual steps in the subtraction algorithm, and we'll use play money to show the steps. Have your child arrange the play money on the Place-Value Chart.

When we subtract dollars and cents, we start with the digits that stand for pennies. 9 is greater than 5, so we don't need to trade. What's 9 minus 5? *4.* Remove 5 pennies and write 4 as shown.

Next, we subtract the digits that stand for dimes. 1 is less than 4, so we need more dimes before we subtract. Let's trade 1 dollar for 10 dimes. Trade 1 one-dollar bill for 10 dimes. **Now, we have 6 one-dollar bills.** Cross out the 7 and write 6 above it. **We have 11 dimes.** Cross out the 1 and write 11 above it.

Now, we're ready to subtract the dimes. What's 11 minus 4? *7.* Remove 4 dimes and write 7 as shown.

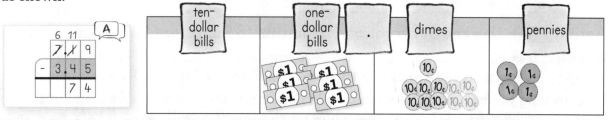

Now, we subtract the digits that stand for one-dollar bills. What's 6 minus 3? *3.* Remove 3 one-dollar bills and write 3 as shown. **The last step is to write the dollar sign and decimal point.** Write a dollar sign and decimal point as shown.

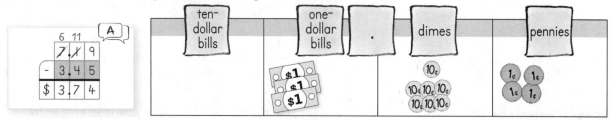

How much money do you have left? *$3.74.* **We estimated that the answer would be around $4, so that seems like a reasonable answer.**

Show your child the second problem in part A ($9.00 – $6.32). **This time, let's pretend you have $9.00 and buy the paint set for $6.32.** Have your child round each number to the nearest dollar and estimate the difference.

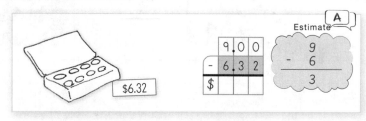

Now, let's find the exact amount you'll have left. The top number has zeros, so we'll need to be extra careful with the trading. Model $9 with one-dollar bills on the Place-Value Chart.

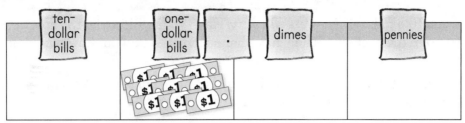

We start with the digits that stand for pennies. We need to subtract 2 pennies, but we don't have any pennies. We don't have any dimes either! How can we get some dimes and pennies? *By trading a one-dollar bill.*

First, we trade 1 one-dollar bill for 10 dimes. Trade 1 one-dollar bill for 10 dimes. Record the trade as shown.

Next, we trade 1 dime for 10 pennies. Have your child trade 1 dime for 10 pennies. Record the trade as shown.

Now, we're ready to subtract! Have your child complete the problem. Use play money to model the steps.

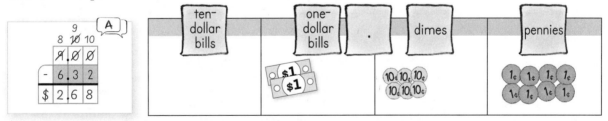

Activity (B): Subtract to Find a Gift Card Balance

Let's pretend you have a gift card with a balance of $9.50 for the art supply store. There are so many things you can buy: beads, craft sticks, googly eyes, pipe cleaners, clay, and pompoms!

If you'd like to make this activity more hands-on, set up a Pretend Store with household items instead. Use the printed prices.

What would you like to buy? *Answers will vary.* Have your child write the cost of her chosen item below $9.50 in the first grid. Then, have her subtract to find out how much money she'll have left after buying that item.

For example, if your child chooses the modeling clay, have her write $2.36 in the grid. Then, have her subtract to find that she'll have $7.14 left.

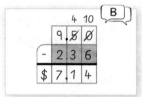

Sample first choice.

Write the difference on the top line of the next grid. **You have this much money left on the gift card.** Have your child choose another item and subtract to find how much money is left on the gift card. Repeat until the "balance" is less than $1.59 (and your child no longer has enough money to buy another item).

Independent Practice and Review

Have your child complete the Lesson 7.7 Practice and Review workbook pages.

The Practice section is short, since your child practiced lots of subtraction with money in the Lesson Activities.

Lesson 7.8
Enrichment (Optional)

Purpose	Materials
• Practice memory work • Understand money arithmetic in real-life situations • Add and subtract real-life money amounts • Summarize what your child has learned and assess your child's progress	• *Follow the Money!,* written and illustrated by Loreen Leedy • Toy catalog or access to a website with items your child would like to buy

Warm-up: Review Memory Work

Quiz your child on all memory work through Unit 7. See pages 527-528 for the full list.

Math Picture Book: *Follow the Money!*

Read *Follow the Money!,* written and illustrated by Loreen Leedy. As you read, give your child a chance to solve the problems before you read the answers. Also talk about how the transactions in the story match the written equations.

Follow the Money! introduces multiplying money. Discuss how the multiplication equations match the equal-groups situations in the story, but don't ask your child to solve these problems on his own. He will learn how to multiply money amounts in later grades.

Enrichment Activity: Add and Subtract Prices

Have your child choose two items he would like to pretend to buy from a toy catalog or website. Have him use the addition algorithm to figure out the total cost of both items. Then, have him use the subtraction algorithm to figure out the difference between the two prices. For example, if he chooses an item that costs $37.49 and an item that costs $18.99:

Total Cost	Difference in Prices
37.49	37.49
+18.99	−18.99
$56.48	$18.50

Unit Wrap-up

Have your child complete the Unit 7 Wrap-up.

Unit 7 Answer Key

7.1 Practice

Practice 🔹 Round each price to the nearest dollar.

$2.09	$2.19	$2.49	$2.59	$2.79	$2.89
$2	$2	$2	$3	$3	$3

$3.17	$6.94	$8.50	$12.64	$38.07	$46.39
$3	$7	$9	$13	$38	$46

Complete with <, >, or =.

$2.47 $<$ $2.74

$2.40 $>$ $2.04

$2.00 $=$ $2

$0.02 $<$ $0.20

$2.02 $>$ $2.00

Complete. Use a dollar sign and decimal point for each amount.

Coins	Value
4 pennies	$0.04
4 nickels	$0.20
4 dimes	$0.40
4 quarters	$1.00

Solve.

Gabe has 4 dimes and 6 pennies. Sarah has 3 dimes and 3 nickels. Who has more money? How much more?

Gabe: 46 ¢
Sarah: 45 ¢
Gabe, 1 ¢ more

Gisele has 3 quarters. Eli has 5 dimes, 4 nickels, and 2 pennies. Who has more money? How much more?

Gisele: 75 ¢
Eli: 72 ¢
Gisele, 3 ¢ more

7.1 Review

Review 🔹 Write mixed numbers to match the shapes.

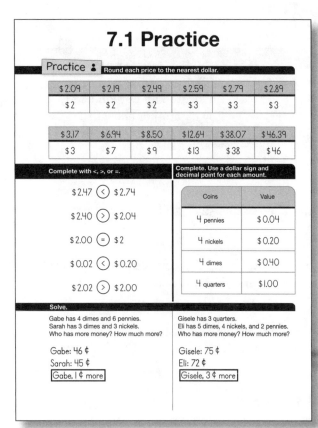

$2\frac{3}{4}$ $1\frac{3}{8}$

Complete.

36 +6 42 +6 48 +6 54 +6 60

42 +7 49 +7 56 +7 63 +7 70

48 +8 56 +8 64 +8 72 +8 80

Complete.   **Match pairs that equal 100.**

25 + 50 = 75

75 + 25 = 100

150 + 25 = 175

50 + 150 = 200

200 + 250 = 450

38 — 72
48 — 82
28 — 52
18 — 62

7.2 Practice

Practice 🔹 Complete.

$	¢	$	¢	$	¢
$2.00	200 ¢	$4.00	400 ¢	$9.25	925 ¢
$2.09	209 ¢	$4.06	406 ¢	$5.07	507 ¢
$2.45	245 ¢	$4.10	410 ¢	$6.15	615 ¢
$2.50	250 ¢	$4.32	432 ¢	$8.91	891 ¢
$2.99	299 ¢	$4.57	457 ¢	$3.79	379 ¢

Use the chart to solve.

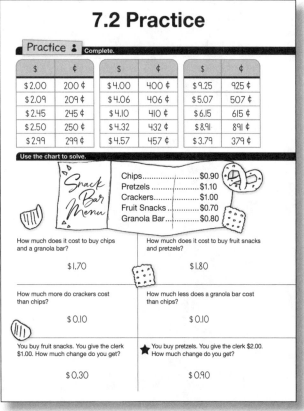

Snack Bar Menu

Chips.....................$0.90
Pretzels $1.10
Crackers................$1.00
Fruit Snacks $0.70
Granola Bar...........$0.80

How much does it cost to buy chips and a granola bar?

$1.70

How much does it cost to buy fruit snacks and pretzels?

$1.80

How much more do crackers cost than chips?

$0.10

How much less does a granola bar cost than chips?

$0.10

You buy fruit snacks. You give the clerk $1.00. How much change do you get?

$0.30

⭐ You buy pretzels. You give the clerk $2.00. How much change do you get?

$0.90

7.2 Review

Review 🔹 Complete.

×	3	×	10	×	9	×	4	×	2
9		10		5		3		9	
27		100		45		12		18	

×	5	×	7	×	10	×	4	×	1
8		4		7		9		8	
40		28		70		36		8	

Complete.

52 − 47 = 5

51 − 46 = 5

50 − 45 = 5

94 − 88 = 6

84 − 78 = 6

74 − 68 = 6

Solve.

You give the clerk $30. How much change do you get?

$16   Change $ 14

You give the clerk $50. How much change do you get?

$39   Change $ 11

Unit 7 Answer Key

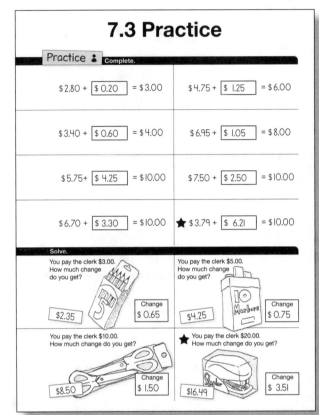

7.3 Practice

Practice · Complete.

$2.80 + $ 0.20 = $3.00	$4.75 + $ 1.25 = $6.00
$3.40 + $ 0.60 = $4.00	$6.95 + $ 1.05 = $8.00
$5.75 + $ 4.25 = $10.00	$7.50 + $ 2.50 = $10.00
$6.70 + $ 3.30 = $10.00	★ $3.79 + $ 6.21 = $10.00

Solve.

You pay the clerk $3.00. How much change do you get?
Change $ 0.65
$2.35

You pay the clerk $5.00. How much change do you get?
$4.25
Change $ 0.75

You pay the clerk $10.00. How much change do you get?
$8.50
Change $ 1.50

★ You pay the clerk $20.00. How much change do you get?
$16.49
Change $ 3.51

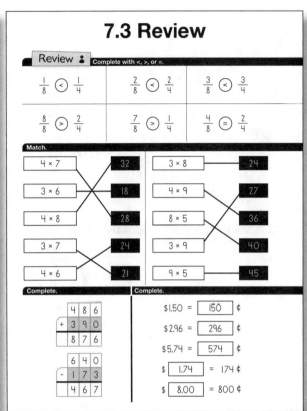

7.3 Review

Review · Complete with <, >, or =.

$\frac{1}{8}$ < $\frac{1}{4}$ $\frac{2}{8}$ < $\frac{2}{4}$ $\frac{3}{8}$ < $\frac{3}{4}$

$\frac{8}{8}$ > $\frac{2}{4}$ $\frac{7}{8}$ > $\frac{1}{4}$ $\frac{4}{8}$ = $\frac{2}{4}$

Match.

4 × 7 — 32
3 × 6 — 18
4 × 8 — 28
3 × 7 — 24
4 × 6 — 21

3 × 8 — 24
4 × 9 — 27
8 × 5 — 36
3 × 9 — 40
9 × 5 — 45

Complete.

$$\begin{array}{r} 4\ 8\ 6 \\ +\ 3\ 9\ 0 \\ \hline 8\ 7\ 6 \end{array}$$

$$\begin{array}{r} 6\ 4\ 0 \\ -\ 1\ 7\ 3 \\ \hline 4\ 6\ 7 \end{array}$$

Complete.

$1.50 = 150 ¢
$2.96 = 296 ¢
$5.74 = 574 ¢
$ 1.74 = 174 ¢
$ 8.00 = 800 ¢

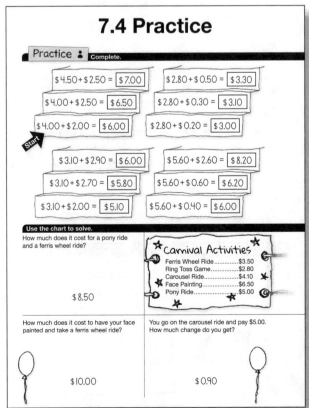

7.4 Practice

Practice · Complete.

$4.50 + $2.50 = $7.00
$4.00 + $2.50 = $6.50
$4.00 + $2.00 = $6.00 **Start**
$3.10 + $2.90 = $6.00
$3.10 + $2.70 = $5.80
$3.10 + $2.00 = $5.10

$2.80 + $0.50 = $3.30
$2.80 + $0.30 = $3.10
$2.80 + $0.20 = $3.00
$5.60 + $2.60 = $8.20
$5.60 + $0.60 = $6.20
$5.60 + $0.40 = $6.00

Use the chart to solve.

How much does it cost for a pony ride and a ferris wheel ride?

$8.50

☆ Carnival Activities ☆
Ferris Wheel Ride..............$3.50
Ring Toss Game................$2.80
Carousel Ride....................$4.10
Face Painting.....................$6.50
Pony Ride...........................$5.00

How much does it cost to have your face painted and take a ferris wheel ride?
$10.00

You go on the carousel ride and pay $5.00. How much change do you get?
$0.90

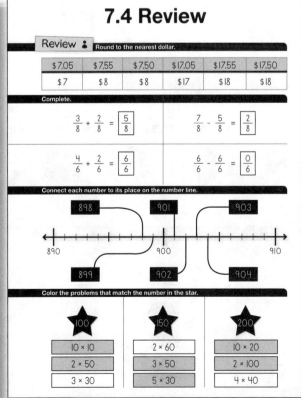

7.4 Review

Review · Round to the nearest dollar.

$7.05	$7.55	$7.50	$17.05	$17.55	$17.50
$7	$8	$8	$17	$18	$18

Complete.

$\frac{3}{8} + \frac{2}{8} = \frac{5}{8}$ $\frac{7}{8} - \frac{5}{8} = \frac{2}{8}$

$\frac{4}{6} + \frac{2}{6} = \frac{6}{6}$ $\frac{6}{6} - \frac{6}{6} = \frac{0}{6}$

Connect each number to its place on the number line.

898   901   903
890 ——————— 900 ——————— 910
899   902   904

Color the problems that match the number in the star.

★ 100
10 × 10
2 × 50
3 × 30

★ 150
2 × 60
3 × 50
5 × 30

★ 200
10 × 20
2 × 100
4 × 40

Unit 7 Answer Key

7.5 Practice

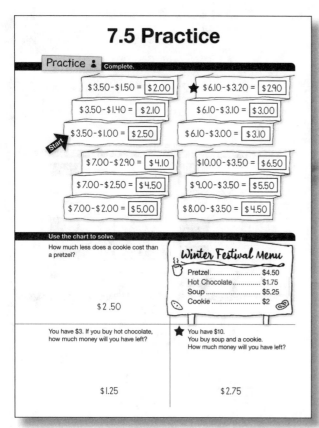

Practice 👤 Complete.

$3.50 - $1.50 = **$2.00**

$3.50 - $1.40 = **$2.10**

Start $3.50 - $1.00 = **$2.50**

★ $6.10 - $3.20 = **$2.90**

$6.10 - $3.10 = **$3.00**

$6.10 - $3.00 = **$3.10**

$7.00 - $2.90 = **$4.10**

$7.00 - $2.50 = **$4.50**

$7.00 - $2.00 = **$5.00**

$10.00 - $3.50 = **$6.50**

$9.00 - $3.50 = **$5.50**

$8.00 - $3.50 = **$4.50**

Use the chart to solve.

How much less does a cookie cost than a pretzel?

$2.50

Winter Festival Menu

Pretzel $4.50
Hot Chocolate $1.75
Soup $5.25
Cookie $2

You have $3. If you buy hot chocolate, how much money will you have left?

$1.25

★ You have $10.
You buy soup and a cookie.
How much money will you have left?

$2.75

7.5 Review

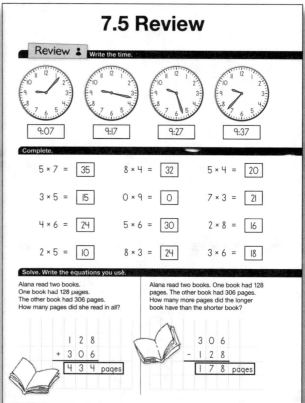

Review 👤 Write the time.

9:07   9:17   9:27   9:37

Complete.

$5 \times 7 =$ **35** $8 \times 4 =$ **32** $5 \times 4 =$ **20**

$3 \times 5 =$ **15** $0 \times 9 =$ **0** $7 \times 3 =$ **21**

$4 \times 6 =$ **24** $5 \times 6 =$ **30** $2 \times 8 =$ **16**

$2 \times 5 =$ **10** $8 \times 3 =$ **24** $3 \times 6 =$ **18**

Solve. Write the equations you use.

Alana read two books. One book had 128 pages. The other book had 306 pages. How many pages did she read in all?

```
  1 2 8
+ 3 0 6
  4 3 4  pages
```

Alana read two books. One book had 128 pages. The other book had 306 pages. How many more pages did the longer book have than the shorter book?

```
  3 0 6
- 1 2 8
  1 7 8  pages
```

7.6 Practice/Review

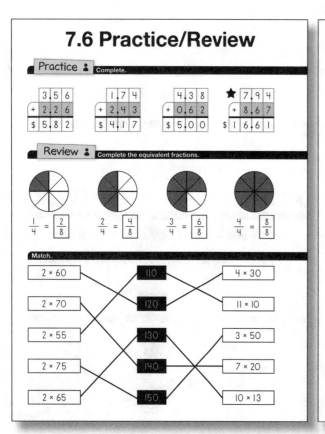

Practice 👤 Complete.

```
  3.5 6
+ 2.2 6
$ 5.8 2
```

```
  1.7 4
+ 2.4 3
$ 4.1 7
```

```
  4.3 8
+ 0.6 2
$ 5.0 0
```

★
```
  7.9 4
+ 8.6 7
$ 16.6 1
```

Review 👤 Complete the equivalent fractions.

$\frac{1}{4} = \frac{2}{8}$ $\frac{2}{4} = \frac{4}{8}$ $\frac{3}{4} = \frac{6}{8}$ $\frac{4}{4} = \frac{8}{8}$

Match.

2 × 60 ——— 110 ——— 4 × 30

2 × 70 ——— 120 ——— 11 × 10

2 × 55 ——— 130 ——— 3 × 50

2 × 75 ——— 140 ——— 7 × 20

2 × 65 ——— 150 ——— 10 × 13

7.7 Practice/Review

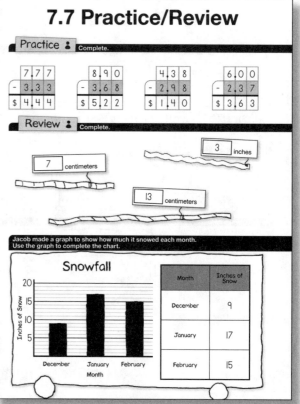

Practice 👤 Complete.

```
  7.7 7
- 3.3 3
$ 4.4 4
```

```
  8.9 0
- 3.6 8
$ 5.2 2
```

```
  4.3 8
- 2.9 8
$ 1.4 0
```

```
  6.0 0
- 2.3 7
$ 3.6 3
```

Review 👤 Complete.

7 centimeters

3 inches

13 centimeters

Jacob made a graph to show how much it snowed each month. Use the graph to complete the chart.

Snowfall

Month	Inches of Snow
December	9
January	17
February	15

Unit 7 Answer Key

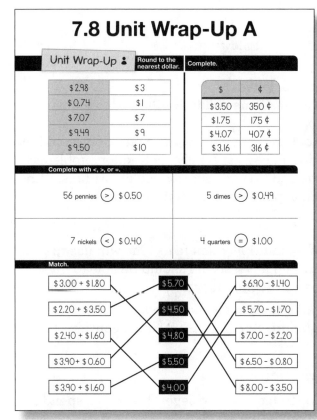

7.8 Unit Wrap-Up A

Unit Wrap-Up — **Round to the nearest dollar.**   **Complete.**

$2.98	$3
$0.74	$1
$7.07	$7
$9.49	$9
$9.50	$10

$	¢
$3.50	350 ¢
$1.75	175 ¢
$4.07	407 ¢
$3.16	316 ¢

Complete with <, >, or =.

56 pennies (>) $0.50   5 dimes (>) $0.49

7 nickels (<) $0.40   4 quarters (=) $1.00

Match.

$3.00 + $1.80	**$5.70**	$6.90 - $1.40
$2.20 + $3.50	**$4.50**	$5.70 - $1.70
$2.40 + $1.60	**$4.80**	$7.00 - $2.20
$3.90 + $0.60	**$5.50**	$6.50 - $0.80
$3.90 + $1.60	**$4.00**	$8.00 - $3.50

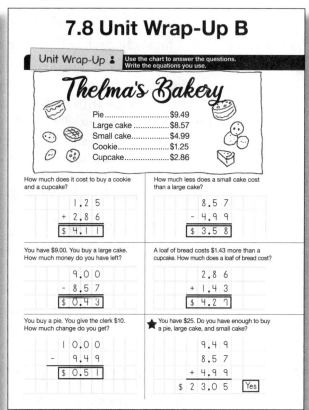

7.8 Unit Wrap-Up B

Unit Wrap-Up — **Use the chart to answer the questions. Write the equations you use.**

Thelma's Bakery

Pie $9.49
Large cake $8.57
Small cake................ $4.99
Cookie...................... $1.25
Cupcake................... $2.86

How much does it cost to buy a cookie and a cupcake?

```
    1 . 2 5
  + 2 . 8 6
  $ 4 . 1 1
```

How much less does a small cake cost than a large cake?

```
    8 . 5 7
  - 4 . 9 9
  $ 3 . 5 8
```

You have $9.00. You buy a large cake. How much money do you have left?

```
    9 . 0 0
  - 8 . 5 7
  $ 0 . 4 3
```

A loaf of bread costs $1.43 more than a cupcake. How much does a loaf of bread cost?

```
    2 . 8 6
  + 1 . 4 3
  $ 4 . 2 7
```

You buy a pie. You give the clerk $10. How much change do you get?

```
   1 0 . 0 0
  -  9 . 4 9
   $ 0 . 5 1
```

★ **You have $25. Do you have enough to buy a pie, large cake, and small cake?**

```
     9 . 4 9
     8 . 5 7
   + 4 . 9 9
 $ 2 3 . 0 5    Yes
```

Unit 7 Checkpoint

What to Expect at the End of Unit 7

By the end of Unit 7, most children will be able to do the following:

- Round money amounts to the nearest dollar.
- Convert dollars to cents, and convert cents to dollars.
- Add up to make change with dollars and cents. Some children will need to model these problems with money.
- Solve mental addition and subtraction problems with dollars and cents. Some children will still need to model these problems with money, especially subtraction problems.
- Add and subtract money amounts with the addition and subtraction algorithms. Some children will need help lining up the decimal points or subtracting across a zero.

Is Your Child Ready to Move on?

In Unit 8, your child will learn the ×6, ×7, ×8, and ×9 multiplication facts. She will use the ×5 and ×10 facts as stepping stones to these challenging facts, so she should be able to find answers to the ×5 or ×10 facts within 3-5 seconds before moving on.

Your child does not need to have the ×5 or ×10 facts completely mastered, and she does not need to have full fluency with the ×3 or ×4 facts before starting Unit 8. She'll continue to practice them throughout the unit.

What to Do If Your Child Needs More Practice

If your child can't find the answers to the ×5 and ×10 facts within several seconds, spend a day or two practicing these facts before moving on to Unit 8.

Activities for Practicing the ×5 and ×10 Facts

- Multiplication Cover Up (×5) (Lesson 2.7)
- Review ×5 Facts on the Clock (Lesson 3.2)
- Tic-Tac-Toe Crash (×10) (Lesson 2.5)

Unit 8
Multiplication, Part 3

Overview

In Units 2 and 4, your child learned the ×1, ×2, ×3, × 4, ×5, and ×10 facts. In this unit, he will use these facts as stepping stones to learn the final multiplication facts. He'll also learn to convert weeks to days and solve two-step multiplication word problems.

This unit is the final multiplication unit in *Third Grade Math with Confidence*, but **your child is not expected to fully master all the multiplication facts by the end of the unit.** He'll continue to practice them throughout the rest of the year, and he'll further reinforce them as he studies area and division. See the Unit 8 checkpoint for more details.

What Your Child Will Learn

In this unit, your child will learn to:

- Find answers for the ×6, ×7, ×8, and ×9 facts
- Multiply and add to find the total of equal groups and extra objects
- Multiply 6, 7, 8, and 9 by multiples of 10 (for example, 9 × 70 or 6 × 60)
- Multiply to convert weeks to days
- Solve two-step multiplication word problems

Lesson List

Lesson 8.1	×6 Facts	Lesson 8.6	Multiply Tens
Lesson 8.2	Multiply and Add	Lesson 8.7	×7 Facts and Convert Weeks to Days
Lesson 8.3	×9 Facts		
Lesson 8.4	Two-Step Word Problems	Lesson 8.8	Multiply and Add to Convert Weeks and Days to Days
Lesson 8.5	×8 Facts		
		Lesson 8.9	Enrichment (Optional)

Extra Materials Needed for Unit 8

- Calendar, optional
- For optional Enrichment Lesson:
  - × *The Best of Times: Math Strategies that Multiply,* written by Greg Tang and illustrated by Harry Briggs. Scholastic Press, 2002.
  - × Varies, depending on which activity you choose. See Lesson 8.9 (page 266) for options.

Teaching Math with Confidence:
Two Ways to Find Answers for the Remaining Multiplication Facts

Your child has already studied 84 of the 100 multiplication facts from 1×1 to 10×10. In this unit, he will study the remaining 16 multiplication facts and review the facts he's learned so far. As in Unit 4, you'll teach your child to use the multiplication facts he already knows as stepping stones to find answers for the new facts.

One way to find the answers is to use a related fact from a different multiplication table. You'll teach your child to use this approach for the x6, x9, and x8 facts.

- **×6 facts:** Add 1 group to the corresponding ×5 fact to solve the ×6 fact. For example, 5 × 7 is 5 groups of 7. So, you can add 1 more group of 7 to 35 to find that 6 × 7 is 42.

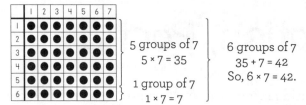

5 groups of 7
5 × 7 = 35

1 group of 7
1 × 7 = 7

6 groups of 7
35 + 7 = 42
So, 6 × 7 = 42.

- **×9 facts:** Subtract 1 group from the corresponding ×10 fact to solve the ×9 fact. For example, 10 × 8 is 10 groups of 8. So, you can subtract 1 group of 8 from 80 to find that 9 × 8 is 72.

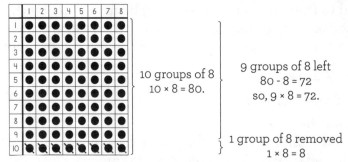

10 groups of 8
10 × 8 = 80.

9 groups of 8 left
80 - 8 = 72
so, 9 × 8 = 72.

1 group of 8 removed
1 × 8 = 8

- **×8 facts:** Double the related ×4 fact to find the ×8 fact. For example, 4 × 7 equals 4 groups of 7. 8 × 7 equals 8 groups of 7. So, you can double 28 to find that 8 × 7 is 56.

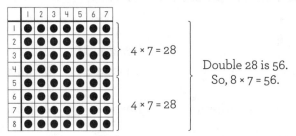

4 × 7 = 28

4 × 7 = 28

Double 28 is 56.
So, 8 × 7 = 56.

Another way to find answers is to use the facts within the same table. For example, say you want to find 7 × 7. If you know 5 × 7 = 35, you can add 7 to 35 twice to find that 7 × 7 = 49.

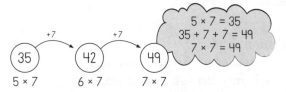

5 × 7 = 35
35 + 7 + 7 = 49
7 × 7 = 49

+7   +7

35   42   49
5 × 7   6 × 7   7 × 7

This method is like skip-counting by 7s, starting at 35. It's an efficient way to use skip-counting to solve multiplication problems, and it's fine for your child to use this approach for all multiplication facts. This approach is especially helpful for the x7 facts, since they do not have a straightforward strategy like the x6, x9, and x8 facts. You'll leave these facts for last so your child can use facts he already knows within the x7 table to help find their answers.

Children often find these last 16 multiplication facts the most difficult to learn, so don't be discouraged if your child finds this unit challenging. Demonstrate the strategies as much as your child needs, allow him to use the dot array as he solves the practice exercises, and reassure him that full fluency will come with more practice.

Lesson 8.1
×6 Facts

Purpose	Materials
• Practice ×5 facts • Introduce ×6 facts • Use ×5 facts to find answers to ×6 facts	• Dot array and L-cover (Blackline Master 5) • Playing cards • Counters

Memory Work
- **What is another name for 12 p.m.?** *Noon.*
- **What is another name for 12 a.m.?** *Midnight.*

In this lesson, you will demonstrate two different ways your child can use related multiplication facts to find answers to the ×6 facts. See the Unit 8 **Teaching Math with Confidence** for more on these two approaches.

Warm-up (A): Practice ×5 Facts

Do a brief oral review of the following ×5 facts. Encourage your child to respond as quickly as possible for each fact.

- 5 × 6 = *30*
- 5 × 9 = *45*
- 5 × 7 = *35*

- 5 × 5 = *25*
- 5 × 10 = *50*
- 5 × 8 = *40*

This activity prepares your child to use the ×5 facts to figure out the ×6 facts.

Activity (A): Introduce ×6 Facts

We're beginning the last unit on multiplication today. You have only 16 multiplication facts left to study! You'll learn the rest of them in this unit.

Show your child the list of ×6 facts in part A. **You have already learned most of the ×6 table.** Have your child complete the ×6 facts that she has already learned: 6 × 1, 6 × 2, 6 × 3, 6 × 4, 6 × 5, and 6 × 10.

			A
6 × 1 = 6		6 × 6 = ☐	
6 × 2 = 12		6 × 7 = ☐	
6 × 3 = 18		6 × 8 = ☐	
6 × 4 = 24		6 × 9 = ☐	
6 × 5 = 30		6 × 10 = 60	

There are only 4 of the ×6 facts left to learn. One way to figure out the rest of the ×6 facts is to use the ×6 facts you already know as stepping stones. Slide the L-cover over the dot array to show 6 × 5. **You know 6 times 5 is 30.** Slide the L-cover to show 6 × 6. **You can add 30 plus 6 to find 6 × 6. What's 6 × 6?** *36.* Write 36 in the blank.

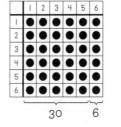

30   6

6 × 6 = 36 **A**

Continue in the same way with the other new ×6 facts. Encourage your child to add 6 to the previous product to find each new total.

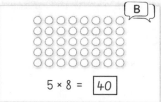

What patterns do you notice? *Sample answers: Some of the answers are the numbers from the ×3 table. All of the products are even.*

Activity (B): Use ×5 Facts to Find Answers to ×6 Facts

Use a piece of paper to cover the completed ×6 table in part A. **Another way to find answers to the ×6 facts is to use the ×5 facts you already know as stepping stones.**

Show your child the first array in part B. **Let's pretend you made an array with 5 rows. You put 8 marbles in each row. What's 5 times 8?** *40.* Write 40 in the blank.

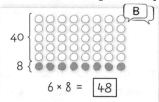

Show your child the next array. **Then, you add another row to the array. Now, the array has 6 rows of 8. How many marbles are in the array now?** *48.* **How do you know?** *Sample answer: The array had 40 marbles, and I added 8. 40 plus 8 equals 48.* Write 48 in the blank.

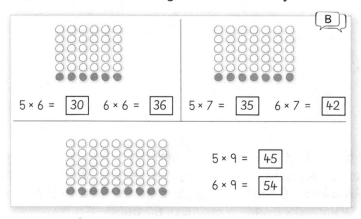

Have your child use the same approach to complete part B. Encourage her to imagine first creating an array with 5 rows and then adding 1 row to the array.

Activity (C): Play Tic-Tac-Toe Crash (×6)

The multiples of 6 are in order on the Tic-Tac-Toe Crash game board. Let's say you wanted to find the answer to 6 times 4. How can you use the way the game board is arranged to find the answer? *Sample answer: I could look for the 4th multiple.* **What's the answer to 6 times 4?** *24.*

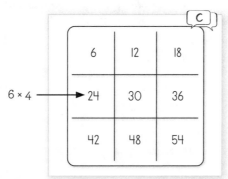

Play Tic-Tac-Toe Crash. See Lesson 2.5 (page 64) for general directions. On your turn, flip over the top card. Multiply the card by 6, say the matching multiplication fact, and place a counter on the box with the matching product. For example, if you flip over a 7, say "6 times 7 equals 42" and place a counter on 42.

Independent Practice and Review

Have your child complete the Lesson 8.1 Practice and Review workbook pages.

If your child is tired after completing the Lesson Activities and Practice pages, you may want to have her complete the Review page at a different time of day.

Lesson 8.2
Multiply and Add

Purpose	Materials
• Practice naming the multiples of 6 • Review how to use the ×5 facts to find answers to the ×6 facts • Practice ×6 facts • Learn to multiply and add to find a total quantity	• Multiplication Strategies chart (Blackline Master 6) • Counters • Dot array and L-cover (Blackline Master 5) • Playing cards

Memory Work   · **How many centimeters equal 1 meter?** *100.*

In this unit, you'll spend two lessons on each new set of multiplication facts. In the first lesson, you'll introduce the new set of facts and teach your child a strategy for finding their answers. In the second lesson, you'll
review the strategy, practice the facts, and teach a related multiplication concept. If your child doesn't have
the stamina to cover so much material in one day, split these lessons over two days.

Warm-up: Practice Naming the Multiples of 6

Name the multiples of 6 in order. *6, 12, 18…* Write each multiple on a piece of paper as your
child says it. Encourage him to add 6 to the previous multiple in order to find the next one.
Stop him when he reaches 60.

6, 12, 18, 24, 30, 36, 42, 48, 54, 60

Writing the numbers as your child says them helps him begin to visually recognize the multiples in addition
to naming them orally.

**Knowing the multiples of a number by heart makes it easier to find answers to the related
multiplication facts. We'll practice naming multiples often in this unit to help you learn
the new multiplication facts.**

Activity (A): Practice Using the ×5 Facts to Find ×6 Facts

In the last lesson, you learned how to use the ×5 facts to find answers for the ×6 facts. Read
aloud the ×6 strategy on the Multiplication Strategies chart (Blackline Master 6). Briefly discuss the example.

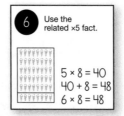

**Today, you'll practice the ×6 facts some more. You'll also learn how to combine multiplica-
tion and addition to find totals.**

Show your child the first pair of problems. Slide the L-cover over the dot array to show 6 × 7.
Draw a ring around 5 groups of 7. **What's 5 times 7?** *35.* Write 35 in the blank.

6 times 7 is 7 more than 35. So, what's 6 times 7? *42.* Write 42 in the blank. If your child's
not sure, suggest he add 35 plus 7.

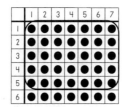

$$5 \times 7 = \boxed{35}$$
$$6 \times 7 = \boxed{42}$$

Have your child use the same approach to complete part A. Model each problem with the dot array and encourage him to use the matching ×5 fact to figure out the ×6 fact.

$$5 \times 8 = \boxed{40} \qquad 5 \times 9 = \boxed{45}$$
$$6 \times 8 = \boxed{48} \qquad 6 \times 9 = \boxed{54}$$

Activity (B): Play Multiplication Bingo (×6)

Use the game boards to play Multiplication Bingo. See Lesson 2.4 (page 61) for general directions. Have your child turn over the top card and multiply the number on the card times 6. For example, if the card is a 5: *6 times 5 equals 30.* Then, each of you uses a counter to cover a square containing that product on your game board.

Activity (C): Multiply and Add to Find a Total

Let's pretend that you work at a bakery and sell cookies. One day, a customer buys 4 boxes of chocolate cookies. Each box has 6 cookies. She also buys 3 sugar cookies.

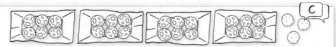

To find the total number of cookies, we can multiply and then add. The boxes have equal numbers of cookies, so first we multiply to find the number of chocolate cookies. What multiplication problem matches the boxes of chocolate cookies? *4 times 6.* Write 4 and 6 in the blanks.

$$\boxed{4} \times \boxed{6} + \boxed{} = \boxed{}$$

Then, we add on the 3 sugar cookies. Write 3 in the blank. **When multiplication and addition are in the same equation, mathematicians have agreed that we multiply before we add. What's 4 times 6?** *24.* **24 plus 3?** *27.* **So, there are a total of 27 cookies.** Write 27 in the blank.

$$\boxed{4} \times \boxed{6} + \boxed{3} = \boxed{27}$$

Have your child complete the equations in part C.

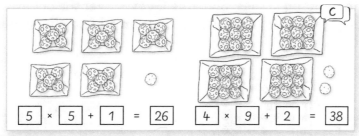

$$\boxed{5} \times \boxed{5} + \boxed{1} = \boxed{26} \qquad \boxed{4} \times \boxed{9} + \boxed{2} = \boxed{38}$$

> Your child will learn about the order of operations in future grades. In this book, all of the equations that combine addition and multiplication have the multiplication written before the addition so that your child can simply complete the equations from left to right.

Independent Practice and Review

Have your child complete the Lesson 8.2 Practice and Review workbook pages. Your child may use the dot array as needed to complete the multiplication practice exercises.

Lesson 8.3
×9 Facts

Purpose	Materials
• Practice subtracting single-digit numbers from multiples of 10 • Introduce ×9 facts • Use ×10 facts to figure out ×9 facts	• Dot array and L-cover (Blackline Master 5) • Playing cards • Counters

Memory Work
- **What do we call the result when we multiply two numbers?** *The product.*
- **What do we call the numbers in a multiplication equation that we multiply together?** *Factors.*

Warm-up: Subtract from Multiples of 10

Ask your child the following subtraction questions orally:

- **50 minus 5?** *45.*
- **90 minus 9?** *81.*
- **60 minus 6?** *54.*

- **80 minus 8?** *72.*
- **70 minus 7?** *63.*

This activity prepares your child to use subtraction to find answers to the ×9 facts.

Activity (A): Introduce ×9 Facts

Show your child the list of ×9 facts in part A. **You have already learned a lot of the multiplication facts in the ×9 table!** Have your child complete the ×9 facts that she has already learned: 9 × 1, 9 × 2, 9 × 3, 9 × 4, 9 × 5, 9 × 6, and 9 × 10.

9 × 1 =	9		9 × 6 =	54
9 × 2 =	18		9 × 7 =	
9 × 3 =	27		9 × 8 =	
9 × 4 =	36		9 × 9 =	
9 × 5 =	45		9 × 10 =	90

There are only 3 of these facts left to learn. One way to find their answers is to use the other ×9 facts as stepping stones. Slide the L-cover over the dot array to show 9 × 6. **9 times 6 is 54.** Slide the L-cover to show 9 × 7. **You can add 54 plus 9 to find 9 times 7. What's 9 times 7?** *63.* Write 63 in the blank.

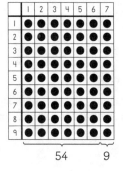

54   9

9 × 7 = 63

Continue in the same way with the other new ×9 facts. Encourage your child to add 9 to the previous product to find each new total.

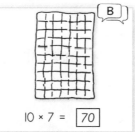

What patterns do you notice? *Sample answers: Some of the answers are the products from the ×3 and ×6 tables. The products alternate odd and even. The digits in each product add up to 9.*

Activity (B): Use ×10 Facts to Find Answers to ×9 Facts

Use a piece of paper to cover the completed ×9 table in part A. **Another way to find answers to the ×9 facts is to use the ×10 facts as stepping stones.**

Show your child the first array in part B. **Let's pretend you made an array with 10 rows. You put 7 tiles in each row. What's 10 times 7?** *70.* Write 70 in the blank.

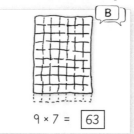

Show your child the next array. **Then, you subtract a row from the array. Now, the array has 9 rows of 7. How many tiles are in the array now?** *63.* **How do you know?** *Sample answer: The array had 70 tiles, and I subtracted 7. 70 minus 7 equals 63.* Write 63 in the blank.

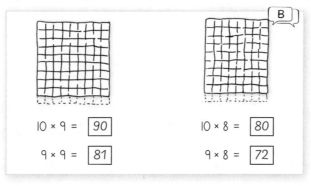

Have your child complete part B. Encourage her to imagine first creating an array with 10 rows and then subtracting 1 row from the array.

Activity (C): Play Multiplication Crash

The multiples of 9 are in order on the Multiplication Crash game board. Let's say you wanted to find the answer to 9 times 6. How can you use the way the game board is arranged to find the answer? *Sample answer: I could look for the 6th multiple. There are 5 multiples in each row, so I know it's the first multiple in the second row.* **What's 9 times 6?** *54.*

9 × 6

Play Multiplication Crash. See Lesson 2.3 (page 60) for general directions. On your turn, flip over the top card. Multiply the card by 9, say the matching multiplication fact, and place a counter on the matching square. For example, if you flip over a 7, say "9 times 7 equals 63" and place a counter on 63.

Independent Practice and Review

Have your child complete the Lesson 8.3 Practice and Review workbook pages.

> Cover the game board at the top of the page so that your child can't use the multiples of 9 to help solve the word problems. Encourage her to use the answers to the ×10 equations to find the answers to the ×9 equations instead.

Lesson 8.4
Two-Step Word Problems

Purpose	Materials
• Practice naming multiples of 9 • Practice using the ×10 facts to find answers to the ×9 facts • Practice ×9 facts • Solve two-step multiplication word problems	• Multiplication Strategies chart (Blackline Master 6) • Dot array and L-cover (Blackline Master 5) • Die • Counters

Memory Work
- **What do we call the top number in a fraction?** *The numerator.*
- **What do we call the bottom number in a fraction?** *The denominator.*
- **What does the numerator tell?** *The number of parts.*
- **What does the denominator tell?** *How many equal parts the whole was split into.*

Warm-up: Practice Naming the Multiples of 9

Name the multiples of 9 in order. *9, 18, 27...* Write each multiple on a piece of paper as your child says it. Encourage him to add 9 to the previous multiple in order to find the next one. Stop him when he reaches 90.

9, 18, 27, 36, 45, 54, 63, 72, 81, 90

Activity (A): Practice Using the ×10 Facts to Find ×9 Facts

In the last lesson, you learned the ×9 facts. Read aloud the ×9 strategy on the Multiplication Strategies chart (Blackline Master 6). Briefly discuss the example.

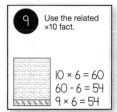

Today, you'll practice the ×9 facts more and solve two-step multiplication word problems.

Show your child the first pair of problems. Slide the L-cover over the dot array to show 10 × 8. **What's 10 times 8?** *80.* Write 80 in the blank.

9 times 8 is 8 less than 80. Cross out 1 row of 8. **So, what's 9 times 8?** *72.* Write 72 in the blank. If your child's not sure, suggest he subtract 80 minus 8.

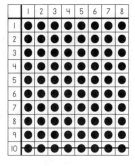

Have your child use the same approach to complete part A. Model each problem with the dot array and encourage him to use the ×10 fact to figure out the corresponding ×9 fact.

$$10 \times 7 = \boxed{70} \qquad 10 \times 9 = \boxed{90} \quad \text{\small A}$$
$$9 \times 7 = \boxed{63} \qquad 9 \times 9 = \boxed{81}$$

Activity (B): Play Climb and Slide

Play Climb and Slide. See Lesson 3.3 (page 90) for full directions. Use the dot array to model the problems as needed.

Activity (C): Solve Two-Step Multiplication Word Problems

Have your child read aloud the first word problem. Remind him to follow the steps for reading word problems. **What's our goal in this problem?** *Find how many hair bows Allie bought.*

> Allie bought 6 packs of plain hair bows.
> Each pack had 5 hair bows.
> She also bought 2 fancy hair bows.
> How many hair bows did she buy in all? 　　**C**

Let's make a quick sketch to help solve the problem. Allie bought 6 packs with 5 bows each. So, I'll draw 6 boxes and write 5 in each one. Draw 6 small boxes and write 5 in each one. **She bought 2 fancy hair bows.** Write "+2" next to the boxes.

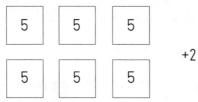

Now, I'm ready to solve. First, I'll multiply 6 times 5 to find how many hair bows are in the boxes. Write "6 × 5 = 30". **Next, I'll add on the 2 fancy hair bows.** Write "30 + 2 = 32". **She bought 32 bows.** Write "bows" after the 32 and draw a box around the complete answer.

$$6 \times 5 = 30$$
$$30 + 2 = \boxed{32 \text{ bows}}$$

> You could also write "6 × 5 + 2 = 32" to solve the problem. Demonstrate writing two separate equations for the word problems in this lesson to reinforce the idea that your child should think through each step of the problem. Allow your child to write equations for the word problems on the Practice and Review pages either way.

Have your child read aloud the second word problem. **What's our goal in this problem?** *Find how much more Tyler's parents spent on adult tickets than child tickets.*

> Tyler's parents bought tickets
> to a play. They bought 4 adult tickets for
> $10 each. They bought 3 child tickets for
> $5 each. How much more did they spend
> on adult tickets than child tickets? 　　**C**

We first need to know how much they spent on adult tickets and how much they spent on child tickets. There are a lot of numbers to keep straight in this problem, so let's write out the important information.

How much did they spend on adult tickets? *$40.* **How do you know?** *Sample answer: I multiplied 4 times 10.* Write "Adult tickets" and "4 × 10 = 40" as shown. **How much did they spend**

on child tickets? *$15.* **How do you know?** *Sample answer: I multiplied 3 times 5.* Write "Child tickets" and "3 × 5 = 15" as shown.

Adult tickets
4 × 10 = 40

Child tickets
3 × 5 = 15

How can we find out how much more they spent on adult tickets than child tickets? *Subtract 40 minus 15.* If your child's not sure, remind him he can subtract the smaller number from the larger number to find the difference.

Write "40 − 15 = " and have your child complete the equation. Remind him to label and draw a box around the complete answer.

40 − 15 = $25

Independent Practice and Review

Have your child complete the Lesson 8.4 Practice and Review workbook pages. Your child may use the dot array as needed to complete the multiplication practice exercises.

Lesson 8.5
×8 Facts

Purpose	Materials
• Practice doubling two-digit numbers • Introduce ×8 facts • Double ×4 facts to figure out ×8 facts	• Dot array and L-cover (Blackline Master 5) • Playing cards • Counters

Memory Work
- **How many inches equal 1 foot?** *12.*
- **How many feet equal 1 yard?** *3.*
- **How many inches equal 1 yard?** *36.*

Warm-up: Double Two-Digit Numbers

Ask your child the following questions orally:

- **What's double 40?** *80.*
- **What's double 24?** *48.*
- **What's double 32?** *64.*
- **What's double 28?** *56.*
- **What's double 36?** *72.*

This activity prepares your child to double answers to the ×4 facts to find answers to the ×8 facts.

Activity (A): Introduce ×8 Facts

Show your child the list of ×8 facts. **You have already learned a lot of the multiplication facts in the ×8 table!** Have your child complete the ×8 facts that she has already learned: 8 × 1, 8 × 2, 8 × 3, 8 × 4, 8 × 5, 8 × 6, 8 × 9, and 8 × 10.

$$
\begin{array}{ll}
8 \times 1 = \boxed{8} & 8 \times 6 = \boxed{48} \\
8 \times 2 = \boxed{16} & 8 \times 7 = \boxed{} \\
8 \times 3 = \boxed{24} & 8 \times 8 = \boxed{} \\
8 \times 4 = \boxed{32} & 8 \times 9 = \boxed{72} \\
8 \times 5 = \boxed{40} & 8 \times 10 = \boxed{80}
\end{array}
$$

Your child has learned strategies for these facts, but she is not expected to have full fluency with all of them yet.

There are only 2 of these facts left to learn. One way to find their answers is to use the other ×8 facts as stepping stones. Slide the L-cover over the dot array to show 8 × 6. **8 times 6 is 48.** Slide the L-cover to show 8 × 7. **You can add 48 plus 8 to find 8 times 7. What's 8 times 7?** *56.* Write 56 in the blank.

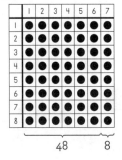

$$8 \times 7 = \boxed{56}$$

Repeat with 8 × 8.

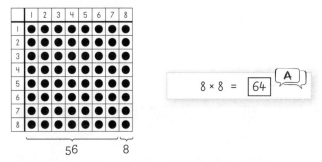

What pattern do you notice? *Sample answers: Some of the answers are the products from the ×4 table. The products are all even.*

Activity (B): Use ×4 Facts to Find Answers to ×8 Facts

Use a piece of paper to cover the completed ×8 table in part A. **Another way to find answers to the ×8 facts is to use the ×4 facts as stepping stones.**

Let's pretend you made an array with 4 rows. You put 8 marbles in each row. What's 4 times 8? *32.* Write 32 in the blank.

Then, you decided to double your array and added 4 more rows. How many marbles do you add to the array? *32.* **So, how many marbles are in the array now?** *64.* **How do you know?** *Sample answer: The array had 32 marbles, so I doubled 32.* Write 64 in the blank.

┌─────────────────────────────┐
│   8   (B)   │
│ 4 { ○○○○○○○○   │
│   ○○○○○○○○   4 × 8 = [32]│
│ 4 { ●●●●●●●●   8 × 8 = [64]│
│   ●●●●●●●●   │
└─────────────────────────────┘

Have your child use the same approach to solve the other problems in part B. Encourage her to imagine first creating an array with 4 rows and then doubling the array.

┌──┐
│   7   6   (B)   │
│ 4 { ○○○○○○○   4 { ○○○○○○   │
│   ○○○○○○○   4 × 7 = [28]   ○○○○○○   4 × 6 = [24]   │
│ 4 { ●●●●●●●   8 × 7 = [56] 4 { ●●●●●●   8 × 6 = [48]   │
│   ●●●●●●●   ●●●●●●   │
└──┘

Activity (C): Play Multiplication Cover Up (×8)

Use a piece of paper to cover parts A and B. **The multiples of 8 are in order on the Multiplication Cover Up game board. Let's say you wanted to find the answer to 8 times 9. How can you use the way the game board is arranged to find the answer?** *Sample answer: I could look for the 9th multiple. There are 10 multiples on the board, so I know the 9th one is second to last.* **What's 8 times 9?** *72.*

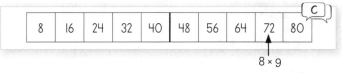

Play Multiplication Cover Up (×8). See Lesson 2.7 (page 69) for general directions. Multiply the number on your card by 8, say the matching multiplication fact, and place a counter on the matching square on game board. For example, if you flip over a 7, say "8 times 7 equals 56" and place a counter on 56.

Independent Practice and Review

Have your child complete the Lesson 8.5 Practice and Review workbook pages.

Lesson 8.6
Multiply Tens

Purpose	Materials
• Practice identifying the multiples of 8 • Practice doubling the ×4 facts to find answers to the ×8 facts • Practice ×8 facts • Review mentally multiplying groups of tens	• Multiplication Strategies chart (Blackline Master 6) • Dot array and L-cover (Blackline Master 5) • Playing cards • Counters

Memory Work • **What do we call numbers that have a whole number and a fraction?** *Mixed numbers.*

Warm-up: Practice Naming the Multiples of 8

Name the multiples of 8 in order. *8, 16, 24…* Write each multiple on a piece of paper as your child says it. Encourage him to add 8 to each previous multiple to find the next multiple. Stop him when he reaches 80.

8, 16, 24, 32, 40, 48, 56, 64, 72, 80

Activity (A): Practice Using the ×4 Facts to Find ×8 Facts

In the last lesson, you learned the ×8 facts. Read aloud the ×8 strategy on the Multiplication Strategies chart (Blackline Master 6). Briefly discuss the example.

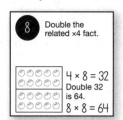

Today, you'll practice the ×8 facts and practice multiplying one-digit numbers times groups of 10.

Show your child the first pair of problems. Slide the L-cover over the dot array to show 8 × 7. Draw a ring around 4 rows of 7. **What's 4 times 7?** *28.* Write 28 in the blank.

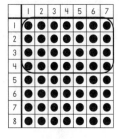

8 times 7 is double 4 times 7. Draw a ring around the other 4 rows of 7. **So, what's 8 times 7?** *56.* Write 56 in the blank. If your child's not sure, suggest he double 28.

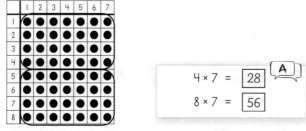

Have your child complete part A. Model each problem with the dot array and encourage him to use the matching ×4 fact to figure out the ×8 fact.

$$4 \times 9 = \boxed{36} \qquad 4 \times 8 = \boxed{32}$$
$$8 \times 9 = \boxed{72} \qquad 8 \times 8 = \boxed{64}$$

Activity (B): Play Escape the Maze (×8)

Play Escape the Maze (×8). Use the same general directions as in Escape the Maze (×3), but multiply each card by 8. See Lesson 6.1 (page 173) for full directions. Use the dot array to model the problems as needed.

Activity (C): Review Multiplying Tens

Even though your child already learned how to multiply one-digit numbers by multiples of ten, he may feel intimidated at first by the large numbers in the problems in part C. This brief review activity is meant to reassure him that he can use the same strategy for larger numbers.

In Unit 5, you learned how to multiply one-digit numbers times multiples of ten. Point to 4 × 80. **We have 4 groups. Each group has 8 tens. What's 4 times 8?** *32.* **So, we have 32 tens.** Write 32 in the blank. **How much do 32 tens equal?** *320.* **So, 8 times 40 equals 320.** Write 320 in the blank.

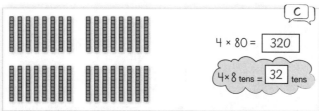

You can use the same reasoning with bigger numbers, too! Have your child complete part C.

$$5 \times 80 = \boxed{400} \qquad 7 \times 60 = \boxed{420} \qquad 9 \times 90 = \boxed{810}$$
$$5 \times 8 \text{ tens} = \boxed{40} \text{ tens} \qquad 7 \times 6 \text{ tens} = \boxed{42} \text{ tens} \qquad 9 \times 9 \text{ tens} = \boxed{81} \text{ tens}$$

Independent Practice and Review

Have your child complete the Lesson 8.6 Practice and Review workbook pages. Your child may use the dot array as needed to complete the multiplication practice exercises.

Lesson 8.7
×7 Facts and Convert Weeks to Days

Purpose	Materials
• Review telling time to the minute • Introduce ×7 facts • Use the ×7 facts to convert weeks to days	• Clock • Dot array and L-cover (Blackline Master 5) • Counters • Playing cards • Calendar, optional

Memory Work • **How many months are in a year?** *12.*
  • **How many days are in a week?** *7.*

Warm-up: Review Telling Time to the Minute

Set a clock to the following times and have your child tell each time: 6:00, 6:02, 6:11, 6:20, 6:29, 6:30, 6:43, 6:45, 6:57, 7:00.

Activity (A): Introduce ×7 Facts

Today, you'll practice the ×7 facts. You'll also learn how to use multiplication to convert weeks to days.

Show your child the list of ×7 facts. **You have now learned nearly all the multiplication facts! The only table you have left to study is the ×7 table.** Have your child complete the × 7 facts that she has already studied: 7×1, 7×2, 7×3, 7×4, 7×5, 7×6, 7×8, 7×9, and 7×10.

$$1 \times 7 = \boxed{7} \qquad 6 \times 7 = \boxed{42} \;\;\text{A}$$
$$2 \times 7 = \boxed{14} \qquad 7 \times 7 = \boxed{}$$
$$3 \times 7 = \boxed{21} \qquad 8 \times 7 = \boxed{56}$$
$$4 \times 7 = \boxed{28} \qquad 9 \times 7 = \boxed{63}$$
$$5 \times 7 = \boxed{35} \qquad 10 \times 7 = \boxed{70}$$

Your child has learned strategies for these facts, but she is not expected to have full fluency with all of them yet.

7 times 7 is the only fact left to study! A good way to find the answer is to use the other ×7 facts as stepping stones. Slide the L-cover over the dot array to show 7×6. **7 times 6 is 42.** Slide the L-cover to show 7×7. **You can add 42 plus 7 to find 7 times 7. What's 7 times 7?** *49.* Write 49 in the blank.

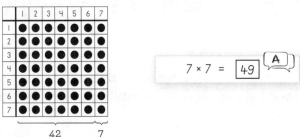

$$7 \times 7 = \boxed{49} \;\;\text{A}$$

You've learned that there are lots of different ways you can use the facts you already know to find the answers. You can use whatever stepping stone works best for you when you solve multiplication problems.

Activity (B): Play Multiplication Crash

Use a piece of paper to cover part A. **The multiples of 7 are in order on the Multiplication Crash game board. Let's say you wanted to find the answer to 7 times 7. How can you use the way the game board is arranged to find the answer?** *Sample answer: I could look for the 7th multiple. There are 5 multiples in each row, so I know it's the second multiple in the second row.*

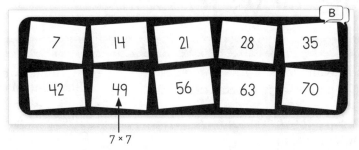

7 × 7

Play Multiplication Crash. See Lesson 2.3 (page 60) for general directions. On your turn, flip over the top card. Multiply the card by 7, say the matching multiplication fact, and place a counter on the matching square. For example, if you flip over a 5, say "7 times 5 equals 35" and place a counter on 35.

Activity (C): Convert Weeks to Days

Let's pretend that you're planning to go to an exciting event in 3 weeks. What event should we pretend you're going to? *Answers will vary.* **Let's find how many days away that is!**

3 weeks are 3 groups of 7 days. So, we can multiply 3 times 7 to find how many days are in 3 weeks. What's 3 times 7? *21.* **3 weeks equal 21 days.** Write 21 in both blanks.

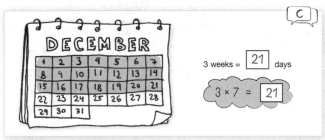

Have your child complete part B in the same way.

If you have time, show your child a real calendar. Choose an event in the next couple of months and tell your child how many weeks away the event is. Then, have your child multiply by 7 to convert the weeks to days. For example: **Grandma is coming in about 6 weeks! How many days equal 6 weeks?** *42 days.*

Independent Practice and Review

Have your child complete the Lesson 8.7 Practice and Review workbook pages.

Both word problems on Practice 8.7 have the same answer. This is to nudge your child to notice that 7 × 8 and 8 × 7 have the same product.

Lesson 8.8
Multiply and Add to Convert Weeks and Days to Days

Purpose	Materials
• Practice identifying the multiples of 7 • Review multiplication strategies in the context of the multiplication table • Multiply and add to convert weeks and days to days • Practice multiplying and adding	• Multiplication Strategies chart (Blackline Master 6) • Dot array and L-cover (Blackline Master 5), optional • Calendar, optional • Playing cards

Memory Work	• **How many hours are in a day?** *24.* • **How many minutes are in an hour?** *60.* • **How many seconds are in a minute?** *60.*

Warm-up: Practice Naming the Multiples of 7

Name the multiples of 7 in order. *7, 14, 21…* Write each multiple on a piece of paper as your child says it. Encourage your child to add 7 to the previous multiple to find the next multiple. Stop him when he reaches 70.

7, 14, 21, 28, 35, 42, 49, 56, 63, 70

Activity (A): Review Multiplication Strategies on the Multiplication Table

In this unit, you've studied the ×6, ×7, ×8, and ×9 facts. Today, we'll review the strategies you've learned. You'll also learn how to convert weeks and days to days.

Read aloud the strategy at the top of the Multiplication Strategies chart (Blackline Master 6). Briefly discuss the example. **This strategy works for any of the multiplication facts. It's especially helpful for the ×7 facts, since there's not a more specific strategy for them.**

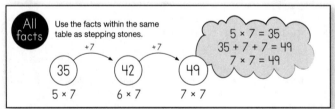

At the beginning of this unit, you had already studied most of the multiplication facts. Now, you've learned how to find answers for the last 16 multiplication facts. We'll use the strategies to complete the missing answers in this multiplication chart.

×	6	7	8	9	10
5	30	35	40	45	50
6					60
7					70
8					80
9					90
10	60	70	80	90	100

First, you learned how to use the ×5 facts as stepping stones to figure out the ×6 facts. Point to the box for 6 × 6. **5 times 6 equals 30. How can you use that to help figure out 6 times 6?** *Sample answer: I can add 6 to 30.* **What's 6 times 6?** *36.* If your child's unsure, use the dot array to model the connection (as in Lesson 8.1). Write 36 in the blank.

×	6	7	8	9	10
5	30	35	40	45	50
6	36				60
7					70
8					80
9					90
10	60	70	80	90	100

Repeat with the other facts in the ×6 row (6 × 7, 6 × 8, and 6 × 9). **We can multiply in any order. So, you can use the same strategies for the facts in the ×6 column.** Have your child complete 7 × 6, 8 × 6, and 9 × 6.

×	6	7	8	9	10
5	30	35	40	45	50
6	36	42	48	54	60
7	42				70
8	48				80
9	54				90
10	60	70	80	90	100

Next, you learned how to use the ×10 facts as stepping stones to figure out the ×9 facts. Point to the box for 9 × 8. **10 times 8 equals 80. How can you use that fact to figure out 9 times 8?** *Sample answer: I can subtract 8 from 80.* **What's 9 times 8?** *72.* If your child's unsure, use the dot array to model the connection (as in Lesson 8.3). Write 72 in the blank.

×	6	7	8	9	10
5	30	35	40	45	50
6	36	42	48	54	60
7	42				70
8	48				80
9	54		72		90
10	60	70	80	90	100

Repeat with the other facts in the ×9 row (9 × 7 and 9 × 9). **We can multiply in any order. So, you can use the same strategies for the facts in the ×9 column.** Have your child complete 7 × 9 and 8 × 9.

×	6	7	8	9	10
5	30	35	40	45	50
6	36	42	48	54	60
7	42			63	70
8	48			72	80
9	54	63	72	81	90
10	60	70	80	90	100

That left only 4 facts! You learned that you can double the ×4 facts to find the ×8 facts. Or, you can use the other facts you know as stepping stones to figure them out. Have your child complete the final 4 facts using whichever strategy he prefers.

×	6	7	8	9	10
5	30	35	40	45	50
6	36	42	48	54	60
7	42	49	56	63	70
8	48	56	64	72	80
9	54	63	72	81	90
10	60	70	80	90	100

A

Activity (B): Convert Weeks and Days to Days

In the last lesson, we pretended that you were planning to go to an exciting event in 3 weeks. Often, events aren't a whole number of weeks away. Today, let's pretend that the exciting event is 3 weeks and 1 day away. We'll multiply and add to convert 3 weeks and 1 day to days.

Each week has 7 days, so first we multiply 3 times 7 to find how many days are in 3 weeks. Then, we add on the 1 extra day. What's 3 times 7? *21.* **Plus 1?** *22.* **So, 3 weeks and 1 day equal 22 days.** Write 22 in both blanks.

3 weeks, 1 day = 22 days

$3 × 7 + 1 =$ 22

Have your child complete the rest of the exercises in part B. Your child may solve the problems mentally or write an equation for each problem.

2 weeks, 4 days = 18 days   5 weeks, 2 days = 37 days

4 weeks, 5 days = 33 days   10 weeks, 6 days = 76 days

B

If you have time, show your child a real calendar. Choose an event in the next couple of months and tell your child how many weeks and days away the event is. Then, have your child multiply and add to convert the weeks to days. For example: **Your birthday is in 4 weeks and 5 days! How many days away is your birthday?** *33 days.*

Activity (C): Play Multiply and Add

Play Multiply and Add.

Multiply and Add

Materials: 2 decks of playing cards, with 10s, jacks, queens, and kings removed (72 cards total)

Object of the Game: Score more points than the other player.

Shuffle the cards and place the stack face down on the table. On your turn, take 3 cards off the top of the deck. Use the digits on the cards to fill in the blanks in the first equation on your scorecard. Then, multiply and add the numbers. This total is your score.

The best strategy is to look for an equation with as high a value as possible.

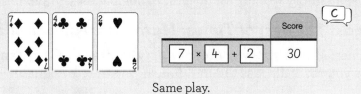

Same play.

Play then passes to the other player. Continue until both players have completed all 5 rounds. Add up each player's total points. The player with more points wins.

To make this game more challenging, have your child take 4 cards and choose which 3 of the cards to use.

Independent Practice and Review

Have your child complete the Lesson 8.8 Practice and Review workbook pages. Your child may use the dot array as needed to complete the multiplication practice exercises.

Lesson 8.9
Enrichment (Optional)

Purpose	Materials
• Practice memory work • Summarize strategies for finding answers to the multiplication facts • Practice the multiplication facts that your child finds most challenging • Summarize what your child has learned and assess your child's progress	• *The Best of Times: Math Strategies That Multiply,* written by Greg Tang and illustrated by Harry Briggs • Varies, depending on which activity you choose

Warm-up: Review Memory Work

Quiz your child on all memory work through Unit 8. See pages 527-528 for the full list.

Math Picture Book: *The Best of Times: Math Strategies that Multiply*

Read *The Best of Times: Math Strategies that Multiply*, written by Greg Tang and illustrated by Harry Briggs. As you read, discuss the multiplication strategies and how they match the illustrations.

Some of the strategies presented in this book differ from the ones you've introduced in Unit 8. Point out that it's fine for your child to use any strategy that helps her find answers accurately and quickly.

Enrichment Activity: Choose Your Own Math Fact Practice

You've worked hard on the ×6, ×7, ×8, and ×9 multiplication facts in this unit! Today, you get to practice them in a different way!

Choose 8-10 of the multiplication facts that your child finds most challenging. Have your child choose one of the following ways to practice these facts:

- Fold a piece of paper (or draw lines on a piece of paper) to make a 2×4 grid. Have your child tape a small slip of paper or place a sticky note in each box. Have her write a multiplication problem on each slip of paper or sticky note. Have her write the answer underneath. Then, have her use this lift-the-flap to quiz herself on the tricky facts.
- Spread pudding on a tray, shaving cream on a counter, or finger paint on a large sheet of paper. Have your child use her finger to write each multiplication fact (with its answer) in the goo.
- Write the multiplication facts' products in chalk outside. Name one of the facts and have your child run to the answer. (Or, if you prefer to do the activity inside, write each product on a piece of paper and tape it to the floor.)
- Name a multiplication fact and toss a ball to your child. Have her say the answer as she catches the ball.
- Make a Multiplication Memory game. Write the multiplication problems on one set of index cards and their answers on another set of index cards. Turn all the cards face-down. On your turn, flip over 2 cards. If the cards match, keep the pair. If the cards don't match, turn them back over. Take turns until you have found pairs for every card. Whoever has the most cards wins.

Unit Wrap-up

Have your child complete the Unit 8 Wrap-up.

Unit 8 Answer Key

8.1 Practice

Tic-Tac-Toe Crash (×6)

6	12	18
24	30	36
42	48	54

Practice Complete.

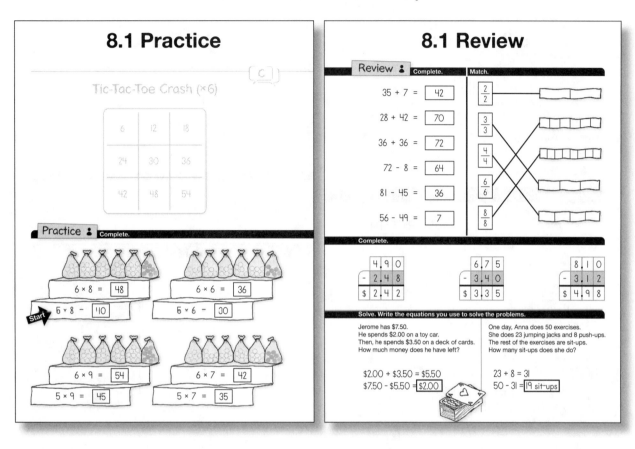

6 × 8 = 48   6 × 6 = 36

6 × 8 = 110   6 × 6 = 00

6 × 9 = 54   6 × 7 = 42

5 × 9 = 45   5 × 7 = 35

8.1 Review

Review Complete.   Match.

35 + 7 = 42

28 + 42 = 70

36 + 36 = 72

72 − 8 = 64

81 − 45 = 36

56 − 49 = 7

Complete.

| 4.90 |
| − 2.48 |
| $ 2.42 |

| 6.75 |
| − 3.40 |
| $ 3.35 |

| 8.10 |
| − 3.12 |
| $ 4.98 |

Solve. Write the equations you use to solve the problems.

Jerome has $7.50. He spends $2.00 on a toy car. Then, he spends $3.50 on a deck of cards. How much money does he have left?

$2.00 + $3.50 = $5.50
$7.50 − $5.50 = $2.00

One day, Anna does 50 exercises. She does 23 jumping jacks and 8 push-ups. The rest of the exercises are sit-ups. How many sit-ups does she do?

23 + 8 = 31
50 − 31 = 19 sit-ups

8.2 Practice

Practice Complete.

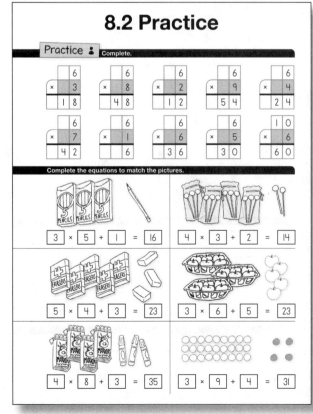

Complete the equations to match the pictures.

3 × 5 + 1 = 16   4 × 3 + 2 = 14

5 × 4 + 3 = 23   3 × 6 + 5 = 23

4 × 8 + 3 = 35   3 × 9 + 4 = 31

8.2 Review

Review Complete.

$\frac{7}{8} + \frac{1}{8} = \frac{8}{8}$ ★ $\frac{6}{8} + \frac{2}{8} = \frac{8}{8}$

$\frac{5}{8} + \frac{3}{8} = \frac{8}{8}$ ★ $\frac{4}{8} + \frac{4}{8} = \frac{8}{8}$

Solve.

You pay the clerk $5.00. How much change do you get?

$3.75   Change $ 1.25

You pay the clerk $10.00. How much change do you get?

$7.95   Change $ 2.05

Write the time.

10:30   12:47   3:22   8:50

Complete.

| 5.32 |
| + 0.89 |
| $ 6.21 |

| 8.32 |
| − 0.89 |
| $ 7.43 |

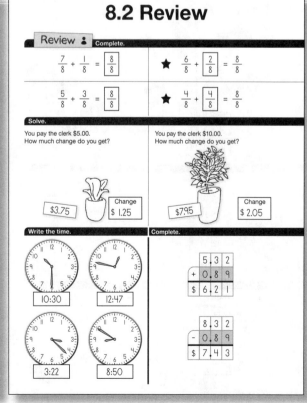

Unit 8 Answer Key

8.3 Practice

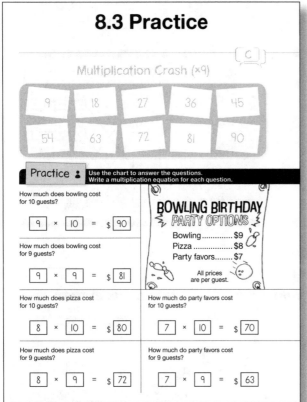

Multiplication Crash (×9)

| 9 | 18 | 27 | 36 | 45 |
| 54 | 63 | 72 | 81 | 90 |

Practice — Use the chart to answer the questions. Write a multiplication equation for each question.

How much does bowling cost for 10 guests?

9 × 10 = $ 90

How much does bowling cost for 9 guests?

9 × 9 = $ 81

BOWLING BIRTHDAY PARTY OPTIONS

Bowling $9
Pizza $8
Party favors........ $7

All prices are per guest.

How much does pizza cost for 10 guests?

8 × 10 = $ 80

How much do party favors cost for 10 guests?

7 × 10 = $ 70

How much does pizza cost for 9 guests?

8 × 9 = $ 72

How much do party favors cost for 9 guests?

7 × 9 = $ 63

8.3 Review

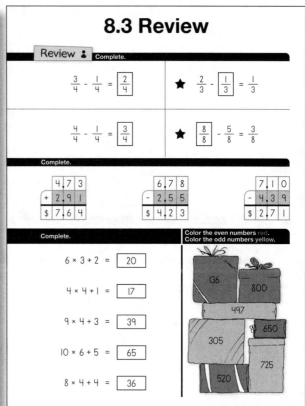

Review — Complete.

$\frac{3}{4} - \frac{1}{4} = \frac{2}{4}$ ★ $\frac{2}{3} - \frac{1}{3} = \frac{1}{3}$

$\frac{4}{4} - \frac{1}{4} = \frac{3}{4}$ ★ $\frac{8}{8} - \frac{5}{8} = \frac{3}{8}$

Complete.

	4	7	3
+	2	9	1
$	7	6	4

	6	7	8
-	2	5	5
$	4	2	3

	7	1	0
-	4	3	9
$	2	7	1

Complete.

6 × 3 + 2 = 20

4 × 4 + 1 = 17

9 × 4 + 3 = 39

10 × 6 + 5 = 65

8 × 4 + 4 = 36

Color the even numbers red.
Color the odd numbers yellow.

136 800 497 650 305 725 520

8.4 Practice

Practice — Color the multiples in order from Start to End.

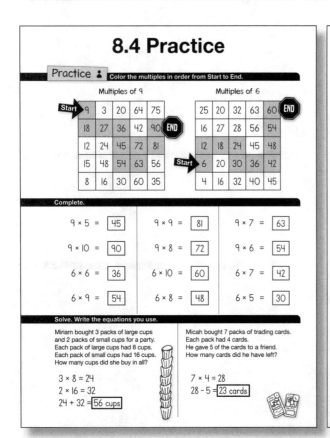

Multiples of 9

Start → | 9 | 3 | 20 | 64 | 75 |
| 18 | 27 | 36 | 42 | 90 | END
12	24	45	72	81
15	48	54	63	56
8	16	30	60	35

Multiples of 6

| 25 | 20 | 32 | 63 | 60 | END
| 16 | 27 | 28 | 56 | 54 |
| 12 | 18 | 24 | 45 | 48 |
Start → | 6 | 20 | 30 | 36 | 42 |
| 4 | 16 | 32 | 40 | 45 |

Complete.

9 × 5 = 45   9 × 9 = 81   9 × 7 = 63

9 × 10 = 90   9 × 8 = 72   9 × 6 = 54

6 × 6 = 36   6 × 10 = 60   6 × 7 = 42

6 × 9 = 54   6 × 8 = 48   6 × 5 = 30

Solve. Write the equations you use.

Miriam bought 3 packs of large cups and 2 packs of small cups for a party. Each pack of large cups had 8 cups. Each pack of small cups had 16 cups. How many cups did she buy in all?

3 × 8 = 24
2 × 16 = 32
24 + 32 = 56 cups

Micah bought 7 packs of trading cards. Each pack had 4 cards. He gave 5 of the cards to a friend. How many cards did he have left?

7 × 4 = 28
28 - 5 = 23 cards

8.4 Review

Review — Complete.

$3.50 + $2.20 = $5.70

$6.80 + $1.30 = $8.10

$3.50 + $3.50 = $7.00

$4.00 - $1.00 = $3.00

$4.00 - $1.50 = $2.50

$4.00 - $2.50 = $1.50

Complete with <, >, or =.

$\frac{8}{8}$ ⊙> $\frac{6}{8}$

$\frac{1}{2}$ ⊙< $\frac{5}{6}$

$\frac{2}{4}$ ⊙= $\frac{3}{6}$

$\frac{1}{3}$ ⊙> $\frac{1}{8}$

$\frac{0}{4}$ ⊙= $\frac{0}{8}$

Draw a shape to match.

Many answers are possible.

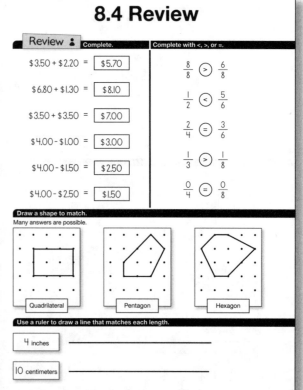

Quadrilateral   Pentagon   Hexagon

Use a ruler to draw a line that matches each length.

4 inches

10 centimeters

Unit 8 Answer Key

8.5 Practice

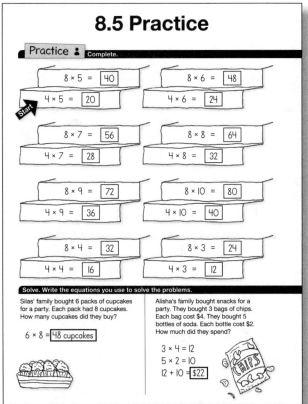

8.5 Review

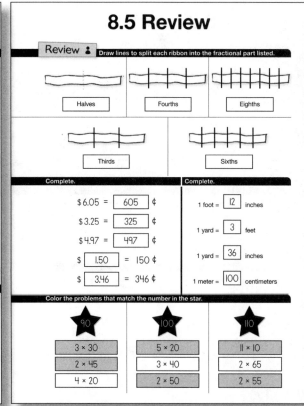

8.6 Practice

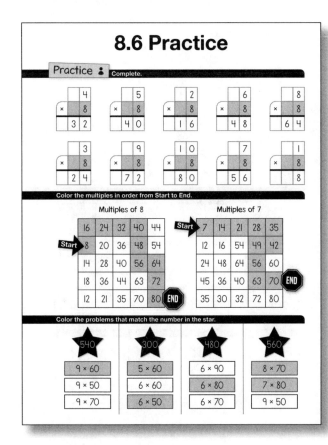

8.6 Review

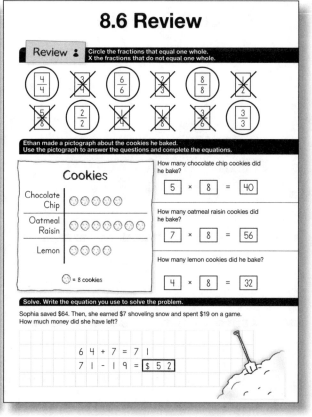

Unit 8 Answer Key

8.7 Practice

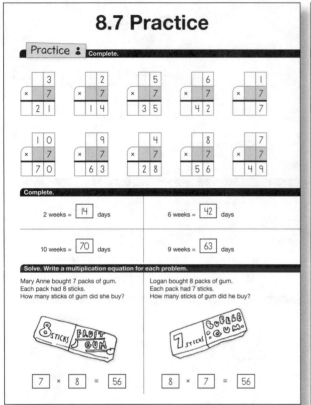

8.7 Review

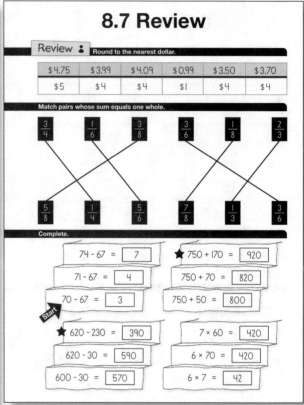

8.8 Practice

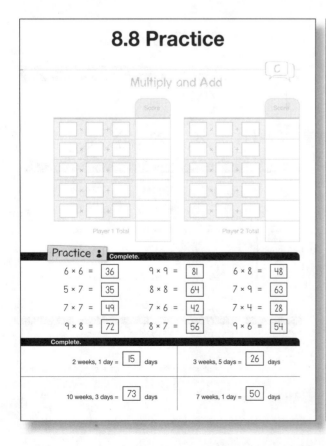

8.8 Review

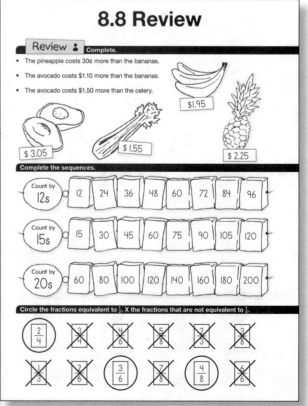

Unit 8 Answer Key

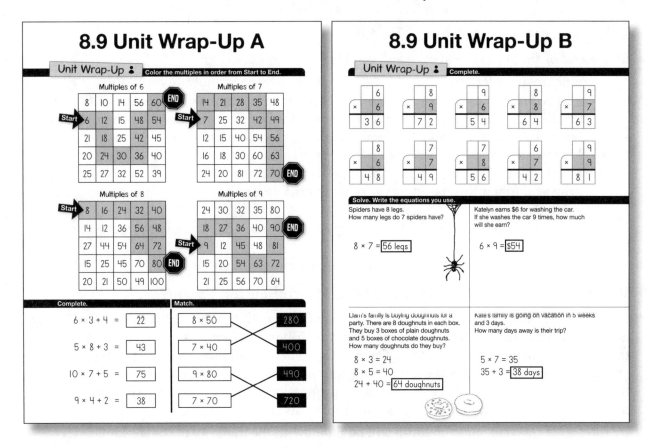

8.9 Unit Wrap-Up A

Unit Wrap-Up 👤 Color the multiples in order from Start to End.

Multiples of 6

8	10	14	56	60	END
6	**12**	15	**48**	**54**	
21	**18**	25	**42**	45	
20	**24**	**30**	**36**	**40**	
25	27	32	52	39	

Start → 6

Multiples of 7

14	**21**	**28**	**35**	48
7	25	32	**42**	**49**
12	15	**40**	**54**	**56**
16	18	30	**60**	**63**
24	20	81	72	**70** END

Start → 7

Multiples of 8

8	**16**	**24**	**32**	**40**
14	12	**36**	**56**	**48**
27	44	**54**	**64**	**72**
15	25	45	**70**	**80** END
20	21	50	49	100

Start → 8

Multiples of 9

24	30	32	35	**80**
18	**27**	**36**	**40**	**90** END
9	12	**45**	**48**	**81**
15	20	**54**	**63**	**72**
21	25	56	70	64

Start → 9

Complete.

$6 \times 3 + 4 =$ 22

$5 \times 8 + 3 =$ 43

$10 \times 7 + 5 =$ 75

$9 \times 4 + 2 =$ 38

Match.

8×50 — 280

7×40 — 400

9×80 — 490

7×70 — 720

8.9 Unit Wrap-Up B

Unit Wrap-Up 👤 Complete.

	6			8			9			8			9
×	6		×	9		×	6		×	8		×	7
3	6		7	2		5	4		6	4		6	3

	8			7			7			6			9
×	6		×	7		×	8		×	7		×	9
4	8		4	9		5	6		4	2		8	1

Solve. Write the equations you use.

Spiders have 8 legs. How many legs do 7 spiders have?

$8 \times 7 =$ 56 legs

Katelyn earns $6 for washing the car. If she washes the car 9 times, how much will she earn?

$6 \times 9 =$ $54

Liam's family is buying doughnuts for a party. There are 8 doughnuts in each box. They buy 3 boxes of plain doughnuts and 5 boxes of chocolate doughnuts. How many doughnuts do they buy?

$8 \times 3 = 24$
$8 \times 5 = 40$
$24 + 40 =$ 64 doughnuts

Kate's family is going on vacation in 5 weeks and 3 days. How many days away is their trip?

$5 \times 7 = 35$
$35 + 3 =$ 38 days

Unit 8 Checkpoint

What to Expect at the End of Unit 8

By the end of Unit 8, most children will be able to do the following:

- Find answers for the ×6, ×7, ×8, and ×9 facts, mostly accurately. Many children will take 5-10 seconds or more to figure out these tricky facts. Some will know the facts with smaller factors (like 4 × 7 or 9 × 5) fairly fluently, but most will need much more practice to become fluent with the facts with larger factors (like 9 × 8 or 6 × 7).
- Multiply and add to find totals.
- Multiply 6, 7, 8, and 9 by multiples of 10 (for example, 9 × 70 or 6 × 60). Some children will feel intimidated by these problems and still need parent help in order to solve them.
- Multiply to convert weeks to days, or multiply and add to convert weeks and days to days.
- Solve two-step word problems that involve multiplication.

What If My Child Isn't Fluent with the Multiplication Facts Yet?

It takes a long time for children to become fully fluent with the multiplication facts. **Your child is not expected to have mastered the multiplication facts yet.** Even though this is the final multiplication unit in *Third Grade Math with Confidence*, he'll continue to play multiplication games in the warm-ups and complete multiplication practice exercises on the Review worksheets. He'll also revisit multiplication in other contexts, and he'll apply the multiplication facts "backward" as he studies division.

By the end of the year, most children will be fluent with the majority of the multiplication facts. Don't worry if there are some tricky ones (like 8 × 7 or 9 × 6) that still take him a while to figure out. Most children will not become completely automatic with these more challenging facts until early in fourth grade, and you'll do a thorough review of multiplication at the beginning of fourth grade. In fourth grade, your child will also learn the ×11 and ×12 facts.

Is Your Child Ready to Move on?

In Unit 9, your child will study length, perimeter, and area. He does not need to have mastered any specific skills before moving on to Unit 9.

Unit 9
Length, Perimeter, and Area

Overview

In Unit 9, you will review length and introduce your child to perimeter and area. She will first use rulers and unit squares to directly measure perimeter and area. Then, she'll learn to calculate perimeter and area based on sketches and logical reasoning. She'll also learn to solve perimeter and area word problems.

You'll focus on shapes composed of rectangles and squares in third grade. In future grades, your child will learn to find the area of more complex shapes.

Children often enjoy exploring these new concepts and find this unit a welcome break after the challenging multiplication facts in Unit 8. Your child will continue to practice multiplication in the warm-up activities and Review workbook pages.

What Your Child Will Learn

In this unit, your child will learn to:

- Review metric and U.S. customary units for measuring length
- Measure length to the nearest quarter-inch or half-inch and write lengths with mixed numbers
- Understand that perimeter is the distance around the edge of a shape
- Measure to find an object's perimeter
- Add the lengths of an object's sides to find its perimeter
- Understand that area is the amount of space that a shape covers
- Multiply length times width to find the area of rectangles
- Split shapes into rectangular parts and add or subtract the areas of the parts to find total area
- Solve perimeter and area word problems

Lesson List

Lesson 9.1	Measure with Half-Inches	Lesson 9.7	Measure Area with Square Centimeters
Lesson 9.2	Measure with Quarter-Inches	Lesson 9.8	Multiply to Find Area
Lesson 9.3	Measure with Centimeters	Lesson 9.9	Find the Area of Larger Rectangles
Lesson 9.4	Add to Find Perimeter		
Lesson 9.5	Use Multiplication to Find Perimeter	Lesson 9.10	Measure Area with Other Units
Lesson 9.6	Perimeter Word Problems	Lesson 9.11	Area Word Problems
		Lesson 9.12	Enrichment (Optional)

Extra Materials Needed for Unit 9

- Scissors
- Tape
- Colored pencils or markers
- 3 books of varying sizes
- Masking tape or yarn
- Yardstick and meterstick, optional
- Map of your town (either paper or on a map app), optional

- For optional Enrichment Lesson:
    × *Bigger, Better, Best!,* written by Stuart J. Murphy and illustrated by Marsha Winborn. HarperCollins, 2002.
    × Tape measure

Teaching Math with Confidence: Developing Conceptual Understanding of Perimeter and Area

In this unit, you'll introduce your child to two new ways to measure two-dimensional shapes: perimeter and area. The *perimeter* of a shape is the distance around its outside edge, while the *area* is the amount of space the shape covers.

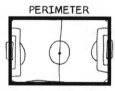 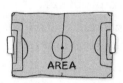

Perimeter measures the "outside" of an object, while area measures the "inside" of the object.

In first and second grade, your child learned how to measure length with a variety of units. Perimeter is closely related to length, so you'll introduce this concept first. Your child will learn how to measure around the outside edge of a shape and add the length of the sides to find the shape's perimeter. Once she has learned to measure perimeter concretely, you'll teach her to interpret diagrams and calculate perimeter without directly measuring the object.

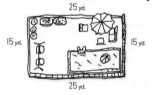

25 + 15 + 25 + 15 = 80 yd.

Then, you'll introduce your child to the concept of area. When she was in kindergarten and first grade, she first learned to measure length by concretely repeating units like paper clips or pattern blocks. You'll introduce area in a similar way. She will first measure area by covering rectangles with unit blocks (from your set of base-ten blocks) and finding how many blocks it takes to cover each rectangle. Unit blocks make a convenient manipulative for measuring area, since each unit block covers 1 square centimeter. As your child creates arrays to cover the rectangles, you'll show her how she can use multiplication as a short-cut for finding area.

Each side of the unit block is 1 centimeter long.
So, the bottom side of the block covers an area of 1 square centimeter.

The main goal of this unit is for your child to develop a solid conceptual understanding of what perimeter and area mean, not memorize formulas. She will learn how to calculate the perimeter and area of rectangles in this unit, but these techniques will naturally arise from the examples and exercises. She'll study area and perimeter more abstractly (and learn formulas for area and perimeter) in future grades.

Lesson 9.1
Measure with Half-Inches

Purpose	Materials
• Practice multiplication facts • Review benchmarks for inch, foot, yard, and mile • Make a paper ruler marked in half-inch increments • Measure and draw lines to the nearest half-inch	• Playing cards • Paper ruler (Blackline Master 8), cut out • Scissors • Tape • Colored pencils or markers

Memory Work
- **How many inches equal 1 foot?** *12.*
- **How many feet equal 1 yard?** *3.*
- **How many inches equal 1 yard?** *36.*

Children are often confused by the many fractional tick marks on a standard ruler. In this lesson, your child will make her own paper ruler for measuring to the nearest half-inch. Constructing the ruler herself will help her better understand the meaning of the tick marks on a regular ruler and prepare her to use one with confidence.

Measuring with half-inches previews understanding fractions as numbers on the number line. Even if your family uses the metric system, make sure you still teach this lesson, so that your child has the chance to practice mixed numbers in the context of length.

Warm-up: Play Multiplication War (Advanced Version)

Play Multiplication War (Advanced Version).

This advanced version of Multiplication War includes more multiplication facts than the version you played earlier in the year.

Multiplication War (Advanced Version)

Materials: Deck of playing cards with jacks, queens, and kings removed (40 cards total)

Object of the Game: Win the most cards.

Shuffle together the cards. Deal them face down into two piles.

On your turn, flip over the top two cards in your pile. Find the product of the numbers. For example, if you flip over a 6 and a 7, the product is 42. Then, the other player flips over their top two cards and finds the product of the cards. Whoever has the greater product wins all 4 cards.

The player who flipped over the two 8s wins the cards, since 64 is greater than 42.

If the products are equal, leave the cards face-up on the table and have both players flip over another two cards from their piles. Whoever has the greater product wins all the face-up cards.

Play until the piles run out. Whoever has won more cards wins the game.

Challenge Version: Use only the 5s, 6s, 7s, 8s, and 9s from 2 decks of cards to give your child lots of practice with challenging multiplication facts like 7 × 8 or 9 × 6.

Activity (A): Review Inch, Foot, Yard, and Mile

Today, we'll review inches, feet, yards, and miles. Then, you'll make a paper ruler and learn how to measure with half-inches. Have your child identify whether each item is typically about an inch, a foot, or a yard long. Write the correct unit below each picture.

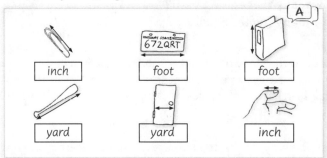

These pictures show ways to remember the length of an inch, foot, and yard.

- **An inch is about as long as a paper clip, or the distance from the first knuckle on your thumb to the tip of your thumb.** Have your child hold her thumb and first finger about one inch apart.
- **12 inches equal 1 foot. A foot is about as long as a license plate, or the height of a binder.** Have your child hold her hands about one foot apart.
- **3 feet equal 1 yard. A yard is about as long as a baseball bat, or about as wide as a doorway.** Have your child hold her hands about one yard apart.

1 mile is 5,280 feet long. I don't think you can hold your hands that far apart! Tell your child the length of some familiar trips in miles. For example: **The walk to the library is about 1 mile. Our bike ride last week was 4 miles long. Grandma and Grandpa's house is about 10 miles away.**

Your child does not need to memorize how many feet equal a mile.

Activity: Make a Paper Ruler with Half-Inch Marks

We're going to make a paper ruler. Show your child the paper ruler from Blackline Master 8. **This ruler is marked in inches.**

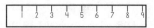

Real-life lengths aren't always a whole number of inches. Let's mark this ruler so that we can use it to measure half-inches, too. Use a colored pencil or maker to draw a mark halfway between the end of the ruler and the 1-inch mark. **This mark splits the inch into 2 equal parts. So, each part is half of an inch.** Have your child use the same colored pencil or marker to draw half-inch marks between the lines on the rest of the ruler.

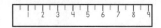

Using a marker or colored pencil to draw the half-inch marks makes them easier to see. You'll use a different color to mark the quarter-inch marks in the next lesson. Encourage your child to draw the half-inch marks a little shorter than the inch marks, just as on a regular ruler. It's okay if your child's marks aren't exactly in the right place, as long as they divide each inch into 2 roughly equal parts.

Activity (B): Measure Bugs with Half-Inches

Let's use the paper ruler to measure the lengths of these bugs. Demonstrate how to use the paper ruler to measure the length of the grasshopper. Line up the left end of the ruler with the left end of the grasshopper. Point to the 2 1/2-inch mark. **From the 0-inch mark to the 2-inch mark is 2 inches. From the 2-inch mark to this mark is half of an inch. So, how far is it from the end of the ruler to this mark?** *2 1/2 inches.* Write 2 1/2 in the blank.

Have your child use the paper ruler to measure the rest of the bugs.

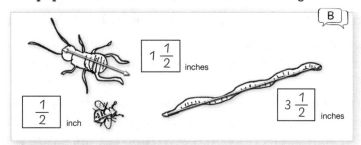

Activity (C): Draw Lines with Half-Inches

I want to draw a line that is 3 and one-half inches long. Which tick mark is 3 and one-half inches from the end of the ruler? *Child points to tick mark shown below.* Use the paper ruler to draw a 3 1/2 inch long line.

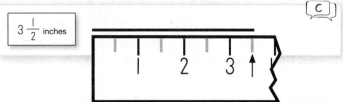

Have your child draw lines to match the rest of the measurements in part C.

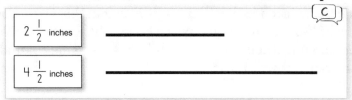

Independent Practice and Review

Have your child complete the Lesson 9.1 Practice and Review workbook pages.

Lesson 9.2
Measure with Quarter-Inches

Purpose	Materials
• Practice multiplication facts • Approximate an inch, a foot, and a yard and introduce abbreviations for each unit • Measure lines and objects with quarter-inches • Compare the paper ruler with a standard ruler	• Playing cards • Paper ruler (from Lesson 9.1) • Colored pencils or markers • 3 books of varying sizes • 1-foot ruler

Memory Work	• **What do we call numbers that have a whole number and a fraction?** *Mixed numbers.*

Your child will measure the length and width of 3 books in this lesson. Use books whose dimensions are 12 inches or less so that your child can measure them with a standard 1-foot ruler.

Warm-up: Play Multiplication War (Advanced Version)

Play Multiplication War (Advanced Version). See Lesson 9.1 (pages 275-276) for directions.

Activity (A): Introduce Abbreviations for Inch, Foot, Yard, and Mile

In the last lesson, we reviewed inches, feet, yards, and miles. We often use abbreviations when we don't want to write out an entire word. What abbreviations do you know? *Answers will vary.*

Show your child part A. **These are the abbreviations we use for inch, foot, yard, and mile. They start with a lower-case letter, and they have a period after them. You can use these abbreviations to label your answers instead of writing out the entire word.**

Unit	inch	foot	yard	mile
Abbreviation	in.	ft.	yd.	mi.

Activity: Add Quarter-Inch Marks to the Paper Ruler

In the last lesson, you learned how to measure with half-inches. Today, you'll learn how to measure with quarter-inches. Quarter means the same as one-fourth. A quarter-inch is one-fourth of an inch, just like a quarter-hour is one-fourth of an hour and a quarter coin is one-fourth of a dollar.

Let's mark the paper ruler so that we can use it to measure quarter-inches. We need to split each inch into 4 equal parts. Each inch on the ruler is already split in half. If we split each half into 2 equal parts, each inch will be split into fourths. Use a colored pencil or maker to split the first half-inch into 2 equal parts. (Use a different color than you used for half-inch marks in Lesson 9.1.) Then, have your child use the same colored pencil or marker to add quarter-inch marks to the rest of the ruler.

Encourage your child to draw the quarter-inch marks a little shorter than the half-inch marks, just as on a regular ruler. It's okay if your child's marks aren't exactly in the right place, as long as they divide each inch into 4 roughly equal parts.

Activity (B): Measure Lines with Quarter-Inches

Show your child part B. Have your child use the paper ruler to measure the first ribbon. **How long is the ribbon?** *3 inches.* Write 3 in the blank.

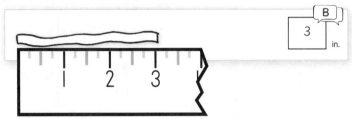

Have your child measure the second ribbon and complete the blank. If he has trouble reading the quarter-inch marks, point to the 3 1/4-inch mark and say: **From the end of the ruler to the 3-inch mark is 3 inches. From the 3-inch mark to this mark is one-fourth of an inch. So, how far is it from the 0-inch mark to this mark?** *Three and one-fourth inches.* Write 3 1/4 in the blank.

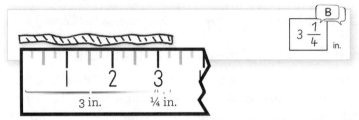

Then, have your child measure the third ribbon. **One-half and two-fourths are equivalent to each other. We can think of this ribbon as 3 and one-half inches long or 3 and two-fourths inches long. In everyday conversation, we usually use the simpler fraction with smaller numbers, so we'll say the ribbon is 3 and one-half inches long.** Write 3 1/2 in the blank. Have your child use the paper ruler to measure the rest of the ribbons.

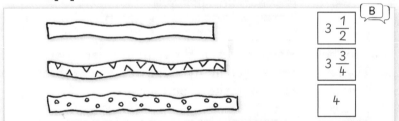

Activity (C): Measure Books to the Nearest Quarter-Inch

Place 3 paperback books on the table. Spread them out and align them at different angles to make it more difficult to compare their heights and widths. **Let's pretend that the books are glued to the table, so we can't move them. Which book looks the tallest? Which book looks the shortest? Which book looks the widest? Which book looks the narrowest?** *Answers will vary.*

Pretending the books are glued to the table gives your child practice at visually estimating and measuring the length of fixed items.

Have your child use the paper ruler to measure the height and width of each book. Help him tilt the ruler as needed to align it along the books' edges. Record the measurements in the chart in part C. Discuss whether your child's predictions were correct.

	Height (in.)	Width (in.)	C
Book 1	$6\frac{3}{4}$	$6\frac{3}{4}$	
Book 2	$8\frac{1}{2}$	$5\frac{1}{2}$	
Book 3	$6\frac{3}{4}$	$4\frac{1}{4}$	

Sample answers.

Help your child round the measurements to the nearest quarter-inch as needed. For example: **The height of this book is between 9 ½ and 9 ¾ inches. It's closer to 9 ¾ inches, so we'll round the length to 9 ¾ inches.**

Activity: Compare the Paper Ruler with a Real Ruler

Show your child the paper ruler and a standard 1-foot ruler. **What's different about the two rulers?** *Possible answers: They are made of different materials. The paper ruler only has a few lines, but the other ruler has a lot of lines. The paper ruler is shorter than a real ruler.*

What do the two rulers have in common? *Possible answers: They both have lines. They both have marks every inch.*

Place the paper ruler on top of the regular ruler so your child can see that the marks on the paper ruler line up with many of the marks on the standard ruler.

Have your child point to the half-inch marks on the regular ruler. Then, have him point to the quarter-inch marks. **The regular ruler has many more tick marks than the paper ruler! The other tick marks split each inch into eighths or sixteenths.**

This discussion is meant as an introduction to the eighth-inch and sixteenth-inch marks. Your child is not expected to measure with eighths or sixteenths in third grade.

Independent Practice and Review

Have your child complete the Lesson 9.2 Practice and Review workbook pages. Your child may use either the paper ruler or a standard ruler for the measuring exercises.

Lesson 9.3
Measure with Centimeters

Purpose	Materials
• Practice multiplication facts • Review centimeter, meter, and kilometer and introduce abbreviations for them • Measure shapes' sides in centimeters • Use reasoning to find the length of shapes' sides	• Playing cards • 30-cm ruler • Colored pencils or markers

Memory Work • **How many centimeters equal 1 meter?** *100.*

Don't skip lessons on the metric system, even if your family lives in the U.S. and mostly uses the U.S. customary system. The metric system is the main system of measurement throughout the rest of the world, and knowing the metric system is crucial for success in science classes in later grades. You'll find a mix of metric units and U.S. customary units throughout *Math with Confidence* so that your child is comfortable with both measurement systems.

Warm-up: Play Multiplication War (Advanced Version)

Play Multiplication War (Advanced Version). See Lesson 9.1 (pages 275-276) for directions.

Activity (A): Review Centimeter, Meter, and Kilometer

In the last lesson, we reviewed inches, feet, yards, and miles. These units are used in the United States, and sometimes in the United Kingdom and Canada. But in most of the world, people use a measurement system called the metric system. Today, we'll review metric units of length: centimeters, meters, and kilometers.

Show your child part A. Have your child identify whether each item is typically about a centimeter or meter long. Write the correct unit below each picture.

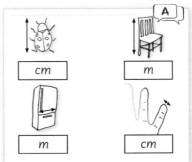

These pictures show ways to remember the length of a centimeter or meter.

- **A centimeter is about as wide as your pinky finger, or as long as a ladybug. It's about half as long as an inch.** Have your child hold her thumb and forefinger about one centimeter apart.
- **100 centimeters equal 1 meter. A meter is a little longer than a yard. Refrigerators are usually about a meter wide, and kitchen chairs are often about a meter high.** Have your child hold his hands about one meter apart.

1 kilometer is 1,000 meters long. A kilometer is a little longer than half of a mile. Tell your child the length of some familiar distances in kilometers. For example: **The bike race that I did was 30 kilometers long. Uncle Charlie and Aunt Louise live about 100 kilometers away.**

Show your child the abbreviation chart. **We use these abbreviations for centimeter, meter, and kilometer. We write metric abbreviations with lower-case letters, and we don't write a period after them.**

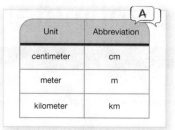

Activity (B): Measure Shapes' Sides in Centimeters

Point to the bottom side of the first rectangle. **How many centimeters long do you think this side is?** *Answers will vary.* Demonstrate how to measure the side in centimeters with a ruler. **This side is 3 centimeters long.** Write 3 in the blank. Repeat with the left side of the rectangle. You should find that it is 5 centimeters long.

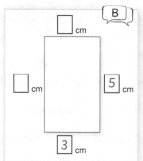

Point to the top side of the rectangle. **How long do you think this side is?** *3 centimeters.* **How do you know?** *It's the same length as the bottom side.* Have your child use a ruler to check the length and label it. Repeat with the right side.

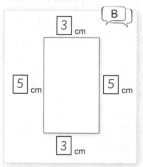

Have your child find the length of each side of the other rectangle in the same way.

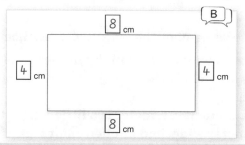

This activity prepares your child to find the perimeter of squares and rectangles in Lesson 9.4.

Activity (C): Use Reasoning to Find Side Lengths

In this shape, some of the lengths are already labeled. We can use reasoning to find the other side lengths. Point to the right side of the first shape. **I can use the labeled sides to figure out the length of this side.** Use a colored pencil or marker to trace the left side. **I know the left side is 5 centimeters.** Trace the other 2 vertical sides with the same color. **These two sides added together equal the left side, so their sum must be 5 centimeters. The labeled side is 1 centimeter long, so how long must the missing side be?** *4 centimeters.* Have your child measure the missing side to check her answer. Write 4 in the blank.

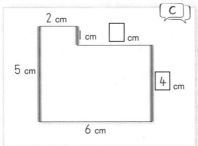

Use a different colored pencil or marker to trace the bottom side. **The bottom side is 6 centimeters long.** Trace the other 2 horizontal sides with the same color. **These two sides added together equal the bottom side, so their sum must be 6 centimeters. The labeled side is 2 centimeters long, so how long must the missing side be?** *4 centimeters.* Have your child measure the missing side to check her answer. Write 4 in the blank.

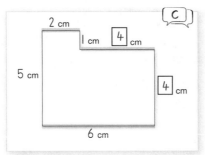

Have your child use similar reasoning to find the missing sides in the other shape. Have her trace the sides with colored pencils or markers as needed to help see the relationships between the sides.

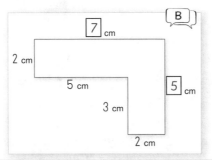

Shapes with straight lines and right angles (like the ones in part C) are called *rectilinear* shapes. Your child will find the perimeter and area of many rectilinear shapes in this unit.

Independent Practice and Review

Have your child complete the Lesson 9.3 Practice and Review workbook pages.

Lesson 9.4
Add to Find Perimeter

Purpose	Materials
• Practice ×6 facts • Introduce the concept of perimeter • Measure around the outside of an object to find its perimeter • Add side lengths to find perimeter	• Playing cards • 1-foot (30-centimeter) ruler

Memory Work · **Name the multiples of 6 in order.** *6, 12, 18…* Stop your child when he reaches 60.

Warm-up: Play Over Under (×6)

Play one round of Over Under (×6).

Over Under is a fast-paced game that gives your child focused practice with one multiplication table. It's similar to Old Maid, in that you lay aside one card at the beginning of the game and this card determines the ultimate winner. You'll play Over Under with the 7, 8, and 9 multiplication tables later in the unit.

Over Under (×6)

Materials: Deck of cards, with jacks, queens, and kings removed (40 cards total)
Object of the Game: Win the most cards.

Remove one card from the deck without looking and place it aside. You will not use this card.

Remove one card from the deck before playing.

Shuffle the remaining cards and place them face-down. Decide which player is "Over" and which player is "Under."

Take turns flipping over a card from the pile and multiplying the number on the card by 6. If the product is less than 32, the player who is "Under" wins the card. If the product is greater than 32, the player who is "Over" wins the card.

For example, if the card is an 8, say, "8 times 6 equals 48." The player who is "Over" wins the card.

Continue until you have used all the cards. Whoever has won more cards wins the game.

Activity (A): Measure Perimeter in Centimeters

You already know how to measure length. Today, you'll learn how to measure around the outside of an object to find its perimeter.

The perimeter of an object is the distance around its outside edge. Underline "rim" in perimeter. **When you find the perimeter of an object, you measure how long the "rim" of the object is.**

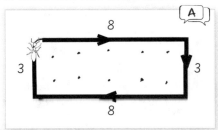

Perimeter [A]
The distance around the outside edge

Let's pretend an ant finds this cracker at a picnic and crawls all the way around the edge. Have your child trace the ant's path with his finger. **About how many centimeters do you think the ant will travel?** *Answers will vary.*

Let's measure the perimeter of the cracker to see how far the ant travels. Have your child use a ruler to measure and label each side in centimeters.

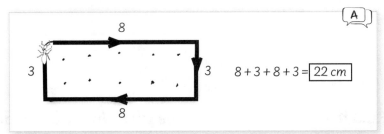

> Your child does not need to include the units when measuring shapes' sides in this unit. Writing every unit is too much writing for many third graders, and the labeled answer boxes make it clear which measurement system he is using.

To find the perimeter, we add all the side lengths. Write "8 + 3 + 8 + 3 =" in the space next to the cracker. **What is the sum of the side lengths?** *22 centimeters.* Complete the equation with "22 cm" and draw a box around your answer. **The ant travels 22 centimeters around the perimeter of the cracker.**

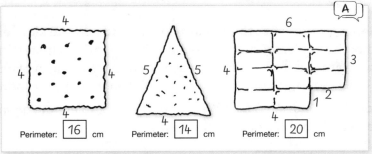

Have your child measure and label the sides of the items in part A in centimeters. Then, have him find the perimeter of each item. He may write the equations or find the sums mentally.

> Measuring and labeling helps your child remember to include every side. He may use logical reasoning to identify some of the lengths, but make sure he labels every side.

Activity (B): Add Side Lengths to Find Perimeter with Other Units

We can also measure perimeter with other units. Let's pretend we want to build a fence around this yard. We need to know its perimeter so that we know how much fencing we'll need.

To find the perimeter, we add up the length of every side. We'll start at the top left corner and add the side lengths in order to make sure we don't miss any. Draw a star at the top left corner of the diagram to mark your starting place. Trace your finger clockwise around the rectangle. Have your child tell the length of each side as you trace it. As he tells you the length of each side, record the length in an addition equation.

What's the total of all the sides? *80 yards.* Write "80 yd." to complete the equation. **So, it would take 80 yards of fencing to build a fence that goes all the way around this yard.**

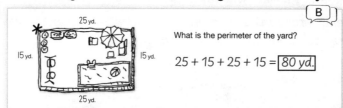

Children often forget to include some of the sides when finding perimeter, especially when they tackle more complex shapes. Labeling the starting point and tracing every side helps prevent this common mistake.

Have your child find the perimeter of the other objects in part B in the same way. Discuss the real-life meaning of perimeter for each object. For the poster: **You need to know the perimeter of a poster if you want to build a frame for it.** For the garden: **If you wanted to build a border around this garden, you'd need to know its perimeter.**

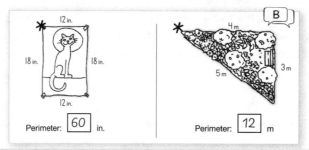

Your child may add the side lengths mentally or write equations.

Activity (C): Find the Perimeter of Shapes with Unlabeled Sides

Let's pretend we want to build a guinea pig cage that's 2 feet wide and 3 feet long. We would need to know the cage's perimeter to know how much material to buy for the sides of the cage.

To find the perimeter, let's start at the top left corner and add the side lengths in order again. Draw a star at the top left corner of the diagram to mark your starting place. Trace your finger clockwise around the cage. Have your child tell the length of each side as you trace it. As he tells you the length of each side, record the length in an addition equation.

What's the total of all the sides? *10 feet.* Write "10 ft." to complete the equation. **So, it would take 10 feet of material to build sides for the cage.**

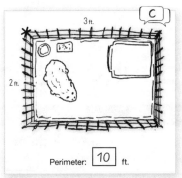

$3 + 2 + 3 + 2 = 10$ ft.

Sometimes, children look at a diagram like this guinea pig cage, and they say that the perimeter is 5 feet. Why do you think they might say that? *Sample answer: Because they just add the printed numbers and don't make sure to include every side.* **Make sure you include every side when you find perimeter, even if not all the sides are labeled.**

Show your child the park map. **The course for this fun run goes around the perimeter of the park. Let's find the perimeter of the park to see how long the fun run is.** Have your child find the perimeter of the park. Remind him to include every side.

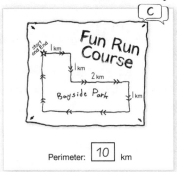

The left side of the park is 2 km and the bottom side is 3 km.
So, the total perimeter equals 1 + 1 + 2 + 1 + 3 + 2, or 10 km.

Independent Practice and Review

Have your child complete the Lesson 9.4 Practice and Review workbook pages. He may write down the equations he uses or solve the problems mentally.

Lesson 9.5
Use Multiplication to Find Perimeter

Purpose	Materials
• Practice multiplication facts • Multiply to find the perimeter of shapes with equal sides	• 2 decks of playing cards

Memory Work	• **How many sides does a triangle have?** *3.* • **How many sides does a hexagon have?** *6.* • **How many sides does an octagon have?** *8.* • **How many sides does a pentagon have?** *5.* • **How many sides does a quadrilateral have?** *4.*

Warm-up: Play Multiplication Least to Greatest

Play Multiplication Least to Greatest.

In this game, players take turns playing pairs of cards and naming their product. Each new product must be greater than the previous product. This makes the game slightly more challenging than Multiplication War, because your child must not only find the products but also reason about them and compare them. If your child finds this game too challenging, it's fine to play Multiplication War instead.

Multiplication Least to Greatest

Materials: 2 decks of cards, with jacks, queens, and kings removed (80 cards total)

Object of the Game: Win the most cards.

Shuffle the cards and deal 5 cards to both players. Place the rest of the deck in a face-down pile.

Choose who will go first. Player 1 chooses two cards from his hand, places them face-up on the table, and names the product. For example, if he plays a 4 and a 9, the product is 36. Then, Player 1 picks up two new cards to replenish his hand.

Player 2 then chooses any two cards from her hand whose product is greater than Player 1's product. (The products may not be equal.) She places her cards on top of Player 1's cards, names their product, and takes two new cards to replenish her hand. For example, if Player 1 played a 4 and a 9, Player 2 can play any two cards with a product greater than 36.

If Player 1 plays a 4 and 9, Player 2 may play any pair of cards whose product is greater than 36.

Continue alternating turns until one player can no longer play a greater product. The player who last played takes all of the face-up cards. The player who was unable to play new cards chooses two cards from their hand and starts a new round.

Play until you have used all the cards. Whoever has won the most cards wins the game.

Cooperative Variation: Take turns playing pairs of cards. Try to play as many cards as possible before one player can no longer play a greater product. Count how many cards both players played, and see if you can play more cards in the next round.

Activity (A): Multiply to Find the Perimeter of Shapes with Equal Sides

In the last lesson, you learned how to add to find perimeter. Today, you'll learn how to use multiplication to add the side lengths more quickly.

Let's pretend we want to put baseboards around the edge of this room. We need to find the perimeter of the room to know what length of baseboard to buy. What addition equation tells the perimeter of this room? *4 plus 4 plus 4 plus 4.* Write the equation below next to the diagram and have your child complete it: 4 + 4 + 4 + 4 = 16 m.

What multiplication problem could you use to find the perimeter instead? *4 times 4.* If your child isn't sure, point out that you added 4 groups of 4 to find the perimeter. Write the equation next to the diagram and have your child complete it: 4 × 4 = 16 m.

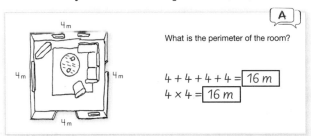

Have your child write multiplication equations to find the perimeters of the other rooms in part A.

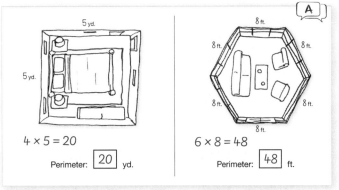

Activity (B): Multiply to Find Perimeter of Rectangles

Show your child the dining room in part B. **What addition equation tells the perimeter of the room?** *15 plus 9 plus 15 plus 9.* Write the equation on a piece of scrap paper and have your child complete it: 15 + 9 + 15 + 9 = 48 ft.

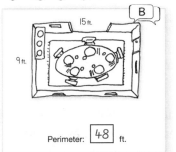

It's fine if your child tells you the addends for the equation in a different order as long as she includes all 4 sides.

In math, there is often more than one way to solve a problem. Multiplication is a faster way to add equal groups. So, if any of the sides are the same length, we can use multiplication to find the perimeter more quickly. Here's one way to multiply to find the perimeter.

- Point to the shorter sides of the dining room. **The shorter sides are each 9 feet long, so I multiply 2 times 9 to find the total length of the shorter sides.** Write 2 × 9 = 18 on a piece of scrap paper.
- **The 2 longer sides are each 15 feet long, so I multiply 2 times 15 to find the total length of the longer sides.** Write 2 × 15 = 30.
- **Last, I add the products together to find the total of all the sides.** Write 18 + 30 = 48 ft.

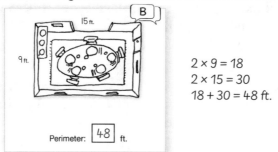

$2 \times 9 = 18$
$2 \times 15 = 30$
$18 + 30 = 48$ ft.

Or, here's another way to use multiplication to find the perimeter.

- **One long side is 15 feet, and one short side is 9 feet.** Trace the two labeled sides with your pencil to identify them. **So, one long side plus one short side equals 24 feet.** Write 15 + 9 = 24 on a piece of scrap paper.
- **There is one more long side and one more short side that I need to include.** Trace the two unlabeled sides with your pencil to identify them. **So, I can multiply 2 times 24 to find the total perimeter.** Write 2 × 24 = 48 ft.

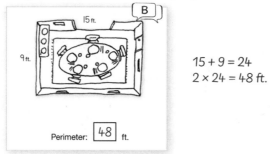

$15 + 9 = 24$
$2 \times 24 = 48$ ft.

Have your child find the perimeter of the garage in the same way. Encourage her to use multiplication.

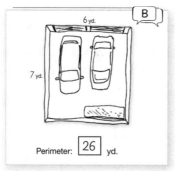

Independent Practice and Review

Have your child complete the Lesson 9.5 Practice and Review workbook pages. Encourage her to use multiplication where possible. She may write out her equations or find the perimeters mentally.

Lesson 9.6
Perimeter Word Problems

Purpose	Materials
• Practice ×7 facts • Draw pictures to solve perimeter word problems • Subtract to find the length of an unknown side in perimeter problems	• Playing cards

Memory Work · **Name the multiples of 7 in order.** *7, 14, 21...* Stop your child when he reaches 70.

Warm-up: Play Over Under (×7)

Play one round of Over Under (×7). Use the same basic directions as Over Under (×6) from Lesson 9.4 (page 284). Multiply each card by 7. If the product is less than 40, the player who is "Under" wins the card. If the product is greater than 40, the player who is "Over" wins the card.

Activity (A): Draw Pictures to Solve Perimeter Word Problems

In the last few lessons, you've learned how to find perimeter. Today, you'll solve perimeter word problems.

Have your child read aloud the first word problem in part A. Remind him to follow the steps for reading word problems. **What's our goal in this problem?** *Find the perimeter of the poster.*

Let's make a quick sketch to help solve the problem. First, I'll draw a rectangle to stand for the poster. Draw a rectangle as shown. **Next, I'll label the sides.** Write 20 in. next to the longer side and 15 in. next to the shorter side. **Now, we're ready to solve!** Have your child find the perimeter of the rectangle.

Kaya made a poster 20 inches long and 15 inches wide. What is the perimeter of the poster?

15 in. | 20 in. | 20 + 15 + 20 + 15 = $\boxed{70 \text{ in.}}$ | A

Other equations are possible. Allow your child to use any method that makes sense to him to find the perimeter, as in Lesson 9.5.

Have your child solve the other word problem in part A in the same way. If he's not sure how to draw a sketch, suggest he draw a hexagon and write 4 next to each side. Encourage him to use multiplication to solve the problem, as in Lesson 9.5.

Ja'shon helps his parents build a chicken coop with 6 sides. Each side is 4 feet long. What is the perimeter of the chicken coop?

4 ft. $4 \times 6 = \boxed{24 \text{ ft.}}$ A

Activity (B): Subtract to Find the Length of a Missing Side

Have your child read aloud the first word problem in part B. **What's our goal in this problem?** *Find the length of the shortest side of the garden.* **This problem is a lot like the part-total word problems that you solved earlier in the year! You know the total and some of the parts, and you want to find a missing part.**

First, I'll add 12 plus 13 to find out how much fence they use for the two longer sides of the garden. Write "12 + 13 = 25".

Now, I'll subtract 30 minus 25 to find how many feet of fence they used for the shortest side. Write "30 – 25 = 5." **So, the shortest side of the garden is 5 feet long.** Write "ft." after the 5 and draw a box around the complete answer.

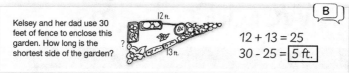

Have your child solve the other word problem in part B in the same way.

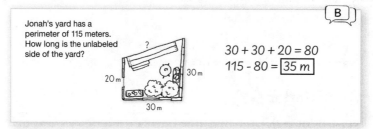

Independent Practice and Review

Have your child complete the Lesson 9.6 Practice and Review workbook pages. For the first two problems, encourage him to draw a sketch to help visualize the problems.

Sample sketches for the first two problems.

Lesson 9.7
Measure Area with Square Centimeters

Purpose	Materials
• Practice multiplication facts • Introduce the concept of area • Measure area concretely with square centimeters	• 2 decks of playing cards • Dot array and L-cover (Blackline Master 5), optional • 30-centimeter ruler • Base-ten blocks

Memory Work	• **What does perimeter measure?** *The distance around the outside edge of a shape.*

Unit blocks (from base-ten block sets) are typically 1 centimeter long on each side. Each block covers one square centimeter, so they are a handy way to measure area in square centimeters. In future grades, your child will stack the unit blocks in multiple layers to measure volume. For now, you'll only use one layer of cubes at a time (and focus on how much two-dimensional space they cover) to help your child understand area.

1 cm
1 cm

Each unit block covers an area of 1 square centimeter.

Warm-up: Play Multiplication Least to Greatest

Play Multiplication Least to Greatest. See Lesson 9.5 (pages 288-289) for directions.

Activity (A): Introduce Area

In the last few lessons, you learned how to measure the distance around a shape to find its perimeter. Today, you'll learn how to measure the space inside a shape to find its area.

Let's pretend we're helping build a soccer field. The perimeter of the soccer field is the distance around the outside edge. We need to know the perimeter if we want to build a fence around the outside edge of the field. Have your child trace around the outside of the field with her finger.

The *area* of the soccer field is the amount of land that it covers. We need to know the area of the field if we want to order the right amount of sod or fake grass to cover the entire inside of the field. Have your child sweep her finger over the inside of the field.

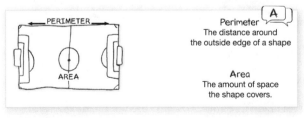

PERIMETER

AREA

A

Perimeter
The distance around
the outside edge of a shape

Area
The amount of space
the shape covers.

Activity (B): Measure Area with Square Centimeters

Which of the first two tiles do you think has a greater perimeter? *Answers will vary.* **Let's measure them to find out!** Have your child measure the side of each tile in centimeters and find its perimeter. **Which tile has a greater perimeter?** *They're equal!*

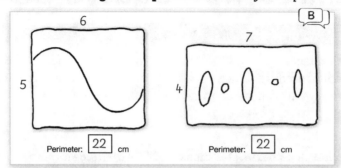

Which tile do you think has a greater area and covers more of the floor or wall? *Answers will vary.* **To measure the inside of the shapes, we'll use the unit blocks from our base-ten blocks.**

Place a unit block on a piece of scrap paper. Trace around the block and have your child color the area inside the tracing. **Each side of the unit block is 1 centimeter long. The block covers a square that is 1 centimeter on each side, so we call this amount of area a square centimeter.**

The bottom side of the unit block covers an area of 1 square centimeter.

Let's see how many square centimeters fit inside each tile. Help your child cover each tile with unit blocks. Push the blocks together so there are no spaces between them.

The unit blocks make an array inside each tile! How many rows of blocks cover the first tile? *5.* **How many columns?** *6.* **So, how many square centimeters does it take to cover the first tile?** *30.* If your child starts to count each block individually, encourage her to multiply 5 times 6 to find the answer instead. **The first tile has an area of 30 square centimeters.** Write 30 in the blank.

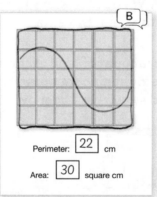

You will teach your child more about multiplying to find area in the next lesson.

How many rows of blocks cover the second tile? *4.* **How many columns?** *7.* **So, how many square centimeters does it take to cover the second tile?** *28.* Encourage her to multiply 4 times 7 to find the answer. **The second tile has an area of 28 square centimeters.** Write 28 in the blank.

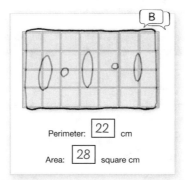

Which tile has the greater area? *The first tile.* **Even though both tiles have the same perimeter, the first tile covers more of the wall or floor.**

Show your child the second pair of tiles in part B. Have her predict which tile has the greater perimeter and which tile has the greater area. Then, have her find the area and perimeter of each tile in the same way as above.

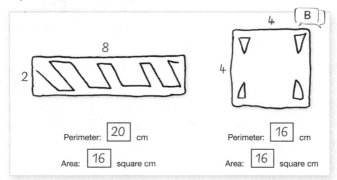

Which tile has the greater perimeter? *The tile on the left.* **Which tile has the greater area?** *They're equal.* **Even though the tile on the left has a greater perimeter than the tile on the right, they both cover the same amount of the wall or floor.**

> Some children will immediately realize that they can multiply length times width to find the areas of the rectangles. Others will need to physically fill each shape with unit blocks before recognizing that they can multiply to find the area. Follow your child's lead, and allow her to use whichever method makes more sense to her at this point. She'll learn to multiply to find area in the next lesson. See the Unit 9 **Teaching Math with Confidence** for more on the importance of developing conceptual understanding of area before memorizing formulas.

Independent Practice and Review

Have your child complete the Lesson 9.7 Practice and Review workbook pages.

> The shapes on the Practice page have a 1-cm grid so that your child doesn't have to physically arrange blocks on top of each rectangle. If your child has trouble using the grid to find the area, allow her to cover the rectangles with unit blocks instead.

Lesson 9.8
Multiply to Find Area

Purpose	Materials
• Practice ×8 facts • Multiply to find the area of rectangles • Split shapes into rectangular parts and add or subtract the areas of the parts to find total area	• Playing cards • Base-ten blocks

Memory Work • **Name the multiples of 8 in order.** *8, 16, 24...* Stop your child when he reaches 80.

Warm-up: Play Over Under (×8)

Play one round of Over Under (×8). Use the same directions as Over Under (×6) from Lesson 9.4 (page 284). Multiply each card by 8. If the product is less than 45, the player who is "Under" wins the card. If the product is greater than 45, the player who is "Over" wins the card.

Activity (A): Multiply to Find the Area of Rectangles

In the last lesson, you learned to measure area. Today, you'll learn how to use multiplication, addition, and subtraction to find area.

The grid lines on this page are 1 centimeter apart. How long is the longer side of the rectangle? *5 centimeters.* **How long is the shorter side of the rectangle?** *4 centimeters.* Label each side as shown. **How do we find the rectangle's perimeter?** *Sample answer: Add up the sides.* Have your child write and solve an equation to find the rectangle's perimeter. **What's the perimeter?** *18 centimeters.* Write 18 in the blank.

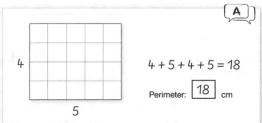

Your child may write any equation that accurately finds the perimeter of the rectangle.

Now, let's find the area of the rectangle. The small squares are 1 centimeter wide and 1 centimeter long, so each small square has an area of 1 square centimeter. Place a unit block inside one of the squares to show that the unit block covers the square exactly.

How many rows of square centimeters cover the rectangle? *4.* **How many columns?** *5.* **So, what multiplication equation tells the area of the rectangle?** *5 times 4 or 4 times 5.* Write "4 × 5 =" in the space and have your child complete the equation. **What's the area of the rectangle?** *20 square centimeters.* Write 20 in the blank.

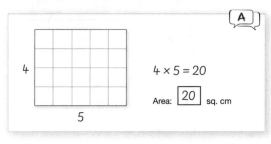

Point to the answer blank and units. **The abbreviation "sq." stands for square. So, we read the answer as "20 square centimeters."**

The square centimeters make an array inside the rectangle. So, we can multiply the length times the width to find the area. Have your child complete part A. Encourage her to multiply to find the areas.

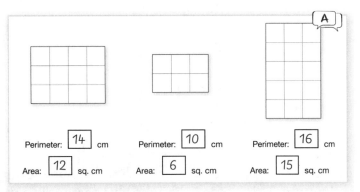

Activity (B): Add and Subtract Areas

Discuss how the shapes in part B are related to the rectangles in part A.

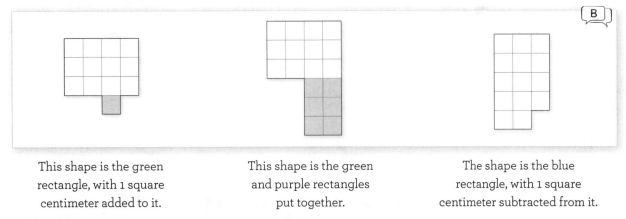

This shape is the green rectangle, with 1 square centimeter added to it.

This shape is the green and purple rectangles put together.

The shape is the blue rectangle, with 1 square centimeter subtracted from it.

Let's find the area of the first shape. You already found that the green rectangle in part A has an area of 12 square centimeters. Draw a line as shown and write 12 in the middle of the 3×4 rectangle. Point to the single square on the bottom side. **What's the area of this part of the shape?** *1 square centimeter.* Write 1 in the middle of the single square.

We know the area of both parts of the shape. So, we can add them together to find the total area. What's the total area of the shape? *13 square centimeters.* Write 13 in the blank.

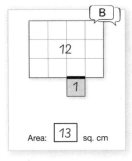

Point to the second shape. **You already found that the green rectangle in part A has an area of 12 square centimeters, and that the purple rectangle has an area of 6 square centimeters.** Draw a line as shown. Write 12 in the middle of the green rectangle and 6 in the middle of the purple rectangle. **How can you find the area of this shape?** *Add the areas of the smaller rectangles.* **What's the total area?** *18 square centimeters.* Write 18 in the blank.

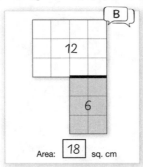

Point to the third shape in part B. **You already found that the blue rectangle in part A has an area of 15 square centimeters. This shape is like the blue rectangle, but 1 square centimeter is missing.** Write 15 in the middle of the shape. Draw dotted lines as shown and write 1 in the middle of the resulting square. **How can you find the area of this shape?** *Subtract 1 from the area of the original rectangle.* **What's the area of the shape?** *14 square centimeters.* Write 14 in the blank.

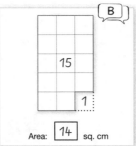

If your child is curious about how the perimeter of the new shapes differs from the perimeter from the original shapes, encourage him to find the perimeters and compare them.

Independent Practice and Review

Have your child complete the Lesson 9.8 Practice and Review workbook pages. Encourage your child to use the relationships between the shapes to find their areas. For example, for the first row: *I can add the area of the yellow rectangle and the area of the blue rectangle to find the area of the last rectangle in the row.*

Lesson 9.9
Find the Area of Larger Rectangles

Purpose	Materials
• Practice multiplication facts • Split large rectangles into parts and add the parts to find the total area	• 2 decks of playing cards

Memory Work	• **What does area measure?** *The amount of space that a shape covers.* • **What does perimeter measure?** *The distance around the outside edge of a shape.*

Warm-up: Play Multiplication Least to Greatest

Play Multiplication Least to Greatest. See Lesson 9.5 (pages 288-289) for directions.

Activity (A): Split a Large Rectangle to Find Its Area

In the last lesson, you learned how to split shapes into parts to find their area. Today, you'll learn how to split a large rectangle into parts to find its area.

The rectangles in part A are all 13 centimeters long and 4 centimeters wide. We'll split the rectangle several different ways and see which way you like best for finding the area.

Point to the first rectangle. **Let's find the area of each of the smaller rectangles and then add them.** Have your child multiply 4 times 6 and 4 times 7 to find the area of each smaller rectangle. Write these areas in the blanks in the middle of the smaller rectangles.

How can you find the area of the whole rectangle? *Add 24 plus 28.* **What's the area of the whole rectangle?** *52 square centimeters.* Write 52 in the blank.

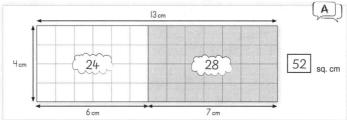

The second rectangle is 13 centimeters long and 4 centimeters wide, too. Let's try a different way to find the area. Have your child multiply 2 times 13 to find the area of each smaller rectangle. Write these areas in the blanks.

How can you find the area of the whole rectangle this time? *Sample answers: Add 26 plus 26. Double 26.* **What's the area of the whole rectangle?** *52 square centimeters.* Write 52 in the blank.

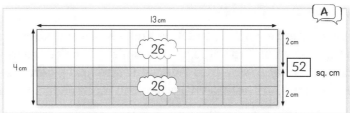

Let's try one more way to find the area of the rectangle. Have your child multiply 4 times 10 and 4 times 3 to find the area of each smaller rectangle. Write these areas in the blanks.

How can you find the area of the whole rectangle this time? *Add 40 plus 12.* **What's the area of the whole rectangle?** *52 square centimeters.* Write 52 in the blank.

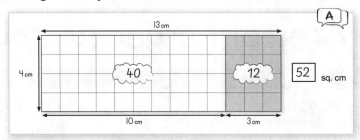

There are many different ways to split the rectangle into smaller parts. But, no matter how you split it, the area doesn't change!

Which way did you like best for finding the area? *Answers will vary.* **Many children like the last way, because they find it easier to multiply by 10 than by the other numbers.**

In fourth grade, your child will learn how to mentally multiply two-digit numbers by one-digit numbers. You'll use a similar visual model to help her understand the steps in this skill.

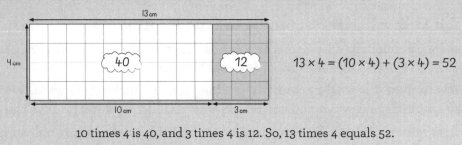

$$13 \times 4 = (10 \times 4) + (3 \times 4) = 52$$

10 times 4 is 40, and 3 times 4 is 12. So, 13 times 4 equals 52.

Activity (B): Split a Large Rectangle to Find Its Area

This rectangle is 14 centimeters long and 5 centimeters wide. How would you like to split it into smaller parts to find the area? *Answers will vary.* If your child isn't sure, suggest she draw a line to split it into a 5×10 rectangle and a 5×4 rectangle.

Have your child find the area of each smaller rectangle and write it in the middle of the smaller rectangle. Then, have her add to find the area of the entire rectangle.

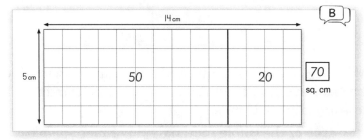

Your child may choose to split the rectangle a different way.

Independent Practice and Review

Have your child complete the Lesson 9.9 Practice and Review workbook pages. Encourage your child to look for an "easy way" to split the rectangles to make the multiplication easier: **You could split the 12-centimeter side into 7 centimeters and 5 centimeters, but splitting it into 10 centimeters and 2 centimeters will make the multiplication a lot easier.**

Lesson 9.10
Measure Area with Other Units

Purpose	Materials
• Practice multiplication facts • Introduce square inches and compare them with square centimeters • Introduce square meters, square kilometers, square feet, square yards, and square miles • Use a variety of units to calculate area	• Dot array and L-cover (Blackline Master 5), optional • Base-ten blocks • Masking tape or yarn • 1-foot (30-cm) ruler • Yardstick and meterstick, optional • Map of your town (either paper or on a map app), optional

Memory Work	
	• **How many inches equal 1 foot?** *12.* • **How many feet equal 1 yard?** *3.* • **How many inches equal 1 yard?** *36.* • **How many centimeters equal 1 meter?** *100.* • **How many meters equal 1 kilometer?** *1,000.*

In this lesson, you will use masking tape or yarn to outline a square foot, square yard, and square meter to help your child concretely understand the size of each unit. You'll need some open floor space for these outlines.

The lesson suggests using masking tape or yarn to create the square unit outlines. If it's a nice day, you can draw the outlines with chalk outside instead.

Warm-up: Practice Multiplication Facts

Do a brief oral review of the following facts.

These multiplication facts are arranged in related pairs. Encourage your child to use the first multiplication fact in each pair to help find the answer to the second multiplication fact. For example: **10 times 8 is 80. 9 times 8 is 1 group of 8 less than 80, so subtract 80 minus 8 to find the answer.** Use the dot array to model the relationships as needed.

- $10 \times 8 = 80$. $9 \times 8 = 72$.
- $10 \times 6 = 60$. $9 \times 6 = 54$.
- $10 \times 9 = 90$. $9 \times 9 = 81$.
- $10 \times 7 = 70$. $9 \times 7 = 63$.
- $4 \times 7 = 28$. $8 \times 7 = 56$.

- $4 \times 6 = 24$. $8 \times 6 = 48$.
- $4 \times 8 = 32$. $8 \times 8 = 64$.
- $5 \times 7 = 35$. $6 \times 7 = 42$.
- $6 \times 7 = 42$. $7 \times 7 = 49$.

Activity (A): Compare Square Centimeters and Square Inches

In the last few lessons, you have learned how to measure area with square centimeters. Each side of this square is 1 centimeter long, so it covers an area of 1 square centimeter.

Today, you will learn about other units for measuring area. The first one is square inches. Point to the square inch. **Each side of this square is 1 inch long, so it covers an area of 1 square inch. Square inches cover a lot more area than square centimeters.**

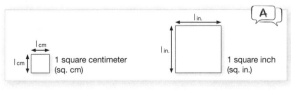

Have your child use the grid lines to find the area of both rectangles in part A. Make sure your child writes the correct units for each answer.

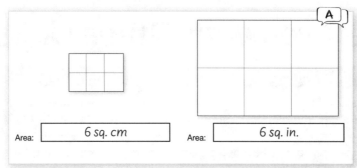

Area: 6 sq. cm   Area: 6 sq. in.

The rectangle on the left covers a lot less space than the rectangle on the right! How can both rectangles have an area of 6? *Sample answer: The rectangle on the left has an area of 6 square centimeters, but the rectangle on the right has an area of 6 square inches.*

Activity: Construct Other Area Units with Tape or Yarn

Imagine if we tried to measure the area of this room with square inches or square centimeters. It would take thousands of square inches or square centimeters to cover the whole floor! It often makes more sense to use units that are larger than square inches or square centimeters.

In the U.S. customary system, we measure length with inches, feet, yards, and miles. You already know what a square inch looks like. Let's see how much space 1 square foot, 1 square yard, and 1 square mile cover.

First, let's make a square with sides that are each 1 foot long. With your child, measure 4 one-foot lengths of masking tape or yarn. Tape them to the floor in the shape of a square.

Next, let's make a square with sides that are each 1 yard long. Measure 3 one-yard lengths of masking tape or yarn, and tape them to the floor in the shape of a square. (If you don't have a yardstick, measure 3 feet.)

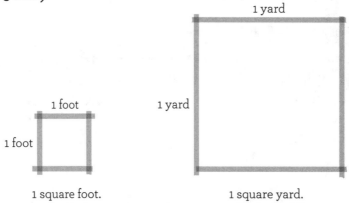

1 square foot.   1 square yard.

What do you notice about the square foot and square yard? Do they look like you expected? *Answers will vary.* **144 square inches fit inside 1 square foot. 9 square feet or 1,296 inches fit inside 1 square yard!**

A square mile covers a square that's one mile on each side. I don't think our floor is big enough to show a square mile! If you have time, show your child the approximate size of a square mile on a map of your town.

In the metric system, we measure length with centimeters, meters, and kilometers. You already know what a square centimeter looks like. Let's make a square with sides that are each 1 meter long to see what a square meter looks like. With your child, measure 4 one-meter lengths of masking tape or yarn. If you don't have a meterstick, measure out 100 centimeters of tape or yarn instead. Tape them to the floor in the shape of a square.

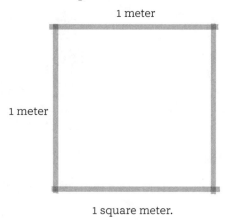

1 square meter.

What do you notice about the square meter? Does it look like you expected? *Answers will vary.* 10,000 square centimeters fit inside 1 square meter!

Have your child compare the sizes of the square meter and square yard. Which covers more area, a square meter or a square yard? *A square meter.* Meters are longer than yards, so a square meter covers more area than a square yard.

A square kilometer covers a square that's one kilometer on each side. A kilometer is shorter than a mile, so a square kilometer covers less area than a square mile. If you have time, show your child the approximate size of a square kilometer on a map of your town.

Activity (B): Find Area with a Variety of Units

Let's pretend we want to buy carpet for this room. We would need to find the area of the room to know how much carpet to buy.

The lengths of the walls are labeled in meters. I'll draw lines to see how many square meters fit in the room. Draw lines as shown to split the diagram into 20 small squares.

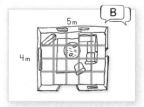

Space the lines as equally as possible, but don't worry if they're a little crooked or uneven.

What multiplication equation can we use to find the area of the room? *4 times 5, or 5 times 4.* Write the equation next to the diagram and have your child complete it: 4 × 5 = 20. **Each of the 20 small squares stands for 1 square meter.** Write "sq. m" next to 20 and draw a box around the answer.

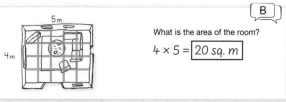

How could I have solved this problem without drawing so many lines? *Sample answer: You could just multiply 4 times 5.* **To find the area of a rectangle, multiply the rectangle's length times its width.**

Have your child complete part B. Make sure he includes the correct unit for each area.

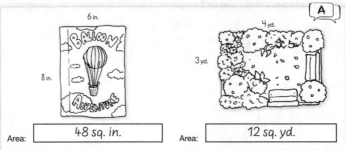

Independent Practice and Review

Have your child complete the Lesson 9.10 Practice and Review workbook pages.

Lesson 9.11
Area Word Problems

Purpose	Materials
• Practice ×9 facts • Draw pictures to solve area word problems • Solve two-step area word problems	• Playing cards

Memory Work · **Name the multiples of 9 in order.** *9, 18, 27...* Stop your child when she reaches 90.

Warm-up: Play Over Under (×9)

Play one round of Over Under (×9). Use the same directions as Over Under (×6) from Lesson 9.4 (page 284). Multiply each card by 9. If the product is less than 50, the player who is "Under" wins the card. If the product is greater than 50, the player who is "Over" wins the card.

Activity (A): Draw Pictures to Solve Area Word Problems

In the last few lessons, you've learned how to find the area of shapes. Today, you'll solve area word problems.

Have your child read aloud the first word problem in part A. Remind her to follow the steps for reading word problems. **What's our goal in this problem?** *Find the area of the poster.*

Let's make a quick sketch to help solve the problem. First, I'll draw a rectangle to stand for the poster. Draw a rectangle as shown. **Next, I'll label the sides.** Write 10 next to the longer side and 6 next to the shorter side. **Now, we're ready to solve!** Have your child multiply to find the area of the rectangle.

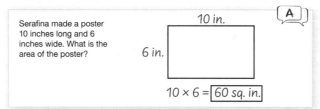

Have your child solve the other word problem in part A in the same way.

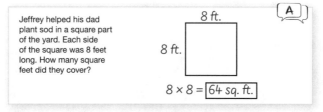

Activity (B): Solve Two-Step Area Word Problems

Have your child read aloud the first word problem in part B. **What's our goal in this problem?** *Find the area of the rug.*

This problem has more than one step. We need to find the length of the longer side of the rug before we can find its area. First, I'll add 6 plus 4 to find the length of that side. Write "6 + 4 = 10". Write 10 next to one of the longer sides.

Now, I'll multiply 10 times 6 to find the area of the rug. Write "10 × 6 = 60" in the blank space. **So, the rug has an area of 60 square feet.** Write "sq. ft." after the 60 and draw a box around the complete answer.

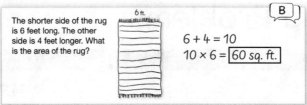

Have your child solve the other word problem in part B in the same way.

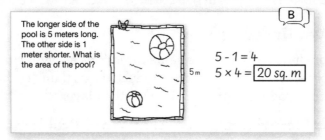

Independent Practice and Review

Have your child complete the Lesson 9.11 Practice and Review workbook pages. For the first two problems, encourage your child to draw sketches to help visualize the problems.

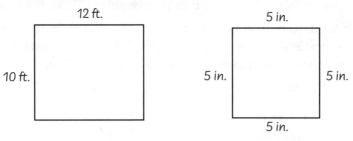

Sample sketches for the first two problems.

Lesson 9.12
Enrichment (Optional)

Purpose	Materials
• Practice memory work • Understand area in a real-life context • Measure the perimeter and area of a room • Summarize what your child has learned and assess your child's progress	• *Bigger, Better, Best!,* written by Stuart J. Murphy and illustrated by Marsha Winborn • Tape measure

Warm-up: Review Memory Work

Quiz your child on all memory work through Unit 9. See pages 527-528 for the full list.

Math Picture Book: *Bigger, Better, Best!*

Read *Bigger, Better, Best!,* written by Stuart J. Murphy and illustrated by Marsha Winborn. As you read, discuss the creative units the children use to measure area.

Enrichment Activity: Measure the Perimeter and Area of a Room

You have learned a lot about perimeter and area in this unit! Today, we'll measure the perimeter and area of your bedroom.

Help your child make a rough sketch of his bedroom. Use a tape measure to measure the length of each wall. Round each length to the nearest foot or meter, and label the sketch accordingly. Then, help your child find the perimeter and area of the room.

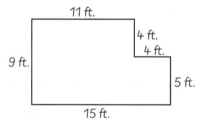

If your family uses the metric system, use meters and square meters for this activity. If your family uses the U.S. customary system, use feet and square feet.

If any of the lengths are greater than 10, help your child split the room into smaller areas, find the area of each part, and then add them to find the total area (as in Lesson 9.9).

Unit Wrap-up

Have your child complete the Unit 9 Wrap-up.

Unit 9 Answer Key

9.1 Practice

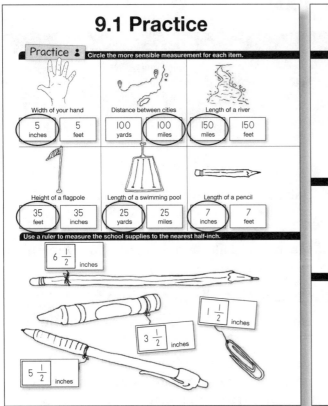

Practice 👤 Circle the more sensible measurement for each item.

Width of your hand	Distance between cities	Length of a river
(5 inches) 5 feet	100 yards (100 miles)	(150 miles) 150 feet

Height of a flagpole	Length of a swimming pool	Length of a pencil
(35 feet) 35 inches	(25 yards) 25 miles	(7 inches) 7 feet

Use a ruler to measure the school supplies to the nearest half-inch.

$6\frac{1}{2}$ inches

$1\frac{1}{2}$ inches

$3\frac{1}{2}$ inches

$5\frac{1}{2}$ inches

9.1 Review

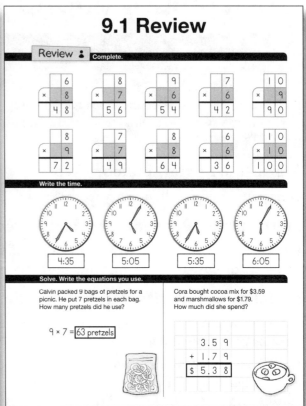

Review 👤 Complete.

× 6 / 8 = 48	× 8 / 7 = 56	× 9 / 6 = 54	× 7 / 6 = 42	× 10 / 9 = 90
× 8 / 9 = 72	× 7 / 7 = 49	× 8 / 8 = 64	× 6 / 6 = 36	× 10 / 10 = 100

Write the time.

4:35   5:05   5:35   6:05

Solve. Write the equations you use.

Calvin packed 9 bags of pretzels for a picnic. He put 7 pretzels in each bag. How many pretzels did he use?

$9 \times 7 = \boxed{63 \text{ pretzels}}$

Cora bought cocoa mix for $3.59 and marshmallows for $1.79. How much did she spend?

```
    3 . 5  9
 +  1 . 7  9
  $ 5 . 3  8
```

9.2 Practice

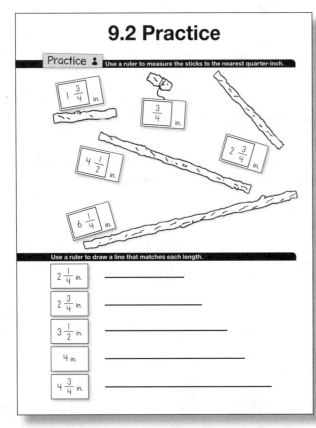

Practice 👤 Use a ruler to measure the sticks to the nearest quarter-inch.

$1\frac{3}{4}$ in.

$\frac{3}{4}$ in.

$4\frac{1}{2}$ in.

$2\frac{3}{4}$ in.

$6\frac{1}{4}$ in.

Use a ruler to draw a line that matches each length.

$2\frac{1}{4}$ in. _____

$2\frac{3}{4}$ in. _____

$3\frac{1}{2}$ in. _____

4 in. _____

$4\frac{3}{4}$ in. _____

9.2 Review

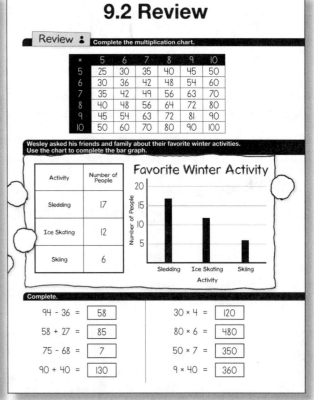

Review 👤 Complete the multiplication chart.

×	5	6	7	8	9	10
5	25	30	35	40	45	50
6	30	36	42	48	54	60
7	35	42	49	56	63	70
8	40	48	56	64	72	80
9	45	54	63	72	81	90
10	50	60	70	80	90	100

Wesley asked his friends and family about their favorite winter activities. Use the chart to complete the bar graph.

Activity	Number of People
Sledding	17
Ice Skating	12
Skiing	6

Favorite Winter Activity

Complete.

94 − 36 = 58   30 × 4 = 120

58 + 27 = 85   80 × 6 = 480

75 − 68 = 7   50 × 7 = 350

90 + 40 = 130   9 × 40 = 360

Unit 9 Answer Key

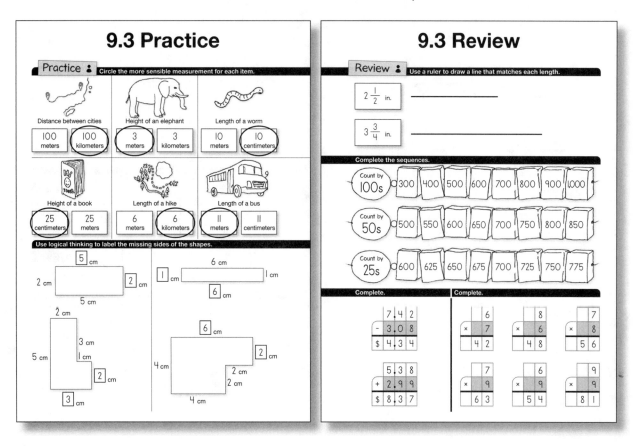

9.3 Practice

Practice | Circle the more sensible measurement for each item.

Distance between cities: 100 meters / **(100 kilometers)**

Height of an elephant: **(3 meters)** / 3 kilometers

Length of a worm: 10 meters / **(10 centimeters)**

Height of a book: **(25 centimeters)** / 25 meters

Length of a hike: 6 meters / **(6 kilometers)**

Length of a bus: **(11 meters)** / 11 centimeters

Use logical thinking to label the missing sides of the shapes.

Rectangle: top **5** cm, 2 cm, **2** cm, 5 cm

1 cm, 6 cm, 1 cm, **6** cm

L-shape: 2 cm, **3** cm, 5 cm, 1 cm, **2** cm, **3** cm

6 cm, **2** cm, 2 cm, 2 cm, 4 cm, 4 cm

9.3 Review

Review | Use a ruler to draw a line that matches each length.

$2\frac{1}{2}$ in. _____

$3\frac{3}{4}$ in. _____

Complete the sequences.

Count by 100s: 300 400 500 600 700 800 900 1,000

Count by 50s: 500 550 600 650 700 750 800 850

Count by 25s: 600 625 650 675 700 725 750 775

Complete.

```
  7 4 2
- 3 0 8
$ 4 3 4
```

```
  5 3 8
+ 2 9 9
$ 8 3 7
```

Complete.

```
   6        8        7
×  7      × 6      × 8
  4 2      4 8      5 6
```

```
   7        6        9
×  9      × 9      × 9
  6 3      5 4      8 1
```

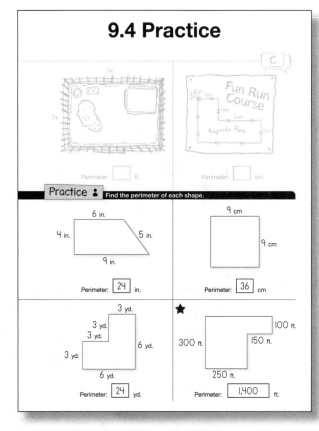

9.4 Practice

Perimeter: [ ] ft.

Fun Run Course — Bayside Park   Perimeter: [ ] km

Practice | Find the perimeter of each shape.

6 in., 4 in., 5 in., 9 in. — Perimeter: **24** in.

9 cm, 9 cm — Perimeter: **36** cm

3 yd., 3 yd., 3 yd., 6 yd., 3 yd., 6 yd. — Perimeter: **24** yd.

★ 100 ft., 150 ft., 300 ft., 250 ft. — Perimeter: **1,400** ft.

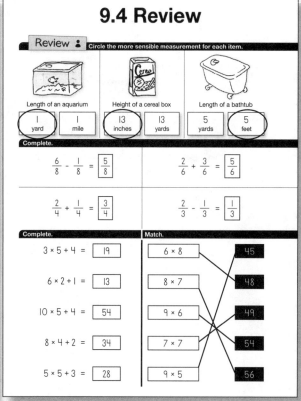

9.4 Review

Review | Circle the more sensible measurement for each item.

Length of an aquarium: **(1 yard)** / 1 mile

Height of a cereal box: **(13 inches)** / 13 yards

Length of a bathtub: 5 yards / **(5 feet)**

Complete.

$\frac{6}{8} - \frac{1}{8} = \frac{5}{8}$

$\frac{2}{6} + \frac{3}{6} = \frac{5}{6}$

$\frac{2}{4} + \frac{1}{4} = \frac{3}{4}$

$\frac{2}{3} - \frac{1}{3} = \frac{1}{3}$

Complete.

$3 \times 5 + 4 = \boxed{19}$

$6 \times 2 + 1 = \boxed{13}$

$10 \times 5 + 4 = \boxed{54}$

$8 \times 4 + 2 = \boxed{34}$

$5 \times 5 + 3 = \boxed{28}$

Match.

6 × 8	45
8 × 7	48
9 × 6	49
7 × 7	54
9 × 5	56

Unit 9 Answer Key

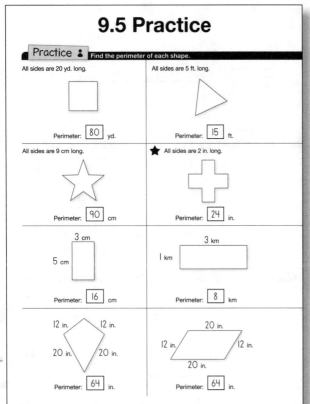

9.5 Practice

Practice 👤 Find the perimeter of each shape.

All sides are 20 yd. long.

Perimeter: 80 yd.

All sides are 5 ft. long.

Perimeter: 15 ft.

All sides are 9 cm long.

Perimeter: 90 cm

All sides are 2 in. long.

Perimeter: 24 in.

3 cm
5 cm

Perimeter: 16 cm

3 km
1 km

Perimeter: 8 km

12 in.   12 in.
20 in.   20 in.

Perimeter: 64 in.

20 in.
12 in.   12 in.
20 in.

Perimeter: 64 in.

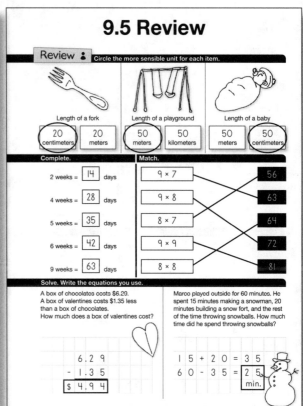

9.5 Review

Review 👤 Circle the more sensible unit for each item.

Length of a fork: (20 centimeters)   20 meters
Length of a playground: (50 meters)   50 kilometers
Length of a baby: 50 meters   (50 centimeters)

Complete.

2 weeks = 14 days
4 weeks = 28 days
5 weeks = 35 days
6 weeks = 42 days
9 weeks = 63 days

Match.

9 × 7 — 63
9 × 8 — 72
8 × 7 — 56
9 × 9 — 81
8 × 8 — 64

Solve. Write the equations you use.

A box of chocolates costs $6.20. A box of valentines costs $1.35 less than a box of chocolates. How much does a box of valentines cost?

```
  6.2 9
- 1.3 5
$ 4.9 4
```

Marco played outside for 60 minutes. He spent 15 minutes making a snowman, 20 minutes building a snow fort, and the rest of the time throwing snowballs. How much time did he spend throwing snowballs?

```
1 5 + 2 0 = 3 5
6 0 - 3 5 = 2 5  min.
```

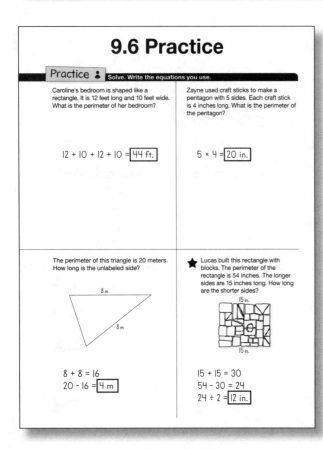

9.6 Practice

Practice 👤 Solve. Write the equations you use.

Caroline's bedroom is shaped like a rectangle. It is 12 feet long and 10 feet wide. What is the perimeter of her bedroom?

12 + 10 + 12 + 10 = 44 ft.

Zayne used craft sticks to make a pentagon with 5 sides. Each craft stick is 4 inches long. What is the perimeter of the pentagon?

5 × 4 = 20 in.

The perimeter of this triangle is 20 meters. How long is the unlabeled side?

8 m
8 m

8 + 8 = 16
20 - 16 = 4 m

Lucas built this rectangle with blocks. The perimeter of the rectangle is 54 inches. The longer sides are 15 inches long. How long are the shorter sides?

15 in.
15 in.

15 + 15 = 30
54 - 30 = 24
24 ÷ 2 = 12 in.

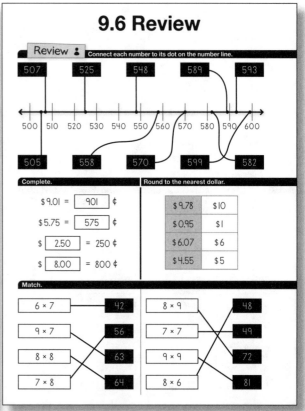

9.6 Review

Review 👤 Connect each number to its dot on the number line.

507   525   548   589   593
500 510 520 530 540 550 560 570 580 590 600
505   558   570   599   582

Complete.

$9.01 = 901 ¢
$5.75 = 575 ¢
$ 2.50 = 250 ¢
$ 8.00 = 800 ¢

Round to the nearest dollar.

$9.78 $10
$0.95 $1
$6.07 $6
$4.55 $5

Match.

6 × 7 — 42
9 × 7 — 56
8 × 8 — 63
7 × 8 — 64

8 × 9 — 48
7 × 7 — 49
9 × 9 — 72
8 × 6 — 81

Unit 9 Answer Key

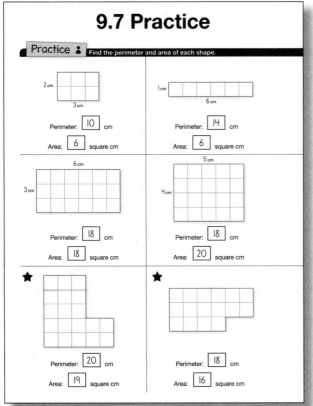

9.7 Practice

Practice 👤 Find the perimeter and area of each shape.

Perimeter: 10 cm
Area: 6 square cm

Perimeter: 14 cm
Area: 6 square cm

Perimeter: 18 cm
Area: 18 square cm

Perimeter: 18 cm
Area: 20 square cm

★
Perimeter: 20 cm
Area: 19 square cm

★
Perimeter: 18 cm
Area: 16 square cm

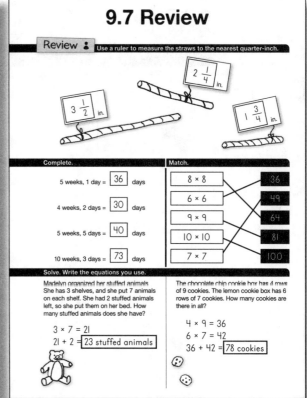

9.7 Review

Review 👤 Use a ruler to measure the straws to the nearest quarter-inch.

$2\frac{1}{4}$ in.

$3\frac{1}{2}$ in.

$1\frac{3}{4}$ in.

Complete.

5 weeks, 1 day = 36 days

4 weeks, 2 days = 30 days

5 weeks, 5 days = 40 days

10 weeks, 3 days = 73 days

Match.

8 × 8	36
6 × 6	49
9 × 9	64
10 × 10	81
7 × 7	100

Solve. Write the equations you use.

Madelyn organized her stuffed animals. She has 3 shelves, and she put 7 animals on each shelf. She had 2 stuffed animals left, so she put them on her bed. How many stuffed animals does she have?

$3 \times 7 = 21$
$21 + 2 = \boxed{23 \text{ stuffed animals}}$

The chocolate chip cookie box has 4 rows of 9 cookies. The lemon cookie box has 6 rows of 7 cookies. How many cookies are there in all?

$4 \times 9 = 36$
$6 \times 7 = 42$
$36 + 42 = \boxed{78 \text{ cookies}}$

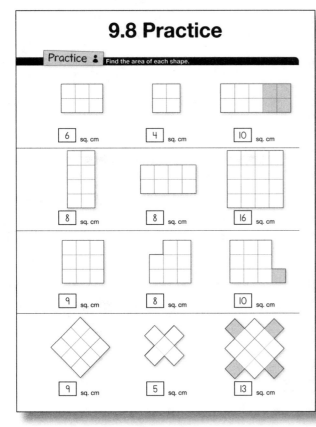

9.8 Practice

Practice 👤 Find the area of each shape.

6 sq. cm

4 sq. cm

10 sq. cm

8 sq. cm

8 sq. cm

16 sq. cm

9 sq. cm

8 sq. cm

10 sq. cm

9 sq. cm

5 sq. cm

13 sq. cm

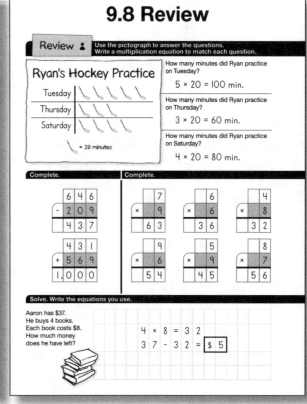

9.8 Review

Review 👤 Use the pictograph to answer the questions.
Write a multiplication equation to match each question.

Ryan's Hockey Practice

Tuesday	\\\\\
Thursday	\\\
Saturday	\\\\

= 20 minutes

How many minutes did Ryan practice on Tuesday?
$5 \times 20 = 100$ min.

How many minutes did Ryan practice on Thursday?
$3 \times 20 = 60$ min.

How many minutes did Ryan practice on Saturday?
$4 \times 20 = 80$ min.

Complete.

```
  6 4 6
- 2 0 9
  4 3 7
```

```
  4 3 1
+ 5 6 9
1,0 0 0
```

Complete.

```
    7
  × 9
  6 3
```

```
    6
  × 6
  3 6
```

```
    4
  × 8
  3 2
```

```
    9
  × 6
  5 4
```

```
    5
  × 9
  4 5
```

```
    8
  × 7
  5 6
```

Solve. Write the equations you use.

Aaron has $37.
He buys 4 books.
Each book costs $8.
How much money does he have left?

$4 \times 8 = 32$
$37 - 32 = \boxed{\$5}$

Unit 9 Answer Key

9.9 Practice

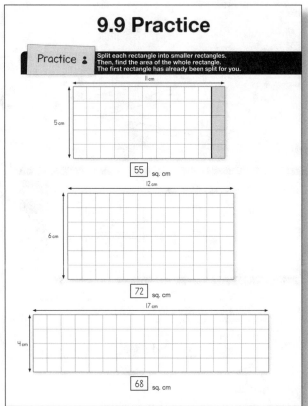

Practice 👤 Split each rectangle into smaller rectangles. Then, find the area of the whole rectangle. The first rectangle has already been split for you.

11 cm / 5 cm → **55** sq. cm

12 cm / 6 cm → **72** sq. cm

17 cm / 4 cm → **68** sq. cm

9.9 Review

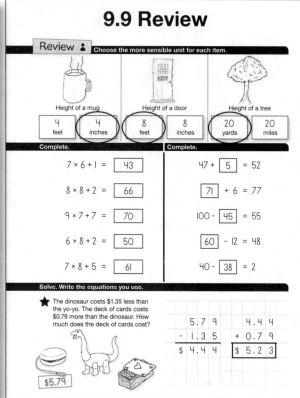

Review 👤 Choose the more sensible unit for each item.

Height of a mug: 4 feet / **4 inches** (circled)
Height of a door: **8 feet** (circled) / 8 inches
Height of a tree: **20 yards** (circled) / 20 miles

Complete.

$7 \times 6 + 1 =$ **43**
$8 \times 8 + 2 =$ **66**
$9 \times 7 + 7 =$ **70**
$6 \times 8 + 2 =$ **50**
$7 \times 8 + 5 =$ **61**

$47 +$ **5** $= 52$
71 $+ 6 = 77$
$100 -$ **45** $= 55$
60 $- 12 = 48$
$40 -$ **38** $= 2$

Solve. Write the equations you use.

⭐ The dinosaur costs $1.35 less than the yo-yo. The deck of cards costs $0.79 more than the dinosaur. How much does the deck of cards cost?

5.79
$- 1.35$
$\$4.44$

4.44
$+ 0.79$
$\$5.23$

$5.79

9.10 Practice

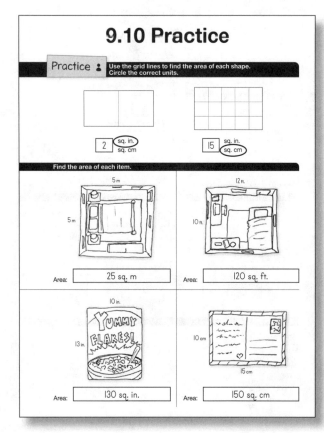

Practice 👤 Use the grid lines to find the area of each shape. Circle the correct units.

2 sq. in. / **sq. cm**
15 sq. in. / **sq. cm** (circled)

Find the area of each item.

5 m / 5 m → Area: **25 sq. m**
12 ft. / 10 ft. → Area: **120 sq. ft.**

10 in. / 13 in. → Area: **130 sq. in.**
10 cm / 15 cm → Area: **150 sq. cm**

9.10 Review

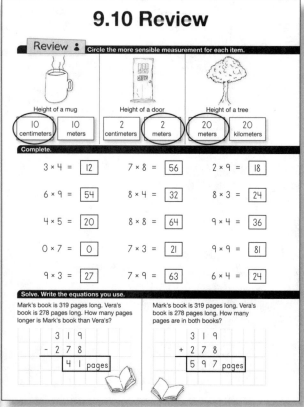

Review 👤 Circle the more sensible measurement for each item.

Height of a mug: **10 centimeters** (circled) / 10 meters
Height of a door: 2 centimeters / **2 meters** (circled)
Height of a tree: **20 meters** (circled) / 20 kilometers

Complete.

$3 \times 4 =$ **12**
$6 \times 9 =$ **54**
$4 \times 5 =$ **20**
$0 \times 7 =$ **0**
$9 \times 3 =$ **27**

$7 \times 8 =$ **56**
$8 \times 4 =$ **32**
$8 \times 8 =$ **64**
$7 \times 3 =$ **21**
$7 \times 9 =$ **63**

$2 \times 9 =$ **18**
$8 \times 3 =$ **24**
$9 \times 4 =$ **36**
$9 \times 9 =$ **81**
$6 \times 4 =$ **24**

Solve. Write the equations you use.

Mark's book is 319 pages long. Vera's book is 278 pages long. How many pages longer is Mark's book than Vera's?

$3 1 9$
$- 2 7 8$
4 1 pages

Mark's book is 319 pages long. Vera's book is 278 pages long. How many pages are in both books?

$3 1 9$
$+ 2 7 8$
5 9 7 pages

Unit 9 Answer Key

9.11 Practice

Practice 👤 Solve. Write the equations you use.

Caroline's bedroom is shaped like a rectangle. It is 12 feet long and 10 feet wide. What is the area of her bedroom?

$12 × 10 = \boxed{120 \text{ sq. ft.}}$

Zayne used 4 craft sticks to make a square. Each craft stick is 5 inches long. What is the area of the square?

$5 × 5 = \boxed{25 \text{ sq. in.}}$

The shorter side of the pool is 4 yards long. The other side is 3 yards longer. What is the area of the pool?

4 yd.

$4 + 3 = 7$
$7 × 4 = \boxed{28 \text{ sq. yd.}}$

★ The perimeter of this garden bed is 14 feet. What is its area?

3 ft.

$3 × 3 = 6$
$14 - 6 = 8$
$8 ÷ 2 = 4 \text{ ft.}$ ← length of longer side
$3 × 4 = \boxed{12 \text{ sq. ft.}}$

9.11 Review

Review 👤 Use the numbers to complete the blanks. You will use each number once.

| 1 | 2 | 3 | 4 | 5 | 6 | 7 | 8 | 9 |

$\boxed{2} × 8 = 16$ $3 × \boxed{4} = 12$ $10 × \boxed{9} = 90$

$\boxed{5} × 4 = 20$ $6 × \boxed{3} = 18$ $3 × \boxed{8} = 24$

$\boxed{7} × 5 = 35$ $10 × \boxed{6} = 60$ $17 × \boxed{1} = 17$

Complete.

×7	
7	49
9	63
6	42
8	56

×8	
6	48
8	64
9	72
7	56

×9	
9	81
7	63
8	72
6	54

Copy the shapes.

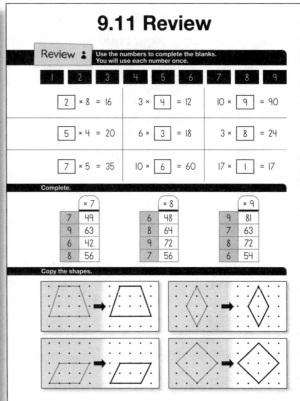

9.12 Unit Wrap-Up A

Unit Wrap-Up 👤 Use a ruler to measure the sticks to the nearest quarter-inch.

$4\frac{1}{2}$ in.

$2\frac{1}{4}$ in.

$3\frac{3}{4}$ in.

Circle the more sensible unit for each item.

Area of a rug: **40 sq. ft.** / 40 sq. in.

Area of a sticky note: **25 sq. cm** / 25 sq. m

Area of a parking lot: 300 sq. m / **300 sq. km**... **300 sq. m** / 300 sq. km

Find the perimeter. Include the correct unit.

14 cm, 10 cm, 10 cm

Perimeter: 34 cm

7 in., 6 in., 3 in., 10 in.

Perimeter: 32 in

All sides are 6 m.

Perimeter: 18 m

9.12 Unit Wrap-Up B

Unit Wrap-Up 👤 Find the area. Include the correct unit.

8 yd., 5 yd.
Area: 40 sq. yd.

5 cm, 6 cm
Area: 29 sq. cm

3 in., 5 in., 2 in., 6 in.
Area: 21 sq. in.

Split the rectangle into smaller rectangles. Then, find the area of the whole rectangle.

13 cm, 5 cm
$\boxed{65}$ sq. cm

Solve. Write the equations you use.

Hannah's kitchen is 20 ft. long and 18 ft. wide. What is the perimeter of the kitchen?

$20 + 18 + 20 + 18 = \boxed{76 \text{ ft.}}$

The shorter side of the sandbox is 8 ft. long. The other side is 2 ft. longer. What is the perimeter of the sandbox?

8 ft., 10 ft.

$8 + 10 + 8 + 10 = \boxed{36 \text{ ft.}}$

Unit 9 Checkpoint

What to Expect at the End of Unit 9

By the end of Unit 9, most children will be able to do the following:

- Approximate metric and U.S. customary length units and choose a reasonable unit for real-life measurements.
- Use a ruler to measure to the nearest quarter- or half-inch and write mixed numbers for these lengths. Some children will still feel confused by the many lines on standard rulers and prefer to use the paper ruler they made in Lessons 9.1 and 9.2.
- Understand that perimeter is the distance around the edge of a shape and know how to measure around the edge of an object to find its perimeter.
- Add the lengths of an object's sides to find its perimeter. Many children will sometimes need a reminder to include every side, especially if some sides are not labeled.
- Understand that area is the amount of space that a shape covers and use centimeter cubes to directly measure area.
- Multiply length times width to find the area of rectangles.
- Split shapes into rectangular parts and add or subtract the areas of the parts to find total area. Many children will still need help dividing large rectangles into manageable parts.
- Draw sketches to solve perimeter and area word problems, and solve perimeter and area word problems that involve two steps.

Is Your Child Ready to Move on?

In Unit 10, you will introduce your child to division. She will learn to use multiplication to find answers to division problems, and she'll begin to master the ÷2, ÷5, and ÷10 facts.

Your child will build on the ×2, ×5, and ×10 facts in Unit 10. If she can't find the answers to these facts within several seconds, spend a day or two practicing them before starting Unit 10. **If you practice these multiplication facts for a few days and find that your child does not have them fully mastered, move on to Unit 10 anyway.** Children vary in how long it takes them to develop speed and fluency with the multiplication facts, and your child will continue to practice them as she studies division in Unit 10.

Activities for Practicing the ×2, ×5, and ×10 Facts

- Multiplication Crash (×2) (Lesson 2.3)
- Multiplication Bingo (×2) (Lesson 2.4)
- Multiplication Cover Up (×5) (Lesson 2.7)
- Review ×5 Facts on the Clock (Lesson 3.2)
- Tic-Tac-Toe Crash (×10) (Lesson 2.5)

Unit 10
Division, Part 1

Overview

In Unit 10, you will introduce your child to the concept of division and teach him how to use multiplication to find answers to division problems. He'll begin to master the ÷2, ÷5, and ÷10 facts, and he'll learn two different ways to apply division to real-life situations.

This unit is the first of three division units in *Third Grade Math with Confidence*. Your child will learn the ÷3 and ÷4 facts in Unit 12, and then he'll tackle the rest of the division facts in Unit 15. By the end of the year, he should have a solid understanding of division and many of the division facts memorized. **Your child is not expected to fully master all the division facts by the end of third grade.** He'll do a thorough review of the division facts in fourth grade before he applies division to problems with larger numbers.

What Your Child Will Learn

In this unit, your child will learn to:

- Write division equations with the ÷ sign to match two different types of division situations
- Understand how to use multiplication to find answers to division problems
- Find answers for the ÷2, ÷5, and ÷10 facts
- Solve simple division word problems
- Solve division problems with remainders

Lesson List

Lesson 10.1	Introduce Division	Lesson 10.5	÷10 Facts
Lesson 10.2	÷2 Facts	Lesson 10.6	÷5 Facts
Lesson 10.3	Use Multiplication to Solve Division Problems	Lesson 10.7	Division Vocabulary and Word Problems
Lesson 10.4	Use Division to Find the Number of Equal Groups	Lesson 10.8	Remainders
		Lesson 10.9	Enrichment (Optional)

Extra Materials Needed for Unit 10

- 6 small boxes or bowls
- Paper clip
- For optional Enrichment Lesson:
    - *The Doorbell Rang*, written by Pat Hutchins. Greenwillow Books, 1989.
    - 20-25 small snacks, such as blueberries, chocolate chips, or pieces of cereal (optional)

Teaching Math with Confidence: Two Ways to Understand Division

You'll introduce your child to division in this unit. One of the most challenging aspects of division is that we use division to find answers in two different types of equal-groups contexts. Sometimes, we want to find the *size* of each group. Other times, we want to find the *number* of groups. For example:

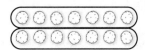

You have 14 cookies.
You split them equally with your brother.
How many do each of you get?

14 ÷ 2 = 7 cookies

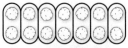

You have 14 cookies.
You put 2 in each box.
How many boxes do you fill?

14 ÷ 2 = 7 boxes

Both problems have 7 as an answer, but the 7 means something different in each problem. The answer to the first problem is 7 cookies, but the answer to the second problem is 7 boxes. You find the size of each group in the first problem, and you find the number of groups in the second problem.

Knowing both interpretations of division makes it easier for children learn the division facts, since some division facts are easier to solve if you imagine finding the size of each group and others are easier to solve if you visualize finding the number of groups. For example, in this unit, your child will learn the ÷2, ÷5, and ÷10 facts. Children usually prefer to find the size of each group for the ÷2 facts. But they usually find it more intuitive to find the number of groups when solving the ÷5 and ÷10 facts.

The lessons in this unit often use contexts that nudge your child towards using one of the interpretations of division. However, when your child solves numerical problems (without a real-life context), he can use whichever interpretation makes more sense to him. By developing deep conceptual understanding of both meanings of division, he'll be able to confidently solve a wide range of real-life problems.

Lesson 10.1
Introduce Division

Purpose	Materials
• Practice multiplication facts • Understand division as dividing a quantity into equal groups and finding the size of each group • Write division equations with the ÷ sign	• 2 decks of playing cards • Counters • 6 small boxes or bowls

Memory Work · **Name the multiples of 6 in order.** *6, 12, 18...* Stop your child when she reaches 60.

Many lessons in this unit are similar to the introductory multiplication lessons in Unit 2. Using similar contexts and examples in both units highlights the relationship between multiplication and division.

Warm-up: Play Multiplication Greatest to Least

Play Multiplication Greatest to Least. Play is the same as in Multiplication Least to Greatest. The only difference is that each new product must be less than the previous product. For example, if Player 1 plays a 4 and a 9, Player 2 can play any two cards with a product less than 36. See Lesson 9.5 (pages 288-289) for the directions for Multiplication Least to Greatest.

Learning to find products that are less than a given number prepares your child to solve division problems with remainders.

Activity: Divide Counters to Find the Size of Each Group

Today, we'll start a brand-new math topic: division! Division is a very important math skill, like multiplication. We'll spend a lot of time on it throughout the rest of this year.

What does it mean to divide something? *Sample answer: It means to share it. It means to take something and split it.* Briefly discuss a few real-life examples of division from your child's life. For example: **When you go to gymnastics, the coach divides the students into equal groups of kids. You and your brother divided the candies into 2 equal groups so that you each got the same number.**

When we divide a number, we split the number into equal groups. Let's pretend that you bake cookies to give away to friends. You split them into equal groups so that each friend gets the same number of cookies.

One day, you bake 8 cookies and you give the cookies to 2 friends. Place 8 counters and 2 small boxes or bowls on the table. Have your child split the counters equally between the 2 boxes. If your child's not sure what to do, suggest she deal out one counter per box (like dealing cards) until she has dealt out all the counters. **How many cookies does each friend get?** *4.*

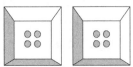

You divided the 8 cookies into 2 equal groups. You put 4 cookies in each group. We say that 8 divided by 2 equals 4.

8 divided by 2 can also be interpreted as "If I have 8 cookies and split them into groups of 2, how many groups will I make?" Your child will learn this interpretation in Lesson 10.4. See the Unit 10 **Teaching Math with Confidence** (page 316) for more on these two different ways to understand division.

Repeat with the following quantities and equal groups. Model each problem with counters and small boxes or bowls.

- **You bake 9 cookies for 3 friends. How many cookies does each friend get?** *3.* **9 divided by 3 equals 3.**
- **You bake 8 cookies for 4 friends. How many cookies does each friend get?** *2.* **8 divided by 4 equals 2.**
- **You bake 5 cookies for 5 friends. How many cookies does each friend get?** *1.* **5 divided by 5 equals 1.**
- **You bake 5 cookies for 1 friend. How many cookies does the friend get?** *5.* **5 divided by 1 equals 5.**

These problems give your child a concrete understanding of division before you introduce written division equations. Make sure to model them with counters.

Activity (A): Introduce the Division Sign

One day, you bake 12 cookies for 3 friends. Place 12 counters and 3 small boxes or bowls on the table. Have your child split the counters equally between the 3 boxes. **How many cookies does each friend get?** *4.*

Show your child part A. **When we multiply, we put equal groups together. We multiply the number of groups times the size of each group to find the total. You made 3 groups, and you put 4 cookies in each group. 3 times 4 equals 12.**

Multiplication

$3 \times 4 = 12$

number of groups   size of each group   total

Division is the opposite of multiplication. When we divide, we split a total into equal groups. In this problem, you divided the total by the number of groups. The answer is the size of the groups. You started with 12 cookies and divided them into 3 equal groups. You put 4 cookies in each group.

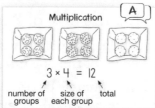

Division

$12 \div 3 = 4$

total   number of groups   size of each group

Point to the division sign in $12 \div 3$. **This sign is called the division sign. It means to divide the first number by the second number. We read this equation as "12 divided by 3 equals 4."**

Point to the next problem. **The next day, you bake 12 cookies for 6 friends.** Have your child split 12 counters equally between 6 boxes. **How many does each friend get?** *2.* Write 2 in the blank. Have your child draw a ring around each group of 2 cookies on the page.

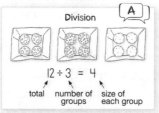

$12 \div 6 = \boxed{2}$

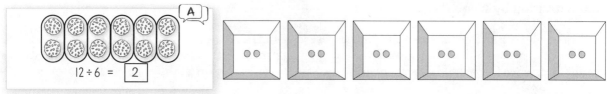

Have your child complete part A. Model each problem with counters. Then, have your child draw a ring around the cookies on the workbook page to match.

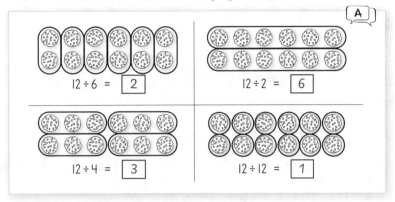

Your child may draw the rings around the cookies in a different way.

All of these problems begin with 12 cookies so that you can use the same 12 counters for every exercise (and don't have to spend lots of time counting out counters). For the last problem, your child can simply separate the counters on the table rather than using 12 separate boxes.

Activity (B): Write Division Equations

Point to the top row of the chart in part B. **Let's pretend you have 6 cookies for 3 friends.**

Have your child take 6 counters and arrange them in 3 equal groups. **What division problem matches the situation?** *6 divided by 3.* **How many cookies does each person get?** *2.* Write the matching division equation in the chart.

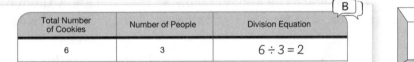
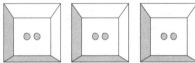

Complete part B. Have your child model each problem with counters and write the matching equation in the chart.

Total Number of Cookies	Number of People	Division Equation
6	3	$6 \div 3 = 2$
10	2	$10 \div 2 = 5$
10	5	$10 \div 5 = 2$
0	4	$0 \div 4 = 0$
15	15	$15 \div 15 = 1$

If your child is confused by the idea of dividing 0 cookies, say: **If you have 0 cookies, no one will get any!** Your child will learn more about dividing with 0 in Unit 12.

Independent Practice and Review

Have your child complete the Lesson 10.1 Practice and Review workbook pages. If your child has trouble, have her first divide real counters into equal groups before drawing circles on the page. For example, for 16 ÷ 8, give her 16 counters and have her split the counters into 8 equal groups.

Lesson 10.2
÷2 Facts

Purpose	Materials
• Practice finding half of numbers • Introduce ÷2 facts • Split numbers in half to find answers to ÷2 facts	• Counters • Coin

Memory Work · **Name the multiples of 9 in order.** *9, 18, 27...* Stop your child when he reaches 90.

Warm-up: Find Half

Have your child mentally find half of the following numbers.

- **What's half of 6?** *3.*
- **What's half of 12?** *6.*
- **What's half of 10?** *5.*
- **What's half of 16?** *8.*
- **What's half of 14?** *7.*

- **What's half of 18?** *9.*
- **What's half of 20?** *10.*
- **What's half of 30?** *15.*
- **What's half of 40?** *20.*

Activity (A): Split Numbers in Half to Find Answers to ÷2 Facts

In the last lesson, you learned what division means. Today, you'll start learning the division facts. The division facts are the division problems from 1 ÷ 1 up to 100 ÷ 10. Over the course of this year and next year, you'll learn the division facts so that you know them by heart, just like the addition, subtraction, and multiplication facts. Today, we'll focus on the ÷2 facts.

Read aloud the word problem in part A: *You have 14 cookies. You split them equally with your brother. How many do each of you get?*

To find the answer, we divide 14 by 2. Dividing by 2 is just like splitting the total in half. What's half of 14? *7.* **So, 14 divided by 2 equals 7.** Write 7 in both blanks. Have your child draw a ring around each group of 7 cookies on the page.

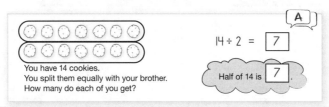

If your child is confused or unsure, place 14 counters on the table and have your child physically divide the counters into 2 equal groups.

Have your child complete the rest of the problems in the same way. Encourage him to think of splitting each total in half. Model the problems with counters if needed.

16 ÷ 2 = **8**	20 ÷ 2 = **10**	8 ÷ 2 = **4**
10 ÷ 2 = **5**	6 ÷ 2 = **3**	4 ÷ 2 = **2**
2 ÷ 2 = **1**	18 ÷ 2 = **9**	12 ÷ 2 = **6**

Activity (B): Play Division Race (÷2)

Play Division Race (÷2).

This fast-moving, luck-based game provides lots of practice with the ÷2 facts.

Division Race (÷2)

Materials: Counters; coin

Object of the Game: Be the first player to reach the end of the racecourse.

Choose which player will be heads and which will be tails. Have each player choose a counter as a game token and place it on the matching starting space.

Have one player flip the coin. (Either you or your child can do this.) If the coin shows heads, the "heads" player moves his game token to the next space and divides the number on the space by 2. For example, if you land on 16, say "16 divided by 2 equals 8."

If the coin shows tails, the "tails" player moves her game token to the next space and divides the number on the space by 2.

Continue flipping the coin and moving the counters until one player reaches the final space on the race course. The first player to reach the end wins.

Independent Practice and Review

Have your child complete the Lesson 10.2 Practice and Review workbook pages.

Lesson 10.3
Use Multiplication to Solve Division Problems

Purpose	Materials
• Practice multiplication facts • Write multiplication and division fact families for arrays • Use multiplication to find answers to division problems	• 2 decks of playing cards • Dot array and L-cover (Blackline Master 5)

Memory Work · **Name the multiples of 7 in order.** *7, 14, 21...* Stop your child when she reaches 70.

In this lesson, you will help your child understand the relationship between multiplication and division so she can use multiplication to solve division problems.

Warm-up: Play Multiplication Greatest to Least

Play Multiplication Greatest to Least. See Lesson 10.1 (page 317) for directions.

Activity (A): Write Multiplication and Division Equations to Match Arrays

In Unit 2, you learned how to write multiplication equations to match arrays. Today, you'll learn how to write division equations to match arrays. You'll also learn more about how multiplication and division are related.

Show your child the 3×5 array in part A. **How many rows are in this array?** *3.* **How many columns are in this array?** *5.*

You learned in Unit 2 that we can multiply the number of rows times the number of columns to find the total number of muffins. Or, we can multiply the number of columns times the number of rows to find the total. What two multiplication equations match this array of muffins? *3 times 5 equals 15. 5 times 3 equals 15.* Write both matching multiplication equations in the blanks.

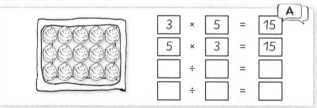

We can also write two division equations to match this array. One way is to divide the total number of muffins by the number of rows to find the number of columns. There are 15 muffins in all, and there are 3 rows. Write 15 and 3 in the blanks. **What's 15 divided by 3?** *5.* Write 5 in the blank.

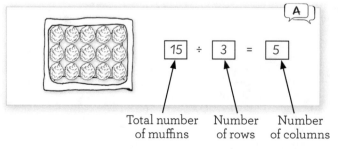

Total number of muffins   Number of rows   Number of columns

Another way is to divide the total number of muffins by the number of columns to find the number of rows. There are 15 muffins in all, and there are 5 columns. Write 15 and 5 in the blanks. **What's 15 divided by 5?** *3.* Write 3 in the blank.

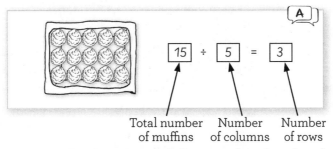

Total number   Number   Number
of muffins   of columns   of rows

These four equations are a multiplication and division fact family. They show the multiplication and division relationships between 3, 5, and 15.

$3 \times 5 = 15$
$5 \times 3 = 15$
$15 \div 3 = 5$
$15 \div 5 = 3$

Have your child write multiplication and division equations to match the other arrays in part A. For the 4×4 array, point out that the fact family only has 2 equations: **If the factors are the same, the fact family has only two equations.**

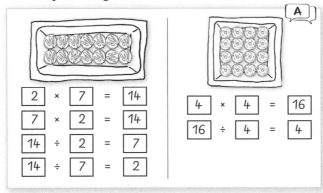

$2 \times 7 = 14$
$7 \times 2 = 14$
$14 \div 2 = 7$
$14 \div 7 = 2$

$4 \times 4 = 16$
$16 \div 4 = 4$

If your child writes the numbers in the division equations in the wrong order, say: **Mathematicians have agreed that we always start division problems with the total.** Avoid saying that division equations must always begin with the greater number, since this rule doesn't always hold. For example, 1 ÷ 2 = 1/2 is a perfectly valid equation.

Activity (B): Use Multiplication to Solve Division Problems

Show your child the open package of cookies in part B. **This package has 18 cookies. The cookies are arranged in 3 rows. Let's find how many cookies are in each row.**

Point to the division equation. **We could imagine splitting 18 cookies into 3 groups to find how many cookies are in each row. It's hard to imagine splitting up so many cookies, though! Instead, let's use the matching multiplication fact to find the answer. 3 times what equals 18?** *6.* Write 6 in the multiplication equation. **So, what does 18 divided by 3 equal?** *6.* Write 6 in the division equation.

$18 \div 3 = 6$
$3 \times 6 = 18$

If your child doesn't immediately know the missing factor in the multiplication problem, don't suggest that she skip-count from zero to find the answer. Instead, encourage her to try a number for the missing factor and then adjust her next guess based on whether the product is less than, equal to, or greater than 18. For example: **What's 4 times 3?** *12.* **Too low. How about 5 times 3?** *15.* **Still too low. How about 6 times 3?** *18.* **That's it!** This approach encourages her to use her multiplication knowledge as efficiently as possible to solve division problems.

18 divided by 3 equals 6, so the cookies must be arranged in 3 rows of 6. Have your child show 3 rows of 6 on the dot array. **3 times 6 equals 18, so 18 divided by 3 equals 6.**

Modeling the matching array on the dot array visually reinforces the connection between the multiplication and division problems.

Repeat with the rest of the division problems in part B. Frame each problem as in the above example, and have your child use the multiplication problem to solve the related division problem. For example, for 20 ÷ 5: **There are 20 cookies in the box. They're arranged in 5 rows. We want to find how many cookies are in each row.** After your child solves each problem, model the matching array on the dot array.

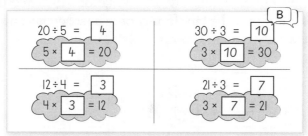

Independent Practice and Review

Have your child complete the Lesson 10.3 Practice and Review workbook pages.

Lesson 10.4
Use Division to Find the Number of Equal Groups

Purpose	Materials
• Understand division as dividing a quantity into equal groups and finding the number of groups • Practice finding answers to simple division problems	• Counters • 6 small boxes or bowls • Die

Memory Work • **Name the multiples of 8 in order.** *8, 16, 24...* Stop your child when he reaches 80.

In Lesson 10.1, your child learned to use division to find the size of equal groups. For example, he split 8 cookies into 2 equal groups and found that each group has 4 cookies. In this lesson, your child will learn that we can also use division to find the number of equal groups. For example, if you split 8 cookies into groups of 2, you get 4 equal groups. See the Unit 10 **Teaching Math with Confidence** (page 316) for more on these two ways to interpret division equations.

Warm-up: Divide Counters to Find the Number of Groups

Let's pretend again that you bake cookies to give away to friends. You split them into equal groups so that each friend gets the same number of cookies.

One day, you bake 8 cookies. You put 2 cookies in each box and give each friend a box. Give your child 8 counters. Place 6 small boxes or bowls on the table. Have him put 2 counters in each box until he has used up all the counters. (He will not fill every box.) **How many friends get a box of cookies?** *4.*

You divided 8 cookies into groups of 2, and you made 4 groups. 8 divided by 2 equals 4.

This activity develops concrete understanding of this new way to understand division. Make sure to model these problems with counters so that your child has plenty of hands-on practice before he tackles written equations.

Repeat with the following quantities and equal groups. Model each problem with counters and small boxes or bowls.

- **You bake 10 cookies. You put 2 cookies in each box. How many friends get cookies?** *5.* **10 divided by 2 equals 5.**
- **You bake 15 cookies. You put 3 cookies in each box. How many friends get cookies?** *5.* **15 divided by 3 equals 5.**
- **You bake 9 cookies. You put 3 cookies in each box. How many friends get cookies?** *3.* **9 divided by 3 equals 3.**
- **You bake 4 cookies. You put 1 cookie in each box. How many friends get cookies?** *4.* **4 divided by 1 equals 4.**
- **You bake 4 cookies. You put 4 cookies in each box. How many friends get cookies?** *1.* **4 divided by 4 equals 1.**

Activity (A): Use Division to Find the Number of Groups

You have already learned how to use division to find the size of equal groups. Today, you'll learn how to use division to find the **number of equal groups.**

Let's pretend there are 12 children at a class. Put 12 counters on the table. **The instructor splits the children into groups of 2.** Have your child arrange the counters in groups of 2. **How many groups does he make?** 6.

To make this activity more fun, pretend that the children are at an activity your child participates in (such as art class, sports practice, or religious education). Use the name of your child's instructor. For example: **Miss Jenna splits the kids in the painting class into groups of 2.**

Show your child part A. Have him draw rings around groups of 2 people. **We divided 12 by 2 and made 6 groups. So, what's 12 divided by 2?** 6. Write 6 in the blank.

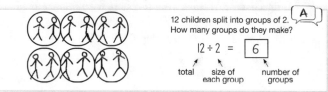

When we divide, we split a total into equal groups. In this problem, we divide the total by the size of each of group. The answer is the number of groups.

Some children may resist the idea that division can be applied in this new way. If so, simply demonstrate this way to use division and move on. Most children become more accepting of this new way to use division after a little more exposure to it. You'll continue to reinforce this concept over the next several lessons.

At the next class, the instructor splits the children into groups of 4. Have your child arrange the 12 counters in groups of 4. **How many groups does he make?** 3. Write 3 in the blank. Have your child draw a ring around each group of 4 people on the page.

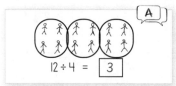

Have your child complete part A. Model each problem with counters before your child draws rings in the workbook.

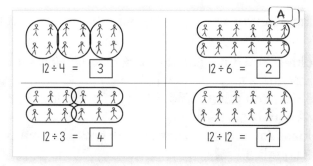

Your child may draw the rings in a different way,
but the number of children in each group should match the sample answers.

Activity (B): Play Treasure Hunt

Play Treasure Hunt. See Lesson 6.5 (page 188) for directions. Encourage your child to use related multiplication facts to find the answers to the division problems on the game board. For example, for 20 ÷ 4: **4 times what equals 20?** *5.* **So, what does 20 divided by 4 equal?** *5.* He may also model the problems with counters if needed.

Independent Practice and Review

Have your child complete the Lesson 10.4 Practice and Review workbook pages.

Lesson 10.5
÷10 Facts

Purpose	Materials
• Practice finding the correct number of dimes to match a money amount • Use place value to find answers to ÷10 facts • Practice ÷10 and ÷2 facts	• Play money • Counters

Memory Work · **Name the multiples of 4 in order.** *4, 8, 12...* Stop your child when she reaches 40.

Warm-up: Use Dimes to Show Money Amounts

Place a handful of dimes on the table. **May I have 60 cents, please?** *Child gives you 6 dimes.* If your child starts to count by 10s, encourage her to use place-value thinking instead. **How do you know how many dimes to give me?** *Sample answers: I know 6 times 10 equals 60. 60 has a 6 in the tens-place, so I know it has 6 tens.*

Have your child give you the following amounts of money in dimes.

- **May I have 50 cents, please?** *Child gives you 5 dimes.*
- **May I have 90 cents, please?** *Child gives you 9 dimes.*
- **May I have 80 cents, please?** *Child gives you 8 dimes.*
- **May I have 40 cents, please?** *Child gives you 4 dimes.*
- **May I have 100 cents, please?** *Child gives you 10 dimes.*
- **May I have 130 cents, please?** *Child gives you 13 dimes.*
- **May I have 160 cents, please?** *Child gives you 16 dimes.*

This activity previews dividing by 10.

Activity (A): Introduce ÷10 Facts

Today, you'll learn the ÷10 facts. Show your child part A. **Let's pretend we're decorating for a big party. We have 70 balloons, and we want to put 10 balloons in each bunch. What times 10 equals 70?** *7.* Write 7 in the blank. **So, what's 70 divided by 10?** *7.* Write 7 in the blank. **We can make 7 bunches of balloons.**

Place value helps find answers for the ÷10 facts. 7 groups of 10 equal 70, so 70 divided by 10 equals 7. Have your child complete the rest of the ÷10 facts. Encourage her to use place-value thinking to find the answers.

90 ÷ 10 = 9	40 ÷ 10 = 4	60 ÷ 10 = 6
30 ÷ 10 = 3	10 ÷ 10 = 1	100 ÷ 10 = 10
50 ÷ 10 = 5	20 ÷ 10 = 2	80 ÷ 10 = 8

Activity (B): Play Four in a Row

Play Four in a Row. See Lesson 3.1 (page 85) for directions.

The game board includes both ÷2 and ÷10 facts so that your child can practice both.

Independent Practice and Review

Have your child complete the Lesson 10.5 Practice and Review workbook pages.

Lesson 10.6
÷5 Facts

Purpose	Materials
• Practice finding the correct number of nickels to match a money amount • Practice ÷5 facts	• Play money • Base-ten blocks • Counters • Paper clip

Memory Work · **Name the multiples of 3 in order.** *3, 6, 9...* Stop your child when he reaches 30.

Warm-up: Use Nickels to Show Money Amounts

Arrange 6 nickels in a 2×3 array on the table. **How much are these nickels worth?** *30¢.* **How do you know?** *Sample answers: I know 6 times 5 equals 30. I counted by 5s.*

If your child doesn't mention it, point out that he could look at the pairs of nickels to find the total value: **Each pair of nickels equals 10¢. There are 3 pairs of nickels, so that means there's 30¢.**

Show your child the following arrangements of nickels. Have him tell you the value of the nickels in each array.

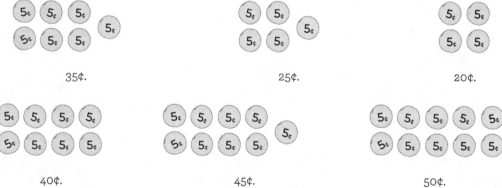

35¢.   25¢.   20¢.

40¢.   45¢.   50¢.

This activity previews the strategy your child will use to learn the ÷5 facts.

Activity (A): Introduce ÷5 Facts

In the last lesson, you learned the ÷10 facts. Today, you'll learn the ÷5 facts.

Point to 10 ÷ 5 and place 1 rod on the table. **Let's pretend that the rods are chocolate bars. Each bar has 10 squares of chocolate. I want to divide the 10 squares of chocolate into groups of 5.** Pretend to cut the rod into groups of 5 squares. **How many groups of 5 equal 10?** 2. Write 2 in the blank.

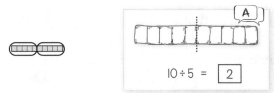

$$10 ÷ 5 = \boxed{2}$$

Point to 20 ÷ 5 and place another rod on the table. **I want to divide the 20 squares of chocolate into groups of 5.** Have your child pretend to cut each rod into groups of 5 squares. **How many groups of 5 equal 20?** 4. Write 4 in the blank.

$$20 ÷ 5 = \boxed{4}$$

Repeat with 30 ÷ 5 and 40 ÷ 5. Model each problem with rods and have your child pretend to cut each rod into groups of 5 squares.

$$30 ÷ 5 = \boxed{6}$$
$$40 ÷ 5 = \boxed{8}$$

Point to 15 ÷ 5. Place 1 rod and 5 unit blocks on the table. **I want to divide these 15 squares of chocolate into groups of 5. We can use 10 ÷ 5 as a stepping stone for finding the answer.** Pretend to cut the rod into 2 groups of 5 squares. **How many groups of 5 equal 10?** 2. **So, how many groups of 5 equal 15?** 3. Write 3 in the blank.

$$15 ÷ 5 = \boxed{3}$$

Point to 25 ÷ 5 and place another rod on the table. **I want to divide the 25 squares of chocolate into groups of 5.** Have your child pretend to cut each rod into groups of 5 squares. **How many groups of 5 equal 20?** 4. **So, how many groups of 5 equal 25?** 5. Write 5 in the blank.

$$25 ÷ 5 = \boxed{5}$$

Repeat with 35 ÷ 5 and 45 ÷ 5. Model each problem with base-ten blocks. Encourage your child to use 30 ÷ 5 and 40 ÷ 5 as stepping stones for finding the answers.

$$35 ÷ 5 = \boxed{7}$$
$$45 ÷ 5 = \boxed{9}$$

Activity (B): Play Spin and Cover

Use the game boards in part B to play Spin and Cover.

Spin and Cover

Materials: Paper clip, counters

Object of the Game: Cover all of your stars before the other player.

Place one end of the paper clip in the center of the spinner. Place the point of a pencil through the paper clip so that it touches the very center of the circle.

On your turn, hold the pencil upright and spin the paper clip. Solve the division problem in the space the paper clip lands on and place a counter on the matching star. For example, if the paper clip stops on 35 ÷ 5, cover the star with a 7.

Then, have the other player spin and cover his matching star. If the spinner lands on a division problem for which the answer is already covered, say the answer to the problem but do not place a new counter.

Continue until one player covers all of his stars. Whoever covers all of their stars first wins the game.

Independent Practice and Review

Have your child complete the Lesson 10.6 Practice and Review workbook pages. If your child has trouble, encourage him to draw lines dividing each rod into 2 groups of 5 to help find the answers.

20 ÷ 5 = 4

Each ten can be split into 2 groups of 5. So, 20 divided by 5 equals 4.

The problems are arranged so that your child can use the problems on the left side of the page as stepping stones for finding the answers to the problems on the right side of the page.

Lesson 10.7
Division Vocabulary and Word Problems

Purpose	Materials
• Practice ÷5 facts • Introduce dividend, divisor, and quotient • Solve division word problems	• Playing cards • Counters

Memory Work
- **What do we call the result when we add numbers together?** *The sum.*
- **What do we call the result when we subtract a number from another number?** *The difference.*
- **What do we call the result when we multiply numbers together?** *The product.*

Warm-up (A): Play Division Crash (÷5)

Play Division Crash (÷5).

Division Crash (÷5)

Materials: Deck of playing cards with jacks, queens, and kings removed (40 cards total); 10 counters of two different colors each

Object of the Game: Have the most counters on the game board at the end of the game.

Shuffle the cards and place the stack face down on the table. Give 10 counters of one color to one player and 10 counters of a different color to the other player.

On your turn, flip over the top card. Find the division problem whose quotient equals the card, and place a counter on the matching square. For example, if you flip over a 7, place a counter on 35 ÷ 5.

If the other player already has a counter on the square, you may "crash" into their counter, remove it, and place your own counter on the square. Continue until all the squares are filled. Whoever has more counters on the board at the end wins the game.

Activity (B): Introduce Division Vocabulary

Today, you'll learn some important division vocabulary words. You'll also solve division word problems.

Show your child part B. **The first number in a division problem is called the *dividend*, and the second number is called the *divisor*. The dividend is the number to be divided. The divisor is the number we divide by. We call the result of division the *quotient*.**

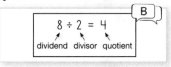

Have your child say each word aloud. Then, cover the words with your hand or a slip of paper and have your child try to recall the name of each number in the equation.

Children often have trouble remembering *divisor* and *dividend*, since the words sound so similar. One way to remember it is that the dividend is on the front *end* of the horizontal equation. Divisor ends in *-or* like *actor*, and it *acts* on the dividend when it divides it up. Your child will practice these tricky vocabulary words more as memory work.

Activity (C): Solve Division Word Problems

Show your child part C. **What do you remember about the steps for reading word problems?** *Sample answer: You read them twice and imagine what's happening.*

Have your child read the first word problem, identify the goal, and then read the problem again slowly.

What's the goal in this problem? *Find how many lollipops each friend gets.* **This is a problem about splitting a total into equal groups, so we can use division to solve it. What division problem tells how many lollipops each friend will get?** *20 ÷ 5.* Write "20 ÷ 5 =" and have your child complete the equation. Remind her to label and box the complete answer.

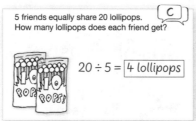

Have your child read aloud the second word problem. **What's the goal in this problem?** *Find how many goodie bags you can make.* Have her write an equation to match the problem and complete the equation.

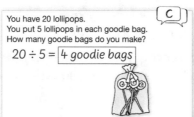

What do these two word problems have in common? *Sample answer: They're both about equal groups of lollipops. They have the same numbers.*

How are these two word problems different? *Sample answer: You find the size of the groups in the first problem, but you find the number of groups in the second problem. The units for the answers are different.*

In the first problem, you knew the *number* of groups and used division to find the *size* of the groups. In the second problem, you knew the *size* of the groups and used division to find the *number* of groups. We can use division to solve both kinds of problems.

Have your child write division equations to solve the final two word problems in part B.

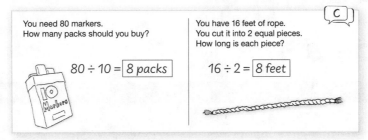

Independent Practice and Review

Have your child complete the Lesson 10.7 Practice and Review workbook pages.

Lesson 10.8
Remainders

Purpose	Materials
• Practice ÷5 facts • Introduce remainders • Solve division problems with remainders	• Counters • Die

Memory Work	• **What do we call the result when we divide two numbers?** *The quotient.* • **What do we call the number to be divided?** *The dividend.* • **What do we call the number we divide by?** *The divisor.*

This lesson provides a simple, concrete introduction to remainders. Your child will explore remainders more and solve more challenging remainder problems in Units 12 and 15.

Warm-up: Practice ÷5 Facts

Do a brief oral review of the ÷5 facts.

- $20 \div 5 = 4$
- $40 \div 5 = 8$
- $15 \div 5 = 3$
- $50 \div 5 = 10$
- $45 \div 5 = 9$

- $5 \div 5 = 1$
- $25 \div 5 = 5$
- $35 \div 5 = 7$
- $10 \div 5 = 2$
- $30 \div 5 = 6$

Activity (A): Introduce Remainders

In this unit, you've learned a lot about division. In all the problems so far, you've been able to divide the quantities evenly, with nothing left over. In real life, division problems don't always work out evenly! Today, you'll learn to solve problems where an amount remains after you divide.

Let's pretend that you work at a bakery and sell cookies. One day, you bake 13 cookies. Place 13 counters on the table. **You package the cookies in boxes, with 4 cookies in each box.** Have your child arrange the counters in groups of 4.

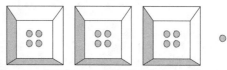

How many boxes do you fill? *3.* **After you fill the boxes, how many cookies do you have left?** *1.* Point to the leftover counter. **The amount left over after division is called the** *remainder,* **because it's the part that remains.**

Show your child part A. **We divided 13 cookies into groups of 4. We made 3 groups and had 1 cookie left.** Have your child draw a circle around each group of 4 cookies on the page.

So, 13 divided by 4 equals 3, with a remainder of 1. Here's how we write the answer for the horizontal equation. Write "3 R1" in the blank. **The R stands for remainder.**

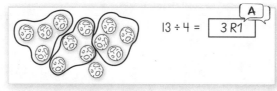

In the next problem, you have 11 cookies and put 2 cookies in each box. Place 11 counters on the table and have your child arrange them in groups of 2. Then, have your child draw a circle around each group of 2 cookies on the page. **How many boxes do you fill?** *5.* **After you fill the boxes, how many cookies do you have left?** *1.* Write "5 R1" to complete the problem.

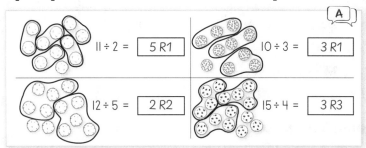

Have your child complete part A. Use counters to model the problems as needed.

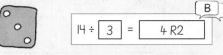

Activity (B): Play Roll and Divide

Play Roll and Divide. Use counters to model the problems as needed.

Roll and Divide

Materials: Die

Object of the Game: Create remainders that are as large as possible so that the sum of your remainders is greater than your opponent's sum.

Roll and Divide has 5 rounds. On your turn, roll the die. Write the number on the die as the divisor in the first blank division equation on your scorecard. Then, solve the problem. For example, if you roll a 3 in the first round:

14 ÷ 3 = 4 R2

Sample first play.

The remainder is your score for that round. If there is no remainder, your score is 0.

Play until both players have completed the entire scorecard. Find the sum of each player's remainders. Whoever has the greater sum wins the game.

Only write the quotient if a problem does not have a remainder. You do not need to write R0.

Advanced Variation: If your child easily solved the problems in part A, add this problem-solving twist to this game. Instead of completing the problems in order, choose which problem to complete for each roll. For example, if you roll a 6, the best play is to write the 6 in the fourth row and create 16 ÷ 6, since this division problem yields the greatest possible remainder.

Independent Practice and Review

Have your child complete the Lesson 10.8 Practice and Review workbook pages.

Lesson 10.9
Enrichment (Optional)

Purpose	Materials
• Practice memory work • Understand division in the context of sharing cookies • Investigate divisibility • Summarize what your child has learned and assess your child's progress	• *The Doorbell Rang,* by Pat Hutchins • 20-25 small snacks, such as blueberries, chocolate chips, or pieces of cereal (optional)

Warm-up: Review Memory Work

Quiz your child on all memory work through Unit 10. See pages 527-528 for the full list.

Math Picture Book: *The Doorbell Rang*

Read *The Doorbell Rang,* by Pat Hutchins. As you read, have your child tell the division equations that match how the children share the cookies. For example, when 2 children share 12 cookies: *12 divided by 2 equals 6.*

Enrichment Activity: What Numbers of Snacks Can We Divide Evenly?

How many people live in our home? *Answers will vary.* **There are some numbers of snacks that we can divide evenly among our family. Other numbers of snacks can't be divided evenly and have a remainder.**

Today, we'll figure out which numbers of snacks we can share evenly in our home and which numbers of snacks have a remainder. Help your child make a chart showing the results if you divide the numbers 1-25 by the number of people in your home.

1 ÷ 5 = 0 R1	6 ÷ 5 = 1 R1	11 ÷ 5 = 2 R1	16 ÷ 5 = 3 R1	21 ÷ 5 = 4 R1
2 ÷ 5 = 0 R2	7 ÷ 5 = 1 R2	12 ÷ 5 = 2 R2	17 ÷ 5 = 3 R2	22 ÷ 5 = 4 R2
3 ÷ 5 = 0 R3	8 ÷ 5 = 1 R3	13 ÷ 5 = 2 R3	18 ÷ 5 = 3 R3	23 ÷ 5 = 4 R3
4 ÷ 5 = 0 R4	9 ÷ 5 = 1 R4	14 ÷ 5 = 2 R4	19 ÷ 5 = 3 R4	24 ÷ 5 = 4 R4
5 ÷ 5 = 1	10 ÷ 5 = 2	15 ÷ 5 = 3	20 ÷ 5 = 4	25 ÷ 5 = 5

Sample chart for a family of 5. Use the number of people in your home as the divisor in each equation.

After you complete the chart, point to the dividends in the equations with no remainder. **What do all these dividends have in common?** *Sample answer: They're all multiples of the number of people in our home.*

What's the largest dividend on the chart with no remainder? *Answers will vary.* If it's near snack time, give your child this number of small snacks and have your child evenly divide them among the people in your household.

Unit Wrap-up

Have your child complete the Unit 10 Wrap-up.

Unit 10 Answer Key

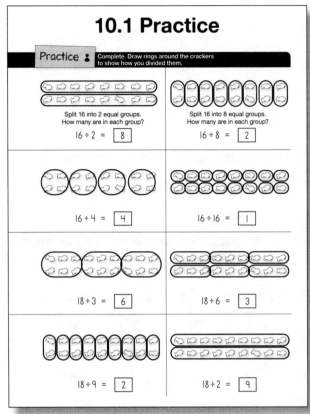

10.1 Practice

Practice — Complete. Draw rings around the crackers to show how you divided them.

Split 16 into 2 equal groups. How many are in each group?

$16 \div 2 = \boxed{8}$

Split 16 into 8 equal groups. How many are in each group?

$16 \div 8 = \boxed{2}$

$16 \div 4 = \boxed{4}$

$16 \div 16 = \boxed{1}$

$18 \div 3 = \boxed{6}$

$18 \div 6 = \boxed{3}$

$18 \div 9 = \boxed{2}$

$18 \div 2 = \boxed{9}$

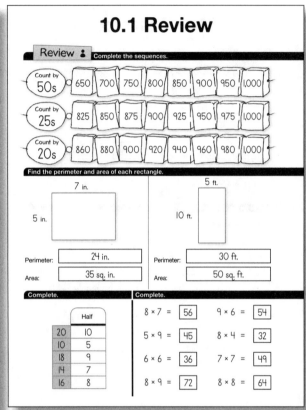

10.1 Review

Review — Complete the sequences.

Count by 50s: 650 | 700 | 750 | 800 | 850 | 900 | 950 | 1,000

Count by 25s: 825 | 850 | 875 | 900 | 925 | 950 | 975 | 1,000

Count by 20s: 860 | 880 | 900 | 920 | 940 | 960 | 980 | 1,000

Find the perimeter and area of each rectangle.

7 in. / 5 in.

Perimeter: 24 in.
Area: 35 sq. in.

5 ft. / 10 ft.

Perimeter: 30 ft.
Area: 50 sq. ft.

Complete.

	Half
20	10
10	5
18	9
14	7
16	8

Complete.

$8 \times 7 = \boxed{56}$ $9 \times 6 = \boxed{54}$

$5 \times 9 = \boxed{45}$ $8 \times 4 = \boxed{32}$

$6 \times 6 = \boxed{36}$ $7 \times 7 = \boxed{49}$

$8 \times 9 = \boxed{72}$ $8 \times 8 = \boxed{64}$

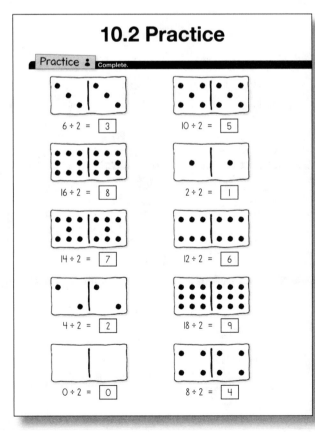

10.2 Practice

Practice — Complete.

$6 \div 2 = \boxed{3}$

$10 \div 2 = \boxed{5}$

$16 \div 2 = \boxed{8}$

$2 \div 2 = \boxed{1}$

$14 \div 2 = \boxed{7}$

$12 \div 2 = \boxed{6}$

$4 \div 2 = \boxed{2}$

$18 \div 2 = \boxed{9}$

$0 \div 2 = \boxed{0}$

$8 \div 2 = \boxed{4}$

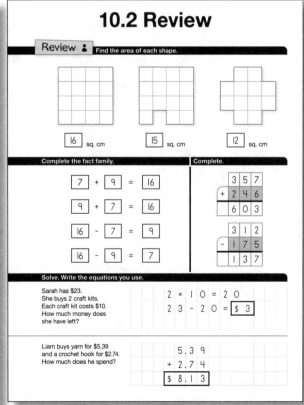

10.2 Review

Review — Find the area of each shape.

16 sq. cm   15 sq. cm   12 sq. cm

Complete the fact family.

$\boxed{7} + \boxed{9} = \boxed{16}$

$\boxed{9} + \boxed{7} = \boxed{16}$

$\boxed{16} - \boxed{7} = \boxed{9}$

$\boxed{16} - \boxed{9} = \boxed{7}$

Complete.

```
  3 5 7
+ 2 4 6
  6 0 3
```

```
  3 1 2
- 1 7 5
  1 3 7
```

Solve. Write the equations you use.

Sarah has $23. She buys 2 craft kits. Each craft kit costs $10. How much money does she have left?

$2 \times 10 = 20$

$23 - 20 = \boxed{\$3}$

Liam buys yarn for $5.39 and a crochet hook for $2.74. How much does he spend?

```
  5.3 9
+ 2.7 4
$ 8.1 3
```

Unit 10 Answer Key

10.3 Practice

Practice 👤 Complete the fact families to match the arrays.

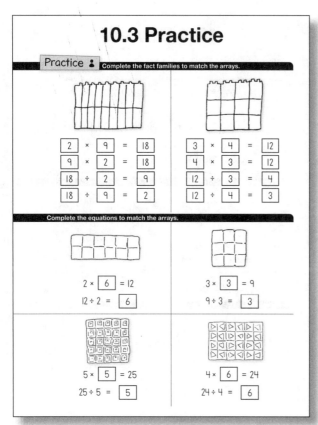

2	×	9	=	18
9	×	2	=	18
18	÷	2	=	9
18	÷	9	=	2

3	×	4	=	12
4	×	3	=	12
12	÷	3	=	4
12	÷	4	=	3

Complete the equations to match the arrays.

2 × **6** = 12
12 ÷ 2 = **6**

3 × **3** = 9
9 ÷ 3 = **3**

5 × **5** = 25
25 ÷ 5 = **5**

4 × **6** = 24
24 ÷ 4 = **6**

10.3 Review

Review 👤 Use the grid lines to find the area of each shape. Circle the correct units.

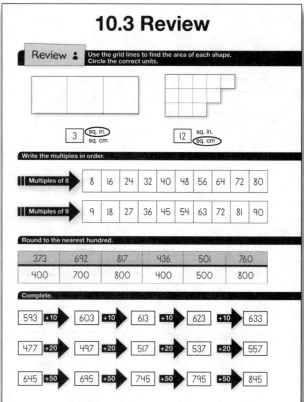

3 (sq. in.) / sq. cm

12 sq. in. / (sq. cm)

Write the multiples in order.

Multiples of 8 → | 8 | 16 | 24 | 32 | 40 | 48 | 56 | 64 | 72 | 80 |

Multiples of 9 → | 9 | 18 | 27 | 36 | 45 | 54 | 63 | 72 | 81 | 90 |

Round to the nearest hundred.

373	692	817	436	501	760
400	700	800	400	500	800

Complete.

| 593 | +10 → | 603 | +10 → | 613 | +10 → | 623 | +10 → | 633 |

| 477 | +20 → | 497 | +20 → | 517 | +20 → | 537 | +20 → | 557 |

| 645 | +50 → | 695 | +50 → | 745 | +50 → | 795 | +50 → | 845 |

10.4 Practice

Practice 👤 Complete. Draw rings around the candies to show how you divided them.

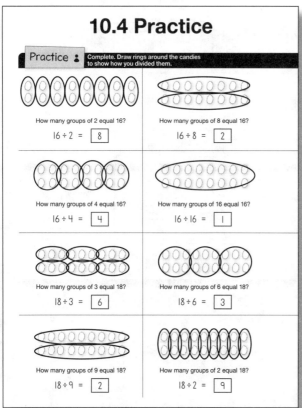

How many groups of 2 equal 16?
16 ÷ 2 = **8**

How many groups of 8 equal 16?
16 ÷ 8 = **2**

How many groups of 4 equal 16?
16 ÷ 4 = **4**

How many groups of 16 equal 16?
16 ÷ 16 = **1**

How many groups of 3 equal 18?
18 ÷ 3 = **6**

How many groups of 6 equal 18?
18 ÷ 6 = **3**

How many groups of 9 equal 18?
18 ÷ 9 = **2**

How many groups of 2 equal 18?
18 ÷ 2 = **9**

10.4 Review

Review 👤 Choose the more sensible unit for each item.

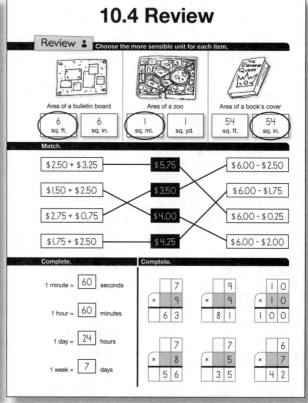

Area of a bulletin board
(**6** sq. ft.) / **6** sq. in.

Area of a zoo
(**1** sq. mi.) / **1** sq. yd.

Area of a book's cover
54 sq. ft. / (**54** sq. in.)

Match.

$2.50 + $3.25 —— $5.75 —— $6.00 - $2.50
$1.50 + $2.50 —— $3.50 —— $6.00 - $1.75
$2.75 + $0.75 —— $4.00 —— $6.00 - $0.25
$1.75 + $2.50 —— $4.25 —— $6.00 - $2.00

Complete.

1 minute = **60** seconds
1 hour = **60** minutes
1 day = **24** hours
1 week = **7** days

Complete.

×	7	
	9	
		6 3

×	9	
	9	
		8 1

×	1 0	
	1 0	
		1 0 0

×	7	
	8	
		5 6

×	7	
	5	
		3 5

×	6	
	7	
		4 2

Unit 10 Answer Key

10.5 Practice

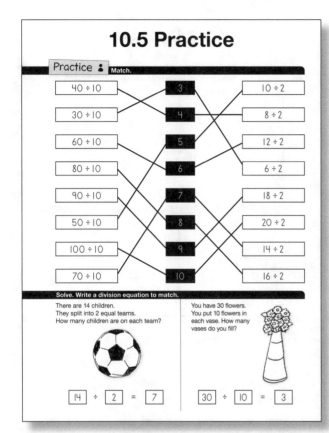

Practice 👤 Match.

40 ÷ 10	3	10 ÷ 2
30 ÷ 10	4	8 ÷ 2
60 ÷ 10	5	12 ÷ 2
80 ÷ 10	6	6 ÷ 2
90 ÷ 10	7	18 ÷ 2
50 ÷ 10	8	20 ÷ 2
100 ÷ 10	9	14 ÷ 2
70 ÷ 10	10	16 ÷ 2

Solve. Write a division equation to match.

There are 14 children. They split into 2 equal teams. How many children are on each team?

14 ÷ 2 = 7

You have 30 flowers. You put 10 flowers in each vase. How many vases do you fill?

30 ÷ 10 = 3

10.5 Review

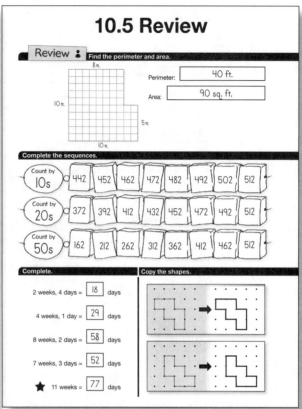

Review 👤 Find the perimeter and area.

Perimeter: 40 ft.
Area: 90 sq. ft.

Complete the sequences.

Count by 10s: 442 452 462 472 482 492 502 512

Count by 20s: 372 392 412 432 452 472 492 512

Count by 50s: 162 212 262 312 362 412 462 512

Complete.

2 weeks, 4 days = 18 days
4 weeks, 1 day = 29 days
8 weeks, 2 days = 58 days
7 weeks, 3 days = 52 days
⭐ 11 weeks = 77 days

Copy the shapes.

10.6 Practice

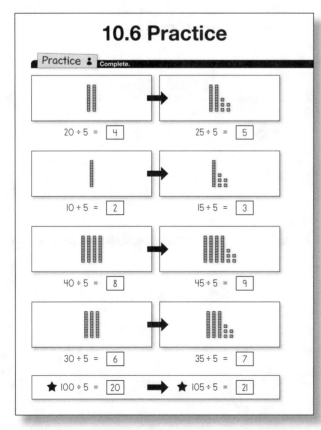

Practice 👤 Complete.

20 ÷ 5 = 4   25 ÷ 5 = 5

10 ÷ 5 = 2   15 ÷ 5 = 3

40 ÷ 5 = 8   45 ÷ 5 = 9

30 ÷ 5 = 6   35 ÷ 5 = 7

⭐ 100 ÷ 5 = 20   ➡ ⭐ 105 ÷ 5 = 21

10.6 Review

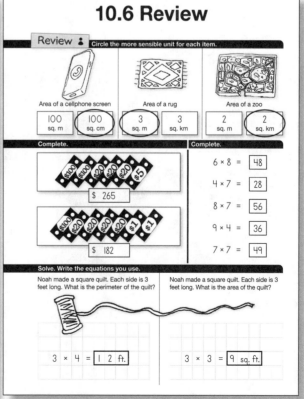

Review 👤 Circle the more sensible unit for each item.

Area of a cellphone screen
100 sq. m   (100 sq. cm)

Area of a rug
(3 sq. m)   3 sq. km

Area of a zoo
2 sq. m   (2 sq. km)

Complete.

$ 265

$ 182

Complete.

6 × 8 = 48
4 × 7 = 28
8 × 7 = 56
9 × 4 = 36
7 × 7 = 49

Solve. Write the equations you use.

Noah made a square quilt. Each side is 3 feet long. What is the perimeter of the quilt?

3 × 4 = 12 ft.

Noah made a square quilt. Each side is 3 feet long. What is the area of the quilt?

3 × 3 = 9 sq. ft.

Unit 10 Answer Key

10.7 Practice

Practice 👤 Complete.

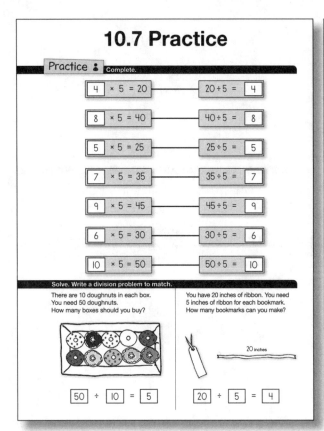

4 × 5 = 20	20 ÷ 5 = 4
8 × 5 = 40	40 ÷ 5 = 8
5 × 5 = 25	25 ÷ 5 = 5
7 × 5 = 35	35 ÷ 5 = 7
9 × 5 = 45	45 ÷ 5 = 9
6 × 5 = 30	30 ÷ 5 = 6
10 × 5 = 50	50 ÷ 5 = 10

Solve. Write a division problem to match.

There are 10 doughnuts in each box. You need 50 doughnuts. How many boxes should you buy?

You have 20 inches of ribbon. You need 5 inches of ribbon for each bookmark. How many bookmarks can you make?

20 inches

50 ÷ 10 = 5

20 ÷ 5 = 4

10.7 Review

Review 👤 Split the rectangle into smaller rectangles. Then, find the area of the whole rectangle.

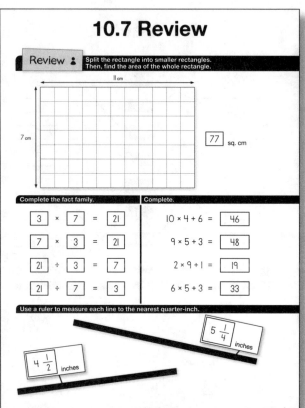

11 cm

7 cm

77 sq. cm

Complete the fact family.

3 × 7 = 21

7 × 3 = 21

21 ÷ 3 = 7

21 ÷ 7 = 3

Complete.

10 × 4 + 6 = 46

9 × 5 + 3 = 48

2 × 9 + 1 = 19

6 × 5 + 3 = 33

Use a ruler to measure each line to the nearest quarter-inch.

$5 \frac{1}{4}$ inches

$4 \frac{1}{2}$ inches

10.8 Practice

Practice 👤 Complete.

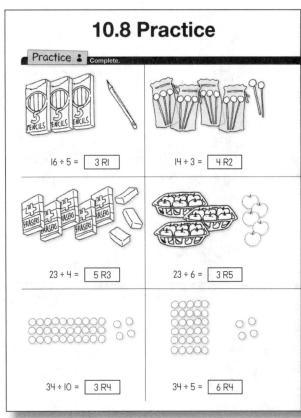

16 ÷ 5 = 3 R1

14 ÷ 3 = 4 R2

23 ÷ 4 = 5 R3

23 ÷ 6 = 3 R5

34 ÷ 10 = 3 R4

34 ÷ 5 = 6 R4

10.8 Review

Review 👤 Complete.

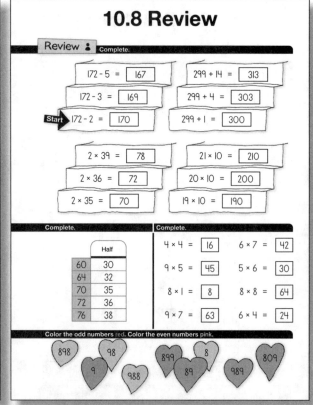

172 − 5 = 167	299 + 14 = 313
172 − 3 = 169	299 + 4 = 303
Start 172 − 2 = 170	299 + 1 = 300

2 × 39 = 78	21 × 10 = 210
2 × 36 = 72	20 × 10 = 200
2 × 35 = 70	19 × 10 = 190

Complete.

	Half
60	30
64	32
70	35
72	36
76	38

Complete.

4 × 4 = 16	6 × 7 = 42
9 × 5 = 45	5 × 6 = 30
8 × 1 = 8	8 × 8 = 64
9 × 7 = 63	6 × 4 = 24

Color the odd numbers red. **Color the even numbers** pink.

898   98   899   8   9   988   89   809   989

Unit 10 Answer Key

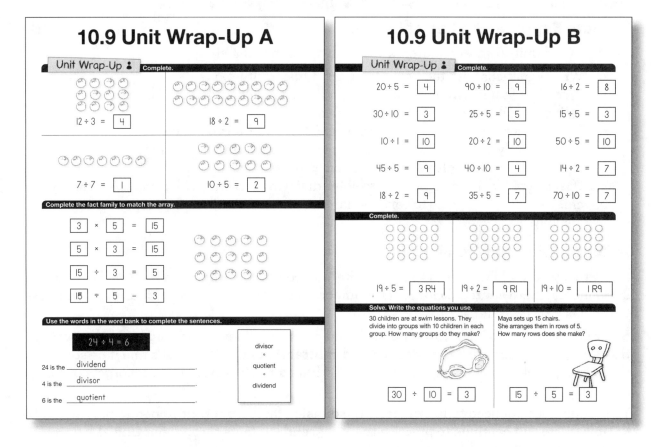

10.9 Unit Wrap-Up A

Unit Wrap-Up 👤 Complete.

$12 \div 3 = \boxed{4}$

$18 \div 2 = \boxed{9}$

$7 \div 7 = \boxed{1}$

$10 \div 5 = \boxed{2}$

Complete the fact family to match the array.

$\boxed{3} \times \boxed{5} = \boxed{15}$

$\boxed{5} \times \boxed{3} = \boxed{15}$

$\boxed{15} \div \boxed{3} = \boxed{5}$

$\boxed{15} \div \boxed{5} = \boxed{3}$

Use the words in the word bank to complete the sentences.

$24 \div 4 = 6$

24 is the ___dividend___.

4 is the ___divisor___.

6 is the ___quotient___.

word bank:
divisor
◦
quotient
◦
dividend

10.9 Unit Wrap-Up B

Unit Wrap-Up 👤 Complete.

$20 \div 5 = \boxed{4}$　　$90 \div 10 = \boxed{9}$　　$16 \div 2 = \boxed{8}$

$30 \div 10 = \boxed{3}$　　$25 \div 5 = \boxed{5}$　　$15 \div 5 = \boxed{3}$

$10 \div 1 = \boxed{10}$　　$20 \div 2 = \boxed{10}$　　$50 \div 5 = \boxed{10}$

$45 \div 5 = \boxed{9}$　　$40 \div 10 = \boxed{4}$　　$14 \div 2 = \boxed{7}$

$18 \div 2 = \boxed{9}$　　$35 \div 5 = \boxed{7}$　　$70 \div 10 = \boxed{7}$

Complete.

$19 \div 5 = \boxed{3\ R4}$　　$19 \div 2 = \boxed{9\ R1}$　　$19 \div 10 = \boxed{1\ R9}$

Solve. Write the equations you use.

30 children are at swim lessons. They divide into groups with 10 children in each group. How many groups do they make?

$\boxed{30} \div \boxed{10} = \boxed{3}$

Maya sets up 15 chairs. She arranges them in rows of 5. How many rows does she make?

$\boxed{15} \div \boxed{5} = \boxed{3}$

Unit 10 Checkpoint

What to Expect at the End of Unit 10

By the end of Unit 10, most children will be able to do the following:

- Write equations with the ÷ sign to match division situations.
- Write fact families for multiplication and division and understand how to use multiplication to find answers to division problems.
- Find answers for the ÷2, ÷5, and ÷10 facts. Most children will know the ÷2 and ÷10 facts fairly fluently, but many will still need more practice with the ÷5 facts.
- Write equations to solve simple division word problems.
- Use concrete objects or pictures to solve division problems with remainders. Many children will not be able to solve remainder problems without first representing them visually.

Is Your Child Ready to Move on?

In Unit 11, your child will learn to read, write, and compare numbers to 10,000. He'll also learn mental math strategies for larger numbers and learn how to round four-digit numbers to the nearest thousand.

Before moving on to Unit 11, your child should be mostly fluent at **adding and subtracting three-digit numbers with the addition and subtraction algorithms.** It's fine if he sometimes has trouble remembering a few of the addition or subtraction facts or forgets one of the steps.

Your child does not need to fully master the division facts from Unit 10 before moving on to Unit 11. He will continue to practice the ÷2, ÷5, and ÷10 facts throughout Unit 11 before working on the ÷3 and ÷4 facts in Unit 12.

What to Do If Your Child Needs More Practice

If your child needs more practice adding and subtracting three-digit numbers, make up a three-digit addition problem and a three-digit subtraction problem for him to solve at the beginning of every lesson in Unit 11. Make sure to include problems that require trading. If needed, model the problems with base-ten blocks and use the Addition and Subtraction Algorithm diagrams (from Blackline Master 4) to remind him of the steps.

Unit 11
Numbers to 10,000

Overview

In this unit, your child will learn about the numbers to 10,000. She'll follow a similar progression as in Unit 5, where she learned about place value in the numbers to 1,000. First, she'll develop number sense with these larger numbers as she compares them, approximates their positions on the number line, and rounds them to the nearest thousand. Then, she'll break apart and put together thousands with mental math, and she'll use the written addition and subtraction algorithms to add four-digit numbers. In fourth grade, your child will extend these skills to even larger numbers.

What Your Child Will Learn

In this unit, your child will learn to:

- Read, write, and compare numbers to 10,000
- Understand place value in four-digit numbers and write four-digit numbers in expanded form
- Round to the nearest thousand
- Use place-value thinking to mentally add and subtract groups of hundreds (for example, 6,700 + 400 or 5,100 – 300)
- Use the addition and subtraction algorithms to add and subtract four-digit numbers
- Subtract to find elapsed time between years

Lesson List

Lesson 11.1   Numbers to 10,000
Lesson 11.2   Compare Numbers to 10,000
Lesson 11.3   Round to the Nearest Thousand
Lesson 11.4   Add Hundreds
Lesson 11.5   Subtract Hundreds

Lesson 11.6   Add and Subtract Four-Digit Numbers
Lesson 11.7   Subtract to Find Elapsed Time Between Years
Lesson 11.8   Enrichment (Optional)

Extra Materials Needed for Unit 11

- 6 dice
- For optional Enrichment Lesson:
    - *How Many Jelly Beans?*, written by Andrea Menotti and illustrated by Yancey Labat. Chronicle Books, 2012.
    - Map app

You will need play thousand-dollar bills for the first time in this unit. If your play money set does not include thousand-dollar bills, use the bills on Blackline Master 13 instead.

Teaching Math with Confidence:
Hooray! Why This Unit Is an Important Milestone

In this unit, your child will learn to add and subtract four-digit numbers. You'll begin by modeling numbers to 10,000 with base-ten blocks, money, expanded form, and the number line. These familiar activities will give your child confidence that she can extend her place-value skills to larger numbers. Four-digit numbers may look intimidating, but she'll quickly discover that she can use the algorithms she's already mastered to add and subtract them.

In future grades, your child will find that she can use these same algorithms to add and subtract numbers in the millions or billions—and that they apply to decimals as well! That's the beauty of the algorithms and place-value system. Once you understand them, you can use these skills and concepts to make sense of both very large and very small numbers.

This unit is an important milestone in the years-long process of raising kids who are capable and confident in math. Your child has come a long way from adding 2 plus 3 in kindergarten, even if she still occasionally forgets an addition fact or gets confused when subtracting across a zero. Make sure to congratulate her on all she's learned about addition and subtraction since then—and take some time to pat yourself on the back for helping her progress from those first simple sums to these challenging multi-digit problems!

Lesson 11.1
Numbers to 10,000

Purpose	Materials
• Review multiplication facts • Represent numbers to 10,000 with base-ten blocks, play money, expanded form, and the number line • Read and write numbers to 10,000 • Reason about place value in numbers to 10,000	• 2 decks of playing cards • Base-ten blocks • Play money

Memory Work • **Name the multiples of 6 in order.** *6, 12, 18…* Stop your child when she reaches 60.

You'll use thousand-dollar bills throughout this unit to make four-digit numbers concrete. If your play money set does not include thousand-dollar bills, use the bills on Blackline Master 13.

Warm-up: Play Multiplication Greatest to Least

Play Multiplication Greatest to Least. See Lesson 10.1 (page 317) for directions.

Activity (A): Represent Numbers to 10,000 in Multiple Ways

You already know a lot about place value in numbers to 1,000. Today, you'll learn about place value in numbers greater than 1,000.

Show your child the large cube from your set of base-ten blocks. **This large cube is the same size as 1,000 unit blocks. You could stack 1,000 unit blocks to make one large cube, but that would take a while! How many hundreds equal 1,000?** *10.* Stack 10 flats to demonstrate that they equal the large cube.

Show your child the 3 large cubes in part A. **Each large cube has a value of 1,000, so 3 large cubes have a value of 3,000.**

We can use place-value thinking to find the value of these base-ten blocks, just like we do with three-digit numbers. Point to each group of blocks as you name its value: **3,000…200…40…7. So, the blocks have a value of 3,247.**

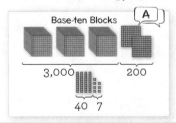

Most sets of base-ten blocks only have 1 large cube, so the lessons use printed illustrations to model four-digit numbers. If you have multiple large cubes, you can model the numbers in this lesson with base-ten blocks as well.

Here's how we write 3,247. Show your child the printed number and point to the 3. **We call this place the thousands-place.** Point to the comma between the 3 and 2. **The comma separates the thousands-place from the hundreds-place and makes it easier to read large numbers.**

comma

Point to the paper bills pictured in part A. **Another way to show 3,247 is to model it with money.** Have your child identify which bills match each digit in the number.

How many digits does 3,247 have? *4.* **We can write four-digit number in expanded form, just like you did with smaller numbers. Remember, when you write a number in expanded form, you s-t-r-e-t-c-h the number to show the value of each of its digits.**

- Point to the 3 in 3,247. **Which part of the expanded form matches this digit?** *3,000.*
- Point to the 2 in 3,247. **Which part of the expanded form matches this digit?** *200.*
- Point to the 4 in 3,247. **Which part of the expanded form matches this digit?** *40.*
- Point to the 7 in 3,247. **Which part of the expanded form matches this digit?** *7.*

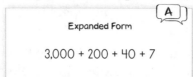

Point to the number line. **We can also show 3,247 on the number line.** Point to 3,240 and count the tick marks until you reach 3,247: **3,240, 3,241, 3,242...**

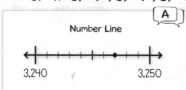

Show your child the next exercise. **What's the value of these base-ten blocks?** *2,153.* Have your child write 2,153 in the blank. Also have her write 2,153 in expanded form in the blank and draw a dot at the matching tick mark on the number line. Then, have her complete the final exercise in the same way.

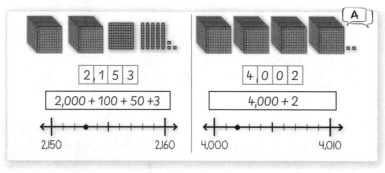

Make sure your child writes a comma between the thousands-place and hundreds-place in each number.

Have your child also model 2,153 and 4,002 with play money. Have her use only thousand-dollar, hundred-dollar, ten-dollar, and one-dollar bills to reinforce the place-value meaning of the digits.

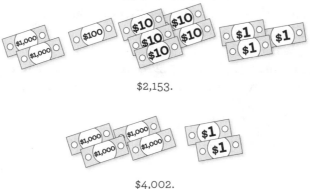

$2,153.

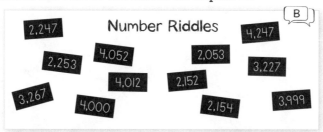

$4,002.

Activity (B): Number Riddles

Show your child the numbers in part B. **We read four-digit numbers from left to right, just like we write them. We say "thousand" when we reach the comma.**

Demonstrate how to read 2,247 aloud. Point to each digit as you read it, and point to the comma when you say "thousand." **Two thousand two hundred forty-seven.**

Have your child read aloud the rest of the numbers in part B.

Number Riddles

2,247   4,052   2,053   4,247
2,253   3,227
4,012   2,152
3,267   2,154
4,000   3,999

Reading the numbers aloud gives your child practice with reading and understanding four-digit numbers. It also familiarizes your child with the numbers so she's ready to solve riddles about them.

Now, I'm going to ask you some riddles about these numbers. I'll only use each number once, so cross off each number after you use it.

Children often have trouble keeping four-digit numbers in their working memory, so make sure to point to each number in part A as you tell your child a riddle about the number. If your child has trouble with the riddles, use the matching base-ten block diagram to help her find the answers. For example, to find a number that is 1 more than 2,153, point to the base-ten blocks that represent 2,153 in part A. **Imagine adding 1 unit block to this group of base-ten blocks.**

- Point to 2,153 in part A. **This number is 1 more than 2,153.** *2,154.*
- **This number is 1 less than 2,153.** *2,152.*

- **This number is 100 more than 2,153.** *2,253.*
- **This number is 100 less than 2,153.** *2,053.*
- Point to 3,247 in part A. **This number is 20 less than 3,247.** *3,227.*
- **This number is 1,000 more than 3,247.** *4,247.*
- **This number is 1,000 less than 3,247.** *2,247.*
- Point to 4,002 in part A. **This number is 10 more than 4,002.** *4,012.*
- **This number is 2 less than 4,002.** *4,000.*
- **This number is 3 less than 4,002.** *3,999.*
- **This number is between 3,260 and 3,270 on the number line.** *3,267.*
- **This number is between 4,050 and 4,060 on the number line.** *4,052.*

Independent Practice and Review

Have your child complete the Lesson 11.1 Practice and Review workbook pages.

Lesson 11.2
Compare Numbers to 10,000

Purpose	Materials
• Practice naming numbers that come before or after four-digit numbers • Compare numbers to 10,000 • Reason about place value in numbers to 10,000	• Play money • 2 decks of playing cards

Memory Work
- **What do we call the top number in a fraction?** *The numerator.*
- **What do we call the bottom number in a fraction?** *The denominator.*
- **What does the numerator tell?** *The number of parts.*
- **What does the denominator tell?** *How many equal parts the whole was split into.*

Warm-up (A): Name Numbers that Come Before or After

Point to 3,678 and have your child read the number aloud: *Three thousand six hundred seventy-eight.* **What number comes after 3,678?** *3,679.* **What number comes before 3,678?** *3,677.*

Repeat with the other numbers in part A.

- **What number comes after 5,070?** *5,071.* **What number comes before 5,070?** *5,069.*
- **What number comes after 4,000?** *4,001.* **What number comes before 4,000?** *3,999.*
- **What number comes after 6,999?** *7,000.* **What number comes before 6,999?** *6,998.*

Activity (B): Compare Numbers to 10,000 with Play Money

In the last lesson, you learned how to read and write numbers greater than 1,000. Today, you'll learn to compare these numbers.

Show your child part B. **Let's pretend you wanted to buy one of these computers. How much does each computer cost?** *$1,899 or $2,015.* If needed, remind your child to say "thousand" for the comma.

Let's use play money to show how much each computer costs. Place thousand-dollar bills, hundred-dollar bills, ten-dollar bills, and one-dollar bills on the table. Have your child model each price with play money. If he has trouble, encourage him to use place-value thinking. For example: **There's a 2 in the thousands-place in $2,015, so use 2 thousand-dollar bills.**

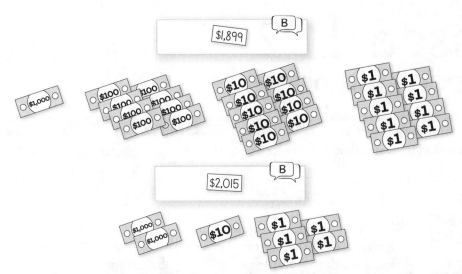

Which computer costs more? *The one that costs $2,015.* **Which computer costs less?** *The one that costs $1,899.* **How do you know?** *Sample answer: 899 is less than 1,000. So 1,899 must be less than any number greater than 2,000.* Write < in the blank.

1,899 < 2,015

Have your child complete the other exercises in part A with < or > and briefly explain how he knows which number is greater. Use play money to model the numbers if he has trouble comparing any of the numbers.

4,600 < 4,700	9,265 > 9,256
8,791 > 891	3,100 > 3,040

Activity (C): Prepare to Play Four-Digit War

We're going to play War to practice comparing four-digit numbers. You'll get four cards and use them to make a four-digit number. Whoever has the greater number wins all the cards.

Before we play, let's first investigate how to arrange the cards to make the greatest number possible. Place a 2, 8, 5 and 7 from a deck of playing cards on the table. (Any suit is fine.) **Here's one way to arrange the cards.** Make the number 7,528 from the cards and have your child read the number aloud. Write 7,528 in one of the blanks.

Have your child try arranging the cards 3 more ways. Have him record each four-digit number in the blanks.

Sample answers. Your child may arrange the cards and digits a different way.

If your child has trouble reading the numbers he creates with the playing cards, write a comma on a slip of paper and insert the comma between the card in the thousands-place and the card in the hundreds-place.

There are 24 different ways to arrange these cards, so we won't try to find all of them! Ask your child to find the greatest possible number that he can create with the cards. Give him time to experiment and try some possibilities. If he's stuck, say: **We want to have as many thousands as possible. Which digit would give us the greatest number of thousands?** *8.* Then, repeat with hundreds, tens, and ones. **The greatest possible number is 8,752.** Write 8,752 in the blank.

Then, ask him to find the least possible number that he can create with the cards. If he's stuck, say: **We want to have as few thousands as possible. Which digit would give us the fewest number of thousands?** *2.* Then, repeat with hundreds, tens, and ones. **The least possible number is 2,578.** Write 2,578 in the blank.

Greatest Possible Number	Least Possible Number	C
8,752	2,578	

Activity: Play Four-Digit War

Play Four-Digit War. Have your child say the numbers aloud as he plays, to practice reading four-digit numbers.

Four-Digit War

Materials: 2 decks of cards, 10s and face cards removed (72 cards total)

Object of the Game: Win the most cards.

Shuffle the cards and deal them face down in two piles. Both players flip over the top 4 cards in their pile and use the digits to make the greatest possible four-digit number. (For example, if you turn over a 5, 9, 2, and 1, some of the numbers you can make are 2,159, 1,952, 5,219, or 9,521. Choose 9,521, since it is the greatest possible number.)

Make the greatest possible four-digit number from your cards.

Whoever has the greater number wins all 8 cards.

If the numbers are equal, leave the cards face-up on the table and have both players make a new four-digit number with the next 4 cards in their piles. Whoever creates the greater number wins all the face-up cards.

Play until the piles run out. Whoever has won more cards wins the game.

Independent Practice and Review

Have your child complete the Lesson 11.2 Practice and Review workbook pages.

Lesson 11.3
Round to the Nearest Thousand

Purpose	Materials
• Practice multiplication facts • Read and compare four-digit numbers on a map • Round four-digit numbers to the nearest thousand	• Playing cards • Counters

Memory Work · **Name the multiples of 9 in order.** *9, 18, 27...* Stop your child when she reaches 90.

Warm-up (A): Play Multiplication Undercover (×7)

Use the game boards in part A to play Multiplication Undercover. Use the same general directions as in Lesson 4.5. Multiply the number on your card by 7, say the matching multiplication fact, and remove the counter from the matching square on your game board.

Activity (B): Read and Compare Distances on a Map

Show your child the map in part B. **This map shows the distances in miles between cities.** Read the name of each city to your child and discuss any background information your child knows about the cities.

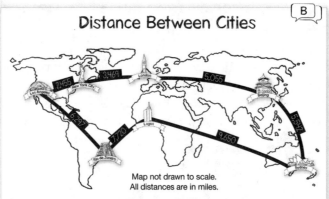

Distance Between Cities

Map not drawn to scale.
All distances are in miles.

Here's the list of landmarks pictured on the map in case you or your child are curious about their names:

- New York City, United States: Statue of Liberty
- Los Angeles, United States: Theme Building
- Rio de Janeiro, Brazil: Metropolitan Cathedral
- Lagos, Nigeria: NECOM House
- Sydney, Australia: Sydney Opera House
- Beijing, China: Temple of Heaven
- London, United Kingdom: Big Ben

Point to each distance and have your child tell the number of miles. For example: **If you flew from New York City to London, how many miles would you travel?** *3,469.*

Which distance on the map is the shortest? *2,455 miles from Los Angeles to New York City.*
Which distance on the map is the longest? *9,650 miles, from Lagos to Sydney.*

In Lesson 11.6, your child will use the same map to plan a trip.

Activity (C): Introduce Rounding to the Nearest Thousand

You have already learned how to round numbers to the nearest ten or hundred. Today, you'll learn how to round numbers to the nearest thousand. When we say the "nearest thousand," we mean the numbers that we say when we count by thousands. Have your child use the numbers printed on the number line to count by thousands up to 10,000: *1,000, 2,000...*

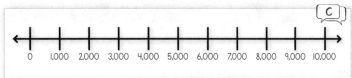

Point to the tick mark labeled 10,000. **This number is 10,000. Can you guess the name of the place the 1 is in?** *Answers will vary.* **The 1 is in the ten-thousands-place. Next year, you'll learn about the ten-thousands-place and numbers greater than 10,000.**

Let's pretend you wanted to fly from Los Angeles to New York City. Your trip would be 2,455 miles.

About where would 2,455 go on the number line? *Child points between 2,000 and 3,000.* **2,455 is between 2,000 and 3,000. Is it closer to 2,000 or 3,000?** *2,000.* **How do you know?** *Answers will vary.*

Here's one way to tell. 2,500 is halfway between 2,000 and 3,000. Draw a tick mark halfway between 2,000 and 3,000 on the number line and label it 2,500. **2,455 is less than 2,500, so it is closer to 2,000 than 3,000. So, 2,455 rounded to the nearest thousand is 2,000. It's about 2,000 miles from Los Angeles to New York City.** Write 2,000 in the chart.

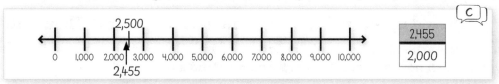

Have your child use the same approach to round the rest of the numbers to the nearest thousand.

2,455	3,469	5,055	5,542	9,650	7,720	6,297
2,000	3,000	5,000	6,000	10,000	8,000	6,000

In fourth grade, your child will learn how to round four-digit numbers to the nearest hundred or ten.

Independent Practice and Review

Have your child complete the Lesson 11.3 Practice and Review workbook pages.

Lesson 11.4
Add Hundreds

Purpose	Materials
• Practice counting by 100s • Add up to find missing addends to the next thousand • Mentally add hundreds to numbers in the thousands	• Play money • 6 dice

Memory Work
- **What does perimeter measure?** *The distance around the outside edge of a shape.*
- **What does area measure?** *The amount of space that a shape covers.*

Warm-up: Count by 100s

Have your child count forward by 100s from the following numbers. Write each number on a piece of scrap paper as he says it, and stop him after he reaches the last number listed. Use play money to model the numbers if needed.

- **Count by 100s from 3,000:** *3,000, 3,100, 3,200, 3,300, 3,400.*
- **Count by 100s from 5,800:** *5,800, 5,900, 6,000, 6,100, 6,200.*
- **Count by 100s from 4,750:** *4,750, 4,850, 4,950, 5,050, 5,150.*

If your child is ready for more challenge, have him count by 50s instead of 100s.

Activity (A): Add Up to Find Missing Addends to the Next Thousand

You've already learned how to mentally add by completing a ten or completing a hundred. Today, you'll learn how to mentally add by completing a thousand.

Show your child part A. **Let's pretend you want to buy something that costs $3,000. You have already saved $2,600.** Briefly discuss what your child might buy that costs $3,000. Give him 2 thousand-dollar bills and 6 hundred-dollar bills.

$$2{,}600 + \boxed{} = 3{,}000$$

Make sure to read 2,600 as "two thousand six hundred" and not "twenty-six hundred." You will introduce your child to this alternate way to read four-digit numbers in Lesson 11.7.

You have 2 thousand-dollar bills and 6 hundred-dollar bills. You need 3 thousand-dollar bills. How many hundreds equal 1 thousand? *10.* **How many more hundred-dollar bills do you need so that your hundred-dollar bills equal $1,000?** *4.* Give your child 4 hundred-dollar bills. **2,600 plus 400 equals 3,000.** Write 400 in the blank.

$$2{,}600 + \boxed{400} = 3{,}000$$

Use play money to model the rest of the problems in part A. Frame each problem in the same way as above. For example, for 4,300 + __ = 5,000: **You want to buy something that costs $5,000. You already have $4,300. How much more money do you need?**

$8{,}900 + \boxed{100} = 9{,}000$	$6{,}500 + \boxed{500} = 7{,}000$
$4{,}300 + \boxed{700} = 5{,}000$	$1{,}200 + \boxed{800} = 2{,}000$

Do not require your child to use play money to find the answers if he can solve the problems without it.

Activity (B): Complete a Thousand to Add Hundreds

Show your child part B. **Let's pretend you have $2,800.** Give your child 2 thousand-dollar bills and 8 hundred-dollar bills. **Then, you earn $500.** Give your child 5 hundred-dollar bills.

Let's complete a thousand to find how much you earned in all. First, I add 2 hundreds to 2,800 to make 3,000. Move 2 hundred-dollar bills as shown. Then, I add on the other 3 hundreds. 3,000 plus 300 equals 3,300. Write 3,300 in the blank.

Have your child complete the other problems in part B. Model them with play money as needed.

8,900 + 400 = 9,300	6,500 + 700 = 7,200
4,300 + 900 = 5,200	1,200 + 900 = 2,100

Activity (C): Play Race to 10,000

Use the scoring guide in part C to play Race to 10,000. Have your child use mental addition to find his new score after each turn.

This game is a simplified version of the classic dice game Farkle (with a little inspiration from Yahtzee). If your child already knows how to play Farkle, you can play Farkle instead.

Race to 10,000

Materials: 6 dice

Object of the Game: Be the first player to reach 10,000 points by rolling dice that show the same number.

Begin a simple scorecard on a separate piece of paper.

Each player takes turns rolling the dice. You may roll the dice up to 3 times per turn. Your goal is to have as many dice showing the same number as possible by the end of the three rolls.

For your first roll, roll all 6 dice. Set aside any dice that show the same number. For example, if you roll 3 fives, set those dice aside. You may only set one group of dice aside. If none of your dice show the same number, don't set any aside and reroll all the dice.

Sample first roll. Set aside the 3 fives.

For your second roll, roll the remaining dice. Set aside any dice that match the ones you already set aside. For example, if you rolled 3 fives on your first roll and 1 five on your second roll, set the additional five aside.

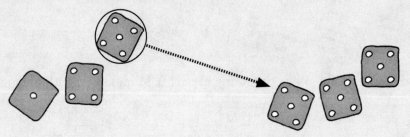

Sample second roll. Set aside the additional 5.

For your third roll, roll the remaining dice. Then, count how many dice show the same number. Use the scoring chart to determine your score and add your score to your previous total.

4 of a Kind = 900 $\boxed{C}$

Sample third roll. Score 900 points, since you have four of a kind.

You may only score one group of dice per turn. For example, if you rolled 3 fives and 3 twos, only score one of the groups. Choose the fives, since they are worth more points.

If you like, you may decide to re-roll dice that you set aside in previous rolls. For example, if you set aside 2 fours after the first roll and then roll 3 twos in your second roll, you may keep the twos and re-roll the fours.

Take turns until one player reaches 10,000 or greater.

Shorter variation: Play until one player reaches 5,000 if you're short on time.

Cooperative variation: Play the game together and keep track of how many rounds it takes for you to reach 10,000. Then, play a second time and see if you can reach 10,000 in fewer rounds.

Independent Practice and Review

Have your child complete the Lesson 11.4 Practice and Review workbook pages.

Lesson 11.5
Subtract Hundreds

Purpose	Materials
• Practice counting backwards by 100s • Subtract hundreds from multiples of 1,000 • Mentally subtract hundreds from numbers in the thousands	• Play money • 6 dice

Memory Work	
	• **What do we call fractions that look different but have the same value?** *Equivalent fractions.* • **What do we call numbers that have a whole number and a fraction?** *Mixed numbers.*

Warm-up: Count Backward by 100s

Have your child count backward by 100s from the following numbers. Write each number on a piece of scrap paper as she says it, and stop her after she reaches the last number listed. Use play money to model the numbers if needed.

- **Count backward by 100s from 6,700:** *6,700, 6,600, 6,500, 6,400, 6,300.*
- **Count backward by 100s from 5,000:** *5,000, 4,900, 4,800, 4,700, 4,600.*
- **Count backward by 100s from 4,390:** *4,390, 4,290, 4,190, 4,090, 3,990.*

> If your child is ready for more challenge, have her count backward by 50s instead of 100s.

Activity (A): Subtract from Multiples of 1,000

In the last lesson, you learned how to mentally add hundreds by completing a thousand. Today, you'll learn how to subtract hundreds by breaking apart a thousand.

Show your child part A. **Let's pretend you have $3,000.** Give her 3 thousand-dollar bills. **You want to buy something that costs $200.** Briefly discuss what your child might buy that costs $200.

$$3,000 - 200 = \boxed{}$$

Looks like you need to trade one of your thousand-dollar bills for hundred-dollar bills! How many hundreds equal 1 thousand? *10.* Help your child trade 1 thousand-dollar bill for 10 hundred-dollar bills.

Then, have your child give you 2 hundred-dollar bills. **How much money do you have left?** *$2,800.* Write 2,800 in the blank.

$$3,000 - 200 = \boxed{2,800}$$

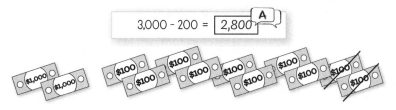

Your child will learn how to use the written algorithms to add and subtract four-digit numbers in Lesson 11.7. Trading the paper bills prepares your child to trade 1 thousand for 10 hundreds in that lesson.

Point to the next problem (4,000 – 600). **This time, let's pretend you have $4,000.** Give your child 4 thousand-dollar bills. **You want to buy something that costs $600. We can use the pairs that make 1,000 to find how much money you have left. 600 and what make 1,000?** *400.* **So, what's 4,000 minus 600?** *3,400.* If your child isn't sure, have her trade the bills as above.

4,000 - 600 = | 3,400 | A

Have your child solve the rest of the problems in part A. Use play money as needed to model the problems.

2,000 - 100 = 1,900	5,000 - 400 = 4,600 A
6,000 - 500 = 5,500	8,000 - 900 = 7,100

Activity (B): Break Apart a Thousand to Subtract Hundreds

Show your child part B. **Let's pretend you have $2,300.** Give your child 2 thousand-dollar bills and 3 hundred-dollar bills. **Then, you buy something that costs $400.**

2,300 - 400 =   B

Let's break apart a thousand to find how much you have left. First, I subtract 3 hundreds from 2,300. That leaves 2,000. Remove 3 hundred-dollar bills. **We want to subtract 4 hundreds, and we have already subtracted 3 hundreds. How many more hundreds do we need to subtract?** *1.* **What's 2,000 minus 100?** *1,900.* Write 1,900 in the blank.

2,300 - 400 = | 1,900 | B

If your child isn't sure, have her trade 1 thousand-dollar bill for 10 hundred-dollar bills and then remove 1 hundred-dollar bill.

Have your child complete the other problems in part B. Model them with play money as needed.

3,100 - 200 = 2,900	5,200 - 500 = 4,700 B
2,600 - 800 = 1,800	4,500 - 700 = 3,800

Activity (C): Play Race to 0

Use the scoring guide in part C to play Race to 0. Have your child use mental subtraction to find her new score after each turn.

Race to 0 is very similar to Race to 10,000. The only difference is that each player begins with 10,000 points and subtracts each new score from the previous total. The first player to reach 0 wins.

Race to Zero

Materials: 6 dice

Object of the Game: Be the first player to reach 0.

Begin a simple scorecard on a piece of paper. Each player starts with 10,000 points.

Dad	Mira
10,000	10,000

Game play is the same as Race to 10,000. See Lesson 11.4 (pages 357-358) for the full description.

After your three rolls, use the scoring chart to determine your score. Subtract this score from your previous total. For example, if you score 600 points on your first turn, subtract 600 from 10,000 to find that your new score is 9,400.

Dad	Mira
10,000	10,000
9,400	8,000

Sample scorecard after both players' first turns.

Play until one player reaches zero (or rolls more points than she has remaining).

Shorter variation: Have each player begin with 5,000 points if you're short on time.

Cooperative variation: Play the game together and keep track of how many rounds it takes for you to reach zero. Then, play a second time and see if you can reach zero in fewer rounds.

Independent Practice and Review

Have your child complete the Lesson 11.5 Practice and Review workbook pages.

Lesson 11.6
Add and Subtract Four-Digit Numbers

Purpose	Materials
• Practice multiplication facts • Add and subtract four-digit numbers with the addition and subtraction algorithms • Solve distance word problems	• Playing cards

Memory Work · **Name the multiples of 8 in order.** *8, 16, 24...* Stop your child when he reaches 80.

In this lesson, your child will learn to add and subtract four-digit numbers with the addition and subtraction algorithms. Most children have little trouble extending these algorithms to four-digit numbers, so this lesson does not include a step-by-step explanation. If your child needs more support, use the Addition Algorithm diagram and Subtraction Algorithm diagram (from Blackline Master 4) to guide him. Model each problem with play money, and demonstrate the trades with paper bills.

Warm-up: Play Over Under (×8)

Play one round of Over Under (×8). Use the same general directions as Over Under (×6) from Lesson 9.4 (page 284). Multiply each card by 8. If the product is less than 45, the player who is "Under" wins the card. If the product is greater than 45, the player who is "Over" wins the card.

Activity (A): Add and Subtract Four-Digit Numbers

You have already learned how to use the addition and subtraction algorithms to add and subtract two- and three-digit numbers. Today, you'll use these algorithms to add and subtract four-digit numbers.

Show your child the first exercise in part A (3,984 + 2,632). **Before we add the numbers, we'll first estimate the sum.** Have your child round each addend to the nearest thousand and estimate the sum.

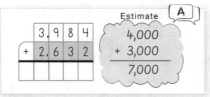

Now, add the numbers to find the exact sum. Use the same steps that you use to add two- or three-digit numbers. Have your child use the addition algorithm to add the numbers. If needed, use play money to model the trading.

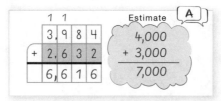

Repeat with the subtraction problem. Have your child estimate the difference and then find the exact difference. If needed, use play money to model the trading.

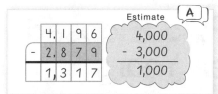

Adding and subtracting four-digit numbers is just like adding and subtracting three-digit numbers. We can even add and subtract numbers in the millions or billions in the exact same way!

See the Unit 11 **Teaching Math with Confidence** (page 346) for more on how this solid foundation in whole number addition and subtraction prepares your child to solve problems involving both large and small numbers in future grades.

Activity (B): Add and Subtract to Solve Distance Word Problems

Show your child part B. **Now, you get to plan a pretend trip! You get to visit three cities. You can only travel between cities that have lines connecting them on the map.** Have your child choose three connected cities to pretend to visit. Write the cities' names in the itinerary.

Let's find the total length of your trip. How far is it from your first city to your second city? *Answers will vary.* **How far is it from your second city to your third city?** *Answers will vary.* Have your child write the numbers in the blank grid and find their sum.

If your child's trip is longer than 10,000 miles, demonstrate how to write a 1 in the ten-thousands-place. Your child will learn to add numbers greater than 10,000 in fourth grade.

Which flight travels a longer distance? *Answers will vary.* **Let's find how much longer the longer flight is than the shorter flight.** Have your child write the longer distance on the top line of the next blank grid and the shorter distance on the middle line. Have him subtract to find the difference between them.

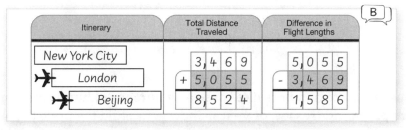

Sample completed first itinerary.

You get to plan one more trip! Have your child choose another three cities. Again, have him find the total length of the trip and the difference between the lengths of the two flights.

Independent Practice and Review

Have your child complete the Lesson 11.6 Practice and Review workbook pages.

Lesson 11.7
Subtract to Find Elapsed Time Between Years

Purpose	Materials
• Practice counting by 500s • Name four-digit numbers as multiples of 100 (i.e., "sixteen hundred") • Read years and organize dates on a timeline • Use subtraction to find elapsed time between years	• Play money

Memory Work · **Name the multiples of 7 in order.** *7, 14, 21...* Stop your child when she reaches 70.

In Lesson 11.6, your child learned to add and subtract four-digit numbers with the written algorithms. In this lesson, she'll practice subtracting across zero in four-digit numbers as she finds elapsed time between years.

Warm-up: Count by 500s

Have your child count forward by 500s to 10,000: *500, 1,000, 1,500....*

Activity (A): Learn Two Ways to Name Multiples of 100

In this unit, you've learned how to read and write four-digit numbers. Today, you'll learn another way to read four-digit numbers. You'll also subtract to find how long ago some inventions were made.

Have your child read aloud the numbers printed in part A: *One thousand five hundred. Four thousand two hundred. One thousand nine hundred.* **These four-digit numbers all have zeros in both the tens-place and ones-place.** Underline the zeros in each number.

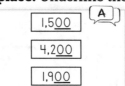

People sometimes think of numbers like these as a number of hundreds, especially when the numbers are prices, addresses, or years. Show your child the price tag with $1500.

This item costs 1,500 dollars. If you wanted to pay for this item in cash, how many hundred-dollar bills would you need? *15.* **One thousand five hundred equals 15 hundreds, so people sometimes read this price as "fifteen hundred."**

If your child has trouble grasping that 1,500 equals 15 hundreds, use play money to show 15 hundreds. **How many hundreds equal 1 thousand?** *10.* **How many hundreds equal 500?** *5.* So, 15 hundreds equal 1,500.

Read the other numbers aloud as well. **We read this this address as "forty-two hundred." We read this year as "nineteen hundred."**

How people read four-digit numbers varies regionally and often depends on how formal the situation is. Most children learn these customary ways to name four-digit numbers through everyday experience.

Activity (B): Read Years and Label Years on a Timeline

Show your child the timeline in part B. **This special kind of number line is called a timeline. We use timelines to put events in order.**

Point to 1600. **The first year marked on this timeline is 1600.** (Read 1600 as "sixteen hundred.") Have your child read the other years marked on the timeline in the same way. For 2000, say: **We read this year as "two thousand" and not "twenty hundred," even though 20 hundreds do equal 2,000!**

How many years are between each tick mark on this timeline? *100 years.* If your child's not sure, ask: **Sixteen hundred plus what equals seventeen hundred?** *1 hundred.*

Briefly discuss each event pictured, and demonstrate how to read each year.

- Telescope: **Sixteen hundred eight.**
- Telephone: **Eighteen hundred seventy-six.**
- Television: **Nineteen hundred twenty-seven.**
- Sewing machine: **Seventeen hundred ninety.**
- Steam engine: **Seventeen hundred sixty-five.**
- Airplane: **Nineteen hundred three.**

Then, have your child draw a line to match each event to its place on the timeline.

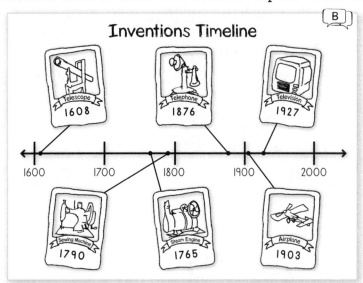

These dates reflect general consensus among historians, although some of them are disputed.

Activity (C): Subtract to Find Elapsed Time

What year is it now? *Answers will vary.* **About where would the current year go on the timeline?** *Child points to the far right of the timeline.* Draw a dot at the approximate position and label the dot with the current year.

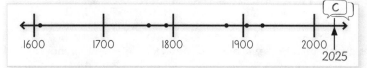

Sample tick mark and label for current year. Use your current year to label your tick mark.

What year was the telephone invented? *1876.* **Let's figure out how many years ago the telephone was invented. We'll use the subtraction algorithm.**

We want to know the difference between the current year and 1876. The current year is the greater number, so we'll subtract 1876 from it. Set up a subtraction problem as shown. Demonstrate how to use the subtraction algorithm to solve the problem. Talk through each step, especially subtracting across the zero in the hundreds-place.

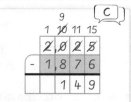

Sample subtraction problem if the current year is 2025. Use your current year for the number on the top line.

See Lesson 5.7 for a sample script to help your child subtract across a zero.

How many years have passed since the telephone was invented? *Sample answer: 149 years. Answers will vary, depending on your current year.* **We say that this number of years has** *elapsed* **since the telephone was invented.**

Your child will learn to calculate elapsed time with minutes and hours in Unit 14. This activity previews the idea of finding how much time has passed and prepares her to learn this challenging skill.

Have your child choose 2 more inventions and subtract to find how long ago each was invented.

Independent Practice and Review

Have your child complete the Lesson 11.7 Practice and Review workbook pages.

Lesson 11.8
Enrichment (Optional)

Purpose	Materials
• Practice memory work • Understand the magnitude of large numbers • Understand numbers to 10,000 in the context of distance • Summarize what your child has learned and assess progress	• *How Many Jelly Beans?*, written by Andrea Menotti and illustrated by Yancey Labat • Map app

Warm-up: Review Memory Work

Quiz your child on all memory work through Unit 11. See pages 527-528 for the full list.

Math Picture Book: *How Many Jelly Beans?*

Read *How Many Jelly Beans?*, written by Andrea Menotti and illustrated by Yancey Labat. As you read, discuss how the smaller groups of jelly beans relate to the larger groups of jelly beans. For example: **The children counted by 25s to make a group of 100 jelly beans.**

Enrichment Activity: Plan a 10,000 Mile (or Kilometer) Trip

Let's pretend you won a free 10,000-mile trip! You can go to multiple destinations, but your entire trip must be less than 10,000 miles. This includes traveling back home.

If your family uses the metric system, use kilometers instead of miles for this activity.

Have your child choose a place he'd like to visit. Use a map app to find the round-trip distance to the place. If the distance is longer than 10,000 miles, have him try a different destination. If the total distance is shorter than 10,000, encourage him to add another destination. For example: **It's only about 2,000 miles to New York City and back, so you can travel to another place, too!**

Use the following options to adjust the complexity of the activity based on how much time you have and what skills you'd like your child to practice:

- If you're short on time, plot all the destinations in a map app (with your home as the final destination). Have the map app find the total length of the trip.
- If you'd like your child to practice estimation, plot each leg of the trip separately in a map app. Have your child round each distance to the nearest hundred or thousand and add to find the approximate total distance.
- If you'd like your child to practice the written addition algorithm, plot each leg of the trip separately in a map app. Have your child add the distances on a piece of paper to find the exact total distance.

Unit Wrap-up

Have your child complete the Unit 11 Wrap-up.

Unit 11 Answer Key

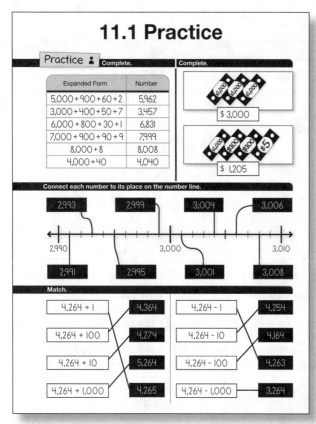

11.1 Practice

Practice Complete.

Expanded Form	Number
5,000+900+60+2	5,962
3,000+400+50+7	3,457
6,000+800+30+1	6,831
7,000+900+90+9	7,999
8,000+8	8,008
4,000+40	4,040

Complete.

$ 3,000

$ 1,205

Connect each number to its place on the number line.

2,993   2,999   3,004   3,006

2,990   3,000   3,010

2,991   2,995   3,001   3,008

Match.

4,264 + 1 → 4,364
4,264 + 100 → 4,274
4,264 + 10 → 5,264
4,264 + 1,000 → 4,265

4,264 - 1 → 4,254
4,264 - 10 → 4,164
4,264 - 100 → 4,263
4,264 - 1,000 → 3,264

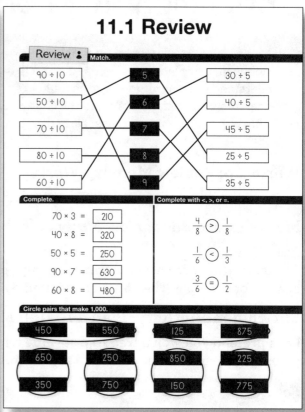

11.1 Review

Review Match.

90 ÷ 10   5
50 ÷ 10   6
70 ÷ 10   7
80 ÷ 10   8
60 ÷ 10   9

30 ÷ 5
40 ÷ 5
45 ÷ 5
25 ÷ 5
35 ÷ 5

Complete.

70 × 3 = 210
40 × 8 = 320
50 × 5 = 250
90 × 7 = 630
60 × 8 = 480

Complete with <, >, or =.

$\frac{4}{8} > \frac{1}{8}$

$\frac{1}{6} < \frac{1}{3}$

$\frac{3}{6} = \frac{1}{2}$

Circle pairs that make 1,000.

450	550	125	875
650	250	850	225
350	750	150	775

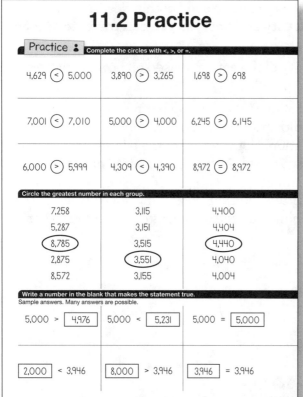

11.2 Practice

Practice Complete the circles with <, >, or =.

4,629 < 5,000   3,890 > 3,265   1,698 > 698

7,001 < 7,010   5,000 > 4,000   6,245 > 6,145

6,000 > 5,999   4,309 < 4,390   8,972 = 8,972

Circle the greatest number in each group.

7,258	3,115	4,400
5,287	3,151	4,404
(8,785)	3,515	(4,440)
2,875	(3,551)	4,040
8,572	3,155	4,004

Write a number in the blank that makes the statement true.
Sample answers. Many answers are possible.

5,000 > 4,976   5,000 < 5,231   5,000 = 5,000

2,000 < 3,946   8,000 > 3,946   3,946 = 3,946

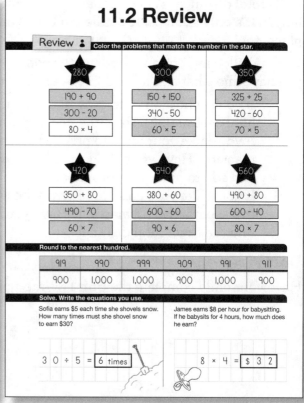

11.2 Review

Review Color the problems that match the number in the star.

⭐ 280
190 + 90
300 - 20
80 × 4

⭐ 300
150 + 150
340 - 50
60 × 5

⭐ 350
325 + 25
420 - 60
70 × 5

⭐ 420
350 + 80
490 - 70
60 × 7

⭐ 540
380 + 60
600 - 60
90 × 6

⭐ 560
490 + 80
600 - 40
80 × 7

Round to the nearest hundred.

919	990	999	909	991	911
900	1,000	1,000	900	1,000	900

Solve. Write the equations you use.

Sofia earns $5 each time she shovels snow. How many times must she shovel snow to earn $30?

30 ÷ 5 = 6 times

James earns $8 per hour for babysitting. If he babysits for 4 hours, how much does he earn?

8 × 4 = $ 3 2

Unit 11 Answer Key

11.3 Practice

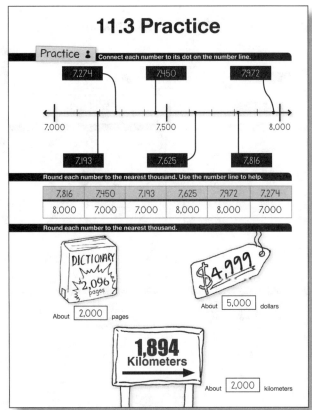

11.3 Review

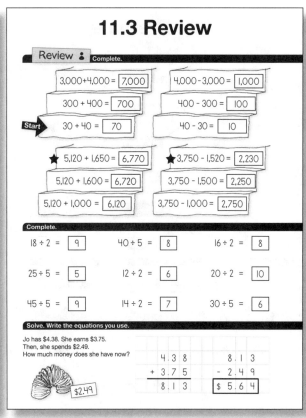

11.4 Practice

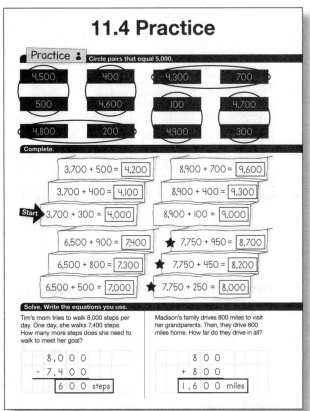

11.4 Review

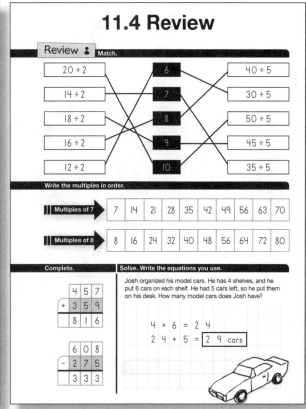

Unit 11 Answer Key

11.5 Practice

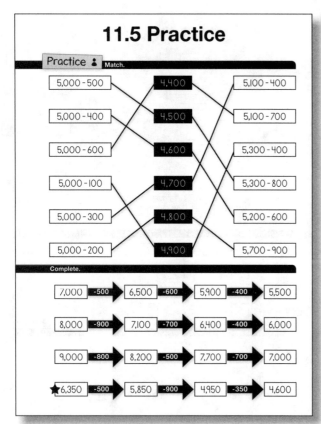

Practice — Match.

5,000 - 500 → 4,400 ← 5,100 - 400
5,000 - 400 → 4,500 ← 5,100 - 700
5,000 - 600 → 4,600 ← 5,300 - 400
5,000 - 100 → 4,700 ← 5,300 - 800
5,000 - 300 → 4,800 ← 5,200 - 600
5,000 - 200 → 4,900 ← 5,700 - 900

Complete.

7,000 −500 → 6,500 −600 → 5,900 −400 → 5,500

8,000 −900 → 7,100 −700 → 6,400 −400 → 6,000

9,000 −800 → 8,200 −500 → 7,700 −700 → 7,000

★6,350 −500 → 5,850 −900 → 4,950 −350 → 4,600

11.5 Review

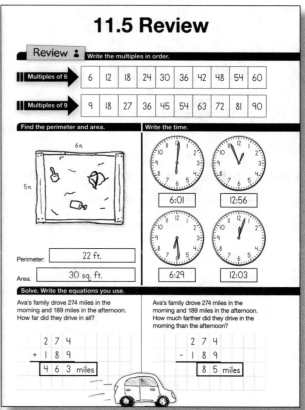

Review — Write the multiples in order.

Multiples of 6	6	12	18	24	30	36	42	48	54	60
Multiples of 9	9	18	27	36	45	54	63	72	81	90

Find the perimeter and area.

Perimeter: 22 ft.
Area: 30 sq. ft.

Write the time.

6:01   12:56
6:29   12:03

Solve. Write the equations you use.

Ava's family drove 274 miles in the morning and 189 miles in the afternoon. How far did they drive in all?

```
  2 7 4
+ 1 8 9
  4 6 3  miles
```

Ava's family drove 274 miles in the morning and 189 miles in the afternoon. How much farther did they drive in the morning than the afternoon?

```
  2 7 4
- 1 8 9
    8 5  miles
```

11.6 Practice

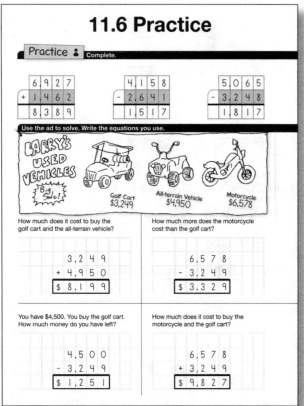

Practice — Complete.

```
  6,9 2 7
+ 1,4 6 2
  8,3 8 9
```

```
  4,1 5 8
- 2,6 4 1
  1,5 1 7
```

```
  5,0 6 5
- 3,2 4 8
  1,8 1 7
```

Use the ad to solve. Write the equations you use.

LARRY'S USED VEHICLES — Big Sale!

Golf Cart $3,249   All-terrain Vehicle $4,950   Motorcycle $6,578

How much does it cost to buy the golf cart and the all-terrain vehicle?

```
  3,2 4 9
+ 4,9 5 0
$ 8,1 9 9
```

How much more does the motorcycle cost than the golf cart?

```
  6,5 7 8
- 3,2 4 9
$ 3,3 2 9
```

You have $4,500. You buy the golf cart. How much money do you have left?

```
  4,5 0 0
- 3,2 4 9
$ 1,2 5 1
```

How much does it cost to buy the motorcycle and the golf cart?

```
  6,5 7 8
+ 3,2 4 9
$ 9,8 2 7
```

11.6 Review

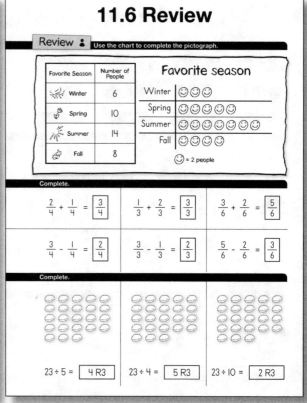

Review — Use the chart to complete the pictograph.

Favorite Season	Number of People
Winter	6
Spring	10
Summer	14
Fall	8

Favorite season

Winter ☺☺☺
Spring ☺☺☺☺☺
Summer ☺☺☺☺☺☺☺
Fall ☺☺☺☺

☺ = 2 people

Complete.

$$\frac{2}{4} + \frac{1}{4} = \frac{3}{4}$$ $$\frac{1}{3} + \frac{2}{3} = \frac{3}{3}$$ $$\frac{3}{6} + \frac{2}{6} = \frac{5}{6}$$

$$\frac{3}{4} - \frac{1}{4} = \frac{2}{4}$$ $$\frac{3}{3} - \frac{1}{3} = \frac{2}{3}$$ $$\frac{5}{6} - \frac{2}{6} = \frac{3}{6}$$

Complete.

$23 \div 5 =$ 4 R3 $23 \div 4 =$ 5 R3 $23 \div 10 =$ 2 R3

Unit 11 Answer Key

11.7 Practice

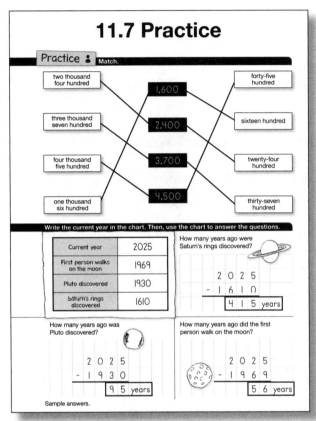

11.7 Review

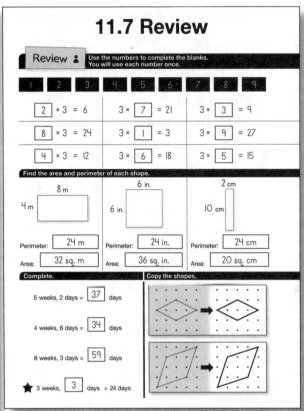

11.8 Unit Wrap-Up A

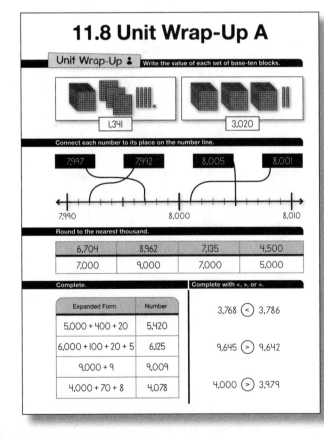

11.8 Unit Wrap-Up B

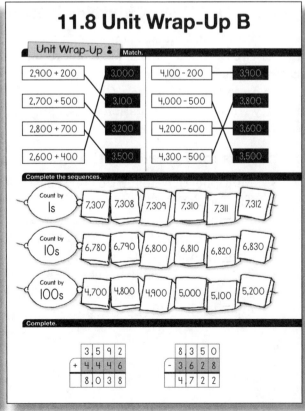

Unit 11 Checkpoint

What to Expect at the End of Unit 11

By the end of Unit 11, most children will be able to do the following:

- Read, write, and compare numbers to 10,000.
- Write four-digit numbers in expanded form and model them with base-ten blocks or play money.
- Round numbers to the nearest thousand.
- Mentally add up to identify missing addends to the next thousand (as in 5,600 + __ = 6,000).
- Use place-value thinking to mentally solve problems like 3,800 + 500 or 4,100 – 300. Many children will still find these problems quite challenging and need to model them with play money.
- Use the addition and subtraction algorithms to add and subtract four-digit numbers. Many children will still need help when subtracting across zero.
- Subtract to find elapsed time between years. Some children will have only a hazy understanding of the concept of elapsed time. Many children will still need help setting up the subtraction problems correctly.

Is Your Child Ready to Move on?

In Unit 12, your child will learn the ÷3, ÷4, and ÷6 facts. Before moving on to Unit 12, your child should understand the concept of division and be able to use multiplication to solve division problems. She will use the ×3, ×4, and ×6 facts as stepping stones to the related division facts, so she should also be able to find answers to the ×3, ×4, and ×6 facts within several seconds.

What to Do If Your Child Needs More Practice

If your child can't find the answers to the ×3, ×4, and ×6 facts within several seconds, spend a day or two practicing these facts before moving on to Unit 12. **If you practice these multiplication facts for a day or two and find that your child does not have them fully mastered, move on to Unit 12 anyway.** Children vary in how long it takes them to develop speed and fluency with the multiplication facts, and your child will continue to practice them as she studies division in Unit 12.

Activities for Practicing the ×3, ×4, and ×6 Facts

- Multiplication Cover-Up (×3) (Lesson 4.1)
- Tic-Tac-Toe Crash (×3) (Lesson 4.2)
- Multiplication Crash (×4) (Lesson 4.4)
- Multiplication Undercover (×4) (Lesson 4.5)
- Dice Tic-Tac-Toe (Lesson 4.6)
- Tic-Tac-Toe Crash (×6) (Lesson 8.1)
- Multiplication Bingo (×6) (Lesson 8.2)
- Over Under (×6) (Lesson 9.4)

Unit 12
Division, Part 2

Overview

In Unit 10, you introduced your child to the concept of division and taught him to write division equations. He also began to master the ÷2, ÷5, and ÷10 facts. In this unit, your child will use the ×3, ×4, and ×6 facts as stepping stones to learn the ÷3, ÷4, and ÷6 facts. You'll also gently introduce him to the long division algorithm and teach him how to interpret remainders in context.

This unit is the second of three division units in *Third Grade Math with Confidence.* Your child will tackle the rest of the division facts in Unit 15.

What Your Child Will Learn

In this unit, your child will learn to:

- Find answers for the ÷3, ÷4, and ÷ 6 facts
- Divide small numbers with the long division algorithm
- Solve division word problems with remainders and interpret remainders in context

Lesson List

Lesson 12.1	÷3 Facts	Lesson 12.6	Two Ways to Write Division
Lesson 12.2	Investigate Dividing with 1 and 0	Lesson 12.7	Preview Long Division
		Lesson 12.8	Introduce Long Division
Lesson 12.3	÷4 Facts	Lesson 12.9	Interpret Remainders
Lesson 12.4	Division Word Problems	Lesson 12.10	Enrichment (Optional)
Lesson 12.5	÷6 Facts		

Extra Materials Needed for Unit 12

- For optional Enrichment Lesson:
    - × *Divide and Ride*, written by Stuart J. Murphy and illustrated by George Ulrich. HarperCollins, 1997

Teaching Math with Confidence:
Why Introduce Long Division with Simple Problems?

In Unit 12, you'll teach your child more division facts and introduce him to the long division algorithm. Like the addition and subtraction algorithms, the long division algorithm is an efficient, reliable, and step-by-step method for solving division problems. However, children often find long division much more challenging to learn than the other algorithms, for several reasons:

- Long division has many steps to remember, and the steps are recorded in a counter-intuitive order. Instead of moving from right to left like the addition and subtraction algorithms, you have to toggle between recording numbers above the dividend and below the dividend.
- Long division requires excellent estimation skills, number sense, and fluency with the multiplication and division facts. If children don't have the facts memorized, they spend so much of their working memory on these subskills that they have trouble remembering the steps.

- Long division is often taught with little conceptual understanding, so children don't grasp the meaning behind each step.

To avoid this frustration, *Math with Confidence* spreads long division instruction over third and fourth grade. This year, you'll give your child a gentle introduction to long division with small numbers. Next year, you'll teach him how to use long division to divide larger numbers. Once he's had plenty of time to master the steps with small numbers, the larger numbers won't feel so overwhelming. Here's how you'll take the stress out of long division as you teach it in this unit:

- You'll use only two-digit numbers as dividends, and all of the quotients will be less than 10. That way, your child will only have to perform 3 steps to solve each problem.
- All of the long division problems use the easier multiplication facts, like 4×3 or 5×5. Your child has practiced these facts since Unit 4, so he likely knows most of them automatically. This will allow him to use his working memory to focus on the long division process, not the multiplication facts. You've also given him practice at estimating products and comparing a product to another number (for example, in games like Multiplication Greatest to Least), so he's well-prepared with the number skills necessary for long division.
- You'll focus on conceptual understanding as much as procedural fluency. You'll use counters to make the steps concrete, and you'll use a familiar division context (packing items into boxes) to help your child connect the steps to what he already knows about division.

Long division may feel unnecessarily complicated for the simple problems in this unit, especially for children who can easily solve these problems in their heads. If your child resists writing out the steps, reassure him that there are only a few problems to solve with long division in each lesson. Next year, this practice will pay off as he tackles complicated, multi-digit long division problems with confidence.

Lesson 12.1
÷3 Facts

Purpose	Materials
• Review ×3 facts • Practice ÷3 facts	• Counters • Die

Memory Work · **Name the multiples of 3 in order.** *3, 6, 9...* Stop your child when she reaches 30.

Warm-up: Review ×3 Facts

In Unit 4, you learned the ×3 facts. Today, you'll use the ×3 facts to find answers to the ÷3 facts. Do a brief oral review of the following ×3 facts. Encourage your child to respond as quickly as possible for each fact.

- 4 × 3 = *12*
- 7 × 3 = *21*
- 10 × 3 = *30*
- 5 × 3 = *15*

- 3 × 3 = *9*
- 9 × 3 = *27*
- 6 × 3 = *18*
- 8 × 3 = *24*

Activity (A): Introduce ÷3 Facts

Let's pretend you're making crafts and have 12 pompoms. You want to put 3 pompoms on each craft, so you divide 12 by 3 to find how many crafts you can make.

12 divided by 3 means "How many groups of 3 equal 12?" What times 3 equals 12? *4*. Write 4 in the multiplication equation blank. **So, what does 12 divided by 3 equal?** *4*. Write 4 in the division equation blank. Have your child draw circles around each group of 3 pompoms to confirm her answer.

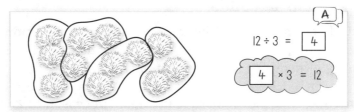

Have your child complete part A. Encourage her to use multiplication to find the answers.

6 ÷ 3 = 2	9 ÷ 3 = 3	3 ÷ 3 = 1
15 ÷ 3 = 5	18 ÷ 3 = 6	30 ÷ 3 = 10
21 ÷ 3 = 7	27 ÷ 3 = 9	24 ÷ 3 = 8

If your child has trouble using multiplication to find the answers (or begins skip-counting), demonstrate how to use the dot array to find the answer more efficiently. For example, for 27 ÷ 3: **We want to know what times 3 equals 27. Let's try some numbers.** Slide the L-cover to show 5 rows of 3. **What's 5 times 3?** *15.* **Hmm, too low!**

Slide the L-cover to show 8 rows of 3. **What's 8 times 3?** *24.* **Still too low!**

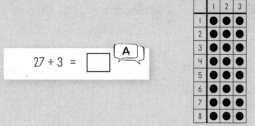

We need 1 more group of 3 to make 27. Slide the L-cover to show 9 rows of 3. **9 groups of 3 equal 27, so what does 27 divided by 3 equal?** *9.*

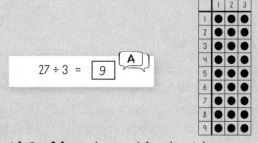

See the Unit 2 **Teaching Math with Confidence** (page 52) for why it's better to avoid relying on skip-counting.

Activity (B): Play Climb and Slide

Play Climb and Slide. Encourage your child to use related multiplication facts to find the answers to the division problems in the game. Use the dot array as needed to model the problems. See Lesson 3.3 (page 90) for full directions.

 Save the Climb and Slide game board to use again in Lesson 12.2.

Independent Practice and Review

Have your child complete the Lesson 12.1 Practice and Review workbook pages.

Lesson 12.2
Investigate Dividing with 1 and 0

Purpose	Materials
• Practice ÷3 facts • Review division vocabulary • Learn that any non-zero number divided by 1 equals the number • Learn that zero divided by any number equals zero • Learn that you cannot divide by zero	• Climb and Slide game board (from Lesson 12.1) • Counters • Die

Memory Work
- **What do we call the result when we multiply two numbers?** *The product.*
- **What do we call the numbers in a multiplication equation that we multiply together?** *Factors.*

Warm-up: Play Climb and Slide

Use the game board from Lesson 12.1 to play Climb and Slide. Encourage your child to use related multiplication facts to find the answers to the division problems in the game. Use the dot array as needed to model the problems. See Lesson 3.3 (page 90) for directions.

You do not need to save the Climb and Slide game board after this lesson.

Activity (A): Review Division Vocabulary

Show your child the equation in part A. **In Unit 10, you learned some important division vocabulary words.**

- Point to the 9. **What do we call the number to be divided?** *The dividend.*
- Point to the 2. **What do we call the number we divide by?** *The divisor.*
- Point to the 4. **What do we call the result when we divide two numbers?** *The quotient.*
- Point to the 1. **What do we call an amount that is left over after division?** *The remainder.*

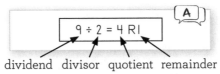

dividend divisor quotient remainder

Activity (B): Investigate Dividing with 1

Today, we'll investigate dividing with 0 and 1. Show your child part B and read the first problem aloud: *There is 1 brownie. 3 friends want to share it equally. How many brownies does each person get?*

How can you split 1 brownie between 3 people? *Sample answer: Cut the brownie into thirds.* **Each person will only get one-third of the brownie!** Draw lines dividing the brownie into thirds, as shown. Write 1/3 in the blank.

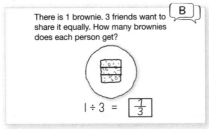

This example is introduced simply as contrast with the next problem. Your child will learn to solve division problems with fractional answers in future grades. He is not expected to solve these problems independently in third grade.

Read the next problem aloud: ***There are 3 brownies. 1 friend wants to eat them all by himself! How many brownies does he get?*** If 1 person eats 3 brownies by himself, how many brownies does he get? *3.* So, what's 3 divided by 1? *3.* Write 3 in the blank.

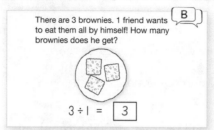

What do you notice about the dividend and quotient? *The dividend and quotient are the same!* **Any number divided by 1 just equals the number, so that makes it easy to divide by 1.** Have your child use the same approach to solve the rest of the problems in part B.

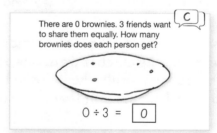

Activity (C): Investigate Dividing with 0

Show your child part C and read the first problem aloud: ***There are 0 brownies. 3 friends want to share them equally. How many brownies does each person get?***

What a silly problem! How many brownies does each friend get if there aren't any brownies? *0.* Write 0 in the blank.

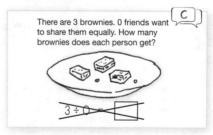

Zero divided by any other number equals zero. No matter how many people share the brownies, they'll all get zero.

Read the next problem aloud: ***There are 3 brownies. 0 friends want to share them equally. How many brownies does each person get?***

This problem is even sillier! It's not possible to share brownies with 0 people, no matter how many brownies there are. Mathematicians say that dividing by zero is "undefined." You can't divide by 0. X out the equation.

For the rest of the problems in part B, have your child solve the problems that involve dividing zero by another number. Have him X out the problems that involve dividing a non-zero number by zero.

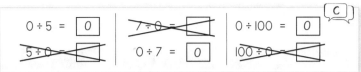

If you have a calculator handy, show your child what happens when you try to divide by zero. Calculator apps typically show "cannot divide by 0." Handheld calculators usually show "E," which stands for "Error."

Independent Practice and Review

Have your child complete the Lesson 12.2 Practice and Review workbook pages.

Lesson 12.3
÷4 Facts

Purpose	Materials
• Review ×4 facts • Practice ÷4 facts	• Counters • Die

Memory Work · **Name the multiples of 4 in order.** *4, 8, 12...* Stop your child when she reaches 40.

Warm-up (A): Review ×4 Facts

In Unit 4, you learned the ×4 facts. Today, you'll use the ×4 facts to find answers to the ÷4 facts. Do a brief oral review of the following ×4 facts. Encourage your child to respond as quickly as possible for each fact.

- 4 × 4 = *16*
- 8 × 4 = *32*
- 3 × 4 = *12*
- 5 × 4 = *20*

- 7 × 4 = *28*
- 10 × 4 = *40*
- 6 × 4 = *24*
- 9 × 4 = *36*

Activity (A): Introduce ÷4 Facts

Let's pretend you're building toy cars and have 16 more wheels. You want to put 4 wheels on each toy car. So, you divide 16 by 4 to find how many more cars you can build.

16 divided by 4 means "How many groups of 4 equal 16?" Let's use multiplication to find the answer. What times 4 equals 16? 4. Write 4 in the multiplication equation blank. **So, what does 16 divided by 4 equal?** 4. Write 4 in the division equation blank. Have your child draw circles around each group of 4 wheels to confirm her answer.

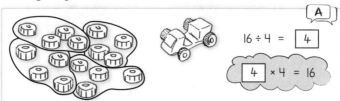

Have your child complete part A. Encourage her to use multiplication to find the answers.

12 ÷ 4 = 3	20 ÷ 4 = 5	32 ÷ 4 = 8
24 ÷ 4 = 6	8 ÷ 4 = 2	4 ÷ 4 = 1
28 ÷ 4 = 7	40 ÷ 4 = 10	36 ÷ 4 = 9

If your child has trouble using multiplication to find the answers (or begins skip-counting), demonstrate how to use the dot array to find the answer more efficiently. For example, for 28 ÷ 4: **We want to know what times 4 equals 28. Let's try some numbers.** Slide the L-cover to show 5 rows of 4. **What's 5 times 4?** *20.* **Hmm, too low!**

28 ÷ 4 = ☐

Slide the L-cover to show 8 rows of 4. **What's 8 times 4?** *32.* **That's too high!**

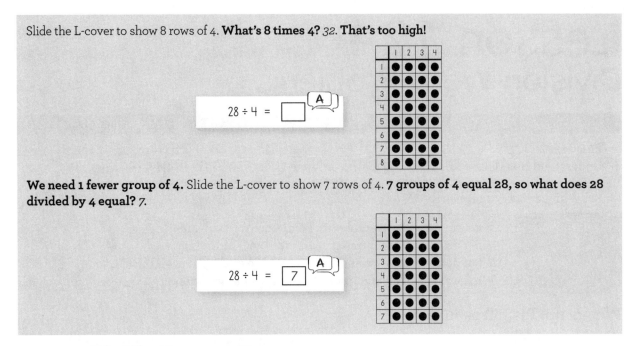

We need 1 fewer group of 4. Slide the L-cover to show 7 rows of 4. **7 groups of 4 equal 28, so what does 28 divided by 4 equal?** *7.*

Activity (B): Play Treasure Hunt

Play Treasure Hunt. See Lesson 6.5 (page 188) for directions. Encourage your child to use related multiplication facts to find the answers, and model the problems on the dot array as needed.

 Save the Treasure Hunt game board to use again in Lesson 12.4.

Independent Practice and Review

Have your child complete the Lesson 12.3 Practice and Review workbook pages.

Lesson 12.4
Division Word Problems

Purpose	Materials
• Practice ÷4 facts • Understand that division can be used to find either a number of groups or how many are in each group • Solve division word problems	• Treasure Hunt game board (from Lesson 12.3) • Counters • Die

Memory Work	• **What do we call the number to be divided?** *The dividend.* • **What do we call the number we divide by?** *The divisor.* • **What do we call the result when we divide two numbers?** *The quotient.* • **What do we call an amount that is left over after division?** *The remainder.*

Warm-up: Play Treasure Hunt

Use the game board from Lesson 12.3 to play Treasure Hunt. See Lesson 6.5 (page 188) for directions. Encourage your child to use related multiplication facts to find the answers to the division problems in the game.

You do not need to save the Treasure Hunt game board after this lesson.

Activity (A): Review Two Ways to Use Division

In Unit 10, you learned we can use division to answer two different kinds of equal-group questions. Read aloud the first word problem in part A: *12 children split into 2 groups. How many children are in each group?* **What's 12 divided by 2?** *6.* Write 6 in the blank.

So, how many children are in each group? *6.* **In this problem, we knew the number of groups. We divided to find the size of each group.**

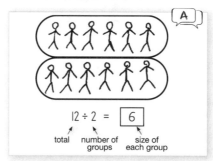

Read aloud the second word problem in part A: *12 children split into groups of 2. How many groups do they make?* **What's 12 divided by 2?** *6.* Write 6 in the blank.

So, how many groups do they make? *6.* **In this problem, we knew the size of each group. We divided to find the number of groups.**

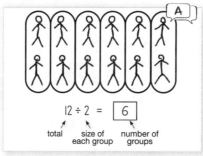

Activity (B): Solve Division Word Problems

We can use division to find either the size of each equal group or the number of equal groups. In part B, we'll use division to find answers to both types of word problems.

Have your child read aloud the first word problem. **What's the goal in this problem?** *Find how many children are in each group.*

Have your child read the problem again slowly. **What equation matches the problem?** *30 divided by 5.* Have your child write the equation in the space provided and solve. **So, how many children are in each group?** *6.* Have your child write "children" after the 6 and draw a box around the final answer. Then, have your child solve the rest of the word problems.

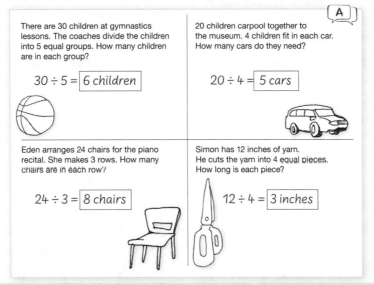

If your child has trouble writing an equation to match the first three word problems, use counters to model the problems. For example, if he has trouble with the first problem, place 30 counters on the table and have him split the counters into 5 equal groups.

If your child has trouble with the final word problem about yarn, draw a simple sketch. **Simon has 12 inches of yarn, and he cuts it into 4 equal pieces. You can think of each piece of yarn as a group of inches. We want to find how many inches are in each piece.**

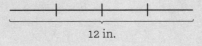

12 in.

Independent Practice and Review

Have your child complete the Lesson 12.4 Practice and Review workbook pages.

Lesson 12.5
÷6 Facts

Purpose	Materials
• Review ×6 facts • Practice ÷6 facts	• Counters • Die

Memory Work · **Name the multiples of 6 in order.** *6, 12, 18...* Stop your child when she reaches 60.

Warm-up: Review ×6 Facts

In Unit 8, you learned the ×6 facts. Today, you'll use the ×6 facts to find answers to the ÷6 facts. Do a brief oral review of the following ×6 facts. Encourage your child to respond as quickly as possible for each fact.

- • 4 × 6 = *24*
- • 5 × 6 = *30*
- • 7 × 6 = *42*
- • 3 × 6 = *18*

- • 6 × 6 = *36*
- • 10 × 6 = *60*
- • 9 × 6 = *54*
- • 8 × 6 = *48*

Activity (A): Introduce ÷6 Facts

Let's pretend you're building insects from clay and toothpicks. You have 42 more toothpicks. Insects have 6 legs, so you need 6 toothpicks for each one. Let's divide 42 by 6 to find how many more insects you can build.

This activity uses a challenging dividend (42) so that you have a reason to discuss how to use the dot array to help find the answer. Most children need this extra support for some of the ÷6 facts (and many of the ÷7, ÷8, and ÷9 facts in Unit 14), so it's important to demonstrate how to use this helpful tool. If your child immediately knows the answer to 42 ÷ 6, skip the following demonstration. Instead, ask her to pretend to be the teacher and explain to you how to use the dot array to find the answer.

42 divided by 6 means "How many groups of 6 equal 42?" We want to know what times 6 equals 42. Let's use the dot array to help find the answer. Slide the L-cover to show 5 rows of 6. **What's 5 times 6?** *30.* **Too low!**

Let's add another group of 6. Slide the L-cover to show 6 rows of 6. **What's 6 times 6?** *36.* That's still too low, but it's closer.

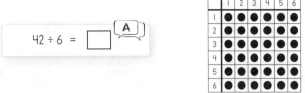

Let's add 1 more group of 6. Slide the L-cover to show 7 rows of 6. **What's 7 times 6?** *42.* That's it! **7 times 6 equals 42, so 42 divided by 6 equals 7.** Write 7 in both blanks.

Have your child complete part A. If she doesn't immediately know the missing factors in the multiplication problems, have her use the dot array to help find the answers.

60 ÷ 6 = 10	12 ÷ 6 = 2	24 ÷ 6 = 4
30 ÷ 6 = 5	6 ÷ 6 = 1	36 ÷ 6 = 6
54 ÷ 6 = 9	48 ÷ 6 = 8	18 ÷ 6 = 3

Activity (B): Play Dice Tic-Tac-Toe

Play Dice Tic-Tac-Toe. Have your child use the dot array to help find the answers, if needed. See Lesson 4.6 (page 128) for directions.

Independent Practice and Review

Have your child complete the Lesson 12.5 Practice and Review workbook pages.

Lesson 12.6
Two Ways to Write Division

Purpose	Materials
• Practice ÷6 facts • Learn to write division problems with a division bracket • Practice reading and solving division problems written with a division bracket	• Counters • Die

Memory Work	
	• **How many sides does a triangle have?** *3.* • **How many sides does a hexagon have?** *6.* • **How many sides does an octagon have?** *8.* • **How many sides does a pentagon have?** *5.* • **How many sides does a quadrilateral have?** *4.*

Warm-up: Practice ÷6 Facts

Do a brief oral review of the ÷6 facts. Encourage your child to use related multiplication facts to help find the answers.

- 24 ÷ 6 = *4*
- 36 ÷ 6 = *6*
- 18 ÷ 6 = *3*
- 60 ÷ 6 = *10*

- 54 ÷ 6 = *9*
- 30 ÷ 6 = *5*
- 42 ÷ 6 = *7*
- 48 ÷ 6 = *8*

Activity (A): Introduce the Division Bracket at the Chocolate Shop

You have already learned how to write division problems with a division sign. Today, you'll learn another way to write division problems.

Let's pretend you work at a chocolate shop, and I'm the customer. I'll tell you how many chocolates I want and how many chocolates I would like you to pack in each box.

Show your child part A. **I'd like 20 striped chocolates. Please put 4 in each box.** Have your child take 20 counters and organize them into groups of 4. **How many groups of 4 can you make?** *5.*

> Make sure to model this problem with counters. It will help your child concretely understand the numbers in the following conversation.

You divided 20 by 4 to find how many groups you could make. One way to write 20 divided by 4 is with a division sign. Point to the horizontal equation. **What's 20 divided by 4?** *5.* Write 5 in the blank for the horizontal equation.

$$20 ÷ 4 = \boxed{5}\; \text{A}$$

We could also use a division bracket to write the same problem. Point to the second version of the problem. **The division bracket means to divide the number inside the bracket by the number outside the bracket. We read this problem as "20 divided by 4." 20 is the dividend, and 4 is the divisor.** Point to each number as you say it.

20 divided by 4 is 5. Write 5 above the division bracket, directly above the 0. **We write the quotient on top of the bracket. The ones-place for the quotient goes right above the ones-place for the number inside the bracket. The grid on the paper helps me line up the digits.**

$$\begin{array}{r} 5 \\ 4\,\overline{)\,2\ 0} \end{array}$$

Developing the habit of aligning the digits will make it easier for your child to organize his work when he learns multi-digit long division in fourth grade.

People sometimes call the division bracket a division house. Imagine the total amount living inside the house. The number to divide by comes knocking on the door—and then you write the quotient on the roof!

So, how many boxes of striped chocolates do I get? 5. Have your child pretend to package the chocolates and give you 5 boxes of striped chocolates.

I really like chocolate, so I have a few more orders! Next, I'd like 15 caramel chocolates, with 5 chocolates in each box. What division problem matches the order? *15 divided by 5.* Use the following conversation to demonstrate how to write the problem with a division bracket.

- **First, I write the total number of chocolates. I'll write it in the middle of the blank area so I have plenty of space.** Write 15 as shown.
- **Next, I draw a division bracket around the 15.** Draw a division bracket around the 15.
- **I want to divide 15 by 5, so I write 5 outside the bracket. It's the number that's knocking on the door of the division house, wanting to divide up the 15 inside the house!** Write 5 to the left of the bracket.
- **What's 15 divided by 5?** *3.* **15 divided by 5 is 3, so I write 3 on top of the house. I line up the 3 with the ones-place for 15.** Write 3 above the bracket, directly above the 5.

15 Caramel Chocolates
(5 in each box)

$$\begin{array}{r} 3 \\ 5\,\overline{)\,1\ 5} \end{array}$$

Repeat with the final two orders. Have your child write a division problem with the division bracket to match each order.

14 Cherry Chocolates
(7 in each box)

$$\begin{array}{r} 2 \\ 7\,\overline{)\,1\ 4} \end{array}$$

24 Dark Chocolates
(6 in each box)

$$\begin{array}{r} 4 \\ 6\,\overline{)\,2\ 4} \end{array}$$

The vertical part of the division bracket can be written with a curved or straight line. Children typically find it easier to draw straight lines, so this book always uses that convention.

Activity (B): Play Dice Tic-Tac-Toe

Play Dice Tic-Tac-Toe. See Lesson 4.6 (page 128) for directions. Have your child read each problem aloud so that he practices reading division problems written with the division bracket.

$$3\,\overline{)\,27}$$ 27 divided by 3 equals 9.

Independent Practice and Review

Have your child complete the Lesson 12.6 Practice and Review workbook pages.

Lesson 12.7
Preview Long Division

Purpose	Materials
• Find products that are less than a given number • Preview how to record steps in long division	• 2 decks of playing cards • Counters

Memory Work	• **How many inches equal 1 foot?** *12.* • **How many feet equal 1 yard?** *3.* • **How many inches equal 1 yard?** *36.* • **How many centimeters equal 1 meter?** *100.* • **How many meters equal 1 kilometer?** *1,000.*

This lesson provides a gentle introduction to the long division algorithm. You'll introduce this process in the context of a chocolate shop to help your child concretely understand the meaning of each step. She'll learn more about long division in Lesson 12.8.

Warm-up (A): Play Hit the Target

Play Hit the Target.

Hit the Target

Materials: 4s, 5s, 6s, 7s, 8s, 9s, and 10s from 2 decks of cards (56 cards total)

Object of the Game: Win the most points by playing pairs of cards whose product is closer to the target number than your opponent's.

Shuffle the cards and deal 5 cards to both players. Place the rest of the deck in a face-down pile.

This game is played in 5 rounds. Each round has a target number (printed in order on the targets on the game board.) In each round, both players play a pair of cards whose product is as close to the target number as possible. The product may not be greater than the target number. Whoever's product is closer to the target number wins a point.

Sample first round. Player 1 plays 4 and 10, for a product of 40. Player 2 plays a 7 and 5, for a product of 35. Player 1 wins the round, because 40 is closer to 41 than 35 is.

If you have no pairs of cards whose products are less than or equal to the target number, you may discard and draw new cards until you are able to play. If both players play the same product, both players win a point.

After you play, discard the face-up cards. Replenish your hand with 2 new cards from the face-down pile. Continue until you have played all 5 rounds. Whoever wins more points wins the game.

Activity (B): Subtract to Find Leftover Chocolates at the Chocolate Shop

In the last lesson, you learned how to write division problems with a division bracket. Today, you'll learn more about division and remainders. We'll pretend again that you work at a chocolate shop, and I'm the customer.

Show your child part B. **I'd like 23 striped chocolates today. Please put 4 in each box.** Have your child take 23 counters and organize them into as many groups of 4 as possible. (She will have 3 left over.) Have her pretend to put each group of 4 into a box. **How many boxes can you fill?** *5.* Write 5 as shown.

To make this activity more concrete, have your child put each group of 4 counters into a small bowl or the cups in a muffin pan.

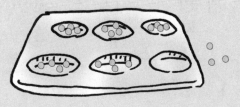

How many chocolates are in the full boxes? *20.* **How do you know?** *Sample answer: 5 times 4 equals 20.* **5 times 4 equals 20, so there are 20 chocolates in the full boxes.** Write 20 as shown.

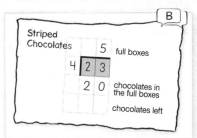

How many chocolates are left? *3.* **How do you know?** *Sample answers: 23 minus 20 equals 3. I see 3 counters left over.* Write a minus sign and horizontal line as shown. **23 minus 20 equals 3, so there are 3 left.** Write 3 as shown.

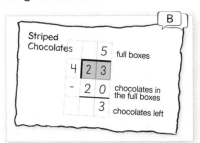

How many boxes of striped chocolates did you pack? *5.* **How many striped chocolates were left over?** *3.*

Asking this question ensures that your child pays attention to the underlying meaning of the answer.

I have a few more orders today! Help your child solve the rest of the problems in part B. Model each problem with counters, and frame each problem in the same way as above. For example: **I'd like 16 caramel chocolates, with 5 in each box.**

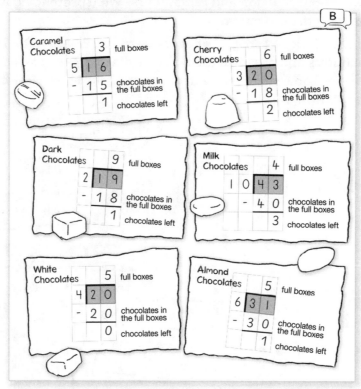

For 20 ÷ 4, point out that there is no remainder: **You can evenly divide the white chocolates into boxes, without any left over.**

Independent Practice and Review

Have your child complete the Lesson 12.7 Practice and Review workbook pages.

Lesson 12.8
Introduce Long Division

Purpose	Materials
• Practice ÷6 facts • Use hands-on materials to understand the long division algorithm	• Counters • Die

Memory Work	• **What do we call the top number in a fraction?** *The numerator.* • **What do we call the bottom number in a fraction?** *The denominator.* • **What does the numerator tell?** *The number of parts.* • **What does the denominator tell?** *How many equal parts the whole was split into.*

In this lesson, your child will learn the first three steps in the long division algorithm. He will learn the fourth step in the division algorithm ("bring down") when he learns to divide larger numbers in fourth grade. See the Unit 12 **Teaching Math with Confidence** (pages 373-374) for more on why *Math with Confidence* spreads long division instruction over both third and fourth grades.

Warm-up: Practice ÷6 Facts

Do a brief oral review of the ÷6 facts.

- 18 ÷ 6 = *3*
- 30 ÷ 6 = *5*
- 36 ÷ 6 = *6*
- 60 ÷ 6 = *10*
- 54 ÷ 6 = *9*

- 42 ÷ 6 = *7*
- 6 ÷ 6 = *1*
- 12 ÷ 6 = *2*
- 24 ÷ 6 = *4*
- 48 ÷ 6 = *8*

Activity (A): Practice Long Division

You have already learned the step-by-step algorithms for addition and subtraction. Today, you'll learn three steps in the division algorithm. People also call this process *long division*. You'll see that it has the same steps we used to pack chocolates at the chocolate shop!

We will solve these problems with 3 steps: divide, multiply, subtract. I'll show you how to use the steps to divide 22 by 3. Place 22 counters on the table.

 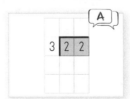

The first step is to divide. I think, "How many groups of 3 can I make from 22?" I want to make as many groups as possible, without going over 22. How many groups of 3 can I make? *7.* If your child isn't sure, encourage him to try out some numbers and multiply them by 3. For example: *3 times 5 is 15. That's 7 less than 22, so I can make some more groups of 3. Or, 8 times 3 is 24. 24 is greater than 22, so that's too many groups.*

Organize the counters in 7 groups of 3, with 1 left over. Write 7 as shown.

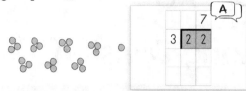

Next, I multiply to find out how many are in the groups. 7 times 3 is 21, so I write 21 on the next line. Point to 7 and 3 as you say them, and write 21 as shown.

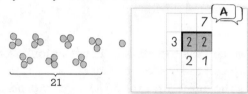

Last, I subtract to find how many are left. Write a minus sign and horizontal line as shown. **22 minus 21 equals 1, so there is a remainder of 1.** Write 1 as shown.

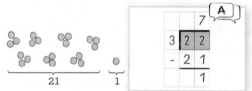

Have your child complete the rest of the problems in part A in the same way. Have him model each problem with counters and use the steps.

	8		5		6		7	
2	1 7	5	2 7	3	2 0	4	3 1	
	- 1 6		- 2 5		- 1 8		- 2 8	
	1		2		2		3	

Your child can use either mental math or the subtraction algorithm for the subtraction step.

Cover the steps in Part A with your hand or a piece of paper. **Can you remember the three steps in order?** *Divide, multiply, subtract.* If your child can't remember, allow him to peek before telling them to you.

It takes a lot of steps to solve problems this way. No wonder it's called long division! Next year, you'll learn another step in the division algorithm, and you'll learn how to use long division to divide larger numbers.

Some children resist learning long division because they can easily find the quotients and remainders mentally. If your child does this, praise his mental math skills. Explain that practicing the steps in long division with smaller numbers prepares him to solve problems with larger numbers that are difficult to divide mentally. If he's interested, demonstrate how you can use long division to solve a more challenging problem.

Activity (B): Play Roll and Divide

Play Roll and Divide

Roll and Divide

Materials: Die

Object of the Game: Create the greatest remainders possible to score more points than your opponent.

On your turn, roll the die. Write the number on the die as the divisor in the first long division problem on your scorecard. Then, solve the problem. The remainder is your score for that round. If there is no remainder, your score is 0.

For example, if you roll a 3 in the first round, write 3 as the divisor. $19 \div 3 = 6$ R1, so your score is 1.

Play until both players have completed their entire scorecard. Find the sum of each player's remainders. Whoever has the greater sum wins the game.

Advanced Variation: If your child easily grasped the steps in long division, add this problem-solving twist to this game. Instead of completing the problems in order, choose which problem to complete for each roll. Try to choose a problem that will yield the greatest possible remainder.

Independent Practice and Review

Have your child complete the Lesson 12.8 Practice and Review workbook pages.

Lesson 12.9
Interpret Remainders

Purpose	Materials
• Find products that are less than a given number • Practice long division • Learn how to interpret remainders in a sensible way depending on the context	• 2 decks of playing cards • Counters

Memory Work	
	• **What do we call the number to be divided?** *The dividend.* • **What do we call the number we divide by?** *The divisor.* • **What do we call the result when we divide two numbers?** *The quotient.* • **What do we call an amount that is left over after division?** *The remainder.*

In real life, solving problems with remainders is more complex than simply writing "R4" after the quotient. Depending on the context, we deal with remainders in different ways. In this lesson, you'll teach your child to interpret remainders according to context.

Warm-up: Play Multiplication Greatest to Least

Play Multiplication Greatest to Least. Use 2 decks of cards with jacks, queens, and kings removed. See Lesson 10.1 (page 317) for directions.

Activity (A): Practice Long Division

In the last lesson, you learned three steps in the long division algorithm. Cover the steps in Part A with your hand or a piece of paper. **Can you remember the three steps in order?** *Divide, multiply, subtract.* If your child can't remember, allow her to peek before telling them to you.

Have your child use the steps to complete the problems in part A. Use counters as needed to model the steps.

Activity (B): Interpret Remainders in a Sensible Way

The word problems in this lesson are very similar to the word problems your child solved in in Lesson 12.4. This allows your child to focus on interpreting the remainder rather than understanding new division situations.

Today, you'll learn more about solving word problems with remainders. Read aloud the first word problem: *There are 32 children at gymnastics lessons. The teachers divide the children into 5 groups. They make the groups as even as possible. How many children are in each group?* **What equation matches the problem?** *32 divided by 5.*

You already solved that problem in part A! Point to the matching problem in part A. **You already found that 32 divided by 5 equals 6, with a remainder of 2.** Place 32 counters on the table. Have your child split them into 5 groups of 6, with 2 counters left over.

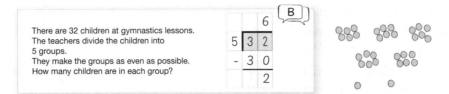

Make sure to model the problem with counters so that your child can concretely see the groups and the remainder.

What is the goal of this problem? *Find how many children are in each group.* **Are there 6 remainder 2 children in each group?** *No!* **In real life, what do you think the instructors would do with the 2 extra children?** *Sample answer: They would have each of the 2 children just join a group.*

To make the groups as even as possible, the instructors would probably have the last 2 children each join a group. Add each of the leftover counters to one of the groups. **So, each group will have 6 or 7 children.** Write "6 or 7 children" in the space below the problem and draw a box around it. **It's funny to have 2 answers, isn't it? But that's the most logical way to handle the remainder in this problem.**

Read aloud the next word problem: ***23 children carpool together to the museum. 4 children fit in each car. How many cars do they need?***

What equation matches the problem? *23 divided by 4.* Point to the matching problem in part A. **You found that 23 divided by 4 equals 5, with a remainder of 3.** Place 23 counters on the table. Have your child split them into 5 groups of 4, with 3 counters left over.

What is the goal of this problem? *Find how many cars they need.* **Should we tell the children that they need 5 remainder 3 cars?** *No!* **Why not?** *Sample answer: It doesn't make sense!*

5 remainder 3 isn't a good answer for this word problem, because it doesn't tell how many cars the children need. Imagine that each counter is a child who wants to go to the museum. How many cars do they need to make sure every child has a ride? *6 cars.*

So, the answer to this problem is 6 cars. Write "6 cars" in the space below the problem and draw a box around it. **We round up to find the answer for this problem.**

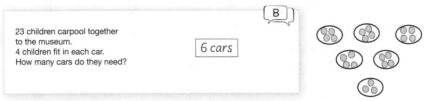

Read aloud the next word problem: ***Eden arranges 25 chairs for the piano recital. She makes 3 rows. Then, she puts away any extra chairs. How many chairs are in each row?*** **What equation matches the problem?** *25 divided by 3.*

You already found that 25 divided by 3 equals 8, with a remainder of 1. Point to the matching problem in part A. Place 25 counters on the table. Have your child arrange them in 3 rows of 8, with 1 counter left to the side.

What's the goal in this problem? *Find how many chairs are in each row.* **Are there 8 remainder 1 chairs in each row?** *No!* **How many chairs are in each row?** *8.* Write "8 chairs" in the space below the problem and draw a box around it. **In this problem, we drop the remainder, because the word problem doesn't ask about it.**

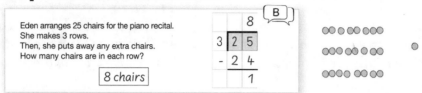

Read aloud the final word problem: *Simon has 20 inches of yarn. He cuts the yarn into 6-inch-long pieces. How much yarn is left over?*

You already found that 20 divided by 6 equals 3, with a remainder of 2. Point to the matching problem in part A. **What's the goal in this problem?** *Find how much yarn is left over.* **Are 3 remainder 2 inches of yarn left over?** *No!* **How many inches of yarn are left over?** *2 inches.*

Write "2 inches" in the space below the problem and draw a box around it. **This word problem doesn't ask about the quotient. Instead, the remainder is the answer!**

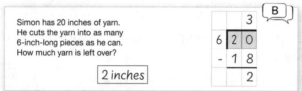

If your child is confused, draw a simple sketch of the situation. Or, if you have time, model the problem with real yarn so your child can see that 2 inches remain after you cut 3 six-inch pieces.

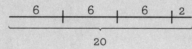

Independent Practice and Review

Have your child complete the Lesson 12.9 Practice and Review workbook pages. If your child has trouble solving the word problems, encourage her to model the problems with counters or draw a sketch.

Lesson 12.10
Enrichment (Optional)

Purpose	Materials
• Practice memory work • Understand division and remainders in the context of children at an amusement park • Create division word problems about a real-life group of people • Summarize what your child has learned and assess your child's progress	• *Divide and Ride,* written by Stuart J. Murphy and illustrated by George Ulrich

Warm-up: Review Memory Work

Quiz your child on all memory work through Unit 12. See pages 527-528 for the full list.

Math Picture Book: *Divide and Ride*

Read *Divide and Ride,* written by Stuart J. Murphy and illustrated by George Ulrich. As you read, discuss how the division equations match the ways the children divide into groups.

Enrichment Activity: Create Your Own Division Word Problems

You've solved a lot of division word problems in this unit! Today, you get to make up your own division word problems.

Choose a community of people that your child knows, such as your extended family, a sports team, a homeschool co-op, or an enrichment class. Help your child make up and solve some real-life word problems that might arise in the group.

Encourage him to create some word problems in which he finds the number of groups and some in which he finds the size of the groups. For example, if your child goes to a robotics class with 18 students, he might make up word problems like the following:

- If the teacher split the class into 3 groups, how many students would be in each group?
- If the teacher split the class into pairs, how many pairs would there be?
- If one student were absent and the teacher split the class into 3 groups, how many students would be in each group?
- If one student were absent and the teacher split the class into pairs, how many pairs would there be?
- If the class carpools to a tournament and 4 children can ride in each car, how many cars will they need?
- If the class carpools to a tournament and 6 children can ride in each minivan, how many minivans will they need?

Unit Wrap-up (Optional)

Have your child complete the Unit 12 Wrap-up.

Unit 12 Answer Key

12.1 Practice

Practice 👤 Complete.

4 × 3 = 12
12 ÷ 3 = 4

2 × 3 = 6
6 ÷ 3 = 2

5 × 3 = 15
15 ÷ 3 = 5

8 × 3 = 24
24 ÷ 3 = 8

1 × 3 = 3
3 ÷ 3 = 1

10 × 3 = 30
30 ÷ 3 = 10

9 × 3 = 27
27 ÷ 3 = 9

3 × 3 = 9
9 ÷ 3 = 3

7 × 3 = 21
21 ÷ 3 = 7

6 × 3 = 18
18 ÷ 3 = 6

12.1 Review

Review 👤 Draw a shape to match.

Many answers are possible.

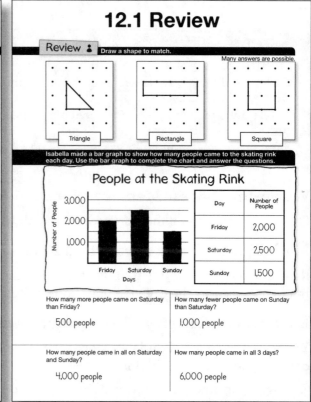

Triangle   Rectangle   Square

Isabella made a bar graph to show how many people came to the skating rink each day. Use the bar graph to complete the chart and answer the questions.

People at the Skating Rink

Day	Number of People
Friday	2,000
Saturday	2,500
Sunday	1,500

How many more people came on Saturday than Friday?

500 people

How many fewer people came on Sunday than Saturday?

1,000 people

How many people came in all on Saturday and Sunday?

4,000 people

How many people came in all 3 days?

6,000 people

12.2 Practice

Practice 👤 Complete the problems that can be solved. Cross out the problems that cannot be solved.

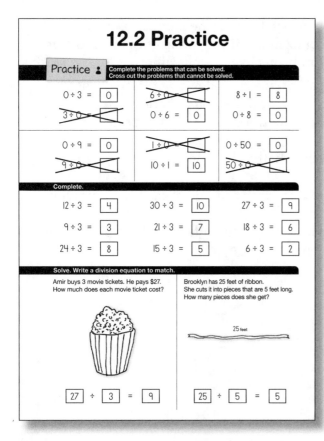

0 ÷ 3 = 0
~~3 ÷ 0~~

~~6 ÷ 0~~
0 ÷ 6 = 0
~~10 ÷ 0~~

8 ÷ 1 = 8
0 ÷ 8 = 0

0 ÷ 9 = 0
~~9 ÷ 0~~

~~1 ÷ 0~~
10 ÷ 1 = 10

0 ÷ 50 = 0
~~50 ÷ 0~~

Complete.

12 ÷ 3 = 4   30 ÷ 3 = 10   27 ÷ 3 = 9

9 ÷ 3 = 3   21 ÷ 3 = 7   18 ÷ 3 = 6

24 ÷ 3 = 8   15 ÷ 3 = 5   6 ÷ 3 = 2

Solve. Write a division equation to match.

Amir buys 3 movie tickets. He pays $27. How much does each movie ticket cost?

27 ÷ 3 = 9

Brooklyn has 25 feet of ribbon. She cuts it into pieces that are 5 feet long. How many pieces does she get?

25 feet

25 ÷ 5 = 5

12.2 Review

Review 👤 Use the numbers to complete the blanks. You will use each number once.

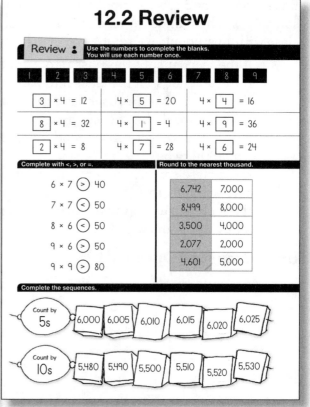

| 1 | 2 | 3 | 4 | 5 | 6 | 7 | 8 | 9 |

3 × 4 = 12   4 × 5 = 20   4 × 4 = 16

8 × 4 = 32   4 × 1 = 4   4 × 9 = 36

2 × 4 = 8   4 × 7 = 28   4 × 6 = 24

Complete with <, >, or =.

6 × 7 (>) 40

7 × 7 (<) 50

8 × 6 (<) 50

9 × 6 (>) 50

9 × 9 (>) 80

Round to the nearest thousand.

6,742	7,000
8,499	8,000
3,500	4,000
2,077	2,000
4,601	5,000

Complete the sequences.

Count by 5s: 6,000 | 6,005 | 6,010 | 6,015 | 6,020 | 6,025

Count by 10s: 5,480 | 5,490 | 5,500 | 5,510 | 5,520 | 5,530

Unit 12 Answer Key

12.3 Practice

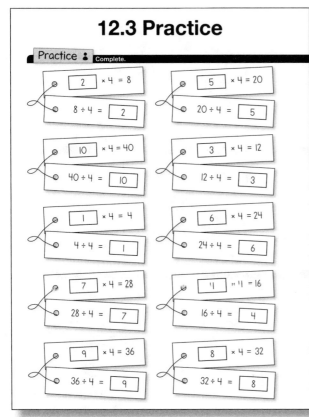

Practice 👤 Complete.

$2 \times 4 = 8$
$8 \div 4 = 2$

$5 \times 4 = 20$
$20 \div 4 = 5$

$10 \times 4 = 40$
$40 \div 4 = 10$

$3 \times 4 = 12$
$12 \div 4 = 3$

$1 \times 4 = 4$
$4 \div 4 = 1$

$6 \times 4 = 24$
$24 \div 4 = 6$

$7 \times 4 = 28$
$28 \div 4 = 7$

$4 \times 4 = 16$
$16 \div 4 = 4$

$9 \times 4 = 36$
$36 \div 4 = 9$

$8 \times 4 = 32$
$32 \div 4 = 8$

12.3 Review

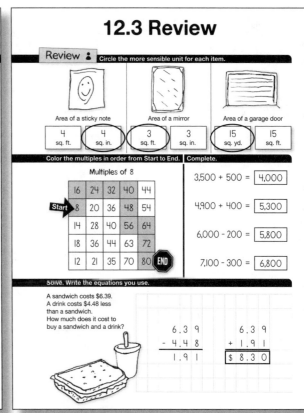

Review 👤 Circle the more sensible unit for each item.

Area of a sticky note: 4 sq. ft. / **(4 sq. in.)**

Area of a mirror: 3 sq. ft. / **(3 sq. in.)**

Area of a garage door: **(15 sq. yd.)** / 15 sq. ft.

Color the multiples in order from Start to End. | Complete.

Multiples of 8

16	24	32	40	44
8	20	36	48	54
14	28	40	56	64
18	36	44	63	72
12	21	35	70	80

Start → 8 ... END 80

$3,500 + 500 = 4,000$

$4,900 + 400 = 5,300$

$6,000 - 200 = 5,800$

$7,100 - 300 = 6,800$

Solve. Write the equations you use.

A sandwich costs $6.39. A drink costs $4.48 less than a sandwich. How much does it cost to buy a sandwich and a drink?

$$\begin{array}{r} 6.39 \\ -4.48 \\ \hline 1.91 \end{array}$$

$$\begin{array}{r} 6.39 \\ +1.91 \\ \hline \$8.30 \end{array}$$

12.4 Practice

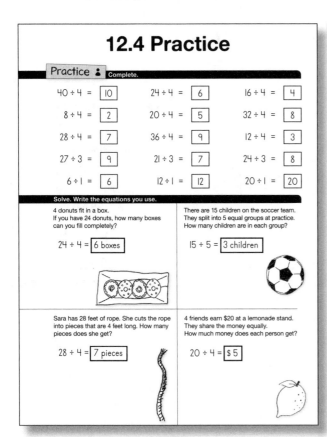

Practice 👤 Complete.

$40 \div 4 = 10$ $24 \div 4 = 6$ $16 \div 4 = 4$

$8 \div 4 = 2$ $20 \div 4 = 5$ $32 \div 4 = 8$

$28 \div 4 = 7$ $36 \div 4 = 9$ $12 \div 4 = 3$

$27 \div 3 = 9$ $21 \div 3 = 7$ $24 \div 3 = 8$

$6 \div 1 = 6$ $12 \div 1 = 12$ $20 \div 1 = 20$

Solve. Write the equations you use.

4 donuts fit in a box. If you have 24 donuts, how many boxes can you fill completely?

$24 \div 4 = 6$ boxes

There are 15 children on the soccer team. They split into 5 equal groups at practice. How many children are in each group?

$15 \div 5 = 3$ children

Sara has 28 feet of rope. She cuts the rope into pieces that are 4 feet long. How many pieces does she get?

$28 \div 4 = 7$ pieces

4 friends earn $20 at a lemonade stand. They share the money equally. How much money does each person get?

$20 \div 4 = \$5$

12.4 Review

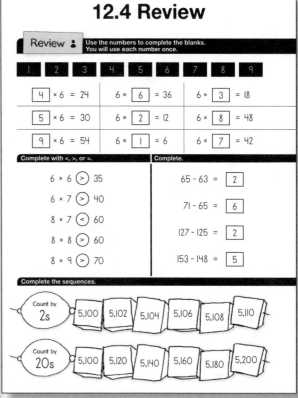

Review 👤 Use the numbers to complete the blanks. You will use each number once.

| 1 | 2 | 3 | 4 | 5 | 6 | 7 | 8 | 9 |

$4 \times 6 = 24$ $6 \times 6 = 36$ $6 \times 3 = 18$

$5 \times 6 = 30$ $6 \times 2 = 12$ $6 \times 8 = 48$

$9 \times 6 = 54$ $6 \times 1 = 6$ $6 \times 7 = 42$

Complete with <, >, or =.

$6 \times 6 > 35$

$6 \times 7 > 40$

$8 \times 7 < 60$

$8 \times 8 > 60$

$8 \times 9 > 70$

Complete.

$65 - 63 = 2$

$71 - 65 = 6$

$127 - 125 = 2$

$153 - 148 = 5$

Complete the sequences.

Count by 2s: 5,100 5,102 5,104 5,106 5,108 5,110

Count by 20s: 5,100 5,120 5,140 5,160 5,180 5,200

Unit 12 Answer Key

12.5 Practice

Practice ⏺ Complete.

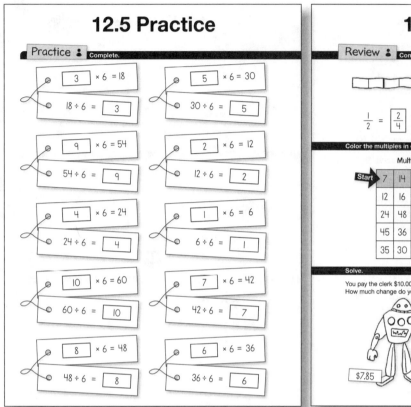

3 × 6 = 18	5 × 6 = 30
18 ÷ 6 = 3	30 ÷ 6 = 5
9 × 6 = 54	2 × 6 = 12
54 ÷ 6 = 9	12 ÷ 6 = 2
4 × 6 = 24	1 × 6 = 6
24 ÷ 6 = 4	6 ÷ 6 = 1
10 × 6 = 60	7 × 6 = 42
60 ÷ 6 = 10	42 ÷ 6 = 7
8 × 6 = 48	6 × 6 = 36
48 ÷ 6 = 8	36 ÷ 6 = 6

12.5 Review

Review ⏺ Complete the equivalent fractions.

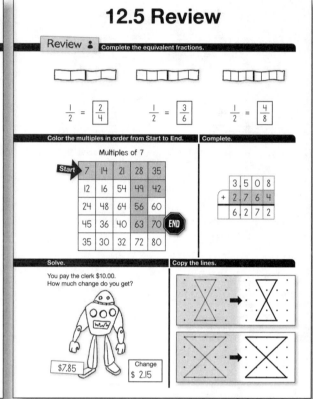

$\frac{1}{2} = \frac{2}{4}$ $\frac{1}{2} = \frac{3}{6}$ $\frac{1}{2} = \frac{4}{8}$

Color the multiples in order from Start to End. | Complete.

Multiples of 7

Start →
7	14	21	28	35
12	16	54	49	42
24	48	64	56	60
45	36	40	63	70	END
35	30	32	72	80

$$\begin{array}{r} 3{,}5\;0\;8 \\ +\;2{,}7\;6\;4 \\ \hline 6{,}2\;7\;2 \end{array}$$

Solve. | Copy the lines.

You pay the clerk $10.00.
How much change do you get?

$7.85   Change $ 2.15

12.6 Practice

Practice ⏺ Complete.

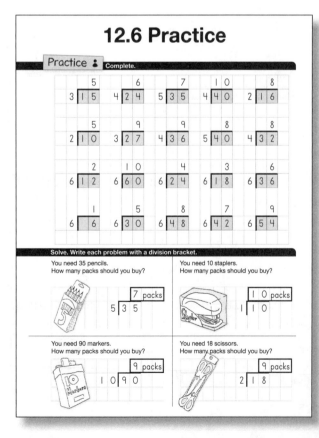

5	6	7	10	8
3)15	4)24	5)35	4)40	2)16

5	9	9	8	8
2)10	3)27	4)36	5)40	4)32

2	10	4	3	6
6)12	6)60	6)24	6)18	6)36

1	5	8	7	9
6)6	6)30	6)48	6)42	6)54

Solve. Write each problem with a division bracket.

You need 35 pencils.
How many packs should you buy?

7 packs
5)35

You need 10 staplers.
How many packs should you buy?

10 packs
1)10

You need 90 markers.
How many packs should you buy?

9 packs
10)90

You need 18 scissors.
How many packs should you buy?

9 packs
2)18

12.6 Review

Review ⏺ Complete.

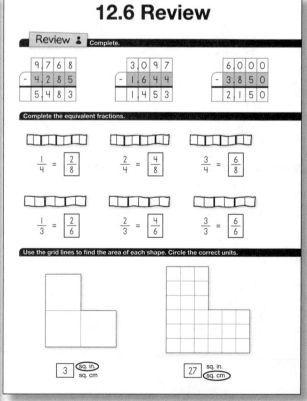

$$\begin{array}{r} 9{,}7\;6\;8 \\ -\;4{,}2\;8\;5 \\ \hline 5{,}4\;8\;3 \end{array}$$ $$\begin{array}{r} 3{,}0\;9\;7 \\ -\;1{,}6\;4\;4 \\ \hline 1\;4\;5\;3 \end{array}$$ $$\begin{array}{r} 6{,}0\;0\;0 \\ -\;3{,}8\;5\;0 \\ \hline 2\;1\;5\;0 \end{array}$$

Complete the equivalent fractions.

$\frac{1}{4} = \frac{2}{8}$ $\frac{2}{4} = \frac{4}{8}$ $\frac{3}{4} = \frac{6}{8}$

$\frac{1}{3} = \frac{2}{6}$ $\frac{2}{3} = \frac{4}{6}$ $\frac{3}{3} = \frac{6}{6}$

Use the grid lines to find the area of each shape. Circle the correct units.

3 sq. in.
sq. cm

27 sq. in.
sq. cm

Unit 12 Answer Key

12.7 Practice

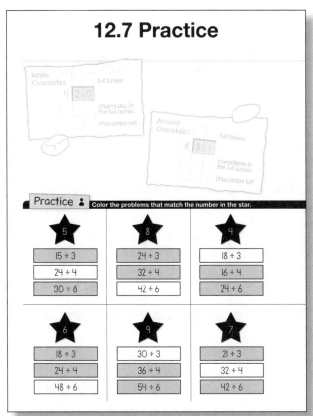

White Chocolates

4 | 2 | 0   full boxes

chocolates in the full boxes

chocolates left

Almond Chocolates

6 | 3 | 1   full boxes

chocolates in the full boxes

chocolates left

Practice — Color the problems that match the number in the star.

⭐ 5

15 ÷ 3
24 ÷ 4
30 ÷ 6

⭐ 8

24 ÷ 3
32 ÷ 4
42 ÷ 6

⭐ 4

18 ÷ 3
16 ÷ 4
24 ÷ 6

⭐ 6

18 ÷ 3
24 ÷ 4
48 ÷ 6

⭐ 9

30 ÷ 3
36 ÷ 4
54 ÷ 6

⭐ 7

21 ÷ 3
32 ÷ 4
42 ÷ 6

12.7 Review

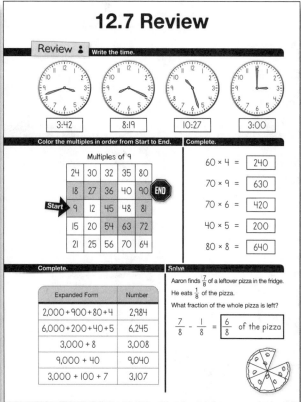

Review — Write the time.

3:42   8:19   10:27   3:00

Color the multiples in order from Start to End.

Multiples of 9

24	30	32	35	80
18	27	36	40	90	END
9	12	45	48	81
15	20	54	63	72
21	25	56	70	64

Start →

Complete.

60 × 4 = 240
70 × 9 = 630
70 × 6 = 420
40 × 5 = 200
80 × 8 = 640

Complete.

Expanded Form	Number
2,000 + 900 + 80 + 4	2,984
6,000 + 200 + 40 + 5	6,245
3,000 + 8	3,008
9,000 + 40	9,040
3,000 + 100 + 7	3,107

Solve.

Aaron finds $\frac{7}{8}$ of a leftover pizza in the fridge. He eats $\frac{1}{8}$ of the pizza. What fraction of the whole pizza is left?

$\frac{7}{8} - \frac{1}{8} = \frac{6}{8}$ of the pizza

12.8 Practice

Practice — Complete. Follow the steps.

1. Divide
2. Multiply
3. Subtract

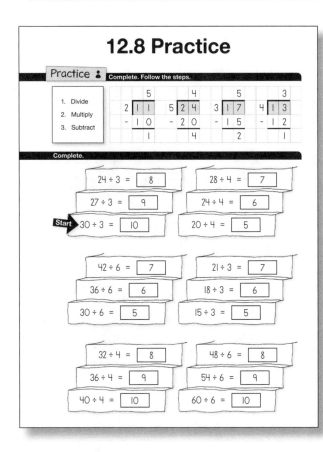

	5		4		5		3
2	1 1	5	2 4	3	1 7	4	1 3
	- 1 0		- 2 0		- 1 5		- 1 2
	1		4		2		1

Complete.

24 ÷ 3 = 8   28 ÷ 4 = 7
27 ÷ 3 = 9   24 ÷ 4 = 6
Start → 30 ÷ 3 = 10   20 ÷ 4 = 5

42 ÷ 6 = 7   21 ÷ 3 = 7
36 ÷ 6 = 6   18 ÷ 3 = 6
30 ÷ 6 = 5   15 ÷ 3 = 5

32 ÷ 4 = 8   48 ÷ 6 = 8
36 ÷ 4 = 9   54 ÷ 6 = 9
40 ÷ 4 = 10   60 ÷ 6 = 10

12.8 Review

Review — Find the perimeter and area of each rectangle.

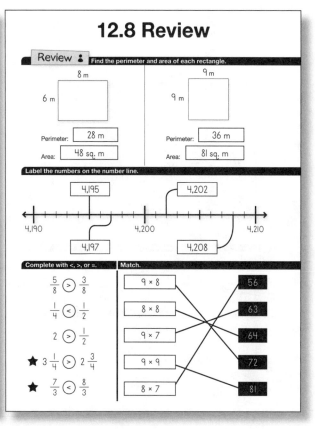

8 m / 6 m

Perimeter: 28 m
Area: 48 sq. m

9 m / 9 m

Perimeter: 36 m
Area: 81 sq. m

Label the numbers on the number line.

4,195   4,202

4,190   4,200   4,210

4,197   4,208

Complete with <, >, or =.

$\frac{5}{8}$ > $\frac{3}{8}$

$\frac{1}{4}$ < $\frac{1}{2}$

2 > $\frac{1}{2}$

⭐ $3\frac{1}{4}$ > $2\frac{3}{4}$

⭐ $\frac{7}{3}$ < $\frac{8}{3}$

Match.

9 × 8		56
8 × 8		63
9 × 7		64
9 × 9		72
8 × 7		81

Unit 12 Answer Key

12.9 Practice

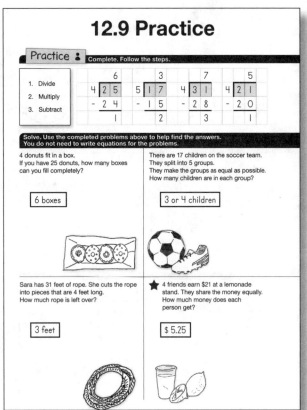

12.9 Review

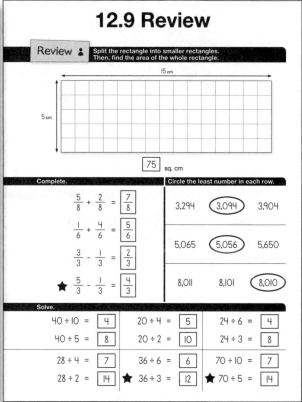

12.10 Unit Wrap-Up A

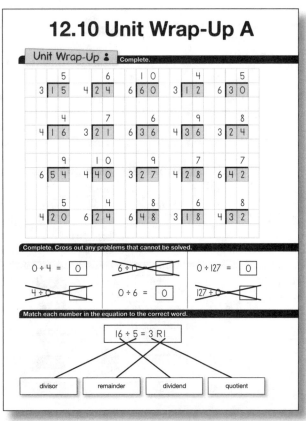

12.10 Unit Wrap-Up B

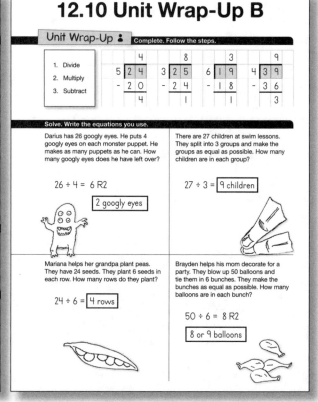

Unit 12 Checkpoint

What to Expect at the End of Unit 12

By the end of Unit 12, most children will be able to do the following:

- Find answers for the ÷3, ÷4, and ÷6 facts. Most children will be fairly fluent with the facts with smaller dividends (like 12 ÷ 3 or 16 ÷ 4) but need more practice with facts with larger dividends (27 ÷ 3 or 48 ÷ 6).
- Use the long division process to solve division problems. Many children will need coaching and guidance to solve these problems.
- Solve division word problems with remainders and understand that there are multiple ways to interpret remainders, depending on the context. Most children will still be working on interpreting remainders in context, and your child will work on this more in Unit 15.

Is Your Child Ready to Move on?

In Unit 13, your child will study geometry. He does not need to fully master the division facts from Unit 12 before moving on to Unit 13. He will continue to practice the ÷3, ÷4, and ÷6 facts before working on the rest of the division facts in Unit 15.

This page is intentionally left blank.

Unit 13
Geometry

Overview

In Unit 13, you will teach your child to identify right angles, squares, rectangles, and rhombuses. She'll develop her spatial skills as she visualizes flipping, turning, and sliding shapes, and she'll learn to identify faces, edges, and vertices in three-dimensional shapes.

Children often enjoy this shift in focus from numbers to spatial skills. Your child will continue to practice arithmetic in the warm-up activities and review pages, especially the multiplication and division facts.

What Your Child Will Learn

In this unit, your child will learn to:

- Identify right angles and tell whether other angles are larger or smaller than a right angle
- Identify, describe, and draw squares, rectangles, and rhombuses
- Use spatial skills to visualize flips, turns, and slides
- Name three-dimensional shapes (cones, cubes, cylinders, rectangular prisms, triangular prisms, and pyramids) and identify faces, edges, and vertices

Lesson List

Lesson 13.1   Right Angles

Lesson 13.2   Rectangles, Squares, and Rhombuses

Lesson 13.3   Explore Pentominoes

Lesson 13.4   Flips, Turns, and Slides

Lesson 13.5   3-D Shapes

Lesson 13.6   Enrichment (Optional)

Extra Materials Needed for Unit 13

- Two pencils
- Paper
- Marker
- Scissors
- Tape
- Highlighter or wide marker
- For optional Enrichment Lesson:
  - × *Which One Doesn't Belong? Playing with Shapes*, written by Christopher Danielson. Charlesbridge, 2019.
  - × Contact paper (self-adhesive, clear vinyl)
  - × Black construction paper
  - × Tissue paper in assorted colors

This unit requires several blackline masters. You may want to cut them apart before the lessons to make the lessons go more quickly.

Teaching Math with Confidence: Developing Spatial Skills with Pentominoes

In Lessons 13.3 and 13.4, your child will develop her spatial skills as she explores pentominoes. These 12 simple shapes are each composed of 5 squares, put together in different configurations.

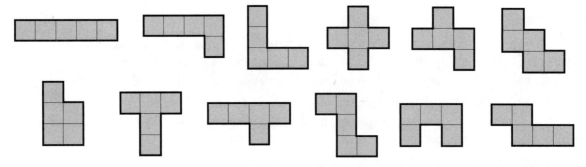

In the first pentomino lesson, your child will use unit blocks (from your set of base-ten blocks) to find as many different pentominoes as she can. A pentomino is considered "different" from the other pentominoes if you cannot flip, slide, or turn one of the other pentominoes to match it. For example, each of the following shapes is considered the same pentomino, since you can move the first pentomino in the row into any of these positions.

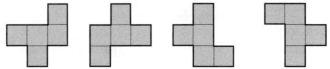

These four shapes are all the same pentomino, oriented in four different ways.

After your child has created as many pentominoes as possible from unit blocks, you'll use paper pentominoes (from Blackline Master 10) to explore the results of flipping, sliding, and turning the shapes. Your child will put them together to create larger shapes. She'll also predict the results of flips, slides, and turns and use the paper pentominoes to check her predictions.

Hands-on experience with pentominoes will help your child grow in her ability to understand, remember, and manipulate spatial relationships. These fun puzzles prepare her to visualize and reason about more complex spatial relationships as she studies geometry in future grades.

Lesson 13.1
Right Angles

Purpose	Materials
• Create angles • Identify right angles • Tell whether angles are larger or smaller than a right angle	• Two pencils • Paper • Marker • Clock

Memory Work	• **How many minutes are in an hour?** *60.* • **How many seconds are in a minute?** *60.*

Warm-up: Make Angles with Pencils

We're starting a new unit on geometry today! Geometry is the study of shapes and lines. What do you remember about shapes that you learned in younger grades? *Answers will vary.*

Today, you'll learn about angles. When two lines meet, they form an angle. Arrange two pencils in a V on the table, with their points touching. **These two pencils meet in a letter V shape to form an angle. The angle is the space between the pencils.**

The space between the pencils is the angle.

If I move the pencils to make the V narrower, the angle between them becomes smaller. Move the pencils to make the V narrower. (Keep the points of the pencils touching.)

If I move the pencils to make the V wider, the angle between them becomes larger. Move the pencils to make the V larger.

Give your child a minute to move the pencils and explore the angles she can make between them.

Activity (A): Identify Whether Angles are Smaller, Larger, or Equal to Right Angles

Move the pencils to match the right angle in part A. **This is a right angle. A right angle is an angle that looks like the corner of a piece of paper.**

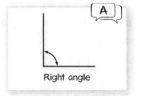

Right angle

Many things around the house have right angles. I wonder if you can find 10 different things with right angles without even moving! With your child, look around the room for items with right angles, like windows, doors, walls, photos on the wall, bookshelves, tables, or this book.

Some angles are smaller than right angles, and some angles are larger than right angles. Have your child move the pencils to match the other two angles in part A.

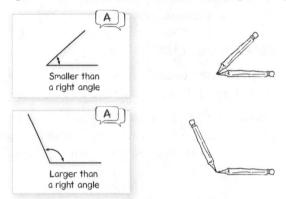

Let's look at the angles that the hands on the clock form. Set a clock for 12:00. **At 12 o'clock, the hands on the clock are on top of each other.** Have your child gradually move the minute hand forward. When the minute hand reaches the 1, ask: **Is the angle between the minute hand and hour hand smaller, larger, or equal to a right angle?** *Smaller.*

Have your child continue to move the minute hand forward. When the minute hand reaches each printed number, ask her to tell whether the hands form an angle that's smaller, larger, or equal to a right angle. Stop when the minute hand reaches the 6.

The angle between the hands is smaller than a right angle.

The angle between the hands is a right angle.

The angle between the hands is larger than a right angle.

The angle between the hands is larger than a right angle.

The angle between the hands is larger than a right angle.

One way to tell whether an angle is smaller than a right angle, larger than a right angle, or equal to a right angle is to compare it to the corner of a piece of paper. Tear off a corner of a piece of paper. Use a marker to highlight the 2 straight sides of the corner.

You can also use the corner of a square tile or pattern block to check whether the angles are right angles.

Align one edge of the corner with the hour hand on the first printed clock. **Is this angle smaller, larger, or equal to a right angle?** *Smaller.*

Repeat with the other two clocks. Align the paper corner as shown to help your child identify whether the hands on the printed clocks form angles that are smaller than a right angle, larger than a right angle, or equal to a right angle.

This angle is larger than a right angle.   This angle is a right angle.

Activity (B): Identify Whether Shapes' Angles are Smaller than a Right Angle, Larger Than a Right Angle, or Equal to a Right Angle

The sides of shapes meet to form angles, too. How many angles does the first triangle have? *3.* Point to each angle and have your child tell whether it is smaller, larger, or equal to a right angle. If your child isn't sure, have her use the torn-off corner of a piece to check (as in the previous activity). **How many right angles does the first triangle have?** *0.* Write 0 in the answer blank. Repeat with the rest of the shapes in part B.

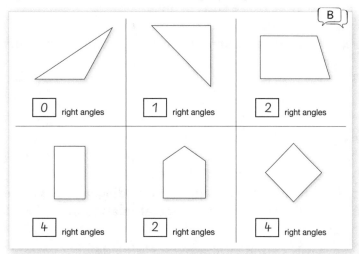

The final shape is more challenging because none of its sides are oriented horizontally. If your child has trouble finding the right angles in this shape, tilt the paper until one side of the shape is oriented horizontally.

Independent Practice and Review

Have your child complete the Lesson 13.1 Practice and Review workbook pages.

Lesson 13.2
Rectangles, Squares, and Rhombuses

Purpose	Materials
• Practice identifying whether angles are smaller than a right angle, larger than a right angle, or equal to a right angle • Sort quadrilaterals based on their sides and angles • Identify and draw rectangles, squares, and rhombuses	• Two pencils • Quadrilateral Cards (Blackline Master 9), cut apart on the dotted lines

Memory Work
- **What is another name for 12 a.m.?** *Midnight.*
- **What is another name for 12 p.m.?** *Noon.*

Warm-up: Practice Identifying Whether Angles are Smaller Than a Right Angle, Larger Than a Right Angle, or Equal to a Right Angle

In the last lesson, you learned about angles. Arrange pencils to create the following angles. Have your child tell whether each angle is smaller than a right angle, larger than a right angle, or equal to a right angle.

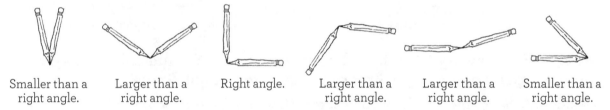

| Smaller than a right angle. | Larger than a right angle. | Right angle. | Larger than a right angle. | Larger than a right angle. | Smaller than a right angle. |

Activity (A): Sort Quadrilaterals Based on Their Sides and Angles

Spread the Quadrilateral Cards (from Blackline Master 9) on the table. **Today, we'll sort these quadrilaterals based on their sides and angles.**

- **How many sides do all of these shapes have?** *4.*
- **How many angles do all of these shapes have?** *4.*
- **What do we call shapes with 4 straight, closed sides?** *Quadrilaterals.*

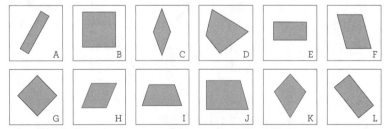

Show your child part A. **This diagram is called a Venn diagram. It's named after a mathematician who used these diagrams to show logical relationships. We'll use this Venn diagram to sort shapes.**

- **We'll put shapes with 4 right angles on the left side.**
- **We'll put shapes with 4 equal sides on the right side.**
- **If any of the shapes have 4 right angles and 4 equal sides, we'll put them in the middle where the circles overlap.**

Show your child shape A. **Does this shape have 4 right angles?** *Yes.* **Does this shape have 4 equal sides?** *No.* Put the shape card on the left side of the Venn diagram.

If your child can't tell that shape A has 4 right angles, tilt the card so that one side is oriented horizontally.

Show your child shape B. **Does this shape have 4 right angles?** *Yes.* **Does it have 4 equal sides?** *Yes.* Put the card in the middle part of the Venn diagram.

Show your child shape C. **Does this shape have 4 right angles?** *No.* **Does it have 4 equal sides?** *Yes.* If your child's not sure, say: **The left half and right half look like they match. The top half and bottom half look identical, too, so the sides must all be the same length.**

Put the card on the right side of the Venn diagram.

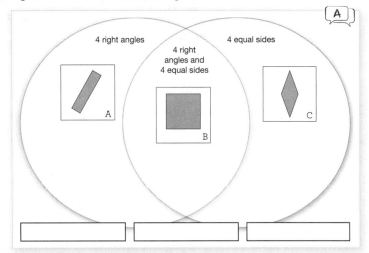

If your child is skeptical that the sides are the same lengths, show him how to use your fingers to compare the lengths of the sides of the first rhombus. Hold your fingers apart the same length as one side. Then, keep your fingers in the same position and compare the distance between your fingers to the length of the other sides of the rhombus.

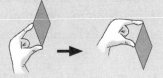

Show your child shape D. **Does this shape have 4 right angles?** *No.* **Does it have 4 equal sides?** *No.* **This card doesn't belong on the Venn diagram.** Put the card off to the side.

Discuss and sort the rest of the shape cards in the same way. Encourage your child to tilt the cards to help check whether they have 4 right angles or 4 equal sides. Overlap the cards as needed.

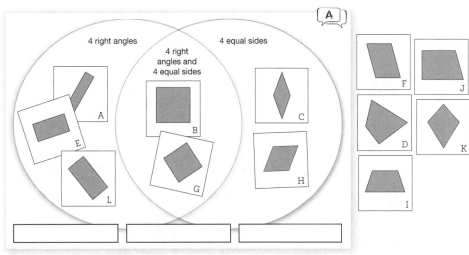

Activity (A): Learn Definitions for Rectangles, Squares, and Rhombuses

Point to the cards on the left side of the Venn diagram. (Spread them out if needed so your child can see all of them.) **These shapes all have 4 right angles. What do we call these shapes?** *Rectangles.* Write "Rectangles" in the box below the left section of the Venn diagram.

Point to the cards in the middle of the Venn diagram. **These shapes all have 4 right angles and 4 equal sides. What do we call these shapes?** *Squares.* Write "Squares" in the box below the middle section.

Point to the cards on the right side of the Venn diagram. **These shapes all have 4 equal sides. We call shapes with 4 equal sides** *rhombuses.* **In everyday life, we sometimes call them diamonds.** Write "Rhombuses" in the box below the right section.

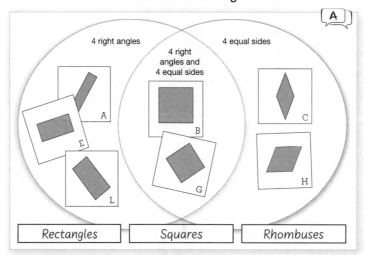

Use these questions to briefly compare and contrast the categories:

- **What do rectangles and squares have in common?** *They have 4 right angles.*
- **What do squares and rhombuses have in common?** *They have 4 equal sides.*
- **What do rectangles, squares, and rhombuses all have in common?** *They all have 4 sides.*

Activity (B): Draw Rectangles, Squares, and Rhombuses

Now, we'll draw more exaples of these shapes. Have your child draw 3 rectangles in the first box, 3 squares in the second box, and 3 rhombuses in the third box. Encourage him to make the shapes look as different from each other as possible.

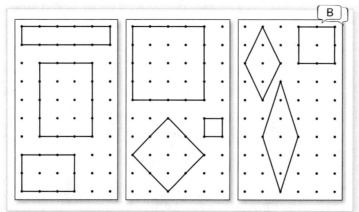

Sample rectangles, squares, and rhombuses. The name of each type of shape is written above the box in part A.

Drawing rhombuses can be challenging. If your child has trouble, draw the left half of one of the sample rhombuses above and have your child draw a right half to match.

In everyday life, we typically use the most specific name possible for shapes. But, mathematically speaking, squares fit the definitions of both rectangles and rhombuses. So, every square is simultaneously a square, a rectangle, and a rhombus.

Your child could technically draw 3 squares for all 3 boxes. If he does this, praise him for his understanding of the relationships between the definitions and ask him to draw a couple of rectangles that aren't squares (or a couple of rhombuses that aren't squares) as well.

Independent Practice and Review

Have your child complete the Lesson 13.2 Practice and Review workbook pages.

Lesson 13.3
Explore Pentominoes

Purpose	Materials
• Practice telling time to the minute • Develop spatial skills by finding all possible pentominoes • Develop spatial skills by completing pentomino puzzles	• Clock • Pentominoes (Blackline Master 10) • Base-ten blocks • Scissors

Memory Work
- **How many days are in a week?** *7.*
- **How many hours are in a day?** *24.*

Your child will investigate pentominoes in this lesson and the next. Pentominoes are simple shapes made from 5 squares. These basic shapes can be put together to create surprisingly complex designs and spatial challenges. See the Unit 13 **Teaching Math with Confidence** for more on the benefits of exploring pentominoes.

Warm-up: Review Telling Time to the Minute

Set a clock to the following times and have your child tell each time: 6:00, 6:15, 6:17, 6:25, 6:29, 6:30, 6:31, 6:45, 6:50, 6:53, 7:00.

Activity (A): Sketch All Possible Pentominoes

In the last lesson, you learned about rectangles, squares, and rhombuses. What do we call shapes with 4 right angles? *Rectangles.* **What do we call shapes with 4 equal sides?** *Rhombuses.* **What do we call shapes with 4 right angles and 4 equal sides?** *Squares.*

Have you ever used dominoes? *Answers will vary.* **Today, we'll explore a special kind of domino called pentominoes. They're made by putting together 5 squares. The prefix "pent-" in pentominoes means "five," just like in the word pentagon.** Read aloud the pentomino rules to your child.

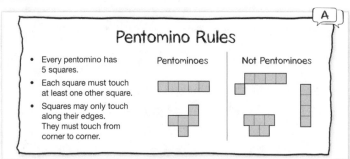

Have your child tell why each of the examples listed under "Not Pentominoes" doesn't fit the rules.

The leftmost square touches another square on a corner, not an edge.

This shape only has 4 squares.

The edges of the squares do not touch from corner to corner.

There are 12 different pentominoes possible with these rules. Let's see how many we can find! We'll make each pentomino from blocks and then draw it on the grid paper. There are 2 sample pentominoes already drawn on the grid paper.

Give your child 5 unit blocks from your set of base-ten blocks. Have her experiment with putting together the blocks to make pentominoes that are different from the ones on the paper. Once she finds a new pentomino, have her sketch it on the grid paper.

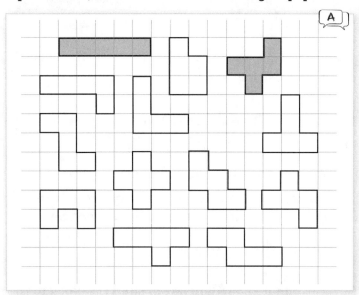

All possible pentominoes.

Each new pentomino is considered "different" from the previous pentominoes if you cannot flip, slide, or turn one of the previous pentominoes to match it. For example, each of the following shapes is considered the same pentomino.

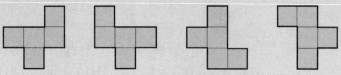

Give your child some time to explore possible arrangements of the blocks and find as many pentominoes as possible. It's fine if she doesn't find all of them. Once she's found as many as she can, show her Blackline Master 10. Have her identify which of these pentominoes she found. Have her draw any missing pentominoes on the grid paper.

Help your child cut out the pentominoes on Blackline Master 10. She will need them for the Practice page and for the next lesson.

If you own the board game Blokus, you may use the plastic pentominoes from the game instead of cutting out the pentominoes on Blackline Master 10. Do not use the pieces with 1, 2, 3, or 4 squares.

Independent Practice and Review

Have your child use the cut-apart pentominoes to complete the Lesson 13.3 Practice and Review workbook pages.

If you are using plastic pentominoes from the board game Blokus: These pentominoes do not fit the squares on Practice page 13.3. Instead, have your child use the pentominoes to create the same shape next to the page. Then, have her draw the matching dividing lines on the page.

 Save the cut-apart pentominoes for Lesson 13.4 and 13.6.

Lesson 13.4
Flips, Turns, and Slides

Purpose	Materials
• Introduce turns with clock hands • Introduce flips, turns, and slides • Develop spatial skills • Visualize the results of flipping, sliding, and turning pentominoes	• Clock • Pentominoes (cut out from Blackline Master 10 in Lesson 13.3)

Memory Work
- How many minutes equal a half-hour? *30.*
- How many minutes equal a quarter-hour? *15.*

Warm-up: Introduce Turns with Clock Hands

In this lesson, you'll learn how to turn pentominoes a quarter-turn or half-turn in either direction. We'll warm up by practicing these turns with clock hands.

Fractional turns can be confusing to children, so you'll first practice them in the familiar context of half- and quarter-hours.

Set a clock to 4:00. **Turn the minute hand halfway around the clock to the right.** *Child turns the minute hand forward until it points to the 6.* **What time does the clock show now?** *4:30.* **You turned the clock forward a half-hour. You turned the minute hand a half-turn to the right.**

Set the clock to 4:00. **This time, turn the minute hand halfway around the clock to the left.** *Child turns the minute hand backwards until it points to the 6.* **What time does the clock show now?** *3:30.* **You turned the clock backward a half-hour. You turned the minute hand a half-turn to the left.**

Set the clock to 4:00. **This time, turn the minute hand one-quarter of the way around the clock to the right. Remember, one-quarter means the same as one-fourth.** *Child turns the minute hand forwards until it points to the 3.* **What time does the clock show now?** *4:15.* **You turned the clock forward a quarter-hour. You turned the minute hand a quarter-turn to the right.**

Set the clock to 4:00. **Last, turn the minute hand one-quarter of the way around the clock to the left.** *Child turns the minute hand backwards until it points to the 9.* **What time does the clock show now?** *3:45.* **You turned the clock backward a quarter-hour. You turned the minute hand a quarter-turn to the left.**

Activity: Introduce Flips, Turns, and Slides

In the last lesson, you created pentominoes. In this lesson, we'll explore what happens when we flip, slide, or turn the pentominoes. Flips, turns, and slides in math mean the same thing as they mean in everyday life.

One way to move the pentomino is to slide it. Slide the L-shaped pentomino around the table in a zig-zag. **No matter how you slide the pentomino, it always looks the same.** Have your child try sliding the pentomino on the table, too.

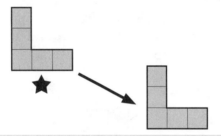

The starting position for the pentomino is marked with a star in these diagrams.

Another way to move the pentomino is to flip it. I can flip it horizontally to the left or to the right. Demonstrate flipping the pentomino horizontally to the left or to the right.

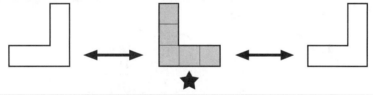

The blank side of the pentomino will face up after you flip it, so you won't see the dividing lines.

Or, I can flip the pentomino vertically upwards or downwards. Flip the pentomino vertically both upwards and downwards from its original position.

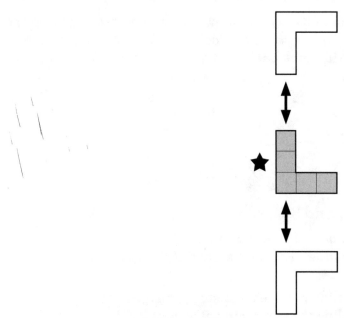

Another way to move the pentomino is to turn it. I can turn it to the left or to the right, and I can turn it a little or a lot. Demonstrate turning the pentomino to the right or to the left by varying amounts. **The pentomino looks different depending on how much I turn it. I can turn it just a little. Or, I can turn it all the way around until it gets back to its original position!** Have your child try turning the pentomino, too.

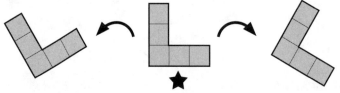

Align the pentomino as shown on the table. **We often describe turns with fractions, just like we did with the clock. It makes it easier to visualize the turns if you imagine one part of the shape like a minute hand pointing to the 12. For this shape, let's pretend that the vertical part is pointing to the 12 on a clock.**

Demonstrate a half-turn to the right. **This is a half-turn to the right. It's called a half-turn, because the pentomino turns halfway around. If the pentomino were on a clock, the part that we imagined pointing to the 12 on a clock now points to the 6.**

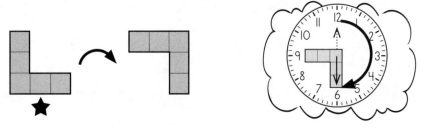

Half-turn to the right.

Return the pentomino to its starting position. **Turn the pentomino a half-turn to the left.** *Child turns the pentomino as shown.*

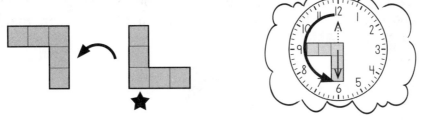

Half-turn to the left.

Return the pentomino to its starting position. Demonstrate a quarter-turn to the right. **This is a quarter-turn to the right. If the pentomino were on a clock, the part that we imagined pointing to the 12 on a clock now points to the 3.**

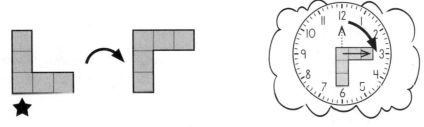

Quarter-turn to the right.

Return the pentomino to its starting position. **Turn the pentomino a quarter-turn to the left.** *Child turns the pentomino as shown.*

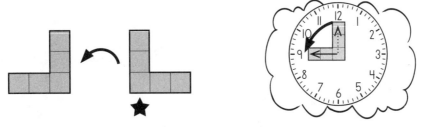

Quarter-turn to the left.

The pentomino's orientation changes depending on how we flip, slide, or turn it. But, it's always the same pentomino, no matter how it looks!

Activity (A): Predict the Results of Flips, Turns, and Slides

`Show your child part A. Draw a dot on the L-shaped paper pentomino to match the printed pentomino.

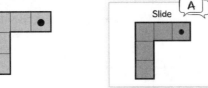

Place the L-shaped paper pentomino on the top printed shape in the "Slide" column. **I'm going to slide the pentomino down the page. Imagine how the pentomino will move and where the square with the dot will go.** Have your child predict which square in the bottom printed pentomino will contain the dot. Have him draw an X in the square that he predicts will contain the dot.

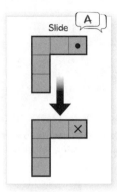

Sample prediction.

Slide the pentomino down until it matches the printed outline. **Is the square with the dot on top of the square with the X?** *Answers will vary.* If your child's prediction was incorrect, have him draw an X on the correct square.

Repeat with the "Flip" and "Turn" columns.

- For the "Flip" column: **This time, I'm going to flip the pentomino vertically. Imagine how the pentomino will move and where the square with the dot will go.**
- For the "Turn" column: **Last, I'm going to turn the pentomino a quarter-turn to the right. Imagine how the pentomino will move and where the square with the dot will go.**

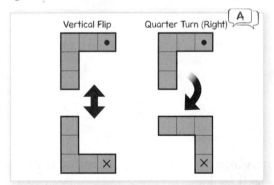

Activity (B): Predict How Pentominoes Will Look After Flips, Turns, and Slides

Place the matching paper pentomino on the printed shape in the first row. Draw a dot on the paper pentomino to match the printed dot. **How do you think this pentomino will look after we slide it?** *Answers will vary.* Have your child draw his prediction on the grid paper. Have him draw an X in the square that he predicts will contain the dot.

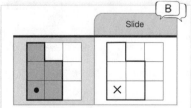

Sample prediction. Your child may also draw the shape on the right side of the grid.

Have your child draw the predicted shape lightly in pencil so that it's easy to change if it's incorrect.

Slide the pentomino to the right to see if the result matches your child's prediction. If he's incorrect, have him erase his prediction and draw the actual result instead.

Children vary widely in their ability to visualize flips, slides, and turns. If your child struggles with these visualizations or feels frustrated by them, skip having him predict the results of each move. Instead, simply have him flip, slide, or turn the paper pentomino and draw the result.

Repeat with the other two columns. Then, repeat with the rest of the pentominoes in the chart.

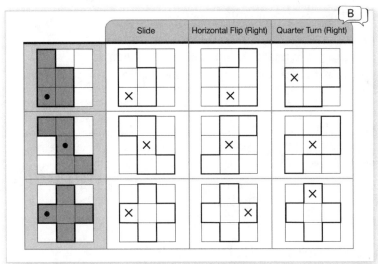

Use the following questions to discuss the results:

- **What happened to the dot in the center of the Z shape in the middle row?** *Sample answer: It stayed in the center each time.* **The shape looks different after you slide, flip, or turn it. But the square in the center stays in the same place.**
- **What happened to the dot in the pentomino shaped like a plus sign in the bottom row?** *It moved positions.* **The shape looks the same after you slide, flip, or turn it. But, the square with the dot moves positions.**

Independent Practice and Review

Have your child complete the Lesson 13.4 Practice page. Have him first visualize each slide, flip, and turn, and draw his prediction. Then, have him use the matching paper pentomino to check his prediction.

If your child finds it difficult to predict the results, he may flip, slide, or turn the paper pentomino and draw the result instead.

Lesson 13.5
3-D Shapes

Purpose	Materials
• Practice counting forwards with time intervals • Fold nets into three-dimensional shapes • Learn names for three-dimensional shapes • Identify faces, edges, and vertices in three-dimensional shapes	• Clock • Nets (Blackline Master 11), cut out according to the directions • Tape • Highlighter or wide marker

Memory Work
- **Are times in the morning a.m. or p.m.?** *A.m.*
- **Are times in the afternoon and evening a.m. or p.m.?** *P.m.*

In this lesson, you and your child will fold and tape nets to create 3-D shapes. This hands-on experience builds your child's spatial skills and helps her understand the relationships between 2-D and 3-D shapes. Depending on your child's folding and taping skills, it can be quite time-consuming. Cut out the shapes on Blackline Master 11 in advance to make the lesson flow more smoothly. Or, split the lesson over two days if it runs too long:

- Day 1: Fold and tape the nets to match the printed shapes in part A of the Lesson Activities. Have your child complete the Review page only.
- Day 2: Use the 3-D shapes to complete the chart in part B. Have your child complete the Practice page.

Warm-up: Count Forwards with the Clock

Have your child count forwards from each of the following times. Use a real clock to model each time, and have your child turn the clock's hands to match each time as she says it.

- Set the clock to 11:30. **Count forwards by 10 minutes, from 11:30 to 12:30.** *11:30, 11:40, 11:50…*
- Set the clock to 12:30. **Count forwards by 15 minutes, from 12:30 to 2:00.** *12:30, 12:45, 1:00…*
- Set the clock to 2:05. **Count forwards by 30 minutes, from 2:05 to 5:05.** *2:05, 2:35, 3:05…*

Activity (A): Fold Nets to Create 3-D Shapes

Shapes like rectangles, squares, and triangles are flat, like a piece of paper. We call flat shapes *two-dimensional*.

Show your child the cut-out nets from Blackline Master 11. **These are special shapes called nets. They're flat right now, but we'll fold and tape them to create *three-dimensional* shapes that take up space.**

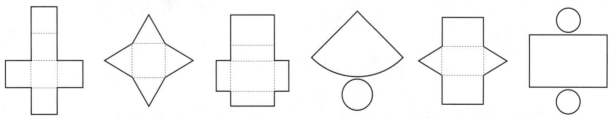

3-D is an abbreviation for three-dimensional. 3-D movies make you feel like the characters are moving in space, not flat on a screen. Briefly discuss any experiences your child has had with 3-D movies or pictures.

Show your child the following net. **We're going to fold and tape this net to create a 3-D shape.** Show your child the printed 3-D shapes in part A. **Which 3-D shape do you think this net will become?** *Answers will vary.* **Let's find out!**

To fold the net into a 3-D shape, first fold the paper along each of the dotted lines. Make each fold upward, away from the table. Then, gently fold the squares inward to create a cube and tape the sides together. **Which 3-D shape did we make?** *A cube.*

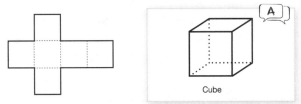

Repeat with the rest of the nets. Have your child first predict which printed 3-D shape the net will become. Then, fold and tape the net to create a 3-D shape and find the matching shape in part A.

> Making predictions about the nets helps build your child's spatial skills. Don't worry if she has trouble visualizing the final 3-D shape. She'll study nets and 3-D shapes more in older grades.

Activity (B): Identify Faces, Edges, and Vertices in 3-D Shapes

We use faces, edges, and vertices to identify 3-D shapes. Place the cube on the table. *Faces* **are the sides of a 3-D shape. The squares in the net became the faces of this cube. Try to count the faces of the cube without touching it. How many faces do you count?** *Answers may vary. 6 is the correct number.* If your child's answer is incorrect, don't tell her the correct answer yet.

> Counting the number of faces (or edges or vertices) without touching the shape develops your child's ability to distinguish the different parts of 3-D shapes. It also encourages her to count the parts in an organized way.

Let's check your prediction. Use a highlighter or wide marker to make a dot in the middle of each face of the cube. Count as you make each dot: **1, 2, 3, 4, 5, 6. The cube has 6 faces.** Write 6 in the chart.

	Faces	Edges	Vertices
Cube	6		

Edges **are the lines where the faces meet. Try to count the edges of the cube without touching it. How many edges do you count?** *Answers may vary. 12 is the correct number.*

Let's check your prediction. Use a highlighter or wide marker to highlight the middle of each edge of the cube. Count as you highlight each edge: **1, 2, 3, ..., 12. The cube has 12 edges.** Write 12 in the chart.

	Faces	Edges	Vertices
Cube	6	12	

A *vertex* **is a point where two or more edges meet. You can think of them as the corners of the shape. When we have more than one vertex, we call them vertices.**

Try to count the vertices of the cube without touching it. How many vertices do you count? *Answers may vary. 8 is the correct number.*

> The word vertex comes from Latin. The unusual ending of vertices is due to the way Latin changes noun endings to make them plural. Vertices is pronounced VUR-tuh-seez.

Let's check your prediction. Use a highlighter or wide marker to draw a dot on each vertex of the cube. Count as you draw each dot: **1, 2, 3, …, 8. The cube has 8 vertices.** Write 8 in the chart.

	Faces	Edges	Vertices
Cube	6	12	8

Repeat with the rest of the 3-D shapes listed in the chart. Have your child predict the number of faces, edges, and vertices without touching the shape. Then, have her use the highlighter or marker to mark and count the actual number of faces, edges, or vertices.

	Faces	Edges	Vertices
Cube	6	12	8
Rectangular prism	6	12	8
Triangular prism	5	9	6
Pyramid	5	8	5

Believe it or not, there's a lot of controversy in math over how to count cylinders' and cones' faces and edges! Some fields of math require faces to be flat and edges to be straight, while others allow for curved faces and edges. It depends on the context and the specific use for the mathematical properties in question.

Your child will learn to calculate the surface area of 3-D solids in older grades. For now, she simply needs to understand that 2-D nets can be assembled to create cones and cylinders. If your child is interested in finding the number of faces, edges, and vertices for the cylinder and cone, discuss the question both ways:

- For the cylinder: **If we count curved faces and curved edges, the cylinder has 3 faces and 2 edges. If we only count flat faces and straight edges, the cylinder has 2 faces and 0 edges.**
- For the cone: **If we count curved faces and curved edges, the cone has 2 faces. The circle around the base of the cone is 1 continuous edge. If we only count flat faces and straight edges, the cone has 1 face and 0 edges.**

Independent Practice and Review

Have your child complete the Lesson 13.5 Practice and Review workbook pages.

Lesson 13.6
Enrichment (Optional)

Purpose	Materials
• Practice memory work • Describe and reason about shapes with both informal language and formal geometric vocabulary • Make a suncatcher craft with a variety of quadrilaterals • Summarize what your child has learned and assess your child's progress	• *Which One Doesn't Belong? Playing with Shapes,* by Christopher Danielson • Contact paper (self-adhesive, clear vinyl) • Black construction paper • Tissue paper in assorted colors

As with all enrichment activities, feel free to adjust this activity based on the materials you have available.

- If you don't have contact paper, you can use wax paper for the base of the suncatcher instead. Mix 2 parts glue with 1 part water. Brush a thin layer onto the wax paper before your child adds the construction paper strips and tissue paper pieces. After your child finishes adding tissue paper, brush another thin layer onto the back of the piece.
- If you don't have black construction paper and tissue paper, make quadrilateral chalk art instead. Help your child use masking tape to create a grid of lines on the pavement. Color in the resulting spaces with chalk and remove the masking tape to show your design.

Warm-up: Review Memory Work

Quiz your child on all memory work through Unit 13. See pages 527-528 for the full list.

Math Picture Book: *Which One Doesn't Belong? Playing with Shapes*

Read *Which One Doesn't Belong? Playing with Shapes,* by Christopher Danielson. As you discuss which shapes don't belong, encourage your child to use both informal language and the geometric vocabulary he learned in this unit to explain his thinking.

Enrichment Activity: Make a Quadrilateral Suncatcher

Today, we'll make a suncatcher with quadrilaterals and other shapes!

Cut a large rectangle out of a piece of black construction paper. Leave the outside edges of the paper intact to create a frame. Cut the inner rectangle into long, thin strips.

Cut a piece of contact paper twice as large as the construction paper frame. Peel the back off half the contact paper and place the frame on the sticky half of the contact paper.

Have your child arrange 6 - 8 of the black construction paper strips across the frame. Have him place each strip so that it reaches all the way from one edge of the frame to another edge. Encourage him to arrange the strips to create a variety of different shapes. Cut off any ends that overhang the frame.

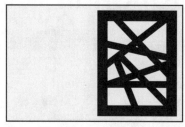

Tear tissue paper into small pieces and have your child stick them to the contact paper. (It's fine for the pieces to overlap each other and the black paper strips.) Have him continue until he fills the entire frame with tissue paper.

Trim off the overhanging ends of the tissue paper. Peel off the back of the rest of the contact paper and fold it over the back of the project. Cut off any extra contact paper and hang the suncatcher in a sunny window.

Unit Wrap-up (Optional)

Have your child complete the Unit 13 Wrap-up.

You do not need to save the paper pentominoes after your child completes the Unit Wrap-up.

Unit 13 Answer Key

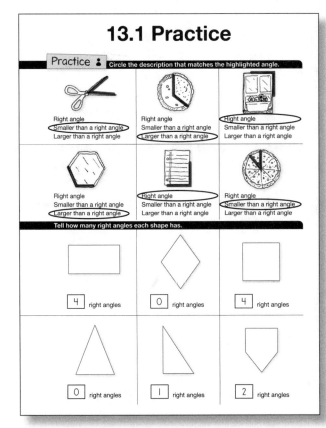

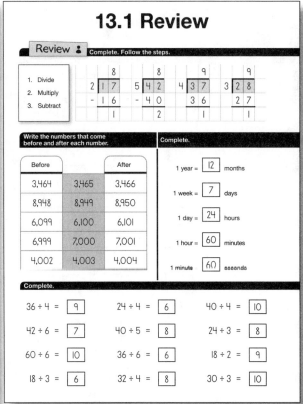

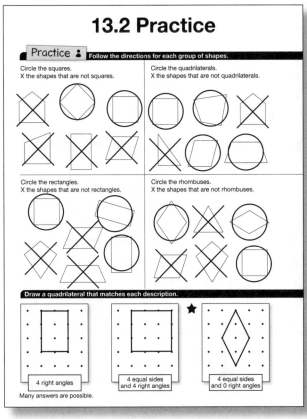

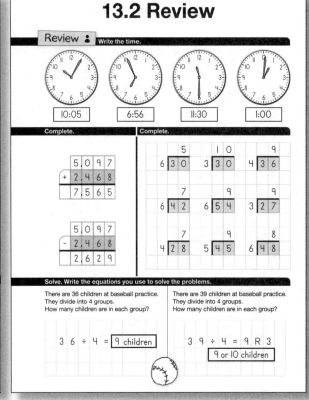

Unit 13 Answer Key

13.3 Practice

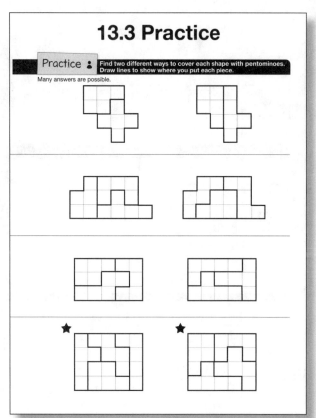

13.3 Review

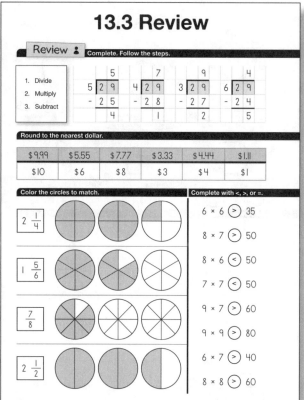

13.4 Practice

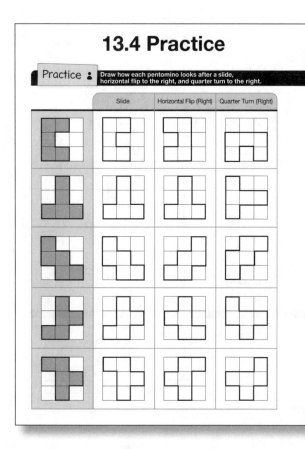

13.4 Review

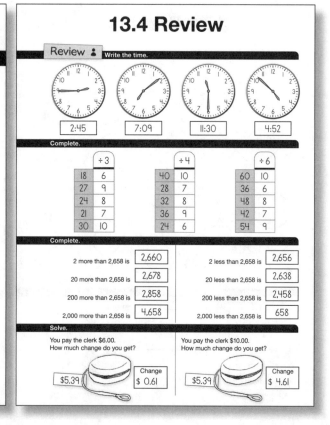

Unit 13 Answer Key

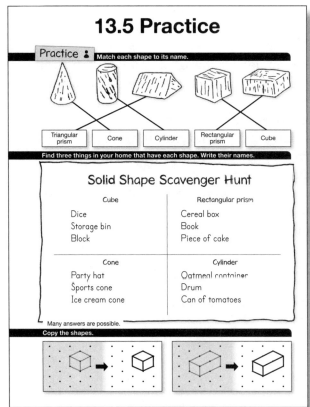

13.5 Practice

Practice 👤 Match each shape to its name.

Triangular prism | Cone | Cylinder | Rectangular prism | Cube

Find three things in your home that have each shape. Write their names.

Solid Shape Scavenger Hunt

Cube	Rectangular prism
Dice	Cereal box
Storage bin	Book
Block	Piece of cake

Cone	Cylinder
Party hat	Oatmeal container
Sports cone	Drum
Ice cream cone	Can of tomatoes

Many answers are possible.

Copy the shapes.

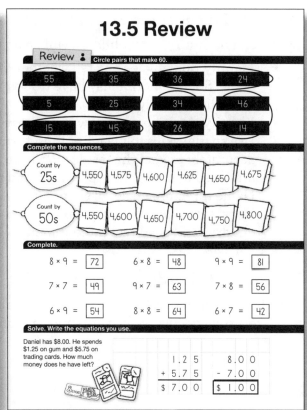

13.5 Review

Review 👤 Circle pairs that make 60.

55	35	36	24
5	25	34	46
15	45	26	14

Complete the sequences.

Count by 25s: 4,550 | 4,575 | 4,600 | 4,625 | 4,650 | 4,675

Count by 50s: 4,550 | 4,600 | 4,650 | 4,700 | 4,750 | 4,800

Complete.

$8 \times 9 =$ 72 $6 \times 8 =$ 48 $9 \times 9 =$ 81

$7 \times 7 =$ 49 $9 \times 7 =$ 63 $7 \times 8 =$ 56

$6 \times 9 =$ 54 $8 \times 8 =$ 64 $6 \times 7 =$ 42

Solve. Write the equations you use.

Daniel has $8.00. He spends $1.25 on gum and $5.75 on trading cards. How much money does he have left?

```
  1 . 2 5        8 . 0 0
+ 5 . 7 5      - 7 . 0 0
$ 7 . 0 0      $ 1 . 0 0
```

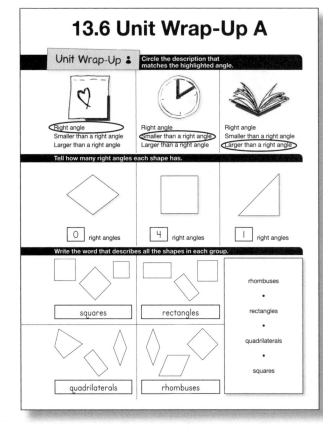

13.6 Unit Wrap-Up A

Unit Wrap-Up 👤 Circle the description that matches the highlighted angle.

Right angle
Smaller than a right angle
Larger than a right angle

Right angle
Smaller than a right angle
Larger than a right angle

Right angle
Smaller than a right angle
Larger than a right angle

Tell how many right angles each shape has.

0 right angles   4 right angles   1 right angles

Write the word that describes all the shapes in each group.

squares   rectangles

• rhombuses
• rectangles
• quadrilaterals
• squares

quadrilaterals   rhombuses

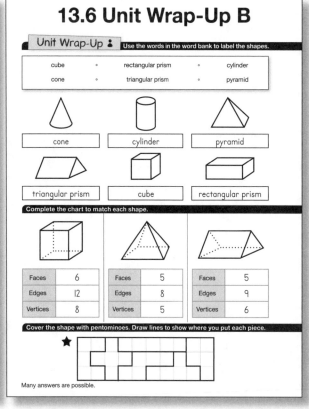

13.6 Unit Wrap-Up B

Unit Wrap-Up 👤 Use the words in the word bank to label the shapes.

| cube | ∘ | rectangular prism | ∘ | cylinder |
| cone | ∘ | triangular prism | ∘ | pyramid |

cone   cylinder   pyramid

triangular prism   cube   rectangular prism

Complete the chart to match each shape.

Faces	6		Faces	5		Faces	5
Edges	12		Edges	8		Edges	9
Vertices	8		Vertices	5		Vertices	6

Cover the shape with pentominoes. Draw lines to show where you put each piece.

★

Many answers are possible.

Unit 13 Checkpoint

What to Expect at the End of Unit 13

By the end of Unit 13, most children will be able to do the following:

- Identify right angles and tell whether other angles are larger or smaller than a right angle. Some children may have trouble identifying right angles if one side is not oriented horizontally.
- Identify, describe, and draw squares, rectangles, and rhombuses.
- Use spatial skills to visualize flips, turns, and slides. Some children will be able to accurately predict the results of flips, turns, and slides. Others will struggle with this and need to model the flips, turns, and slides concretely.
- Name three-dimensional shapes (cones, cubes, cylinders, rectangular prisms, triangular prisms, and pyramids). Understand and identify faces, edges, and vertices. Some children will need real three-dimensional shapes in order to identify faces, edges, and vertices.

Is Your Child Ready to Move on?

In Unit 14, your child will learn to calculate elapsed time. Your child does not need to have mastered any specific skills before moving on to Unit 14.

Unit 14
Elapsed Time

Overview

Your child will learn how to solve problems that involve elapsed time. He'll first turn the hands on a clock to solve these problems, and then he'll progress to solving them mentally or with timeline sketches.

What Your Child Will Learn

In this unit, your child will learn to:

- Review telling time to the minute
- Describe times with *past* or *to*
- Find times that are a certain number of minutes before or after a given time
- Find the number of minutes that elapse between two times
- Find times that are a certain number of hours and minutes before or after a given time
- Find the number of hours and minutes that elapse between two times
- Find how much time has elapsed before or after midnight or noon
- Solve elapsed time word problems

Lesson List

Lesson 14.1 Review Telling Time
Lesson 14.2 Minutes Past and To the Hour
Lesson 14.3 Elapsed Time with Minutes, Part 1
Lesson 14.4 Elapsed Time with Minutes, Part 2
Lesson 14.5 Elapsed Time with Hours and Minutes

Lesson 14.6 Times Before and After Noon or Midnight
Lesson 14.7 Elapsed Time Across Noon or Midnight
Lesson 14.8 Elapsed Time Word Problems
Lesson 14.9 Enrichment (Optional)

Extra Materials Needed for Unit 14

- For optional Enrichment Lesson:
    - *How Do You Know What Time It Is?*, written and illustrated by Robert E. Wells. Albert Whitman & Company, 2002.
    - Paper plate
    - Pencil
    - Tape, optional

You will also need a clock with hands for this unit. Your clock should have:

- Clear, easy-to-read numbers (no Roman numerals!)
- Tick marks along the edge for each minute
- Hands your child can easily move.

If your family's clocks don't meet these criteria, you may want to buy an inexpensive, geared teaching clock (sometimes called a "Judy clock") to make these lessons easier to teach.

Teaching Math with Confidence: Using Real Clocks, Mental Math, and Timeline Sketches to Teach Elapsed Time

In *Second Grade Math with Confidence*, you taught your child to tell time to the minute. This year, he will learn to solve problems about elapsed time. Although there is a written algorithm for calculating elapsed time, it's rarely used in real life. You've probably never pulled out a piece of paper to figure out when the movie will be over or when you need to leave to get to gymnastics on time! Instead, you will teach your child to solve elapsed time problems mentally. Just as with other mental math topics, you'll start with concrete, hands-on methods before you introduce more abstract techniques.

First, you'll model elapsed time directly on a clock. Your child will physically turn the hands of the clock so that he concretely understands the structure of these problems. For example, when he moves the minute hand from 1:20 to 1:35, he'll be able to see that the minute hand moves through 15 minutes on the clock.

Start Time	End Time	Number of Minutes
1:20	1:35	15

Next, you'll introduce him to mental strategies for solving simple elapsed time problems. He'll imagine jumping forward or backward on the clock, and he'll learn how to add or subtract small numbers of minutes or hours.

Once your child becomes comfortable with the concept of elapsed time and solving simple problems in his head, you'll teach him to draw timeline sketches to model and solve more complex problems. Timeline sketches are like number lines, but they show times rather than numbers. They allow your child to see all the relevant information at a glance, and they help him keep track of his thinking as he works through each problem.

For example, in Lesson 14.8, your child will find how much time elapses between 12:50 p.m. and 2:40 p.m. You'll demonstrate how to draw a timeline sketch like the following to organize the information. Then, your child will use the sketch to keep track of his thinking as he solves the problem. For example: *12:50 to 1:50 is 1 hour. 1:50 to 2:00 is 10 minutes, and 2:00 to 2:40 is 40 minutes. So, there's a total of 1 hour 50 minutes between these two times.*

The baby naps from 12:50 p.m. until 2:40 p.m. How long does the baby nap?

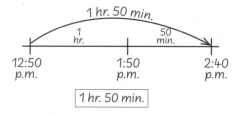

Children often find elapsed time a very challenging skill. As you move through this unit, adjust the level of support based on your child's needs. Allow him to use whichever method makes the most sense to him as he solves elapsed time problems.

Lesson 14.1
Review Telling Time

Purpose	Materials
• Review how to tell time to the minute • Find times that are earlier or later than a given time	• Clock

Memory Work	• **How many minutes equal a half-hour?** *30.* • **How many minutes equal a quarter-hour?** *15.*

If your child can confidently tell time to the minute, have her label the minutes on the printed clock in part A. Then, skip the rest of the activity and move on to part B.

Warm-up (A): Review Telling Time to the Minute

We're beginning a new unit on time today. In this unit, you'll learn how to find how long an activity lasts, or how to find its start time or end time. Today, we'll review how to tell time so you're ready to solve more complicated problems.

Show your child the printed clock in part A. **Which hand is the hour hand?** *Child points to shorter hand.* **Which hour is the minute hand?** *Child points to longer hand.* **What time does this clock show?** *7:00.*

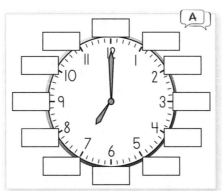

The minute hand tells us how many minutes have passed since the start of the hour. When the minute hand points to the 12, it is zero minutes past the hour. Write :00 in the blank above the 12.

The printed numbers tell how many groups of 5 minutes have passed since the start of the hour. Earlier in the year, you learned that you can multiply the printed number by 5 to find out how many minutes have passed since the start of the hour. Have your child count by 5s (or multiply the printed numbers by 5) to label the minutes on the clock.

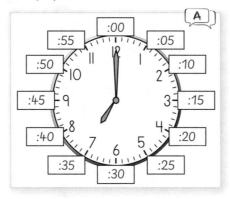

Point to the tick mark on the printed clock for 4 minutes past the hour. **When the minute hand points to this tick mark, how many minutes have passed since the start of the hour? 4. How do you know?** *Sample answers: It's 4 tick marks past the start of the hour. It's 1 tick mark before 5 minutes.* Then, have your child identify the tick marks on the printed clock for 13, 29, 46 and 58 minutes past the hour.

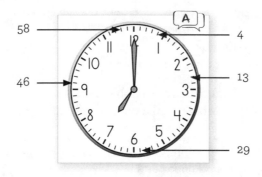

If your child struggles to identify the tick marks, encourage her to think of the clock as a number line wrapped around the edge of the clock. For example: **On the number line, 13 is 3 tick marks after 10. This tick mark is 3 tick marks after 10 minutes, so it must be 13 minutes past the hour.**

Show your child a real clock and have her identify the hour hand and minute hand. Set the clock to the following times and have your child tell each time.

- 1:15
- 1:14
- 2:40
- 2:38
- 3:55

- 4:00
- 5:05
- 5:07
- 5:59

If your child struggles to identify the hour, encourage her to think of each hour as "owning" part of the clock. For example, for 2:40, lightly shade the part of the clock between the 2 and the 3. **The 2 o'clock hour owns this part of the clock. If the hour hand is in this area, the hour is 2.**

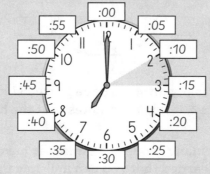

Activity (B): Find Times that are Earlier or Later Than a Given Time

Let's pretend we're assistants at a science museum. The director started to fill out the schedule for the live demonstrations, and now it's our job to finish it. Briefly read the name of each demonstration and discuss your child's experiences with live demonstrations or science museums.

The first tornado vortex demonstration each morning is at 9:25. Set a clock for 9:25. **The next one is 5 minutes later.** Have your child turn the clock forward 5 minutes. **What time is 5 minutes later than 9:25?** *9:30.* Write 9:30 in the chart. Fill the rest of the morning slots in the same way.

The last tornado vortex demonstration each afternoon is at 3:05. Set a clock for 3:05. **The second-to-last tornado vortex demonstration is 5 minutes earlier.** Have your child turn the clock backward 5 minutes. **What time is 5 minutes earlier than 3:05?** *3:00.* Write 3:00 in the chart. Fill the rest of the afternoon slots in the same way.

Repeat with the lightning demonstration schedule. Set the clock to each printed time and then have your child move the hands either 10 minutes forward or 10 minutes backward to complete the charts.

Lightning every 10 min.	Morning	10:40	10:50	11:00	11:10
	Afternoon	1:50	2:00	2:10	2:20

For the chemistry morning schedule, say: **We want to find the time that is 30 minutes later than 9:20. 30 minutes is half of an hour. When half an hour passes, the minute hand moves half of the way around the clock. So, you can just turn the minute hand halfway around the clock to find the time that's 30 minutes later.** Have your child move the minute hand halfway around the clock to find the time 30 minutes later than 9:20. Have her find the rest of the morning times in the same way.

If your child has trouble remembering the minute hand's starting position, place a small sticky note or piece of tape at the starting position before she moves the minute hand.

For the chemistry afternoon schedule, set the clock to 1:30. Have your child turn the minute hand backward halfway around the clock to find each time.

For the reptile talk morning schedule, say: **We want to find the time that is 15 minutes later than 10:45. 15 minutes is one-quarter of an hour, or one-fourth of an hour. When a quarter hour passes, the minute hand moves one-fourth of the way around the clock. So, you can just turn the minute hand one-fourth of the way around the clock to find the time that's 15 minutes later.** Have your child move the minute hand one-fourth of the way around the clock to find the time 15 minutes later than 10:45. Have her find the rest of the morning times in the same way.

For the reptile talk afternoon schedule, set the clock to 4:30. Have your child turn the minute hand backward one-fourth of the way around the clock to find each time.

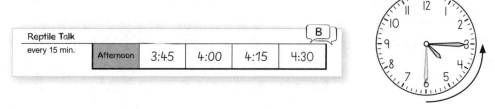

Independent Practice and Review

Have your child complete the Lesson 14.1 Practice and Review workbook pages. Your child may model the problems on a real clock as needed.

Lesson 14.2
Minutes Past and To the Hour

Purpose	Materials
• Review telling time • Use *past* and *to* to describe times • Identify the number of minutes before or after the hour	• Clock

Memory Work	• **How many hours are in a day?** *24.* • **How many minutes are in an hour?** *60.* • **How many seconds are in a minute?** *60.*

In this lesson, your child will learn to identify the number of minutes before or after the hour and tell time with phrases like *quarter past 6* or *twenty to 10*. Knowing the number of minutes before or after the hour is an essential stepping-stone for solving elapsed time problems. Your child will build on this skill as he solves more complex problems throughout the rest of the unit.

Warm-up: Practice Telling Time

Set the clock to the following times and have your child tell each time.

- 3:58
- 4:02
- 5:05

- 4:55
- 6:52
- 7:01

Children often have trouble telling the hour when the hour hand is just before or after the start of an hour. If your child has trouble with these tricky times, encourage him to consider the minute hand's position as he finds the hour. For example, for 3:58: **The minute hand isn't back to the top of the clock, so the new hour hasn't started yet. The hour hand must be just before the new hour, too.**

Activity (A): Describe Times with *To* and *Past*

In the last lesson, we reviewed how to tell time. You also found times that were earlier or later than a given time. Today, you'll learn how to use the words *to* and *past* to tell time.

Show your child part A. Set a clock to 9:00. **Turn the minute hand 5 minutes past 9:00.** *Child sets clock to 9:05.* **What time does the clock show now?** *9:05.* **People sometimes call 9:05 *5 past 9*, since it's 5 minutes after 9 o'clock.** *Write 9:05 in the chart.*

Turn the minute hand so that the clock shows 10 past 9. *Child sets clock to 9:10.* **What time does the clock show now?** *9:10.* Write 9:10 in the chart.

Set the clock to 9:15. **When the minute hand travels from 9:00 to 9:15, it travels one-fourth or one-quarter of the way around the clock. 9:15 is called** *quarter past 9,* **because it's a quarter of an hour after 9 o'clock.** Write 9:15 in the chart. Repeat with 20 past 9 and 25 past 9.

	A
quarter past 9	9:15
20 past 9	9:20
25 past 9	9:25

Set the clock to 9:30. **When the minute hand travels from 9:00 to 9:30, it travels halfway around the clock. 9:30 is called** *half past 9,* **because it's half an hour after 9 o'clock.** Write 9:30 in the chart.

	A
half past 9	9:30

We use *past* **to describe times up to 30 minutes past the hour. We use** *to* **for times that are less than 30 minutes before the next hour.**

The next time in the chart is *25 to 10.* **This means 25 minutes before 10 o'clock.** Set the clock to 10:00. **Turn the minute hand 25 minutes before 10 o'clock.** *Child sets clock to 9:35.* **What time does the clock show now?** *9:35.* Write 9:35 in the chart.

Continue in the same way for the rest of the times in the chart. For 9:45, say: **9:45 is called** *quarter to 10,* **because it's a quarter of an hour before 10 o'clock.**

	A
25 to 10	9:35
20 to 10	9:40
quarter to 10	9:45
10 to 10	9:50
5 to 10	9:55
10 o'clock	10:00

Activity (B): Time Riddles

I'm going to describe these times with words like *past* and *to.* Set the clock to the time I describe. Then, find the time on the page. I'll only use each time once, so cross off each time after you use it.

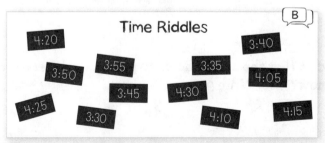

Time Riddles

4:20 3:50 3:55 3:45 4:25 3:30 3:35 4:30 4:10 3:40 4:05 4:15

Setting the clock to match each time previews using the clock to solve elapsed time problems. Your child will learn more about elapsed time with minutes in Lessons 14.3 and 14.4.

- **Half past 4.** *4:30.*
- **Half past 3.** *3:30.*
- **Quarter past 4.** *4:15.*
- **Quarter to 4.** *3:45.*
- **5 past 4.** *4:05.*
- **5 to 4.** *3:55.*
- **20 to 4.** *3:40.*
- **20 past 4.** *4:20.*
- **10 past 4.** *4:10.*
- **25 past 4.** *4:25.*
- **10 to 4.** *3:50.*
- **25 to 4.** *3:35.*

Independent Practice and Review

Have your child complete the Lesson 14.2 Practice and Review workbook pages. Your child may model the problems on a real clock as needed.

Lesson 14.3
Elapsed Time with Minutes, Part 1

Purpose	Materials
• Practice telling time with *to* or *past* • Find times that are a certain number of minutes later than a given time • Find the number of minutes that elapse between two times	• Clock • Die

Memory Work	• **What do we call an angle that looks like the corner of a piece of paper?** *A right angle.*

Elapsed time problems have 3 components: start time, end time, and amount of time that elapses between these two times. If you know any two of these components, you can use them to find the other missing component. In this lesson, your child will learn to find end times and elapsed times. She'll learn to find start times in Lesson 14.4.

Warm-up: Practice Telling Time with *To* or *Past*

In the last lesson, you learned how to identify times before and after the hour. Set a clock to the following times. Have your child first tell each time using hours and minutes. Then, have her tell the time using *to* or *past*.

- 8:10. *Eight ten. 10 past 8.*
- 8:15. *Eight fifteen. Quarter past 8.*
- 8:20. *Eight twenty. 20 past 8.*
- 8:30. *Eight thirty. Half past 8.*

- 8:35. *Eight thirty-five. 25 to 9.*
- 8:45. *Eight forty-five. Quarter to 9.*
- 8:55. *Eight fifty-five. 5 to 9.*
- 9:05. *Nine oh five. 5 past 9.*

Activity (A): Solve Elapsed Time Problems in a Piano Practice Log

Today, you'll begin to solve problems about elapsed time. Elapsed time is the time that passes between when you start doing something and stop doing something. Briefly discuss several recent examples when you calculated the start time or end time for an event, or when you calculated the elapsed time for an activity. For example: **I had to figure out when we should leave for the doctor so that we would get to the appointment on time. When I make soup, I look at the cooking time in the recipe to figure out when it will be ready.**

Show your child the piano practice log in part A. **Eleanor's piano teacher asks her to fill out a practice log every time she practices. This log shows how much she practiced over two weeks. She wrote down most of the information, but she forgot to complete every part of the chart. We'll fill it in.** Briefly discuss any experience your child has with completing practice logs for a sport or instrument.

Day	Start Time	End Time	Number of Minutes
Monday	2:20		20

Eleanor's Piano Practice Log

This lesson assumes that all times in the piano practice log are daytime hours. You'll teach your child to find elapsed time with a.m. and p.m. in Lessons 14.6 and 14.7.

On Monday, Eleanor started practicing at 2:20. Set a clock to 2:20. **She practiced for 20 minutes. Let's count by 5s to find when she stopped practicing.** Show your child how to start at 2:20 and count by 5s: **5, 10, 15, 20. What time did she stop practicing?** *2:40.* Write 2:40 in the blank.

Day	Start Time	End Time	Number of Minutes
Monday	2:20	2:40	20

Jumping forward 20 minutes on the clock is like adding 20 minutes. She started practicing at 20 minutes past the hour, and she practiced for 20 minutes. 20 plus 20 equals 40, so she stopped practicing 40 minutes past the hour.

20 + 20 = 40.

Use the following questions to help your child complete the practice log for Tuesday, Thursday, and Sunday.

- For Tuesday: **She started practicing at 35 minutes past the hour, and she practiced for 25 minutes. What's 35 plus 25?** *60.* **60 minutes equal 1 hour, so she must have stopped practicing at the end of the hour.**

Tuesday	1:35	2:00	25

- For Thursday: **What's 55 plus 15?** *70.* **Hours only have 60 minutes, so we can't just add the minutes to find when she stopped practicing! Instead, let's make two jumps. First, let's jump 5 minutes from 3:55 to 4:00. Then, let's jump 10 more minutes past 4. What time is 10 minutes past 4?** *4:10.*

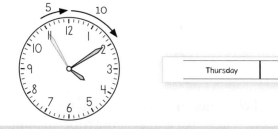

Thursday	3:55	4:10	15

Jumping forward twice is similar to the way your child learned to mentally add in two steps in Unit 1.

- For Sunday: **She practiced a whole hour! The minute hand turns all the way around the clock in one hour.** Set the clock to 11:30 and have your child turn the minute hand forward 1 full circle around the clock. **What time did she stop?** *12:30.* **11:30 and 12:30 are 1 hour apart. They have the same minutes, but different hours.**

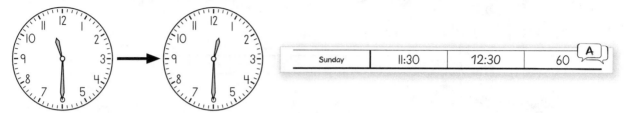

The next Monday, Eleanor started practicing at 1:20. Set a clock to 1:20. **She stopped practicing at 1:35. Where will the minute hand point when she's done practicing at 1:35?** *Child points to the 7.* Have your child continue pointing to the 7 while you demonstrate how to count by 5s from 1:20 to 1:35: **5, 10, 15. 15 minutes pass from 1:20 to 1:35.** Write 15 in the blank.

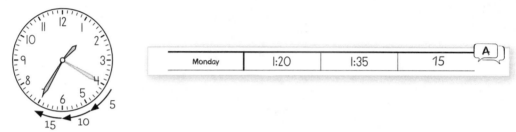

When two times have the same hour, you can subtract to find the difference between the minutes. Eleanor started practicing at 20 minutes past the hour, and she stopped practicing at 35 minutes past the same hour. The difference between 35 and 20 is 15, so there's 15 minutes between the two times.

35 minus 20 equals 15.

Use the following questions to help your child complete the practice log for Wednesday, Friday, and Saturday.

- For Wednesday: **2:40 is 20 minutes to 3. So, 20 minutes elapse between 2:40 and 3 o'clock.**

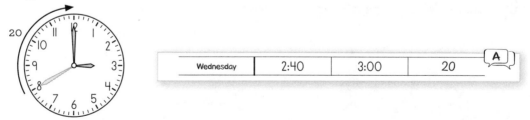

- For Friday: **Let's make two jumps to find how much time passes between 2:40 and 3:05. 20 minutes elapse from 2:40 to 3:00. 5 minutes elapse from 3:00 to 3:05. 20 plus 5 equals 25, so she practiced for 25 minutes.**

| | Friday | 2:40 | 3:05 | 25 | A |

- For Saturday: **12:45 and 1:45 have the same minutes but different hours. That means there's a whole number of hours between them.** Set the clock to 12:45 and show your child how you turn the minute hand 1 full circle around the clock to reach 1:45. **I turned the minute hand 1 full circle around the clock. 1 hour passes between 12:45 and 1:45, so she practiced for 60 minutes.**

| | Saturday | 12:45 | 1:45 | 60 | A |

Activity (B): Play Race to 2:00

Play Race to 2:00.

The game directions suggest that your child use a clock to model the times on her scorecard. She may find the new times mentally if she prefers. If you have two clocks, you may model your time on a clock as well.

Race to 2:00

Materials: Die; clock

Object of the Game: Be the first player to reach 2:00.

Both players start with 12:00 on their scorecards. On your turn, roll the die and find the corresponding number of minutes on the game board. Add the number of minutes to the time on your scorecard and record your new time on your scorecard.

When your child plays, have her model the times with a real clock. Set the clock to 12:00 before her first turn, and then have her move the minute hand on the clock forward by that number of minutes she rolls. For example, if your child rolls a 4 on her first turn, have her move the clock forward 20 minutes to 12:20 and write 12:20 on her scorecard.

■ = 20 minutes

| Player 1 | B |
| 12:00 |
| 12:20 |

Take turns rolling the die, finding your new time, and recording your new time. Continue until one player reaches 2:00 or goes past 2:00.

Independent Practice and Review

Have your child complete the Lesson 14.3 Practice and Review workbook pages. Your child may model the problems on a real clock as needed.

Lesson 14.4
Elapsed Time with Minutes, Part 2

Purpose	Materials
• Practice counting backwards with time intervals • Find times that are a certain number of minutes earlier than a given time	• Clock • Die

Memory Work
- **What do we call a quadrilateral with 4 right angles?** *A rectangle.*
- **What do we call a quadrilateral with 4 right angles and 4 equal sides?** *A square.*

In the previous lesson, your child learned to find end times and elapsed times. In this lesson, he'll work backward to find start times.

Warm-up: Count Backwards with the Clock

Have your child count backwards from each of the following times. Use a real clock to model each time, and have your child turn the clock's hands to match each time as he says it.

- Set a clock to 5:45. **Count backwards by 5 minutes, from 5:45 to 4:45.** *5:45, 5:40, 5:35...*
- Set a clock to 4:45. **Count backwards by 10 minutes, from 4:45 to 3:45.** *4:45, 4:35, 4:25...*
- Set a clock to 3:45. **Count backwards by 30 minutes, from 3:45 to 1:45.** *3:45, 3:15, 2:45...*

Activity (A): Find When to Leave for Family Activities

Show your child part A. **This family has a busy week! They made a list of their plans. They wrote down when they need to arrive at each activity and how long it takes to get to each activity. Let's figure out when they need to leave for each activity so that they arrive on time.**

The first activity is gymnastics. They need to arrive at 2:30. Set a clock to 2:30. **The drive takes 20 minutes. So, let's count backward by 5s to find when they need to leave for gymnastics.** Show your child how to start at 2:30 and count backward by 5s: **5, 10, 15, 20. What time do they need to leave for gymnastics?** *2:10.* Write 2:10 in the blank.

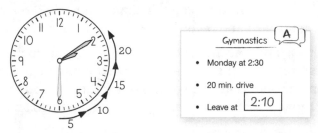

Jumping backward 20 minutes on the clock is like subtracting 20 minutes. They need to arrive at gymnastics at 30 minutes past the hour, and the drive takes 20 minutes. 30 minus 20 equals 10, so they need to leave at 10 minutes past the hour.

$30 - 20 = 10.$

Use these questions to help your child complete the rest of the blanks in part A.

- For library story hour: **They need to arrive at 10:00, and it takes 15 minutes to bike to the library. What time is 15 minutes to 10?** *9:45.*

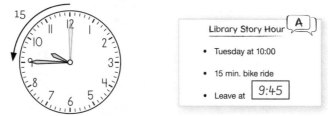

- For the dentist appointment: **They need to arrive at 11:10, and it takes 25 minutes to drive to the dentist. Let's jump backward twice to find when they need to leave. First, let's jump 10 minutes from 11:10 to 11:00. Then, let's jump backward 15 more minutes. What time is 15 minutes to 11?** *10:45.*

- For visiting Aunt Claire: **It takes a whole hour to get to Aunt Claire's house, and they want to arrive at 1:30.** Set the clock to 1:30 and have your child turn the minute hand backward 1 full circle around the clock. **What time is an hour earlier than 1:30?** *12:30.* **1:30 and 12:30 are 1 hour apart. They have the same minutes, but different hours.**

- For the park play date: **They need to arrive at the park at 1:15, and it takes 20 minutes to walk. Let's jump backward twice to find when they need to leave. First, let's jump 15 minutes from 1:15 to 1:00. Then, let's jump backward 5 more minutes. What time is 5 minutes to 1?** *12:55.*

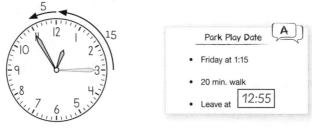

For the final blank space on the calendar, choose one of your family's activities. Write the name of the activity, when the activity occurs, and how long it takes to get to the activity. (Round the times to the nearest 5 minutes.) Have your child figure out when you need to leave in order to arrive on time.

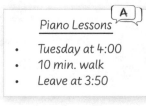

Piano Lessons

- *Tuesday at 4:00*
- *10 min. walk*
- *Leave at 3:50*

Sample activity.

Activity (B): Play Race to 12:00

Play Race to 12:00.

Race to 12:00 is the same as Race to 2:00, but in reverse.

Race to 12:00

Materials: Die; clock

Object of the Game: Be the first player to reach 12:00.

Both players start with 2:00 on their scorecards. On your turn, roll the die and find the corresponding number of minutes on the game board. Subtract the number of minutes from 2:00 and record your new time on your scorecard.

When your child plays, have him model the times with a real clock. Set the clock to 2:00 before his first turn, and then have him move the minute hand on the clock backward by the number of minutes he rolls.

For example, if he rolls a 4 on his first turn, he moves the clock backward 20 minutes to 1:40 and writes 1:40 on the scorecard.

= 20 minutes

Player 1
2:00
1:40

Sample first turn if your child rolls a 4.

Take turns rolling the die, finding your new time, and recording your new time. Continue until one player reaches 12:00 or goes past 12:00.

Independent Practice and Review

Have your child complete the Lesson 14.4 Practice and Review workbook pages. Your child may model the problems on a real clock as needed.

Lesson 14.5
Elapsed Time with Hours and Minutes

Purpose	Materials
• Practice multiplication facts • Find times that are a certain number of hours and minutes later than a given time • Find the number of hours and minutes that elapse between two times	• Playing cards • Counters

Memory Work
- **What do we call a quadrilateral with 4 equal sides?** *A rhombus.*
- **What do we call a quadrilateral with 4 right angles and 4 equal sides?** *A square.*

Warm-up (A): Play Multiplication Undercover (×8)

Use the game boards in part A to play Multiplication Undercover. Use the same general directions as in Lesson 4.5. Multiply the number on your card by 8, say the matching multiplication fact, and remove the counter from the matching square on your game board.

Activity (B): Make a Day Camp Schedule

In the last two lessons, you solved elapsed time problems with minutes. Today, you'll learn how to solve elapsed time problems with hours and minutes.

The camp director is making the schedule for the day. We'll help him fill in the rest of the schedule. Briefly discuss any experience your child has with day camp or the activities on the schedule.

Camp starts at 8:00 in the morning. Set a clock to 8:00. **Outdoor skills lasts for 1 hour and 10 minutes, so it will end 1 hour and 10 minutes later than 8:00.**

Jumping forward 1 hour and 10 minutes is like adding 1 hour and 10 minutes. First, let's add the hours. What time is 1 hour after 8:00? *9:00.* Have your child turn the minute hand forward 1 hour.

Now, let's add the minutes. What time is 10 minutes after 9:00? *9:10.* Have your child turn the minute hand forward 10 minutes more.

Adding the hours and minutes separately is similar to the way your child learned to add the tens and ones separately when she solved mental addition problems in Unit 1.

Outdoor skills ends at 9:10, so Capture the Flag will begin at 9:10. Write 9:10 as the end time for Outdoor Skills and the start time for Capture the Flag.

Have your child turn the hands on the clock to complete the rest of the day camp schedule. Encourage her to first add the hours and then add the minutes for each activity.

Activity	Start Time	End Time
Outdoor Skills (1 hr. 10 min.)	8:00	9:10
Capture the Flag (1 hr. 15 min.)	9:10	10:25
Hike (1 hr. 45 min.)	10:25	12:10
Lunch and Sing-along (50 min.)	12:10	1:00
Afternoon Choice Time (3 hr. 30 min.)	1:00	4:30

B

Activity (B): Find Elapsed Time for Camp Activities

Show your child the list of activity choices in part B. **In the afternoons, the campers get to choose which activities they want to do. They can choose more than one activity each day, but each activity is only available at certain times.** Briefly discuss which activities your child would like to choose from the list.

Swimming starts at 1:00 and goes until 4:00. Set a clock to 1:00. **The hour hand will point to the 4 at the end of swimming. How many hours pass from 1:00 to 4:00?** *3 hours.* If your child isn't sure, point out that the hour hand goes through 3 hours from 1:00 to 4:00. Write "3 hr." in the blank.

Have your child check her answer by turning the clock's hands until they reach 4:00. Have her count how many full circles the minute hand makes as she turns the hands.

Activity	Start Time	End Time	Length of Activity
Swimming	1:00	4:00	3 hr.

B

You could also subtract to find the difference between the hours. What's 4 minus 1? *3.* **There are 3 hours between 1 o'clock and 4 o'clock.**

> Subtracting to find the difference doesn't work if one time is a.m. and the other time is p.m. Your child will learn how to calculate times that involve a.m. or p.m. in Lessons 14.6 and 14.7.

Use the following questions to guide your child as she finds the length of each activity in the chart. Use a clock to model the questions.

- For canoeing: **2:30 and 4:30 have the same minutes, so they must be a whole number of hours apart.** Set the clock to 2:30 and have your child turn the clock's hands until they reach 4:30. **How many hours pass from 2:30 to 4:30?** *2.*

| Canoeing | 2:30 | 4:30 | 2 hr. |

- For archery: **Archery goes from 2:00 to 3:40. How many hours pass from 2:00 to 3:00?** *1 hour.* **How many minutes pass from 3:00 to 3:40?** *40 minutes.* **So, 1 hour and 40 minutes pass from 2:00 to 3:40.**

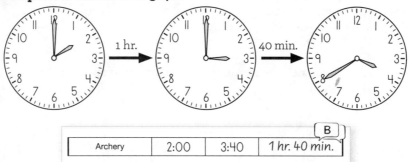

| Archery | 2:00 | 3:40 | *1 hr. 40 min.* |

- For crafts: **Crafts are available from 1:30 to 2:45. How many hours pass from 1:30 to 2:30?** *1 hour.* **How many minutes pass from 2:30 to 2:45?** *15 minutes.* **So, 1 hour and 15 minutes pass from 1:30 to 2:45.**

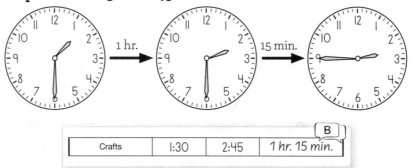

| Crafts | 1:30 | 2:45 | *1 hr. 15 min.* |

- For rock climbing: **Rock climbing is open from 2:45 to 4:25. How many hours pass from 2:45 to 3:45?** *1 hour.* **How many minutes pass from 3:45 to 4:25?** *40 minutes.* **So, 1 hour and 40 minutes pass from 2:45 to 4:25.**

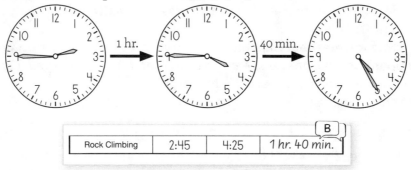

| Rock Climbing | 2:45 | 4:25 | *1 hr. 40 min.* |

Independent Practice and Review

Have your child complete the Lesson 14.5 Practice and Review workbook pages. Your child may model the problems on a real clock as needed.

Lesson 14.6
Times Before and After Noon or Midnight

Purpose	Materials
• Review noon, midnight, a.m., and p.m. • Find how much time has elapsed before or after noon or midnight	• None

Memory Work	• **What do we call the result when we multiply two numbers?** *The product.* • **What do we call the result when we divide two numbers?** *The quotient.*

In this lesson, you'll teach your child how to find the amount of time before or after noon or midnight. This will prepare him to solve elapsed time problems that cross noon or midnight in Lessons 14.7 and 14.8.

Warm-up (A): Review Noon, Midnight, A.M, and P.M.

This timeline shows one day. Each day is divided into 24 hours.

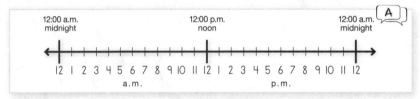

Use the following questions to review midnight, noon, a.m., and p.m.:

- **Each day begins at 12:00 a.m., or midnight. What are you usually doing at midnight?** *Sleeping!* Point to midnight on the timeline.
- **We use a.m. for times before noon. What are some things you usually do before noon?** *Sample answers: Wake up. Eat breakfast. Have my math lesson.* Have your child identify the approximate location for each event on the timeline.
- **12 o'clock p.m. is the middle of the day. We also call it noon. What do you usually do at noon?** *Sample answers: Eat lunch. Finish my spelling workbook. Play outside.* Point to noon on the timeline.
- **We use p.m. for times that happen after noon. What are some things you usually do after noon?** *Sample answers: Make a craft. Eat dinner. Go to bed.* Have him identify the approximate location for each event on the timeline.
- **The next day begins at midnight, at 12:00 a.m.** Point to midnight on the timeline.

Activity (B): Find Elapsed Time Before Midnight

New Year's Eve is on December 31st each year. The new year starts at midnight, at 12:00 a.m. Have you ever stayed up until midnight on New Year's Eve? Briefly discuss how your family celebrates New Year's Eve.

Show your child the first chart in part B. **Let's pretend it's New Year's Eve! It's 7:00 p.m. and you want to know how many hours it is until midnight. We'll use the timeline in part A to help figure it out.**

Point to the 7 on the right-hand half of the timeline in part A. Count the spaces between 7 and 12 on the timeline: **1, 2, 3, 4, 5. There are 5 hours between 7 and 12. Write "5 hr." in the chart.**

The timeline from part A is enlarged for clarity.

If your child counts the tick marks (rather than the spaces between them), point out that the tick marks simply indicate one specific time. Each space between a pair of tick marks is the hour that passes between those two times.

You could also subtract to find the difference. What's 12 minus 7? *5.* **So, there are 5 hours between midnight and 7:00 p.m.**

How many hours pass between 8:00 p.m. and midnight? *4.* Your child may count hours on the timeline or subtract to find the answer. Write "4 hr." in the chart.

The next one is a little trickier! We want to know how long it is from 8:30 p.m. to 12:00 midnight. About where on the timeline would 8:30 go? *Child points to approximate position shown below.* **Let's find the elapsed time in two jumps. How long is it from 8:30 to 9:00?** *30 minutes.* **How long is it from 9:00 to 12:00?** *3 hours.* **So, how long is it in all from 8:30 to 12:00?** *3 hours and 30 minutes.* **Write "3 hr. 30 min." in the chart.** Help your child use the timeline to complete the chart.

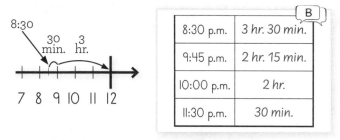

Activity (B): Find Elapsed Time After Midnight

Let's pretend it's midnight now. Happy New Year! Show your child the second chart in part B. **Let's pretend you stay up very late and want to know how long it has been since midnight.**

The new day starts at midnight. About where on the timeline would 12:30 a.m. go? *Child points to approximate position for 12:30.* **How long is it from 12:00 a.m. to 12:30 a.m.?** *30 minutes.* **Write "30 min." in the chart.**

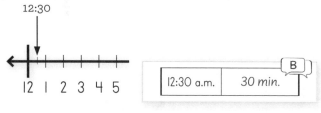

How many hours pass between 12:00 a.m. and 1:00 a.m.? *1.* Write "1 hr." in the chart.

How much time passes between 12:00 a.m. and 1:45 a.m.? *1 hour and 45 minutes.* If your child isn't sure, say: **We just found that 1 hour passes from 12:00 a.m. to 1:00 a.m. How many minutes pass from 1:00 a.m. to 1:45 a.m.?** *45.* **So, 1 hour and 45 minutes pass from 12:00 a.m. to 1:45 a.m.** Write "1 hr. 45 min." in the chart.

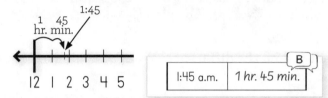

Complete the rest of the chart in the same way. Once you finish, ask: **What relationship do you notice between the times and the number of hours and minutes past midnight?** *Sample answer: Except for 12:30, the hours and minutes for each time tells how much time has passed since midnight.*

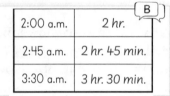

Independent Practice and Review

Have your child complete the Lesson 14.6 Practice and Review workbook pages. Your child may model the problems on a real clock as needed.

Lesson 14.7
Elapsed Time Across Noon or Midnight

Purpose	Materials
• Practice finding elapsed time before or after noon • Understand that elapsed time problems have three components: start time, end time, and elapsed time • Use timeline sketches to solve elapsed time problems with hours and minutes	• Clock

Memory Work	• **What do we call the number to be divided?** *The dividend.* • **What do we call the number we divide by?** *The divisor.* • **What do we call an amount that is left over after division?** *The remainder.*

You'll teach your child to draw timeline sketches to solve elapsed time problems in this lesson. See the Unit 14 **Teaching Math with Confidence** for an introduction to this helpful tool.

Warm-up (A): Tell Times Before and After Noon

In the last lesson, we used a timeline to find how long it was until midnight or how long it had been since midnight. You can use the same kind of thinking to find how long it is before noon or after noon. Ask your child the following questions. Point to each time on the timeline in part A as you say it.

- **1:00 p.m. is how many hours after noon?** *1 hour.*
- **3:00 p.m. is how many hours after noon?** *3 hours.*
- **4:00 p.m. is how many hours after noon?** *4 hours.*
- **6:00 p.m. is how many hours after noon?** *6 hours.*
- **11:00 a.m. is how many hours before noon?** *1 hour.*
- **10:00 a.m. is how many hours before noon?** *2 hours.*
- **8:00 a.m. is how many hours before noon?** *4 hours.*
- **6:00 a.m. is how many hours before noon?** *6 hours.*

Activity (B): Draw Timeline Sketches to Complete a Volunteer Log

The animal shelter asks volunteers to record how long they spend helping at the shelter. The volunteers write down when they start, when they end, and how long they spend at the shelter. Briefly discuss your child's experiences with animal shelters or volunteering.

Some of the volunteers forgot to complete every part of the chart, so we'll help fill it in. Elapsed time problems have three parts: the start time, the end time, and how much time elapses between the start time and end time. We'll use timeline sketches to organize the information and solve the problems.

The first volunteer started at 11:00 a.m. and volunteered for 2 hours and 45 minutes. We know the start time and elapsed time. We want to find the end time. Show your child the first timeline sketch in part B.

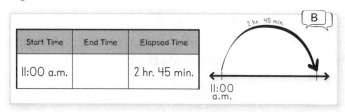

First, let's add the hours. What time is 2 hours after 11:00 a.m.? *1:00 p.m.* If your child isn't sure, have her use the timeline in part A to figure it out. Draw a tick mark and label the tick mark "1:00 p.m." Write "2 hr." above the timeline as shown.

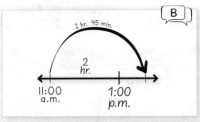

Try to draw the tick mark roughly where it would go if all the times on the timeline were marked. But, don't worry about putting the tick mark in the exact right spot. The main goal is to keep track of your problem-solving process, not to draw a perfectly proportioned timeline.

Now, let's add the minutes. Write "45 min." above the timeline as shown. **What time is 45 minutes after 1:00 p.m.?** *1:45 p.m.* Label the final tick mark "1:45 p.m." **So, 2 hours and 45 minutes after 11:00 a.m. is 1:45 p.m. That's when the volunteer left.** Write "1:45 p.m." in the chart.

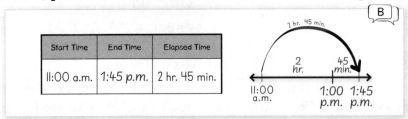

If your child finds the timeline sketch confusing, model the problem on a clock as well. Set the clock to 11:00 and have your child turn the hands forward 2 hours and 45 minutes. As she turns the hands, discuss how the hands match the timeline sketch: **After you turn the hands forward 2 hours, the clock is at 1:00. When you turn the hands forward another 45 minutes, the clock is at 1:45.**

The next volunteer started at 11:30 a.m. and left at 2:00 p.m. We know the start time and end time, and we want to find the elapsed time.

Let's find the elapsed time in two jumps. Draw a tick mark on the timeline as shown. Label it "12:00 p.m." **How long is it from 11:30 a.m. to 12:00 p.m.?** *30 minutes.* Write "30 min." above the timeline as shown.

How long is it from noon to 2:00 p.m.? *2 hours.* Write "2 hr." above the timeline as shown.

So, how much time passes in all from 11:30 a.m. to 2:00 p.m.? *2 hours and 30 minutes.* Draw an arrow as shown. Label the arrow "2 hr. 30 min." **The volunteer stayed for 2 hours and 30 minutes.** Write "2 hr. 30 min." in the chart.

The third volunteer stayed for 2 hours and 15 minutes and left at 3:45. We know the end time and elapsed time. We want to find the start time.

First, let's subtract the hours. What time is 2 hours before 3:45 p.m.? *1:45 p.m.* Draw a tick mark as shown. Label the tick mark "1:45 p.m." Write "2 hr." above the timeline as shown.

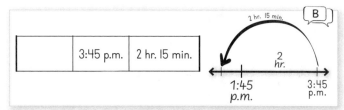

Now, let's subtract the minutes. Write "15 min." above the timeline as shown. **What time is 15 minutes before 1:45 p.m.?** *1:30 p.m.* Label the leftmost tick mark "1:30 p.m." **So, 2 hours and 15 minutes before 3:45 p.m. is 1:30 p.m. That's when the volunteer arrived.** Write "1:30 p.m." in the chart.

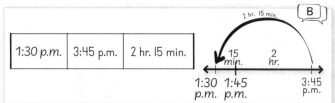

Have your child complete the rest of the chart in the same way. As you work:

- Make sure to have her identify what she is looking for in each problem before solving: **Are you trying to find the start time, end time, or elapsed time?**
- Help your child draw a timeline sketch for each problem on scrap paper. Sample sketches are shown below, but your child may also make different jumps on the time-lines as she solves the problems. She may also take more than 2 jumps.
- If your child is confused by the timeline sketches or struggles with a problem, model the problem on a clock as well.
- If your child grasps the problems quickly and can solve them mentally, don't require her to draw a timeline sketch for every problem.

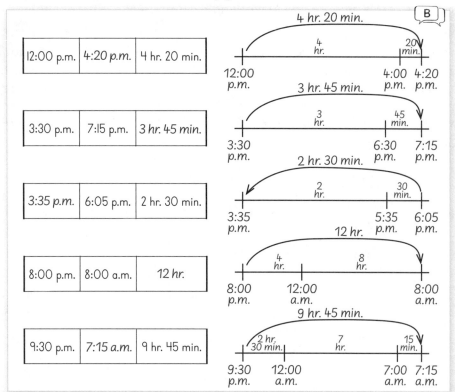

Independent Practice and Review

Have your child complete the Lesson 14.7 Practice and Review workbook pages. Your child may model the problems on a real clock as needed.

Lesson 14.8
Elapsed Time Word Problems

Purpose	Materials
• Practice finding elapsed time with hours and minutes • Use timeline sketches to organize information in word problems and solve	• Counters

Memory Work
- **What is another name for 12 a.m.?** *Midnight.*
- **What is another name for 12 p.m.?** *Noon.*

Warm-up (A): Elapsed Time Tic-Tac-Toe

Play Elapsed Time Tic-Tac-Toe. Your child may solve the problems mentally or draw timeline sketches on scrap paper.

Elapsed Time Tic-Tac-Toe

Materials: Counters of two different colors each

Object of the Game: Be the first player to fill 3 boxes in a row, either horizontally, vertically, or diagonally.

Place a counter on 7:30 and a counter on 10:00. (These counters may be any color.) Give 8 counters of one color to one player and 8 counters of a different color to the other player.

On your turn, move one of the counters on the Start or End chart. (You do not have to move a counter, but you may only move one. It must stay on the same chart.) Calculate the elapsed time between the two times covered on the chart. For example, if one counter is on 7:45 and the other counter is on 10:30, the elapsed time is 2 hours 45 minutes. Use one of your counters to cover the box with 2 hours 45 minutes on the tic-tac-toe board.

Start	End
7:00	9:30
7:15	9:45
7:30	10:00
7:45	10:15
8:00	10:30
8:15	10:45

All times are a.m.

2 hr. 45 min.	3 hr. 15 min.	1 hr. 30 min.	2 hr. 30 min.
3 hr.	2 hr.	2 hr. 45 min.	3 hr. 30 min.
2 hr. 30 min.	1 hr. 45 min.	2 hr.	1 hr. 15 min.
3 hr. 45 min.	2 hr. 15 min.	3 hr.	2 hr. 15 min.

Sample play.

Play then passes to the other player. Continue until one player covers 3 boxes in a row on the tic-tac-toe board, either horizontally, vertically, or diagonally.

Activity (B): Solve Time Word Problems

In the last lesson, you used timeline sketches to complete a volunteer log. Today, you'll use timeline sketches to organize the information in word problems and solve them.

Do you remember the three parts of time problems? *Start time, end time, and elapsed time.* If your child can't remember, have him look back at the volunteer log in Lesson 14.7. **Time word problems are a lot easier if you look for these three parts before you try to solve them.**

Have your child read aloud the first word problem. **What times does the problem mention?** *1:45 p.m. and 2 hours and 20 minutes.* Have your child underline both times in the printed problem.

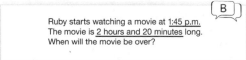

Is 1:45 p.m. the start time, end time, or elapsed time? *Start time.* **Is 2 hours and 20 minutes the start time, end time, or elapsed time?** *Elapsed time.*

What are we trying to find out? *When the movie will be over.* **Is that the start time, end time, or elapsed time?** *End time.*

Let's draw a timeline sketch to match the problem. Draw a horizontal line in the blank space next to the problem. **What's the start time?** *1:45 p.m* Draw a tick mark as shown and label it "1:45 p.m."

What's the elapsed time? *2 hours and 20 minutes.* Draw an arrow as shown and label it "2 hr. 20 min." Draw a tick mark at the end of the arrow. **Our goal is to find the end time.**

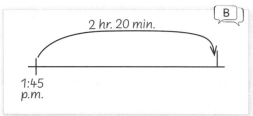

Have your child use the timeline sketch to find the end time. If he's not sure how to start, suggest he add the hours first, and then the minutes. **So, when will the movie be over?** *4:05 p.m.* Write "4:05 p.m." and draw a box around it.

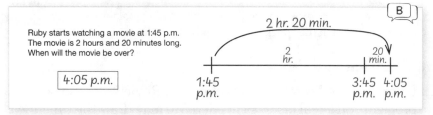

Sample timeline sketch. It's fine if your child chooses to break the elapsed time into different jumps than shown.

Have your child solve the other word problems in the same way. Make sure he underlines the important information and identifies what he's trying to find before he starts solving each problem.

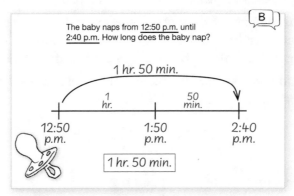

In this problem, you know the start time and end time. Your goal is to find the elapsed time.

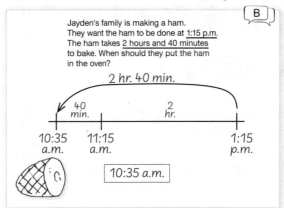

In this problem, you know the end time and elapsed time. Your goal is to find the start time.

Your child may draw the timeline sketches on scrap paper if he needs more room.

If your child can easily solve these problems mentally, he does not need to draw the matching timeline sketches. If he has trouble understanding how to draw the sketches, have him turn the hands on a real clock to solve the problems instead. Draw timeline sketches to match his problem-solving process so that he begins to see the connection between the concrete clock and more abstract timeline sketches.

Independent Practice and Review

Have your child complete the Lesson 14.8 Practice and Review workbook pages. Your child may model the problems on a real clock as needed. He may draw the timeline sketches on scrap paper if he needs more room.

Lesson 14.9
Enrichment (Optional)

Purpose	Materials
• Practice memory work • Understand that time-keeping has become more precise throughout history • Make a sundial • Summarize what your child has learned and assess your child's progress	• *How Do You Know What Time It Is?*, written and illustrated by Robert E. Wells • Paper plate • Pencil • Tape, optional

Warm-up: Review Memory Work

Quiz your child on all memory work through Unit 14. See pages 527-528 for the full list.

Math Picture Book: *How Do You Know What Time It Is?*

Read *How Do You Know What Time It Is?*, written and illustrated by Robert E. Wells. As you read, discuss the different tools that people have used throughout history to measure time. Discuss how life would be different if you didn't have clocks that can measure to the minute or second.

Enrichment Activity: Make a Sundial

To make your sundial, you'll need a day where you expect it to be sunny for at least several hours. If possible, begin this activity in the morning so that you can mark most of the hours before it gets dark. If you start later in the day, you can continue recording hours the next morning.

People in ancient times used sundials to tell the times. Sundials weren't as accurate as our clocks, but they gave people a general idea of what time it was.

Have your child mark a dot on the bottom of a paper plate, directly in the center. Help your child poke a pencil through the plate at this spot, from the top side of the plate to the bottom side. If your pencil is wobbly, secure it with a few pieces of tape.

We can use the pencil's shadow to make a sundial. Place the sundial outside in a sunny spot where you can leave it for several hours. At the beginning of every hour, trace the pencil's shadow and label the hour. Repeat for as many hours as you have sunlight.

The next day, place the sundial in the same spot and facing the same direction. Periodically have your child look at the sundial's shadow and estimate the time. Then, compare the estimate to a real clock.

It looks like it's about 10:30.

Unit Wrap-up (Optional)

Have your child complete the Unit 14 Wrap-up. Your child may draw the timeline sketches on scrap paper if she needs more room.

Unit 14 Answer Key

14.1 Practice

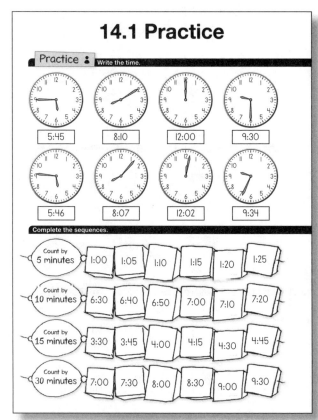

Practice 👤 **Write the time.**

5:45	8:10	12:00	9:30
5:46	8:07	12:02	9:34

Complete the sequences.

Count by 5 minutes: 1:00, 1:05, 1:10, 1:15, 1:20, 1:25

Count by 10 minutes: 6:30, 6:40, 6:50, 7:00, 7:10, 7:20

Count by 15 minutes: 3:30, 3:45, 4:00, 4:15, 4:30, 4:45

Count by 30 minutes: 7:00, 7:30, 8:00, 8:30, 9:00, 9:30

14.1 Review

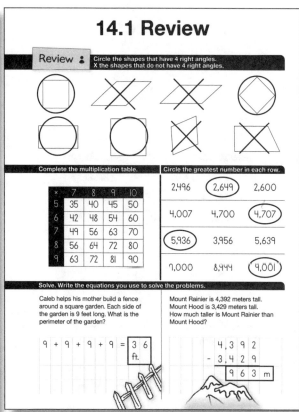

Review 👤 **Circle the shapes that have 4 right angles. X the shapes that do not have 4 right angles.**

Complete the multiplication table.

×	7	8	9	10
5	35	40	45	50
6	42	48	54	60
7	49	56	63	70
8	56	64	72	80
9	63	72	81	90

Circle the greatest number in each row.

2,496	(2,649)	2,600
4,007	4,700	(4,707)
(5,936)	3,956	5,639
1,000	8,444	(4,001)

Solve. Write the equations you use to solve the problems.

Caleb helps his mother build a fence around a square garden. Each side of the garden is 9 feet long. What is the perimeter of the garden?

$9 + 9 + 9 + 9 = $ 36 ft.

Mount Rainier is 4,392 meters tall. Mount Hood is 3,429 meters tall. How much taller is Mount Rainier than Mount Hood?

```
  4,3 9 2
- 3,4 2 9
  9 6 3  m
```

14.2 Practice

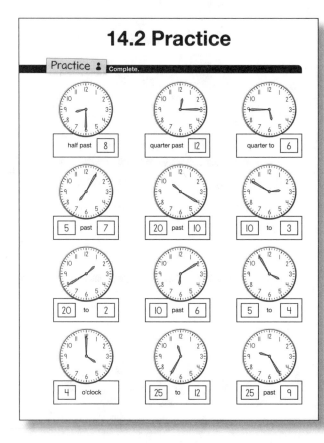

Practice 👤 **Complete.**

half past 8	quarter past 12	quarter to 6
5 past 7	20 past 10	10 to 3
20 to 2	10 past 6	5 to 4
4 o'clock	25 to 12	25 past 9

14.2 Review

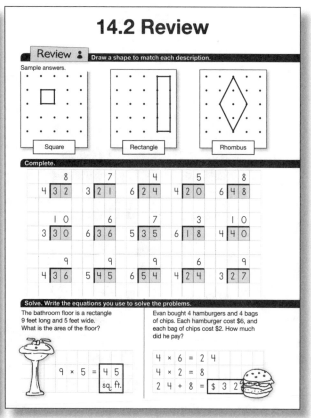

Review 👤 **Draw a shape to match each description.**

Sample answers.

Square	Rectangle	Rhombus

Complete.

8	7	4	5	8
4 [3 2]	3 [2 1]	6 [2 4]	4 [2 0]	6 [4 8]

10	6	7	3	10
3 [3 0]	6 [3 6]	5 [3 5]	6 [1 8]	4 [4 0]

9	9	9	6	9
4 [3 6]	5 [4 5]	6 [5 4]	4 [2 4]	3 [2 7]

Solve. Write the equations you use to solve the problems.

The bathroom floor is a rectangle 9 feet long and 5 feet wide. What is the area of the floor?

$9 \times 5 = $ 45 sq. ft.

Evan bought 4 hamburgers and 4 bags of chips. Each hamburger cost $6, and each bag of chips cost $2. How much did he pay?

$4 \times 6 = 24$
$4 \times 2 = 8$
$24 + 8 = $ $32

Unit 14 Answer Key

14.3 Practice

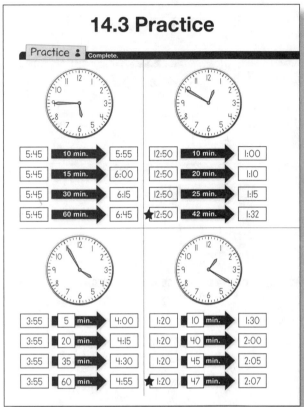

14.3 Review

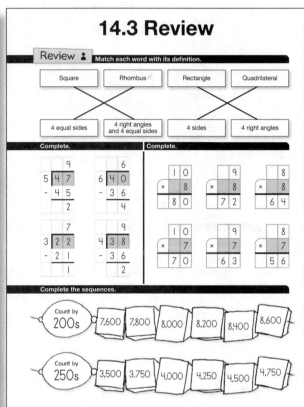

14.4 Practice

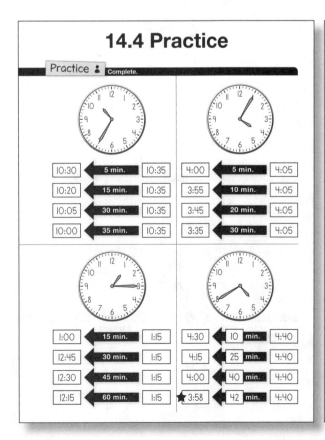

14.4 Review

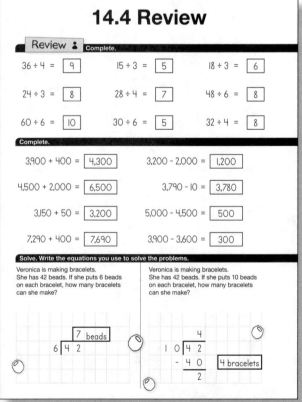

Unit 14 Answer Key

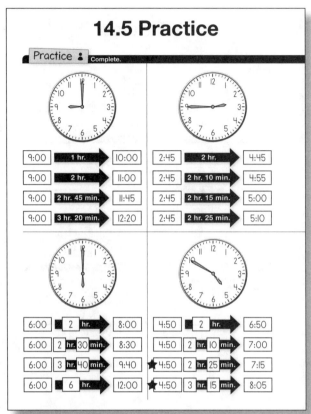

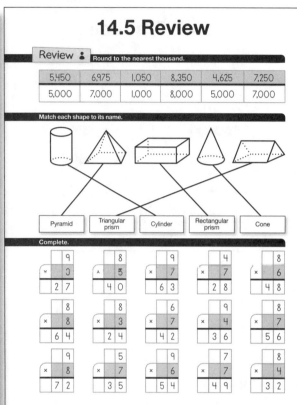

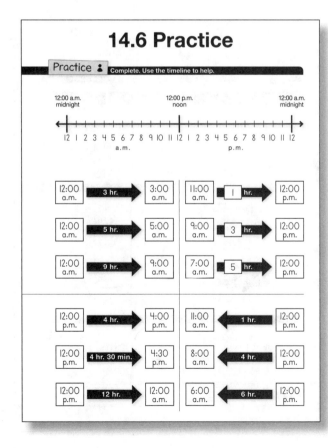

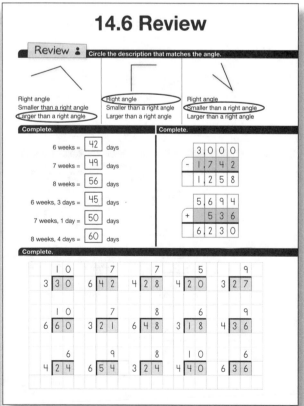

Unit 14 Answer Key

14.7 Practice

Practice 🙎 Complete. Use the timelines to help.

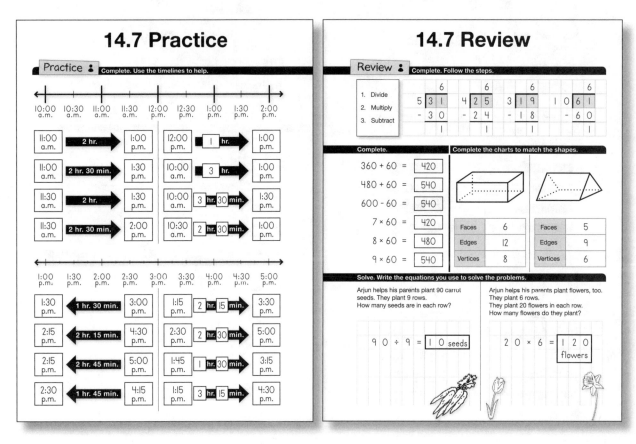

10:00 10:30 11:00 11:30 12:00 12:30 1:00 1:30 2:00
a.m. a.m. a.m. a.m. p.m. p.m. p.m. p.m. p.m.

11:00 a.m.	→ 2 hr. →	1:00 p.m.		12:00 p.m.	1 hr. →	1:00 p.m.
11:00 a.m.	→ 2 hr. 30 min. →	1:30 p.m.		10:00 a.m.	3 hr. →	1:00 p.m.
11:30 a.m.	→ 2 hr. →	1:30 p.m.		10:00 a.m.	3 hr. 30 min. →	1:30 p.m.
11:30 a.m.	→ 2 hr. 30 min. →	2:00 p.m.		10:30 a.m.	2 hr. 30 min. →	1:00 p.m.

1:00 1:30 2:00 2:30 3:00 3:30 4:00 4:30 5:00
p.m. p.m. p.m. p.m. p.m. p.m. p.m. p.m. p.m.

1:30 p.m.	← 1 hr. 30 min.	3:00 p.m.		1:15 p.m.	← 2 hr. 15 min.	3:30 p.m.
2:15 p.m.	← 2 hr. 15 min.	4:30 p.m.		2:30 p.m.	← 2 hr. 30 min.	5:00 p.m.
2:15 p.m.	← 2 hr. 45 min.	5:00 p.m.		1:45 p.m.	← 1 hr. 30 min.	3:15 p.m.
2:30 p.m.	← 1 hr. 45 min.	4:15 p.m.		1:15 p.m.	← 3 hr. 15 min.	4:30 p.m.

14.7 Review

Review 🙎 Complete. Follow the steps.

1. Divide
2. Multiply
3. Subtract

	6			6			6			6
5	3 1		4	2 5		3	1 9		10	6 1
−	3 0		−	2 4		−	1 8		−	6 0
	1			1			1			1

Complete.

$360 + 60 = \boxed{420}$

$480 + 60 = \boxed{540}$

$600 - 60 = \boxed{540}$

$7 \times 60 = \boxed{420}$

$8 \times 60 = \boxed{480}$

$9 \times 60 = \boxed{540}$

Complete the charts to match the shapes.

Faces	6
Edges	12
Vertices	8

Faces	5
Edges	9
Vertices	6

Solve. Write the equations you use to solve the problems.

Arjun helps his parents plant 90 carrot seeds. They plant 9 rows. How many seeds are in each row?

$90 \div 9 = \boxed{1\ 0}$ seeds

Arjun helps his parents plant flowers, too. They plant 6 rows. They plant 20 flowers in each row. How many flowers do they plant?

$20 \times 6 = \boxed{1\ 2\ 0}$ flowers

14.8 Practice

Practice 🙎 Complete. Use the timeline sketches to help.

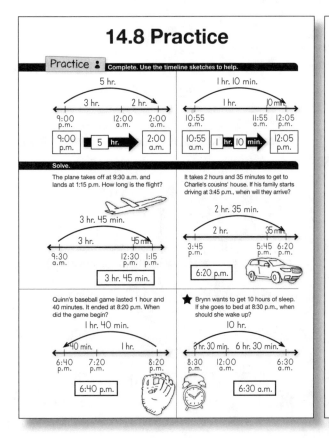

5 hr.
3 hr. / 2 hr.
9:00 p.m. 12:00 a.m. 2:00 a.m.

| 9:00 p.m. | → 5 hr. → | 2:00 a.m. |

1 hr. 10 min.
1 hr. / 10 min.
10:55 a.m. 11:55 a.m. 12:05 p.m.

| 10:55 a.m. | → 1 hr. 10 min. → | 12:05 p.m. |

Solve.

The plane takes off at 9:30 a.m. and lands at 1:15 p.m. How long is the flight?

3 hr. 45 min.
3 hr. / 45 min.
9:30 a.m. 12:30 p.m. 1:15 p.m.

| 3 hr. 45 min. |

It takes 2 hours and 35 minutes to get to Charlie's cousins' house. If his family starts driving at 3:45 p.m., when will they arrive?

2 hr. 35 min.
2 hr. / 35 min.
3:45 p.m. 5:45 p.m. 6:20 p.m.

| 6:20 p.m. |

Quinn's baseball game lasted 1 hour and 40 minutes. It ended at 8:20 p.m. When did the game begin?

1 hr. 40 min.
40 min. / 1 hr.
6:40 p.m. 7:20 p.m. 8:20 p.m.

| 6:40 p.m. |

⭐ Brynn wants to get 10 hours of sleep. If she goes to bed at 8:30 p.m., when should she wake up?

10 hr.
3 hr. 30 min. / 6 hr. 30 min.
8:30 p.m. 12:00 a.m. 6:30 a.m.

| 6:30 a.m. |

14.8 Review

Review 🙎 Use the numbers to complete the blanks. You will use each number once.

| 1 | 2 | 3 | 4 | 5 | 6 | 7 | 8 | 9 |

$\boxed{2} \times 7 = 14$ $7 \times \boxed{4} = 28$ $7 \times \boxed{7} = 49$

$\boxed{8} \times 7 = 56$ $7 \times \boxed{1} = 7$ $7 \times \boxed{3} = 21$

$\boxed{5} \times 7 = 35$ $7 \times \boxed{9} = 63$ $7 \times \boxed{6} = 42$

Complete.

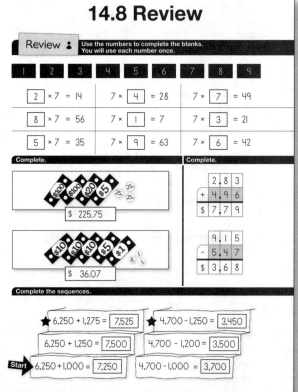

$100, $100, $20, $5, 25¢, 25¢, 25¢

$ 225.75

$10, $10, $10, $5, $1, 1¢, 1¢, 5¢

$ 36.07

Complete.

	2	8	3
+	4	9	6
$	7	7	9

	9	1	5
−	5	4	7
$	3	6	8

Complete the sequences.

★ $6,250 + 1,275 = \boxed{7,525}$ ★ $4,700 - 1,250 = \boxed{3,450}$

$6,250 + 1,250 = \boxed{7,500}$ $4,700 - 1,200 = \boxed{3,500}$

Start ▶ $6,250 + 1,000 = \boxed{7,250}$ $4,700 - 1,000 = \boxed{3,700}$

Unit 14 Answer Key

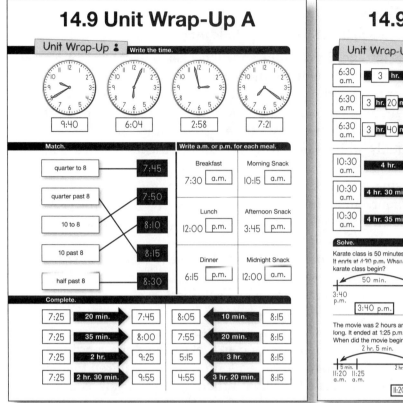

14.9 Unit Wrap-Up A

Unit Wrap-Up — Write the time.

9:40   6:04   2:58   7:21

Match.

quarter to 8 — 7:45
quarter past 8 — 7:50
10 to 8 — 8:10
10 past 8 — 8:15
half past 8 — 8:30

Write a.m. or p.m. for each meal.

Breakfast	Morning Snack
7:30 a.m.	10:15 a.m.

Lunch	Afternoon Snack
12:00 p.m.	3:45 p.m.

Dinner	Midnight Snack
6:15 p.m.	12:00 a.m.

Complete.

7:25 → 20 min. → 7:45   8:05 ← 10 min. ← 8:15
7:25 → 35 min. → 8:00   7:55 ← 20 min. ← 8:15
7:25 → 2 hr. → 9:25   5:15 ← 3 hr. ← 8:15
7:25 → 2 hr. 30 min. → 9:55   4:55 ← 3 hr. 20 min. ← 8:15

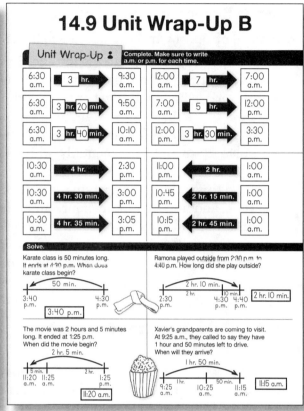

14.9 Unit Wrap-Up B

Unit Wrap-Up — Complete. Make sure to write a.m. or p.m. for each time.

6:30 a.m. → 3 hr. → 9:30 a.m.   12:00 a.m. → 7 hr. → 7:00 a.m.
6:30 a.m. → 3 hr. 20 min. → 9:50 a.m.   7:00 a.m. → 5 hr. → 12:00 p.m.
6:30 a.m. → 3 hr. 40 min. → 10:10 a.m.   12:00 p.m. → 3 hr. 30 min. → 3:30 p.m.

10:30 a.m. → 4 hr. → 2:30 p.m.   11:00 a.m. ← 2 hr. ← 1:00 p.m.
10:30 a.m. → 4 hr. 30 min. → 3:00 p.m.   10:45 a.m. ← 2 hr. 15 min. ← 1:00 a.m.
10:30 a.m. → 4 hr. 35 min. → 3:05 p.m.   10:15 a.m. ← 2 hr. 45 min. ← 1:00 a.m.

Solve.

Karate class is 50 minutes long. It ends at 4:30 p.m. When does karate class begin?

50 min.
3:40 p.m. ‿ 4:30 p.m.

3:40 p.m.

Ramona played outside from 2:30 p.m. to 4:40 p.m. How long did she play outside?

2 hr. 10 min.
2:30 p.m. — 2 hr. — 4:30 p.m. — 10 min. — 4:40 p.m.

2 hr. 10 min.

The movie was 2 hours and 5 minutes long. It ended at 1:25 p.m. When did the movie begin?

2 hr. 5 min.
11:20 a.m. — 5 min. — 11:25 a.m. — 2 hr. — 1:25 p.m.

11:20 a.m.

Xavier's grandparents are coming to visit. At 9:25 a.m., they called to say they have 1 hour and 50 minutes left to drive. When will they arrive?

1 hr. 50 min.
9:25 a.m. — 1 hr. — 10:25 a.m. — 50 min. — 11:15 a.m.

11:15 a.m.

Unit 14 Checkpoint

What to Expect at the End of Unit 14

By the end of Unit 14, most children will be able to do the following:

- Confidently tell time to the minute. Some children will occasionally have trouble telling the time when the minute hand is close to the top of the clock.
- Describe times with *past* or *to*, including *quarter past, quarter to,* or *half past.*
- Find times that are a certain number of minutes before or after a given time, and find the number of minutes that elapse between two times. Some children will be able to solve these problems mentally, while others will need to turn the hands on a clock to figure them out.
- Find times that are a certain number of hours and minutes before or after a given time, and find how many hours and minutes have elapsed between two times. Many children will need help drawing a timeline sketch and solving these problems, especially ones that involve crossing midnight or noon.
- Solve elapsed time word problems. Most children will be able to identify the three parts of elapsed time problems within these word problems, but some will need help translating this information to a timeline sketch and solving.

Is Your Child Ready to Move on?

In Unit 15, you will introduce your child to the ÷7, ÷8, and ÷9 facts. These challenging division facts (and their related multiplication facts) take a long time for children to master, and your child is not expected to become fully fluent with them in third grade. **It's fine to move on to Unit 15 even if your child doesn't immediately know the answers to the ×7, ×8, and ×9 facts yet.**

Unit 15
Division, Part 3

Overview

In Units 10 and 12, your child learned many of the division facts. In this unit, you'll introduce her to the remaining ÷7, ÷8, and ÷9 facts. You'll also teach her how to divide by 7 to convert days to weeks and how to use division to solve perimeter and area problems.

This unit is the final division unit in *Third Grade Math with Confidence*. **Your child is not expected to fully master all the division facts by the end of the year.** She'll continue to practice them throughout the rest of the year, and she'll review them thoroughly in *Fourth Grade Math with Confidence*. See the Unit 15 checkpoint for more details.

What Your Child Will Learn

In this unit, your child will learn to:

- Find answers for the ÷7, ÷8, and ÷9 facts
- Divide by 7 to convert days to weeks
- Use division to solve perimeter and area problems

Lesson List

Lesson 15.1	÷7 Facts	Lesson 15.5	÷9 Facts
Lesson 15.2	Convert Days to Weeks	Lesson 15.6	Divide Area to Find a Missing Side Length
Lesson 15.3	÷8 Facts		
Lesson 15.4	Divide Perimeter to Find Side Lengths	Lesson 15.7	Enrichment (Optional)

Extra Materials Needed for Unit 15

- Calendar, optional
- Yarn
- Scissors
- For optional Enrichment Lesson:
  - × *A Remainder of One*, written by Elinor Pinczes and illustrated by Bonnie MacKain
  - × Varies, depending on which activity you choose

Teaching Math with Confidence: Gradual Division Fact Mastery

Children often find the division facts much more difficult than the multiplication facts, especially the tricky ÷7, ÷8, and ÷ 9 facts in this unit. Some third-graders will readily master these challenging division facts, but others will need much more practice before they achieve full fluency. Consider this unit an introduction to the ÷7, ÷8, and ÷9 facts, and don't worry if your child doesn't fully master them by the end of the year. Even if she doesn't become fully fluent with the division facts now, the strategies and practice will prepare her to master the division facts thoroughly in fourth grade.

Lesson 15.1
÷7 Facts

Purpose	Materials
• Review ×7 facts • Practice ÷7 facts	• Dot array and L-cover (Blackline Master 5) • Counters • Die

Memory Work	• **Are times in the morning a.m. or p.m.?** *A.m.* • **Are times in the afternoon and evening a.m. or p.m.?** *P.m.*

Warm-up: Practice ×7 Facts

In Unit 8, you learned the ×7 facts. Today, you'll use the ×7 facts to find answers to the ÷7 facts. Do a brief oral review of the following ×7 facts. Encourage your child to respond as quickly as possible for each fact.

- 4 × 7 = 28
- 8 × 7 = 56
- 3 × 7 = 21
- 5 × 7 = 35

- 7 × 7 = 49
- 10 × 7 = 70
- 6 × 7 = 42
- 9 × 7 = 63

Activity (A): Introduce ÷7 Facts

Show your child part A. **Let's pretend you're making bunches of balloons for a party. You have 56 balloons, and you put 7 balloons in each bunch.**

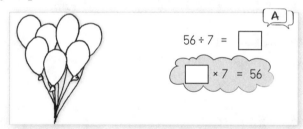

If your child immediately knows the answer to 56 ÷ 7, skip the following demonstration. Instead, ask her to pretend to be the teacher and explain to you how to use the dot array to find the answer.

56 divided by 7 means "How many groups of 7 equal 56?" We want to know what times 7 equals 56. Let's use the dot array to help find the answer. Slide the L-cover to show 5 rows of 7. **What's 5 times 7?** *35.* **Too low!**

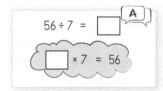

Let's add another 2 more groups of 7. Slide the L-cover to show 7 rows of 7. **What's 7 times 7?** *49.* **That's still too low, but it's closer.**

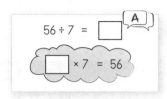

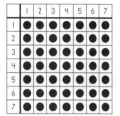

Let's add 1 more group of 7. Slide the L-cover to show 8 rows of 7. **What's 8 times 7?** *56.* **That's it! 8 times 7 equals 56, so 56 divided by 7 equals 8.** Write 8 in both blanks.

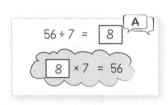

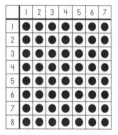

Have your child complete part A. Use the dot array to model the problems as needed.

14 ÷ 7 = 2	28 ÷ 7 = 4	35 ÷ 7 = 5
42 ÷ 7 = 6	7 ÷ 7 = 1	49 ÷ 7 = 7
21 ÷ 7 = 3	70 ÷ 7 = 10	63 ÷ 7 = 9

Activity (B): Play Dice Tic-Tac-Toe

Play Dice Tic-Tac-Toe. Have your child use the dot array as needed. See Lesson 4.6 (page 128) for directions.

Independent Practice and Review

Have your child complete the Lesson 15.1 Practice and Review workbook pages.

Lesson 15.2
Convert Days to Weeks

Purpose	Materials
• Practice ÷7 facts • Use the ÷7 facts to convert days to weeks	• Dot array and L-cover (Blackline Master 5), optional • Playing cards • Counters • Calendar, optional

Memory Work
- **What do we call the top number in a fraction?** *The numerator.*
- **What do we call the bottom number in a fraction?** *The denominator.*

Warm-up (A): Play Division Bingo (÷7)

In the last lesson, you worked on the ÷7 facts. Today, you'll practice these facts more and use them to convert days to weeks. Play Division Bingo (÷7).

If your child finds this game confusing, write a simple equation like the following on a piece of paper. Place the playing card in the quotient position. **We want to find the number that we can divide by 7 to equal 6. So, we multiply 7 times 6 to find that number.**

$$\square \div 7 = \boxed{6}$$

Division Bingo (÷7)

Materials: Deck of playing cards with jacks, queens, and kings removed (40 cards total); counters

Object of the Game: Be the first player to fill in an entire column, row, or diagonal.

Shuffle the cards and place the stack face down on the table. Have each player choose which game board to use.

Turn over the top card. Both players look for a dividend on their game board that equals the number on the card when you divide it by 7. Then, each player uses a counter to cover a square containing that dividend on their game board. For example, if the card is a 5, both players cover a 35, since 35 ÷ 7 = 5.

Continue until one player wins by filling an entire column, row, or diagonal.

Activity (B): Convert Days to Weeks

Show your child the first exercise in part B. **Let's pretend that you're planning to go to an exciting event in 28 days. What event should we pretend you're going to?** *Answers will vary.* **Let's find how many weeks away that is!**

1 week equals 7 days. So, we can divide 28 by 7 to find how many weeks equal 28 days. What's 28 divided by 7? *4.* **28 days equal 4 weeks.** Write 4 in both blanks. Show your child the printed calendar in part B. **From April 1st to April 28th is 4 weeks.**

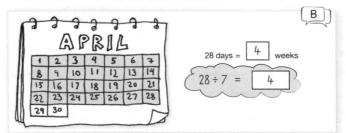

Now, let's pretend that the exciting event is 30 days away. We can divide 30 by 7 to find how many weeks and days equal 30 days. What's 30 divided by 7? *4, with a remainder of 2.* If your child isn't sure, say: **You already found that 28 divided by 7 is 4. 30 is 2 more than 28, so 30 divided by 7 is 4 with a remainder of 2.** Write "4 R2" in the division equation blank.

So, 30 days equal 4 weeks and 2 days. Write 4 and 2 in the blanks. Point to the printed calendar. **From April 1st to April 30th is 4 weeks and 2 days.**

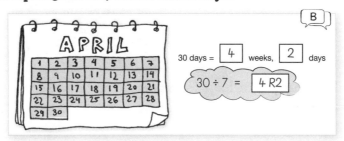

Have your child complete part B in the same way.

If you have time, show your child a real calendar. Choose an event in the next couple of months and tell your child how many days away the event is. Then, have your child divide by 7 to convert the days to weeks. For example: **Memorial Day is 25 days away. How many weeks away is that?** *3 weeks and 4 days.* Repeat with several events.

Independent Practice and Review

Have your child complete the Lesson 15.2 Practice and Review workbook pages.

Lesson 15.3
÷8 Facts

Purpose	Materials
• Review ×8 facts • Practice ÷8 facts	• Dot array and L-cover (Blackline Master 5) • Counters • Die

Memory Work	• **What does area measure?** *The amount of space that a shape covers.* • **What does perimeter measure?** *The distance around the outside edge of a shape.*

Warm-up: Practice ×8 Facts

In Unit 8, you learned the ×8 facts. Today, you'll use the ×8 facts to find answers to the ÷8 facts. Do a brief oral review of the following ×8 facts. Encourage your child to respond as quickly as possible for each fact.

- 5 × 8 = 40
- 4 × 8 = 32
- 6 × 8 = 48
- 8 × 8 = 64

- 3 × 8 = 24
- 7 × 8 = 56
- 10 × 8 = 80
- 9 × 8 = 72

Activity (A): Introduce ÷8 Facts

Let's pretend you're making goodie bags for a party. You have 64 pieces of candy, and you put 8 pieces in each goodie bag.

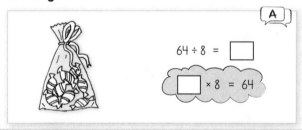

If your child immediately knows the answer to 64 ÷ 8, skip the following demonstration. Instead, ask her to pretend to be the teacher and explain to you how to use the dot array to find the answer.

64 divided by 8 means "How many groups of 8 equal 64?" We want to know what times 8 equals 64. Let's use the dot array to help find the answer. Slide the L-cover to show 10 rows of 8. **What's 10 times 8?** *80.* **Too high!**

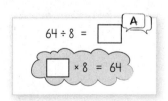

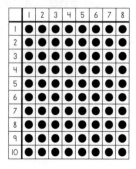

Let's subtract 1 group of 8. Slide the L-cover to show 9 rows of 8. **What's 9 times 8?** *72.*
That's still too high, but it's closer.

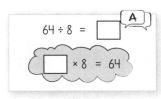

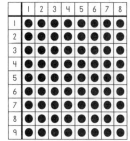

Let's subtract 1 more group of 8. Slide the L-cover to show 8 rows of 8. **What's 8 times 8?** *64.*
That's it! 8 times 8 equals 64, so 64 divided by 8 equals 8. Write 8 in both blanks.

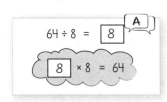

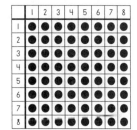

Have your child complete part A. Use the dot array to model the problems as needed.

24 ÷ 8 = 3	32 ÷ 8 = 4	80 ÷ 8 = 10
56 ÷ 8 = 7	16 ÷ 8 = 2	72 ÷ 8 = 9
40 ÷ 8 = 5	48 ÷ 8 = 6	8 ÷ 8 = 1

Activity (B): Play Climb and Slide

Play Climb and Slide. Encourage your child to use related multiplication facts to find the answers to the division problems in the game. Use the dot array as needed. See Lesson 3.3 (page 90) for full directions.

Independent Practice and Review

Have your child complete the Lesson 15.3 Practice and Review workbook pages.

If your child has trouble with the time sequences on the Review page, have her model them with a real clock.

Lesson 15.4
Divide Perimeter to Find Side Lengths

Purpose	Materials
• Practice ÷8 facts • Divide the perimeter of shapes with equal sides to find the length of each side	• Counters • Playing cards • Dot array and L-cover (Blackline Master 5), optional • Yarn • Scissors • Ruler

Memory Work	• **How many sides does a triangle have?** *3.* • **A quadrilateral?** *4.* • **A pentagon?** *5.* • **A hexagon?** *6.* • **An octagon?** *8.*

Warm-up (A): Play Division Crash (÷8)

Play Division Crash (÷8). See Lesson 10.7 (page 333) for directions. Encourage your child to use related multiplication facts to find the answers, and model the problems on the dot array as needed.

> If your child finds this game confusing, write a simple equation like the following on a piece of paper. Place the playing card in the quotient position. **We want to find the number that we can divide by 8 to equal 6. So, we multiply 8 times 6 to find that number.**
>
> $$\square \div 8 = \boxed{6 \blacklozenge}$$

Activity (B): Divide Perimeter to Find Side Length

In Unit 9, you learned how to find perimeter. How do we usually find perimeter? *Sample answer: Add up the length of all the sides.*

Show your child part B. **This perimeter problem is a little different than the ones you solved in Unit 9. In this problem, we know the perimeter and want to find the length of each side. All the sides have an equal length. We'll use yarn to help us find the length of each side.**

The perimeter is 15 centimeters. Have your child measure and cut a 15-cm length of yarn. Place the yarn on top of the pentagon's outline.

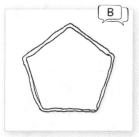

Placing yarn exactly on top of an outline is difficult. It's fine if the yarn only roughly covers the pentagon's edges.

How many sides does the pentagon have? *5.* **If you cut the yarn into 5 equal pieces, how long will each piece be?** *3 centimeters.* **How do you know?** *Sample answer: 15 divided by 5 equals 3.* Have your child use a ruler to measure and cut the yarn into 5 3-cm-long pieces.

3 cm

The pentagon has 5 equal sides and a perimeter of 15 centimeters. So, just like we divided the yarn into 5 equal pieces, we can divide the perimeter by 5 to find the length of each side. Write "15 ÷ 5 =" in the space below the problem. Place each of the small pieces of yarn along one of the sides of the pentagon.

So, how long is each side of the pentagon? *3 centimeters.* Complete the equation and write 3 cm in the blank.

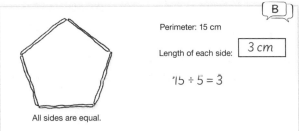

> B
>
> Perimeter: 15 cm
>
> Length of each side: $\boxed{3\ cm}$
>
> $15 ÷ 5 = 3$
>
> All sides are equal.

When we know the perimeter of a shape with equal sides, we can divide the perimeter by the number of sides to find how long each side is. This only works if the shape has equal sides, though! Have your child identify the number of sides in each shape in part B. Then, have him write a division equation to find the length of each side.

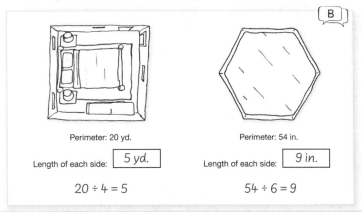

> B
>
> Perimeter: 20 yd.
>
> Length of each side: $\boxed{5\ yd.}$
>
> $20 ÷ 4 = 5$
>
> Perimeter: 54 in.
>
> Length of each side: $\boxed{9\ in.}$
>
> $54 ÷ 6 = 9$

All sides are equal in these shapes.

Independent Practice and Review

Have your child complete the Lesson 15.4 Practice and Review workbook pages.

Lesson 15.5
÷9 Facts

Purpose	Materials
• Review ×9 facts • Practice ÷9 facts	• Dot array and L-cover (Blackline Master 5) • Counters • Die

Memory Work	• **What do we call fractions that look different but have the same value?** *Equivalent fractions.* • **What do we call numbers that have a whole number and a fraction?** *Mixed numbers.*

Warm-up: Practice ×9 Facts

Today, you'll use the ×9 facts to find answers to the ÷9 facts. Do a brief oral review of the following ×9 facts. Encourage your child to respond as quickly as possible for each fact.

- 5 × 9 = *45*
- 6 × 9 = *54*
- 4 × 9 = *36*
- 10 × 9 = *90*

- 8 × 9 = *72*
- 7 × 9 = *63*
- 9 × 9 = *81*
- 3 × 9 = *27*

Activity (A): Introduce ÷9 Facts

Show your child part A. **Let's pretend you're planting green bean seeds in the garden. You have 36 seeds, and you want to plant 9 seeds in each row.**

If your child immediately knows the answer to 36 ÷ 9, skip the following demonstration. Instead, have her pretend to be the teacher and explain how to use the dot array to find the answer.

36 divided by 9 means "How many groups of 9 equal 36?" We want to know what times 9 equals 36. Let's use the dot array to help find the answer. Slide the L-cover to show 5 rows of 9. **What's 5 times 9?** *45.* **Too high!**

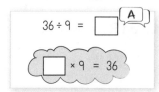

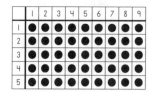

Let's subtract 1 group of 9. Slide the L-cover to show 4 rows of 9. **What's 4 times 9?** *36.* **4 times 9 equals 36, so 36 divided by 9 equals 4.** Write 4 in both blanks.

Have your child complete part A. Model the problems with the dot array as needed.

$18 \div 9 = \boxed{2}$ $90 \div 9 = \boxed{10}$ $72 \div 9 = \boxed{8}$

$81 \div 9 = \boxed{9}$ $9 \div 9 = \boxed{1}$ $63 \div 9 = \boxed{7}$

$27 \div 9 = \boxed{3}$ $45 \div 9 = \boxed{5}$ $54 \div 9 = \boxed{6}$

Activity (B): Play Treasure Hunt

Play Treasure Hunt. See Lesson 6.5 (page 188) for directions. Encourage your child to use related multiplication facts to find the answers, and model the problems on the dot array as needed.

Independent Practice and Review

Have your child complete the Lesson 15.5 Practice and Review workbook pages.

Lesson 15.6
Divide Area to Find a Missing Side Length

Purpose	Materials
• Practice ÷9 facts • Divide area to find the length of a missing side	• Counters • Playing cards • Base-ten blocks

| Memory Work | • **What do we call an angle that looks like the corner of a piece of paper?** *A right angle.*
• **What do we call a quadrilateral with 4 right angles?** *A rectangle.*
• **What do we call a quadrilateral with 4 right angles and 4 equal sides?** *A square.*
• **What do we call a quadrilateral with 4 equal sides?** *A rhombus.* |

Warm-up (A): Play Escape the Maze (÷9)

Play Escape the Maze (÷9). On your turn, flip over the top card. Figure out what number divided by 9 equals that number. For example, if you draw a 7: **63 divided by 9 equals 7.** If your counter is connected to a square with 63, you may move your counter to that square. See Lesson 6.1 (page 173) for full directions.

Activity (B): Divide Area to Find the Length of a Missing Side

In Unit 9, you learned how to find the area of rectangles. How do we usually find the area of a rectangle? *Sample answer: Multiply the length times the width.*

This area problem is a little different than the ones you solved in Unit 9. In this problem, we know the rectangle's area and width. We want to find the rectangle's length.

While it may be obvious to adults that you can divide to find the missing side in this problem, many children are still developing an understanding of the relationship between multiplication and division. Using unit blocks to model the problem makes this relationship more concrete.

This rectangle has an area of 24 square centimeters. Place 24 unit blocks on the table.

The rectangle is 3 centimeters wide, so we need to divide the 24 blocks into 3 rows to cover the rectangle. What's 24 divided by 3? *8.* Write "24 ÷ 3 =" in the space next to the rectangle. **So, each row will have 8 blocks in it. How long must the rectangle be?** *8 centimeters.* Arrange the unit blocks in 3 rows of 8 inside the rectangle. Complete the equation and write 8 in the blank.

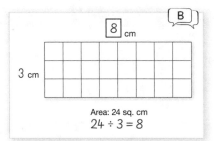

Multiplication and division are the opposite of each other. Length times width equals area, so we can divide area by width to find length. When you know the area and the length of one side of a rectangle, you can divide to find the other side length.

Have your child solve the other problems in part B. Count out unit blocks to match each area and have your child use division to find the number of blocks to place in each row.

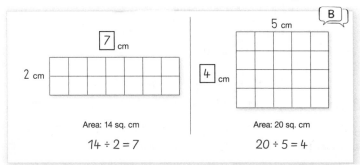

If your child immediately understands why he should divide, you do not need to cover the rectangles with unit blocks.

Independent Practice and Review

Have your child complete the Lesson 15.6 Practice and Review workbook pages.

Lesson 15.7
Enrichment (Optional)

Purpose	Materials
• Practice memory work • Understand division and remainders in the context of ants marching in formation • Practice the division facts that your child finds most challenging • Summarize what your child has learned and assess your child's progress	• *A Remainder of One,* written by Elinor Pinczes and illustrated by Bonnie MacKain • Varies, depending on which activity you choose

Warm-up: Review Memory Work

Quiz your child on all memory work through Unit 15. See pages 527-528 for the full list.

Math Picture Book: *A Remainder of One*

Read *A Remainder of One,* written by Elinor Pinczes and illustrated by Bonnie MacKain. As you read, have your child tell the division equation that matches how the ants divide. For example, when the 25 ants divide into pairs: *25 divided by 2 equals 12, with a remainder of one.*

Enrichment Activity: Choose Your Own Math Fact Practice

You've worked hard on the division facts! Today, you get to practice them in a different way!

Choose 8-10 of the division facts that your child finds most challenging. Have your child choose one of the following ways to practice these facts:

- Fold a piece of paper (or draw lines on a piece of paper) to make a 2×4 grid. Have your child tape a small slip of paper or place a sticky note in each box. Have her write a division problem on each slip of paper or sticky note. Have her write the answer underneath. Then, have her use this lift-the-flap to quiz herself on the tricky facts.
- Spread pudding on a tray, shaving cream on a counter, or finger paint on a large sheet of paper. Have your child use her finger to write each division fact (with its answer) in the goo.
- Write the division facts' answers in chalk outside. Name one of the facts and have your child run to the answer. (Or, if you prefer to do the activity inside, write each answer on a piece of paper and tape it to the floor.)
- Name a division fact and toss a ball to your child. Have her say the answer as she catches the ball.
- Make a Division Memory game. Write the division problems on one set of index cards and their answers on another set of index cards. Turn all the cards face-down. On your turn, flip over 2 cards. If the cards match, keep the pair. If the cards don't match, turn them back over. Take turns until you have found pairs for every card. Whoever has the most cards wins.

Unit Wrap-up (Optional)

Have your child complete the Unit 15 Wrap-up.

Unit 15 Answer Key

15.1 Practice

Practice ▸ Complete and match the equations.

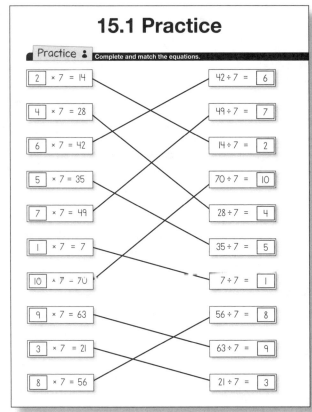

$2 \times 7 = 14$	$42 \div 7 = 6$
$4 \times 7 = 28$	$49 \div 7 = 7$
$6 \times 7 = 42$	$14 \div 7 = 2$
$5 \times 7 = 35$	$70 \div 7 = 10$
$7 \times 7 = 49$	$28 \div 7 = 4$
$1 \times 7 = 7$	$35 \div 7 = 5$
$10 \times 7 = 70$	$7 \div 7 = 1$
$9 \times 7 = 63$	$56 \div 7 = 8$
$3 \times 7 = 21$	$63 \div 7 = 9$
$8 \times 7 = 56$	$21 \div 7 = 3$

15.1 Review

Review ▸ Complete the two missing sides for each square.

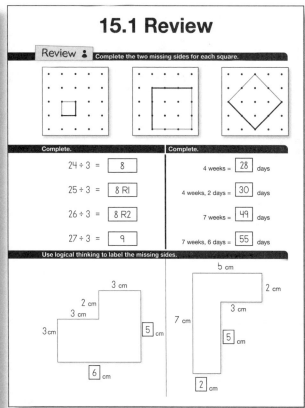

Complete.

$24 \div 3 = 8$

$25 \div 3 = 8\ R1$

$26 \div 3 = 8\ R2$

$27 \div 3 = 9$

Complete.

4 weeks = 28 days

4 weeks, 2 days = 30 days

7 weeks = 49 days

7 weeks, 6 days = 55 days

Use logical thinking to label the missing sides.

15.2 Practice

Practice ▸ Complete.

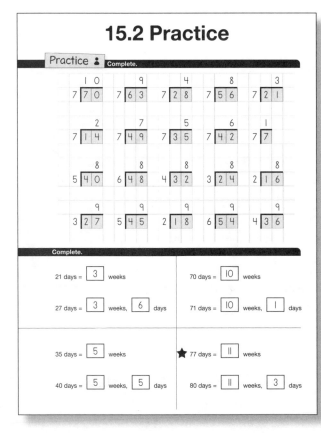

Complete.

21 days = 3 weeks

27 days = 3 weeks, 6 days

35 days = 5 weeks

40 days = 5 weeks, 5 days

70 days = 10 weeks

71 days = 10 weeks, 1 days

★ 77 days = 11 weeks

80 days = 11 weeks, 3 days

15.2 Review

Review ▸ Color the multiples in order from Start to End.

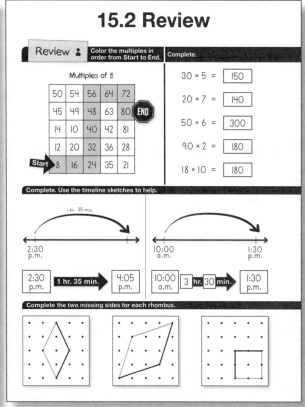

Multiples of 8

Complete.

$30 \times 5 = 150$

$20 \times 7 = 140$

$50 \times 6 = 300$

$90 \times 2 = 180$

$18 \times 10 = 180$

Complete. Use the timeline sketches to help.

2:30 p.m. — 1 hr. 35 min. → 4:05 p.m.

10:00 a.m. — 3 hr. 30 min. → 1:30 p.m.

Complete the two missing sides for each rhombus.

Unit 15 Answer Key

15.3 Practice

Practice · Complete and match the equations.

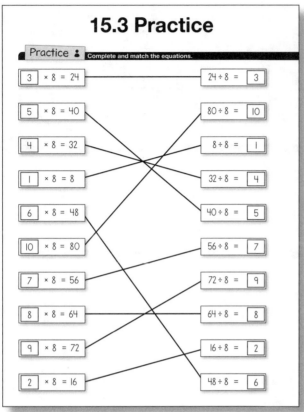

3 × 8 = 24   24 ÷ 8 = 3
5 × 8 = 40   80 ÷ 8 = 10
4 × 8 = 32   8 ÷ 8 = 1
1 × 8 = 8   32 ÷ 8 = 4
6 × 8 = 48   40 ÷ 8 = 5
10 × 8 = 80   56 ÷ 8 = 7
7 × 8 = 56   72 ÷ 8 = 9
8 × 8 = 64   64 ÷ 8 = 8
9 × 8 = 72   16 ÷ 8 = 2
2 × 8 = 16   48 ÷ 8 = 6

15.3 Review

Review · Find the perimeter of each shape.

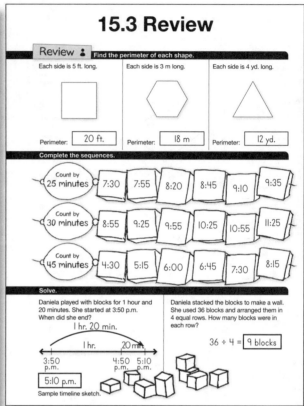

Each side is 5 ft. long.   Perimeter: 20 ft.
Each side is 3 m long.   Perimeter: 18 m
Each side is 4 yd. long.   Perimeter: 12 yd.

Complete the sequences.

Count by 25 minutes: 7:30, 7:55, 8:20, 8:45, 9:10, 9:35

Count by 30 minutes: 8:55, 9:25, 9:55, 10:25, 10:55, 11:25

Count by 45 minutes: 4:30, 5:15, 6:00, 6:45, 7:30, 8:15

Solve.

Daniela played with blocks for 1 hour and 20 minutes. She started at 3:50 p.m. When did she end?

1 hr. 20 min.

1 hr.   20 min.

3:50 p.m.   4:50 p.m.   5:10 p.m.

5:10 p.m.

Sample timeline sketch.

Daniela stacked the blocks to make a wall. She used 36 blocks and arranged them in 4 equal rows. How many blocks were in each row?

36 ÷ 4 = 9 blocks

15.4 Practice

Practice · Complete.

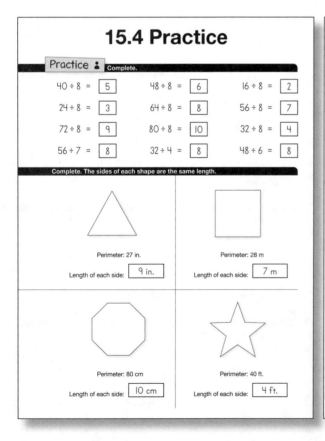

40 ÷ 8 = 5   48 ÷ 8 = 6   16 ÷ 8 = 2
24 ÷ 8 = 3   64 ÷ 8 = 8   56 ÷ 8 = 7
72 ÷ 8 = 9   80 ÷ 8 = 10   32 ÷ 8 = 4
56 ÷ 7 = 8   32 ÷ 4 = 8   48 ÷ 6 = 8

Complete. The sides of each shape are the same length.

Perimeter: 27 in.   Length of each side: 9 in.

Perimeter: 28 m   Length of each side: 7 m

Perimeter: 80 cm   Length of each side: 10 cm

Perimeter: 40 ft.   Length of each side: 4 ft.

15.4 Review

Review · Circle the more sensible unit for each item.

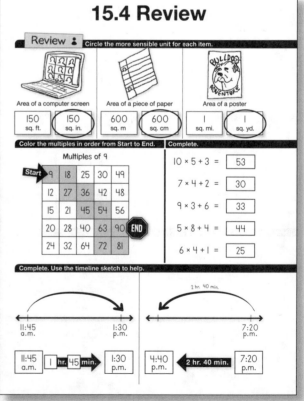

Area of a computer screen: 150 sq. ft. / **150 sq. in.**

Area of a piece of paper: 600 sq. m / **600 sq. cm**

Area of a poster: 1 sq. mi. / **1 sq. yd.**

Color the multiples in order from Start to End.

Multiples of 9

Start→ 9	18	25	30	49
12	27	36	42	48
15	21	45	54	56
20	28	40	63	90 END
24	32	64	72	81

Complete.

10 × 5 + 3 = 53
7 × 4 + 2 = 30
9 × 3 + 6 = 33
5 × 8 + 4 = 44
6 × 4 + 1 = 25

Complete. Use the timeline sketch to help.

11:45 a.m. → 1:30 p.m.

2 hr. 40 min.

7:20 p.m.

11:45 a.m. → 1 hr. 45 min. → 1:30 p.m.

4:40 p.m. ← 2 hr. 40 min. ← 7:20 p.m.

Unit 15 Answer Key

15.5 Practice

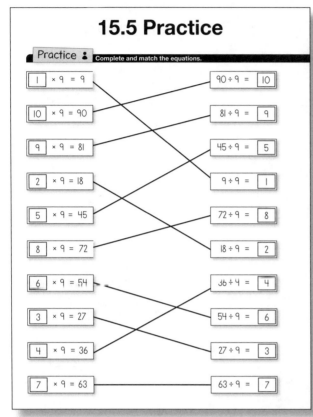

Practice 👤 Complete and match the equations.

$1 \times 9 = 9$

$10 \times 9 = 90$

$9 \times 9 = 81$

$2 \times 9 = 18$

$5 \times 9 = 45$

$8 \times 9 = 72$

$6 \times 9 = 54$

$3 \times 9 = 27$

$4 \times 9 = 36$

$7 \times 9 = 63$

$90 \div 9 = 10$

$81 \div 9 = 9$

$45 \div 9 = 5$

$9 \div 9 = 1$

$72 \div 9 = 8$

$18 \div 9 = 2$

$36 \div 4 = 4$

$54 \div 9 = 6$

$27 \div 9 = 3$

$63 \div 9 = 7$

15.5 Review

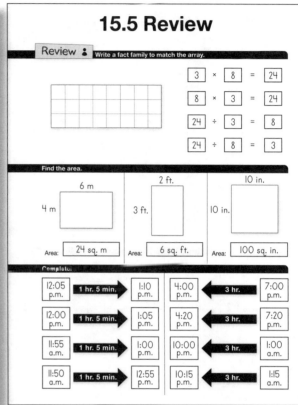

Review 👤 Write a fact family to match the array.

$3 \times 8 = 24$

$8 \times 3 = 24$

$24 \div 3 = 8$

$24 \div 8 = 3$

Find the area.

6 m, 4 m — Area: 24 sq. m

2 ft., 3 ft. — Area: 6 sq. ft.

10 in., 10 in. — Area: 100 sq. in.

Complete.

12:05 p.m.	1 hr. 5 min.	1:10 p.m.	4:00 p.m.	3 hr.	7:00 p.m.
12:00 p.m.	1 hr. 5 min.	1:05 p.m.	4:20 p.m.	3 hr.	7:20 p.m.
11:55 a.m.	1 hr. 5 min.	1:00 p.m.	10:00 p.m.	3 hr.	1:00 a.m.
11:50 a.m.	1 hr. 5 min.	12:55 p.m.	10:15 p.m.	3 hr.	1:15 a.m.

15.6 Practice

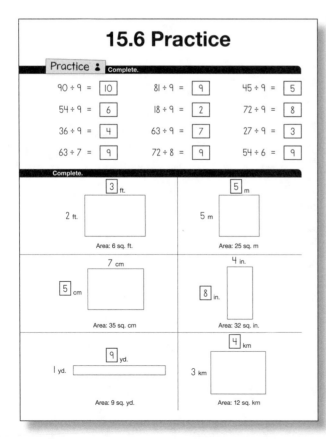

Practice 👤 Complete.

$90 \div 9 = 10$ $81 \div 9 = 9$ $45 \div 9 = 5$

$54 \div 9 = 6$ $18 \div 9 = 2$ $72 \div 9 = 8$

$36 \div 9 = 4$ $63 \div 9 = 7$ $27 \div 9 = 3$

$63 \div 7 = 9$ $72 \div 8 = 9$ $54 \div 6 = 9$

Complete.

3 ft., 2 ft. — Area: 6 sq. ft.

5 m, 5 m — Area: 25 sq. m

7 cm, 5 cm — Area: 35 sq. cm

4 in., 8 in. — Area: 32 sq. in.

9 yd., 1 yd. — Area: 9 sq. yd.

4 km, 3 km — Area: 12 sq. km

15.6 Review

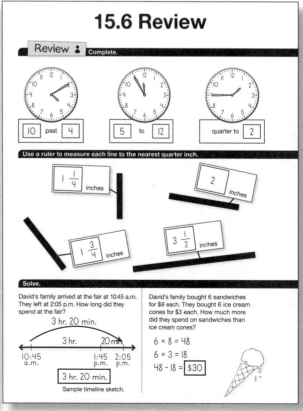

Review 👤 Complete.

10 past 4

5 to 12

quarter to 2

Use a ruler to measure each line to the nearest quarter inch.

$1\frac{1}{4}$ inches

2 inches

$1\frac{3}{4}$ inches

$3\frac{1}{2}$ inches

Solve.

David's family arrived at the fair at 10:45 a.m. They left at 2:05 p.m. How long did they spend at the fair?

3 hr. 20 min.

3 hr.   20 min.

10:45 a.m.   1:45 p.m.   2:05 p.m.

3 hr. 20 min.

Sample timeline sketch.

David's family bought 6 sandwiches for $8 each. They bought 6 ice cream cones for $3 each. How much more did they spend on sandwiches than ice cream cones?

$6 \times 8 = 48$

$6 \times 3 = 18$

$48 - 18 = \$30$

Unit 15 Answer Key

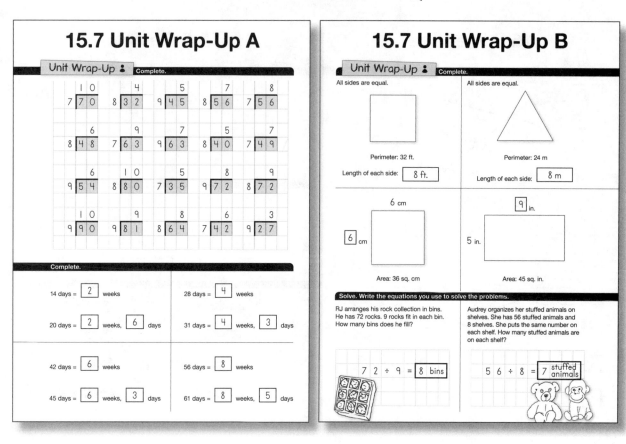

15.7 Unit Wrap-Up A

Unit Wrap-Up **Complete.**

1 0	4	5	7	8
7 ⟌7 0	8 ⟌3 2	9 ⟌4 5	8 ⟌5 6	7 ⟌5 6
6	9	7	5	7
8 ⟌4 8	7 ⟌6 3	9 ⟌6 3	8 ⟌4 0	7 ⟌4 9
6	1 0	5	8	9
9 ⟌5 4	8 ⟌8 0	7 ⟌3 5	9 ⟌7 2	8 ⟌7 2
1 0	9	8	6	3
9 ⟌9 0	9 ⟌8 1	8 ⟌6 4	7 ⟌4 2	9 ⟌2 7

Complete.

14 days = 2 weeks   28 days = 4 weeks

20 days = 2 weeks, 6 days   31 days = 4 weeks, 3 days

42 days = 6 weeks   56 days = 8 weeks

45 days = 6 weeks, 3 days   61 days = 8 weeks, 5 days

15.7 Unit Wrap-Up B

Unit Wrap-Up **Complete.**

All sides are equal.

Perimeter: 32 ft.

Length of each side: 8 ft.

All sides are equal.

Perimeter: 24 m

Length of each side: 8 m

6 cm

6 cm

Area: 36 sq. cm

9 in.

5 in.

Area: 45 sq. in.

Solve. Write the equations you use to solve the problems.

RJ arranges his rock collection in bins. He has 72 rocks. 9 rocks fit in each bin. How many bins does he fill?

7 2 ÷ 9 = 8 bins

Audrey organizes her stuffed animals on shelves. She has 56 stuffed animals and 8 shelves. She puts the same number on each shelf. How many stuffed animals are on each shelf?

5 6 ÷ 8 = 7 stuffed animals

Unit 15 Checkpoint

What to Expect at the End of Unit 15

By the end of Unit 15, most children will be able to do the following:

- Find answers for the ÷7, ÷8, and ÷9 facts. Most children will be fairly fluent with the facts with smaller dividends and divisors (like 21 ÷ 7 or 32 ÷ 8) but need more practice with facts with larger dividends and divisors (63 ÷ 9 or 56 ÷ 8).
- Divide by 7 to convert days to weeks.
- Use division to solve area and perimeter problems. Some children will still be working on understanding why they can use division for these problems.

Is Your Child Ready to Move on?

In Unit 16, your child will study weight and capacity. She does not need to master the division facts from Unit 15 before moving on to Unit 16. It usually takes children a long time to become fully fluent with these facts. She will continue to practice the ÷7, ÷8, and ÷9 facts in Unit 16, and she'll work on them more in *Fourth Grade Math with Confidence.*

This page is intentionally left blank.

Unit 16
Weight and Capacity

Overview

Your child will learn how to estimate and measure weight and capacity with both U.S. customary units (ounces/pounds and cups/pints/quarts/gallons) and metric units (grams/kilograms and milliliters/liters). He will also learn how to read scales and beakers.

These fun, hands-on lessons make a great way to end the year. Your child will continue to practice the difficult division facts from Unit 15 in the review workbook pages. In the final lessons, you and your child will review what he has learned and celebrate completing the book.

What Your Child Will Learn

In this unit, your child will learn to:

- Understand the approximate size of an ounce, pound, gram, and kilogram
- Estimate weight with ounces, pounds, grams, and kilograms
- Understand the approximate size of a cup, pint, quart, gallon, milliliter, and liter
- Estimate and measure capacity with cups and milliliters
- Read scales and beakers
- Solve weight and capacity word problems

Lesson List

Lesson 16.1   Ounces and Pounds
Lesson 16.2   Grams and Kilograms
Lesson 16.3   Cups, Pints, Quarts, and Gallons
Lesson 16.4   Milliliters and Liters
Lesson 16.5   Enrichment (Optional)

Lesson 16.6   Review Addition and Subtraction
Lesson 16.7   Review Multiplication and Division
Lesson 16.8   Review Measurement
Lesson 16.9   Review Fractions and Geometry

> The optional enrichment lesson for this unit is in the middle of the unit so you can wrap up your study of weight and capacity before moving on to the end-of-year review lessons.

Note for Families Living Outside the U.S.

If you live outside the U.S., your child may rarely encounter pounds or cups in his everyday life. However, future levels of *Math with Confidence* will sometimes use these units in review word problems, so it's helpful for your child to be at least acquainted with them. You do not need to teach the full lessons on U.S. weight and capacity units, but you should at least teach your child the basic benchmarks for these units. Look for notes at the beginning of Lessons 16.1 and 16.3 for how to do this. You may also want to teach Lesson 16.2 before 16.1 (so that your child is familiar with metric weight units before tackling U.S. units) and teach Lesson 16.4 before 16.3 (so that your child learns about milliliters and liters before cups, pints, quarts, and gallons).

Lesson 16.3 focuses on the relationships between cups, pints, quarts, and gallons. If you live in the U.K., note that the imperial versions of these units are different from the U.S. versions. (For example, 1 imperial cup equals 284 milliliters, while 1 U.S. cup equals 237 milliliters.) However, the relationships between the units are the same in both systems, so you can teach Lesson 16.3 as written.

Extra Materials Needed for Unit 16

- Object that weighs about 1 ounce, such as a slice of bread, AA battery, or a stack of 5 quarters
- Object that weighs about 1 pound, such as a loaf of bread, can of vegetables, or box of pasta
- 5 pantry items of varying weights, with tape or a sticky note covering the items' labeled weights
- Kitchen scale or postal scale that measures in pounds and ounces, optional
- 5 small household objects, optional
- Object that weighs about 1 gram, such as a paper clip, 1-dollar bill, or thumbtack
- Object that weighs about 1 kilogram, such as a pair of adult shoes, a pineapple, or your child's student workbook
- Kitchen scale or postal scale that measures in kilograms and grams, optional
- Blue marker or colored pencil
- 1-cup measuring cup
- 1-pint and 1-quart measuring cups, optional
- Water
- 5 containers of varying capacities
- Eyedropper, optional
- 1-liter container (such as a large water bottle or measuring cup), optional
- Variety of food and personal care items, with capacity labeled in milliliters
- Colored pencils and markers
- For optional Enrichment Lesson:
  - *Room for Ripley*, written by Stuart J. Murphy and illustrated by Sylvie Wickstrom. HarperCollins, 1999.
  - Honey
  - Blue dishwashing soap
  - Water
  - Vegetable oil
  - Rubbing alcohol (also known as surgical spirit)
  - Food coloring
  - Tall, clear glass or glass jar
  - Measuring cup that measures in milliliters
  - Small bowls and spoons for mixing

Teaching Math with Confidence:
Understanding the Magnitude of Weight and Capacity Units

In this unit, your child will learn about weight and capacity units, both in the U.S. customary system and the metric system. You can't see each individual pound or liter in most real-life situations, and so children often have trouble grasping the magnitude of these units. You'll use a variety of hands-on activities to help your child develop a concrete sense of these units.

First, each lesson provides examples of household objects roughly equal to the unit. For example, your child will learn that one AA battery typically weighs about an ounce, and that many water bottles hold about 1 liter of water. Knowing these benchmarks gives him a basis of comparison as he begins to estimate weights and capacities.

Then, you'll give your child many opportunities to estimate the weight or capacity of pantry or personal care items around your house. Each time, you'll also tell him the exact weight or capacity so that he knows how close his estimate was. This feedback will help him refine his guesses and become more precise in his estimates.

Developing a sense of the magnitude of units is an essential part of learning about measurement. With a strong grasp of the size of these units, your child will be well-prepared to solve measurement word problems, find equivalencies, and use fractions and decimals to describe quantities in future grades.

Lesson 16.1
Ounces and Pounds

Purpose	Materials
• Practice division facts • Introduce ounces and pounds • Estimate weight in ounces and pounds and compare with actual weight • Measure weight in ounces and pounds with a scale (optional)	• Dot array and L-cover (Blackline Master 5), optional • Object that weighs about 1 ounce, such as a slice of bread, AA battery, or a stack of 5 quarters • Object that weighs about 1 pound, such as a loaf of bread, can of vegetables, or box of pasta • 5 pantry items of varying weights, with tape or a sticky note covering the items' labeled weights (See note below for more information) • Kitchen scale or postal scale that measures in pounds and ounces, optional • 5 small household objects, optional

Memory Work

- **What do we call the number to be divided?** *The dividend.*
- **What do we call the number we divide by?** *The divisor.*
- **What do we call the result when we divide two numbers?** *The quotient.*
- **What do we call an amount that is left over after division?** *The remainder.*

If you live outside the U.S. and do not use ounces or pounds, teach Lesson 16.2 before Lesson 16.1. If you do not have any pantry items labeled with ounces or pounds, skip part B on the Lesson Activities page.

You need 5 pantry items of varying weights for this lesson. Try to include 2 items that are lighter than a pound, 1 item equal to a pound, and 2 items heavier than a pound. Before the lesson, cover the printed weight for each item with a sticky note or piece of masking tape. See the Unit 16 **Teaching Math with Confidence** for the benefits of using concrete objects for measurement activities.

Warm-up: Practice Division Facts

Do a brief oral review of the following division facts. Allow your child to model the facts with the dot array as needed.

- $30 \div 6 = 5$
- $49 \div 7 = 7$
- $48 \div 8 = 6$

- $72 \div 9 = 8$
- $42 \div 7 = 6$

Activity (A): Introduce Pounds and Ounces

In this unit, you'll learn how to estimate and measure weight. When we measure something's weight, we measure how heavy it is.

Today, you'll learn about measuring weight with pounds and ounces. Pounds and ounces are part of the same measuring system as inches, feet, yards, and miles. These units are used in the United States, and sometimes in the United Kingdom and Canada.

Your child will learn about measuring with grams and kilograms in Lesson 16.2.

These pictures show ways to remember about how heavy an ounce and pound are. A slice of bread weighs about as much as an ounce. Have your child hold one hand out. Place an object that weighs about 1 ounce in her hand, such as a slice of bread, an AA battery, or a stack of 5 quarters. **How does an ounce feel?** *Sample answer: Pretty light!*

16 ounces equal 1 pound. A small loaf of bread usually weighs about one pound. Have your child hold one hand out. Place an object that weighs about 1 pound in her hand, such as a loaf of bread, can of vegetables, or box of pasta. **How does 1 pound feel?** *Sample answer: It's more than an ounce, but it's still pretty light!*

Show your child the abbreviation next to each unit. **We use these abbreviations for ounces and pounds.**

Your child may wonder why these abbreviations use letters that aren't in the written-out words. The abbreviation "oz." comes from the medieval Italian version of ounce, onza. The abbreviation "lb." comes from the ancient Roman unit libra pondo, which means "a pound by weight." English simply took the "lb." from the first word of this phrase.

Have your child identify whether each of the objects pictured in part A is roughly 1 pound or 1 ounce. Write "1 lb." or "1 oz." below each object.

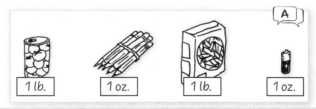

Pencils are surprisingly light! Wooden pencils typically weigh 0.2 ounces each, so 5 pencils equal 1 ounce.

Activity (B): Read Scales in Pounds and Ounces

We measure weight with a scale. Some have a hand like a clock, and others are digital. Show your child the scales in part B.

When you use a scale with a hand, you first have to figure out what each tick mark stands for. Point to the tick mark for 4 oz. on the first scale. **There are 4 spaces from 0 to 4 ounces on this scale. 4 divided by 4 equals 1, so each tick mark on this scale stands for 1 ounce. How much does the pear weigh?** *5 ounces.* Write "5 oz." in the blank.

Point to the tick mark for 4 oz. on the next scale. **On this scale, there are 2 spaces from 0 to 4 ounces. What's 4 divided by 2?** *2.* **So, each tick mark on this scale stands for 2 ounces. How much does the apple weigh?** *6 ounces.* Write "6 oz." in the blank.

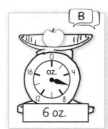

Point to the tick mark for 1 lb. on the final scale. **The tick marks on this scale are labeled in pounds. How many spaces are there from 0 to 1 pound?** *2.* **How many ounces equal 1 pound?** *16.* **So, we can divide 16 by 2 to find how many ounces each tick mark represents. What's 16 divided by 2?** *8.* **So, each tick mark on this scale stands for 8 ounces. How much does this pineapple weigh?** *2 pounds, 8 ounces.* Write "2 lb. 8 oz." in the blank.

If your child says that the pineapple weighs 40 ounces, explain that this is another correct way to describe the weight.

Activity (C): Estimate Weight in Pounds and Ounces

Place 5 pantry items of varying weights on the table. Make sure you've covered their printed weights with tape or sticky notes so that your child can't see them.

Have your child hold each item and put them in order from lightest to heaviest according to how they feel. If she has trouble deciding between two items, have her hold one item in each hand and ask: **Which item feels like it pushes down more on your hand?**

Sample items in order from lightest to heaviest.

Write the names of the items in the chart in part C in the order your child arranged them. Have her estimate the weight of the first item and write the estimate in the chart. Then, remove the sticky note or piece of tape from the item to reveal the item's actual weight. Discuss how close your child's estimate is to the actual weight. For example: **You estimated 4 ounces for the ramen noodles, and they actually weigh 3 ounces. That's pretty close!**

Repeat with the rest of the items. Encourage your child to use the previous items' weights to refine her estimates. For example: **Does this item feel a lot heavier or just a little heavier than the previous item?**

Item	Estimated Weight	Actual Weight
Ramen noodles	4 oz.	3 oz.
Tuna	8 oz.	12 oz.
Pasta	1 lb.	1 lb.
Cereal	2 lb.	1 lb. 10 oz.
Rice	4 lbs.	5 lbs.

Activity: Measure Weight in Pounds and Ounces (Optional)

Skip this activity if you do not own a scale that measures in pounds and ounces.

Show your child a scale the measures in pounds and ounces. If your scale has tick marks, discuss what each tick mark on the scale represents. If your scale is digital, show your child how to turn on the scale and select a unit (if applicable). Demonstrate how to use the scale to weigh the 1-ounce and 1-pound objects that you used earlier in the lesson.

If your scale uses decimals, explain that the digits on the left side of the decimal point tell the whole number of ounces or pounds. The digits on the right side tell if there is also a fractional number of ounces or pounds. Your child will learn about decimals in *Fourth Grade Math with Confidence*.

Have your child choose 5 small items from around the house and weigh them with the scale. Have her estimate the weight of each object before weighing it.

Independent Practice and Review

Have your child complete the Lesson 16.1 Practice and Review workbook pages.

Lesson 16.2
Grams and Kilograms

Purpose	Materials
• Practice division facts • Introduce grams and kilograms • Estimate weight in grams or kilograms and compare with actual weight • Measure weight in grams and kilograms with a scale (optional)	• Dot array and L-cover (Blackline Master 5), optional • Object that weighs about 1 gram, such as a paper clip, one-dollar bill, or thumbtack • Object that weighs about 1 kilogram, such as a pair of adult shoes, a pineapple, or this Instructor Guide • 5 pantry items of varying weights, with tape or a sticky note covering the items' labeled weights (See note below for more information.) • Kitchen scale or postal scale that measures in kilograms and grams, optional

Memory Work   • **How many ounces equal 1 pound?** *16.*

You will again need 5 pantry items of varying weights for this lesson. Use different items than you used in Lesson 16.1 for some variety. Try to include a range of weights, from very light items (like a spice packet) up to quite heavy items (like an unopened bag of flour or sugar). Before the lesson, cover the printed weight for each item with a sticky note or piece of masking tape.

Warm-up: Practice Division Facts

Do a brief oral review of the following division facts. Allow your child to model the facts with the dot array as needed.

- $72 \div 8 = 9$
- $45 \div 5 = 9$
- $56 \div 8 = 7$

- $36 \div 6 = 6$
- $64 \div 8 = 8$

Activity (A): Introduce Kilograms and Grams

In the last lesson, you learned how to measure weight with pounds and ounces. Today, you'll learn to measure weight with kilograms and grams. Kilograms and grams are part of the metric measurement system, like centimeters, meters, and kilometers. These units are used all over the world.

Technically, kilograms and grams measure mass, not weight. Mass is the amount of matter in an object, while weight measures how much force gravity exerts on the object. In everyday life, we use the two terms interchangeably, so *Math with Confidence* doesn't address this subtle distinction.

These pictures show ways to remember about how heavy a gram and kilogram are. A paper clip weighs about 1 gram. Have your child hold one hand out. Place an object that weighs about 1 gram in his hand, such as a paper clip, one-dollar bill, or thumbtack. **How does 1 gram feel?** *Sample answer: Very light!*

1,000 grams equal 1 kilogram. This Instructor Guide weighs about 1 kilogram. Have your child hold one hand out. Place an object that weighs about 1 kilogram in his hand. **How does 1 kilogram feel?** *Sample answer: A lot heavier than a gram!*

If you do not have a printed Instructor Guide, you can use a large paperback book instead.

Show your child the abbreviation next to each unit. **We don't write a period after the abbreviations for grams and kilograms, just like with centimeters, meters, and kilometers.**

Have your child identify whether each of the objects pictured in part A is roughly 1 gram or 1 kilogram. Write "1 g" or "1 kg" below each object.

Activity (B): Read Scales in Kilograms and Grams

Show your child the scales in part B. **Remember, when you use a scale with a hand, you first have to figure out what each tick mark stands for.** Point to the tick mark for 500 g on the first scale. **There are 5 spaces from 0 to 500 grams on this scale. 500 divided by 5 equals 100, so each tick mark on this scale stands for 100 grams. How much does the basket of strawberries weigh?** *300 grams.* Write "300 g" in the blank.

Your child has not yet learned how to perform mental division with the numbers to 1,000, so he's not expected to independently calculate what each tick mark represents. Some children may be able to use place-value knowledge to figure out these answers, but it's also fine for you to simply tell him what the tick marks represent.

Point to the tick mark for 500 g on the second scale. **There are 2 spaces from 0 to 500 grams on this scale. 500 divided by 2 equals 250, so each tick mark on this scale stands for 250 grams. How much does the bunch of lettuce weigh?** *750 grams.* Write "750 g" in the blank.

Point to the tick mark for 1 kg on the final scale. **The tick marks on this scale are labeled in kilograms. How many spaces are there from 0 to 1 kilogram?** *5.* **1,000 grams equal 1 kilogram. 1,000 divided by 5 equals 200, so each tick mark on this scale stands for 200 grams. How much does this cantaloupe weigh?** *2 kilograms, 600 grams.* Write "2 kg, 600 g" in the blank.

If your child says that the cantaloupe weighs 2,600 grams, explain that this is another correct way to describe the weight.

Activity (C): Estimate Weight in Kilograms and Grams

Place 5 pantry items of varying weights on the table. Make sure you've covered their printed weights with tape or sticky notes so that your child can't see them.

Have your child hold each item and put them in order from lightest to heaviest according to how they feel. If he has trouble deciding between two items, have him hold one item in each hand and ask: **Which item feels like it pushes down more on your hand?**

Sample items in order from lightest to heaviest.

Write the name of each item in the chart in the order your child arranged them. Have him estimate the weight of the first item and write the estimate in the chart. Then, remove the sticky note or piece of tape from the item to reveal the item's actual weight. Discuss how close your child's estimate is to the actual weight. For example: **You estimated 100 grams for the spice packet, and it actually weighs 30 grams. Wow, it's very light!**

Repeat with the rest of the items. Encourage your child to use the previous items' weights to refine his estimates. For example: *This item feels twice as heavy as the last item. The last item was 200 grams, so I estimate that this item is about 400 grams.*

Item	Estimated Weight	Actual Weight
Spice packet	100 g	30 g
Snack bag of chips	50 g	80 g
Can of vegetables	300 g	425 g
Tortilla chips	500 g	481 g
Flour	2 kg	2 kg 260 g

Activity: Measure Weight in Kilograms and Grams (Optional)

Skip this activity if you do not own a scale that measures in kilograms and grams.

Show your child a scale that measures in kilograms and grams. If your scale has tick marks, discuss what each tick mark on the scale represents. If your scale is digital, show your child how to turn on the scale and select grams or kilograms. Demonstrate how to use the scale to weigh the 1-gram and 1-kilogram objects that you used earlier in the lesson.

If your scale uses decimals, explain that the digits on the left side of the decimal point tell the whole number of grams or kilograms. The digits on the right side tell if there is also a fractional number of grams or kilograms.

Have your child choose 5 small items from around the house and weigh them with the scale. Have him estimate the weight of each object before weighing it.

Independent Practice and Review

Have your child complete the Lesson 16.2 Practice and Review workbook pages.

Lesson 16.3
Cups, Pints, Quarts, and Gallons

Purpose	Materials
• Practice division facts • Introduce cups, pints, quarts, and gallons • Introduce equivalencies for cups, pints, quarts, and gallons • Estimate and measure capacity	• Dot array and L-cover (Blackline Master 5), optional • Blue marker or colored pencil • 1-cup measuring cup • 1-pint and 1-quart measuring cups (optional) • Water • 5 containers of varying capacities

Memory Work · **How many grams equal 1 kilogram?** *1,000.*

If you live outside the U.S. and do not use cups, pints, quarts, and gallons, teach Lesson 16.4 before Lesson 16.3. If you do not own a 1-cup measuring cup, skip part C on the Lesson Activities page.

This lesson involves pouring water; you may want to teach it near a sink (and in a place where it's easy to clean up any water that spills!) You and your child will look for 5 containers with varying capacities in the scavenger hunt in this lesson. You do not need to gather the containers in advance.

Warm-up: Practice Division Facts

Do a brief oral review of the following division facts. Allow your child to model the facts with the dot array as needed.

- $54 \div 9 = 6$
- $63 \div 7 = 9$
- $42 \div 6 = 7$

- $81 \div 9 = 9$
- $35 \div 7 = 5$

Activity (A): Introduce Cups, Pints, Quarts, and Gallons

In last few lessons, you learned how to estimate and measure weight. Today, you'll learn how to measure capacity. When we measure a container's capacity, we measure how much it can hold.

Today, you'll learn about measuring capacity with cups, pints, quarts, and gallons. They're part of the same measuring system as inches, feet, yards, miles, ounces, and pounds. These units are used in the United States, and sometimes in the United Kingdom and Canada.

Your child will learn about measuring with milliliters and liters in Lesson 16.4.

Show your child part A. Use the questions below to discuss cups, pints, quarts, and gallons.

- **We often use cups to measure ingredients for cooking. Have you ever measured ingredients in cups? What did you measure?** *Answers will vary.*
- **2 cups equal 1 pint.** Describe some real-life examples of pints. For example: **Cream sometimes comes in pints. We buy pints of blueberries at the farmer's market. When I make jam, I can it in pint jars.**
- **2 pints equal 1 quart.** Describe some real-life examples of quarts. For example: **Juice sometimes comes in quart containers. The large boxes of strawberries at the farmer's market are quart boxes. When Grandpa cans peaches, he puts them in quart jars.**

- **4 quarts equal 1 gallon.** Share several real-life examples where your family uses gallons: For example: **Milk comes in gallon containers. When I put gas in the car, I usually put in around 10 gallons. When we painted the living room, we used 1 gallon of paint.**

Show your child the abbreviation next to each unit. **We use these abbreviations for cups, pints, quarts, and gallons.**

If you have any pint, quart, or gallon-sized food items in your kitchen or refrigerator, use them to concretely show your child the size of each unit. Dairy products (like milk and cream) often come in these units. Vinegar, sports drinks, and chicken stock are also often packaged in pints or quarts.

Activity (B): Explore Equivalencies Between Cups, Pints, Quarts, and Gallons

Show your child the printed 1-quart measuring cup. **The lines on measuring cups tell us how much liquid is in them. We'll use this measuring cup to see how cups, pints, and quarts are related.**

If you own a similar 1-quart measuring cup, show it to your child. Pour water in it as you demonstrate the relationships between the units in the rest of the activity.

We want to find out how many cups equal 1 pint. Let's pretend we poured 1 pint of water into this cup. Have your child use a blue marker or colored pencil to color the measuring cup up to the 1-pint line. **How many cups equal 1 pint?** *2.* If your child's not sure, point out that the line is labeled in both cups and pints. Write 2 in the blank.

Next, we want to find out how many cups equal 1 quart. Have your child use a blue marker or colored pencil to color the measuring cup up to the 1-quart line. **How many cups equal 1 quart?** *4.* If your child's not sure, point out that the line is labeled in both cups and pints. Write 4 in the blank.

Next, we want to find out how many pints equal 1 quart. How many pints equal 1 quart? *2.* If your child's not sure, draw dark lines across the measuring cup as shown. **Each pint equals 2 cups. 4 cups equal 1 quart, so that means that 2 pints equal 1 quart.** Write 2 in the blank.

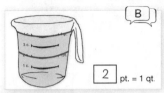

Let's pretend you wanted to use the 1-quart measuring cup to fill a gallon container. It takes 4 quarts of water to make a gallon. Have your child use a blue marker or colored pencil to color all 4 measuring cups up to the 1-quart line.

Each quart holds 4 cups. So, how many cups of water does it take to make a gallon? *16.* If your child's not sure, suggest she multiply 4 times 4. Write 16 in the blank.

How many *pints* equal 1 gallon? *8.* **How do you know?** *Sample answer: There are 2 pints in each quart, and there are 4 quarts. 2 times 4 equals 8, so there are 8 pints.* If your child's not sure, draw dark lines across the measuring cups as shown. **Each quart holds 2 pints. So, you can multiply 2 times 4 to find the number of quarts in a gallon.** Write 8 in the blank.

Activity (C): Capacity Scavenger Hunt with Cups, Pints, Quarts, and Gallons

Show your child part C. **We're going to go on a Capacity Scavenger Hunt! Let's see if we can find kitchen containers that fit each category.** Have your child choose a container that she thinks fits each category. Then, use water and measuring cups to check whether she is correct. Use whatever measuring cups you have, and use the equivalencies listed in part B to help convert between units.

For example, if she guesses that a cereal bowl has a capacity larger than 1 cup and less than 1 pint, have her pour 1 cup of water into the bowl. If all the water fits, the bowl has a capacity larger than 1 cup.

To see if the cereal bowl has a capacity less than a pint, have your child pour 2 cups of water into the bowl (since 2 cups equal 1 pint). If not all the water fits, the bowl has a capacity less than 1 pint. If all the water fits, the bowl has a capacity greater than 1 pint.

If you own a 1-pint measuring cup, you can have your child pour 1 pint of water into the bowl instead to check whether its capacity is less than a pint.

As your child finds containers that fit the categories in part C, write the name of each container in the chart.

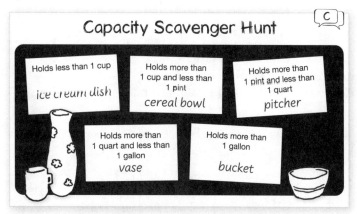

Independent Practice and Review

Have your child complete the Lesson 16.3 Practice and Review workbook pages.

Lesson 16.4
Milliliters and Liters

Purpose	Materials
• Practice division facts • Introduce milliliters and liters • Use lines on a beaker to measure in milliliters • Become familiar with quantities in milliliters	• Dot array and L-cover (Blackline Master 5), optional • Eyedropper, optional • Water, optional • 1-liter container (such as a large water bottle or measuring cup), optional • Variety of food and personal care items, with capacity labeled in milliliters

Memory Work
- **How many cups equal 1 pint?** *2.*
- **How many pints equal 1 quart?** *2.*
- **How many quarts equal 1 gallon?** *4.*

This lesson introduces your child to milliliters and liters. If possible, use real items to show your child the size of these units. Suggested items:

- Chemistry sets or baby medicines often come with an eyedropper that measures in milliliters.
- If you own a 1-quart measuring cup, it may be labeled in liters and milliliters on the other side.
- Sport drink bottles and large water bottles sometimes hold 1 liter.

You and your child will look for food and personal care items labeled in milliliters as part of a scavenger hunt in this lesson. You do not need to gather these items in advance.

Warm-up: Practice Division Facts

Do a brief oral review of the following division facts. Allow your child to model the facts with the dot array as needed.

- $48 \div 6 = 8$
- $56 \div 7 = 8$
- $81 \div 9 = 9$

- $54 \div 6 = 9$
- $63 \div 7 = 9$

Activity (A): Introduce Milliliters and Liters

In the last lesson, you learned how to measure capacity with cups, pints, quarts, and gallons. Today, you'll learn to measure capacity with milliliters and liters. Milliliters and liters are part of the metric system.

When we measure something's capacity, we measure how much it can hold. Show your child part A. **An eyedropper can't hold very much! This eyedropper holds just 1 milliliter of liquid.** If you have an eyedropper, show your child how to use it to measure 1 milliliter of liquid.

1 milliliter equals a little less than 1/4 teaspoon. If you don't have an eyedropper, measure 1/4 teaspoon of water and show your child how little liquid that is.

1,000 milliliters equal 1 liter. A small pitcher holds about 1 liter. Soda often comes in 2-liter bottles, so 1 liter is about half of a large bottle of soda. If you have a container that holds 1 liter, have your child fill the container with water to concretely see a liter.

Show your child the abbreviation next to each unit. **We use these abbreviations for milliliters and liters. We use a capital L for liters so the abbreviation doesn't get confused with the number 1.**

1 liter is a little more than 1 quart. If you own a measuring cup that measures in both liters and quarts, show your child the lines for both measurements. Point out how close the two measurements are.

Activity (B): Read Beakers in Milliliters

Scientists often use milliliters when they measure chemicals for experiments. How much liquid is in the first beaker? *350 milliliters.* Write "350 ml" in the blank.

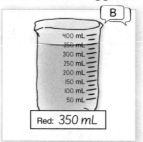

Point to the tick mark for 50 ml on the next beaker. **On this scale, there are 2 spaces from 150 to 200 milliliters. 200 minus 150 equals 50. 50 divided by 2 equals 25. So, each tick mark on this beaker stands for 25 milliliters. How much liquid is in this beaker?** *175 milliliters.* Write "175 ml" in the blank.

Point to the last beaker. **How much liquid is in this beaker?** *900 milliliters.* Write "900 ml" in the blank.

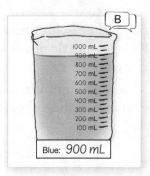

Activity (C): Capacity Scavenger Hunt with Milliliters and Liters

We're going to go on a milliliter and liter scavenger hunt! Let's see if we can find containers of liquid in our home that fit each category. Walk around your home with your child and look for a food or personal care item that fits each category. Have your child record the name of each item and its capacity.

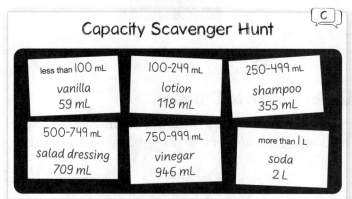

If you live in the U.S., you'll usually find the metric capacity in parentheses after the U.S. customary capacity.

Independent Practice and Review

Have your child complete the Lesson 16.4 Practice and Review workbook pages.

Lesson 16.5
Enrichment (Optional)

Purpose	Materials
• Practice memory work • Understand cups, pints, quarts, and gallons in the context of a fish bowl • Measure in milliliters to make a rainbow craft • Summarize what your child has learned and assess your child's progress	• *Room for Ripley,* written by Stuart J. Murphy and illustrated by Sylvie Wickstrom • Honey • Blue dishwashing soap • Water • Vegetable oil • Rubbing alcohol • Food coloring • Tall, clear glass or glass jar • Measuring cup that measures in milliliters • Small bowls and spoons for mixing

This optional enrichment lesson is in the middle of the unit so you can wrap up your study of weight and capacity before moving on to the end-of-the-year review and celebration lessons.

Make sure your glass or glass jar can hold 450 milliliters (approximately 1 pint) before beginning. If you do not own a measuring cup that measures in milliliters, you can use U.S. customary cups for the enrichment activity instead. See the directions below for U.S. customary measurements.

Warm-up: Review Memory Work

Quiz your child on all memory work through Unit 16. See pages 527-528 for the full list.

Math Picture Book: *Room for Ripley*

Read *Room for Ripley,* written by Stuart J. Murphy and illustrated by Sylvie Wickstrom. As you read, point out the relationships between the cups, pints, quarts, and gallons of water in the fish bowl.

Enrichment Activity: Make a Liquid Rainbow

You will use 5 different liquids in this activity. Each new liquid has a lower density than the previous ones, so each new layer stays on top of the previous layer.

We're going to measure in milliliters to make a liquid rainbow today!

The bottom layer of the rainbow is purple. Have your child measure 50 milliliters (or 1/4 cup) of honey and dump it in a small bowl. Add several drops of red and blue food coloring and mix to make the honey purple. Then, pour the purple honey into the bottom of a tall, clear glass.

Try to pour the honey straight into the center of the glass so that there are no streaks of purple along the sides of the glass.

The next layer of the rainbow is blue. Have your child measure 100 milliliters (or 1/3 cup) of blue dish soap. Then, have her pour it very slowly and gently on top of the honey.

> Make sure your child pours very slowly and gently so that the layers stay separate.

The next layer of the rainbow is green. Have your child measure 100 milliliters (or 1/3 cup) of water and pour it into a small bowl. Add several drops of green food coloring and mix to make the water green. Then, pour the green water carefully on top of the dish soap.

The next layer of the rainbow is yellow. Have your child measure 150 milliliters (or 1/2 cup) of vegetable oil and pour it carefully on top of the water.

The last layer of the rainbow is red. Have your child measure 50 milliliters of rubbing alcohol and pour it into a small bowl. Add several drops of red food coloring and mix to make the rubbing alcohol red. Then, pour the rubbing alcohol slowly and gently along the side of the cup to make a layer on top of the oil.

> Pour the rubbing alcohol along the side of the glass so that it lands very gently on top of the oil.

Unit Wrap-up (Optional)

Have your child complete the Unit 16 Wrap-up.

Lesson 16.6
Review Addition and Subtraction

Purpose	Materials
• Review memory work • Celebrate what your child has learned about addition and subtraction • Create a board game to practice mental math	• Counters • Die

Memory Work See the warm-up activity for memory work review.

In the daily routine of lessons, it can be easy to forget how much progress your child has made since the start of the year. The final four lessons give both you and your child a chance to look back and celebrate how much he has learned.

Warm-up: Review Memory Work

In this lesson and the next three lessons, we'll review and celebrate all that you've learned this year. Each day, we'll review some memory work.

- Write the < sign. **What does this sign mean?** *Less than.*
- Write the > sign. **What does this sign mean?** *Greater than.*
- **If a number has 1, 3, 5, 7, or 9 in the ones-place, is the number even or odd?** *Odd.*
- **If a number has 0, 2, 4, 6, or 8 in the ones-place, is the number even or odd?** *Even.*
- **What do we call the result when we add numbers together?** *The sum.*
- **What do we call the result when we subtract a number from another number?** *The difference.*

Activity: Celebrate What Your Child Has Learned About Addition and Subtraction

You have learned so much in math this year! Today, we'll look back at how much you've learned about addition and subtraction.

At the beginning of the year, we reviewed addition and subtraction. With your child, flip through the Unit 1 workbook pages.

If you no longer have the workbook pages, flip through the matching lessons in the Instructor Guide and have your child look at the workbook answer keys instead.

You learned how to solve mental math problems and word problems. Page through the Unit 3 workbook pages. **You added and subtracted three- and four-digit numbers and money with the addition and subtraction algorithms.** Page through the Unit 5, Unit 7, and Unit 11 workbook pages.

Next year, you'll learn about numbers that are greater than 10,000.

Briefly discuss any concepts that were especially difficult for your child, and remind him how far he has come in his math learning. For example: **Remember how hard it was for you to subtract across zero? Now that you've practiced those problems so much, you have no problem solving them!**

Activity (A): Make Your Own Math Game

We've played a lot of math games this year. Today, you get to make your own math game!
Show your child the blank game board in part A. Have him choose numbers to complete the addition and subtraction problems on the board.

Encourage your child to choose numbers that are slightly challenging for him to solve mentally, but not frustrating.

For the blank squares, have your child choose and write an action. For example, he might choose actions such as the following:

- Go forward 3 spaces.
- Go backward 1 space.
- Lose a turn.
- Take an extra turn.
- Do 10 jumping jacks.
- Spin in a circle while you solve the next problem.

If you have time, your child may choose a theme and decorate the game board as well. For example, he might draw volcanoes and dinosaurs around the board for a prehistoric theme, or he might draw flowers and rainbows for a spring theme.

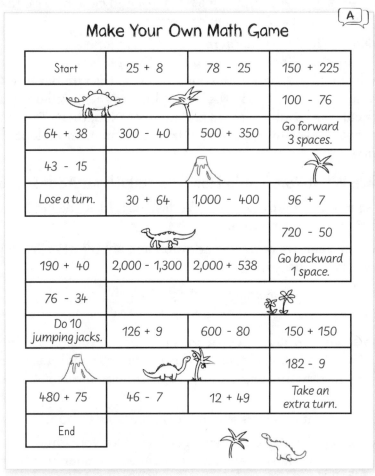

Sample game board.

Once he finishes the game board, use the following rules to play the game.

Make Your Own Math Game

Materials: 2 different-colored counters to use as game tokens; die

Object of the Game: Be the first player to reach the Finish square.

Each player chooses a counter to use as a game token and places it on the Start Square.

On your turn, roll the die and advance your token the corresponding number of squares. If there is a math problem on the square, say the answer to the problem. If there is an action on the square, complete the action.

The first player to reach Finish wins the game.

Independent Practice and Review

Have your child complete the Lesson 16.6 Practice and Review workbook pages.

Lesson 16.7
Review Multiplication and Division

Purpose	Materials
• Review memory work • Celebrate what your child has learned about multiplication and division this year • Practice naming multiples in order	• Colored pencils or markers

Memory Work See the warm-up activity for memory work review.

Warm-up: Review Memory Work

Today, we'll review memory work about multiplication and division.

- **What do we call the result when we multiply two numbers?** *The product.*
- **Name the multiples of 8 in order.** *8, 16, 24...* Stop your child when she reaches 80. **What do we call the numbers in a multiplication equation that we multiply together?** *Factors.*
- **What do we call the number to be divided?** *The dividend.*
- **What do we call the number we divide by?** *The divisor.*
- **What do we call the result when we divide two numbers?** *The quotient.*
- **What do we call an amount that is left over after division?** *The remainder.*

Activity: Celebrate What Your Child Has Learned About Multiplication and Division

Today, we'll celebrate how much you've learned about multiplication and division. At the beginning of the year, you learned what it means to multiply, and you worked on the ×1, ×2, ×5, and ×10 facts. With your child, flip through the Unit 2 workbook pages.

Then, you learned the rest of the multiplication facts. You also learned how to solve multiplication word problems. Page through the Unit 4, Unit 8, and Unit 9 workbook pages.

Once you understood multiplication well, you learned about division. First, you worked on the ÷1, ÷2, ÷5, and ÷10 facts. Page through the Unit 10 workbook pages.

You learned how to solve problems with long division and remainders. You solved lots of different kinds of division word problems. Page through the Unit 12 and Unit 15 workbook pages.

Next year, you'll learn how to multiply and divide larger numbers with the multiplication and division algorithms! You'll also learn more strategies for mental multiplication and division.

Briefly discuss any concepts that were especially difficult for your child, and remind her of how far she has come in her math learning. For example: **Remember how hard it was for you to figure out the ×7 facts at first? You worked really hard on them, and now you can figure them out in just a few seconds!**

Activity (A): Multiplication Art

Today, we'll use the patterns in the multiplication tables to make art! Show your child part A. **These circles are like dot-to-dot activities. You start at zero and connect the dots that match the ones-place in the multiples of the number listed.**

Point to the circle labeled "Multiples of 1." **This circle is for the multiples of 1. Start at 0. Say the multiples of 1 aloud, and connect the dots that match the ones-place in each number you say.** *1, 2, 3...* Stop your child when she reaches 10 and her pencil returns to 0.

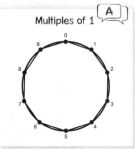

Multiples of l

1, 2, 3, 4, 5,

6, 7, 8, 9, 10.

Point to the circle labeled "Multiples of 2." **This circle is for the multiples of 2. This time, start at 0 and say the multiples of 2 aloud. Connect the dots that match the ones-place in each number you say.** *2, 4, 6...* Stop your child when she reaches 20 (the tenth multiple of 2) and her pencil returns to 0.

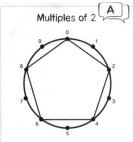

Multiples of 2

2, 4, 6, 8, 10,

12, 14, 16, 18, 20.

Have your child complete the rest of the dot-to-dot circles in the same way. Have her name the multiples aloud, and draw lines connecting the digits in the ones-places in each number. After your child connects the dots, discuss any patterns that she notices. For example: *The ones-digits in the multiples of 5 just go back and forth between 0 and 5. The ones-digits in the multiples of 9 go down by 1 each time.*

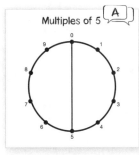

Multiples of 5

5, 10, 15, 20, 25,

30, 35, 40, 45, 50.

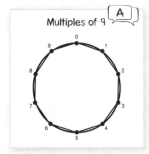

Multiples of 9

9, 18, 27, 36, 45,

54, 63, 72, 81, 90.

Then, have your child use colored pencils or markers to color in the designs she created.

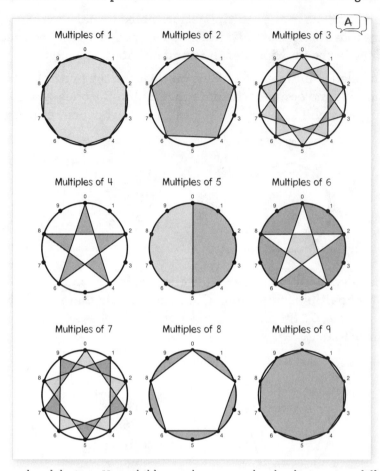

Sample completed designs. Your child may choose to color the designs in a different way.

Independent Practice and Review

Have your child complete the Lesson 16.7 Practice and Review workbook pages.

Lesson 16.8
Review Measurement

Purpose	Materials
• Review memory work • Celebrate what your child has learned about time, length, area, perimeter, weight, and capacity • Review abbreviations for units of measurement • Sort units by measurement system and the attribute that they measure	• None

Memory Work   See the warm-up activity for memory work review.

Warm-up: Review Memory Work

Today, we'll review the memory work about length, area, perimeter, time, weight, and capacity.

- **How many centimeters equal 1 meter?** *100.*
- **How many meters equal 1 kilometer?** *1,000.*
- **How many inches equal 1 foot?** *12.*
- **How many feet equal 1 yard?** *3.*
- **How many inches equal 1 yard?** *36.*
- **What does area measure?** *The amount of space that a shape covers.*
- **What does perimeter measure?** *The distance around the outside edge of a shape.*
- **How many months are in a year?** *12.*
- **How many days are in a week?** *7.*
- **How many hours are in a day?** *24.*
- **How many minutes are in an hour?** *60.*
- **How many seconds are in a minute?** *60.*
- **Are times in the morning a.m. or p.m.?** *A.m.*
- **Are times in the afternoon and evening a.m. or p.m.?** *P.m.*
- **What is another name for 12 a.m.?** *Midnight.*
- **What is another name for 12 p.m.?** *Noon.*
- **How many minutes equal a half-hour?** *30.*
- **How many minutes equal a quarter-hour?** *15.*
- **How many ounces equal 1 pound?** *16.*
- **How many grams equal 1 kilogram?** *1,000.*
- **How many cups equal 1 pint?** *2.*
- **How many pints equal 1 quart?** *2.*
- **How many quarts equal 1 gallon?** *4.*
- **How many milliliters equal 1 liter?** *1,000.*

The weight and capacity memory work in this unit is new, so don't worry if your child hasn't memorized it yet. He'll work on these items more in *Fourth Grade Math with Confidence*.

Activity: Celebrate What Your Child Has Learned About Measurement

You've learned how to measure in so many different ways this year! Today, we'll look back at how much you've learned about measurement.

In Unit 9, we reviewed how to measure length, and you learned how to measure perimeter and area. With your child, flip through the Unit 9 workbook pages.

In Unit 14, you reviewed how to tell time. You learned how to calculate elapsed time and solve elapsed time word problems. Page through the Unit 14 workbook pages.

Finally, in this unit, you learned how to measure weight and capacity. Look over the Unit 16 workbook pages. Next year, you'll learn more about how to convert between different units in measurement problems. You'll also learn more about area and perimeter.

Briefly discuss any concepts that were especially difficult for your child, and remind him of how far he has come in his math learning. For example: Remember how confusing elapsed time was at first? You worked hard to learn to make timeline sketches, and now you can solve elapsed time word problems!

Activity (A): Review Units of Measurement

Show your child the list of abbreviations in part A. Look at how many different units of measurement you learned about this year! Point to each abbreviation and have your child tell what it stands for.

We use these units to measure length, area, weight, capacity, and time. Some of these units belong to the U.S. customary measurement system, and some of them belong to the metric measurement system. People all over the world use the same units for time. Have your child identify what each unit is used for and which measurement system it belongs to. Then, write the unit in the correct place on the chart.

	U.S.		Metric	
Length	in.	mi.	cm	m
	ft.	yd.	km	
Area	sq. in.	sq. mi.	sq. cm	sq. m
	sq. ft.	sq. yd.	sq. km	
Weight	lb.	oz.	g	kg
Capacity	qt.	pt.	L	mL
	gal.	c.		
Time	hr.		min.	

Units of time (hours and minutes) are used in both measurement systems, so they are not separated into different categories on the chart.

Independent Practice and Review

Have your child complete the Lesson 16.8 Practice and Review workbook pages.

Lesson 16.9
Review Fractions and Geometry

Purpose	Materials
• Review memory work • Celebrate what your child has learned about fractions and geometry • Create a drawing with straight lines, angles, and quadrilaterals • Reflect on the year and look ahead to fourth grade	• Colored pencils or markers

Memory Work   See the warm-up activity for memory work review.

Warm-up: Review Memory Work

Today, we'll review memory work about fractions and geometry.

- **What do we call the top number in a fraction?** *The numerator.*
- **What does the numerator tell?** *The number of parts.*
- **What do we call the bottom number in a fraction?** *The denominator.*
- **What does the denominator tell?** *How many equal parts the whole was split into.*
- **What do we call fractions that look different but have the same value?** *Equivalent fractions.*
- **What do we call numbers that have a whole number and a fraction?** *Mixed numbers.*
- **How many sides does a triangle have?** *3.*
- **How many sides does a quadrilateral have?** *4.*
- **How many sides does a pentagon have?** *5.*
- **How many sides does a hexagon have?** *6.*
- **How many sides does an octagon have?** *8.*
- **What do we call an angle that looks like the corner of a piece of paper?** *A right angle.*
- **What do we call a quadrilateral with 4 right angles?** *A rectangle.*
- **What do we call a quadrilateral with 4 right angles and 4 equal sides?** *A square.*
- **What do we call a quadrilateral with 4 equal sides?** *A rhombus.*

Activity: Celebrate What Your Child Has Learned About Fractions and Geometry

Today, we'll celebrate how much you've learned about fractions and geometry.

In Unit 6, you learned about fractions. You learned how to write and compare fractions, and you learned how to add and subtract fractions. You also learned about mixed numbers. With your child, flip through the Unit 6 workbook pages.

In Unit 13, you studied geometry. You learned about different kinds of quadrilaterals and explored pentominoes. Page through the Unit 13 workbook pages.

Activity (A): Draw a Picture with Straight Lines, Angles, and Quadrilaterals

Artists sometimes choose to use only straight lines in their art. They might draw horizontal or vertical lines, or they might draw diagonal lines. They might join the lines to create polygons, and they might draw lines that never meet.

If you have time, look online for paintings by Mondrian, Rothko, or Kandinsky. Look for straight and curved lines in their work, as well as different types of angles and quadrilaterals.

Today, we'll review geometry with art. Your challenge is to create an artwork that includes all of these elements. Read aloud the list of geometric elements. Then, have your child draw a picture that includes each element at least once. She may draw the lines freehand or use a ruler.

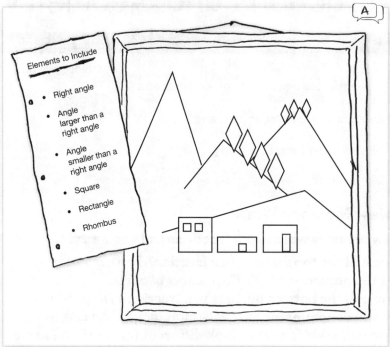

Sample picture design.

Activity (B): Reflect on the Year

Show your child the reflection questions in part B. Have her answer each question in a sentence, or scribe her answers for her. She may also draw pictures to illustrate her answers.

Independent Practice and Review

Have your child complete the Lesson 16.9 Practice page. Then, complete the certificate on workbook page 202 and present it to your child.

Unit 16 Answer Key

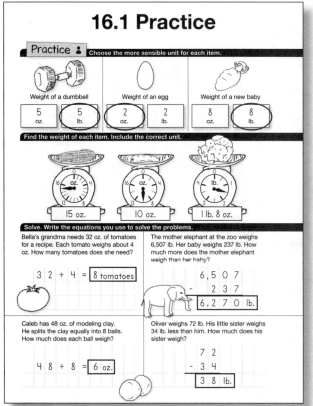

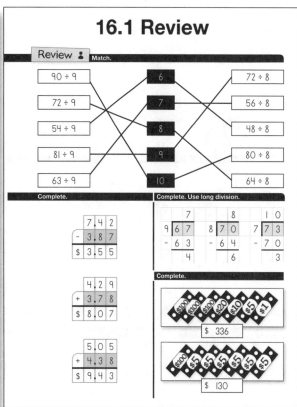

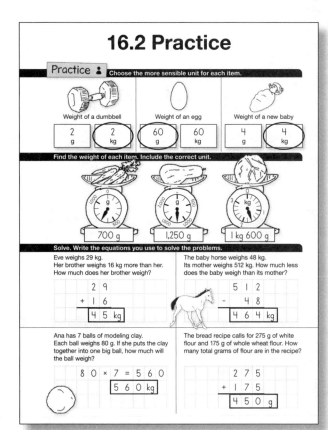

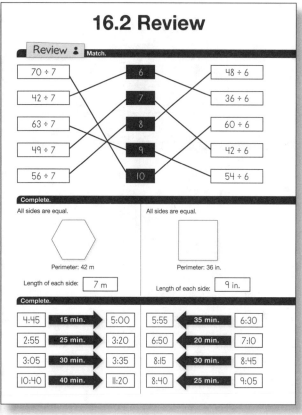

Unit 16 Answer Key

16.3 Practice

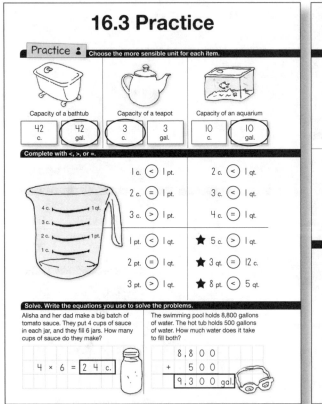

16.3 Review

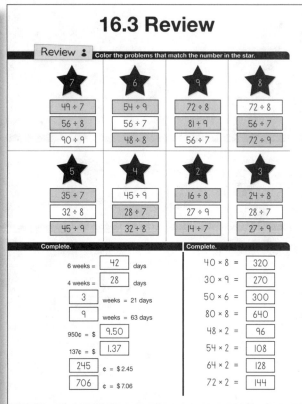

16.4 Practice

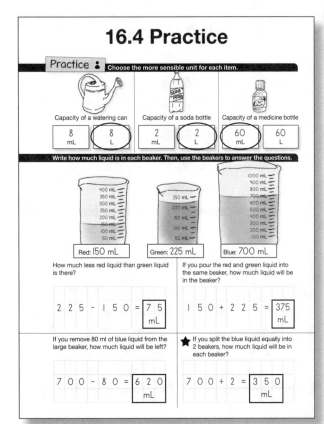

16.4 Review

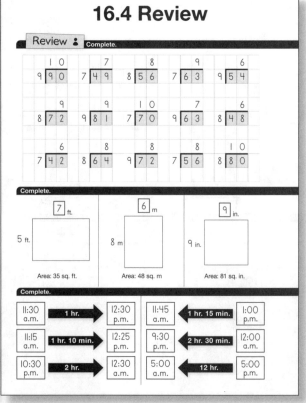

Unit 16 Answer Key

16.5 Unit Wrap-Up A

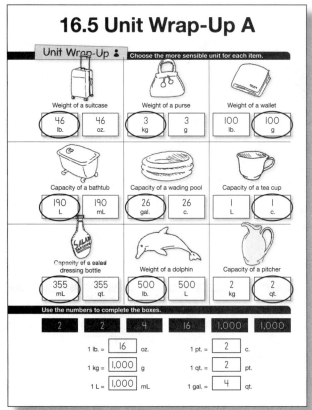

Unit Wrap-Up Choose the more sensible unit for each item.

Weight of a suitcase: (46 lb.) 46 oz.
Weight of a purse: (3 kg) 3 g
Weight of a wallet: 100 lb. (100 g)

Capacity of a bathtub: (190 L) 190 mL
Capacity of a wading pool: 26 gal. 26 c.
Capacity of a tea cup: 1 L (1 c.)

Capacity of a salad dressing bottle: (355 mL) 355 qt.
Weight of a dolphin: (500 lb.) 500 L
Capacity of a pitcher: 2 kg (2 qt.)

Use the numbers to complete the boxes.

2   2   4   16   1,000   1,000

1 lb. = 16 oz.   1 pt. = 2 c.
1 kg = 1,000 g   1 qt. = 2 pt.
1 L = 1,000 mL   1 gal. = 4 qt.

16.5 Unit Wrap-Up B

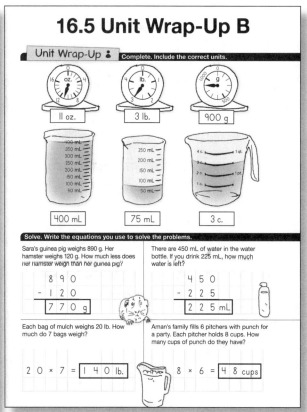

Unit Wrap-Up Complete. Include the correct units.

11 oz.   3 lb.   900 g

400 mL   75 mL   3 c.

Solve. Write the equations you use to solve the problems.

Sara's guinea pig weighs 890 g. Her hamster weighs 120 g. How much less does her hamster weigh than her guinea pig?

```
  8 9 0
- 1 2 0
  7 7 0 g
```

There are 450 mL of water in the water bottle. If you drink 225 mL, how much water is left?

```
  4 5 0
- 2 2 5
  2 2 5 mL
```

Each bag of mulch weighs 20 lb. How much do 7 bags weigh?

20 × 7 = 1 4 0 lb.

Aman's family fills 6 pitchers with punch for a party. Each pitcher holds 8 cups. How many cups of punch do they have?

8 × 6 = 4 8 cups

16.6 Practice

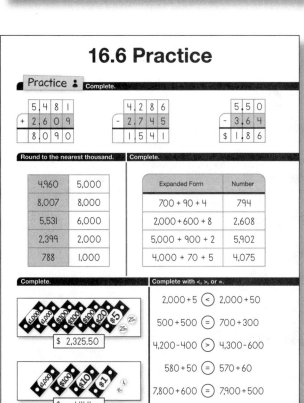

Practice Complete.

```
  5 4 8 1
+ 2 6 0 9
  8 0 9 0
```

```
  4 2 8 6
- 2 7 4 5
  1 5 4 1
```

```
  5 5 0
- 3 6 4
$ 1 8 6
```

Round to the nearest thousand.

4,960	5,000
8,007	8,000
5,531	6,000
2,399	2,000
788	1,000

Complete.

Expanded Form	Number
700 + 90 + 4	794
2,000 + 600 + 8	2,608
5,000 + 900 + 2	5,902
4,000 + 70 + 5	4,075

Complete.

$ 2,325.50

$ 1,111.11

Complete with <, >, or =.

2,000 + 5 < 2,000 + 50
500 + 500 = 700 + 300
4,200 − 400 > 4,300 − 600
580 + 50 = 570 + 60
7,800 + 600 = 7,900 + 500
730 + 80 > 750 + 50

16.6 Review

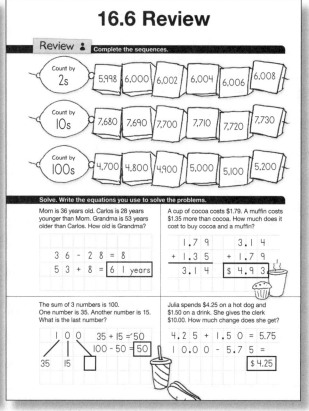

Review Complete the sequences.

Count by 2s: 5,998   6,000   6,002   6,004   6,006   6,008
Count by 10s: 7,680   7,690   7,700   7,710   7,720   7,730
Count by 100s: 4,700   4,800   4,900   5,000   5,100   5,200

Solve. Write the equations you use to solve the problems.

Mom is 36 years old. Carlos is 28 years younger than Mom. Grandma is 53 years older than Carlos. How old is Grandma?

36 − 28 = 8
53 + 8 = 6 1 years

A cup of cocoa costs $1.79. A muffin costs $1.35 more than cocoa. How much does it cost to buy cocoa and a muffin?

```
  1 . 7 9        3 . 1 4
+ 1 . 3 5      + 1 . 7 9
  3 . 1 4      $ 4 . 9 3
```

The sum of 3 numbers is 100. One number is 35. Another number is 15. What is the last number?

```
    1 0 0      35 + 15 = 50
   /    \      100 − 50 = 50
  35    15
```

Julia spends $4.25 on a hot dog and $1.50 on a drink. She gives the clerk $10.00. How much change does she get?

4.25 + 1.50 = 5.75
10.00 − 5.75 =
$ 4.25

Unit 16 Answer Key

16.7 Practice

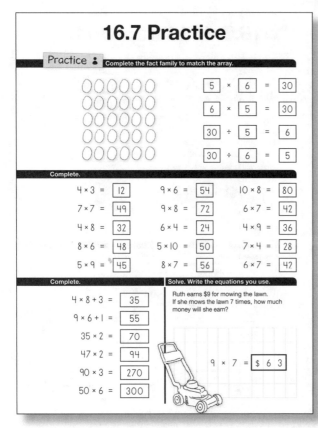

Practice 👤 Complete the fact family to match the array.

5	×	6	=	30
6	×	5	=	30
30	÷	5	=	6
30	÷	6	=	5

Complete.

4 × 3 = 12   9 × 6 = 54   10 × 8 = 80
7 × 7 = 49   9 × 8 = 72   6 × 7 = 42
4 × 8 = 32   6 × 4 = 24   4 × 9 = 36
8 × 6 = 48   5 × 10 = 50   7 × 4 = 28
5 × 9 = 45   8 × 7 = 56   6 × 7 = 42

Complete.

4 × 8 + 3 = 35
9 × 6 + 1 = 55
35 × 2 = 70
47 × 2 = 94
90 × 3 = 270
50 × 6 = 300

Solve. Write the equations you use.

Ruth earns $9 for mowing the lawn. If she mows the lawn 7 times, how much money will she earn?

9 × 7 = $ 6 3

16.7 Review

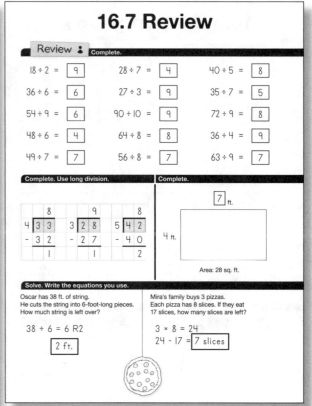

Review 👤 Complete.

18 ÷ 2 = 9   28 ÷ 7 = 4   40 ÷ 5 = 8
36 ÷ 6 = 6   27 ÷ 3 = 9   35 ÷ 7 = 5
54 ÷ 9 = 6   90 ÷ 10 = 9   72 ÷ 9 = 8
48 ÷ 6 = 4   64 ÷ 8 = 8   36 ÷ 4 = 9
49 ÷ 7 = 7   56 ÷ 8 = 7   63 ÷ 9 = 7

Complete. Use long division.

```
    8            9            8
4 | 3 3      3 | 2 8      5 | 4 2
  - 3 2        - 2 7        - 4 0
      1            1            2
```

Complete.

7 ft.

4 ft.

Area: 28 sq. ft.

Solve. Write the equations you use.

Oscar has 38 ft. of string. He cuts the string into 6-foot-long pieces. How much string is left over?

38 ÷ 6 = 6 R2

2 ft.

Mira's family buys 3 pizzas. Each pizza has 8 slices. If they eat 17 slices, how many slices are left?

3 × 8 = 24
24 − 17 = 7 slices

16.8 Practice

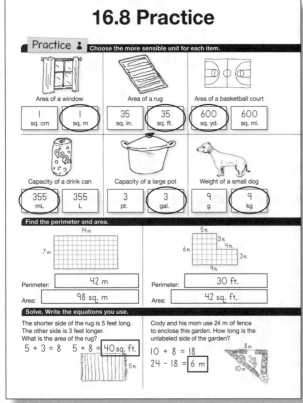

Practice 👤 Choose the more sensible unit for each item.

Area of a window — (1 sq. cm) / **1 sq. m**
Area of a rug — 35 sq. in. / **35 sq. ft.**
Area of a basketball court — **600 sq. yd.** / 600 sq. mi.

Capacity of a drink can — **355 mL** / 355 L
Capacity of a large pot — 3 pt. / **3 gal.**
Weight of a small dog — 9 g / **9 kg**

Find the perimeter and area.

14 m
7 m

Perimeter: 42 m
Area: 98 sq. m

5 ft.
3 ft.
6 ft.
4 ft.
9 ft.
3 ft.

Perimeter: 30 ft.
Area: 42 sq. ft.

Solve. Write the equations you use.

The shorter side of the rug is 5 feet long. The other side is 3 feet longer. What is the area of the rug?

5 + 3 = 8   5 × 8 = 40 sq. ft.

Cody and his mom use 24 m of fence to enclose this garden. How long is the unlabeled side of the garden?

10 + 8 = 18
24 − 18 = 6 m

8 m
5 ft.
10 m

16.8 Review

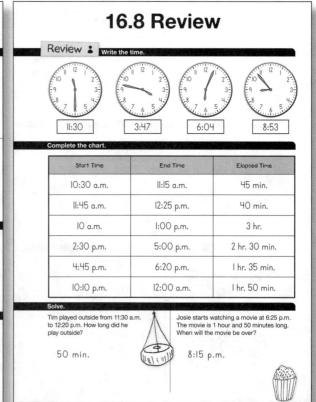

Review 👤 Write the time.

11:30   3:47   6:04   8:53

Complete the chart.

Start Time	End Time	Elapsed Time
10:30 a.m.	11:15 a.m.	45 min.
11:45 a.m.	12:25 p.m.	40 min.
10 a.m.	1:00 p.m.	3 hr.
2:30 p.m.	5:00 p.m.	2 hr. 30 min.
4:45 p.m.	6:20 p.m.	1 hr. 35 min.
10:10 p.m.	12:00 a.m.	1 hr. 50 min.

Solve.

Tim played outside from 11:30 a.m. to 12:20 p.m. How long did he play outside?

50 min.

Josie starts watching a movie at 6:25 p.m. The movie is 1 hour and 50 minutes long. When will the movie be over?

8:15 p.m.

Unit 16 Answer Key

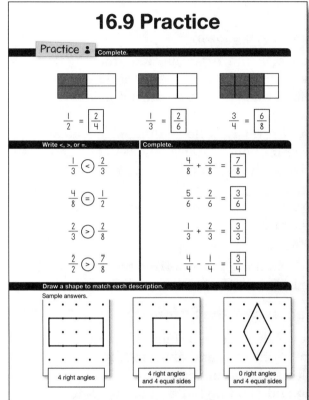

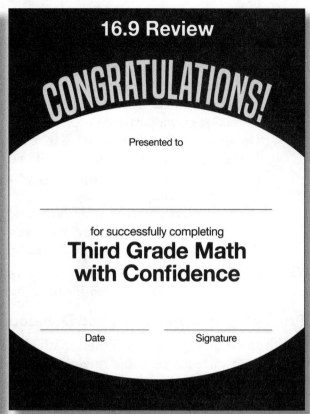

Unit 16 Checkpoint

What to Expect at the End of Unit 16

By the end of Unit 16, most children will be able to do the following:

- Understand the approximate size of an ounce, pound, gram, and kilogram.
- Estimate weight with ounces, pounds, grams, and kilograms. Many children's estimates will still be quite inaccurate, especially when using the measurement system that is less familiar to them.
- Understand the approximate size of a cup, pint, quart, gallon, milliliter, and liter.
- Estimate and measure capacity with cups or milliliters. Many children's estimates will still be quite inaccurate, especially when using the measurement system that is less familiar to them.
- Read measurements on scales and beakers. Some children will need help determining the size of the increment between each tick mark.
- Solve word problems that involve weight or capacity.

Your child does not need to have fully mastered these skills or memorized the weight and capacity equivalents. He will practice them more in *Fourth Grade Math with Confidence*.

Practicing Multiplication and Division Facts over the Summer

Children often forget some of their math skills over the summer. *Fourth Grade Math with Confidence* will provide some review with the multiplication and division facts at the beginning of the year. But the better your child knows his multiplication and division facts, the better prepared he'll be to tackle multiplying and dividing multi-digit numbers in fourth grade.

If you'd like to do a methodical review of the multiplication or division facts over the summer, check out *Multiplication Facts That Stick* or *Division Facts That Stick*. You'll find many games (some familiar and some new), as well as workbook pages to help your child further increase his speed and fluency with the math facts.

Congratulations!

Congratulations on finishing *Third Grade Math with Confidence*! Give yourself a pat on the back for all that you've taught your child this year.

Complete Picture Book List

Reading math picture books together is a fun, cozy, and delightful way to enjoy math. Most of these books relate to what your child will learn in each unit, but some expose your child to other interesting or fun math topics. **These picture books are not required.** You do not need to buy every book or track down every book in your library system. Or, you can use a book on a similar topic as a substitute.

Unit	Book
1	*Fun with Roman Numerals,* written by David A. Adler and illustrated by Edward Miller III. Holiday House, 2009.
2	*2 × 2 = Boo!: A Set of Spooky Multiplication Stories,* by Loreen Leedy. Holiday House, 1995. Alternate selection for families that do not observe Halloween: *Too Many Kangaroo Things to Do,* written by Stuart J. Murphy and illustrated by Kevin O'Malley. HarperCollins, 1996.
3	*Counting on Katherine: How Katherine Johnson Saved Apollo 13,* written by Helaine Becker and illustrated by Dow Phumiruk. Henry Holt and Co., 2018.
4	*Minnie's Diner,* written by Dayle Ann Dodds and illustrated by John Manders. Candlewick, 2007.
5	*Betcha! Estimating,* written by Stuart J. Murphy and illustrated by S. D. Schindler. HarperCollins, 1997.
6	*Fraction Action,* written and illustrated by Loreen Leedy. Holiday House, 1994.
7	*Follow the Money!,* written and illustrated by Loreen Leedy. Holiday House, 2002.
8	*The Best of Times: Math Strategies that Multiply,* written by Greg Tang and illustrated by Harry Briggs. Scholastic Press, 2002.
9	*Bigger, Better, Best,* written by Stuart J. Murphy and illustrated by Marsha Winborn. HarperCollins, 2002.
10	*The Doorbell Rang,* written by Pat Hutchins. Greenwillow Books, 1989.
11	*How Many Jelly Beans?,* written by Andrea Menotti and illustrated by Yancey Labat. Chronicle Books, 2012.
12	*Divide and Ride,* written by Stuart J. Murphy and illustrated by George Ulrich. HarperCollins, 1997.
13	*Which One Doesn't Belong? Playing with Shapes,* written by Christopher Danielson. Charlesbridge, 2019.
14	*How Do You Know What Time It Is?,* written and illustrated by Robert E. Wells. Albert Whitman & Company, 2002.
15	*A Remainder of One,* written by Elinor Pinczes and illustrated by Bonnie MacKain. HMH Books for Young Readers, 2002.
16	*Room for Ripley,* written by Stuart J. Murphy and illustrated by Sylvie Wickstrom. HarperCollins, 1999.

Scope and Sequence

Unit	Objectives
Unit 1 Review Addition and Subtraction	• Round two-digit numbers to the nearest ten • Compare numbers and addition and subtraction expressions with the <, >, and = signs • Find missing numbers in addition and subtraction equations • Solve one- and two-step addition and subtraction word problems • Review adding and subtracting two-digit numbers with the addition and subtraction algorithms • Review bar graphs
Unit 2 Multiplication, Part 1	• Write multiplication equations with the × sign for equal groups and arrays • Understand that you can multiply numbers in any order • Find answers for the ×1, ×2, ×5, and ×10 facts • Understand that any number times zero equals zero • Solve simple multiplication word problems
Unit 3 Mental Math and Word Problems	• Find the value of groups of tens and mentally add tens • Add up to identify missing addends and make change • Review strategies for mentally adding and subtracting one- and two-digit numbers • Mentally find differences between close numbers by adding up • Solve two-step word problems
Unit 4 Multiplication, Part 2	• Find answers for the ×3 and ×4 facts • Mentally multiply two-digit numbers by 2 (for example, 2 × 36) • Use multiplication to interpret pictographs
Unit 5 Numbers to 1,000	• Round three-digit numbers to the nearest hundred • Mentally add up to find missing addends to 1,000 or the next hundred • Use place-value thinking to add and subtract groups of tens (for example, 670 + 40 or 510 – 30) • Use the addition and subtraction algorithms to add and subtract three-digit numbers • Use estimation to check whether answers are reasonable • Solve mental multiplication problems that involve groups of 10 (for example, 4 × 30 or 17 × 10)
Unit 6 Fractions	• Read and write fractions to match pictures and hands-on materials • Identify the numerator and denominator in fractions and understand what each number means • Add and subtract fractions with the same denominator • Use pictures and hands-on materials to find equivalent fractions, including fractions equal to 1/2 or 1 whole • Compare fractions by reasoning about the numerator and denominator or by comparing the fractions to 1/2 • Write mixed numbers to match pictures or hands-on materials

Unit 7 **Money**	• Round prices to the nearest dollar • Convert dollars to cents, and convert cents to dollars • Add up to make change with dollars and cents • Solve mental addition and subtraction problems with money • Use the addition and subtraction algorithms to add and subtract dollars and cents
Unit 8 **Multiplication,** **Part 3**	• Find answers for the ×6, ×7, ×8, and ×9 facts • Multiply and add to find the total of equal groups and extra objects • Multiply 6, 7, 8, and 9 by multiples of 10 (for example, 9 × 70 or 6 × 60) • Multiply to convert weeks to days • Solve two-step multiplication word problems
Unit 9 **Length,** **Perimeter,** **and Area**	• Review metric and U.S. customary units for measuring length • Measure length to the nearest quarter-inch or half-inch and write lengths with mixed numbers • Understand that perimeter is the distance around the edge of a shape • Measure to find an object's perimeter • Add the lengths of an object's sides to find its perimeter • Understand that area is the amount of space that a shape covers • Multiply length times width to find the area of rectangles • Split shapes into rectangular parts and add or subtract the areas of the parts to find total area • Solve perimeter and area word problems
Unit 10 **Division, Part 1**	• Write division equations with the ÷ sign to match two different types of division situations • Understand how to use multiplication to find answers to division problems • Find answers for the ÷2, ÷5, and ÷10 facts • Solve simple division word problems • Solve division problems with remainders
Unit 11 **Numbers to** **10,000**	• Read, write, and compare numbers to 10,000 • Understand place value in four-digit numbers and write four-digit numbers in expanded form • Round to the nearest thousand • Use place-value thinking to mentally add and subtract groups of hundreds (for example, 6,700 + 400 or 5,100 − 300) • Use the addition and subtraction algorithms to add and subtract four-digit numbers • Subtract to find elapsed time between years

Unit 12 Division, Part 2	• Find answers for the ÷3, ÷4, and ÷ 6 facts • Divide small numbers with the long division algorithm • Solve division word problems with remainders and interpret remainders in context
Unit 13 Geometry	• Identify right angles and tell whether other angles are larger or smaller than a right angle • Identify, describe, and draw squares, rectangles, and rhombuses • Use spatial skills to visualize flips, turns, and slides • Name three-dimensional shapes (cones, cubes, cylinders, rectangular prisms, triangular prisms, and pyramids) and identify faces, edges, and vertices
Unit 14 Elapsed Time	• Review telling time to the minute • Describe times with *past* or *to* • Find times that are a certain number of minutes before or after a given time • Find the number of minutes that elapse between two times • Find times that are a certain number of hours and minutes before or after a given time • Find the number of hours and minutes that elapse between two times • Find how much time has elapsed before or after midnight or noon • Solve elapsed time word problems
Unit 15 Division, Part 3	• Find answers for the ÷7, ÷8, and ÷9 facts • Divide by 7 to convert days to weeks • Use division to solve perimeter and area problems
Unit 16 Weight and Capacity	• Understand the approximate size of an ounce, pound, gram, and kilogram • Estimate weight with ounces, pounds, grams, and kilograms • Understand the approximate size of a cup, pint, quart, gallon, milliliter, and liter • Estimate and measure capacity with cups and milliliters • Read scales and beakers • Solve weight and capacity word problems

Complete Memory Work List

You'll find a visual summary of all the memory work on Blackline Master 1 (pages 533-535). Keep this summary in your math binder (or post it near your math lesson area) so your child can refer to it as he learns these important facts and vocabulary words.

Review Memory Work

In Unit 1, your child will review the memory work from *Second Grade Math with Confidence*. Your child is not expected to completely memorize this list by the end of Unit 1, especially if she did not use *Second Grade Math with Confidence*. She'll have many opportunities to practice these items over the course of the year.

Topic	Memory Work
Numbers and Operations	• **What do we call the result when we add numbers together?** *The sum.* • **What do we call the numbers that we add together?** *The addends.* • **What do we call the result when we subtract a number from another number?** *The difference.* • Write the < sign. **What does this sign mean?** *Less than.* • Write the > sign. **What does this sign mean?** *Greater than.* • **If a number has 1, 3, 5, 7, or 9 in the ones-place, is the number even or odd?** *Odd.* • **If a number has 0, 2, 4, 6, or 8 in the ones-place, is the number even or odd?** *Even.*
Time	• **How many months are in a year?** *12.* • **How many days are in a week?** *7.* • **How many hours are in a day?** *24.* • **How many minutes are in an hour?** *60.* • **How many seconds are in a minute?** *60.* • **Are times in the morning a.m. or p.m.?** *A.m.* • **Are times in the afternoon and evening a.m. or p.m.?** *P.m.* • **What is another name for 12 a.m?** *Midnight.* • **What is another name for 12 p.m.?** *Noon.* • **How many minutes equal a half-hour?** *30.* • **How many minutes equal a quarter-hour?** *15.*
Geometry	• **How many sides does a triangle have?** *3.* • **How many sides does a quadrilateral have?** *4.* • **How many sides does a pentagon have?** *5.* • **How many sides does a hexagon have?** *6.* • **How many sides does an octagon have?** *8.*
Measurement	• **How many inches equal 1 foot?** *12.* • **How many feet equal 1 yard?** *3.* • **How many inches equal 1 yard?** *36.* • **How many centimeters equal 1 meter?** *100.*

New Memory Work

New memory work is gradually introduced throughout the year. Note that not all units have new memory work. The Unit 16 memory work is introduced in the last few lessons of the year, so your child isn't expected to fully memorize these items before the end of the year. She'll work on them more in *Fourth Grade Math with Confidence*.

Unit	Memory Work
2	• **What do we call the result when we multiply two numbers?** *The product.* • **What do we call the numbers in a multiplication equation that we multiply together?** *Factors.*
4	• **Name the multiples of X in order.** (Replace X with any number from 1 to 10.) *Answers will vary.* Stop your child when he reaches the tenth multiple.
6	• **What do we call the top number in a fraction?** *The numerator.* • **What does the numerator tell?** *The number of parts.* • **What do we call the bottom number in a fraction?** *The denominator.* • **What does the denominator tell?** *How many equal parts the whole was split into.* • **What do we call fractions that look different but have the same value?** *Equivalent fractions.* • **What do we call numbers that have a whole number and a fraction?** *Mixed numbers.*
9	• **How many meters equal 1 kilometer?** *1,000.* • **What does perimeter measure?** *The distance around the outside edge of a shape.* • **What does area measure?** *The amount of space that a shape covers.*
10	• **What do we call the number to be divided?** *The dividend.* • **What do we call the number we divide by?** *The divisor.* • **What do we call the result when we divide two numbers?** *The quotient.*
12	• **What do we call an amount that is left over after division?** *The remainder.*
13	• **What do we call an angle that looks like the corner of a piece of paper?** *A right angle.* • **What do we call a quadrilateral with 4 right angles?** *A rectangle.* • **What do we call a quadrilateral with 4 right angles and 4 equal sides?** *A square.* • **What do we call a quadrilateral with 4 equal sides?** *A rhombus.*
16	• **How many ounces equal 1 pound?** *16.* • **How many grams equal 1 kilogram?** *1,000.* • **How many cups equal 1 pint?** *2.* • **How many pints equal 1 quart?** *2.* • **How many quarts equal 1 gallon?** *4.* • **How many milliliters equal 1 liter?** *1,000.*

Materials List

What You'll Need in Your Math Kit

You'll use the following materials regularly in *Third Grade Math with Confidence*. Stash them in a box or basket and always keep them ready for your next lesson. (See page 9 in the Introduction for more detailed descriptions of each item.)

- Base-ten blocks (at least 50 units, 20 rods, 10 flats, and 1 large cube)
- 50 small counters
- Coins (20 pennies, 20 nickels, 20 dimes, 10 quarters)
- Play money (20 each of one-dollar bills, ten-dollar bills, and hundred-dollar bills; 10 each of five-dollar bills, twenty-dollar bills, and thousand-dollar bills)
- Clock with hands
- Fraction circles
- 1-foot (or 30-centimeter) ruler, labeled with both inches and centimeters
- 2 packs of playing cards and 2 regular, six-sided dice
- Blank paper
- Pencils
- 1 page protector and 1 dry-erase marker
- Binder with about 10 page protectors, optional

Other Supplies

Besides your Math Kit, you'll also need the following household items. You'll only need most of them once or twice, so you don't need to gather them ahead of time or store them separately. Check the unit overviews for the specific household items you'll need for each unit.

Items marked with an asterisk are needed for the optional enrichment lessons at the end of each unit.

- 6 toothpicks
- White crayon
- Marker or highlighter
- Markers, crayons, or colored pencils
- Small slips of paper
- 5-6 small boxes or bowls
- *24 small snack items, such as raisins, pieces of cereal, or small candies
- Paper clip
- *3 clear jars or bowls
- *3 sets of small objects (such as crackers, blocks, or cotton balls) with 50-150 objects in each set
- Measuring cups (1/4-cup, 1/3-cup, 1/2-cup, and 1-cup)
- Water
- *Ingredients for pumpkin bread or another recipe. See the recipe in Lesson 6.11 (page 204) for suggested ingredients.
- 3 small office items (such as a pencil, eraser, and ruler)
- *Toy catalog or access to a website with items your child would like to buy
- Calendar, optional
- *Varies, depending on which activity you choose. See Lesson 8.9 (page 266) for options.
- Scissors
- Tape
- 3 books of varying sizes
- Masking tape or yarn

- Yardstick and meterstick, optional
- Map of your town (either paper or on a map app), optional
- *Tape measure
- *20-25 small snacks, such as blueberries, chocolate chips, or pieces of cereal (optional)
- 6 dice
- *Map app
- *Contact paper (self-adhesive, clear vinyl)
- *Black construction paper
- *Tissue paper in assorted colors
- *Paper plate
- *Pencil
- *Tape, optional
- Yarn
- Object that weighs about 1 ounce, such as a slice of bread, AA battery, or a stack of 5 quarters
- Object that weighs about 1 pound, such as a loaf of bread, can of vegetables, or box of pasta
- 5 pantry items of varying weights, with tape or a sticky note covering the items' labeled weights
- Kitchen scale or postal scale that measures in pounds and ounces, optional
- 5 small household objects, optional
- Object that weighs about 1 gram, such as a paper clip, 1-dollar bill, or thumbtack
- Object that weighs about 1 kilogram, such as a pair of adult shoes, a pineapple, or your child's student workbook
- Kitchen scale or postal scale that measures in kilograms and grams, optional
- 1-pint and 1-quart measuring cups, optional
- 5 containers of varying capacities
- Eyedropper, optional
- 1-liter container (such as a large water bottle or measuring cup), optional
- Variety of food and personal care items, with capacity labeled in milliliters
- *Honey
- *Blue dishwashing soap
- *Vegetable oil
- *Rubbing alcohol (surgical spirit)
- *Food coloring
- *Tall, clear glass or glass jar
- *Measuring cup that measures in milliliters
- *Small bowls and spoons for mixing

Guide to the Blackline Masters

Digital Copies of Blackline Masters

Prefer to print the Blackline Masters rather than copy them from the book?
Download digital copies of all Math with Confidence Blackline Masters at welltrainedmind.com/mwc.

Frequently-Used Blackline Masters

You'll use these pages often throughout the book. Some are for modeling important concepts, while others provide helpful reference information. Place these pages in page protectors in a binder so they're always available. Encourage your child to refer to them as needed as he completes the Practice and Review pages.

- Memory Work (Blackline Master 1)
- How to Read Word Problems (Blackline Master 2)
- Place-Value Chart (Blackline Master 3)
- Addition and Subtraction Algorithms (Blackline Master 4)
- Dot Array and L-cover (Blackline Master 5)
- Multiplication Strategies (Blackline Master 6)

Short-Term-Use Blackline Masters

These pages give your child hands-on practice with measurement and geometry concepts. You will use them for only a few lessons, and you do not need to save these Blackline Masters after you finish the corresponding unit.

- Paper Ruler (Blackline Master 8), used in Unit 9 only
- Quadrilateral Cards (Blackline Master 9), used in Unit 13 only
- Pentominoes (Blackline Master 10) used in Unit 13 only
- Nets (Blackline Master 11), used in Unit 13 only

Optional Blackline Masters

These blackline masters are optional. If you have real fraction circles, base-ten blocks, and play money, you do not need Blackline Masters 7, 12, and 13. The Subtraction Climb and Slide page is an optional game for practicing the subtraction facts. See the Unit 2 Checkpoint (page 79) for details on whether or not you need it.

- *Fraction Circles (Blackline Master 7)
- *Base-Ten Blocks (Blackline Master 12)
- *Play Money (Blackline Master 13)
- *Subtraction Climb and Slide (Blackline Master 14)

Memory Work (Blackline Master 1)

$3 + 4 = 7$

addends   sum

$7 - 4 = 3$

difference

$5 < 6$

less-than sign

$6 > 5$

greater-than sign

Odd numbers have

1, 3, 5, 7, or 9

in the ones-place.

Even numbers have

0, 2, 4, 6, or 8

in the ones-place.

1 foot = 12 inches

1 yard = 3 feet

1 yard = 36 inches

1 meter = 100 centimeters

1 year = 12 months

1 week = 7 days

1 day = 24 hours

1 hour = 60 minutes

1 minute = 60 seconds

Midnight   Noon   Midnight

12 a.m.   12 p.m.   12 a.m.

Half-hour
30 minutes

Quarter-hour
15 minutes

Triangle
3 sides

Quadrilateral
4 sides

Pentagon
5 sides

Hexagon
6 sides

Octagon
8 sides

$$3 \times 4 = 12$$

factors   product

$$9 \div 4 = 2 \, R \, 1$$

dividend   divisor   quotient   remainder

1 kilometer = 1,000 meters

1 kilogram = 1,000 grams

1 liter = 1,000 milliliters

1 pound = 16 ounces

1 pint = 2 cups

1 quart = 2 pints

1 gallon = 4 quarts

Perimeter measures the distance
around the outside edge of a shape.

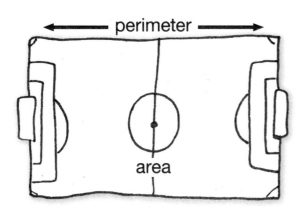

perimeter

area

Area measures the amount of space
that a shape covers.

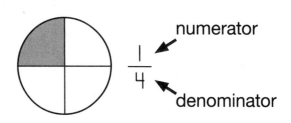

numerator

$$\frac{1}{4}$$

denominator

$$\frac{1}{2} = \frac{2}{4}$$

equivalent fractions

$$2\frac{1}{3}$$

mixed number

Rectangle
4 right angles

Square
4 right angles
4 equal sides

Rhombus
4 equal sides
2 pairs of parallel sides

How to Read Word Problems (Blackline Master 2)

1. Read the problem.

2. Identify the goal.

3. Read the problem again.

   - Read slowly and carefully.
   - Imagine what's happening.
   - Stop after each sentence to make sure you understand it.

4. Solve.

Place-Value Chart (Blackline Master 3)

tens	ones

	thousands
	hundreds

Addition and Subtraction Algorithms (Blackline Master 4)

The Addition Algorithm

∗∗∗ Start with the ones-place.

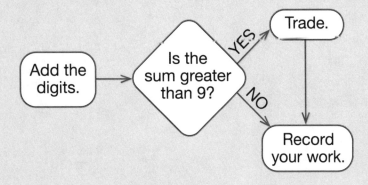

∗∗∗ Follow the steps for all the places.

The Subtraction Algorithm

∗∗∗ Start with the ones-place.

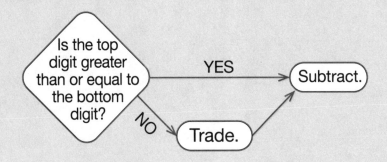

∗∗∗ Follow the steps for all the places.

Dot Array and L-Cover (Blackline Master 5)

	1	2	3	4	5	6	7	8	9	10
1	●	●	●	●	●	●	●	●	●	●
2	●	●	●	●	●	●	●	●	●	●
3	●	●	●	●	●	●	●	●	●	●
4	●	●	●	●	●	●	●	●	●	●
5	●	●	●	●	●	●	●	●	●	●
6	●	●	●	●	●	●	●	●	●	●
7	●	●	●	●	●	●	●	●	●	●
8	●	●	●	●	●	●	●	●	●	●
9	●	●	●	●	●	●	●	●	●	●
10	●	●	●	●	●	●	●	●	●	●

Directions: Cut on the dotted line. You will be left with a gray L.

Multiplication Strategies (Blackline Master 6)

All facts Use the facts within the same table as stepping stones.

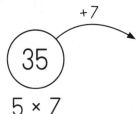

+7   +7

35   42   49

5 × 7   6 × 7   7 × 7

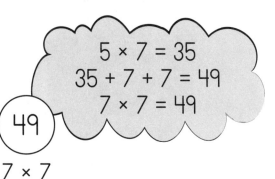

$5 × 7 = 35$
$35 + 7 + 7 = 49$
$7 × 7 = 49$

---

1 Any number times 1 equals the number.

$1 × 6 = 6$

2 Double the number.

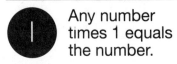

Double 5 is 10.
$2 × 5 = 10$

3 Use the related ×2 fact.

$2 × 8 = 16$
$16 + 8 = 24$
$3 × 8 = 24$

---

4 Double the related ×2 fact.

$2 × 7 = 14$
Double 14 is 28.
$4 × 7 = 28$

5 Make groups of 10.

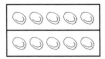

4 groups of 5 equal 2 tens.
$4 × 5 = 20$

6 Use the related ×5 fact.

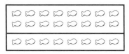

$5 × 8 = 40$
$40 + 8 = 48$
$6 × 8 = 48$

---

8 Double the related ×4 fact.

$4 × 8 = 32$
Double 32 is 64.
$8 × 8 = 64$

9 Use the related ×10 fact.

$10 × 6 = 60$
$60 - 6 = 54$
$9 × 6 = 54$

10 Use place-value thinking.

4 tens = 40
$4 × 10 = 40$

Fraction Circles (Blackline Master 7)

You do not need these if you have plastic or wooden fraction circles.

Directions: Copy this page onto sturdy paper. Color each circle the color listed next to it. Then, cut along the lines.

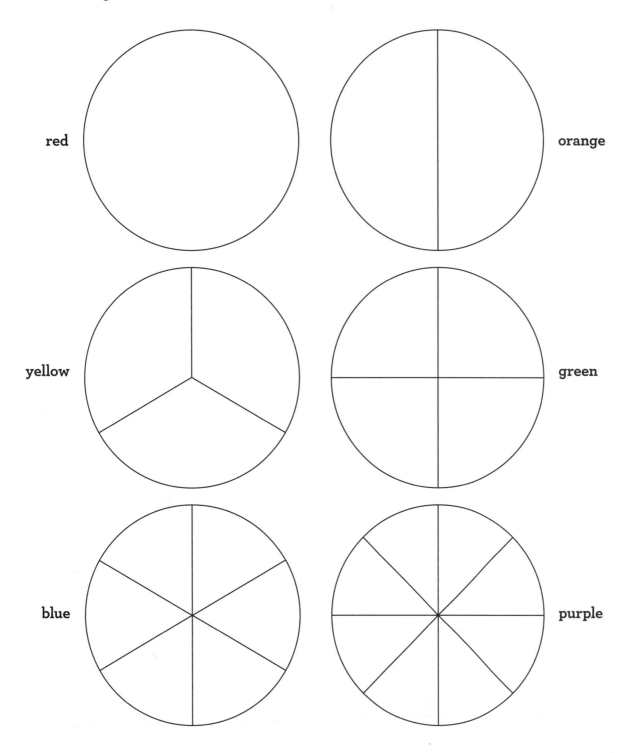

red

orange

yellow

green

blue

purple

Paper Ruler
(Blackline Master 8)

Directions: Cut out the paper ruler on the solid line.

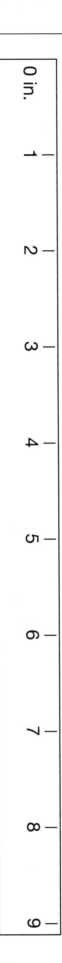

0 in.   1   2   3   4   5   6   7   8   9

Quadrilateral Cards (Blackline Master 9)

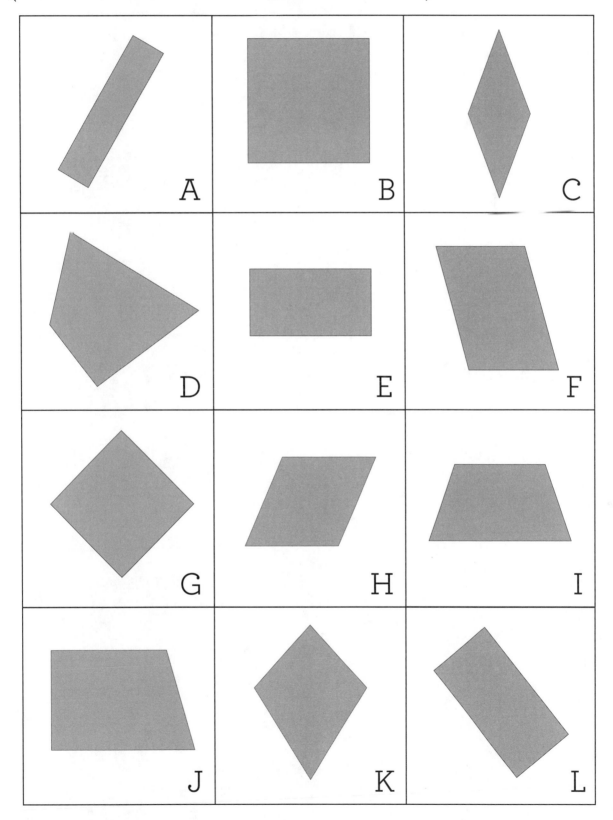

Pentominoes
(Blackline Master 10)

Directions: Copy this page onto sturdy paper. Cut out the pentominoes on the heavy lines.

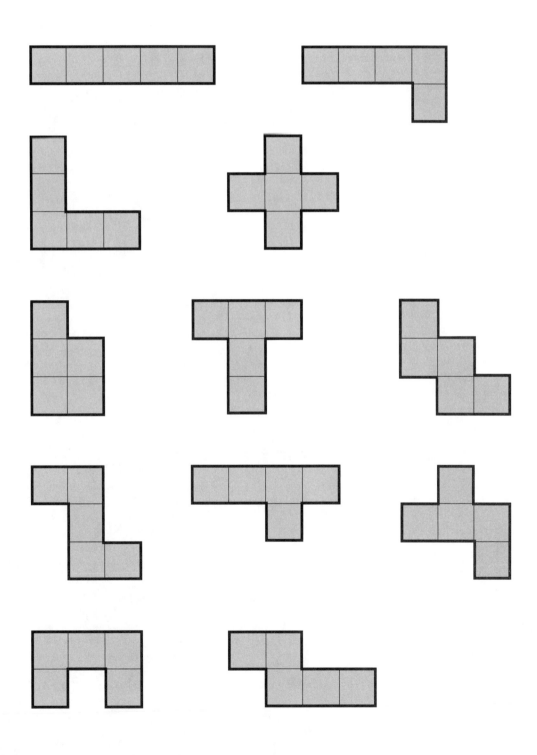

Nets
(Blackline Master 11)

Directions: Copy these pages onto sturdy paper. Cut out along the solid lines.

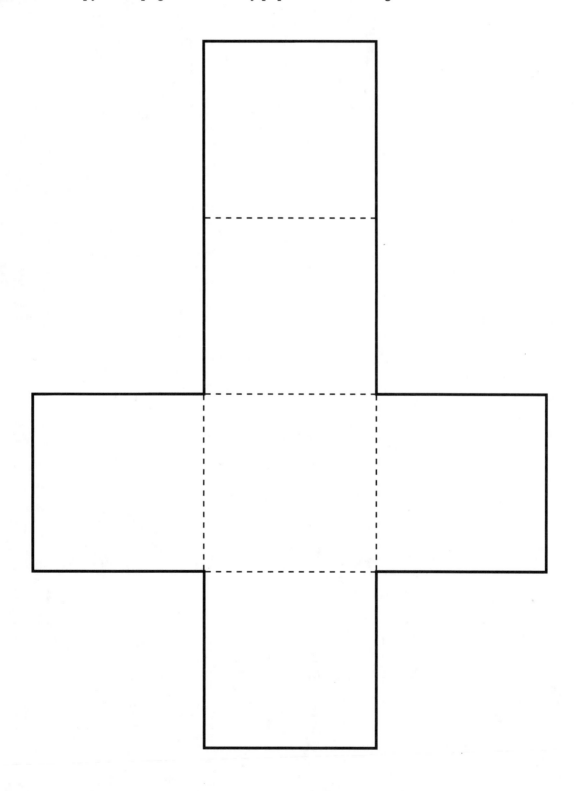

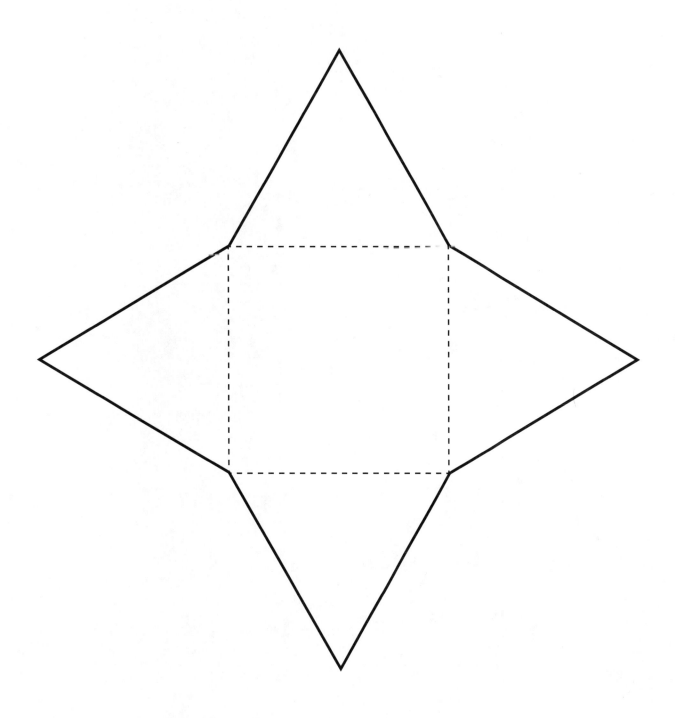

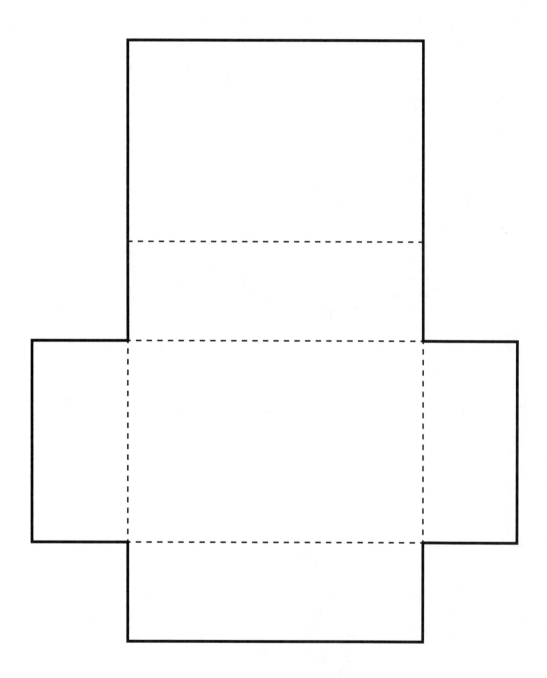

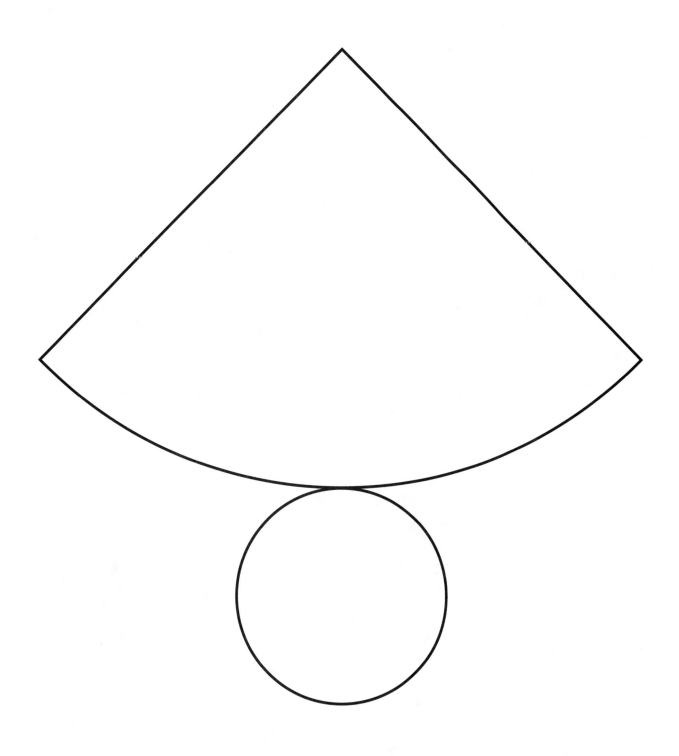

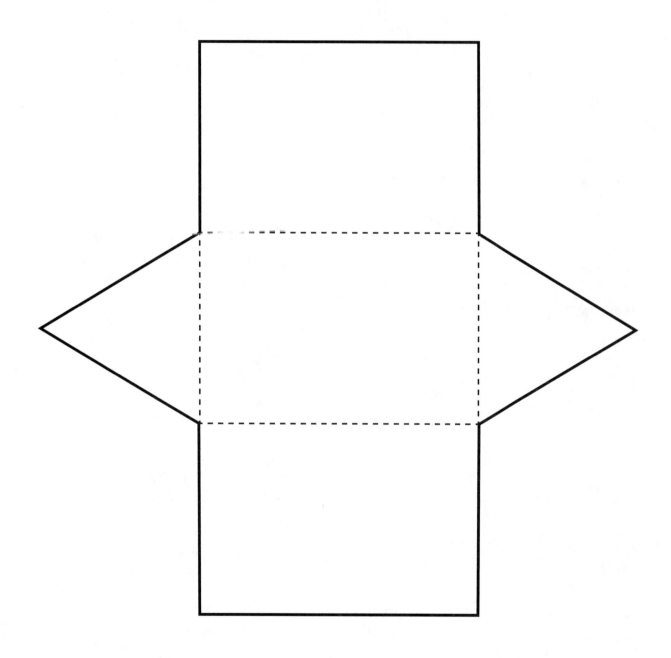

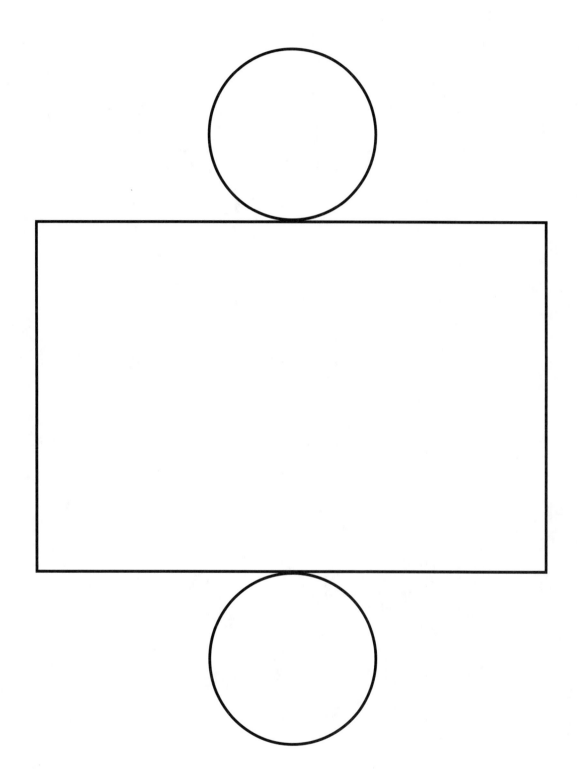

Base-Ten Blocks
(Blackline Master 12)

You do not need these if you have real base-ten blocks.

Directions: Make 5 copies of this page on sturdy paper. Cut out the blocks on the dark lines.

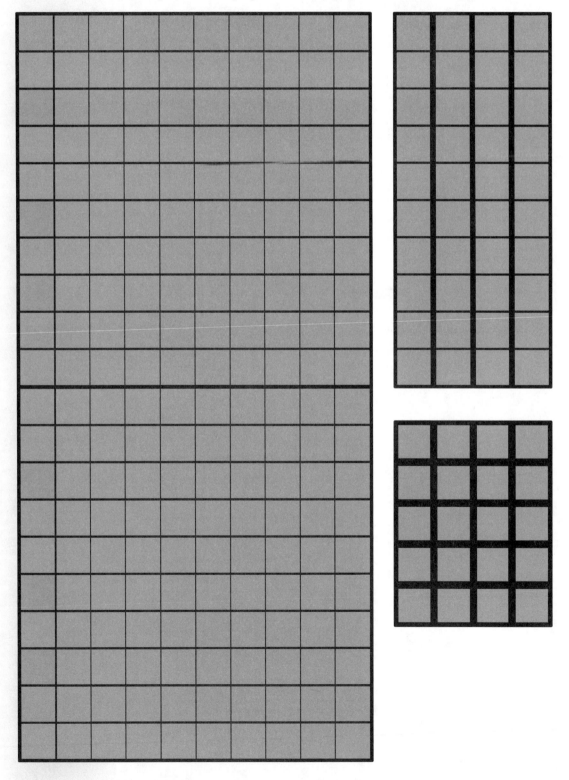

Play Paper Bills for Families Outside the US
(Blackline Master 13)

You do not need these if you have other play money, either from a toy cash register or board game.

Directions: Make 2 copies of this page on sturdy paper and cut out the paper bills.

$1	$1	$1	$1	$1
$5	$5	$5	$5	$5
$10	$10	$10	$10	$10
$20	$20	$20	$20	$20
$100	$100	$100	$100	$100
$1,000	$1,000	$1,000	$1,000	$1,000

Subtraction Climb and Slide (Blackline Master 14)

Use this game as needed to review subtraction facts.

Materials: 2 different-colored counters to use as game tokens; die

Object of the Game: Be the first player to reach the Finish square.

Each player chooses a counter to use as a game token and places it on the Start square.

On your turn, roll the die and advance your token the corresponding number of squares. Say the answer to the problem on your landing square.

If you land on a square at the bottom of a ladder, "climb" the ladder and place your game token on the square at the top of the ladder. If you land on a square at the top of a slide, slide down the slide and place your game token on the square at the bottom of the slide.

The first player to reach Finish wins the game.

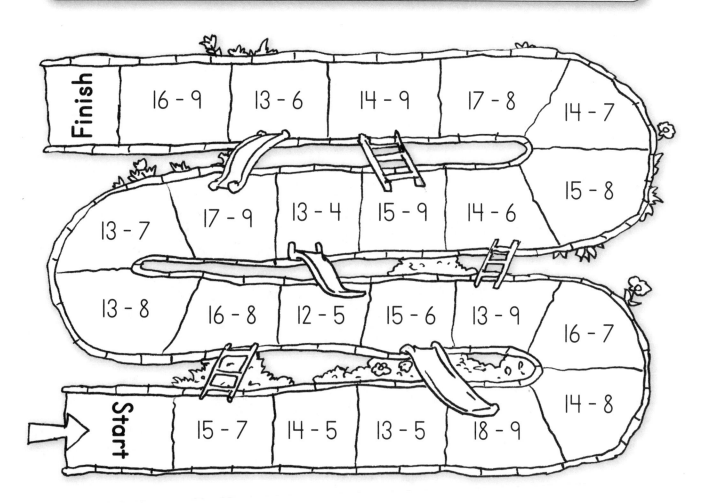

Acknowledgements

Thanks to Itamar Katz, whose design and illustration skills transform my Word document and messy sketches into this clear, easy-to-read Instructor Guide and colorful, whimsical Student Book. These books wouldn't be the same without your thoughtful design suggestions and wonderful drawings, Itamar!

To Shane Klink, who designed the beautiful covers for the series. To Rachael Churchill, whose thorough editing improved the clarity of the Instructor Guide and cleaned up my typos and mistakes.

To Susan Wise Bauer, for her guidance and advice as I honed the vision for the *Math with Confidence* series. To Justin Moore, for his thoughtful clarifying questions and indefatigable copy-editing. And to Melissa Moore, both for her expert project management and for her steadfast support and encouragement as I write this program.

Finally, many thanks to the members of the *Third Grade Math with Confidence* pilot-test group. Thank you for finding the activities that didn't work, the workbook pages that were too long, and the lessons that needed a little more fun! This program is better because of you, and I appreciate all the time you spent giving me feedback, answering my questions, and helping me understand how your kids responded to the lessons. Beyond these practical matters, thank you for your generous encouragement and support. Your commitment to giving your kids an excellent math education motivates and inspires me, and it is an honor to be part of that journey with you.

Cherie Adams
Rebecca Agnew
Megan Anderson
Stella Barnett
Jacquelyn Beaumont
Krista Biggs
Chrissy Blumer
Liz Bolton
Nancy Bradford
Nicole Craig
Jill Cross
Mandi Davidson
Stacie Fox
Lauren Gartland
Julie Gatewood
Bettina Gentry
Lindsey Goetz
Kelly Gouss
Kristy Griggs
Jessica Grime
Tiffany Hafner
Evelyn Hakimian
Susan J. Harmon
Bethany Haugen
Lisa Healy
Donna Hunter

Rhebeka Hyland
Nicky Kester
Christy Kian
Rachel King
Mary Kouf
Jana Krasney
Emily Kuhl
Amy Lerner
Poonam Ligade
Nikki Lindo
Becky Lingen
Melissa Mackey
Amy Martello
The Martoncik Family
Sarah McCormick
Mageda Merbouh-Bangert
Holly Merryman
Sally Metcalfe
Kelly Minner
Sarah Montgomery
Kate Nicolaus
Shannon O'Brien
Kim O'Connor
Lindsay Partridge
Anna Haskins Patton
Angela Penk

Megan Preedin
Sierra Pung
Rebekah Randolph
Jenna Rice
Laura Sandiford
Kathleen Santos
Emily Schindler
Ashley Scofield
Meghan Shaffer
Bethany Shields
Kirsten Shope
Kathy Smerke
Shannon Smith
Rachel Sohn
A. Steele
Sandy Lorraine Tad-y
Johanna Tomlinson
Amanda Troxell
Duski Van Fleet
Sietske Veenman
Sara Watson
Ashley Weaver
Elizabeth Wenzel
Stacy Whitaker
Anna White
Valerie Winkley